FUNDAMENTALS OF COMPUTER GRAPHICS

FUNDAMENTALS OF COMPUTER GRAPHICS

Baraka Mwangi
Zawadi Njeri

Kruger Brentt
Publishers

2026

Kruger Brentt Publishers UK. LTD.
Company Number 9728962

Regd. Office: 68 St Margarets Road, Edgware, Middlesex HA8 9UU

ISBN: 978-1-78715-650-0

Disclaimer:

Every possible effort has been made to ensure that the information contained in this book is accurate at the time of going to press, and the publisher and author cannot accept responsibility for any errors or omissions, however caused. No responsibility for loss or damage occasioned to any person acting, or refraining from action, as a result of the material in this publication can be accepted by the editor, the publisher or the author. The Publisher is not associated with any product or vendor mentioned in the book. The contents of this work are intended to further general scientific research, understanding and discussion only. Readers should consult with a specialist where appropriate.

Every effort has been made to trace the owners of copyright material used in this book, if any. The author and the publisher will be grateful for any omission brought to their notice for acknowledgement in the future editions of the book.

For information on all our publications visit our website at http://krugerbrentt.com/

PREFACE

Computer graphics has emerged as a central discipline within computer science, enabling the creation, representation, and manipulation of visual content across scientific, industrial, and creative domains. From interactive user interfaces and digital imaging to advanced simulations and cinematic visual effects, the field continues to expand through developments in mathematical modeling, rendering algorithms, hardware acceleration, and real-time processing. A solid understanding of the foundational principles of computer graphics is therefore essential for students and practitioners seeking to engage with modern visualization technologies.

Fundamentals of Computer Graphics provides a comprehensive introduction to the key concepts, methodologies, and algorithms that define the discipline. The book covers the mathematical foundations of geometric modeling, transformations, and projections; explores rendering techniques such as shading, illumination, ray tracing, and rasterization; and examines essential topics including texture mapping, animation, and graphical system architectures. Emerging directions—such as real-time graphics, GPU programming, and physically based rendering—are incorporated to reflect ongoing advancements within the field.

This text is intended for students, educators, researchers, and professionals in computer science, digital media, engineering, and related disciplines. By integrating theoretical principles with practical insights and illustrative examples, the book provides a structured and accessible framework for understanding the fundamental mechanisms that govern the creation of visual content in computer graphics.

Baraka Mwangi

Zawadi Njeri

CONTENTS

Chapter 1

Introduction

The term "computer graphics" refers to anything involved in the creation or manipulation of images on a computer, including animated images. It is a very broad field, and one in which changes and advances seem to come at a dizzying pace. It can be difficult for a beginner to know where to start. However, there is a core of fundamental ideas that are part of the foundation of most applications of computer graphics. This book attempts to cover those foundational ideas, or at least as many of them as will fit into a one-semester college-level course. While it is not possible to cover the entire field in a first course - or even a large part of it-this should be a good place to start.

This short chapter provides an overview and introduction to the material that will be covered in the rest of the book, without going into a lot of detail.

1.1 Painting and Drawing

The main focus of this book is three-dimensional (3D) graphics, where most of the work goes into producing a 3D model of a scene. But ultimately, in almost all cases, the end result of a computer graphics project is a two-dimensional image. And of course, the direct production and manipulation of 2D images is an important topic in its own right. Furthermore, a lot of ideas carry over from two dimensions to three. So, it makes sense to start with graphics in 2D.

An image that is presented on the computer screen is made up of pixels. The screen consists of a rectangular grid of pixels, arranged in rows and columns. The pixels are small enough that they are not easy to see individually. In fact, for many very high-resolution displays, they become essentially invisible. At a given time, each pixel can show only one color. Most screens these days use 24 -bit color, where a color can be specified by three 8 -bit numbers, giving the levels of red, green, and blue in the color. Any color that can be shown on the screen is made up of some combination of these three "primary" colors. Other formats are possible, such as grayscale, where each pixel is some shade of gray and the pixel color is given by one number that specifies the level of gray on a black-to-white scale. Typically, 256 shades of gray are used. Early computer screens used indexed color, where only a small set of colors, usually 16 or 256 , could be displayed. For an indexed color display, there is a numbered list of possible colors, and the color of a pixel is specified by an integer giving the position of the color in the list.

In any case, the color values for all the pixels on the screen are stored in a large block of memory known as a frame buffer. Changing the image on the screen requires changing color values that are stored in the frame buffer. The screen is redrawn many times per second, so that almost immediately after the color values are changed in the frame buffer, the colors of the pixels on the screen will be changed to match, and the displayed image will change.

A computer screen used in this way is the basic model of raster graphics. The term "raster" technically refers to the mechanism used on older vacuum tube computer monitors: An electron beam would move along the rows of pixels, making them glow. The beam was moved across the screen by powerful magnets that would deflect the path of the electrons. The stronger the beam, the brighter the glow of the pixel, so the brightness of the pixels could be controlled by modulating the intensity of the electron beam. The color values stored in the frame buffer were used to determine the intensity of the electron beam. (For a color screen, each pixel had a red dot, a green dot, and a blue dot, which were separately illuminated by the beam.)

A modern flat-screen computer monitor is not a raster in the same sense. There is no moving electron beam. The mechanism that controls the colors of the pixels is different for different types of screen. But the screen is still made up of pixels, and the color values for all the pixels are still stored in a frame buffer. The idea of an image consisting of a grid of pixels, with numerical color values for each pixel, defines raster graphics.

Although images on the computer screen are represented using pixels, specifying individual pixel colors is not always the best way to create an image. Another way is to specify the basic geometric objects that it contains, shapes such as lines, circles, triangles, and rectangles. This is the idea that defines vector graphics: Represent an image as a list of the geometric shapes that it contains. To make things more interesting, the shapes can have attributes, such as the thickness of a line or the color that fills a rectangle. Of course, not every image can be composed from simple geometric shapes. This approach certainly wouldn't work for a picture of a beautiful sunset (or for most any other photographic image). However, it works well for many types of images, such as architectural blueprints and scientific illustrations.

In fact, early in the history of computing, vector graphics was even used directly on computer screens. When the first graphical computer displays were developed, raster displays were too slow and expensive to be practical. Fortunately, it was possible to use vacuum tube technology in another way: The electron beam could be made to directly draw a line on the screen, simply by sweeping the beam along that line. A vector graphics display would store a display list of lines that should appear on the screen. Since a point on the screen would glow only very briefly after being illuminated by the electron beam, the graphics display would go through the display list over and over, continually redrawing all the lines on the list. To change the image, it would only be necessary to change the contents of the display list. Of course, if the display list became too long, the image would start to flicker because a line would have a chance to visibly fade before its next turn to be redrawn.

But here is the point: For an image that can be specified as a reasonably small number of geometric shapes, the amount of information needed to represent the image is much smaller using a vector representation than using a raster representation. Consider an image made up of one thousand line segments. For a vector representation of the image, you only need to store the coordinates of two thousand points, the endpoints of the lines. This would take up only a few kilobytes of memory. To store the image in a frame buffer for a raster display would require much more memory. Similarly, a vector display could draw the lines on the screen more quickly than a raster display could copy the the same image from the frame buffer to the screen. (As soon as raster displays became fast and inexpensive, however, they quickly displaced vector displays because of their ability to display all types of images reasonably well.)

The divide between raster graphics and vector graphics persists in several areas of computer graphics. For example, it can be seen in a division between two categories of programs that can be used to create images: painting programs and drawing programs. In a painting program, the image is represented as a grid of pixels, and the user creates an image by assigning colors to pixels. This might be done by using a "drawing tool" that acts like a painter's brush, or even by tools that draw geometric shapes such as lines or rectangles. But the point in a painting program is to color the individual pixels, and it is only the pixel colors that are saved. To make this clearer, suppose that you use a painting program to draw a house, then draw a tree in front of the house. If you then erase the tree, you'll only reveal a blank background, not a house. In fact, the image never really contained a "house" at all - only individually colored pixels that the viewer might perceive as making up a picture of a house.

In a drawing program, the user creates an image by adding geometric shapes, and the image is represented as a list of those shapes. If you place a house shape (or collection of shapes making up a house) in the image, and you then place a tree shape on top of the house, the house is still there, since it is stored in the list of shapes that the image contains. If you delete the tree, the house will still be in the image, just as it was before you added the tree. Furthermore, you should be able to select one of the shapes in the image and move it or change its size, so drawing programs offer a rich set of editing operations that are not possible in painting programs. (The reverse, however, is also true.)

A practical program for image creation and editing might combine elements of painting and drawing, although one or the other is usually dominant. For example, a drawing program might allow the user to include a raster-type image, treating it as one shape. A painting program might let the user create "layers," which are separate images that can be layered one on top of another to create the final image. The layers can then be manipulated much like the shapes in a drawing program (so that you could keep both your house and your tree in separate layers, even if in the image of the house is in back of the tree).

Two well-known graphics programs are Adobe Photoshop and Adobe Illustrator. Photoshop is in the category of painting programs, while Illustrator is more of a drawing program. In the world of free software, the GNU image-processing program, Gimp, is a good alternative to Photoshop, while Inkscape is a reasonably capable free drawing program. Short introductions to Gimp and Inkscape can be found.

The divide between raster and vector graphics also appears in the field of graphics file formats. There are many ways to represent an image as data stored in a file. If the original image is to be recovered from the bits stored in the file, the representation must follow some exact, known specification. Such a specification is called a graphics file format. Some popular graphics file formats include GIF, PNG, JPEG, WebP, and SVG. Most images used on the Web are GIF, PNG, or JPEG, but most browsers also have support for SVG images and for the newer WebP format.

GIF, PNG, JPEG, and WebP are basically raster graphics formats; an image is specified by storing a color value for each pixel. GIF is an older file format, which has largely been superseded by PNG, but you can still find GIF images on the web. (The GIF format supports animated images, so GIFs are often used for simple animations on Web pages.) GIF uses an indexed color model with a maximum of 256 colors. PNG can use either indexed or full 24-bit color, while JPEG is meant for full color images.

The amount of data necessary to represent a raster image can be quite large. However, the data usually contains a lot of redundancy, and the data can be "compressed" to reduce its size. GIF and PNG use lossless data compression, which means that the original image can be recovered perfectly from the compressed data. JPEG uses a lossy data compression algorithm, which means that the image that is recovered from a JPEG file is not exactly the same as the original image; some information has been lost. This might not sound like a good idea, but in fact the difference is often not very noticeable, and using lossy compression usually permits a greater reduction in the size of the compressed data. JPEG generally works well for photographic images, but not as well for images that have sharp edges between different colors. It is especially bad for line drawings and images that contain text; PNG is the preferred format for such images. WebP can use both lossless and lossy compression.

SVG, on the other hand, is fundamentally a vector graphics format (although SVG images can include raster images). SVG is actually an XML-based language for describing twodimensional vector graphics images. "SVG" stands for "Scalable Vector Graphics," and the term "scalable" indicates one of the advantages of vector graphics: There is no loss of quality when the size of the image is increased. A line between two points can be represented at any scale, and it is still the same perfect geometric line. If you try to greatly increase the size of a raster image, on the other hand, you will find that you don't have enough color values for all the pixels in the new image; each pixel from the original image will be expanded to cover a rectangle of pixels in the scaled image, and you will get multi-pixel blocks of uniform color. The scalable nature of SVG images make them a good choice for web browsers and for graphical elements on your computer's desktop. And indeed, some desktop environments are now using SVG images for their desktop icons.

A digital image, no matter what its format, is specified using a coordinate system. A coordinate system sets up a correspondence between numbers and geometric points. In two dimensions, each point is assigned a pair of numbers, which are called the coordinates of the point. The two coordinates of a point are often called its x-coordinate and y-coordinate, although the names " x " and " y " are arbitrary.

A raster image is a two-dimensional grid of pixels arranged into rows and columns. As such, it has a natural coordinate system in which each pixel corresponds to a pair of integers giving the number of the row and the number of the column that contain the pixel. (Even in this simple case, there is some disagreement as to whether the rows should be numbered from top-to-bottom or from bottom-to-top.)

For a vector image, it is natural to use real-number coordinates. The coordinate system for an image is arbitrary to some degree; that is, the same image can be specified using different coordinate systems. I do not want to say a lot about coordinate systems here, but they will be a major focus of a large part of the book, and they are even more important in three-dimensional graphics than in two dimensions.

1.2 Elements of 3D Graphics

When we turn to 3D graphics, we find that the most common approaches have more in common with vector graphics than with raster graphics. That is, the content of an image is specified as a list of geometric objects. The technique is referred to as geometric modeling. The starting point is to construct an "artificial 3D world" as a collection of simple geometric shapes, arranged in three-dimensional space. The objects can have attributes that, combined with global properties of the world, determine the appearance of the objects. Often, the range of basic shapes is very limited, perhaps including only points, line segments, and triangles. A more complex shape such as a polygon or sphere can be built or approximated as a collection of more basic shapes, if it is not itself considered to be basic. To make a two-dimensional image of the scene, the scene is projected from three dimensions down to two dimensions. Projection is the equivalent of taking a photograph of the scene. Let's look at how it all works in a little more detail.

First, the geometry.... We start with an empty 3D space or "world." Of course, this space exists only conceptually, but it's useful to think of it as real and to be able to visualize it in your mind. The space needs a coordinate system that associates each point in the space with three numbers, usually referred to as the x, y, and z coordinates of the point. This coordinate system is referred to as "world coordinates."

We want to build a scene inside the world, made up of geometric objects. For example, we can specify a line segment in the scene by giving the coordinates of its two endpoints, and we can specify a triangle by giving the coordinates of its three vertices. The smallest building blocks that we have to work with, such as line segments and triangles, are called geometric primitives. Different graphics systems make different sets of primitive available, but in many cases only very basic shapes such as lines and triangles are considered primitive. A complex scene can contain a large number of primitives, and it would be very difficult to create the scene by giving explicit coordinates for each individual primitive. The solution, as any programmer should immediately guess, is to chunk together primitives into reusable components. For example, for a scene that contains several automobiles, we might create a geometric model of a wheel. An automobile can be modeled as four wheels together with models of other components. And we could then use several copies of the automobile model in the scene. Note that once a geometric model has been designed, it can be used as a component in more complex models. This is referred to as hierarchical modeling.

Suppose that we have constructed a model of a wheel out of geometric primitives. When that wheel is moved into position in the model of an automobile, the coordinates of all of its primitives will have to be adjusted. So what exactly have we gained by building the wheel? The point is that all of the coordinates in the wheel are adjusted in the same way. That is, to place the wheel in the automobile, we just have to specify a single adjustment that is applied to the wheel as a whole. The type of "adjustment" that is used is called a geometric transform (or geometric transformation). A geometric transform is used to adjust the size, orientation, and position of a geometric object. When making a model of an automobile, we build one wheel. We then apply four different transforms to the wheel model to add four copies of the wheel to the automobile. Similarly, we can add several automobiles to a scene by applying different transforms to the same automobile model.

The three most basic kinds of geometric transform are called scaling, rotation, and translation. A scaling transform is used to set the size of an object, that is, to make it bigger or smaller by some specified factor. A rotation transform is used to set an object's orientation, by rotating it by some angle about some specific axis. A translation transform is used to set the position of an object, by displacing it by a given amount from its original position. In this book, we will meet these transformations first in two dimensions, where they are easier to understand. But it is in 3D graphics that they become truly essential.

Next, appearance.... Geometric shapes by themselves are not very interesting. You have to be able to set their appearance. This is done by assigning attributes to the geometric objects. An obvious attribute is color, but getting a realistic appearance turns out to be a lot more complicated than simply specifying a color for each primitive. In 3D graphics, instead of color, we usually talk about material. The term material here refers to the properties that determine the intrinsic visual appearance of a surface. Essentially, this means how the surface interacts with light that hits the surface. Material properties can include a basic color as well as other properties such as shininess, roughness, and transparency.

One of the most useful kinds of material property is a texture. In most general terms, a texture is a way of varying material properties from point-to-point on a surface. The most common use of texture is to allow different colors for different points. This is often done by using a 2D image as a texture. The image can be applied to a surface so that the image looks like it is "painted" onto the surface. However, texture can also refer to changing values for things like transparency or "bumpiness." Textures allow us to add detail to a scene without using a huge number of geometric primitives; instead, you can use a smaller number of textured primitives.

A material is an intrinsic property of an object, but the actual appearance of the object also depends on the environment in which the object is viewed. In the real world, you don't see anything unless there is some light in the environment. The same is true in 3D graphics: you have to add simulated lighting to a scene. There can be several sources of light in a scene. Each light source can have its own color, intensity, and direction or position. The light from those sources will then interact with the material properties of the objects in the scene. Support for lighting in a graphics system can range from fairly simple to very complex and computationally intensive.

Finally, the image.... In general, the ultimate goal of 3D graphics is to produce 2D images of the 3D world. The transformation from 3D to 2D involves viewing and projection. The world looks different when seen from different points of view. To set up a point of view, we need to specify the position of the viewer and the direction that the viewer is looking. It is also necessary to specify an "up" direction, a direction that will be pointing upwards in the final image. This can be thought of as placing a "virtual camera" into the scene. Once the view is set up, the world as seen from that point of view can be projected into 2D. Projection is analogous to taking a picture with the camera.

The final step in 3D graphics is to assign colors to individual pixels in the 2D image. This process is called rasterization, and the whole process of producing an image is referred to as rendering the scene.

In many cases the ultimate goal is not to create a single image, but to create an animation, consisting a sequence of images that show the world at different times. In an animation, there are small changes from one image in the sequence to the next. Almost any aspect of a scene can change during an animation, including coordinates of primitives, transformations, material properties, and the view. For example, an object can be made to grow over the course of an animation by gradually increasing the scale factor in a scaling transformation that is applied to the object. And changing the view during an animation can give the effect of moving or flying through the scene. Of course, it can be difficult to compute the necessary changes. There are many techniques to help with the computation. One of the most important is to use a "physics engine," which computes the motion and interaction of objects based on the laws of physics. (However, you won't learn about physics engines in this book.)

1.3 Hardware and Software

We will be using OpenGL as the primary basis for 3D graphics programming. The original version of OpenGL was released in 1992 by a company named Silicon Graphics, which was known for its graphics workstations-powerful, expensive computers designed for intensive graphical applications. (Today, you probably have more graphics computing power on your smart phone.) OpenGL is supported by the graphics hardware in most modern computing devices, including desktop computers, laptops, and many mobile devices. This section will give you a bit of background about the history of OpenGL and about the graphics hardware that supports it.

In the first desktop computers, the contents of the screen were managed directly by the CPU. For example, to draw a line segment on the screen, the CPU would run a loop to set the color of each pixel that lies along the line. Needless to say, graphics could take up a lot of the CPU's time. And graphics performance was very slow, compared to what we expect today. So what has changed? Computers are much faster in general, of course, but the big change is that in modern computers, graphics processing is done by a specialized component called a ***GPU***, or Graphics Processing Unit. A GPU includes processors for doing graphics computations; in fact, it can include a large number of such processors that work in parallel to greatly speed up graphical operations. It also includes its own dedicated memory for storing things like images and lists of coordinates. GPU processors have very fast access to data that is stored in GPU memory - much faster than their access to data stored in the computer's main memory.

To draw a line or perform some other graphical operation, the CPU simply has to send commands, along with any necessary data, to the GPU, which is responsible for actually carrying out those commands. The CPU offloads most of the graphical work to the GPU, which is optimized to carry out that work very quickly. The set of commands that the GPU understands make up the API of the GPU. OpenGL is an example of a graphics API, and most GPUs support OpenGL in the sense that they can understand OpenGL commands, or at least that OpenGL commands can efficiently be translated into commands that the GPU can understand.

OpenGL is not the only graphics API. The best-known alternatives are probably the proprietary APIs used by Apple and Microsoft. Apple's MacOS uses an API known as Metal, while Microsoft Windows uses Direct3D. Nevertheless, OpenGL can currently still be used on MacOS and Windows. Furthermore, a newer open API named Vulkan has been defined as a replacement for OpenGL itself. Vulkan is a complex, low-level API designed more for speed and efficiency rather than ease-of-use, and it will likely not completely replace OpenGL for some time, if ever. Metal, Direct3D, and Vulkan are not covered in this textbook. We are using OpenGL since it provides an easier introduction to 3D graphics and because it is still the basis for 3D graphics in Web browsers.

I have said that OpenGL is an API, but in fact it is a series of APIs that have been subject to repeated extension and revision. The current version, in 2021, is 4.6, which was first released in 2017. It is very different from the 1.0 version from 1992. Furthermore, there is a specialized version called OpengGL ES for "embedded systems" such as mobile phones and tablets. And there is also WebGL, for use in Web browsers, which is basically a port of OpenGL ES. It will be useful to know something about how and why OpenGL has changed.

First of all, you should know that OpenGL was designed as a "client/server" system. The server, which is responsible for controlling the computer's display and performing graphics computations, carries out commands issued by the client. Typically, the server is a GPU, including its graphics processors and memory. The server executes OpenGL commands. The client is the CPU in the same computer, along with the application program that it is running. OpenGL commands come from the program that is running on the CPU. However, it is actually possible to run OpenGL programs remotely over a network. That is, you can execute an application program on a remote computer (the OpenGL client), while the graphics computations and display are done on the computer that you are actually using (the OpenGL server).

The key idea is that the client and the server are separate components, and there is a communication channel between those components. OpenGL commands and the data that they need are communicated from the client (the CPU) to the server (the GPU) over that channel. The capacity of the channel can be a limiting factor in graphics performance. Think of drawing an image onto the screen. If the GPU can draw the image in microseconds, but it takes milliseconds to send the data for the image from the CPU to the GPU, then the great speed of the GPU is irrelevant-most of the time that it takes to draw the image is communication time.

For this reason, one of the driving factors in the evolution of OpenGL has been the desire to limit the amount of communication that is needed between the CPU and the GPU. One approach is to store information in the GPU's memory. If some data is going to be used several times, it can be transmitted to the GPU once and stored in memory there, where it will be immediately accessible to the GPU. Another approach is to try to decrease the number of OpenGL commands that must be transmitted to the GPU to draw a given image.

OpenGL draws primitives such as triangles. Specifying a primitive means specifying coordinates and attributes for each of its vertices. In the original OpenGL 1.0, a separate command was used to specify the coordinates of each vertex, and a command was needed each time the value of an attribute changed. To draw a single triangle would require three or more commands. Drawing a complex object made up of thousands of triangles would take many thousands of commands. Even in OpenGL 1.1, it became possible to draw such an object with a single command instead of thousands. All the data for the object would be loaded into arrays, which could then be sent in a single step to the GPU. Unfortunately, if the object was going to be drawn more than once, then the data would have to be retransmitted each time the object was drawn. This was fixed in OpenGL 1.5 with Vertex Buffer Objects. A VBO is a block of memory in the GPU that can store the coordinates or attribute values for a set of vertices. This makes it possible to reuse the data without having to retransmit it from the CPU to the GPU every time it is used.

Similarly, OpenGL 1.1 introduced texture objects to make it possible to store several images on the GPU for use as textures. This means that texture images that are going to be reused several times can be loaded once into the GPU, so that the GPU can easily switch between images without having to reload them.

As new capabilities were added to OpenGL, the API grew in size. But the growth was still outpaced by the invention of new, more sophisticated techniques for doing graphics. Some of these new techniques were added to OpenGL, but the problem is that no matter how many features you add, there will always be demands for new features - as well as complaints that all the new features are making things too complicated! OpenGL was a giant machine, with new pieces always being tacked onto it, but still not pleasing everyone. The real solution was to make the machine programmable. With OpenGL 2.0, it became possible to write programs to be executed as part of the graphical computation in the GPU. The programs are run on the GPU at GPU speed. A programmer who wants to use a new graphics technique can write a program to implement the feature and just hand it to the GPU. The OpenGL API doesn't have to be changed. The only thing that the API has to support is the ability to send programs to the GPU for execution.

The programs are called shaders (although the term does't really describe what most of them actually do). The first shaders to be introduced were vertex shaders and fragment shaders. When a primitive is drawn, some work has to be done at each vertex of the primitive, such as applying a geometric transform to the vertex coodinates or using the attributes and global lighting environment to compute the color of that vertex. A vertex shader is a program that can take over the job of doing such "per-vertex" computations. Similarly, some work has to be done for each pixel inside the primitive. A fragment shader can take over the job of performing such "per-pixel" computations. (Fragment shaders are also called pixel shaders.)

The idea of programmable graphics hardware was very successful-so successful that in OpenGL 3.0, the usual per-vertex and per-fragment processing was deprecated (meaning that its use was discouraged). And in OpenGL 3.1, it was removed from the OpenGL standard, although it is still present as an optional extension. In practice, all the original features of OpenGL are still supported in desktop versions of OpenGL and will probably continue to be available in the future. On the embedded system side, however, with OpenGL ES 2.0 and later, the use of shaders is mandatory, and a large part of the OpenGL 1.1 API has been completely removed. WebGL, the version of OpenGL for use in web browsers, is based on OpenGL ES, and it also requires shaders to get anything at all done. Nevertheless, we will begin our study of OpenGL with version 1.1. Most of the concepts and many of the details from that version are still relevant, and it offers an easier entry point for someone new to 3D graphics programming.

OpenGL shaders are written in ***GLSL*** (OpenGL Shading Language). Like OpenGL itself, GLSL has gone through several versions. We will spend some time later in the course studying GLSL ES, the version used with WebGL and OpenGL ES. GLSL uses a syntax similar to the C programming language.

As a final remark on GPU hardware, I should note that the computations that are done for different vertices are pretty much independent, and so can potentially be done in parallel. The same is true of the computations for different fragments. In fact, GPUs can have hundreds or thousands of processors that can operate in parallel. Admittedly, the individual processors are much less powerful than a CPU, but then typical per-vertex and per-fragment computations are not very complicated. The large number of processors, and the large amount of parallelism that is possible in graphics computations, makes for impressive graphics performance even on fairly inexpensive GPUs.

Chapter 2

Two-Dimensional Graphics

With this chapter, we begin our study of computer graphics by looking at the twodimensional case. Things are simpler, and a lot easier to visualize, in 2D than in 3D, but most of the ideas that are covered in this chapter will also be very relevant to 3D.

The chapter begins with four sections that examine 2D graphics in a general way, without tying it to a particular programming language or graphics API. The coding examples in these sections are written in pseudocode that should make sense to anyone with enough programming background to be reading this book. In the next three sections, we will take quick looks at 2D graphics in three particular languages: Java with Graphics2D, JavaScript with HTML <canvas> graphics, and SVG. We will see how these languages use many of the general ideas from earlier in the chapter.

2.1 Pixels, Coordinates, and Colors

To create a two-dimensional image, each point in the image is assigned a color. A point in 2D can be identified by a pair of numerical coordinates. Colors can also be specified numerically. However, the assignment of numbers to points or colors is somewhat arbitrary. So we need to spend some time studying coordinate systems, which associate numbers to points, and color models, which associate numbers to colors.

2.1.1 Pixel Coordinates

A digital image is made up of rows and columns of pixels. A pixel in such an image can be specified by saying which column and which row contains it. In terms of coordinates, a pixel can be identified by a pair of integers giving the column number and the row number. For example, the pixel with coordinates (3,5) would lie in column number 3 and row number 5 . Conventionally, columns are numbered from left to right, starting with zero. Most graphics systems, including the ones we will study in this chapter, number rows from top to bottom, starting from zero. Some, including OpenGL, number the rows from bottom to top instead.

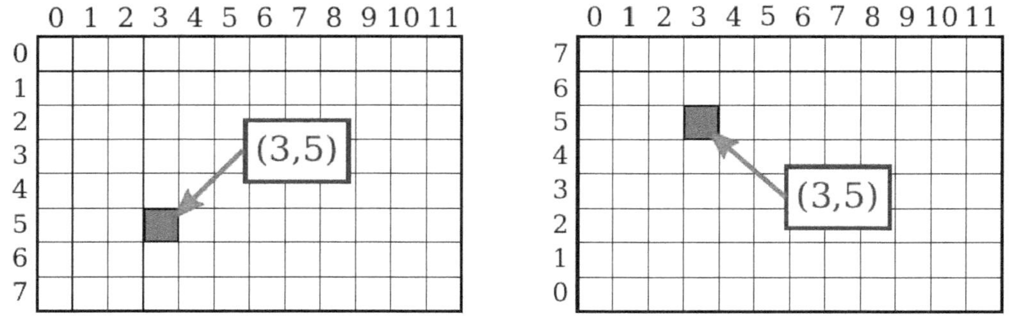

Row and column numbers identify a pixel, not a point. A pixel contains many points; mathematically, it contains an infinite number of points. The goal of computer graphics is not really to color pixels-it is to create and manipulate images. In some ideal sense, an image should be defined by specifying a color for each point, not just for each pixel. Pixels are an approximation. If we imagine that there is a true, ideal image that we want to display, then any image that we display by coloring pixels is an approximation. This has many implications.

Suppose, for example, that we want to draw a line segment. A mathematical line has no thickness and would be invisible. So we really want to draw a thick line segment, with some specified width. Let's say that the line should be one pixel wide. The problem is that, unless the line is horizontal or vertical, we can't actually draw the line by coloring pixels. A diagonal geometric line will cover some pixels only partially. It is not possible to make part of a pixel black and part of it white. When you try to draw a line with black and white pixels only, the result is a jagged staircase effect. This effect is an example of something called "aliasing." Aliasing can also be seen in the outlines of characters drawn on the screen and in diagonal or curved boundaries between any two regions of different color. (The term aliasing likely comes from the fact that ideal images are naturally described in real-number coordinates. When you try to represent the image using pixels, many real-number coordinates will map to the same integer pixel coordinates; they can all be considered as different names or "aliases" for the same pixel.)

Antialiasing is a term for techniques that are designed to mitigate the effects of aliasing. The idea is that when a pixel is only partially covered by a shape, the color of the pixel should be a mixture of the color of the shape and the color of the background. When drawing a black line on a white background, the color of a partially covered pixel would be gray, with the shade of gray depending on the fraction of the pixel that is covered by the line. (In practice, calculating this area exactly for each pixel would be too difficult, so some approximate method is used.) Here, for example, is a geometric line, shown on the left, along with two approximations of that line made by coloring pixels. The lines are greatly magnified so that you can see the individual pixels. The line on the right is drawn using antialiasing, while the one in the middle is not:

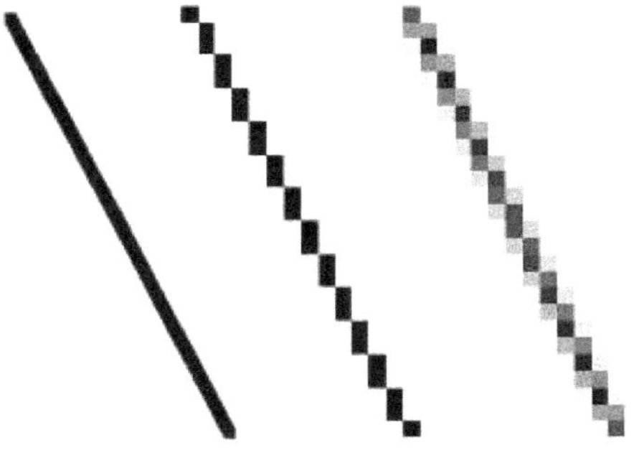

Note that antialiasing does not give a perfect image, but it can reduce the "jaggies" that are caused by aliasing (at least when it is viewed on a normal scale).

There are other issues involved in mapping real-number coordinates to pixels. For example, which point in a pixel should correspond to integer-valued coordinates such as (3,5) ? The center of the pixel? One of the corners of the pixel? In general, we think of the numbers as referring to the top-left corner of the pixel. Another way of thinking about this is to say that integer coordinates refer to the lines between pixels, rather than to the pixels themselves. But that still doesn't determine exactly which pixels are affected when a geometric shape is drawn. For example, here are two lines drawn using HTML canvas graphics, shown greatly magnified. The lines were specified to be colored black with a one-pixel line width:

The top line was drawn from the point (100,100) to the point (120,100). In canvas graphics, integer coordinates corresponding to the lines between pixels, but when a one-pixel line is drawn, it extends one-half pixel on either side of the infinitely thin geometric line. So for the top line, the line as it is drawn lies half in one row of pixels and half in another row. The graphics system, which uses antialiasing, rendered the line by coloring both rows of pixels gray. The bottom line was drawn from the point (100.5,100.5) to (120.5,120.5). In this case, the line lies exactly along one line of pixels, which gets colored black. The gray pixels at the ends of the bottom line have to do with the fact that the line only extends halfway into the pixels at its endpoints. Other graphics systems might render the same lines differently.

The interactive demo c2/pixel-magnifier.html lets you experiment with pixels and antialiasing. Interactive demos can be found on the web pages in the on-line version of this book. If you have downloaded the web site, you can also find the demos in the folder named demos. (Note that in any of the interactive demos that accompany this book, you can click the question mark icon in the upper left for more information about how to use it.)

All this is complicated further by the fact that pixels aren't what they used to be. Pixels today are smaller! The resolution of a display device can be measured in terms of the number of pixels per inch on the display, a quantity referred to as PPI (pixels per inch) or sometimes DPI (dots per inch). Early screens tended to have resolutions of somewhere close to 72 PPI. At that resolution, and at a typical viewing distance, individual pixels are clearly visible. For a while, it seemed like most displays had about 100 pixels per inch, but high resolution displays today can have 200,300 or even 400 pixels per inch. At the highest resolutions, individual pixels can no longer be distinguished.

The fact that pixels come in such a range of sizes is a problem if we use coordinate systems based on pixels. An image created assuming that there are 100 pixels per inch will look tiny on a 400 PPI display. A one-pixel-wide line looks good at 100 PPI, but at 400 PPI, a one-pixel-wide line is probably too thin.

In fact, in many graphics systems, "pixel" doesn't really refer to the size of a physical pixel. Instead, it is just another unit of measure, which is set by the system to be something appropriate. (On a desktop system, a pixel is usually about one one-hundredth of an inch. On a smart phone, which is usually viewed from a closer distance, the value might be closer to 1/160 inch. Furthermore, the meaning of a pixel as a unit of measure can change when, for example, the user applies a magnification to a web page.)

Pixels cause problems that have not been completely solved. Fortunately, they are less of a problem for vector graphics, which is mostly what we will use in this book. For vector graphics, pixels only become an issue during rasterization, the step in which a vector image is converted into pixels for display. The vector image itself can be created using any convenient coordinate system. It represents an idealized, resolution-independent image. A rasterized image is an approximation of that ideal image, but how to do the approximation can be left to the display hardware.

2.1.2 Real-number Coordinate Systems

When doing 2D graphics, you are given a rectangle in which you want to draw some graphics primitives. Primitives are specified using some coordinate system on the rectangle. It should be possible to select a coordinate system that is appropriate for the application. For example, if the rectangle represents a floor plan for a 15 foot by 12 foot room, then you might want to use a coordinate system in which the unit of measure is one foot and the coordinates range from 0 to 15 in the horizontal direction and 0 to 12 in the vertical direction. The unit of measure in this case is feet rather than pixels, and one foot can correspond to many pixels in the image. The coordinates for a pixel will, in general, be real numbers rather than integers. In fact, it's better to forget about pixels and just think about points in the image. A point will have a pair of coordinates given by real numbers.

To specify the coordinate system on a rectangle, you just have to specify the horizontal coordinates for the left and right edges of the rectangle and the vertical coordinates for the top and bottom. Let's call these values left, right, top, and bottom. Often, they are thought of as xmin, xmax, ymin, and ymax, but there is no reason to assume that, for example, top is less than bottom. We might want a coordinate system in which the vertical coordinate increases from bottom to top instead of from top to bottom. In that case, top will correspond to the maximum y-value instead of the minimum value.

To allow programmers to specify the coordinate system that they would like to use, it would be good to have a subroutine such as

```
setCoordinateSystem(left,right,bottom,top)
```

The graphics system would then be responsible for automatically transforming the coordinates from the specfiied coordinate system into pixel coordinates. Such a subroutine might not be available, so it's useful to see how the transformation is done by hand. Let's consider the general case. Given coordinates for a point in one coordinate system, we want to find the coordinates for the same point in a second coordinate system. (Remember that a coordinate system is just a way of assigning numbers to points. It's the points that are real!) Suppose that the horizontal and vertical limits are oldLeft, oldRight, oldTop, and oldBottom for the first coordinate system, and are newLeft, newRight, newTop, and newBottom for the second. Suppose that a point has coordinates (old X, old Y) in the first coordinate system. We want to find the coordinates $(newX, newY)$ of the point in the second coordinate system.

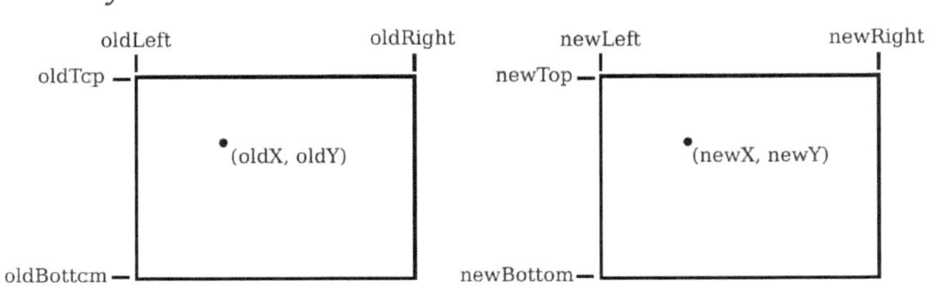

Formulas for new X and new Y are then given by

```
newX = newLeft +
    ((oldX - oldLeft) / (oldRight - oldLeft)) * (newRight - newLeft))
newY = newTop +
    ((oldY - oldTop) / (oldBottom - oldTop)) * (newBotom - newTop)
```

The logic here is that old *X* is located at a certain fraction of the distance from oldLeft to oldRight. That fraction is given by

```
((oldX - oldLeft) / (oldRight - oldLeft))
```

The formula for new *X* just says that new *X* should lie at the same fraction of the distance from newLeft to newRight. You can also check the formulas by testing that they work when old *X* is equal to oldLeft or to oldRight, and when oldY is equal to oldBottom or to oldTop.

As an example, suppose that we want to transform some real-number coordinate system with limits left, right, top, and bottom into pixel coordinates that range from 0 at left to 800 at the right and from 0 at the top 600 at the bottom. In that case, newLeft and newTop are zero, and the formulas become simply

```
newX = ((oldX - left) / (right - left)) * 800
newY = ((oldY - top) / (bottom - top)) * 600
```

Of course, this gives new *X* and new *Y* as real numbers, and they will have to be rounded or truncated to integer values if we need integer coordinates for pixels. The reverse transformation-going from pixel coordinates to real number coordinates-is also useful. For example, if the image is displayed on a computer screen, and you want to react to mouse clicks on the image, you will probably get the mouse coordinates in terms of integer pixel coordinates, but you will want to transform those pixel coordinates into your own chosen coordinate system.

In practice, though, you won't usually have to do the transformations yourself, since most graphics APIs provide some higher level way to specify transforms. We will talk more about this in Section 2.3.

2.1.3 Aspect Ratio

The aspect ratio of a rectangle is the ratio of its width to its height. For example an aspect ratio of 2:1 means that a rectangle is twice as wide as it is tall, and an aspect ratio of 4: 3

means that the width is 4/3 times the height. Although aspect ratios are often written in the form width:height, I will use the term to refer to the fraction width/height. A square has aspect ratio equal to 1 . A rectangle with aspect ratio 5/4 and height 600 has a width equal to 600*(5/4), or 750 .

A coordinate system also has an aspect ratio. If the horizontal and vertical limits for the coordinate system are left, right, bottom, and top, as above, then the aspect ratio is the absolute value of (right - left) / (top - bottom) If the coordinate system is used on a rectangle with the same aspect ratio, then when viewed in that rectangle, one unit in the horizontal direction will have the same apparent length as a unit in the vertical direction. If the aspect ratios don't match, then there will be some distortion. For example, the shape defined by the equation $x^2 + y^2 = 9$ should be a circle, but that will only be true if the aspect ratio of the (x, y) coordinate system matches the aspect ratio of the drawing area.

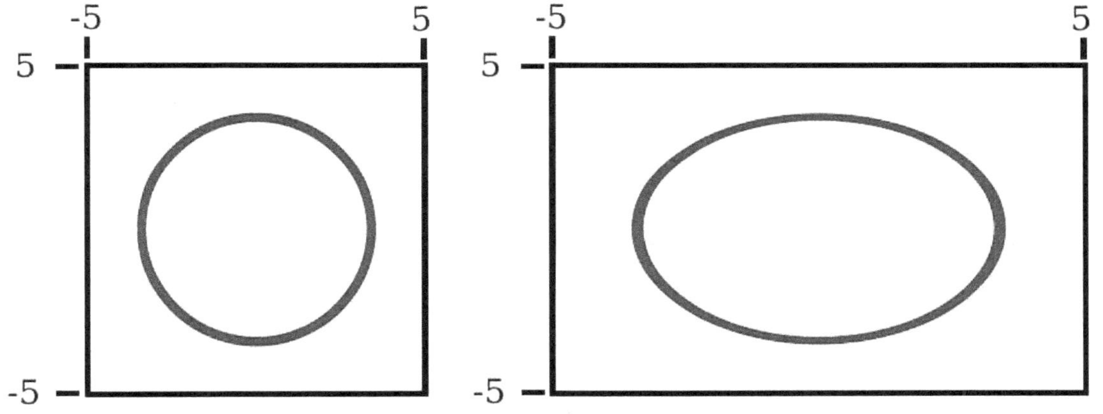

Suppose that x and y coordinates both range from -5 to 5, and we draw a "circle" of radius 3 with center at (0,0). If the drawing area is square, the "circle" looks like a circle; if not, the circle is distorted into an ellipse. The problem occurs when the aspect ratio of the coordinate system does not match the aspect ratio of the drawing area.

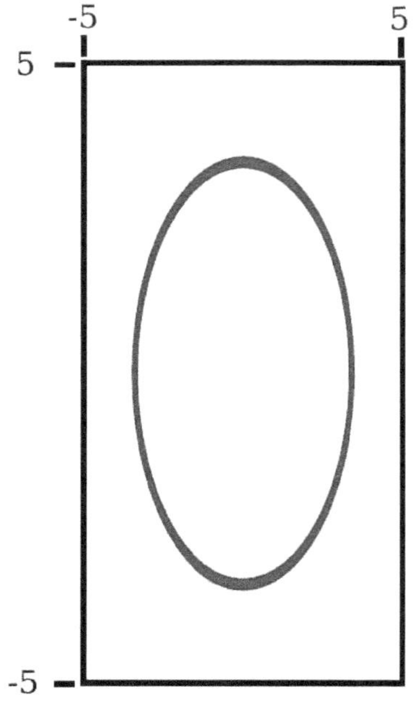

It is not always a bad thing to use different units of length in the vertical and horizontal directions. However, suppose that you want to use coordinates with limits left, right, bottom, and top, and that you do want to preserve the aspect ratio. In that case, depending on the shape of the display rectangle, you might have to adjust the values either of left and right or of bottom and top to make the aspect ratios match:

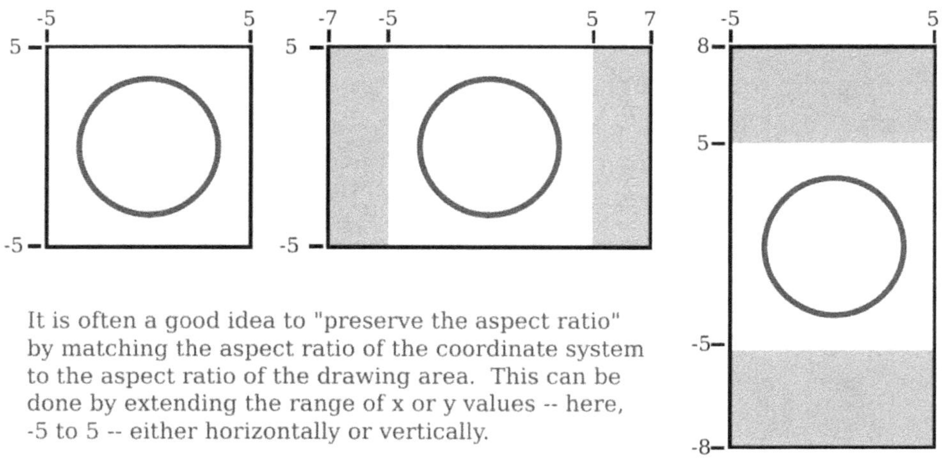

We will look more deeply into geometric transforms later in the chapter, and at that time, we'll see some program code for setting up coordinate systems.

2.1.4 Color Models

We are talking about the most basic foundations of computer graphics. One of those is coordinate systems. The other is color. Color is actually a surprisingly complex topic. We will look at some parts of the topic that are most relevant to computer graphics applications.

The colors on a computer screen are produced as combinations of red, green, and blue light. Different colors are produced by varying the intensity of each type of light. A color can be specified by three numbers giving the intensity of red, green, and blue in the color. Intensity can be specified as a number in the range zero, for minimum intensity, to one, for maximum intensity. This method of specifying color is called the ***RGB*** color model, where RGB stands for Red/Green/Blue. For example, in the RGB color model, the number triple (1,0.5,0.5) represents the color obtained by setting red to full intensity, while green and blue are set to half intensity. The red, green, and blue values for a color are called the color components of that color in the RGB color model.

Light is made up of waves with a variety of wavelengths. A pure color is one for which all the light has the same wavelength, but in general, a color can contain many wavelengthsmathematically, an infinite number. How then can we represent all colors by combining just red, green, and blue light? In fact, we can't quite do that.

You might have heard that combinations of the three basic, or "primary," colors are sufficient to represent all colors, because the human eye has three kinds of color sensors that detect red, green, and blue light. However, that is only an approximation. The eye does contain three kinds of color sensor. The sensors are called "cone cells." However, cone cells do not respond exclusively to red, green, and blue light. Each kind of cone cell responds, to a varying degree, to wavelengths of light in a wide range. A given mix of wavelengths will stimulate each type of cell to a certain degree, and the intensity of stimulation determines the color that we see. A different mixture of wavelengths that stimulates each type of cone cell to the same extent will be perceived as the same color. So a perceived color can, in fact, be specified by three numbers giving the intensity of stimulation of the three types of cone cell. However, it is not possible to produce all possible patterns of stimulation by combining just three basic colors, no matter how those colors are chosen. This is just a fact about the way our eyes actually work; it might have been different. Three basic colors can produce a reasonably large fraction of the set of perceivable colors, but there are colors that you can see in the world that you will never see on your computer screen. (This whole discussion only applies to people who actually have three kinds of cone cell. Color blindness, where someone is missing one or more kinds of cone cell, is surprisingly common.)

The range of colors that can be produced by a device such as a computer screen is called the color gamut of that device. Different computer screens can have different color gamuts, and the same RGB values can produce somewhat different colors on different screens. The color gamut of a color printer is noticeably different - and probably smaller - than the color gamut of a screen, which explain why a printed image probably doesn't look exactly the same as it did on the screen. (Printers, by the way, make colors differently from the way a screen does it. Whereas a screen combines light to make a color, a printer combines inks or dyes. Because of this difference, colors meant for printers are often expressed using a different set of basic colors. A common color model for printer colors is CMYK, using the colors cyan, magenta, yellow, and black.)

In any case, the most common color model for computer graphics is RGB. RGB colors are most often represented using 8 bits per color component, a total of 24 bits to represent a color. This representation is sometimes called " 24 -bit color." An 8 -bit number can represent 2^8, or 256 , different values, which we can take to be the positive integers from 0 to 255 . A color is then specified as a triple of integers (r, g, b) in that range.

This representation works well because 256 shades of red, green, and blue are about as many as the eye can distinguish. In applications where images are processed by computing with color components, it is common to use additional bits per color component, to avoid visual effects that might occur due to rounding errors in the computations. Such applications might use a 16 -bit integer or even a 32 -bit floating point value for each color component. On the other hand, sometimes fewer bits are used. For example, one common color scheme uses 5 bits for the red and blue components and 6 bits for the green component, for a total of 16 bits for a color. (Green gets an extra bit because the eye is more sensitive to green light than to red or blue.) This "16-bit color" saves memory compared to 24-bit color and was more common when memory was more expensive.

There are many other color models besides RGB. RGB is sometimes criticized as being unintuitive. For example, it's not obvious to most people that yellow is made of a combination of red and green. The closely related color models ***HSV*** and ***HSL*** describe the same set of colors as RGB, but attempt to do it in a more intuitive way. (HSV is sometimes called HSB, with the "B" standing for "brightness." HSV and HSB are exactly the same model.)

The "H" in these models stands for "hue," a basic spectral color. As H increases, the color changes from red to yellow to green to cyan to blue to magenta, and then back to red. The value of H is often taken to range from 0 to 360 , since the colors can be thought of as arranged around a circle with red at both 0 and 360 degrees.

The "S" in HSV and HSL stands for "saturation," and is taken to range from 0 to 1 . A saturation of 0 gives a shade of gray (the shade depending on the value of V or L). A saturation of 1 gives a "pure color," and decreasing the saturation is like adding more gray to the color. "V" stands for "value," and "L" stands for "lightness." They determine how bright or dark the color is. The main difference is that in the HSV model, the pure spectral colors occur for V = 1, while in HSL, they occur for L = 0.5.

Let's look at some colors in the HSV color model. The illustration below shows colors with a full range of H -values, for S and V equal to 1 and to 0.5 . Note that for S = V = 1, you get bright, pure colors. S = 0.5 gives paler, less saturated colors. V = 0.5 gives darker colors.

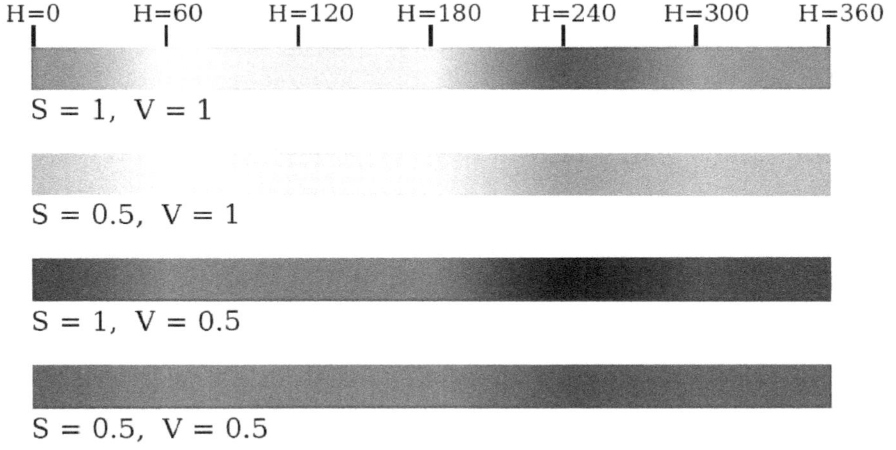

It's probably easier to understand color models by looking at some actual colors and how they are represented. The interactive demo *c2/rgb*-hsv.html lets you experiment with the RGB and HSV color models.

* * *

Often, a fourth component is added to color models. The fourth component is called alpha, and color models that use it are referred to by names such as RGBA and HSLA. Alpha is not a color as such. It is usually used to represent transparency. A color with maximal alpha value is fully opaque; that is, it is not at all transparent. A color with alpha equal to zero is completely transparent and therefore invisible. Intermediate values give translucent, or partly transparent, colors. Transparency determines what happens when you draw with one color (the foreground color) on top of another color (the background color). If the foreground color is fully opaque, it simply replaces the background color. If the foreground color is partly transparent, then it is blended with the background color.

Assuming that the alpha component ranges from 0 to 1 , the color that you get can be computed as

```
new_color = (alpha)*(foreground_color) + (1 - alpha)*(background_color)
```

This computation is done separately for the red, blue, and green color components. This is called alpha blending. The effect is like viewing the background through colored glass; the color of the glass adds a tint to the background color. This type of blending is not the only possible use of the alpha component, but it is the most common.

An RGBA color model with 8 bits per component uses a total of 32 bits to represent a color. This is a convenient number because integer values are often represented using 32 -bit values. A 32 -bit integer value can be interpreted as a 32 -bit RGBA color. How the color components are arranged within a 32 -bit integer is somewhat arbitrary. The most common layout is to store the alpha component in the eight high-order bits, followed by red, green, and blue. (This should probably be called ARGB color.) However, other layouts are also in use.

2.2 Shapes

We have been talking about low-level graphics concepts like pixels and coordinates, but fortunately we don't usually have to work on the lowest levels. Most graphics systems let you work with higher-level shapes, such as triangles and circles, rather than individual pixels and a lot of the hard work with coordinates is done using transforms rather than by working with coordinates directly. In this section and the next, we will look at some of the higher-level capabilities that are typically provided by 2D graphics APIs.

2.2.1 Basic Shapes

In a graphics API, there will be certain basic shapes that can be drawn with one command, whereas more complex shapes will require multiple commands. Exactly what qualifies as a basic shape varies from one API to another. In the WebGL API, for example, the only basic shapes are points, lines, and triangles. In this subsection, I consider lines, rectangles, and ovals to be basic.

By "line," I really mean line segment, that is a straight line segment connecting two given points in the plane. A simple one-pixel-wide line segment, without antialiasing, is the most basic shape. It can be drawn by coloring pixels that lie along the infinitely thin geometric line segment. An algorithm for drawing the line has to decide exactly which pixels to color. One of the first computer graphics algorithms, Bresenham's algorithm for line drawing, implements a very efficient procedure for doing so. I won't discuss such low-level details here, but it's worth looking them up if you want to start learning about what graphics hardware actually has to do on a low level. In any case, lines are typically more complicated. Antialiasing is one complication. Line width is another. A wide line might actually be drawn as a rectangle.

Lines can have other attributes, or properties, that affect their appearance. One question is, what should happen at the end of a wide line? Appearance might be improved by adding a rounded "cap" on the ends of the line. A square cap-that is, extending the line by half of the line width-might also make sense. Another question is, when two lines meet as part of a larger shape, how should the lines be joined? And many graphics systems support lines that are patterns of dashes and dots. This illustration shows some of the possibilities:

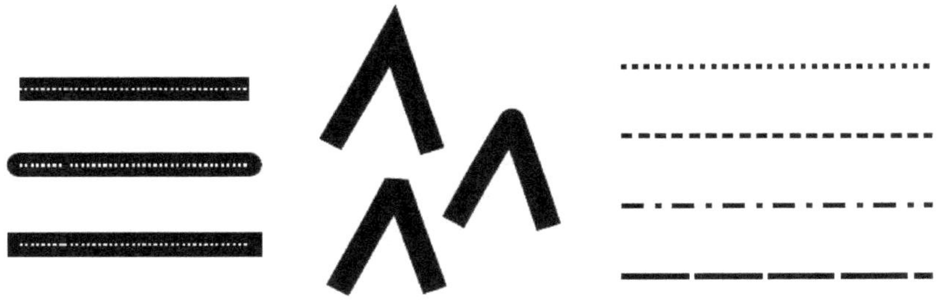

On the left are three wide lines with no cap, a round cap, and a square cap. The geometric line segment is shown as a dotted line. (The no-cap style is called "butt.") To the right are four lines with different patters of dots and dashes. In the middle are three different styles of line joins: mitered, rounded, and beveled.

The basic rectangular shape has sides that are vertical and horizontal. (A tilted rectangle generally has to be made by applying a rotation.) Such a rectangle can be specified with two points, (x1, y1) and (x2, y2), that give the endpoints of one of the diagonals of the rectangle. Alternatively, the width and the height can be given, along with a single base point, (x, y). In that case, the width and height have to be positive, or the rectangle is empty. The base point (x, y) will be the upper left corner of the rectangle if y increases from top to bottom, and it will be the lower left corner of the rectangle if y increases from bottom to top.

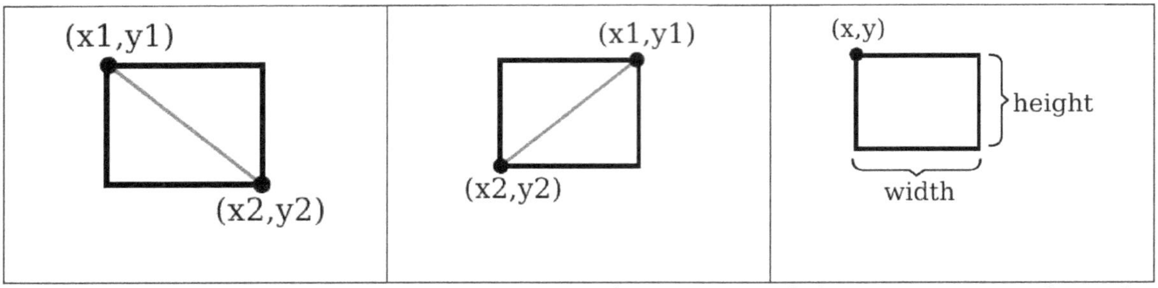

Suppose that you are given points (x1,y1) and (x2,y2), and that you want to draw the rectangle that they determine. And suppose that the only rectangle-drawing command that you have available is one that requires a point (x, y), a width, and a height. For that command, x must be the smaller of x 1 and x 2 , and the width can be computed as the absolute value of x 1 minus x 2 . And similarly for y and the height. In pseudocode,

```
DrawRectangle from points (x1,y1) and (x2,y2):
    x = min( x1, x2 )
    y = min( y1, y2 )
    width = abs( x1 - x2 )
    height = abs( y1 - y2 )
    DrawRectangle( x, y, width, height )
```

A common variation on rectangles is to allow rounded corners. For a "round rect," the corners are replaced by elliptical arcs. The degree of rounding can be specified by giving the horizontal radius and vertical radius of the ellipse. Here are some examples of round rects. For the shape at the right, the two radii of the ellipse are shown:

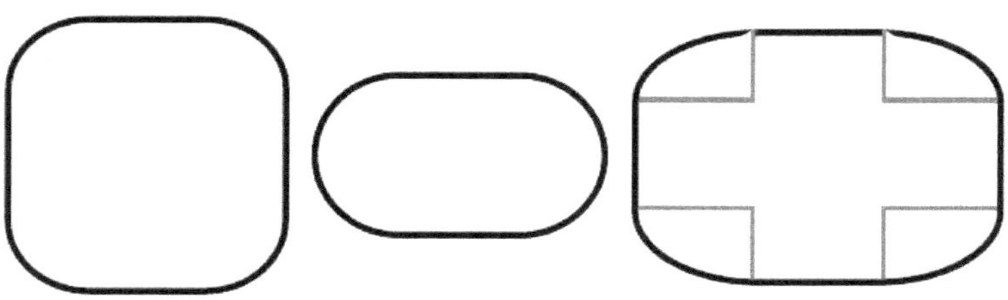

My final basic shape is the oval. (An oval is also called an ellipse.) An oval is a closed curve that has two radii. For a basic oval, we assume that the radii are vertical and horizontal. An oval with this property can be specified by giving the rectangle that just contains it. Or it can be specified by giving its center point and the lengths of its vertical radius and its horizontal radius. In this illustration, the oval on the left is shown with its containing rectangle and with its center point and radii:

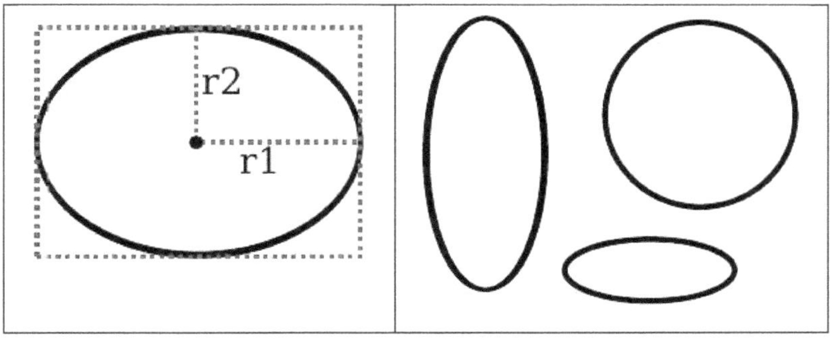

The oval on the right is a circle. A circle is just an oval in which the two radii have the same length.

If ovals are not available as basic shapes, they can be approximated by drawing a large number of line segments. The number of lines that is needed for a good approximation depends on the size of the oval. It's useful to know how to do this. Suppose that an oval has center point (x, y), horizontal radius r 1 , and vertical radius r 2 . Mathematically, the points on the oval are given by

```
( x + r1* cos(angle), y + r2*sin(angle) )
```

where angle takes on values from 0 to 360 if angles are measured in degrees or from 0 to 2π if they are measured in radians. Here sin and cos are the standard sine and cosine functions. To get an approximation for an oval, we can use this formula to generate some number of points and then connect those points with line segments. In pseudocode, assuming that angles are measured in radians and that *pi* represents the mathematical constant π,

```
Draw Oval with center (x,y), horizontal radius r1, and vertical radius
r2:
    for i = 0 to numberOfLines:
        angle1 = i * (2*pi/numberOfLines)
        angle2 = (i+1) * (2*pi/numberOfLines)
        a1 = x + r1* cos(angle1)
        b1 = y + r2*sin(angle1)
        a2 = x + r1* cos(angle2)
```

```
        b2 = y + r2*sin(angle2)
        Draw Line from (x1,y1) to (x2,y2)
```

For a circle, of course, you would just have r1 = r2. This is the first time we have used the sine and cosine functions, but it won't be the last. These functions play an important role in computer graphics because of their association with circles, circular motion, and rotation. We will meet them again when we talk about transforms in the next section.

2.2.2 Stroke and Fill

There are two ways to make a shape visible in a drawing. You can stroke it. Or, if it is a closed shape such as a rectangle or an oval, you can fill it. Stroking a line is like dragging a pen along the line. Stroking a rectangle or oval is like dragging a pen along its boundary. Filling a shape means coloring all the points that are contained inside that shape. It's possible to both stroke and fill the same shape; in that case, the interior of the shape and the outline of the shape can have a different appearance.

When a shape intersects itself, like the two shapes in the illustration below, it's not entirely clear what should count as the interior of the shape. In fact, there are at least two different rules for filling such a shape. Both are based on something called the winding number. The winding number of a shape about a point is, roughly, how many times the shape winds around the point in the positive direction, which I take here to be counterclockwise. Winding number can be negative when the winding is in the opposite direction. In the illustration, the shapes on the left are traced in the direction shown, and the winding number about each region is shown as a number inside the region.

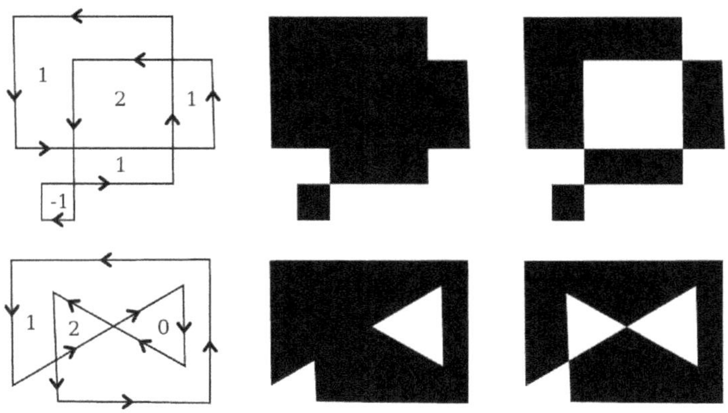

The shapes are also shown filled using the two fill rules. For the shapes in the center, the fill rule is to color any region that has a non-zero winding number. For the shapes shown on the right, the rule is to color any region whose winding number is odd; regions with even winding number are not filled.

There is still the question of what a shape should be filled with. Of course, it can be filled with a color, but other types of fill are possible, including patterns and gradients. A pattern is an image, usually a small image. When used to fill a shape, a pattern can be repeated horizontally and vertically as necessary to cover the entire shape. A gradient is similar in that it is a way for color to vary from point to point, but instead of taking the colors from an image, they are computed. There are a lot of variations to the basic idea, but there is always a line segment along which the color varies. The color is specified at the endpoints of the line segment, and possibly at additional points; between those points, the color is interpolated. The color can also be extrapolated to other points on the line that contains the line segment but lying outside the line segment; this can be done either by repeating the pattern from the line segment or by simply extending the color from the nearest endpoint. For a linear gradient, the color is constant along lines perpendicular to the basic line segment, so you get lines of solid color going in that direction. In a radial gradient, the color is constant along circles centered at one of the endpoints of the line segment. And that doesn't exhaust the possibilities. To give you an idea what patterns and gradients can look like, here is a shape, filled with two gradients and two patterns:

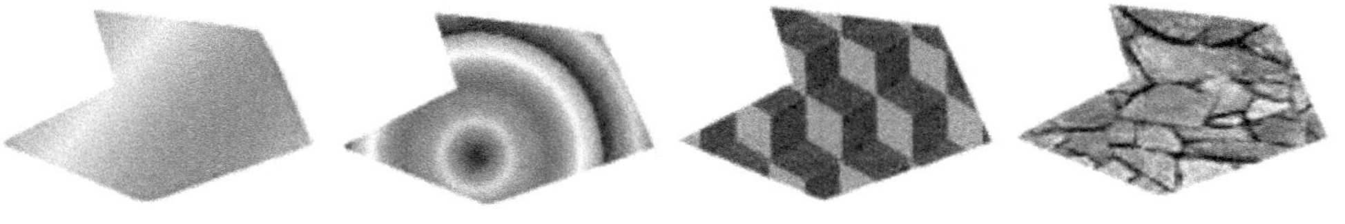

The first shape is filled with a simple linear gradient defined by just two colors, while the second shape uses a radial gradient.

Patterns and gradients are not necessarily restricted to filling shapes. Stroking a shape is, after all, the same as filling a band of pixels along the boundary of the shape, and that can be done with a gradient or a pattern, instead of with a solid color.

Finally, I will mention that a string of text can be considered to be a shape for the purpose of drawing it. The boundary of the shape is the outline of the characters. The text is drawn by filling that shape. In some graphics systems, it is also possible to stroke the outline of the shape that defines the text. In the following illustration, the string "Graphics" is shown, on top, filled with a pattern and, below that, filled with a gradient and stroked with solid black:

2.2.3 Polygons, Curves, and Paths

It is impossible for a graphics API to include every possible shape as a basic shape, but there is usually some way to create more complex shapes. For example, consider polygons. A polygon is a closed shape consisting of a sequence of line segments. Each line segment is joined to the next at its endpoint, and the last line segment connects back to the first. The endpoints are called the vertices of the polygon, and a polygon can be defined by listing its vertices.

In a regular polygon, all the sides are the same length and all the angles between sides are equal. Squares and equilateral triangles are examples of regular polygons. A convex polygon has the property that whenever two points are inside or on the polygon, then the entire line segment between those points is also inside or on the polygon. Intuitively, a convex polygon has no "indentations" along its boundary. (Concavity can be a property of any shape, not just of polygons.)

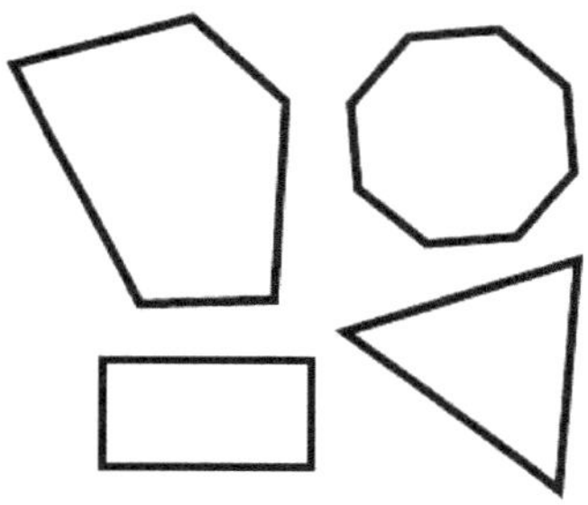

Convex Polygons

Non-convex Polygons

Sometimes, polygons are required to be "simple," meaning that the polygon has no selfintersections. That is, all the vertices are different, and a side can only intersect another side at its endpoints. And polygons are usually required to be "planar," meaning that all the vertices lie in the same plane. (Of course, in 2D graphics, everything lies in the same plane, so this is not an issue. However, it does become an issue in 3D.)

How then should we draw polygons? That is, what capabilities would we like to have in a graphics API for drawing them. One possibility is to have commands for stroking and for filling polygons, where the vertices of the polygon are given as an array of points or as an array of x -coordinates plus an array of y -coordinates. In fact, that is sometimes done; for example, the Java graphics API includes such commands. Another, more flexible, approach is to introduce the idea of a "path." Java, SVG, and the HTML canvas API all support this idea. A path is a general shape that can include both line segments and curved segments. Segments can, but don't have to be, connected to other segments at their endpoints. A path is created by giving a series of commands that tell, essentially, how a pen would be moved to draw the path. While a path is being created, there is a point that represents the pen's current location. There will be a command for moving the pen without drawing, and commands for drawing various kinds of segments. For drawing polygons, we need commands such as

- createPath() - start a new, empty path
- moveTo (x, y) - move the pen to the point (x, y), without adding a segment to the the path; that is, without drawing anything
- lineTo (x, y) - add a line segment to the path that starts at the current pen location and ends at the point (x, y), and move the pen to (x, y)
- closePath() - add a line segment from the current pen location back to the starting point, unless the pen is already there, producing a closed path. (For closePath, I need to define "starting point." A path can be made up of "subpaths" A subpath consists of a series of connected segments. A moveTo always starts a new subpath. A closePath ends the current segment and implicitly starts a new one. So "starting point" means the position of the pen after the most recent moveTo or closePath.)

Suppose that we want a path that represents the triangle with vertices at (100,100), (300,100), and (200,200). We can do that with the commands

```
createPath()
moveTo( 100, 100 )
lineTo( 300, 100 )
lineTo( 200, 200 )
```

```
closePath()
```

The closePath command at the end could be replaced by lineTo (100,100), to move the pen back to the first vertex.

A path represents an abstract geometric object. Creating one does not make it visible on the screen. Once we have a path, to make it visible we need additional commands for stroking and filling the path.

Earlier in this section, we saw how to approximate an oval by drawing, in effect, a polygon with a large number of sides. In that example, I drew each side as a separate line segment, so we really had a bunch of separate lines rather than a polygon. There is no way to fill such a thing. It would be better to approximate the oval with a polygonal path. For an oval with center (x, y) and radii r1 and r2:

```
createPath()
moveTo( x + r1, y )
for i = 1 to numberOfPoints-1
    angle = i * (2*pi/numberOfLines)
    lineTo( x + r1*cos(angle), y + r2*sin(angle) )
closePath()
```

Using this path, we could draw a filled oval as well as stroke it. Even if we just want to draw the outline of a polygon, it's still better to create the polygon as a path rather than to draw the line segments as separate sides. With a path, the computer knows that the sides are part of single shape. This makes it possible to control the appearance of the "join" between consecutive sides, as noted earlier in this section.

I noted above that a path can contain other kinds of segments besides lines. For example, it might be possible to include an arc of a circle as a segment. Another type of curve is a Bezier curve. Bezier curves can be used to create very general curved shapes. They are fairly intuitive, so that they are often used in programs that allow users to design curves interactively. Mathematically, Bezier curves are defined by parametric polynomial equations, but you don't need to understand what that means to use them. There are two kinds of Bezier curve in common use, cubic Bezier curves and quadratic Bezier curves; they are defined by cubic and quadratic polynomials respectively. When the general term "Bezier curve" is used, it usually refers to cubic Bezier curves.

A cubic Bezier curve segment is defined by the two endpoints of the segment together with two control points. To understand how it works, it's best to think about how a pen would draw the curve segment. The pen starts at the first endpoint, headed in the direction of the first control point. The distance of the control point from the endpoint controls the speed of the pen as it starts drawing the curve. The second control point controls the direction and speed of the pen as it gets to the second endpoint of the curve. There is a unique cubic curve that satisfies these conditions.

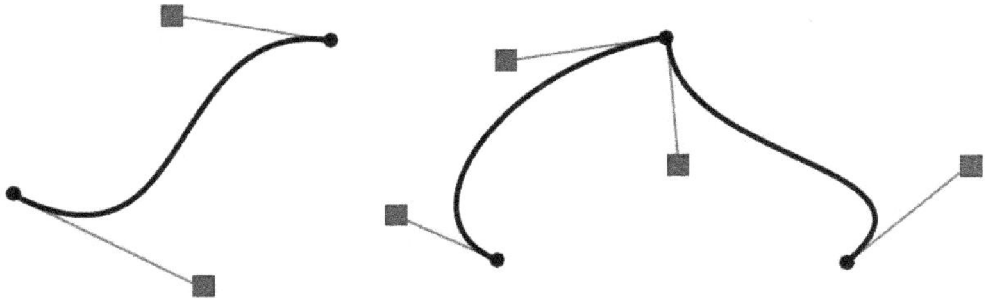

The illustration above shows three cubic Bezier curve segments. The two curve segments on the right are connected at an endpoint to form a longer curve. The curves are drawn as thick black lines. The endpoints are shown as black dots and the control points as blue squares, with a thin red line connecting each control point to the corresponding endpoint. (Ordinarily, only the curve would be drawn, except in an interface that lets the user edit the curve by hand.) Note that at an endpoint, the curve segment is tangent to the line that connects the endpoint to the control point. Note also that there can be a sharp point or corner where two curve segments meet. However, one segment will merge smoothly into the next if control points are properly chosen.

This will all be easier to understand with some hands-on experience. The interactive demo c2/cubic-bezier.html lets you edit cubic Bezier curve segments by dragging their endpoints and control points.

When a cubic Bezier curve segment is added to a path, the path's current pen location acts as the first endpoint of the segment. The command for adding the segment to the path must specify the two control points and the second endpoint. A typical command might look like

```
cubicCurveTo( cx1, cy1, cx2, cy2, x, y )
```

This would add a curve from the current location to point (x, y), using (cx1, cy1) and (cx2, cy2) as the control points. That is, the pen leaves the current location heading towards (cx1,cy1), and it ends at the point (x, y), arriving there from the direction of (cx2, cy2).

Quadratic Bezier curve segments are similar to the cubic version, but in the quadratic case, there is only one control point for the segment. The curve leaves the first endpoint heading in the direction of the control point, and it arrives at the second endpoint coming from the direction of the control point. The curve in this case will be an arc of a parabola.

Again, this is easier to understand this with some hands-on experience. Try the interactive demo c2/quadratic-bezier.html.

2.3 Transforms

In Section 2.1, we discussed coordinate systems and how it is possible to transform coordinates from one coordinate system to another. In this section, we'll look at that idea a little more closely, and also look at how geometric transformations can be used to place graphics objects into a coordinate system.

2.3.1 Viewing and Modeling

In a typical application, we have a rectangle made of pixels, with its natural pixel coordinates, where an image will be displayed. This rectangle will be called the viewport. We also have a set of geometric objects that are defined in a possibly different coordinate system, generally one that uses real-number coordinates rather than integers. These objects make up the "scene" or "world" that we want to view, and the coordinates that we use to define the scene are called world coordinates.

For 2D graphics, the world lies in a plane. It's not possible to show a picture of the entire infinite plane. We need to pick some rectangular area in the plane to display in the image. Let's call that rectangular area the window, or view window. A coordinate transform is used to map the window to the viewport.

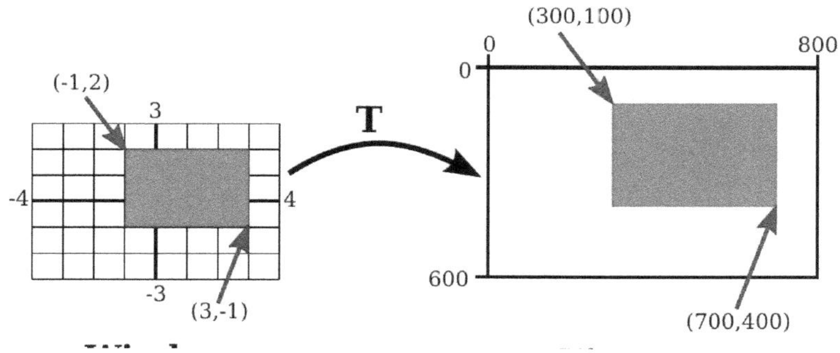

Viewport

In this illustration, **T** represents the coordinate transformation. **T** is a function that takes world coordinates (x, y) in some window and maps them to pixel coordinates $\mathbf{T}(x, y)$ in the viewport. (I've drawn the viewport and window with different sizes to emphasize that they are not the same thing, even though they show the same objects, but in fact they don't even exist in the same space, so it doesn't really make sense to compare their sizes.) In this example, as you can check,

$$T(x, y) = (800 * (x + 4)/8{,}600 * (3 - y)/6)$$

Look at the rectangle with corners at $(-1{,}2)$ and $(3, -1)$ in the window. When this rectangle is displayed in the viewport, it is displayed as the rectangle with corners $\mathbf{T}(-1{,}2)$ and $\mathbf{T}(3, -1)$. In this example, $\mathbf{T}(-1{,}2) = (300{,}100)$ and $\mathbf{T}(3, -1) = (700{,}400)$.

We use coordinate transformations in this way because it allows us to choose a world coordinate system that is natural for describing the scene that we want to display, and it is easier to do that than to work directly with viewport coordinates. Along the same lines, suppose that we want to define some complex object, and suppose that there will be several copies of that object in our scene. Or maybe we are making an animation, and we would like the object to have different positions in different frames. We would like to choose some convenient coordinate system and use it to define the object once and for all. The coordinates that we use to define an object are called object coordinates for the object. When we want to place the object into a scene, we need to transform the object coordinates that we used to define the object into the world coordinate system that we are using for the scene. The transformation that we need is called a modeling transformation. This picture illustrates an object defined in its own object coordinate system and then mapped by three different modeling transformations into the world coordinate system:

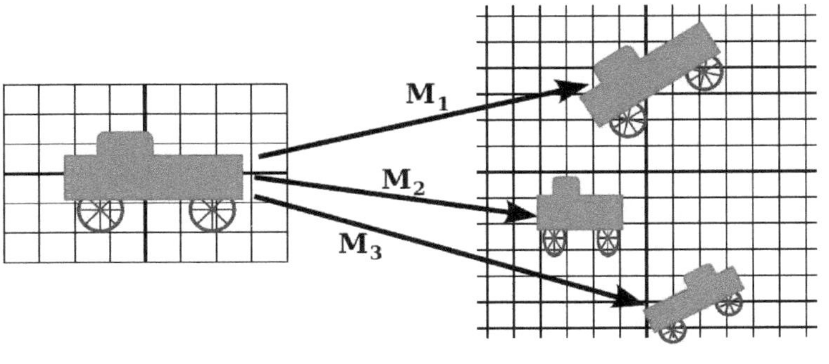

Remember that in order to view the scene, there will be another transformation that maps the object from a view window in world coordinates into the viewport.

Now, keep in mind that the choice of a view window tells which part of the scene is shown in the image. Moving, resizing, or even rotating the window will give a different view of the scene. Suppose we make several images of the same car:

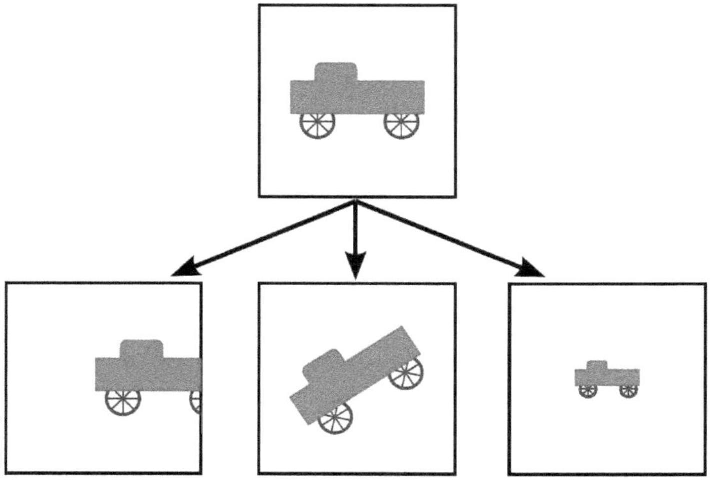

What happened between making the top image in this illustration and making the image on the bottom left? In fact, there are two possibilities: Either the car was moved to the right, or the view window that defines the scene was moved to the left. This is important, so be sure you understand it. (Try it with your cell phone camera. Aim it at some objects, take a step to the left, and notice what happens to the objects in the camera's viewfinder:

They move to the right in the picture!) Similarly, what happens between the top picture and the middle picture on the bottom? Either the car rotated counterclockwise, or the window was rotated clockwise. (Again, try it with a camera-you might want to take two actual photos so that you can compare them.) Finally, the change from the top picture to the one on the bottom right could happen because the car got smaller or because the window got larger. (On your camera, a bigger window means that you are seeing a larger field of view, and you can get that by applying a zoom to the camera or by backing up away from the objects that you are viewing.)

There is an important general idea here. When we modify the view window, we change the coordinate system that is applied to the viewport. But in fact, this is the same as leaving that coordinate system in place and moving the objects in the scene instead. Except that to get the same effect in the final image, you have to apply the opposite transformation to the objects (for example, moving the window to the left is equivalent to moving the objects to the right). So, there is no essential distinction between transforming the window and transforming the object. Mathematically, you specify a geometric primitive by giving coordinates in some natural coordinate system, and the computer applies a sequence of transformations to those coordinates to produce, in the end, the coordinates that are used to actually draw the primitive in the image. You will think of some of those transformations as modeling transforms and some as coordinate transforms, but to the computer, it's all the same.

The on-line version of this section includes the live demo c2/transform-equivalence-2d.html that can help you to understand the equivalence between modeling transformations and viewport transformations. Read the help text in the demo for more information.

We will return to this idea several times later in the book, but in any case, you can see that geometric transforms are a central concept in computer graphics. Let's look at some basic types of transformation in more detail. The transforms we will use in 2D graphics can be written in the form

```
$\mathrm{x} 1=\mathrm{a} * \mathrm{x}+\mathrm{b} *
\mathrm{y}+\mathrm{e}$
$\mathrm{y} 1=\mathrm{c} * \mathrm{x}+\mathrm{d} *
\mathrm{y}+\mathrm{f}$
```

where (x, y) represents the coordinates of some point before the transformation is applied, and $(x1, y1)$ are the transformed coordinates. The transform is defined by the six constants a, b, c, d, e, and f. Note that this can be written as a function **T**, where

```
$T(x, y)=(a * x+b * y+e, c * x+d * y+f)$
```

A transformation of this form is called an affine transform. An affine transform has the property that, when it is applied to two parallel lines, the transformed lines will also be parallel. Also, if you follow one affine transform by another affine transform, the result is again an affine transform.

2.3.2 Translation

A translation transform simply moves every point by a certain amount horizontally and a certain amount vertically. If (x, y) is the original point and ($x1, y1$) is the transformed point, then the formula for a translation is

```
x1 = x + e
y1 = y + f
```

where e is the number of units by which the point is moved horizontally and f is the amount by which it is moved vertically. (Thus for a translation, $a = d = 1$, and $b = c = 0$ in the general formula for an affine transform.) A 2D graphics system will typically have a function such as to apply a translate transformation. The translation would apply to everything that is drawn after the command is given. That is, for all subsequent drawing operations, e would be added to the x -coordinate and f would be added to the y -coordinate. Let's look at an example. Suppose that you draw an "F" using coordinates in which the "F" is centered at (0,0). If you say translate (4,2) before drawing the " F ", then every point of the " F " will be moved horizontally by 4 units and vertically by 2 units before the coordinates are actually used, so that after the translation, the "F" will be centered at (4,2):

```
translate( e, f )
```

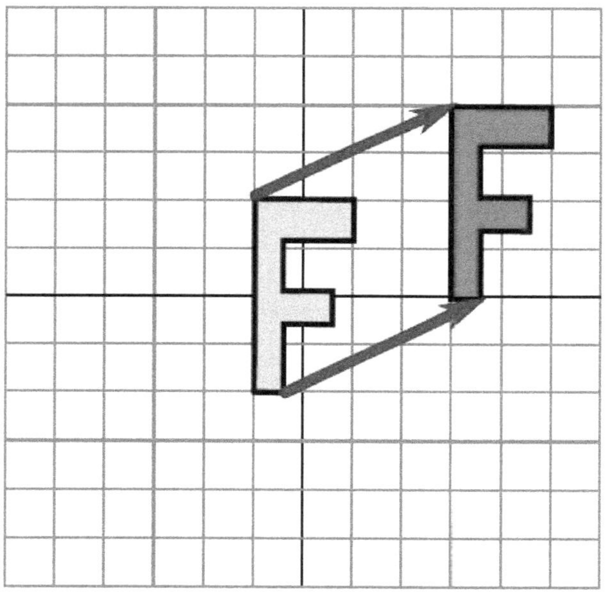

The light gray "F" in this picture shows what would be drawn without the translation; the dark red "F" shows the same "F" drawn after applying a translation by (4,2). The top arrow shows that the upper left corner of the "F" has been moved over 4 units and up 2 units. Every point in the "F" is subjected to the same displacement. Note that in my examples, I am assuming that the y -coordinate increases from bottom to top. That is, the y -axis points up.

Remember that when you give the command translate(e, f), the translation applies to all the drawing that you do after that, not just to the next shape that you draw. If you apply another transformation after the translation, the second transform will not replace the translation. It will be combined with the translation, so that subsequent drawing will be affected by the combined transformation. For example, if you combine translate (4,2) with translate (−1,5), the result is the same as a single translation, translate(3,7). This is an important point, and there will be a lot more to say about it later.

Also remember that you don't compute coordinate transformations yourself. You just specify the original coordinates for the object (that is, the object coordinates), and you specify the transform or transforms that are to be applied. The computer takes care of applying the transformation to the coordinates. You don't even need to know the equations that are used for the transformation; you just need to understand what it does geometrically.

2.3.3 Rotation

A rotation transform, for our purposes here, rotates each point about the origin, (0,0). Every point is rotated through the same angle, called the angle of rotation. For this purpose, angles can be measured either in degrees or in radians. (The 2D graphics APIs for Java and JavaScript that we will look at later in this chapter use radians, but OpenGL and SVG use degrees.) A rotation with a positive angle rotates objects in the direction from the positive x -axis towards the positive y -axis. This is counterclockwise in a coordinate system where the y -axis points up, as it does in my examples here, but it is clockwise in the usual pixel coordinates, where the y-axis points down rather than up. Although it is not obvious, when rotation through an angle of r radians about the origin is applied to the point (x, y), then the resulting point $(x1, y1)$ is given by

```
x1 = cos(r) * x - sin(r) * y
y1 = sin(r) * x + cos(r) * y
```

That is, in the general formula for an affine transform, $e = f = 0, a = d = \cos(r), b = -\sin(r)$, and $c = \sin(r)$. Here is a picture that illustrates a rotation about the origin by the angle negative 135 degrees:

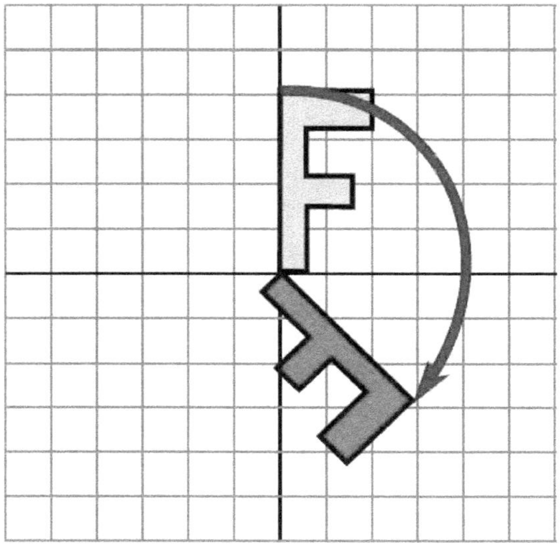

Again, the light gray "F" is the original shape, and the dark red "F" is the shape that results if you apply the rotation. The arrow shows how the upper left corner of the original " F " has been moved.

A 2D graphics API would typically have a command rotate(r) to apply a rotation. The command is used before drawing the objects to which the rotation applies.

2.3.4 Combining Transformations

We are now in a position to see what can happen when you combine two transformations. Suppose that before drawing some object, you say

```
translate(4,0)
rotate(90)
```

Assume that angles are measured in degrees. The translation will then apply to all subsequent drawing. But, because of the rotation command, the things that you draw after the translation are rotated objects. That is, the translation applies to objects that have already been rotated. An example is shown on the left in the illustration below, where the light gray "F" is the original shape, and red "F" shows the result of applying the two transforms to the original. The original "F" was first rotated through a 90 degree angle, and then moved 4 units to the right.

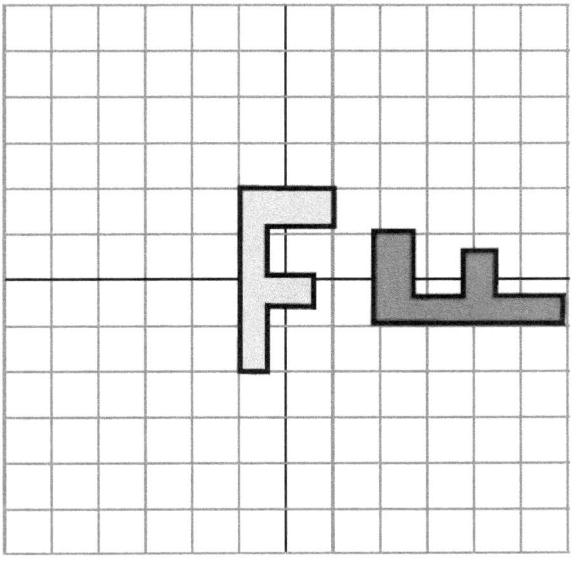

Rotate then translate

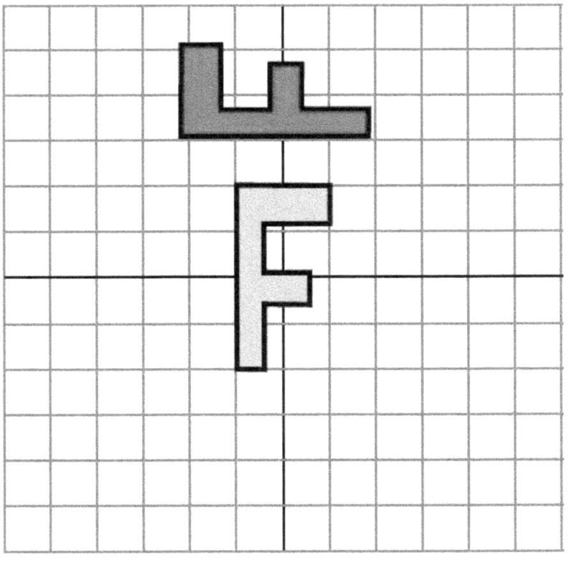

Translate then rotate

Note that transforms are applied to objects in the reverse of the order in which they are given in the code (because the first transform in the code is applied to an object that has already been affected by the second transform). And note that the order in which the transforms are applied is important. If we reverse the order in which the two transforms are applied in this example, by saying

```
rotate(90)
translate(4,0)
```

then the result is as shown on the right in the above illustration. In that picture, the original "F" is first moved 4 units to the right and the resulting shape is then rotated through an angle of 90 degrees about the origin to give the shape that actually appears on the screen.

For another example of applying several transformations, suppose that we want to rotate a shape through an angle r about a point (p, q) instead of about the point (0,0). We can do this by first moving the point (p, q) to the origin, using translate ($-p, -q$). Then we can do a standard rotation about the origin by calling rotate(r). Finally, we can move the origin back to the point (p, q) by applying translate (p, q). Keeping in mind that we have to write the code for the transformations in the reverse order, we need to say

```
translate(p,q)
rotate(r)
translate(-p,-q)
```

before drawing the shape. (In fact, some graphics APIs let us accomplish this transform with a single command such as rotate(r, p, q). This would apply a rotation through the angle r about the point (p, q).)

2.3.5 Scaling

A scaling transform can be used to make objects bigger or smaller. Mathematically, a scaling transform simply multiplies each x -coordinate by a given amount and each y -coordinate by a given amount. That is, if a point (x, y) is scaled by a factor of a in the x direction and by a factor of d in the y direction, then the resulting point $(x1, y1)$ is given by

```
x1 = a * x
y1 = d * y
```

If you apply this transform to a shape that is centered at the origin, it will stretch the shape by a factor of a horizontally and d vertically. Here is an example, in which the original light gray " F " is scaled by a factor of 3 horizontally and 2 vertically to give the final dark red " F ":

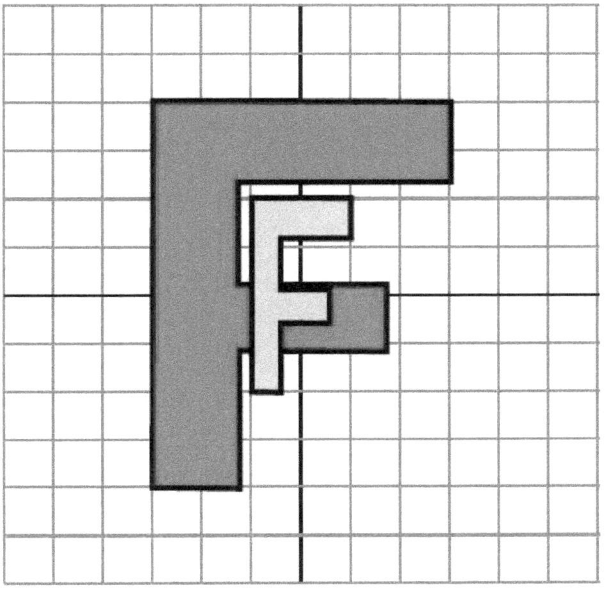

The common case where the horizontal and vertical scaling factors are the same is called uniform scaling. Uniform scaling stretches or shrinks a shape without distorting it.

When scaling is applied to a shape that is not centered at (0,0), then in addition to being stretched or shrunk, the shape will be moved away from 0 or towards 0 . In fact, the true description of a scaling operation is that it pushes every point away from (0,0) or pulls every point towards (0,0). If you want to scale about a point other than (0,0), you can use a sequence of three transforms, similar to what was done in the case of rotation.

A 2D graphics API can provide a function scale (a, d) for applying scaling transformations. As usual, the transform applies to all x and y coordinates in subsequent drawing operations. Note that negative scaling factors are allowed and will result in reflecting the shape as well as possibly stretching or shrinking it. For example, scale $(1, -1)$ will reflect objects vertically, through the x-axis.

It is a fact that every affine transform can be created by combining translations, rotations about the origin, and scalings about the origin. I won't try to prove that, but c2/transforms2 d.html is an interactive demo that will let you experiment with translations, rotations, and scalings, and with the transformations that can be made by combining them.

I also note that a transform that is made from translations and rotations, with no scaling, will preserve length and angles in the objects to which it is applied. It will also preserve aspect ratios of rectangles. Transforms with this property are called "Euclidean." If you also allow uniform scaling, the resulting transformation will preserve angles and aspect ratio, but not lengths.

2.3.6 Shear

We will look at one more type of basic transform, a shearing transform. Although shears can in fact be built up out of rotations and scalings if necessary, it is not really obvious how to do so. A shear will "tilt" objects. A horizontal shear will tilt things towards the left (for negative shear) or right (for positive shear). A vertical shear tilts them up or down. Here is an example of horizontal shear:

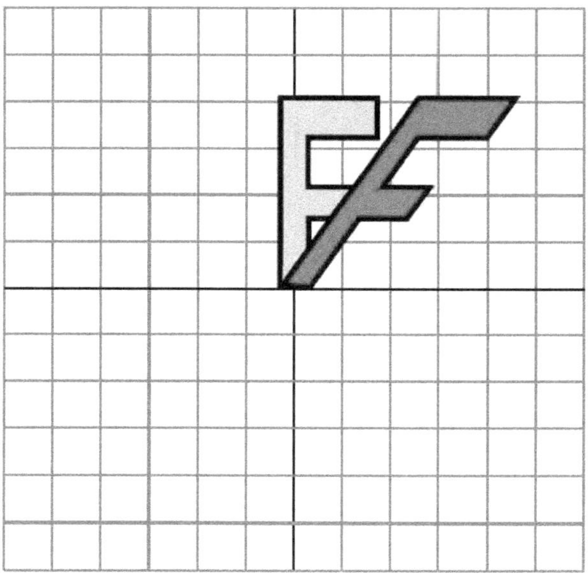

A horizontal shear does not move the x-axis. Every other horizontal line is moved to the left or to the right by an amount that is proportional to the y -value along that line. When a horizontal shear is applied to a point (x, y), the resulting point $(x1, y1)$ is given by

```
x1 = x + b * y
y1 = y
```

for some constant shearing factor b. Similarly, a vertical shear with shearing factor c is given by the equations

```
x1 = x
y1 = c * x + y
```

Shear is occasionally called "skew," but skew is usually specified as an angle rather than as a shear factor.

2.3.7 Window-to-Viewport

The last transformation that is applied to an object before it is displayed in an image is the window-to-viewport transformation, which maps the rectangular view window in the xy-plane that contains the scene to the rectangular grid of pixels where the image will be displayed. I'll assume here that the view window is not rotated; that it, its sides are parallel to the x and y -axes. In that case, the window-to-viewport transformation can be expressed in terms of translation and scaling transforms. Let's look at the typical case where the viewport has pixel coordinates ranging from 0 on the left to width on the right and from 0 at the top to height at the bottom. And assume that the limits on the view window are left, right, bottom, and top. In that case, the window-to-viewport transformation can be programmed as:

```
scale( width / (right-left), height / (bottom-top) );
translate( -left, -top )
```

These should be the last transforms that are applied to a point. Since transforms are applied to points in the reverse of the order in which they are specified in the program, they should be the first transforms that are specified in the program. To see how this works, consider a point (x, y) in the view window. (This point comes from some object in the scene. Several modeling transforms might have already been applied to the object to produce the point (x, y), and that point is now ready for its final transformation into viewport coordinates.) The coordinates (x, y) are first translated by (-left,-top) to give (x-left, y-top). These coordinates are then multiplied by the scaling factors shown above, giving the final coordinates

```
x1 = width / (right-left) * (x-left)
y1 = height / (bottom-top) * (y-top)
```

Note that the point (left,top) is mapped to (0,0), while the point (right,bottom) is mapped to (width,height), which is just what we want.

There is still the question of aspect ratio. As noted in Subsection 2.1.3, if we want to force the aspect ratio of the window to match the aspect ratio of the viewport, it might be necessary to adjust the limits on the window. Here is pseudocode for a subroutine that will do that, again assuming that the top-left corner of the viewport has pixel coordinates (0,0):

```
subroutine applyWindowToViewportTransformation (
            left, right, // horizontal limits on view window
            bottom, top, // vertical limits on view window
            width, height, // width and height of viewport
            preserveAspect // should window be forced to match viewport
aspect?
        )
    if preserveAspect :
        // Adjust the limits to match the aspect ratio of the drawing
area.
        displayAspect = abs(height / width);
        windowAspect = abs(( top-bottom ) / ( right-left ));
        if displayAspect > windowAspect :
                // Expand the viewport vertically.
                excess = (top-bottom) * (displayAspect/windowAspect -
1)
                top = top + excess/2
                bottom = bottom - excess/2
        else if displayAspect < windowAspect :
                // Expand the viewport horizontally.
                excess = (right-left) * (windowAspect/displayAspect -
1)
                right = right + excess/2
                left = left - excess/2
    scale( width / (right-left), height / (bottom-top) )
    translate( -left, -top )
```

2.3.8 Matrices and Vectors

The transforms that are used in computer graphics can be represented as matrices, and the points on which they operate are represented as vectors. Recall that a matrix, from the point of view of a computer scientist, is a two-dimensional array of numbers, while a vector is a onedimensional array. Matrices and vectors are studied in the field of mathematics called linear algebra. Linear algebra is fundamental to computer graphics. In fact, matrix and vector math is built into GPUs. You won't need to know a great deal about linear algebra for this textbook, but a few basic ideas are essential.

The vectors that we need are lists of two, three, or four numbers. They are often written as (x, y), (x, y, z), and (x, y, z, w). A matrix with N rows and M columns is called an "N-by-M matrix." For the most part, the matrices that we need are N -by- N matrices, where N is 2,3 , or 4 . That is, they have 2,3 , or 4 rows and columns, and the number of rows is equal to the number of columns.

If A and B are two N-by-N matrices, then they can be multiplied to give a product matrix $C = AB$. If A is an N -by- N matrix, and v is a vector of length N , then v can be multiplied by A to give another vector $w = Av$. The function that takes v to Av is a transformation; it transforms any given vector of size N into another vector of size N . A transformation of this form is called a linear transformation.

Now, suppose that A and B are N -by- N matrices and v is a vector of length N . Then, we can form two different products: $A(Bv)$ and $(AB)v$. It is a central fact that these two operations have the same effect. That is, we can multiply v by B and then multiply the result by A, or we can multiply the matrices A and B to get the matrix product AB and then multiply v by AB. The result is the same.

Rotation and scaling, as it turns out, are linear transformations. That is, the operation of rotating (x, y) through an angle d about the origin can be done by multiplying (x, y) by a 2 -by- 2 matrix. Let's call that matrix R_d. Similarly, scaling by a factor a in the horizontal direction and b in the vertical direction can be given as a matrix $S_{a,b}$. If we want to apply a scaling followed by a rotation to the point $v = (x, y)$, we can compute either $R_d(S_{a,b}v)$ or ($R_d S_{a,b})v$.

So what? Well, suppose that we want to apply the same two operations, scale then rotate, to thousands of points, as we typically do when transforming objects for computer graphics. The point is that we could compute the product matrix $R_d S_{a,b}$ once and for all, and then apply the combined transform to each point with a single multiplication. This means that if a program says

```
rotate(d)
scale(a,b)
    |
    \mathrm{ - // draw a complex object}
     .
```

the computer doens't have to keep track of two separate operations. It combines the operations into a single matrix and just keeps track of that. Even if you apply, say, 50 transformations to the object, the computer can just combine them all into one matrix. By using matrix algebra, multiple transformations can be handled as efficiently as a single transformation!

This is really nice, but there is a gaping problem: Translation is not a linear transformation. To bring translation into this framework, we do something that looks a little strange at first: Instead of representing a point in 2D as a pair of numbers (x, y), we represent it as the triple of numbers $(x, y, 1)$. That is, we add a one as the third coordinate. It then turns out that we can then represent rotation, scaling, and translation - and hence any affine transformation-on 2D space as multiplication by a 3 -by- 3 matrix. The matrices that we need have a bottom row containing (0,0,1). Multiplying $(x, y, 1)$ by such a matrix gives a new vector $(x1, y1, 1)$. We ignore the extra coordinate and consider this to be a transformation of (x, y) into $(x1, y1)$. For the record, the 3 -by-3 matrices for translation $(T_{a,b})$, scaling $(S_{a,b})$, and rotation (R_d) in 2D are

$$\mathbf{T_{a,b}} = \begin{pmatrix} 1 & 0 & \mathrm{a} \\ 0 & 1 & \mathrm{b} \\ 0 & 0 & 1 \end{pmatrix} \mathbf{S_{a,b}} = \begin{pmatrix} \mathrm{a} & 0 & 0 \\ 0 & \mathrm{b} & 0 \\ 0 & 0 & 1 \end{pmatrix} \mathbf{R_d} = \begin{pmatrix} \cos(\mathrm{d}) & -\sin(\mathrm{d}) & 0 \\ \sin(\mathrm{d}) & \cos(\mathrm{d}) & 0 \\ 0 & 0 & 1 \end{pmatrix}$$

You can compare multiplication by these matrices to the formulas given above for translation, scaling, and rotation. But when doing graphics programming, you won't need to do the multiplication yourself. For now, the important idea that you should take away from this discussion is that a sequence of transformations can be combined into a single transformation. The computer only needs to keep track of a single matrix, which we can call the "current matrix" or "current transformation." To implement transform commands such as translate(a,b) or rotate(d), the computer simply multiplies the current matrix by the matrix that represents the transform.

2.4 Hierarchical Modeling

In this section, we look at how complex scenes can be built from very simple shapes. The key is hierarchical structure. That is, a complex object can be made up of simpler objects, which can in turn be made up of even simpler objects, and so on until it bottoms out with simple geometric primitives that can be drawn directly. This is called hierarchical modeling. We will see that the transforms that were studied in the previous section play an important role in hierarchical modeling.

Hierarchical structure is the key to dealing with complexity in many areas of computer science (and in the rest of reality), so it be no surprise that it plays an important role in computer graphics.

2.4.1 Building Complex Objects

A major motivation for introducing a new coordinate system is that it should be possible to use the coordinate system that is most natural to the scene that you want to draw. We can extend this idea to individual objects in a scene: When drawing an object, use the coordinate system that is most natural for the object.

Usually, we want an object in its natural coordinates to be centered at the origin, (0,0), or at least to use the origin as a convenient reference point. Then, to place it in the scene, we can use a scaling transform, followed by a rotation, followed by a translation to set its size, orientation, and position in the scene. Recall that transformations used in this way are called modeling transformations. The transforms are often applied in the order scale, then rotate, then translate, because scaling and rotation leave the reference point, (0,0), fixed. Once the object has been scaled and rotated, it's easy to use a translation to move the reference point to any desired point in the scene. (Of course, in a particular case, you might not need all three operations.) Remember that in the code, the transformations are specified in the opposite order from the order in which they are applied to the object and that the transformations are specified before drawing the object. So in the code, the translation would come first, followed by the rotation and then the scaling. Modeling transforms are not always composed in this order, but it is the most common usage.

The modeling transformations that are used to place an object in the scene should not affect other objects in the scene. To limit their application to just the one object, we can save the current transformation before starting work on the object and restore it afterwards. How this is done differs from one graphics API to another, but let's suppose here that there are subroutines saveTransform() and restoreTransform() for performing those tasks. That is, saveTransform will make a copy of the modeling transformation that is currently in effect and store that copy. It does not change the current transformation; it merely saves a copy. Later, when restoreTransform is called, it will retrieve that copy and will replace the current modeling transform with the retrieved transform. Typical code for drawing an object will then have the form:

```
saveTransform()
translate(dx,dy) // move object into position
rotate(r) // set the orientation of the object
scale(sx,sy) // set the size of the object
    |
    \mathrm{ - // draw the object, using its natural coordinates}
    |
```

Note that we don't know and don't need to know what the saved transform does. Perhaps it is simply the so-called identity transform, which is a transform that doesn't modify the coordinates to which it is applied. Or there might already be another transform in place, such as a coordinate transform that affects the scene as a whole. The modeling transform for the object is effectively applied in addition to any other transform that was specified previously. The modeling transform moves the object from its natural coordinates into its proper place in the scene. Then on top of that, a coordinate transform that is applied to the scene as a whole would carry the object along with it.

Now let's extend this idea. Suppose that the object that we want to draw is itself a complex entity, made up of a number of smaller objects. Think, for example, of a potted flower made up of pot, stem, leaves, and bloom. We would like to be able to draw the smaller component objects in their own natural coordinate systems, just as we do the main object. For example, we would like to specify the bloom in a coordinate system in which the center of the bloom is at (0,0). But this is easy: We draw each small component object, such as the bloom, in its own coordinate system, and use a modeling transformation to move the sub-object into position within the main object. We are composing the complex object in its own natural coordinate system as if it were a complete scene.

On top of that, we can apply another modeling transformation to the complex object as a whole, to move it into the actual scene; the sub-objects of the complex object are carried along with it. That is, the overall transformation that applies to a sub-object consists of a modeling transformation that places the sub-object into the complex object, followed by the transformation that places the complex object into the scene.

In fact, we can build objects that are made up of smaller objects which in turn are made up of even smaller objects, to any level. For example, we could draw the bloom's petals in their own coordinate systems, then apply modeling transformations to place the petals into the natural coordinate system for the bloom. There will be another transformation that moves the bloom into position on the stem, and yet another transformation that places the entire potted flower into the scene. This is hierarchical modeling.

Let's look at a little example. Suppose that we want to draw a simple 2D image of a cart with two wheels.

This cart is used as one part of a complex scene in an example below. The body of the cart can be drawn as a pair of rectangles. For the wheels, suppose that we have written a subroutine drawWheel() that draws a wheel. This subroutine draws the wheel in its own natural coordinate system. In this coordinate system, the wheel is centered at (0,0) and has radius 1.

In the cart's coordinate system, I found it convenient to use the midpoint of the base of the large rectangle as the reference point. I assume that the positive direction of the *y*-axis points upward, which is the common convention in mathematics. The rectangular body of the cart has width 6 and height 2 , so the coordinates of the lower left corner of the rectangle are (−3,0), and we can draw it with a command such as fillRectangle (−3,0,6,2). The top of the cart is a smaller red rectangle, which can be drawn in a similar way. To complete the cart, we need to add two wheels to the object. To make the size of the wheels fit the cart, they need to be scaled. To place them in the correct positions relative to body of the cart, one wheel must be translated to the left and the other wheel, to the right. When I coded this example, I had to play around with the numbers to get the right sizes and positions for the wheels, and I found that the wheels looked better if I also moved them down a bit. Using the usual techniques of hierarchical modeling, we save the current transform before drawing each wheel, and we restore it after drawing the wheel. This restricts the effect of the modeling transformation for the wheel to that wheel alone, so that it does not affect any other part of the cart. Here is pseudocode for a subroutine that draws the cart in its own coordinate system:

```
subroutine drawCart() :
    saveTransform() // save the current transform
    translate(-1.65,-0.1) // center of first wheel will be at (-1.65,-
0.1)
    scale(0.8,0.8) // scale to reduce radius from 1 to 0.8
    drawWheel() // draw the first wheel
    restoreTransform() // restore the saved transform
    saveTransform() // save it again
    translate(1.5,-0.1) // center of second wheel will be at (1.5,-0.1)
    scale(0.8,0.8) // scale to reduce radius from 1 to 0.8
    drawWheel(g2) // draw the second wheel
    restoreTransform() // restore the transform
    setDrawingColor(RED) // use red color to draw the rectangles
    fillRectangle(-3, 0, 6, 2) // draw the body of the cart
    fillRectangle(-2.3, 1, 2.6, 1) // draw the top of the cart
```

It's important to note that the same subroutine is used to draw both wheels. The reason that two wheels appear in the picture in different positions is that different modeling transformations are in effect for the two subroutine calls.

Once we have this cart-drawing subroutine, we can use it to add a cart to a scene. When we do this, we apply another modeling transformation to the cart as a whole. Indeed, we could add several carts to the scene, if we wanted, by calling the drawCart subroutine several times with different modeling transformations.

You should notice the analogy here: Building up a complex scene out of objects is similar to building up a complex program out of subroutines. In both cases, you can work on pieces of the problem separately, you can compose a solution to a big problem from solutions to smaller problems, and once you have solved a problem, you can reuse that solution in several places.

The demo c2/cart-and-windmills.html uses the cart in an animated scene. Here's one of the frames from that demo:

You can probably guess how hierarchical modeling is used to draw the three windmills in this example. There is a drawWindmill method that draws a windmill in its own coordinate system. Each of the windmills in the scene is then produced by applying a different modeling transform to the standard windmill. Furthermore, the windmill is itself a complex object that is constructed from several sub-objects using various modeling transformations.

It might not be so easy to see how different parts of the scene can be animated. In fact, animation is just another aspect of modeling. A computer animation consists of a sequence of frames. Each frame is a separate image, with small changes from one frame to the next. From our point of view, each frame is a separate scene and has to be drawn separately. The same object can appear in many frames. To animate the object, we can simply apply a different modeling transformation to the object in each frame. The parameters used in the transformation can be computed from the current time or from the frame number. To make a cart move from left to right, for example, we might apply a modeling transformation

```
translate( frameNumber * 0.1, 0 )
```

to the cart, where frameNumber is the frame number. In each frame, the cart will be 0.1 units farther to the right than in the previous frame. (In fact, in the actual program, the translation that is applied to the cart is

```
translate( -3 + 13*(frameNumber % 300) / 300.0, 0 )
```

which moves the reference point of the cart from -3 to 13 along the horizontal axis every 300 frames. In the coordinate system that is used for the scene, the x-coordinate ranges from 0 to 7, so this puts the cart outside the scene for much of the loop.)

The really neat thing is that this type of animation works with hierarchical modeling. For example, the drawWindmill method doesn't just draw a windmill-it draws an animated windmill, with turning vanes. That just means that the rotation applied to the vanes depends on the frame number. When a modeling transformation is applied to the windmill, the rotating vanes are scaled and moved as part of the object as a whole. This is an example of hierarchical modeling. The vanes are sub-objects of the windmill. The rotation of the vanes is part of the modeling transformation that places the vanes into the windmill object. Then a further modeling transformation is applied to the windmill object to place it in the scene.

The file java2d/HierarchicalModeling2D.java contains the complete source code for a Java version of this example. The next section of this book covers graphics programming in Java. Once you are familiar with that, you should take a look at the source code, especially the paintComponent() method, which draws the entire scene. The same example, using the same scene graph API, is implemented in JavaScript in canvas2d/HierarchicalModel2D.html.

2.4.2 Scene Graphs

Logically, the components of a complex scene form a structure. In this structure, each object is associated with the sub-objects that it contains. If the scene is hierarchical, then the structure is hierarchical. This structure is known as a scene graph. A scene graph is a tree-like structure, with the root representing the entire scene, the children of the root representing the top-level objects in the scene, and so on. We can visualize the scene graph for our sample scene:

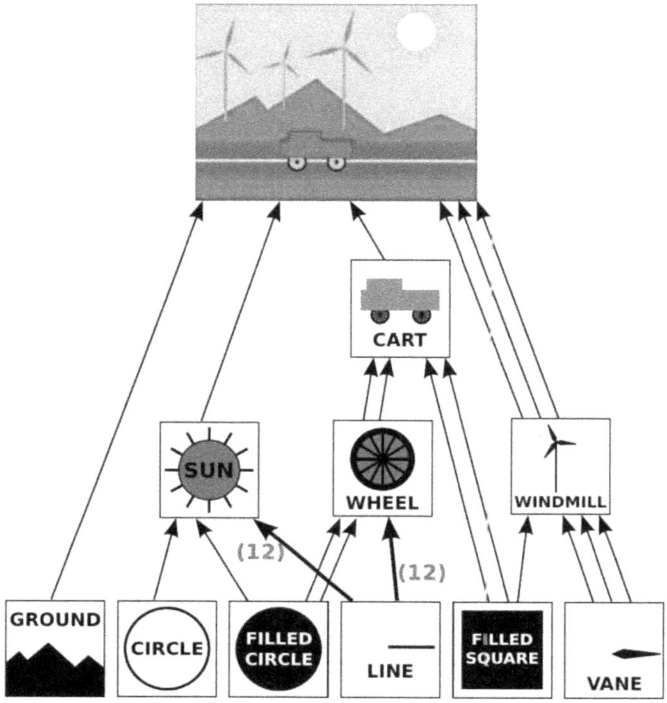

In this drawing, a single object can have several connections to one or more parent objects. Each connection represents one occurrence of the object in its parent object. For example, the "filled square" object occurs as a sub-object in the cart and in the windmill. It is used twice in the cart and once in the windmill. (The cart contains two red rectangles, which are created as squares with a non-uniform scaling; the pole of the windmill is made as a scaled square.) The "filled circle" is used in the sun and is used twice in the wheel. The "line" is used 12 times in the sun and 12 times in the wheel; I've drawn one thick arrow, marked with a 12 , to represent 12 connections. The wheel, in turn, is used twice in the cart. (My diagram leaves out, for lack of space, two occurrences of the filled square in the scene: It is used to make the road and the line down the middle of the road.)

Each arrow in the picture can be associated with a modeling transformation that places the sub-object into its parent object. When an object contains several copies of a sub-object, each arrow connecting the sub-object to the object will have a different associated modeling transformation. The object is the same for each copy; only the transformation differs.

Although the scene graph exists conceptually, in some applications it exists only implicitly. For example, the Java version of the program that was mentioned above draws the image "procedurally," that is, by calling subroutines. There is no data structure to represent the scene graph. Instead, the scene graph is implicit in the sequence of subroutine calls that draw the scene. Each node in the graph is a subroutine, and each arrow is a subroutine call. The various objects are drawn using different modeling transformations. As discussed in Subsection 2.3.8, the computer only keeps track of a "current transformation" that represents all the transforms that are applied to an object. When an object is drawn by a subroutine, the program saves the current transformation before calling the subroutine. After the subroutine returns, the saved transformation is restored. Inside the subroutine, the object is drawn in its own coordinate system, possibly calling other subroutines to draw sub-objects with their own modeling transformations. Those extra transformations will have no effect outside of the subroutine, since the transform that is in effect before the subroutine is called will be restored after the subroutine returns.

It is also possible for a scene graph to be represented by an actual data structure in the program. In an object-oriented approach, the graphical objects in the scene are represented by program objects. There are many ways to build an object-oriented scene graph API. For a simple example implemented in Java, you can take a look at java2d/SceneGraphAPI2D.java. This program draws the same animated scene as the previous example, but it represents the scene with an object-oriented data structure rather than procedurally. The same scene graph API is implemented in JavaScript in the live demo c2/cart-and-windmills.html, and you might take a look at its source code after you read about HTML canvas graphics in Section 2.6.

In the example program, both in Java and in JavaScript, a node in the scene graph is represented by an object belonging to a class named SceneGraphNode. SceneGraphNode is an abstract class, and actual nodes in the scene graph are defined by subclasses of that class. For example, there is a subclass named CompoundObject to represent a complex graphical object that is made up of sub-objects. A variable, obj, of type CompoundObject includes a method obj.add(subobj) for adding a sub-object to the compound object.

When implementing a scene graph as a data structure made up of objects, a decision has to be made about how to handle transforms. One option is to allow transformations to be associated with any node in the scene graph. In this case, however, I decided to use special nodes to represent transforms as objects of type TransformedObject. A TransformedObject is a SceneGraphNode that contains a link to another SceneGraphNode and also contains a modeling transformation that is to be applied to that object. The modeling transformation is given in terms of scaling, rotation, and translation amounts that are instance variables in the object. It is worth noting that these are always applied in the order scale, then rotate, then translate, no matter what order the instance variables are set in the code. If you want to do a translation followed by a rotation, you will need two TransformedObjects to implement it, since a translation plus a rotation in the same TransformedObject would be applied in the order rotate-then-translate. It is also worth noting that the setter methods for the scaling, rotation, and translation have a return value that is equal to the object. This makes it possible to chain calls to the methods into a single statement such as

```
transformedObject.setScale(5,2).setTranslation(3.5,0);
```

and even say things like

```
world.add(
    new
TransformedObject(windmill).setScale(0.4,0.4).setTranslation(2.2,1.3)
);
```

This type of chaining can make for more compact code and can eliminate the need for a lot of extra temporary variables.

Another decision has to be made about how to handle color. One possibility would be to make a ColoredObject class similar to TransformedObject. However, in this case I just added a setColor() method to the main ScreenGraphNode class. A color that is set on a compound object is inherited by any sub-objects, unless a different color is set on the sub-object. In other words, a color on a compound object acts as a default color for its sub-objects, but color can be overridden on the sub-objects.

In addition to compound objects and transformed objects, we need scene graph nodes to represent the basic graphical objects that occupy the bottom level of the scene graph. These are the nodes that do the actual drawing in the end.

For those who are familiar with data structures, I will note that a scene graph is actually an example of a "directed acyclic graph" or "dag." The process of drawing the scene involves a traversal of this dag. The term "acyclic" means that there can't be cycles in the graph. For a scene graph, this is the obvious requirement that an object cannot be a sub-object, either directly or indirectly, of itself.

2.4.3 The Transform Stack

Suppose that you write a subroutine to draw an object. At the beginning of the subroutine, you use a routine such as saveTransform() to save a copy of the current transform. At the end of the subroutine, you call restoreTransform() to reset the current transform back to the value that was saved. Now, in order for this to work correctly for hierarchical graphics, these routines must actually use a stack of transforms. (Recall that a stack is simply a list where items can be added, or "pushed," onto one end of the list and removed, or "popped," from the same end.) The problem is that when drawing a complex object, one subroutine can call other subroutines. This means that several drawing subroutines can be active at the same time, each with its own saved transform. When a transform is saved after another transform has already been saved, the system needs to remember both transforms. When restoreTransform() is called, it is the most recently saved transform that should be restored.

A stack has exactly the structure that is needed to implement these operations. Before you start drawing an object, you would push the current transform onto the stack. After drawing the object, you would pop the transform from the stack. Between those two operations, if the object is hierarchical, the transforms for its sub-objects will have been pushed onto and popped from the stack as needed.

Some graphics APIs come with transform stacks already defined. For example, the original OpenGL API includes the functions glPushMatrix() and glPopMatrix() for using a stack of transformation matrices that is built into OpenGL. The Java Graphics2D API does not include a built-in stack of transforms, but it does have methods for getting and setting the current transform, and the get and set methods can be used with an explicit stack data structure to implement the necessary operations. When we turn to the HTML canvas API for 2D graphics, we'll see that it includes functions named save() and restore() that are actually push and pop operations on a stack. These functions are essential to implementing hierarchical graphics for an HTML canvas.

Let's try to bring this all together by considering how it applies to a simple object in a complex scene: one of the filled circles that is part of the front wheel on the cart in our example scene. Here, I have rearranged part of the scene graph for that scene, and I've added labels to show the modeling transformations that are applied to each object:

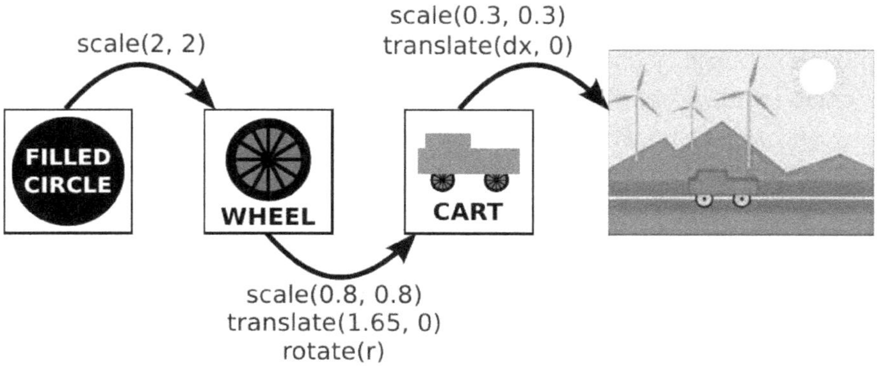

The rotation amount for the wheel and the translation amount for the cart are shown as variables, since they are different in different frames of the animation. When the computer starts drawing the scene, the modeling transform that is in effect is the identity transform, that is, no transform at all. As it prepares to draw the cart, it saves a copy of the current transform (the identity) by pushing it onto the stack. It then modifies the current transform by multiplying it by the modeling transforms for the cart, scale (0.3,0.3) and translate(dx, 0). When it comes to drawing the wheel, it again pushes the current transform (the modeling transform for the cart as a whole) onto the stack, and it modifies the current transform to take the wheel's modeling transforms into account. Similarly, when it comes to the filled circle, it saves the modeling transform for the wheel, and then applies the modeling transform for the circle.

When, finally, the circle is actually drawn in the scene, it is transformed by the combined transform. That transform places the circle directly into the scene, but it has been composed from the transform that places the circle into the wheel, the one that places the wheel into the cart, and the one that places the cart into the scene. After drawing the circle, the computer replaces the current transform with one it pops from the stack. That will be the modeling transform for the wheel as a whole, and that transform will be used for any further parts of the wheel that have to be drawn. When the wheel is done, the transform for the cart is popped. And when the cart is done, the original transform, the identity, is popped. When the computer goes onto the next object in the scene, it starts the whole process again, with the identity transform as the starting point.

This might sound complicated, but I should emphasize that it something that the computer does for you. Your responsibility is simply to design the individual objects, in their own natural coordinate system. As part of that, you specify the modeling transformations that are applied to the sub-objects of that object. You construct the scene as a whole in a similar way. The computer will then put everything together for you, taking into account the many layers of hierarchical structure. You only have to deal with one component of the structure at a time. That's the power of hierarchical design; that's how it helps you deal with complexity.

2.5 Java Graphics2D

In the rest of this chapter, we look at specific implementations of two-dimensional graphics. There are a few new ideas here, but mostly you will see how the general concepts that we have covered are used in several real graphics systems.

In this section, our focus is on the Java programming language. Java remains one of the most popular programming languages. Its standard desktop version includes a sophisticated 2D graphics API, which is our topic here. Before reading this section, you should already know the basics of Java programming. But even if you don't, you should be able to follow most of the discussion of the graphics API itself. (See Section A. 1 in Appendix A for a very basic introduction to Java.)

The graphics API that is discussed here is part of Swing, an API for graphical user interface programming that is included as part of the standard distribution of Java. Many Java programs are now written using an alternative API called JavaFX, which is not part of the standard distribution. JavaFX is not discussed in this textbook. Its graphics API is, in fact, quite similar to the API for HTML canvas graphics, which is discussed in Section 2.6.

The original version of Java had a much smaller graphics API. It was tightly focused on pixels, and it used only integer coordinates. The API had subroutines for stroking and filling a variety of basic shapes, including lines, rectangles, ovals, and polygons (although Java uses the term draw instead of stroke). Its specification of the meaning of drawing operations was very precise on the pixel level. Integer coordinates are defined to refer to the lines between pixels. For example, a 12 -by- 8 pixel grid has x-coordinates from 0 to 12 and y-coordinates from 0 to 8, as shown below. The lines between pixels are numbered, not the pixels.

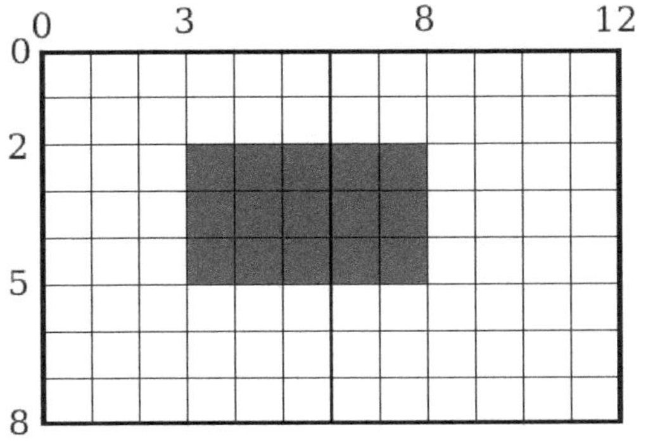

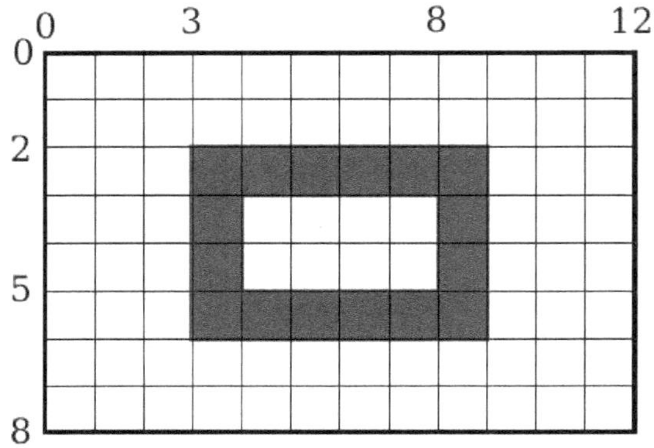

The command fillRect (3,2,5,3) fills the rectangle with upper left corner at (3,2), with width 5 , and with height 3 , as shown on the left above. The command drawRect(3,2,5,3) conceptually drags a "pen" around the outline of this rectangle. However, the pen is a 1 - pixel square, and it is the upper left corner of the pen that moves along the outline. As the pen moves along the right edge of the rectangle, the pixels to the right of that edge are colored; as the pen moves along the bottom edge, the pixels below the edge are colored. The result is as shown on the right above. My point here is not to belabor the details, but to point out that having a precise specification of the meaning of graphical operations gives you very fine control over what happens on the pixel level.

Java's original graphics did not support things like real-number coordinates, transforms, antialiasing, or gradients. Just a few years after Java was first introduced, a new graphics API was added that does support all of these. It is that more advanced API that we will look at here.

2.5.1 Graphics2D

Java is an object-oriented language. Its API is defined as a large set of classes, The actual drawing operations in the original graphics API were mostly contained in the class named Graphics. In the newer Swing API, drawing operations are methods in a class named Graphics2D, which is a subclass of Graphics, so that all the original drawing operations are still available. (A class in Java is contained in a collection of classes known as a "package." Graphics and Graphics2D, for example, are in the package named java.awt. Classes that define shapes and transforms are in a package named java.awt.geom.)

A graphics system needs a place to draw. In Java, the drawing surface is often an object of the class JPanel, which represents a rectangular area on the screen. The JPanel class has a method named paintComponent() to draw its content. To create a drawing surface, you can create a subclass of JPanel and provide a definition for its paintComponent() method. All drawing should be done inside paintComponent(); when it is necessary to change the contents of the drawing, you can call the panel's repaint() method to trigger a call to paintComponent(). The paintComponent() method has a parameter of type Graphics, but the parameter that is passed to the method is actually an object of type Graphics2D, and it can be type-cast to Graphics2D to obtain access to the more advanced graphics capabilities. So, the definition of the paintComponent() method usually looks something like this:

```
protected void paintComponent( Graphics g ) {
    Graphics2D g2;
    g2 = (Graphics2D)g; // Type-cast the parameter to Graphics2D.
        .
        . // Draw using g2.
}
```

In the rest of this section, I will assume that *g*2 is a variable of type Graphics2D, and I will discuss some of the things that you can do with it. As a first example, I note that Graphics2D supports antialiasing, but it is not turned on by default. It can be enabled in a graphics context g_2 with the rather intimidating command

```
g2.setRenderingHint(RenderingHints.KEY_ANTIALIASING,
    RenderingHints.VALUE_ANTIALIAS_ON) ;
```

For simple examples of graphics in complete Java programs, you can look at the sample programs java2d/GraphicsStarter.java and java2d/AnimationStarter.java. They provide very minimal frameworks for drawing static and animated images, respectively, using Graphics2D. The program java2d/EventsStarter.java is a similar framework for working with mouse and key events in a graphics program. You can use these programs as the basis for some experimentation if you want to explore Java graphics.

2.5.2 Shapes

Drawing with the original Graphics class is done using integer coordinates, with the measurement given in pixels. This works well in the standard coordinate system, but is not appropriate when real-number coordinates are used, since the unit of measure in such a coordinate system will not be equal to a pixel. We need to be able to specify shapes using real numbers. The Java package java.awt.geom provides support for shapes defined using real number coordinates. For example, the class Line2D in that package represents line segments whose endpoints are given as pairs of real numbers.

Now, Java has two real number types: double and float. The double type can represent a larger range of numbers than float, with a greater number of significant digits, and double is the more commonly used type. In fact, doubles are simply easier to use in Java. However, float values generally have enough accuracy for graphics applications, and they have the advantage of taking up less space in memory. Furthermore, computer graphics hardware often uses float values internally.

So, given these considerations, the java.awt.geom package actually provides two versions of each shape, one using coordinates of type float and one using coordinates of type double. This is done in a rather strange way. Taking Line2D as an example, the class Line2D itself is an abstract class. It has two subclasses, one that represents lines using float coordinates and one using double coordinates. The strangest part is that these subclasses are defined as nested classes inside Line2D: Line2D.Float and Line2D.Double. This means that you can declare a variable of type Line2D, but to create an object, you need to use Line2D.Double or Line2D.Float:

```
Line2D line1, line2;
line1 = new Line2D.Double(1,2,5,7); // Line from (1.0,2.0) to (5.0,7.0)
line2 = new Line2D.Float(2.7F,3.1F,1.5F,7.1F); // (2.7,3.1) to
(1.5,7.1)
```

Note that when using constants of type float in Java, you have to add "F" as a suffix to the value. This is one reason why doubles are easier in Java. For simplicity, you might want to stick to using Line2D.Double. However, Line2D.Float might give slightly better performance.

Let's take a look at some of the other classes from java.awt.geom. The abstract class Point2D - with its concrete subclasses Point2D.Double and Point2D.Float-represents a point in two dimensions, specified by two real number coordinates. A point is not a shape; you can't fill or stroke it. A point can be constructed from two real numbers ("new Point2D.Double(1.2,3.7)"). If p is a variable of type Point2D, you can use $p.\text{get}X()$ and $p.\text{get}Y()$ to retrieve its coordinates, and you can use p.set $X(x), p.\text{set}Y(y)$, or p.setLocation (x, y) to set its coordinates. If pd is a variable of type Point2D.Double, you can also refer directly to the coordinates as pd.x and pd.y (and similarly for Point2D.Float). Other classes in java.awt.geom offer a similar variety of ways to manipulate their properties, and I won't try to list them all here.

There is a variety of classes that represent geometric shapes, including Line2D, Rectangle2D, RoundRectangle2D, Ellipse2D, Arc2D, and Path2D. All of these are abstract classes, and each of them contains a pair of subclasses such as Rectangle2D.Double and Rectangle2D.Float. Some shapes, such as rectangles, have interiors that can be filled; such shapes also have outlines that can be stroked. Some shapes, such as lines, are purely one-dimensional and can only be stroked.

Aside from lines, rectangles are probably the simplest shapes. A Rectangle2D has a corner point (x,y), a width, and a height, and can be constructed from that data ("new Rectangle2D.Double (x, y, w, h) "). The corner point (x,y) specifies the minimum x and y-values in the rectangle. For the usual pixel coordinate system, (x,y) is the upper left corner. However, in a coordinate system in which the minimum value of y is at the bottom, (x,y) would be the lower left corner. The sides of the rectangle are parallel to the coordinate axes. A variable r of type Rectangle2D.Double has public instance variables r.x, r.y, r.width, and r.height. If the width or the height is less than or equal to zero, nothing will be drawn when the rectangle is filled or stroked. A common task is to define a rectangle from two corner points $(x1,y1)$ and $(x2,y2)$. This can be accomplished by creating a rectangle with height and width equal to zero and then adding the second point to the rectangle. Adding a point to a rectangle causes the rectangle to grow just enough to include that point:

```
Rectangle2D.Double r = new Rectangle2D.Double(x1,y1,0,0);
r.add(x2,y2);
```

The classes Line2D, Ellipse2D, RoundRectangle2D and Arc2D create other basic shapes and work similarly to Rectangle2D. You can check the Java API documentation for details.

The Path2D class is more interesting. It represents general paths made up of segments that can be lines and Bezier curves. Paths are created using methods similar to the moveTo and lineTo subroutines that were discussed in Subsection 2.2.3. To create a path, you start by constructing an object of type Path2D.Double (or Path2D.Float):

```
Path2D.Double p = new Path2D.Double();
```

The path p is empty when it is first created. You construct the path by moving an imaginary "pen" along the path that you want to create. The method p.moveTo(x,y) moves the pen to the point (x,y) without drawing anything. It is used to specify the initial point of the path or the starting point of a new piece of the path. The method p.lineTo (x,y) draws a line from the current pen position to (x,y), leaving the pen at (x,y). The method p.close () can be used to close the path (or the current piece of the path) by drawing a line back to its starting point. For example, the following code creates a triangle with vertices at $(0,5), (2,-3)$, and $(-4,1)$:

```
Path2D.Double p = new Path2D.Double();
p.moveTo(0,5);
p.lineTo(2,-3);
p.lineTo(-4,1);
p.close();
```

You can also add Bezier curve segments to a Path2D. Bezier curves were discussed in Subsection 2.2.3. You can add a cubic Bezier curve to a Path2D p with the method

```
p.curveTo( cx1, cy1, cx2, cy2, x, y );
```

This adds a curve segment that starts at the current pen position and ends at (x, y), using (cx1,cy1) and (cx2,cy2) as the two control points for the curve. The method for adding a quadratic Bezier curve segment to a path is quadTo. It requires only a single control point:

```
p.quadTo( cx, cy, x, y );
```

When a path intersects itself, its interior is determined by looking at the winding number, as discussed in Subsection 2.2.2. There are two possible rules for determining whether a point is interior: asking whether the winding number of the curve about that point is non-zero, or asking whether it is odd. You can set the winding rule used by a Path2D p with

```
p.setWindingRule( Path2D.WIND_NON_ZERO );
p.setWindingrule( Path2D.WIND_EVEN_ODD );
```

The default is WIND_NON_ZERO.

Finally, I will note that it is possible to draw a copy of an image into a graphics context. The image could be loaded from a file or created by the program. I discuss the second possibility later in this section. An image is represented by an object of type Image. In fact, I will assume here that the object is of type BufferedImage, which is a subclass of Image. If img is such an object, then

```
g2.drawImage( img, x, y, null );
```

will draw the image with its upper left corner at the point (x, y). (The fourth parameter is hard to explain, but it should be specified as null for Buffered/mages.) This draws the image at its natural width and height, but a different width and height can be specified in the method:

```
g2.drawImage( img, x, y, width, height, null );
```

There is also a method for drawing a string of text. The method specifies the string and the basepoint of the string. (The basepoint is the lower left corner of the string, ignoring "descenders" like the tail on the letter "g".) For example,

```
g2.drawString( "Hello World", 100, 50 );
```

Images and strings are subject to transforms in the same way as other shapes. Transforms are the only way to get rotated text and images. As an example, here is what can happen when you apply a rotation to some text and an image:

The Space Station

2.5.3 Stroke and Fill

Once you have an object that represents a shape, you can fill the shape or stroke it. The Graphics2D class defines methods for doing this. The method for stroking a shape is called draw:

```
g2.fill(shape);
g2.draw(shape);
```

Here, g^2 is of type Graphics2D, and shape can be of type Path2D, Line2D, Rectangle2D or any of the other shape classes. These are often used on a newly created object, when that object represents a shape that will only be drawn once. For example

```
g2.draw( new Line2D.Double( -5, -5, 5, 5 ) );
```

Of course, it is also possible to create shape objects and reuse them many times. The "pen" that is used for stroking a shape is usually represented by an object of type BasicStroke. The default stroke has line width equal to 1. That's one unit in the current coordinate system, not one pixel. To get a line with a different width, you can install a new stroke with

```
g2.setStroke( new BasicStroke(width) );
```

The width in the constructor is of type float. It is possible to add parameters to the constructor to control the shape of a stroke at its endpoints and where two segments meet. (See Subsection 2.2.1.) For example,

```
g2.setStroke( new BasicStroke( 5.0F,
    BasicStroke.CAP_ROUND, BasicStroke.JOIN_BEVEL) );
```

It is also possible to make strokes out of dashes and dots, but I won't discuss how to do it here.

Stroking or filling a shape means setting the colors of certain pixels. In Java, the rule that is used for coloring those pixels is called a "paint." Paints can be solid colors, gradients, or patterns. Like most things in Java, paints are represented by objects. If paint is such an object, then

```
g2.setPaint(paint);
```

will set paint to be used in the graphics context $g2$ for subsequent drawing operations, until the next time the paint is changed. (There is also an older method, g2.setColor(c), that works only for colors and is equivalent to calling g2.setPaint(c).)

Solid colors are represented by objects of type Color. A color is represented internally as an RGBA color. An opaque color, with maximal alpha component, can be created using the constructor

```
new Color( r, g, b );
```

where r, g, and b are integers in the range 0 to 255 that give the red, green, and blue components of the color. To get a translucent color, you can add an alpha component, also in the range 0 to 255 :

```
new Color( r, b, g, a );
```

There is also a function, Color.getHSBColor (h, s, b), that creates a color from values in the HSB color model (which is another name for HSV). In this case, the hue, saturation, and brightness color components must be given as values of type float. And there are constants to represent about a dozen common colors, such as Color.WHITE, Color.RED, and Color.YELLOW. For example, here is how I might draw a square with a black outline and a light blue interior:

```
Rectangle2D square = new Rectangle2D.Double(-2,-2,4,4);
g2.setPaint( new Color(200,200,255) );
g2.fill( square );
g2.setStroke( new BasicStroke(0.1F) );
g2.setPaint( Color.BLACK );
g2.draw( square );
```

Beyond solid colors, Java has the class GradientPaint, to represent simple linear gradients, and TexturePaint to represent to represent pattern fills. (Image patterns used in a similar way in 3D graphics are called textures.) Gradients and patterns were discussed in Subsection 2.2.2. For these paints, the color that is applied to a pixel depends on the coordinates of the pixel.

To create a TexturePaint, you need a BufferedImage object to specify the image that it will use as a pattern. You also have to say how coordinates in the image will map to drawing coordinates in the display. You do this by specifying a rectangle in that will hold one copy of the image. So the constructor takes the form:

```
new TexturePaint( image, rect );
```

where image is the BufferedImage and rect is a Rectangle2D. Outside that specified rectangle, the image is repeated horizontally and vertically. The constructor for a GradientPaint takes the form

```
new GradientPaint( x1, y1, color1, x2, y2, color2, cyclic )
```

Here, $x1, y1, x2$, and $y2$ are values of type float; color1 and color 2 are of type Color; and cyclic is boolean. The gradient color will vary along the line segment from the point $(x1, y1)$ to the point $(x2, y2)$. The color is color1 at the first endpoint and is color 2 at the second endpoint. Color is constant along lines perpendicular to that line segment. The boolean parameter cyclic says whether or not the color pattern repeats. As an example, here is a command that will install a GradientPaint into a graphics context:

```
g2.setPaint( new GradientPaint( 0,0, Color.BLACK, 200,100, Color.RED,
true ) );
```

You should, by the way, note that the current paint is used for strokes as well as for fills. The sample Java program java2d/PaintDemo.java displays a polygon filled with a GradientPaint or a TexturePaint and lets you adjust their properties. The image files java2d/QueenOfHearts.png and java2d/TinySmiley.png are part of that program, and they must be in the same location as the compiled class files that make up that program when it is run.

2.5.4 Transforms

Java implements geometric transformations as methods in the Graphics2D class. For example, if g^2 is a Graphics2D, then calling g 2.translate (1,3) will apply a translation by (1,3) to objects that are drawn after the method is called. The methods that are available correspond to the transform functions discussed in Section 2.3:

- g2.scale(sx,sy) - scales by a horizontal scale factor sx and a vertical scale factor sy.
- g2.rotate(r) - rotates by the angle r about the origin, where the angle is measured in radians. A positive angle rotates the positive x -axis in the direction of the positive y -axis.
- g2. rotate (r, x, y) - rotates by the angle r about the point (x,y). -g2.translate(dx,dy) - translates by dx horizontally and dy vertically. -g2.shear(sx,sy) - applies a horizontal shear amount sx and a vertical shear amount sy. (Usually, one of the shear amounts is 0 , giving a pure horizontal or vertical shear.)

A transform in Java is represented as an object of the class AffineTransform. You can create a general affine transform with the contstructor

```
AffineTransform trns = new AffineTransform(a,b,c,d,e,f);
```

The transform trns will transform a point (x,y) to the point $(x1,y1)$ given by

```
x1 = a*x + c*y + e
y1 = b*x + d*y + f;
```

You can apply the transform trns to a graphics context $g2$ by calling g2.transform(trns). The graphics context g_2 includes the current affine transform, which is the composition of all the transforms that have been applied. Commands such as g2.rotate and g2.transform modify the current transform. You can get a copy of the current transform by calling g2.getTransform(), which returns an AffineTransform object. You can set the current transform using g2.setTransform(trns). This replaces the current transform in $g2$ with the AffineTransform trns. (Note that g2.setTransform(trns) is different from g2.transform(trns); the first command replaces the current transform in $g2$, while the second modifies the current transform by composing it with trns.)

The getTransform and setTransform methods can be used to implement hierarchical modeling. The idea, as discussed in Section 2.4, is that before drawing an object, you should save the current transform. After drawing the object, restore the saved transform. Any additional modeling transformations that are applied while drawing the object and its sub-objects will have no effect outside the object. In Java, this looks like

```
AffineTransform savedTransform = g2.getTransform();
drawObject();
g2.setTransform( savedTransform );
```

For hierarchical graphics, we really need a stack of transforms. However, if the hierarchy is implemented using subroutines, then the above code would be part of a subroutine, and the value of the local variable savedTransform would be stored on the subroutine call stack. Effectively, we would be using the subroutine call stack to implement the stack of saved transforms.

In addition to modeling transformations, transforms are used to set up the window-toviewport transformation that establishes the coordinate system that will be used for drawing. This is usually done in Java just after the graphics context has been created, before any drawing operations. It can be done with a Java version of the applyWindowToViewportTransformation function from Subsection 2.3.7. See the sample program java2d/GraphicsStarter.java for an example.

***

I will mention one more use for AffineTransform objects: Sometimes, you do need to explicitly transform coordinates. For example, given object coordinates (x, y), I might need to know where they will actually end up on the screen, in pixel coordinates. That is, I would like to transform (x, y) by the current transform to get the corresponding pixel coordinates. The AffineTransform class has a method for applying the affine transform to a point. It works with objects of type Point2D. Here is an example:

```
AffineTransform trns = g2.getTransform();
Point2D.Double originalPoint = new Point2D.Double(x,y);
Point2D.Double transformedPoint = new Point2D.Double();
```

```
trns.transform( originalPoint, transformedPoint );
// transformedPoint nowcontains the pixel coords corresponding to (x,y)
int pixelX = (int)transformedPoint.x;
int pixelY = (int)transformedPoint.y;
```

One way I have used this is when working with strings. Often when displaying a string in a transformed coordinate system, I want to transform the basepoint of a string, but not the string itself. That is, I want the transformation to affect the location of the string but not its size or rotation. To accomplish this, I use the above technique to obtain the pixel coordinates for the transformed basepoint, and then draw the string at those coordinates, using an original, untransformed graphics context.

The reverse operation is also sometimes necessary. That is, given pixel coordinates (px, py), find the point (x, y) that is transformed to (px, py) by a given affine transform. For example, when implementing mouse interaction, you will generally know the pixel coordinates of the mouse, but you will want to find the corresponding point in your own chosen coordinate system. For that, you need an inverse transform. The inverse of an affine transform **T** is another transform that performs the opposite transformation. That is, if $\mathbf{T}(x, y) = (px, py)$, and if **R** is the inverse transform, then $\mathbf{R}(px, py) = (x, y)$. In Java, the inverse transform of an AffineTransform trns can be obtained with

```
AffineTransform inverse = trns.createInverse();
```

(A final note: The older drawing methods from Graphics, such as drawLine, use integer coordinates. It's important to note that any shapes drawn using these older methods are subject to the same transformation as shapes such as Line2D that are specified with real number coordinates. For example, drawing a line with g.drawLine (1,2,5,7) will have the same effect as drawing a Line2D that has endpoints (1.0,2.0) and (5.0,7.0). In fact, all drawing is affected by the transformation of coordinates.)

2.5.5 BufferedImage and Pixels

In some graphics applications, it is useful to be able to work with images that are not visible on the screen. That is, you need what I call an off-screen canvas. You also need a way to quickly copy the off-screen canvas onto the screen. For example, it can be useful to store a copy of the on-screen image in an off-screen canvas. The canvas is the official copy of the image. Changes to the image are made to the canvas, then copied to the screen. One reason to do this is that you can then draw extra stuff on top of the screen image without changing the official copy. For example, you might draw a box around a selected region in the on-screen image. You can do this without damaging the official copy in the off-screen canvas.

To remove the box from the screen, you just have to copy the off-screen canvas image onto the screen.

In Java, an off-screen image can be implemented as an object of type BufferedImage. A BufferedImage represents a region in memory where you can draw, in exactly the same way that you can draw to the screen. That is, you can obtain a graphics context $g2$ of type Graphics2D that you can use for drawing on the image. A BufferedImage is an Image, and you can draw it onto the screen-or into any other graphics context-like any other Image, that is, by using the drawImage method of the graphics context where you want to display the image. In a typical setup, there are variables

```
BufferedImage OSC; // The off-screen canvas.
Graphics2D OSG; // graphics context for drawing to the canvas
```

The objects are created using, for example,

```
OSC = new BufferedImage( 640, 480, BufferedImage.TYPE_INT_RGB );
OSG = OSC.createGraphics();
```

The constructor for BufferedImage specifies the width and height of the image along with its type. The type tells what colors can be represented in the image and how they are stored. Here, the type is TYPE_INT_RGB, which means the image uses regular RGB colors with 8 bits for each color component. The three color components for a pixel are packed into a single integer value.

In a program that uses a BufferedImage to store a copy of the on-screen image, the paintComponent method generally has the form

```
protected void paintComponent(Graphics g) {
    g.drawimage( OSC, 0, 0, null );
    Graphics2D g2 = (Graphics2D)g.create();
        . // Draw extra stuff on top of the image.
}
```

A sample program that uses this technique is javaQd/JavaPixelManipulation.java. In that program, the user can draw lines, rectangles, and ovals by dragging the mouse. As the mouse moves, the shape is drawn between the starting point of the mouse and its current location. As the mouse moves, parts of the existing image can be repeatedly covered and uncovered, without changing the existing image. In fact, the image is in an off-screen canvas, and the shape that the user is drawing is actually drawn by paintComponent over the contents of the canvas. The shape is not drawn to the official image in the canvas until the user releases the mouse and ends the drag operation.

But my main reason for writing the program was to illustrate pixel manipulation, that is, computing with the color components of individual pixels. The Buffered/mage class has methods for reading and setting the color of individual pixels. An image consists of rows and columns of pixels. If *OSC* is a BufferedImage, then

```
int color = OSC.getRGB(x,y)
```

gets the integer that represents the color of the pixel in column number x and row number y. Each color component is stored in an 8-bit field in the integer color value. The individual color components can be extracted for processing using Java's bit manipulation operators:

```
int red = (color >> 16) & 255;
int green = (color >> 8) & 255;
int blue = color & 255;
```

Similarly, given red, green, and blue color component values in the range 0 to 255 , we can combine those component values into a single integer and use it to set the color of a pixel in the image:

```
int color = (red << 16) | (green << 8) | blue;
OSC.setRGB(x,y,color);
```

There are also methods for reading and setting the colors of an entire rectangular region of pixels.

Pixel operations are used to implement two features of the sample program. First, there is a "Smudge" tool. When the user drags with this tool, it's like smearing wet paint. When the user first clicks the mouse, the color components from a small square of pixels surrounding the mouse position are copied into arrays. As the user moves the mouse, color from the arrays is blended into the color of the pixels near the mouse position, while those colors are blended into the colors in the arrays. Here is a small rectangle that has been "smudged":

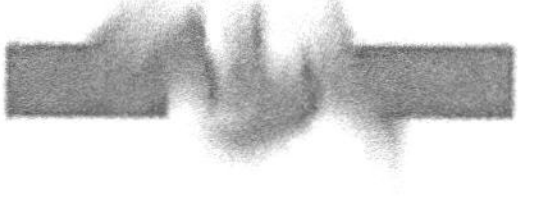

The second use of pixel manipulation is in implementing "filters." A filter, in this program, is an operation that modifies an image by replacing the color of each pixel with a weighted average of the colors of a 3 -by- 3 square of pixels. A "Blur" filter for example, uses equal weights for all pixels in the average, so the color of a pixel is changed to the simple average of the colors of that pixel and its neighbors. Using different weights for each pixel can produce some striking effects.

The pixel manipulation in the sample program produces effects that can't be achieved with pure vector graphics. I encourage you to learn more by looking at the source code. You might also take a look at the live demos in the next section, which implement the same effects using HTML canvas graphics.

2.6 HTML Canvas Graphics

Most modern web browsers support a 2D graphics API that can be used to create images on a web page. The API is implemented using JavaScript, the client-side programming language for the web. I won't cover the JavaScript language in this section. To understand the material presented here, you don't need to know much about it. Even if you know nothing about it at all, you can learn something about its 2D graphics API and see how it is similar to, and how it differs from, the Java API presented in the previous section. (For a short introduction to JavaScript, see Section A. 3 in Appendix A.)

2.6.1 The 2D Graphics Context

The visible content of a web page is made up of "elements" such as headlines and paragraphs. The content is specified using the HTML language. A "canvas" is an HTML element. It appears on the page as a blank rectangular area which can be used as a drawing surface by what I am calling the "HTML canvas" graphics API. In the source code of a web page, a canvas element is created with code of the form

```
<canvas width="800" height="600" id="theCanvas"></canvas>
```

The width and height give the size of the drawing area, in pixels. The id is an identifier that can be used to refer to the canvas in JavaScript.

To draw on a canvas, you need a graphics context. A graphics context is an object that contains functions for drawing shapes. It also contains variables that record the current graphics state, including things like the current drawing color, transform, and font. Here, I will generally use graphics as the name of the variable that refers to the graphics context, but the variable name is, of course, up to the programmer. This graphics context plays the same role in the canvas API that a variable of type Graphics2D plays in Java. A typical starting point is

```
canvas = document.getElementById("theCanvas");
graphics = canvas.getContext("2d");
```

The first line gets a reference to the canvas element on the web page, using its *id*. The second line creates the graphics context for that canvas element. (This code will produce an error in a web browser that doesn't support canvas, so you might add some error checking such as putting these commands inside a try..catch statement.)

Typically, you will store the canvas graphics context in a global variable and use the same graphics context throughout your program. This is in contrast to Java, where you typically get a new Graphics2D context each time the paintComponent() method is called, and that new context is in its initial state with default color and stroke properties and with no applied transform. When a graphics context is global, changes made to the state in one function call will carry over to subsequent function calls, unless you do something to limit their effect. This can actually lead to a fairly common type of bug: For example, if you apply a 30 -degree rotation in a function, those rotations will accumulate each time the function is called, unless you do something to undo the previous rotation before the function is called again.

The rest of this section will be mostly concerned with describing what you can do with a canvas graphics context. But here, for the record, is the complete source code for a very minimal web page that uses canvas graphics:

```
<!DOCTYPE html>
<html>
<head>
<title>Canvas Graphics</title>
<script>
    let canvas; // DOM object corresponding to the canvas
    let graphics; // 2D graphics context for drawing on the canvas
    function draw() {
            // draw on the canvas, using the graphics context
        graphics.fillText("Hello World", 10, 20);
    }
    function init() {
        canvas = document.getElementById("theCanvas");
        graphics = canvas.getContext("2d");
        draw(); // draw something on the canvas
    }
    window.onload = init;
```

```
</script>
</head>
<body>
    <canvas id="theCanvas" width="640" height="480"></canvas>
</body>
</html>
```

For a more complete, though still minimal, example, you can look at the sample page canvas2d/GraphicsStarter.html. (You should look at the page in a browser, but you should also read the source code.) This example shows how to draw some basic shapes using canvas graphics, and you can use it as a basis for your own experimentation. There are also three more advanced "starter" examples: canvas2d/GraphicsPlusStarter.html adds some utility functions for drawing shapes and setting up a coordinate system; canvas2d/AnimationStarter.html adds animation and includes a simple hierarchical modeling example; and canvas2d/EventsStarter.html shows how to respond to keyboard and mouse events.

2.6.2 Shapes

The default coordinate system on a canvas is the usual: The unit of measure is one pixel; (0,0) is at the upper left corner; the *x*-coordinate increases to the right; and the *y*-coordinate increases downward. The range of *x* and *y* values is given by the width and height properties of the <canvas> element. The term "pixel" here for the unit of measure is not really correct. Probably, I should say something like "one nominal pixel." The unit of measure is one pixel at typical desktop resolution with no magnification. If you apply a magnification to a browser window, the unit of measure gets stretched. And on a high-resolution screen, one unit in the default coordinate system might correspond to several actual pixels on the display device.

The canvas API supports only a very limited set of basic shapes. In fact, the only basic shapes are rectangles and text. Other shapes must be created as paths. Shapes can be stroked and filled. That includes text: When you stroke a string of text, a pen is dragged along the outlines of the characters; when you fill a string, the insides of the characters are filled. It only really makes sense to stroke text when the characters are rather large.

Here are the functions for drawing rectangles and text, where graphics refers to the object that represents the graphics context:

- graphics.fillRect (x, y, w, h) - draws a filled rectangle with corner at (*x*, *y*), with width *w* and with height *h*. If the width or the height is less than or equal to zero, nothing is drawn.

- graphics.strokeRect (x, y, w, h) - strokes the outline of the same rectangle.
- graphics.clearRect (x, y, w, h) - clears the rectangle by filling it with fully transparent pixels, allowing the background of the canvas to show. The background is determined by the properties of the web page on which the canvas appears. It might be a background color, an image, or even another canvas.
- graphics.fillText (str, x, y) - fills the characters in the string str. The left end of the baseline of the string is positioned at the point (x, y).
- graphics.strokeText (str, x, y) - strokes the outlines of the characters in the string.

A path can be created using functions in the graphics context. The context keeps track of a "current path." In the current version of the API, paths are not represented by objects, and there is no way to work with more than one path at a time or to keep a copy of a path for later reuse. Paths can contain lines, Bezier curves, and circular arcs. Here are the most common functions for working with paths:

- graphics.beginPath() - start a new path. Any previous path is discarded, and the current path in the graphics context is now empty. Note that the graphics context also keeps track of the current point, the last point in the current path. After calling graphics.beginPath(), the current point is undefined.
- graphics.moveTo (x, y) - move the current point to (x, y), without adding anything to the path. This can be used for the starting point of the path or to start a new, disconnected segment of the path.
- graphics.lineTo (x, y) - add the line segment starting at current point and ending at (x, y) to the path, and move the current point to (x, y).
- graphics.bezierCurveTo(cx1,cy1,c2x,cy2,x,y) - add a cubic Bezier curve to the path. The curve starts at the current point and ends at (x, y). The points $(cx1, cy1)$ and (cx2,cy2) are the two control points for the curve. (Bezier curves and their control points were discussed in Subsection 2.2.3.)
- graphics.quadraticCurveTo(cx,cy,x,y) - adds a quadratic Bezier curve from the current point to (x, y), with control point (cx, cy).
- graphics.arc(x,y,r,startAngle,endAngle) - adds an arc of the circle with center (x, y) and radius r. The next two parameters give the starting and ending angle of the arc. They are measured in radians. The arc extends in the positive direction from the start angle to the end angle. (The positive rotation direction is from the

positive x -axis towards the positive y -axis; this is clockwise in the default coordinate system.) An optional fifth parameter can be set to true to get an arc that extends in the negative direction. After drawing the arc, the current point is at the end of the arc. If there is a current point before graphics.arc is called, then before the arc is drawn, a line is added to the path that extends from the current point to the starting point of the arc. (Recall that immediately after graphics.beginPath(), there is no current point.)

- graphics.closePath() - adds to the path a line from the current point back to the starting point of the current segment of the curve. (Recall that you start a new segment of the curve every time you use moveTo.)

Creating a curve with these commands does not draw anything. To get something visible to appear in the image, you must fill or stroke the path.

The commands graphics.fill() and graphics.stroke() are used to fill and to stroke the current path. If you fill a path that has not been closed, the fill algorithm acts as though a final line segment had been added to close the path. When you stroke a shape, it's the center of the virtual pen that moves along the path. So, for high-precision canvas drawing, it's common to use paths that pass through the centers of pixels rather than through their corners. For example, to draw a line that extends from the pixel with coordinates (100,200) to the pixel with coordinates (300,200), you would actually stroke the geometric line with endpoints (100.5,200.5) and (100.5,300.5). We should look at some examples. It takes four steps to draw a line:

```
graphics.beginPath(); // start a new path
graphics.moveTo(100.5,200.5); // starting point of the new path
graphics.lineTo(300.5,200.5); // add a line to the point (300.5,200.5)
graphics.stroke(); // draw the line
```

Remember that the line remains as part of the current path until the next time you call graphics.beginPath(). Here's how to draw a filled, regular octagon centered at (200,400) and with radius 100 :

```
graphics.beginPath();
graphics.moveTo(300,400);
for (let i = 1; i < 8; i++) {
    let angle = (2*Math.PI)/8 * i;
    let x = 200 + 100*Math.cos(angle);
    let y = 400 + 100*Math.sin(angle);
    graphics.lineTo(x,y);
```

```
}
graphics.closePath();
graphics.fill();
```

The function graphics.arc() can be used to draw a circle, with a start angle of 0 and an end angle of 2* Math.PI. Here's a filled circle with radius 100 , centered at 200,300:

```
graphics.beginPath();
graphics.arc( 200, 300, 100, 0, 2*Math.PI );
graphics.fill();
```

To draw just the outline of the circle, use graphics.stroke() in place of graphics.fill(). You can apply both operations to the same path. If you look at the details of graphics.arc(), you can see how to draw a wedge of a circle:

```
graphics.beginPath();
graphics.moveTo(200,300); // Move current point to center of the
circle.
graphics.arc(200,300,100,0,Math.PI/4); // Arc, plus line from current
point.
graphics.lineTo(200,300); // Line from end of arc back to center of
circle.
graphics.fill(); // Fill the wedge.
```

There is no way to draw an oval that is not a circle, except by using transforms. We will cover that later in this section. But JavaScript has the interesting property that it is possible to add new functions and properties to an existing object. The sample program canvas2d/GraphicsPlusStarter.html shows how to add functions to a graphics context for drawing lines, ovals, and other shapes that are not built into the API.

2.6.3 Stroke and Fill

Attributes such as line width that affect the visual appearance of strokes and fills are stored as properties of the graphics context. For example, the value of graphics.line Width is a number that represents the width that will be used for strokes. (The width is given in pixels for the default coordinate system, but it is subject to transforms.) You can change the line width by assigning a value to this property:

```
graphics.lineWidth = 2.5; // Change the current width.
```

The change affects subsequent strokes. You can also read the current value:

```
saveWidth = graphics.lineWidth; // Save current width.
```

The property graphics.lineCap controls the appearance of the endpoints of a stroke. It can be set to "round", "square", or "butt". The quotation marks are part of the value. For example,

```
graphics.lineCap = "round";
```

Similarly, graphics.lineJoin controls the appearance of the point where one segment of a stroke joins another segment; its possible values are "round", "bevel", or "miter". (Line endpoints and joins were discussed in Subsection 2.2.1.)

Note that the values for graphics.lineCap and graphics.lineJoin are strings. This is a somewhat unusual aspect of the API. Several other properties of the graphics context take values that are strings, including the properties that control the colors used for drawing and the font that is used for drawing text.

Color is controlled by the values of the properties graphics.fillStyle and graphics.strokeStyle. The graphics context maintains separate styles for filling and for stroking. A solid color for stroking or filling is specified as a string. Valid color strings are ones that can be used in CSS, the language that is used to specify colors and other style properties of elements on web pages. Many solid colors can be specified by their names, such as "red", "black", and "beige". An RGB color can be specified as a string of the form " rgb(r, g, b) ", where the parentheses contain three numbers in the range 0 to 255 giving the red, green, and blue components of the color. Hexadecimal color codes are also supported, in the form "#XXYYZZ" where XX, YY, and ZZ are two-digit hexadecimal numbers giving the RGB color components. For example,

```
graphics.fillStyle = "rgb(200,200,255)"; // light blue
graphics.strokeStyle = "#0070A0"; // a darker, greenish blue
```

The style can actually be more complicated than a simple solid color: Gradients and patterns are also supported. As an example, a gradient can be created with a series of steps such as

```
let lineargradient = graphics.createLinearGradient(420,420,550,200);
lineargradient.addColorStop(0,"red");
lineargradient.addColorStop(0.5,"yellow");
lineargradient.addColorStop(1,"green");
graphics.fillStyle = lineargradient; // Use a gradient fill!
```

The first line creates a linear gradient that will vary in color along the line segment from the point (420,420) to the point (550,200). Colors for the gradient are specified by the addColorStop function: the first parameter gives the fraction of the distance from the initial point to the final point where that color is applied, and the second is a string that specifies the color itself. A color stop at 0 specifies the color at the initial point; a color stop at 1 specifies the color at the final point. Once a gradient has been created, it can be used both as a fill style and as a stroke style in the graphics context.

Finally, I note that the font that is used for drawing text is the value of the property graphics.font. The value is a string that could be used to specify a font in CSS. As such, it can be fairly complicated, but the simplest versions include a font-size (such as 20px or 150%) and a font-family (such as serif, sans-serif, monospace, or the name of any font that is accessible to the web page). You can add italic or bold or both to the front of the string. Some examples:

```
graphics.font = "2cm monospace"; // the size is in centimeters
graphics.font = "bold 18px sans-serif";
graphics.font = "italic 150% serif"; // size is 150% of the usual size
```

The default is " 10 px sans-serif," which is usually too small. Note that text, like all drawing, is subject to coordinate transforms. Applying a scaling operation changes the size of the text, and a negative scaling factor can produce mirror-image text.

2.6.4 Transforms

A graphics context has three basic functions for modifying the current transform by scaling, rotation, and translation. There are also functions that will compose the current transform with an arbitrary transform and for completely replacing the current transform:

- graphics.scale(sx,sy) - scale by *sx* in the *x*-direction and *sy* in the *y*-direction.
- graphics.rotate(angle) - rotate by angle radians about the origin. A positive rotation is clockwise in the default coordinate system.
- graphics.translate(tx,ty) - translate by *tx* in the *x*-direction and ty in the *y* direction.
- graphics.transform(a, b, c, d, e, f) - apply the affine transform $\mathrm{x1} = a * x + c * y + e$, and $\mathrm{y1} = \mathrm{b} * \mathrm{x} + \mathrm{d} * \mathrm{y} + \mathrm{f}$.

- graphics.setTransform(a,b,c,d,e,f) - discard the current transformation, and set the current transformation to be $x1 = a * x + c * y + e$, and $y1 = b * x + d * y + f$. Note that there is no shear transform, but you can apply a shear as a general transform. For example, for a horizontal shear with shear factor 0.5 , use

```
graphics.transform(1, 0, 0.5, 1, 0, 0)
```

To implement hierarchical modeling, as discussed in Section 2.4, you need to be able to save the current transformation so that you can restore it later. Unfortunately, no way is provided to read the current transformation from a canvas graphics context. However, the graphics context itself keeps a stack of transformations and provides methods for pushing and popping the current transformation. In fact, these methods do more than save and restore the current transformation. They actually save and restore almost the entire state of the graphics context, including properties such as current colors, line width, and font (but not the current path):

- graphics.save() - push a copy of the current state of the graphics context, including the current transformation, onto the stack.

- graphics.restore() - remove the top item from the stack, containing a saved state of the graphics context, and restore the graphics context to that state. Using these methods, the basic setup for drawing an object with a modeling transform becomes:

```
graphics.save(); // save a copy of the current state
graphics.translate(a,b); // apply modeling transformations
graphics.rotate(r);
graphics.scale(sx,sy);
    .
    \mathrm{ - // Draw the object!}
     .
graphics.restore(); // restore the saved state
```

Note that if drawing the object includes any changes to attributes such as drawing color, those changes will be also undone by the call to graphics.restore(). In hierarchical graphics, this is usually what you want, and it eliminates the need to have extra statements for saving and restoring things like color.

To draw a hierarchical model, you need to traverse a scene graph, either procedurally or as a data structure. It's pretty much the same as in Java. In fact, you should see that the basic concepts that you learned about transformations and modeling carry over to the canvas graphics API. Those concepts apply very widely and even carry over to 3D graphics APIs, with just a little added complexity. The sample web page canvas2d/HierarchicalModel2D.html implements hierarchical modeling using the 2D canvas API.

Now that we know how to do transformations, we can see how to draw an oval using the canvas API. Suppose that we want an oval with center at (x, y), with horizontal radius $r1$ and with vertical radius $r2$. The idea is to draw a circle of radius 1 with center at (0,0), then transform it. The circle needs to be scaled by a factor of $r1$ horizontally and $r2$ vertically. It should then be translated to move its center from (0,0) to (x, y). We can use graphics.save() and graphics.restore() to make sure that the transformations only affect the circle. Recalling that the order of transforms in the code is the opposite of the order in which they are applied to objects, this becomes:

```
graphics.save();
graphics.translate( x, y );
graphics.scale( r1, r2 );
graphics.beginPath();
graphics.arc( 0, 0, 1, 0, Math.PI ); // a circle of radius 1
graphics.restore();
graphics.stroke();
```

Note that the current path is not affected by the calls to graphics.save() and graphics.restore(). So, in the example, the oval-shaped path is not discarded when graphics.restore() is called. When graphics.stroke() is called at the end, it is the oval-shaped path that is stroked. On the other hand, the line width that is used for the stroke is not affected by the scale transform that was applied to the oval. Note that if the order of the last two commands were reversed, then the line width would be subject to the scaling.

There is an interesting point here about transforms and paths. In the HTML canvas API, the points that are used to create a path are transformed by the current transformation before they are saved. That is, they are saved in pixel coordinates. Later, when the path is stroked or filled, the current transform has no effect on the path (although it can affect, for example, the line width when the path is stroked). In particular, you can't make a path and then apply different transformations. For example, you can't make an oval-shaped path, and then use it to draw several ovals in different positions. Every time you draw the oval, it will be in the same place, even if different translation transforms are applied to the graphics context.

The situation is different in Java, where the coordinates that are stored in the path are the actual numbers that are used to specify the path, that is, the object coordinates. When the path is stroked or filled, the transformation that is in effect at that time is applied to the path. The path can be reused many times to draw copies with different transformations. This comment is offered as an example of how APIs that look very similar can have subtle differences.

2.6.5 Auxiliary Canvases

In Subsection 2.5.5, we looked at the sample program javaQd/JavaPixelManipulation.java, which uses a BufferedImage both to implement an off-screen canvas and to allow direct manipulation of the colors of individual pixels. The same ideas can be applied in HTML canvas graphics, although the way it's done is a little different. The sample web application canvas2d/SimplePaintProgram.html does pretty much the same thing as the Java program (except for the image filters).

The on-line version of this section has a live demo version of the program that has the same functionality. You can try it out to see how the various drawing tools work. Don't forget to try the "Smudge" tool! (It has to be applied to shapes that you have already drawn.)

For JavaScript, a web page is represented as a data structure, defined by a standard called the DOM, or Document Object model. For an off-screen canvas, we can use a <canvas> that is not part of that data structure and therefore is not part of the page. In JavaScript, a <canvas> can be created with the function call document.createElement("canvas"). There is a way to add this kind of dynamically created canvas to the DOM for the web page, but it can be used as an off-screen canvas without doing so. To use it, you have to set its width and height properties, and you need a graphics context for drawing on it. Here, for example, is some code that creates a 640 -by- 480 canvas, gets a graphics context for the canvas, and fills the whole canvas with white:

```
OSC = document.createElement("canvas"); // off-screen canvas
OSC.width = 640; // Size of OSC must be set explicitly.
OSC.height = 480;
OSG = OSC.getContext("2d"); // Graphics context for drawing on OSC.
OSG.fillStyle = "white"; // Use the context to fill OSC with white.
OSG.fillRect(0,0,OSC.width,OSC.height);
```

The sample program lets the user drag the mouse on the canvas to draw some shapes. The off-screen canvas holds the official copy of the picture, but it is not seen by the user. There is also an on-screen canvas that the user sees. The off-screen canvas is copied to the on-screen canvas whenever the picture is modified. While the user is dragging the mouse to draw a line, oval, or rectangle, the new shape is actually drawn on-screen, over the contents of the off-screen canvas. It is only added to the off-screen canvas when the user finishes the drag operation. For the other tools, changes are made directly to the off-screen canvas, and the result is then copied to the screen. This is an exact imitation of the Java program.

(The demo version mentioned above actually uses a somewhat different technique to accomplish the same thing. It uses two on-screen canvases, one located exactly on top of the other. The lower canvas holds the actual image. The upper canvas is completely transparent, except when the user is drawing a line, oval, or rectangle. While the user is dragging the mouse to draw such a shape, the new shape is drawn on the upper canvas, where it hides the part of the lower canvas that is beneath the shape. When the user releases the mouse, the shape is added to the lower canvas and the upper canvas is cleared to make it completely transparent again. Again, the other tools operate directly on the lower canvas.)

2.6.6 Pixel Manipulation

The "Smudge" tool in the sample program and demo is implemented by computing with the color component values of pixels in the image. The implementation requires some way to read the colors of pixels in a canvas. That can be done with the function graphics.getPixelData (x, y, w, h), where graphics is a 2D graphics context for the canvas. The function reads the colors of a rectangle of pixels, where (x, y) is the upper left corner of the rectangle, w is its width, and h is its height. The parameters are always expressed in pixel coordinates. Consider, for example

```
colors = graphics.getImageData(0,0,20,10)
```

This returns the color data for a 20 -by-10 rectangle in the upper left corner of the canvas. The return value, colors, is an object with properties colors.width, colors.height, and colors.data. The width and height give the number of rows and columns of pixels in the returned data. (According to the documentation, on a high-resolution screen, they might not be the same as the width and height in the function call. The data can be for real, physical pixels on the display device, not the "nominal" pixels that are used in the pixel coordinate system on the canvas. There might be several device pixels for each nominal pixel. I'm not sure whether this can really happen in practice.)

The value of colors.data is an array, with four array elements for each pixel. The four elements contain the red, blue, green, and alpha color components of the pixel, given as integers in the range 0 to 255 . For a pixel that lies outside the canvas, the four component values will all be zero. The array is a value of type Uint8ClampedArray whose elements are 8-bit unsigned integers limited to the range 0 to 255 . This is one of JavaScript's typed array datatypes, which can only hold values of a specific numerical type. As an example, suppose that you just want to read the RGB color of one pixel, at coordinates (x, y). You can set

```
pixel = graphics.getImageData(x,y,1,1);
```

Then the RGB color components for the pixel are R = pixel.data [0], G = pixel.data [1], and B = pixel.data [2].

The function graphics.putImageData(imageData, x, y) is used to copy the colors from an image data object into a canvas, placing it into a rectangle in the canvas with upper left corner at (x, y). The imageData object can be one that was returned by a call to graphics.getImageData, possibly with its color data modified. Or you can create a blank image data object by calling graphics.createImageData(w, h) and fill it with data.

Let's consider the "Smudge" tool in the sample program. When the user clicks the mouse with this tool, I use OSG.getImageData to get the color data from a 9 -by-9 square of pixels surrounding the mouse location. *OSG* is the graphics context for the canvas that contains the image. Since I want to do real-number arithmetic with color values, I copy the color components into another typed array, one of type Float32Array, which can hold 32-bit floating point numbers. Here is the function that I call to do this:

```
function grabSmudgeData(x, y) { // (x,y) gives mouse location
    let colors = OSG.getImageData(x-5,y-5,9,9);
    if (smudgeColorArray == null) {
        // Make image data & array the first time this function is
called.
        smudgeImageData            =            OSG.createImageData(9,9);
        smudgeColorArray    =    new    Float32Array(colors.data.length);
    }
    for    (let    i    =    0;    i    <    colors.data.length;    i++)    {
          // Copy the color component data into the Float32Array.
        smudgeColorArray[i]              =              colors.data[i];
    }
}
```

The floating point array, smudgeColorArray, will be used for computing new color values for the image as the mouse moves. The color values from this array will be copied into the image data object, smudgeImageData, which will then be used to put the color values into the image. This is done in another function, which is called for each point that is visited as the user drags the Smudge tool over the canvas:

```
function swapSmudgeData(x, y) { // (x,y) is new mouse location
    let colors = OSG.getImageData(x-5,y-5,9,9); // get color data from
image
    for (let i = 0; i < smudgeColorArray.length; i += 4) {
        // The color data for one pixel is in the next four array
locations.
        if (smudgeColorArray[i+3] && colors.data[i+3]) {
                // alpha-components are non-zero; both pixels are in
the canvas;
                // (getImageData() gets 0 for the alpha value at pixel
coordinates
                // that are not actually part of the canvas).
            for (let j = i; j < i+3; j++) { // compute new RGB values
                let newSmudge = smudgeColorArray[j]*0.8 +
colors.data[j]*0.2;
                let newImage = smudgeColorArray[j]*0.2 +
colors.data[j]*0.8;
                smudgeImageData.data[j] = newImage;
                smudgeColorArray[j] = newSmudge;
            }
            smudgeImageData.data[i+3] = 255; // alpha component
        }
        else {
                // one of the alpha components is zero; set the output
                // color to all zeros, "transparent black", which will
have
                // no effect on the color of the pixel in the canvas.
            for (let j = i; j <= i+3; j++) {
                smudgeImageData.data[j] = 0;
            }
        }
    }
    OSG.putImageData(smudgeImageData,x-5,y-5); // copy new colors into
canvas
}
```

In this function, a new color is computed for each pixel in a 9 -by- 9 square of pixels around the mouse location. The color is replaced by a weighted average of the current color of the pixel and the color of the corresponding pixel in the smudgeColorArray. At the same time, the color in smudgeColorArray is replaced by a similar weighted average.

It would be worthwhile to try to understand this example to see how pixel-by-pixel processing of color data can be done. See the source code of the example for more details.

2.6.7 Images

For another example of pixel manipulation, we can look at image filters that modify an image by replacing the color of each pixel with a weighted average of the color of that pixel and the 8 pixels that surround it. Depending on the weighting factors that are used, the result can be as simple as a slightly blurred version of the image, or it can be something more interesting.

The on-line version of this section includes an interactive demo that lets you apply several different image filters to a variety of images.

The filtering operation in the demo uses the image data functions getImageData, createImageData, and putImageData that were discussed above. Color data from the entire image is obtained with a call to getImageData. The results of the averaging computation are placed in a new image data object, and the resulting image data is copied back to the image using putImageData.

The remaining question is, where do the original images come from, and how do they get onto the canvas in the first place? An image on a web page is specified by an element in the web page source such as

```
<img src="pic.jpg" width="400" height="300" id="mypic">
```

The src attribute specifies the URL from which the image is loaded. The optional id can be used to reference the image in JavaScript. In the script,

```
image = document.getElementById("mypic");
```

gets a reference to the object that represents the image in the document structure. Once you have such an object, you can use it to draw the image on a canvas. If graphics is a graphics context for the canvas, then

```
graphics.drawImage(image, x, y);
```

draws the image with its upper left corner at (x, y). Both the point (x, y) and the image itself are transformed by any transformation in effect in the graphics context. This will draw the image using its natural width and height (scaled by the transformation, if any). You can also specify the width and height of the rectangle in which the image is drawn:

```
graphics.drawImage(image, x, y, width, height);
```

With this version of drawImage, the image is scaled to fit the specified rectangle. Now, suppose that the image you want to draw onto the canvas is not part of the web page? In that case, it is possible to load the image dynamically. This is much like making an off-screen canvas, but you are making an "off-screen image." Use the document object to create an img element:

```
newImage = document.createElement("img");
```

An img element needs a src attribute that specifies the URL from which it is to be loaded. For example,

```
newImage.src = "pic2.jpg";
```

As soon as you assign a value to the *src* attribute, the browser starts loading the image. The loading is done asynchronously; that is, the computer continues to execute the script without waiting for the load to complete. This means that you can't simply draw the image on the line after the above assignment statement: The image is very likely not done loading at that time. You want to draw the image after it has finished loading. For that to happen, you need to assign a function to the image's onload property before setting the src. That function will be called when the image has been fully loaded. Putting this together, here is a simple JavaScript function for loading an image from a specified URL and drawing it on a canvas after it has loaded:

```
function loadAndDraw( imageURL, x, y ) {
    let image = document.createElement("img");
    image.onload = doneLoading;
    image.src = imageURL;
    function doneLoading() {
        graphics.drawImage(image, x, y);
    }
}
```

A similar technique is used to load the images in the filter demo. There is one last mystery to clear up. When discussing the use of an off-screen canvas in the SimplePaintProgram example earlier in this section, I noted that the contents of the off-screen canvas have to be copied to the main canvas, but I didn't say how that can be done. In fact, it is done using drawImage. In addition to drawing an image onto a canvas, drawImage can be used to draw the contents of one canvas into another canvas. In the sample program, the command

```
graphics.drawImage( OSC, 0, 0 );
```

is used to draw the off-screen canvas to the main canvas. Here, graphics is a graphics context for drawing on the main canvas, and *OSC* is the object that represents the off-screen canvas.

2.7 SVG: A Scene Description Language

We finish this chapter with a look at one more 2D graphics system: ***SVG***, or Scalable Vector Graphics. So far, we have been considering graphics programming APIs. SVG, on the other hand is a scene description language rather than a programming language. Where a programming language creates a scene by generating its contents procedurally, a scene description language specifies a scene "declaratively," by listing its content. Since SVG is a vector graphics language, the content of of a scene includes shapes, attributes such as color and line width, and geometric transforms. Most of this should be familiar to you, but it should be interesting to see it in a new context.

SVG is an XML language, which means it has a very strict and somewhat verbose syntax. This can make it a little annoying to write, but on the other hand, it makes it possible to read and understand SVG documents even if you are not familiar with the syntax. It's possible that SVG originally stood for "Simple" Vector Graphics, but it is by no means a simple language at this point. I will cover only a part of it here, and there are many parts of the language and many options that I will not mention. My goal is to introduce the idea of a scene description language and to show how such a language can use the same basic ideas that are used in the rest of this chapter.

SVG can be used as a file format for storing vector graphics images, in much the same way that PNG and JPEG are file formats for storing pixel-based images. That means that you can open an SVG file with almost any web browser to view the image. An SVG image can be included in a web page by using it as the src of an element. That's how the SVG examples in the web version of this section are displayed. Since SVG documents are written in plain text, you can create SVG images using a regular text editor, and you can read the source for an SVG image by opening it in a text editor or by viewing the source of the image when it is displayed in a web browser.

2.7.1 SVG Document Structure

An SVG file, like any XML document, starts with some standard code that almost no one memorizes. It should just be copied into a new document. Here is some code that can be copied as a starting point for SVG documents of the type discussed in this section (which, remember use only a subset of the full SVG specification):

```
<?xml version="1.0"?>
<!DOCTYPE svg PUBLIC "-//W3C//DTD SVG 1.1//EN"
    "http://www.w3.org/Graphics/SVG/1.1/DTD/svg11.dtd">
<svg version="1.1" xmlns="http://www.w3.org/2000/svg"
            xmlns:xlink="http://www.w3.org/1999/xlink"
            width="4in" height="4in"
            viewBox="0 0 400 400"
            preserveAspectRatio="xMidYMid">
        <!-- The scene description goes here! -->
</svg>
```

The first three lines say that this is an XML SVG document. The rest of the document is an <svg> element that acts as a container for the entire scene description. You'll need to know a little about XML syntax. First, an XML "element" in its general form looks like this:

```
<elementname attrib1="value1" attrib2="value2">
    ...content...
</elementname>
```

The element starts with a "start tag," which begins with a "<" followed by an identifier that is the name of the tag, and ending with a ">". The start tag can include "attributes," which have the form name ="value". The name is an identifier; the value is a string. The value must be enclosed in single or double quotation marks. The element ends with an "end tag," which has an element name that matches the element name in the start tag and has the form </elementname>. Element names and attribute names are case-sensitive. Between the start and end tags comes the "content" of the element. The content can consist of text and nested elements. If an element has no content, you can replace the " > " at the end of the start tag with "/>", and leave out the end tag. This is called a "self-closing tag." For example,

```
<circle cx="5" cy="5" r="4" fill="red"/>
```

This is an actual SVG element that specifies a circle. It's easy to forget the "/" at the end of a self-closing tag, but it has to be there to have a legal XML document.

Looking back at the SVG document, the five lines starting with <svg are just a long start tag. You can use the tag as shown, and customize the values of the width, height, viewBox, and preserveAspectRatio attributes. The next line is a comment; comments in XML start with "".

The width and height attributes of the <svg> tag specify a natural or preferred size for the image. It can be forced into a different size, for example if it is used in an element on a web page that specifies a different width and height. The size can be specified using units of measure such as in for inches, *cm* for centimeters, and *px*, for pixels, with 90 pixels to the inch. If no unit of measure is specified, pixels are used. There cannot be any space between the number and the unit of measure.

The viewBox attribute sets up the coordinate system that will be used for drawing the image. It is what I called the view window in Subsection 2.3.1. The value for viewBox is a list of four numbers, giving the minimum *x*-value, the minimum *y*-value, the width, and the height of the view window. The width and the height must be positive, so *x* increases from left-to-right, and *y* increases from top-to-bottom. The four numbers in the list can be separated either by spaces or by commas; this is typical for lists of numbers in SVG.

Finally, the preserveAspectRatio attribute tells what happens when the aspect ratio of the viewBox does not match the aspect ratio of the rectangle in which the image is displayed. The default value, "xMidYMid", will extend the limts on the viewBox either horizontally or vertically to preserve the aspect ratio, and the viewBox will appear in the center of the display rectangle. If you would like your image to stretch to fill the display rectangle, ignoring the aspect ratio, set the value of preserveAspectRatio to "none". (The aspect ratio issue was discussed in Subsection 2.3.7.)

Let's look at a complete SVG document that draws a few simple shapes. Here's the document. You could probably figure out what it draws even without knowing any more about SVG:

```
<?xml version="1.0"?>
<!DOCTYPE svg PUBLIC "-//W3C//DTD SVG 1.1//EN"
    "http://www.w3.org/Graphics/SVG/1.1/DTD/svg11.dtd">
<svg version="1.1" xmlns="http://www.w3.org/2000/svg"
        xmlns:xlink="http://www.w3.org/1999/xlink"
        width="300px" height="200px"
        viewBox="0 0 3 2"
        preserveAspectRatio="xMidYMid">
```

```
<rect x="0" y="0" width="3" height="2"
                stroke="blue" fill="none" stroke-width="0.05"/>
<text x="0.2" y="0.5" font-size="0.4" fill="red">Hello World!</text>
<line x1="0.1" y1="0.7" x2="2.9" y2="0.7" stroke-width="0.05"
stroke="blue"/>
<ellipse cx="1.5" cy="1.4" rx=".6" ry=".4" fill="rgb(0,255,180)"/>
<circle cx="0.4" cy="1.4" r="0.3"
            fill="magenta" stroke="black" stroke-width="0.03"/>
<polygon points="2.2,1.7 2.4,1 2.9,1.7"
            fill="none" stroke="green" stroke-width="0.02"/>
</svg>
```

and here's the image that is produced by this example:

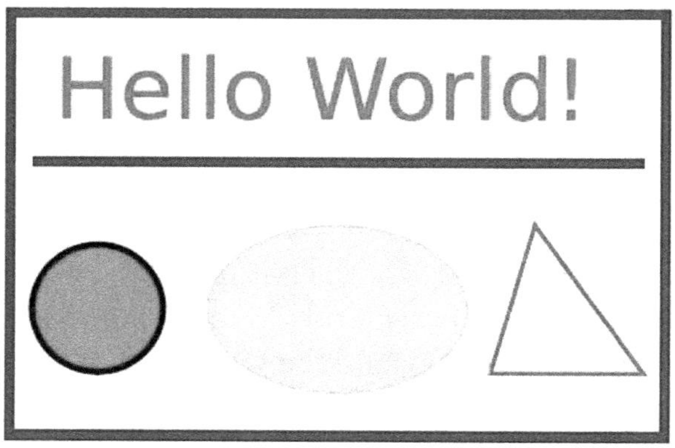

In the drawing coordinate system for this example, *x* ranges from 0 to 3 , and *y* ranges from 0 to 2. All values used for drawing, including stroke width and font size, are given in terms of this coordinate system. Remember that you can use any coordinate system that you find convenient! Note, by the way, that parts of the image that are not covered by the shapes that are drawn will be transparent.

Here's another example, with a larger variety of shapes. The source code for this example has a lot of comments. It uses features that we will discuss in the remainer of this section.

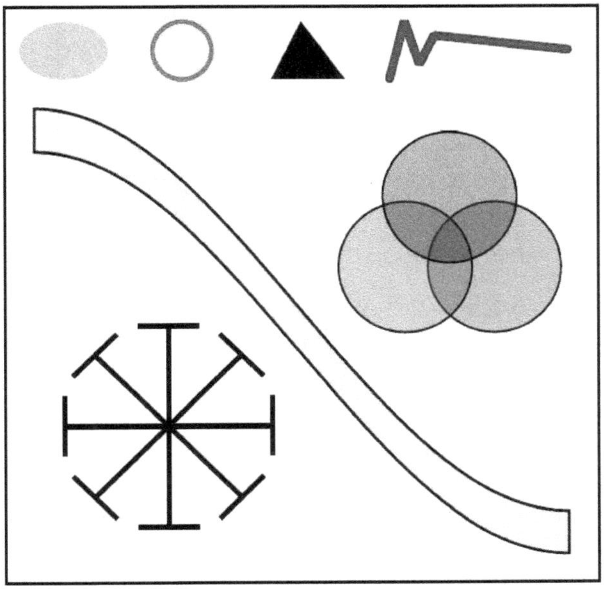

You can take a look at the source code, svg/svg-starter.svg. (For example, open it in a text editor, or open it in a web browser and use the browser's "view source" command.)

2.7.2 Shapes, Styles, and Transforms

In SVG, a basic shape is specified by an element in which the tag name gives the shape, and attributes give the properties of the shape. There are attributes to specify the geometry, such as the endpoints of a line or the radius of a circle. Other attributes specify style properties, such as fill color and line width. (The style properties are what I call attributes elsewhere in this book; in this section, I am using the term "attribute" in its XML sense.) And there is a transform attribute that can be used to apply a geometric transform to the shape.

For a detailed example, consider the rect element, which specifies a rectangle. The geometry of the rectangle is given by attributes named *x*, *y*, width and height in the usual way. The default value for *x* and *y* is zero; that is, they are optional, and leaving them out is the same as setting their value to zero. The width and the height are required attributes. Their values must be non-negative. For example, the element specifies a rectangle with corner at (0,0), width 3 , and height 2 , while

```
<rect x="100" y="200" height="480" width="640"/>
```

gives a rectangle with corner at (100,200), width 640 , and height 480 . (Note, by the way, that the attributes in an XML element can be given in any order.) The rect element also has optional attributes *rx* and *ry* that can be used to make "roundRects," with their corners replaced by elliptical arcs. The values of *rx* and *ry* give the horizontal and vertical radii of the elliptical arcs.

Style attributes can be added to say how the shape should be stroked and filled. The default is to use a black fill and no stroke. (More precisely, as we will see later, the default is for a shape to inherit the values of style attributes from its environment. Black fill and no stroke is the initial environment.) Here are some common style attributes:

- fill - specifies how to fill the shape. The value can be "none" to indicate that the shape is not filled. It can be be a color, in the same format as the CSS colors that are used in the HTML canvas API. For example, it can be a common color name such as "black" or "red", or an RGB color such as " rgb(255,200,180) ". There are also gradient and pattern fills, though I will not discuss them here.
- stroke - specifies how to stroke the shape, with the same possible values as "fill".
- stroke-opacity and fill-opacity - are numbers between 0.0 and 1.0 that specify the opacity of the stroke and fill. Values less than 1.0 give a translucent stroke or fill. The default value, 1.0 , means fully opaque.
- stroke-width - is a number that sets the line width to use for the stroke. Note that the line width is subject to transforms. The default value is " 1 ", which is fine if the coordinate system is using pixels as the unit of measure, but often too wide in custom coordinate systems.
- stroke-linecap - determines the appearance of the endpoints of a stroke. The value can be "square", "round", or "butt". The default is "butt". (See Subsection 2.2.1 for a discussion of line caps and joins.)
- stroke-linejoin - determines the appearance of points where two segments of a stroke meet. The values can be "miter", "round", or "bevel". The default is "miter".

As an example that uses many of these options, let's make a square that is rounded rather than pointed at the corners, with size 1 , centered at the origin, and using a translucent red fill and a gray stroke:

```
<rect x="-0.5" y="-0.5" width="1" height="1"
    rx="0.1" ry="0.1"
    fill="red" fill-opacity="0.5"
    stroke="gray" stroke-width="0.05" stroke-linejoin="round"/>
```

and a simple outline of a rectangle with no fill:

```
<rect width="200" height="100" stroke="black" fill="none"/>
```

The transform attribute can be used to apply a transform or a series of transforms to a shape. As an example, we can make a rectangle tilted 30 degrees from the horizontal:

```
<rect width="100" height="50" transform="rotate(30)"/>
```

The value "rotate(30)" represents a rotation of 30 degrees (not radians!) about the origin, (0,0). The positive direction of rotation, as usual, rotates the positive x -axis in the direction of the positive y-axis. You can specify a different center of rotation by adding arguments to rotate. For example, to rotate the same rectangle about its center

```
<rect width="100" height="50" transform="rotate(30,50,25)"/>
```

Translation and scaling work as you probably expect, with transform values of the form "translate(dx, dy)" and "scale(sx, sy) ". There are also shear transforms, but they go by the names skew X and skew Y, and the argument is a skew angle rather than a shear amount. For example, the transform "skew X(45) " tilts the y-axis by 45 degrees and is equivalent to an x -shear with shear factor 1 . (The function that tilts the y -axis is called skew X because it modifies, or skews, the x -coordinates of points while leaving their y -coordinates unchanged.) For example, we can use skew X to tilt a rectangle and make it into a parallelogram:

```
<rect width="100" height="50" transform="skewX(-30)"/>
```

I used an angle of -30 degrees to make the rectangle tilt to the right in the usual pixel coordinate system.

The value of the transform attribute can be a list of transforms, separated by spaces or commas. The transforms are applied to the object, as usual, in the opposite of the order in which they are listed. So,

```
<rect width="100" height="50"
    transform="translate(0,50) rotate(45) skewX(-30)"/>
```

would first skew the rectangle into a parallelogram, then rotate the parallelogram by 45 degrees about the origin, then translate it by 50 units in the y -direction.

In addition to rectangles, SVG has lines, circles, ellipses, and text as basic shapes. Here are some details. A <line> element represents a line segement and has geometric attributes $x1, y1, x2$, and $y2$ to specify the coordinates of the endpoints of the line segment. These four attributes have zero as default value, which makes it easier to specify horizontal and vertical lines. For example,

```
<line x1="100" x2="300" stroke="black"/>
```

Without the stroke attribute, you wouldn't see the line, since the default value for stoke is "none".

For a <circle> element, the geometric attributes are *cx*, *cy*, and *r* giving the coordinates of the center of the circle and the radius. The center coordinates have default values equal to zero. For an <ellipse> element, the attributes are *cx*, *cy*, *rx*, and *ry*, where *rx* and *ry* give the radii of the ellipse in the x - and y -directions.

A <text> element is a little different. It has attributes *x* and *y*, with default values zero, to specify the location of the basepoint of the text. However, the text itself is given as the content of the element rather than as an attribute. That is, the element is divided into a start tag and an end tag, and the text that will appear in the drawing comes between the start and end tags. For example,

```
<text x="10" y="30">This text will appear in the image</text>
```

The usual stroke and fill attributes apply to text, but text has additional style attributes. The font-family attribute specifies the font itself. Its value can be one of the generic font names "serif", "sans-serif", "monospace", or the name of a specific font that is available on the system. The font-size can be a number giving the (approximate) height of the characters in the coordinate system. (Font size is subject to coordinate and modeling transforms like any other length.) You can get bold and italic text by setting font-weight equal to "bold" and font-style equal to "italic". Here is an example that uses all of these options, and applies some additional styles and a transform for good measure:

```
<text x="10" y="30"
    font-family="sans-serif" font-size="50"
    font-style="italic" font-weight="bold"
    stroke="black" stroke-width="1" fill="rgb(255,200,0)"
    transform="rotate(20)">Hello World</text>
```

2.7.3 Polygons and Paths

SVG has some nice features for making more complex shapes. The <polygon> element makes it easy to create a polygon from a list of coordinate pairs. For example,

```
<polygon points="0,0 100,0 100,75 50,100 0,75"/>
```

creates a five-sided polygon with vertices at (0,0), (100,0), (100,75), (50,100), and (0,75). Every pair of numbers in the points attribute specifies a vertex. The numbers can be separated by either spaces or commas. I've used a mixture of spaces and commas here to make it clear how the numbers pair up. Of course, you can add the usual style attributes for stroke and fill to the polygon element. A <polyline> is similar to a <polygon>, except that it leaves out the last line from the final vertex back to the starting vertex. The difference only shows up when a polyline is stroked; a polyline is filled as if the missing side were added.

The <path> element is much more interesting. In fact, all of the other basic shapes, except text, could be made using path elements. A path can consist of line segments, Bezier curves, and elliptical arcs (although I won't discuss elliptical arcs here). The syntax for specifying a path is very succinct, and it has some features that we have not seen before. A path element has an attribute named *d* that contains the data for the path. The data consists of one or more commands, where each command consists of a single letter followed by any data necessary for the command. The moveTo, lineTo, cubic Bezier, and quadratic Bezier commands that you are already familiar with are coded by the letters M, L, C, and Q . The command for closing a path segment is Z , and it requires no data. For example the path data "M 1020 L 100200 " would draw a line segment from the point (10,20) to the point (100,200). You can combine several connected line segments into one L command. For example, the <polygon> example given above could be created using the <path> element

```
<path d="M 0,0 L 100,0 100,75 50,100 0,75 Z"/>
```

The Z at the end of the data closes the path by adding the final side to the polygon. (Note that, as usual, you can use either commas or spaces in the data.)

The C command takes six numbers as data, to specify the two control points and the final endpoint of the cubic Bezier curve segment. You can also give a multiple of six values to get a connected sequence of curve segements. Similarly, the Q command uses four data values to specify the control point and final endpoint of the quadratic Bezier curve segment. The large, curvy, yellow shape shown in the picture earlier in this section was created as a path with two line segments and two Bezier curve segments:

```
<path
    d="M 20,70 C 150,70 250,350 380,350 L 380,380 C 250,380 150,100
20,100                                                            Z"
    fill="yellow" stroke-width="2" stroke="black"/>
```

SVG paths add flexibility by defining "relative" versions of the path commands, where the data for the command is given relative to the current position. A relative move command, for example, instead of telling where to move, tells how far to move from the current position. The names of the relative versions of the path commands are lower case letters instead of upper case. "M 10,20 " means to move to the point with coordinates (10,20), while "m 10,20 " means to move 10 units horizontally and 20 units vertically from the current position. Similarly, if the current position is (x, y), then the command " 3,5 ", where the first character is a lower case L , draws a line from (x, y) to $(x+3, y+5)$.

2.7.4 Hierarchical Models

SVG would not be a very interesting language if it could only work with individual simple shapes. For complex scenes, we want to be able to do hierarchical modeling, where objects can be constructed from sub-objects, and a transform can be applied to an entire complex object. We need a way to group objects so that they can be treated as a unit. For that, SVG has the <g> element. The content of a <g> element is a list of shape elements, which can be simple shapes or nested <g> elements.

You can add style and transform attributes to a <g> element. The main point of grouping is that a group can be treated as a single object. A transform attribute in a <g> will transform the entire group as a whole. A style attribute, such as fill or font-family, on a <g> element will set a default value for the group, replacing the current default. Here is an example:

```
<g fill="none" stroke="black" stroke-width="2" transform="scale(1,-1)">
    <circle r="98"/>
    <ellipse cx="40" cy="40" rx="20" ry="7"/>
    <ellipse cx="-40" cy="40" rx="20" ry="7"/>
    <line y1="20" y2="-10"/>
    <path d="M -40,-40 C -30,-50 30,-50 40,-40" stroke-width="4"/>
</g>
```

The nested shapes use fill="none" stroke="black" stroke-width=" 2 " for the default values of the attributes. The default can be overridden by specifying a different value for the element, as is done for the stroke-width of the <path> element in this example. Setting transform="scale($1, -1$)" for the group flips the entire image vertically. I do this only because I am more comfortable working in a coordinate system in which y increases from bottom-to-top rather than top-to-bottom. Here is the simple line drawing of a face that is produced by this group:

Now, suppose that we want to include multiple copies of an object in a scene. It shouldn't be necessary to repeat the code for drawing the object. It would be nice to have something like reusable subroutines. In fact, SVG has something very similar: You can define reusable objects inside a <defs> element. An object that is defined inside <defs> is not added to the scene, but copies of the object can be added to the scene with a single command. For this to work, the object must have an id attribute to identify it. For example, we could define an object that looks like a plus sign:

```
<defs>
    <g id="plus" stroke="black">
        <line x1="-20" y1="0" x2="20" y2="0"/>
        <line x1="0" y1="-20" x2="0" y2="20"/>
    </g>
</defs>
```

A <use> element can then be used to add a copy of the plus sign object to the scene. The syntax is

```
<use xlink:href="#plus"/>
```

The value of the xlink:href attribute must be the id of the object, with a "#" character added at the beginning. (Don't forget the #. If you leave it out, the <use> element will simply be ignored.) You can add a transform attribute to the <use> element to apply a transformation to the copy of the object. You can also apply style attributes, which will be used as default values for the attributes in the copy. For example, we can draw several plus signs with different transforms and stroke widths:

```
<use xlink:href="#plus" transform="translate(50,20)" stroke-width="5"/>
<use xlink:href="#plus" transform="translate(0,30) rotate(45)"/>
```

Note that we can't change the color of the plus sign, since it already specifies its own stroke color.

An object that has been defined in the <defs> section can also be used as a sub-object in other object definitions. This makes it possible to create a hierarchy with multiple levels. Here is an example from svg/svg-hierarchy.svg that defines a "wheel" object, then uses two copies of the wheel as sub-objects in a "cart" object:

```
<defs>
<!-- Define an object that represents a wheel centered at (0,0) and
with
        radius 1. The wheel is made out of several filled circles, with
        thin rectangles for the spokes. -->
<g id="wheel">
    <circle cx="0" cy="0" r="1" fill="black"/>
    <circle cx="0" cy="0" r="0.8" fill="lightGray"/>
    <rect x="-0.9" y="-0.05" width="1.8" height=".1" fill="black"/>
    <rect x="-0.9" y="-0.05" width="1.8" height=".1" fill="black"
            transform="rotate(120)"/>
    <rect x="-0.9" y="-0.05" width="1.8" height=".1" fill="black"
            transform="rotate(240)"/>
    <circle cx="0" cy="0" r="0.2" fill="black"/>
</g>
<!-- Define an object that represents a cart made out of two wheels,
        with two rectangles for the body of the cart. -->
<g id="cart">
    <use xlink:href="#wheel" transform="translate(-1.5,-0.1)
scale(0.8,0.8)"/>
    <use xlink:href="#wheel" transform="translate(1.5,-0.1)
scale(0.8,0.8)"/>
    <rect x="-3" y="0" width="6" height="2"/>
    <rect x="-2.3" y="1.9" width="2.6" height="1"/>
</g>
</defs>
```

The SVG file goes on to add one copy of the wheel and four copies of the cart to the image. The four carts have different colors and transforms. Here is the image:

2.7.5 Animation

SVG has a number of advanced features that I won't discuss here, but I do want to mention one: animation. It is possible to animate almost any property of an SVG object, including geometry, style, and transforms. The syntax for animation is itself fairly complex, and I will only do a few examples. But I will tell you enough to produce a fairly complex hierarchical animation like the "cart-and-windmills" example that was discussed and used as a demo in Subsection 2.4.1. An SVG version of that animation can be found in svg/cart-and-windmills.svg. (But note that some web browsers do not implement SVG animations correctly or at all.)

Many attributes of a shape element can be animated by adding an <animate> element to the content of the shape element. Here is an example that makes a rectangle move across the image from left to right:

```
<rect x="0" y="210" width="40" height="40">
    <animate attributeName="x"
    from="0" to="430" dur="7s"
    repeatCount="indefinite"/>
</rect>
```

Note that the <animate> is nested inside the <rect>. The attributeName attribute tells which attribute of the <rect> is being animated, in this case, x. The from and to attributes say that x will take on values from 0 to 430 . The dur attribute is the "duration", that is, how long the animation lasts; the value " 7 s " means " 7 seconds." The attribute repeatCount = "indefinite" means that after the animation completes, it will start over, and it will repeat indefinitely, that is, as long as the image is displayed. If the repeatCount attribute is omitted, then after the animation runs once, the rectangle will jump back to its original position and remain there. If repeatCount is replaced by fill="freeze", then after the animation runs, the rectangle will be frozen in its final position, instead of jumping back to the starting position. The animation begins when the image first loads. If you want the animation to start at a later time, you can add a begin attribute whose value gives the time when the animation should start, as a number of seconds after the image loads.

What if we want the rectangle to move back and forth between its initial and final position? For that, we need something called keyframe animation, which is an important idea in its own right. The from and to attributes allow you to specify values only for the beginning and end of the animation. In a keyframe animation, values are specified at additional times in the middle of the animation. For a keyframe animation in SVG, the from and to attributes are replaced by keyTimes and values. Here is our moving rectangle example, modified to use keyframes:

```
<rect x="0" y="210" width="40" height="40">
    <animate attributeName="x"
    keyTimes="0;0.5;1" values="0;430;0" dur="7s"
    repeatCount="indefinite"/>
</rect>
```

The keyTimes attribute is a list of numbers, separated by semicolons. The numbers are in the range 0 to 1 , and should be in increasing order. The first number should be 0 and the last number should be 1 . A number specifies a time during the animation, as a fraction of the complete animation. For example, 0.5 is a point half-way through the animation, and 0.75 is three-quarters of the way. The values attribute is a list of values, with one value for each key time. In this case, the value for x is 0 at the start of the animation, 430 half-way through the animation, and 0 again at the end of the animation. Between the key times, the value for x is obtained by interpolating between the values specified for the key times. The result in this case is that the rectangle moves from left to right during the first half of the animation and then back from right to left in the second half.

Transforms can also be animated, but you need to use the <animateTransform> tag instead of <animate>, and you need to add a type attribute to specify which transform you are animating, such as "rotate" or "translate". Here, for example, is a transform animation applied to a group:

```
<g transform="scale(0,0)">
    <animateTransform attributeName="transform" type="scale"
        from="0,0" to="0.4,0.7"
        begin="3s" dur="15s" fill="freeze"/>
    <rect x="-15" y="0" width="30" height="40" fill="rgb(150,100,0)"/>
    <polygon points="-60,40 60,40 0,200" fill="green"/>
</g>
```

The animation shows a growing "tree" made from a green triangle and a brown rectangle. In the animation, the transform goes from scale (0,0) to scale (0.4,0.7). The animation starts 3 seconds after the image loads and lasts 15 seconds. At the end of the animation, the tree freezes at its final scale. The transform attribute on the <g> element specifies the scale that is in effect until the animation starts. (A scale factor of 0 collapses the object to size zero, so that it is invisible.) You can find this example, along with a moving rectangle and a keyframe animation, in the sample file svg/first-svg-animation.svg.

You can create animated objects in the <defs> section of an SVG file, and you can apply animation to <use> elements. This makes it possible to create hierarchical animations. A simple example can be found in the sample file svg/hierarchical-animation.svg.

The example shows a rotating hexagon with a rotating square at each vertex of the hexagon. The hexagon is constructed from six copies of one object, with a different rotation applied to each copy. (A copy of the basic object is shown in the image to the right of the hexagon.) The square is defined as an animated object with its own rotation. It is used as a sub-object in the hexagon. The rotation that is applied to the hexagon applies to the square, on top of its own built-in rotation. That's what makes this an example of hierarchical animation.

If you look back at the cart-and-windmills example now, you can probably see how to do the animation. Don't forget to check out the source code, which is surprisingly short!

Chapter-3

OpenGL 1.1: Geometry

It is time to move on to computer graphics in three dimensions, although it won't be until Section 2 of this chapter that we really get into 3D. You will find that many concepts from 2D graphics carry over to 3D, but the move into the third dimension brings with it some new features that take a while to get used to.

Our focus will be OpenGL, a graphics API that was introduced in 1992 and has gone through many versions and many changes since then. OpenGL is a low-level graphics API, similar to the 2D APIs we have covered. It is even more primitive in some ways, but of course it is complicated by the fact that it supports 3D. OpenGL is the basis for WebGL, the current standard for 3D applications on the Web that is covered in Chapter 6 and Chapter 7. There are many competing frameworks for low-level 3D graphics, including Microsoft's Direct3D, Apple's Metal, and Vulkan, which was designed by the creators of OpenGL as a more modern and efficient replacement.

For the next two chapters, the discussion is limited to OpenGL 1.1. OpenGL 1.1 is a large API, and we will only cover a part of it. The goal is to introduce 3D graphics concepts, not to fully cover the API. A significant part of what we cover here has been removed from the most modern versions of OpenGL, including WebGL. However, modern OpenGL in its pure form has a very steep initial learning curve, and it is really not a good starting place for someone who is encountering 3D graphics for the first time. Some additional support is needed-if not OpenGL 1.1 then some similar framework. Since OpenGL 1.1 is still supported, at least by all desktop implementations of OpenGL, it's a reasonable place to start learning about 3D graphics.

This chapter concentrates on the geometric aspects of 3D graphics, such as defining and transforming objects and projecting 3D scenes into 2D images. The images that we produce will look very unrealistic. In the next chapter, we will see how to add some realism by simulating the effects of lighting and of the material properties of surfaces.

3.1 Shapes and Colors in OpenGL 1.1

This section introduces some of the core features of OpenGL. Much of the discussion in this section is limited to 2D. For now, all you need to know about 3D is that it adds a third direction to the x and y directions that are used in 2D. By convention, the third direction is called z. In the default coordinate system, the x and y axes lie in the plane of the image, and the positive direction of the z-axis points in a direction perpendicular to the image.

In the default coordinate system for OpenGL, the image shows a region of 3D space in which x, y, and z all range from minus one to one. To show a different region, you have to apply a transform. For now, we will just use coordinates that lie between -1 and 1 . A note about programming: OpenGL can be implemented in many different programming languages, but the API specification more or less assumes that the language is C. (See Section A. 2 for a short introduction to C .) For the most part, the C specification translates directly into other languages. The main differences are due to the special characteristics of arrays in the C language. My examples will follow the C syntax, with a few notes about how things can be different in other languages. Since I'm following the C API, I will refer to "functions" rather than "subroutines" or "methods." Section 3.6 explains in detail how to write OpenGL programs in C and in Java. You will need to consult that section before you can do any actual programming. The live OpenGL 1.1 demos for this book are written using a JavaScript simulator that implements a subset of OpenGL 1.1. That simulator is discussed in Subsection 3.6.3.

3.1.1 OpenGL Primitives

OpenGL can draw only a few basic shapes, including points, lines, and triangles. There is no built-in support for curves or curved surfaces; they must be approximated by simpler shapes. The basic shapes are referred to as primitives. A primitive in OpenGL is defined by its vertices. A vertex is simply a point in 3D, given by its x, y, and z coordinates. Let's jump right in and see how to draw a triangle. It takes a few steps:

```
glBegin(GL_TRIANGLES);
glVertex2f( -0.7, -0.5 );
glVertex2f( 0.7, -0.5 );
glVertex2f( 0, 0.7 );
glEnd();
```

Each vertex of the triangle is specified by a call to the function glVertex2f. Vertices must be specified between calls to glBegin and glEnd. The parameter to glBegin tells which type of primitive is being drawn. The GL_TRIANGLES primitive allows you to draw more than one triangle: Just specify three vertices for each triangle that you want to draw. Note that using glBegin/glEnd is not the preferred way to specify primitives, even in OpenGL 1.1. However, the alternative, which is covered in Subsection 3.4.2, is more complicated to use. You should consider glBegin/glEnd to be a convenient way to learn about vertices and their properties, but not the way that you will actually do things in modern graphics APIs. (I should note that OpenGL functions actually just send commands to the GPU. OpenGL can save up batches of commands to transmit together, and the drawing won't actually be done until the commands are transmitted. To ensure that that happens, the function glFlush() must be called. In some cases, this function might be called automatically by an OpenGL API, but you might well run into times when you have to call it yourself.)

For OpenGL, vertices have three coordinates. The function glVertex $2f$ specifies the x and y coordinates of the vertex, and the z coordinate is set to zero. There is also a function glVertex3f that specifies all three coordinates. The " 2 " or " 3 " in the name tells how many parameters are passed to the function. The " f " at the end of the name indicates that the parameters are of type float. In fact, there are other "glVertex" functions, including versions that take parameters of type int or double, with named like glVertex2i and glVertex3d. There are even versions that take four parameters, although it won't be clear for a while why they should exist. And, as we will see later, there are versions that take an array of numbers instead of individual numbers as parameters. The entire set of vertex functions is often referred to as "glVertex*", with the "*" standing in for the parameter specification. (The proliferation of names is due to the fact that the C programming language doesn't support overloading of function names; that is, C distinguishes functions only by their names and not by the number and type of parameters that are passed to the function.)

OpenGL 1.1 has ten kinds of primitive. Seven of them still exist in modern OpenGL; the other three have been dropped. The simplest primitive is GL_POINTS, which simply renders a point at each vertex of the primitive. By default, a point is rendered as a single pixel. The size of point primitives can be changed by calling

```
glPointSize(size);
```

where the parameter, size, is of type float and specifies the diameter of the rendered point, in pixels. By default, points are squares. You can get circular points by calling

```
glEnable(GL_POINT_SMOOTH) ;
```

The functions glPointSize and glEnable change the OpenGL "state." The state includes all the settings that affect rendering. We will encounter many state-changing functions. The functions glEnable and glDisable can be used to turn many features on and off. In general, the rule is that any rendering feature that requires extra computation is turned off by default. If you want that feature, you have to turn it on by calling glEnable with the appropriate parameter.

There are three primitives for drawing line segments: GL_LINES, GL_LINE_STRIP, and GL_LINE_LOOP. GL_LINES draws disconnected line segments; specify two vertices for each segment that you want to draw. The other two primitives draw connected sequences of line segments. The only difference is that GL_LINE_LOOP adds an extra line segment from the final vertex back to the first vertex. Here is what you get if use the same six vertices with the four primitives we have seen so far:

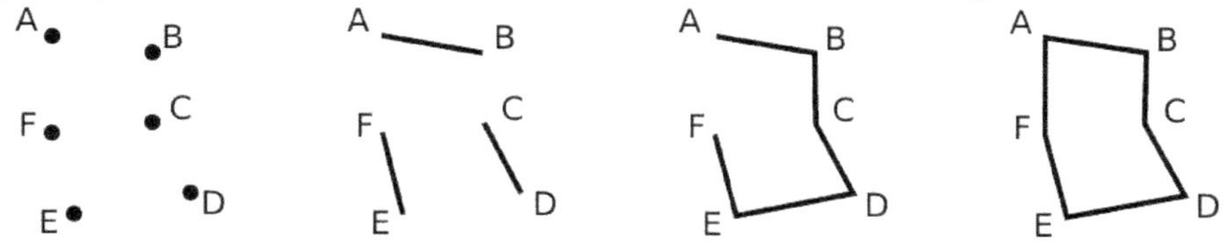

GL_POINTS GL_LINES GL_LINE_STRIP GL_LINE_LOOP

The points A, B, C, D, E, and F were specified in that order. In this illustration, all the points lie in the same plane, but keep in mind that in general, points can be anywhere in 3D space.

The width for line primitives can be set by calling glLineWidth(width). The line width is always specified in pixels. It is not subject to scaling by transformations.

Let's look at an example. OpenGL does not have a circle primitive, but we can approximate a circle by drawing a polygon with a large number of sides. To draw an outline of the polygon, we can use a GL_LINE_LOOP primitive:

```
glBegin( GL_LINE_LOOP );
for (i = 0; i < 64; i++) {
    angle = 6.2832 * i / 64; // 6.2832 represents 2*PI
    x = 0.5* cos(angle);
    y = 0.5 * sin(angle);
    glVertex2f( x, y );
}
glEnd();
```

This draws an approximation for the circumference of a circle of radius 0.5 with center at (0,0). Remember that to learn how to use examples like this one in a complete, running program, you will have to read Section 3.6. Also, you might have to make some changes to the code, depending on which OpenGL implementation you are using.

The next set of primitives is for drawing triangles. There are three of them: GL_TRIANGLES, GL_TRIANGLE_STRIP, and GL_TRIANGLE_FAN.

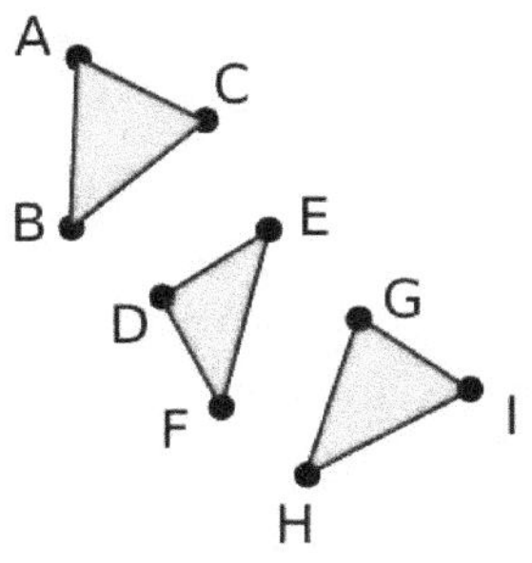

GL_TRIANGLES

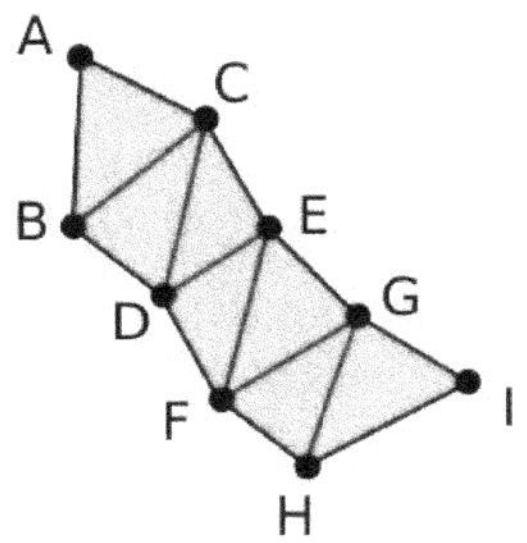

GL_TRIANGLE_STRIP

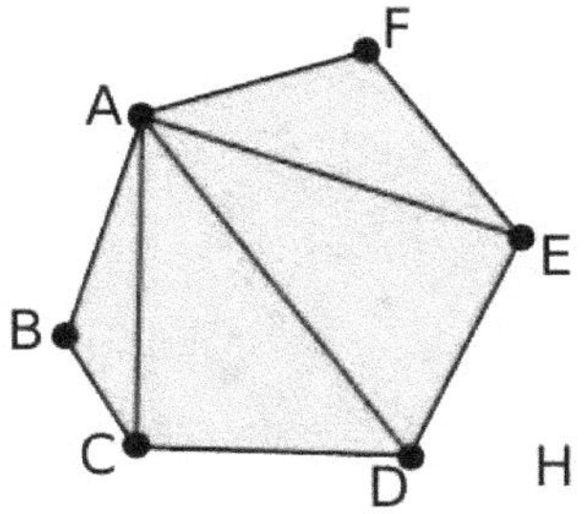

GL_TRIANGLE_FAN

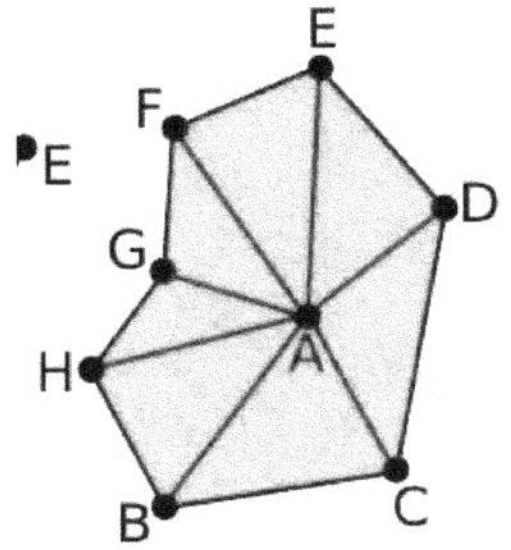

GL_TRIANGLE_FAN

The three triangles on the left make up one GL_TRIANGLES primitive, with nine vertices. With that primitive, every set of three vertices makes a separate triangle. For a GL_TRIANGLE_STRIP primitive, the first three vertices produce a triangle. After that, every new vertex adds another triangle to the strip, connecting the new vertex to the two previous vertices. Two GL_TRIANGLE_FAN primitives are shown on the right. Again for a GL_TRIANGLE_FAN, the first three vertices make a triangle, and every vertex after that adds anther triangle, but in this case, the new triangle is made by connecting the new vertex to the previous vertex and to the very first vertex that was specified (vertex "A" in the picture). Note that Gl_TRIANGLE_FAN can be used for drawing filled-in polygons. In this picture, by the way, the dots and lines are not part of the primitive; OpenGL would only draw the filled-in, green interiors of the figures.

The three remaining primitives, which have been removed from modern OpenGL, are GL_QUADS, GL_QUAD_STRIP, and GL_POLYGON. The name "quad" is short for quadrilateral, that is, a four-sided polygon. A quad is determined by four vertices. In order for a quad to be rendered correctly in OpenGL, all vertices of the quad must lie in the same plane. The same is true for polygon primitives. Similarly, to be rendered correctly, quads and polygons must be convex (see Subsection 2.2.3). Since OpenGL doesn't check whether these conditions are satisfied, the use of quads and polygons is error-prone. Since the same shapes can easily be produced with the triangle primitives, they are not really necessary, but here for the record are some examples:

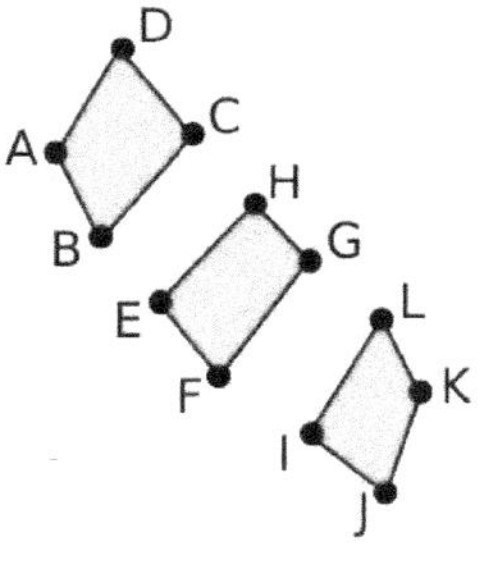

GL_QUADS

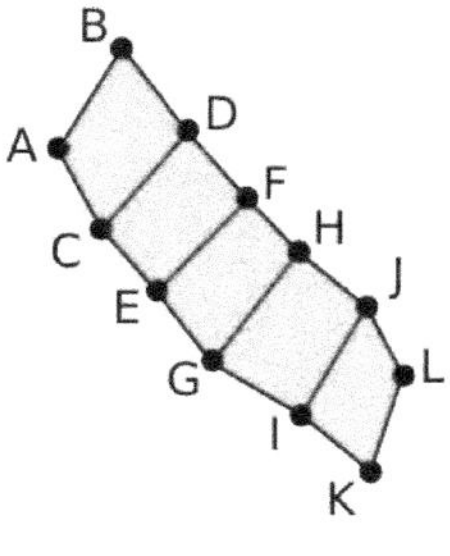

GL_QUAD_STRIP

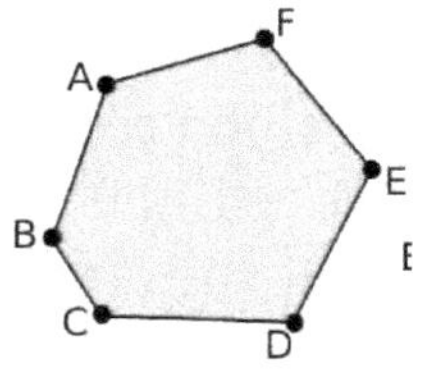

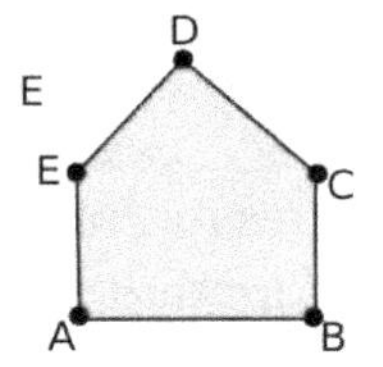

GL_POLYGON

The vertices for these primitives are specified in the order A, B, C, ... Note how the order differs for the two quad primitives: For *GL_QUADS*, the vertices for each individual quad should be specified in counterclockwise order around the quad; for GL_QUAD_STRIP, the vertices should alternate from one side of the strip to the other.

3.1.2 OpenGL Color

OpenGL has a large collection of functions that can be used to specify colors for the geometry that we draw. These functions have names of the form glColor*, where the "" *stands for a suffix that gives the number and type of the parameters. I should warn you now that for realistic 3D graphics, OpenGL has a more complicated notion of color that uses a different set of functions. You will learn about that in the next chapter, but for now we will stick to glColor.*

For example, the function glColor3f has three parameters of type float. The parameters give the red, green, and blue components of the color as numbers in the range 0.0 to 1.0 . (In fact, values outside this range are allowed, even negative values. When color values are used in computations, out-of-range values will be used as given. When a color actually appears on the screen, its component values are clamped to the range 0 to 1 . That is, values less than zero are changed to zero, and values greater than one are changed to one.)

You can add a fourth component to the color by using glColor $4f()$. The fourth component, known as alpha, is not used in the default drawing mode, but it is possible to configure OpenGL to use it as the degree of transparency of the color, similarly to the use of the alpha component in the 2D graphics APIs that we have looked at. You need two commands to turn on transparency:

```
glEnable(GL_BLEND);
glBlendFunc(GL_SRC_ALPHA, GL_ONE_MINUS_SRC_ALPHA);
```

The first command enables use of the alpha component. It can be disabled by calling glDisable(GL_BLEND). When the GL_BLEND option is disabled, alpha is simply ignored. The second command tells how the alpha component of a color will be used. The parameters shown here are the most common; they implement transparency in the usual way. I should note that while transparency works fine in 2D, it is much more difficult to use transparency correctly in 3D.

If you would like to use integer color values in the range 0 to 255, you can use glColor3ub() or glColor4ub to set the color. In these function names, "ub" stands for "unsigned byte." Unsigned byte is an eight-bit data type with values in the range 0 to 255 . Here are some examples of commands for setting drawing colors in OpenGL:

```
glColor3f(0,0,0); // Draw in black.
glColor3f(1,1,1); // Draw in white.
glColor3f(1,0,0); // Draw in full-intensity red.
glColor3ub(1,0,0); // Draw in a color just a tiny bit different from
    // black. (The suffix, "ub" or "f", is important!)
glColor3ub(255,0,0); // Draw in full-intensity red.
glColor4f(1, 0, 0, 0.5); // Draw in transparent red, but only if OpenGL
    // has been configured to do transparency. By
    // default this is the same as drawing in plain red.
```

Using any of these functions sets the value of a "current color," which is part of the OpenGL state. When you generate a vertex with one of the glVertex* functions, the current color is saved along with the vertex coordinates, as an attribute of the vertex. We will see that vertices can have other kinds of attribute as well as color. One interesting point about OpenGL is that colors are associated with individual vertices, not with complete shapes. By changing the current color between calls to glBegin() and glEnd(), you can get a shape in which different vertices have different color attributes. When you do this, OpenGL will compute the colors of pixels inside the shape by interpolating the colors of the vertices. (Again, since OpenGL is extremely configurable, I have to note that interpolation of colors is just the default behavior.) For example, here is a triangle in which the three vertices are assigned the colors red, green, and blue:

This image is often used as a kind of "Hello World" example for OpenGL. The triangle can be drawn with the commands

```
glBegin(GL_TRIANGLES);
glColor3f( 1, 0, 0 ); // red
glVertex2f( -0.8, -0.8 );
glColor3f( 0, 1, 0 ); // green
glVertex2f( 0.8, -0.8 );
glColor3f( 0, 0, 1 ); // blue
glVertex2f( 0, 0.9 );
glEnd();
```

Note that when drawing a primitive, you do not need to explicitly set a color for each vertex, as was done here. If you want a shape that is all one color, you just have to set the current color once, before drawing the shape (or just after the call to glBegin(). For example, we can draw a solid yellow triangle with

```
glColor3ub(255,255,0); // yellow
glBegin(GL_TRIANGLES);
glVertex2f( -0.5, -0.5 );
glVertex2f( 0.5, -0.5 );
glVertex2f( 0, 0.5 );
glEnd();
```

Also remember that the color for a vertex is specified before the call to glVertex* that generates the vertex.

The on-line version of this section has an interactive demo that draws the basic OpenGL triangle, with different colored vertices. That demo is our first OpenGL example. The demo actually uses WebGL, so you can use it as a test to check whether your web browser supports WebGL.

The sample program jogl/FirstTriangle.java draws the basic OpenGL triangle using Java. The program glut/first-triangle.c does the same using the C programming language. And glsim/first-triangle.html is a version that uses my JavaScript simulator, which implements just the parts of OpenGL 1.1 that are covered in this book. Any of those programs could be used to experiment with 2D drawing in OpenGL. And you can use them to test your OpenGL programming environment.

A common operation is to clear the drawing area by filling it with some background color. It is be possible to do that by drawing a big colored rectangle, but OpenGL has a potentially more efficient way to do it. The function

```
glClearColor(r,g,b,a);
```

sets up a color to be used for clearing the drawing area. (This only sets the color; the color isn't used until you actually give the command to clear the drawing area.) The parameters are floating point values in the range 0 to 1 . There are no variants of this function; you must provide all four color components, and they must be in the range 0 to 1 . The default clear color is all zeros, that is, black with an alpha component also equal to zero. The command to do the actual clearing is:

```
glClear( GL_COLOR_BUFFER_BIT );
```

The correct term for what I have been calling the drawing area is the color buffer, where "buffer" is a general term referring to a region in memory. OpenGL uses several buffers in addition to the color buffer. We will encounter the "depth buffer" in just a moment. The glClear command can be used to clear several different buffers at the same time, which can be more efficient than clearing them separately since the clearing can be done in parallel. The parameter to glClear tells it which buffer or buffers to clear. To clear several buffers at once, combine the constants that represent them with an arithmetic OR operation. For example,

```
glClear( GL_COLOR_BUFFER_BIT | GL_DEPTH_BUFFER_BIT );
```

This is the form of glClear that is generally used in 3D graphics, where the depth buffer plays an essential role. For 2D graphics, the depth buffer is generally not used, and the appropriate parameter for glClear is just GL_COLOR_BUFFER_BIT.

3.1.3 glColor and glVertex with Arrays

We have see that there are versions of glColor* and glVertex* that take different numbers and types of parameters. There are also versions that let you place all the data for the command in a single array parameter. The names for such versions end with "v". For example: glColor3fv, glVertex2iv, glColor4ubv, and glVertex3dv. The "v" actually stands for "vector," meaning essentially a one-dimensional array of numbers. For example, in the function call glVertex3fv(coords), coords would be an array containing at least three floating point numbers.

The existence of array parameters in OpenGL forces some differences between OpenGL implementations in different programming languages. Arrays in Java are different from arrays in C, and arrays in JavaScript are different from both. Let's look at the situation in C first, since that's the language of the original OpenGL API.

In C, array variables are a sort of variation on pointer variables, and arrays and pointers can be used interchangeably in many circumstances. In fact, in the C API, array parameters are actually specified as pointers. For example, the parameter for glVertex3fv is of type "pointer to float." The actual parameter in a call to glVertex3fv can be an array variable, but it can also be any pointer that points to the beginning of a sequence of three floats. As an example, suppose that we want to draw a square. We need two coordinates for each vertex of the square. In C, we can put all 8 coordinates into one array and use glVertex2fv to pull out the coordinates that we need:

```
float coords[] = { - 0.5, -0.5, 0.5, -0.5, 0.5, 0.5, -0.5, 0.5};
glBegin(GL_TRIANGLE_FAN);
glVertex2fv(coords); // Uses coords[0] and coords[1].
glVertex2fv(coords + 2); // Uses coords[2] and coords[3].
glVertex2fv(coords + 4); // Uses coords[4] and coords[5].
glVertex2fv(coords + 6); // Uses coords[6] and coords[7].
glEnd();
```

This example uses "pointer arithmetic," in which coords $+N$ represents a pointer to the N -th element of the array. An alternative notation would be & coords $[N]$, where "&" is the address operator, and &coords $[N]$ means "a pointer to coords $[N]$ ". This will all seem very alien to people who are only familiar with Java or JavaScript. In my examples, I will avoid using pointer arithmetic, but I will occasionally use address operators.

As for Java, the people who designed JOGL wanted to preserve the ability to pull data out of the middle of an array. However, it's not possible to work with pointers in Java. The solution was to replace a pointer parameter in the C API with a pair of parameters in the JOGL API-one parameter to specify the array that contains the data and one to specify the starting index of the data in the array. For example, here is how the square-drawing code translates into Java:

```
float[] coords = { - 0.5F, -0.5F, 0.5F, -0.5F, 0.5F, 0.5F, -0.5F, 0.5F
};
```

```
gl2.glBegin(GL2.GL_TRIANGLES);
gl2.glVertex2fv(coords, 0); // Uses coords[0] and coords[1].
gl2.glVertex2fv(coords, 2); // Uses coords[2] and coords[3].
gl2.glVertex2fv(coords, 4); // Uses coords[4] and coords[5].
gl2.glVertex2fv(coords, 6); // Uses coords[6] and coords[7].
gl2.glEnd();
```

There is really not much difference in the parameters, although the zero in the first glVertex2fv is a little annoying. The main difference is the prefixes "gl2" and "GL2", which are required by the object-oriented nature of the JOGL API. I won't say more about JOGL here, but if you need to translate my examples into JOGL, you should keep in mind the extra parameter that is required when working with arrays.

For the record, here are the glVertex* and glColor* functions that I will use in this book. This is not the complete set that is available in OpenGL:

```
glVertex2f( x, y ); glVertex2fv( xyArray );
glVertex2d( x, y ); glVertex2dv( xyArray );
glVertex2i( x, y ); glVertex2iv( xyArray );
glVertex3f( x, y, z ); glVertex3fv( xyzArray );
glVertex3d( x, y, z ); glVertex3dv( xyzArray );
glVertex3i( x, y, z ); glVertex3iv( xyzArray );
glColor3f( r, g, b ); glColor3f( rgbArray );
glColor3d( r, g, b ); glColor3d( rgbArray );
glColor3ub( r, g, b ); glColor3ub( rgbArray );


glColor4f( r, g, b, a); glColor4f( rgbaArray );
glColor4d( r, g, b, a); glColor4d( rgbaArray );
glColor4ub( r, g, b, a); glColor4ub( rgbaArray );
```

For glColor*, keep in mind that the "ub" variations require integers in the range 0 to 255 , while the " f " and " d " variations require floating-point numbers in the range 0.0 to 1.0 .

3.1.4 The Depth Test

An obvious point about viewing in 3D is that one object can be behind another object. When this happens, the back object is hidden from the viewer by the front object. When we create an image of a 3D world, we have to make sure that objects that are supposed to be hidden behind other objects are in fact not visible in the image. This is the hidden surface problem.

The solution might seem simple enough: Just draw the objects in order from back to front. If one object is behind another, the back object will be covered up later when the front object is drawn. This is called the painter's algorithm. It's essentially what you are used to doing in 2D. Unfortunately, it's not so easy to implement. First of all, you can have objects that intersect, so that part of each object is hidden by the other. Whatever order you draw the objects in, there will be some points where the wrong object is visible. To fix this, you would have to cut the objects into pieces, along the intersection, and treat the pieces as separate objects. In fact, there can be problems even if there are no intersecting objects: It's possible to have three non-intersecting objects where the first object hides part of the second, the second hides part of the third, and the third hides part of the first. The painter's algorithm will fail regardless of the order in which the three objects are drawn. The solution again is to cut the objects into pieces, but now it's not so obvious where to cut.

Even though these problems can be solved, there is another issue. The correct drawing order can change when the point of view is changed or when a geometric transformation is applied, which means that the correct drawing order has to be recomputed every time that happens. In an animation, that would mean for every frame.

So, OpenGL does not use the painter's algorithm. Instead, it uses a technique called the depth test. The depth test solves the hidden surface problem no matter what order the objects are drawn in, so you can draw them in any order you want! The term "depth" here has to do with the distance from the viewer to the object. Objects at greater depth are farther from the viewer. An object with smaller depth will hide an object with greater depth. To implement the depth test algorithm, OpenGL stores a depth value for each pixel in the image. The extra memory that is used to store these depth values makes up the depth buffer that I mentioned earlier. During the drawing process, the depth buffer is used to keep track of what is currently visible at each pixel. When a second object is drawn at that pixel, the information in the depth buffer can be used to decide whether the new object is in front of or behind the object that is currently visible there. If the new object is in front, then the color of the pixel is changed to show the new object, and the depth buffer is also updated. If the new object is behind the current object, then the data for the new object is discarded and the color and depth buffers are left unchanged.

By default, the depth test is not turned on, which can lead to very bad results when drawing in 3D. You can enable the depth test by calling

```
glEnable( GL_DEPTH_TEST );
```

It can be turned off by calling glDisable(*GL_DEPTH_TEST*). If you forget to enable the depth test when drawing in 3D, the image that you get will likely be confusing and will make no sense physically. You can also get quite a mess if you forget to clear the depth buffer, using the glClear command shown earlier in this section, at the same time that you clear the color buffer.

The demo c3/first-cube.html in the online version of this section lets you experiment with the depth test. It also lets you see what happens when part of your geometry extends outside the visible range of *z*-values.

Here are are a few details about the implementation of the depth test: For each pixel, the depth buffer stores a representation of the distance from the viewer to the point that is currently visible at that pixel. This value is essentially the *z*-coordinate of the point, after any transformations have been applied. (In fact, the depth buffer is often called the "z-buffer".) The range of possible *z*-coordinates is scaled to the range 0 to 1 . The fact that there is only a limited range of depth buffer values means that OpenGL can only display objects in a limited range of distances from the viewer. A depth value of 0 corresponds to the minimal distance; a depth value of 1 corresponds to the maximal distance. When you clear the depth buffer, every depth value is set to 1 , which can be thought of as representing the background of the image.

You get to choose the range of *z*-values that is visible in the image, by the transformations that you apply. The default range, in the absence of any transformations, is -1 to 1 . Points with *z*-values outside the range are not visible in the image. It is a common problem to use too small a range of *z*-values, so that objects are missing from the scene, or have their fronts or backs cut off, because they lie outside of the visible range. You might be tempted to use a huge range, to make sure that the objects that you want to include in the image are included within the range. However, that's not a good idea: The depth buffer has a limited number of bits per pixel and therefore a limited amount of accuracy. The larger the range of values that it must represent, the harder it is to distinguish between objects that are almost at the same depth. (Think about what would happen if all objects in your scene have depth values between 0.499999 and 0.500001 - the depth buffer might see them all as being at exactly the same depth!)

There is another issue with the depth buffer algorithm. It can give some strange results when two objects have exactly the same depth value. Logically, it's not even clear which object should be visible, but the real problem with the depth test is that it might show one object at some points and the second object at some other points. This is possible because numerical calculations are not perfectly accurate. Here an actual example:

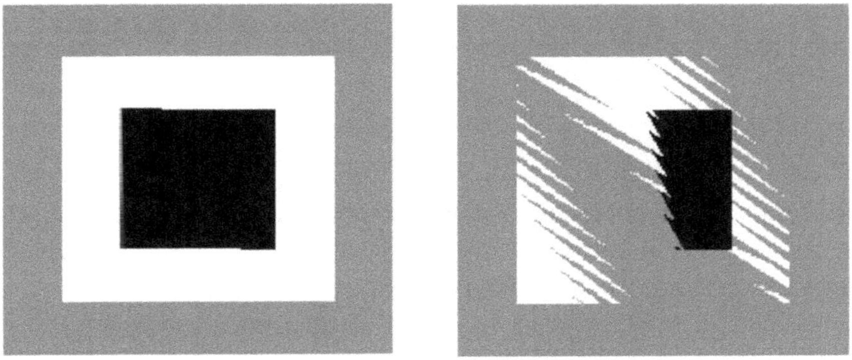

In the two pictures shown here, a gray square was drawn, followed by a white square, followed by a black square. The squares all lie in the same plane. A very small rotation was applied, to force the computer do some calculations before drawing the objects. The picture on the left was drawn with the depth test disabled, so that, for example, when a pixel of the white square was drawn, the computer didn't try to figure out whether it lies in front of or behind the gray square; it simply colored the pixel white. On the right, the depth test was enabled, and you can see the strange result.

Finally, by the way, note that the discussion here assumes that there are no transparent objects. Unfortunately, the depth test does not handle transparency correctly, since transparency means that two or more objects can contribute to the color of the pixel, but the depth test assumes that the pixel color is the color of the object nearest to the viewer at that point. To handle 3D transparency correctly in OpenGL, you pretty much have to resort to implementing the painter's algorithm by hand, at least for the transparent objects in the scene.

3.2 3D Coordinates and Transforms

In Chapter 2, we looked fairly closely at coordinate systems and transforms in twodimensional computer graphics. In this section and the next, we will move that discussion into 3D. Things are more complicated in three dimensions, but a lot of the basic concepts remain the same.

3.2.1 3D Coordinates

A coordinate system is a way of assigning numbers to points. In two dimensions, you need a pair of numbers to specify a point. The coordinates are often referred to as x and y, although of course, the names are arbitrary. More than that, the assignment of pairs of numbers to points is itself arbitrary to a large extent. Points and objects are real things, but coordinates are just numbers that we assign to them so that we can refer to them easily and work with them mathematically. We have seen the power of this when we discussed transforms, which are defined mathematically in terms of coordinates but which have real, useful physical meanings.

In three dimensions, you need three numbers to specify a point. (That's essentially what it means to be three dimensional.) The third coordinate is often called z. The z-axis is perpendicular to both the x-axis and the y-axis.

This image illustrates a 3D coordinate system. The positive directions of the x, y, and z axes are shown as big arrows. The x-axis is green, the y-axis is blue, and the z-axis is red. The on-line version of this section has a demo version of this image in which you drag on the axes to rotate the image.

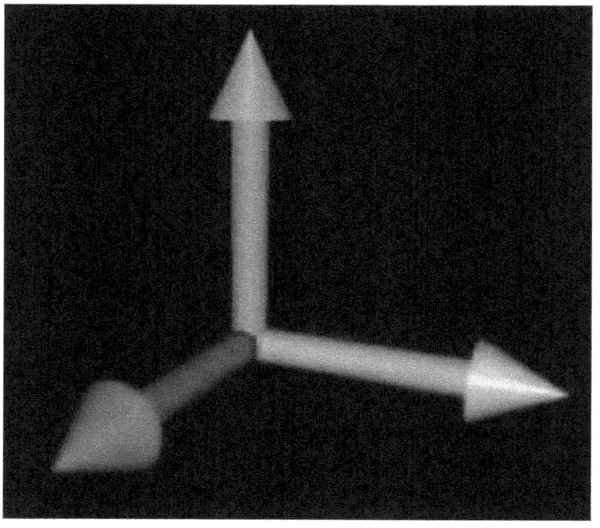

This example is a 2D image, but it has a 3D look. (The illusion is much stronger if you can rotate the image.) Several things contribute to the effect. For one thing, objects that are farther away from the viewer in 3D look smaller in the 2D image. This is due to the way that the 3D scene is "projected" onto 2D. We will discuss projection in the next section. Another factor is the "shading" of the objects. The objects are shaded in a way that imitates the interaction of objects with the light that illuminates them. We will put off a discussion of lighting until Chapter 4. In this section, we will concentrate on how to construct a scene in 3D-what we have referred to as modeling.

OpenGL programmers usually think in terms of a coordinate system in which the x - and y-axes lie in the plane of the screen, and the z-axis is perpendicular to the screen with the positive direction of the z-axis pointing out of the screen towards the viewer. Now, the default coordinate system in OpenGL, the one that you are using if you apply no transformations at all, is similar but has the positive direction of the z-axis pointing into the screen. This is not a contradiction: The coordinate system that is actually used is arbitrary. It is set up by a transformation. The convention in OpenGL is to work with a coordinate system in which the positive z-direction points toward the viewer and the negative z-direction points away from the viewer. The transformation into default coordinates reverses the direction of the z-axis.

This conventional arrangement of the axes produces a right-handed coordinate system. This means that if you point the thumb of your right hand in the direction of the positive z-axis, then when you curl the fingers of that hand, they will curl in the direction from the positive x-axis towards the positive y-axis. If you are looking at the tip of your thumb, the curl will be in the counterclockwise direction. Another way to think about it is that if you curl the figures of your right hand from the positive x to the positive y-axis, then your thumb will point in the direction of the positive z-axis. The default OpenGL coordinate system (which, again, is hardly ever used) is a left-handed system. You should spend some time trying to visualize right- and left-handed coordinates systems. Use your hands!

All of that describes the natural coordinate system from the viewer's point of view, the so-called "eye" or "viewing" coordinate system. However, these eye coordinates are not necessarily the natural coordinates on the world. The coordinate system on the world-the coordinate system in which the scene is assembled-is referred to as world coordinates.

Recall that objects are not usually specified directly in world coordinates. Instead, objects are specified in their own coordinate system, known as object coordinates, and then modeling transforms are applied to place the objects into the world, or into more complex objects. In OpenGL, object coordinates are the numbers that are used in the glVertex* function to specify the vertices of the object. However, before the objects appear on the screen, they are usually subject to a sequence of transformations, starting with a modeling transform.

3.2.2 Basic 3D Transforms

The basic transforms in 3D are extensions of the basic transforms that you are already familiar with from 2D: rotation, scaling, and translation. We will look at the 3D equivalents and see how they affect objects when applied as modeling transforms. We will also discuss how to use the transforms in OpenGL.

Translation is easiest. In 2D, a translation adds some number onto each coordinate. The same is true in 3D; we just need three numbers, to specify the amount of motion in the direction of each of the coordinate axes. A translation by (dx, dy, dz) transforms a point (x, y, z) to the point $(x + dx, y + dy, z + dz)$. In OpenGL, this translation would be specified by the command

```
glTranslatef( dx, dy, dz );
```

or by the command

```
glTranslated( dx, dy, dz );
```

The translation will affect any drawing that is done after the command is given. Note that there are two versions of the command. The first, with a name ending in " f ", takes three float values as parameters. The second, with a name ending in "d", takes parameters of type double. As an example,

```
glTranslatef( 0, 0, 1 );
```

would translate objects by one unit in the z direction. Scaling works in a similar way: Instead of one scaling factor, you need three. The OpenGL command for scaling is glScale*, where the "*" can be either "f" or "d". The command

```
glScalef( sx, sy, sz );
```

transforms a point (x, y, z) to (x^*sx, y^*sy, z^*sz). That is, it scales by a factor of sx in the x direction, sy in the y direction, and sz in the z direction. Scaling is about the origin; that is, it moves points farther from or closer to the origin, (0,0,0). For uniform scaling, all three factors would be the same. You can use scaling by a factor of minus one to apply a reflection. For example,

```
glScalef( 1, 1, -1 );
```

reflects objects through the xy-plane by reversing the sign of the z coordinate. Note that a reflection will convert a right-handed coordinate system into a left-handed coordinate system, and vice versa. Remember that the left/right handed distinction is not a property of the world, just of the way that one chooses to lay out coordinates on the world.

Rotation in 3D is harder. In 2D, rotation is rotation about a point, which is usually taken to be the origin. In 3D, rotation is rotation about a line, which is called the axis of rotation. Think of the Earth rotating about its axis. The axis of rotation is the line that passes through the North Pole and the South Pole. The axis stays fixed as the Earth rotates around it, and points that are not on the axis move in circles about the axis. Any line can be an axis of rotation, but we generally use an axis that passes through the origin. The most common choices for axis of rotation are the coordinates axes, that is, the x-axis, the y-axis, or the z-axis. Sometimes, however, it's convenient to be able to use a different line as the axis.

There is an easy way to specify a line that passes through the origin: Just specify one other point that is on the line, in addition to the origin. That's how things are done in OpenGL: An axis of rotation is specified by three numbers, (ax, ay, az), which are not all zero. The axis is the line through (0,0,0) and (ax, ay, az). To specify a rotation transformation in 3D, you have to specify an axis and the angle of rotation about that axis.

We still have to account for the difference between positive and negative angles. We can't just say clockwise or counterclockwise. If you look down on the rotating Earth from above the North pole, you see a counterclockwise rotation; if you look down on it from above the South pole, you see a clockwise rotation. So, the difference between the two is not well-defined. To define the direction of rotation in 3D, we use the right-hand rule, which says: Point the thumb of your right hand in the direction of the axis - from the point (0,0,0) towards the point (ax, ay, az) that determines the axis. Then the direction of rotation for positive angles is given by the direction in which your fingers curl. I should emphasize that the right-hand rule only works if you are working in a right-handed coordinate system. If you have switched to a left-handed coordinate system, then you need to use a left-hand rule to determine the positive direction of rotation.

The demo c3/rotation-axis.html can help you to understand rotation in three-dimensional space.

The rotation function in OpenGL is glRotatef (r, ax, ay, az). You can also use glRotated. The first parameter specifies the angle of rotation, measured in degrees. The other three parameters specify the axis of rotation, which is the line from (0,0,0) to (ax, ay, az).

Here are a few examples of scaling, translation, and scaling in OpenGL:

```
glScalef(2,2,2); // Uniform scaling by a factor of 2.
glScalef(0.5,1,1); // Shrink by half in the x-direction only.
glScalef(-1,1,1); // Reflect through the yz-plane.
    // Reflects the positive x-axis onto negative x.
glTranslatef(5,0,0); // Move 5 units in the positive x-direction.
glTranslatef(3,5,-7.5); // Move each point (x,y,z) to (x+3, y+5, z-
7.5).
glRotatef(90,1,0,0); // Rotate 90 degrees about the x-axis.
    // Moves the +y axis onto the +z axis
```

```
    // and the +z axis onto the -y axis.
glRotatef (-90, -1,0,0); // Has the same effect as the previous
rotation.
glRotatef(90,0,1,0); // Rotate 90 degrees about the y-axis.
    // Moves the +z axis onto the +x axis
    // and the +x axis onto the -z axis.
glRotatef(90,0,0,1); // Rotate 90 degrees about the z-axis.
    // Moves the +x axis onto the +y axis
    // and the +y axis onto the -x axis.
glRotatef(30,1.5,2,-3); // Rotate 30 degrees about the line through
    // the points (0,0,0) and (1.5,2,-3).
```

Remember that transforms are applied to objects that are drawn after the transformation function is called, and that transformations apply to objects in the opposite order of the order in which they appear in the code.

Of course, OpenGL can draw in 2D as well as in 3D. For 2D drawing in OpenGL, you can draw on the xy-plane, using zero for the z coordinate. When drawing in 2D, you will probably want to apply 2D versions of rotation, scaling, and translation. OpenGL does not have 2D transform functions, but you can just use the 3D versions with appropriate parameters:

- For translation by (dx, dy) in 2D, use glTranslatef $(dx, dy, 0)$. The zero translation in the z direction means that the transform doesn't change the z coordinate, so it maps the xy-plane to itself. (Of course, you could use glTranslated instead of glTranslatef.)
- For scaling by (sx, sy) in 2D, use glScalef($sx, sy, 1$), which scales only in the x and y directions, leaving the z coordinate unchanged.
- For rotation through an angle r about the origin in 2D, use glRotatef ($r, 0,0,1$). This is rotation about the z-axis, which rotates the xy-plane into itself. In the usual OpenGL coordinate system, the z-axis points out of the screen, and the right-hand rule says that rotation by a positive angle will be in the counterclockwise direction in the xy-plane. Since the x-axis points to the right and the y-axis points upwards, a counterclockwise rotation rotates the positive x-axis in the direction of the positive y-axis. This is the same convention that we have used previously for the positive direction of rotation.

3.2.3 Hierarchical Modeling

Modeling transformations are often used in hierarchical modeling, which allows complex objects to be built up out of simpler objects. See Section 2.4. To review briefly: In hierarchical modeling, an object can be defined in its own natural coordinate system, usually using (0,0,0) as a reference point. The object can then be scaled, rotated, and translated to place it into world coordinates or into a more complex object. To implement this, we need a way of limiting the effect of a modeling transformation to one object or to part of an object. That can be done using a stack of transforms. Before drawing an object, push a copy of the current transform onto the stack. After drawing the object and its sub-objects, using any necessary temporary transformations, restore the previous transform by popping it from the stack.

OpenGL 1.1 maintains a stack of transforms and provides functions for manipulating that stack. (In fact it has several transform stacks, for different purposes, which introduces some complications that we will postpone to the next section.) Since transforms are represented as matrices, the stack is actually a stack of matrices. In OpenGL, the functions for operating on the stack are named glPushMatrix() and glPopMatrix().

These functions do not take parameters or return a value. OpenGL keeps track of a current matrix, which is the composition of all transforms that have been applied. Calling a function such as glScalef simply modifies the current matrix. When an object is drawn, using the glVertex* functions, the coordinates that were specified for the object are transformed by the current matrix. There is another function that affects the current matrix: glLoadIdentity(). Calling glLoadIdentity sets the current matrix to be the identity transform, which represents no change of coordinates at all and is the usual starting point for a series of transformations.

When the function glPushMatrix() is called, a copy of the current matrix is pushed onto the stack. Note that this does not change the current matrix; it just saves a copy on the stack. When glPopMatrix() is called, the matrix on the top of the stack is popped from the stack, and that matrix replaces the current matrix. Note that glPushMatrix and glPopMatrix must always occur in corresponding pairs; glPushMatrix saves a copy of the current matrix, and a corresponding call to glPopMatrix restores that copy. Between a call to glPushMatrix and the corresponding call to glPopMatrix, there can be additional calls of these functions, as long as they are properly paired. Usually, you will call glPushMatrix before drawing an object and glPopMatrix after finishing that object. In between, drawing sub-objects might require additional pairs of calls to those functions.

As an example, suppose that we want to draw a cube. It's not hard to draw each face using glBegin/glEnd, but let's do it with transformations. We can start with a function that draws a square in the position of the front face of the cube. For a cube of size 1 , the front face would sit one-half unit in front of the screen, in the plane $z = 0.5$, and it would have vertices at $(-0.5, -0.5, 0.5), (0.5, -0.5, 0.5), (0.5, 0.5, 0.5)$, and $(-0.5, 0.5, 0.5)$. Here is a function that draws the square. The function's parameters are floating point numbers in the range 0.0 to 1.0 that give the RGB color of the square:

```
void square( float r, float g, float b ) {
    glColor3f(r,g,b); // Set the color for the square.
    glBegin(GL_TRIANGLE_FAN);
    glVertex3f(-0.5, -0.5, 0.5);
    glVertex3f(0.5, -0.5, 0.5);
    glVertex3f(0.5, 0.5, 0.5);
    glVertex3f(-0.5, 0.5, 0.5);
    glEnd();
```

To make a red front face for the cube, we just need to call square (1,0,0). Now, consider the right face, which is perpendicular to the x-axis, in the plane $x = 0.5$. To make a right face, we can start with a front face and rotate it 90 degrees about the y-axis. Think about rotating the front face (red) to the position of the right face (green) in this illustration by rotating the red square about the y-axis:

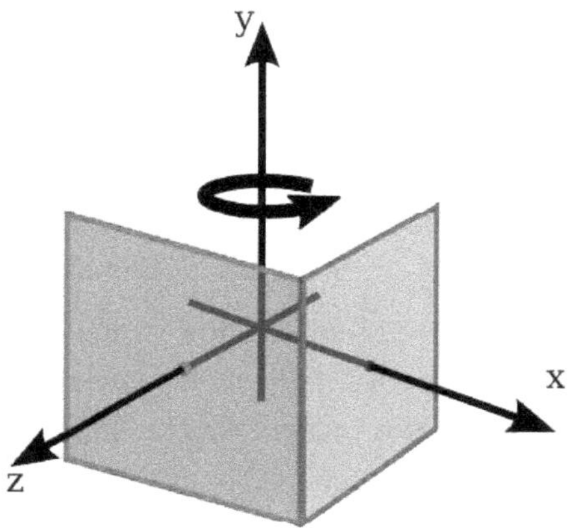

So, we can draw a green right face for the cube with

```
glPushMatrix();
glRotatef(90, 0, 1, 0);
square(0, 1, 0);
glPopMatrix();
```

The calls to glPushMatrix and glPopMatrix ensure that the rotation that is applied to the square will not carry over to objects that are drawn later. The other four faces can be made in a similar way, by rotating the front face about the coordinate axes. You should try to visualize the rotation that you need in each case. We can combine it all into a function that draws a cube. To make it more interesting, the size of the cube is a parameter:

```
void cube(float size) { // Draws a cube with side length = size.
    glPushMatrix(); // Save a copy of the current matrix.
    glScalef(size,size,size); // Scale unit cube to desired size.
    square(1, 0, 0); // red front face
    glPushMatrix();
    glRotatef(90, 0, 1, 0);
    square(0, 1, 0); // green right face
    glPopMatrix();
    glPushMatrix();
    glRotatef(-90, 1, 0, 0);
    square(0, 0, 1); // blue top face
    glPopMatrix();
    glPushMatrix();
    glRotatef(180, 0, 1, 0);
    square(0, 1, 1); // cyan back face
    glPopMatrix();
    glPushMatrix();
    glRotatef(-90, 0, 1, 0);
    square(1, 0, 1); // magenta left face


    glPopMatrix();
    glPushMatrix();
    glRotatef(90, 1, 0, 0);
    square(1, 1, 0); // yellow bottom face
    glPopMatrix();
    glPopMatrix(); // Restore matrix to its state before cube() was
called.
}
```

The sample program glut/unlit-cube.c uses this function to draw a cube, and lets you rotate the cube by pressing the arrow keys. A Java version is jogl/UnlitCube.java, and a web version is glsim/unlit-cube.html. Here is an image of the cube, rotated by 15 degrees about the x-axis and -15 degrees about the y-axis to make the top and right sides visible:

For a more complex example of hierarchical modeling with glPushMatrix and glPopMatrix, you can check out an OpenGL equivalent of the "cart and windmills" animation that was used as an example in Subsection 2.4.1. The three versions of the example are: glut/opengl-cart-and-windmill-2d.c, jogl/CartAndWindmillJogl2D.java, and glsim/opengl-cart-and-windmill.html. This program is an example of hierarchical 2D graphics in OpenGL.

Keep in mind that transformation and matrix functions such as glRotated() and glPushMatrix() are old-fashioned OpenGL. In WebGL and other modern graphics APIs, you will be responsible for managing transforms and matrices on your own. You are quite likely to do that using a software library that provides functions very similar to those that are built into OpenGL 1.1.

3.3 Projection and Viewing

In the previous section, we looked at the modeling transformation, which transforms from object coordinates to world coordinates. However, for 3D computer graphics, you need to know about several other coordinate systems and the transforms between them. We discuss them in this section.

We start with an overview of the various coordinate systems. Some of this is review, and some of it is new.

3.3.1 Many Coordinate Systems

The coordinates that you actually use for drawing an object are called object coordinates. The object coordinate system is chosen to be convenient for the object that is being drawn. A modeling transformation can then be applied to set the size, orientation, and position of the object in the overall scene (or, in the case of hierarchical modeling, in the object coordinate system of a larger, more complex object). The modeling transformation is the first that is applied to the vertices of an object.

The coordinates in which you build the complete scene are called world coordinates. These are the coordinates for the overall scene, the imaginary 3D world that you are creating. The modeling transformation maps from object coordinates to world coordinates.

In the real world, what you see depends on where you are standing and the direction in which you are looking. That is, you can't make a picture of the scene until you know the position of the "viewer" and where the viewer is looking - and, if you think about it, how the viewer's head is tilted. For the purposes of OpenGL, we imagine that the viewer is attached to their own individual coordinate system, which is known as eye coordinates. In this coordinate system, the viewer is at the origin, (0,0,0), looking in the direction of the negative z-axis; the positive direction of the y-axis is pointing straight up; and the x-axis is pointing to the right. This is a viewer-centric coordinate system. In other words, eye coordinates are (almost) the coordinates that you actually want to use for drawing on the screen. The transform from world coordinates to eye coordinates is called the viewing transformation.

If this is confusing, think of it this way: We are free to use any coordinate system that we want on the world. Eye coordinates are the natural coordinate system for making a picture of the world as seen by a viewer. If we used a different coordinate system (world coordinates) when building the world, then we have to transform those coordinates to eye coordinates to find out what the viewer actually sees. That transformation is the viewing transform.

Note, by the way, that OpenGL doesn't keep track of separate modeling and viewing transforms. They are combined into a single transform, which is known as the modelview transformation. In fact, even though world coordinates might seem to be the most important and natural coordinate system, OpenGL doesn't have any representation for them and doesn't use them internally. For OpenGL, only object and eye coordinates have meaning. OpenGL goes directly from object coordinates to eye coordinates by applying the modelview transformation.

We are not done. The viewer can't see the entire 3D world, only the part that fits into the viewport, which is the rectangular region of the screen or other display device where the image will be drawn. We say that the scene is "clipped" by the edges of the viewport. Furthermore, in OpenGL, the viewer can see only a limited range of z-values in the eye coordinate system. Points with larger or smaller z-values are clipped away and are not rendered into the image. (This is not, of course, the way that viewing works in the real world, but it's required by the use of the depth test in OpenGL. See Subsection 3.1.4.) The volume of space that is actually rendered into the image is called the view volume. Things inside the view volume make it into the image; things that are not in the view volume are clipped and cannot be seen. For purposes of drawing, OpenGL applies a coordinate transform that maps the view volume onto a cube. The cube is centered at the origin and extends from -1 to 1 in the x -direction, in the y -direction, and in the z -direction. The coordinate system on this cube is referred to as clip coordinates. The transformation from eye coordinates to clip coordinates is called the projection transformation. At this point, we haven't quite projected the 3D scene onto a 2D surface, but we can now do so simply by discarding the z -coordinate. (The z -coordinate, however, is still needed to provide the depth information that is needed for the depth test.)

Note that clip coordinates are the coordinates will be used if you apply no transformation at all, that is if both the modelview and the projection transforms are the identity. It is a lefthanded coordinate system, with the positive direction of the z-axis pointing into the screen.

We still aren't done. In the end, when things are actually drawn, there are device coordinates, the 2D coordinate system in which the actual drawing takes place on a physical display device such as the computer screen. Ordinarily, in device coordinates, the pixel is the unit of measure. The drawing region is a rectangle of pixels. This is the rectangle that is called the viewport. The viewport transformation takes x and y from the clip coordinates and scales them to fit the viewport.

Let's go through the sequence of transformations one more time. Think of a primitive, such as a line or triangle, that is part of the scene and that might appear in the image that we want to make of the scene. The primitive goes through the following sequence of operations:

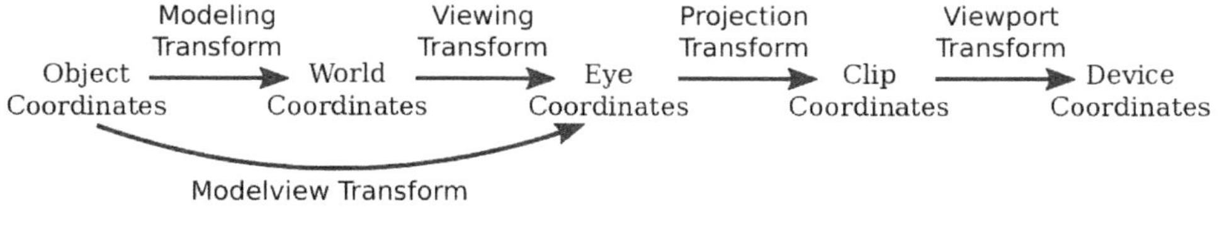

1. The points that define the primitive are specified in object coordinates, using methods such as glVertex3f.

2. The points are first subjected to the modelview transformation, which is a combination of the modeling transform that places the primitive into the world and the viewing transform that maps the primitive into eye coordinates.

3. The projection transformation is then applied to map the view volume that is visible to the viewer onto the clip coordinate cube. If the transformed primitive lies outside that cube, it will not be part of the image, and the processing stops. If part of the primitive lies inside and part outside, the part that lies outside is clipped away and discarded, and only the part that remains is processed further.

4. Finally, the viewport transform is applied to produce the device coordinates that will actually be used to draw the primitive on the display device. After that, it's just a matter of deciding how to color the individual pixels that are part of the primitive.

We need to consider these transforms in more detail and see how to use them in OpenGL 1.1.

3.3.2 The Viewport Transformation

The simplest of the transforms is the viewport transform. It transforms x and y clip coordinates to the coordinates that are used on the display device. To specify the viewport transform, it is only necessary to specify the rectangle on the device where the scene will be rendered. This is done using the glViewport function.

OpenGL must be provided with a drawing surface by the environment in which it is running, such as JOGL for Java or the GLUT library for C. That drawing surface is a rectangular grid of pixels, with a horizontal size and a vertical size. OpenGL uses a coordinate system on the drawing surface that puts (0,0) at the lower left, with y increasing from bottom to top and x increasing from left to right. When the drawing surface is first given to OpenGL, the viewport is set to be the entire drawing surface. However, it is possible for OpenGL to draw to a different rectangle by calling

```
glViewport( x, y, width, height );
```

where (x,y) is the lower left corner of the viewport, in the drawing surface coordinate system, and width and height are the size of the viewport. Clip coordinates from -1 to 1 will then be mapped to the specified viewport. Note that this means in particular that drawing is limited to the viewport. It is not an error for the viewport to extend outside of the drawing surface, though it would be unusual to set up that situation deliberately.

When the size of the drawing surface changes, such as when the user resizes a window that contains the drawing surface, OpenGL does not automatically change the viewport to match the new size. However, the environment in which OpenGL is running might do that for you. (See Section 3.6 for information about how this is handled by JOGL and GLUT.)

glViewport is often used to draw several different scenes, or several views of the same scene, on the same drawing surface. Suppose, for example, that we want to draw two scenes, side-byside, and that the drawing surface is 600 -by- 400 pixels. An outline for how to do that is very simple:

```
glViewport(0,0,300,400); // Draw to left half of the drawing surface.
    . // Draw the first scene.
glViewport(300,0,300,400); // Draw to right half of the drawing
surface.
    .
    - // Draw the second scene.
    .
```

The first glViewport command establishes a 300 -by- 400 pixel viewport with its lower left corner at (0,0). That is, the lower left corner of the viewport is at the lower left corner of the drawing surface. This viewport fills the left half of the drawing surface. Similarly, the second viewport, with its lower left corner at (300,0), fills the right half of the drawing surface.

3.3.3 The Projection Transformation

We turn next to the projection transformation. Like any transform, the projection is represented in OpenGL as a matrix. OpenGL keeps track of the projection matrix separately from the matrix that represents the modelview transformation. The same transform functions, such as glRotatef, can be applied to both matrices, so OpenGL needs some way to know which matrix those functions apply to. This is determined by an OpenGL state property called the matrix mode. The value of the matrix mode is a constant such as GL_PROJECTION or GL_MODELVIEW. When a function such as glRotatef is called, it modifies a matrix; which matrix is modified depends on the current value of the matrix mode. The value is set by calling the function glMatrixMode. The initial value is GL_MODELVIEW. This means that if you want to work on the projection matrix, you must first call

```
glMatrixMode(GL_PROJECTION);
```

If you want to go back to working on the modelview matrix, you must call

```
glMartrixMode(GL_MODELVIEW);
```

In my programs, I generally set the matrix mode to *GL*_PROJECTION, set up the projection transformation, and then immediately set the matrix mode back to GL-

MODELVIEW. This means that anywhere else in the program, I can be sure that the matrix mode is GL_MODELVIEW.

To help you to understand projection, remember that a 3D image can show only a part of the infinite 3D world. The view volume is the part of the world that is visible in the image. The view volume is determined by a combination of the viewing transformation and the projection transformation. The viewing transform determines where the viewer is located and what direction the viewer is facing, but it doesn't say how much of the world the viewer can see. The projection transform does that: It specifies the shape and extent of the region that is in view. Think of the viewer as a camera, with a big invisible box attached to the front of the camera that encloses the part of the world that that camera has in view. The inside of the box is the view volume. As the camera moves around in the world, the box moves with it, and the view volume changes. But the shape and size of the box don't change. The shape and size of the box correspond to the projection transform. The position and orientation of the camera correspond to the viewing transform.

This is all just another way of saying that, mathematically, the OpenGL projection transformation transforms eye coordinates to clip coordinates, mapping the view volume onto the 2 -by- 2 -by- 2 clipping cube that contains everything that will be visible in the image. To specify a projection just means specifying the size and shape of the view volume, relative to the viewer.

There are two general types of projection, perspective projection and orthographic projection. Perspective projection is more physically realistic. That is, it shows what you would see if the OpenGL display rectangle on your computer screen were a window into an actual 3D world (one that could extend in front of the screen as well as behind it). It shows a view that you could get by taking a picture of a 3D world with an ordinary camera. In a perspective view, the apparent size of an object depends on how far it is away from the viewer. Only things that are in front of the viewer can be seen. In fact, ignoring clipping in the *z* direction for the moment, the part of the world that is in view is an infinite pyramid, with the viewer at the apex of the pyramid, and with the sides of the pyramid passing through the sides of the viewport rectangle.

However, OpenGL can't actually show everything in this pyramid, because of its use of the depth test to solve the hidden surface problem. Since the depth buffer can only store a finite range of depth values, it can't represent the entire range of depth values for the infinite pyramid that is theoretically in view. Only objects in a certain range of distances from the viewer can be part of the image. That range of distances is specified by two values, near and far. For a perspective transformation, both of these values must be positive numbers, and far must be greater than near. Anything that is closer to the viewer than the near distance or farther away than the far distance is discarded and does not appear in the rendered image. The volume of space that is represented in the image is thus a "truncated pyramid." This pyramid is the view volume for a perspective projection:

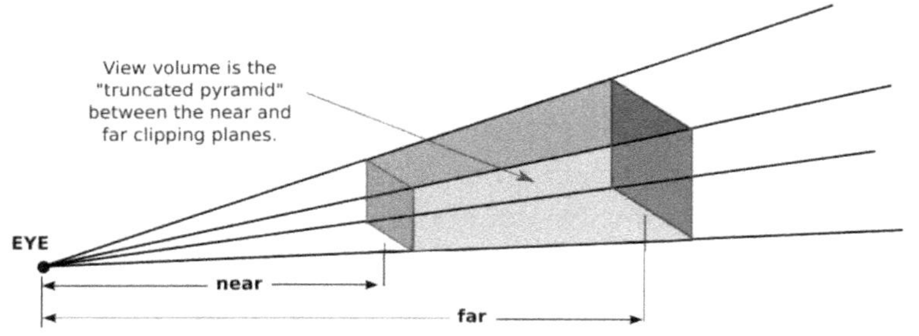

The view volume is bounded by six planes-the four sides plus the top and bottom of the truncated pyramid. These planes are called clipping planes because anything that lies on the wrong side of each plane is clipped away. The projection transformation maps the six sides of the truncated pyramid in eye coordinates to the six sides of the clipping cube in clip coordinates.

In OpenGL, setting up the projection transformation is equivalent to defining the view volume. For a perspective transformation, you have to set up a view volume that is a truncated pyramid. A rather obscure term for this shape is a frustum. A perspective transformation can be set up with the glFrustum command:

```
glFrustum( xmin, xmax, ymin, ymax, near, far );
```

The last two parameters specify the near and far distances from the viewer, as already discussed. The viewer is assumed to be at the origin, (0,0,0), facing in the direction of the negative z -axis. (This is the eye coordinate system.) So, the near clipping plane is at $z = -$ near, and the far clipping plane is at $z = -far$. (Notice the minus signs!) The first four parameters specify the sides of the pyramid: xmin, xmax, ymin, and ymax specify the horizontal and vertical limits of the view volume at the near clipping plane. For example, the coordinates of the upper-left corner of the small end of the pyramid are (xmin, ymax, -near). The x and y limits at the far clipping plane are larger, usually much larger, than the limits specified in the glFrustum command.

Note that x and y limits in glFrustum are usually symmetrical about zero. That is, xmin is usually equal to the negative of xmax and ymin is usually equal to the negative of ymax. However, this is not required. It is possible to have asymmetrical view volumes where the z -axis does not point directly down the center of the view.

Since the matrix mode must be set to GL_PROJECTION to work on the projection transformation, glFrustum is often used in a code segment of the form

```
glMatrixMode(GL_PROJECTION);
glLoadIdentity();
glFrustum( xmin, xmax, ymin, ymax, near, far );
glMatrixMode(GL_MODELVIEW);
```

The call to glLoadIdentity ensures that the starting point is the identity transform. This is important since glFrustum modifies the existing projection matrix rather than replacing it, and although it is theoretically possible, you don't even want to try to think about what would happen if you combine several projection transformations into one.

Compared to perspective projections, orthographic projections are easier to understand: In an orthographic projection, the 3D world is projected onto a 2D image by discarding the *z*-coordinate of the eye-coordinate system. This type of projection is unrealistic in that it is not what a viewer would see. For example, the apparent size of an object does not depend on its distance from the viewer. Objects in back of the viewer as well as in front of the viewer can be visible in the image. Orthographic projections are still useful, however, especially in interactive modeling programs where it is useful to see true sizes and angles, undistorted by perspective.

In fact, it's not really clear what it means to say that there is a viewer in the case of orthographic projection. Nevertheless, for orthographic projection in OpenGL, there is considered to be a viewer. The viewer is located at the eye-coordinate origin, facing in the direction of the negative z -axis. Theoretically, a rectangular corridor extending infinitely in both directions, in front of the viewer and in back, would be in view. However, as with perspective projection, only a finite segment of this infinite corridor can actually be shown in an OpenGL image. This finite view volume is a parallelepiped-a rectangular solid-that is cut out of the infinite corridor by a near clipping plane and a far clipping plane. The value of far must be greater than near, but for an orthographic projection, the value of near is allowed to be negative, putting the "near" clipping plane behind the viewer, as shown in the lower section of this illustration:

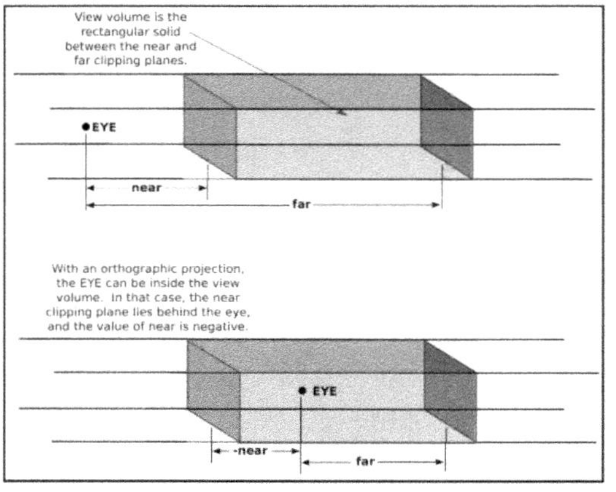

Note that a negative value for near puts the near clipping plane on the positive z-axis, which is behind the viewer.

An orthographic projection can be set up in OpenGL using the glOrtho method, which is has the following form:

```
glOrtho( xmin, xmax, ymin, ymax, near, far );
```

The first four parameters specify the x - and y-coordinates of the left, right, bottom, and top of the view volume. Note that the last two parameters are near and far, not zmin and zmax.

In fact, the minimum z -value for the view volume is -far and the maximum z -value is -near. However, it is often the case that near $= -far$, and if that is true then the minimum and maximum z-values turn out to be near and far after all!

As with glFrustum, glOrtho should be called when the matrix mode is GL_PROJECTION. As an example, suppose that we want the view volume to be the box centered at the origin containing x, y, and z values in the range from -10 to 10 . This can be accomplished with

```
glMatrixMode(GL_PROJECTION);
glLoadIdentity();
glOrtho( -10, 10, -10, 10, -10, 10 );
glMatrixMode(GL_MODELVIEW);
```

Now, as it turns out, the effect of glOrtho in this simple case is exactly the same as the effect of glScalef (0.1,0.1, −0.1), since the projection just scales the box down by a factor of 10 . But it's usually better to think of projection as a different sort of thing from scaling. (The minus sign on the z scaling factor is there because projection reverses the direction of the z-axis, transforming the conventionally right-handed eye coordinate system into OpenGL's left-handed default coordinate system.)

The glFrustum method is not particularly easy to use. There is a library known as ***GLU*** that contains some utility functions for use with OpenGL. The GLU library includes the method gluPerspective as an easier way to set up a perspective projection. The command

```
gluPerspective( fieldOfViewAngle, aspect, near, far );
```

can be used instead of glFrustum. The fieldOfViewAngle is the vertical angle, measured in degrees, between the upper side of the view volume pyramid and the lower side. Typical values are in the range 30 to 60 degrees. The aspect parameter is the aspect ratio of the view, that is, the width of a cross-section of the pyramid divided by its height. The value of aspect should generally be set to the aspect ratio of the viewport. The near and far parameters in gluPerspective have the same meaning as for glFrustum.

3.3.4 The Modelview Transformation

"Modeling" and "viewing" might seem like very different things, conceptually, but OpenGL combines them into a single transformation. This is because there is no way to distinguish between them in principle; the difference is purely conceptual. That is, a given transformation can be considered to be either a modeling transformation or a viewing transformation, depending on how you think about it. (One significant difference, conceptually, is that the same viewing transformation usually applies to every object in the 3D scene, while each object can have its own modeling transformation. But this is not a difference in principle.) We have already seen something similar in 2D graphics (Subsection 2.3.1), but let's think about how it works in 3D.

For example, suppose that there is a model of a house at the origin, facing towards the direction of the positive z-axis. Suppose the viewer is on the positive z-axis, looking back towards the origin. The viewer is looking directly at the front of the house. Now, you might apply a modeling transformation to the house, to rotate it by 90 degrees about the y-axis. After this transformation, the house is facing in the positive direction of the x-axis, and the viewer is looking directly at the left side of the house. On the other hand, you might rotate the viewer by minus 90 degrees about the y-axis. This would put the viewer on the negative x-axis, which would give it a view of the left side of the house. The net result after either transformation is that the viewer ends up with exactly the same view of the house. Either transformation can be implemented in OpenGL with the command

```
glRotatef (90,0,1,0) ;
```

That is, this command represents either a modeling transformation that rotates an object by 90 degrees or a viewing transformation that rotates the viewer by -90 degrees about the y-axis. Note that the effect on the viewer is the inverse of the effect on the object. Modeling and viewing transforms are always related in this way. For example, if you are looking at an object, you can move yourself 5 feet to the left (viewing transform), or you can move the object 5 feet to the right (modeling transform). In either case, you end up with the same view of the object. Both transformations would be represented in OpenGL as

```
glTranslatef(5,0,0);
```

This even works for scaling: If the viewer shrinks, it will look to the viewer exactly the same as if the world is expanding, and vice-versa.

Although modeling and viewing transformations are the same in principle, they remain very different conceptually, and they are typically applied at different points in the code. In general when drawing a scene, you will do the following: (1) Load the identity matrix, for a well-defined starting point; (2) apply the viewing transformation; and (3) draw the objects in the scene, each with its own modeling transformation. Remember that OpenGL keeps track of several transformations, and that this must all be done while the modelview transform is current; if you are not sure of that then before step (1), you should call glMatrixMode (GL_MODELVIEW). During step (3), you will probably use glPushMatrix() and glPopMatrix() to limit each modeling transform to a particular object.

After loading the identity matrix, the viewer is in the default position, at the origin, looking down the negative z-axis, with the positive y-axis pointing upwards in the view. Suppose, for example, that we would like to move the viewer from its default location at the origin back along the positive z -axis to the point (0,0,20). This operation has exactly the same effect as moving the world, and the objects that it contains, 20 units in the negative direction along the z-axis. Whichever operation is performed, the viewer ends up in exactly the same position relative to the objects. Both operations are implemented by the same OpenGL command, glTranslatef (0,0, -20). For another example, suppose that we use two commands

```
glRotatef(90,0,1,0);
glTranslatef (10,0,0) ;
```

to establish the viewing transformation. As a modeling transform, these commands would first translate an object 10 units in the positive x-direction, then rotate the object 90 degrees about the y-axis. This would move an object originally at (0,0,0) to $(0,0,-10)$, placing the object 10 units directly in front of the viewer. (Remember that modeling transformations are applied to objects in the order opposite to their order in the code.)

What do these commands do as a viewing transformation? The effect on the view is the inverse of the effect on objects. The inverse of "translate 90 then rotate 10 " is "rotate -10 then translate -90 ." That is, to do the inverse, you have to undo the rotation before you undo the translation. The effect as a viewing transformation is first to rotate the view by -90 degrees about the y-axis (which would leave the viewer at the origin, but now looking along the positive x-axis), then to translate the viewer by -10 along the x-axis (backing up the viewer to the point $(-10,0,0)$). An object at the point (0,0,0) would thus be 10 units directly in front of the viewer. (You should think about how the two interpretations affect the view of a house that starts out at (0,0,0). The transformation affects which side of the house the viewer is looking at, as well as how far away from the house the viewer is located).

Note, by the way, that the order in which viewing transformations are applied is the same as the order in which they occur in the code.

The on-line version of this section includes the live demo c3/transform-equivalence-3d.html that can help you to understand the equivalence between modeling and viewing. This picture, taken from that demo, visualizes the view volume as a translucent gray box. The scene contains eight cubes, but not all of them are inside the view volume, so not all of them would appear in the rendered image:

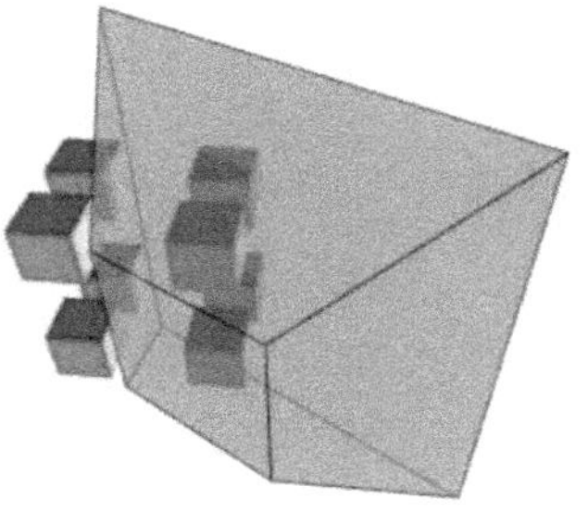

In this case, the projection is a perspective projection, and the view volume is a frustum. This picture might have been made either by rotating the frustum towards the right (viewing transformation) or by rotating the cubes towards the left (modeling transform). Read the help text in the demo for more information

It can be difficult to set up a view by combining rotations, scalings, and translations, so OpenGL provides an easier way to set up a typical view. The command is not part of OpenGL itself but is part of the GLU library.

The GLU library provides the following convenient method for setting up a viewing transformation:

```
gluLookAt( eyeX,eyeY,eyeZ, refX,refY,refZ, upX,upY,upZ );
```

This method places the viewer at the point (eyeX, eyeY, eyeZ), looking towards the point (refX, refY, refZ). The viewer is oriented so that the vector (upX, upY, upZ) points upwards in the viewer's view. For example, to position the viewer on the negative x-axis, 10 units from the origin, looking back at the origin, with the positive direction of the y-axis pointing up as usual, use

```
gluLookAt( -10,0,0, 0,0,0, 0,1,0);
```

With all this, we can give an outline for a typical display routine for drawing an image of a 3D scene with OpenGL 1.1:

```
// possibly set clear color here, if not set elsewhere
glClear( GL_COLOR_BUFFER_BIT | GL_DEPTH_BUFFER_BIT );


// possibly set up the projection here, if not done elsewhere
glMatrixMode( GL_MODELVIEW );
glLoadIdentity();
gluLookAt( eyeX,eyeY,eyeZ, refX,refY,refZ, upX,upY,upZ ); // Viewing
transform
glPushMatrix();
    .
    - // apply modeling transform and draw an object
    -
glPopMatrix();
glPushMatrix();
    .
    \mathrm{ - // apply another modeling transform and draw another
object}
    -
glPopMatrix();
```

3.3.5 A Camera Abstraction

Projection and viewing are often discussed using the analogy of a camera. A real camera is used to take a picture of a 3D world. For 3D graphics, it useful to imagine using a virtual camera to do the same thing. Setting up the viewing transformation is like positioning and pointing the camera. The projection transformation determines the properties of the camera: What is its field of view, what sort of lens does it use? (Of course, the analogy breaks for OpenGL in at least one respect, since a real camera doesn't do clipping in its *z*-direction.)

I have written a camera utility to implement this idea. The camera is meant to take over the job of setting the projection and view. Instead of doing that by hand, you set properties of the camera. The API is available for both C and Java. The two versions are somewhat different because the Java version is object-oriented. I will discuss the C implementation first. (See Section 3.6 for basic information about programming OpenGL in C and Java. For an example of using a camera in a program, see the polyhedron viewer example in the next section. Note also that there is a version of the camera for use with my JavaScript simulator for OpenGL; it is part of the simulator library glsim/glsim.js and has an API almost identical to the Java API.)

In C, the camera is defined by the sample .c file, glut/camera.c and a corresponding header file, glut/camera.h. Full documentation for the API can be found in the header file. To use the camera, you should #include "camera.h" at the start of your program, and when you compile the program, you should include camera.c in the list of files that you want to compile. The camera depends on the GLU library and on C's standard math library, so you have to make sure that those libraries are available when it is compiled. To use the camera, you should call

```
cameraApply();
```

to set up the projection and viewing transform before drawing the scene. Calling this function replaces the usual code code for setting up the projection and viewing transformations. It leaves the matrix mode set to GL_MODELVIEW.

The remaining functions in the API are used to configure the camera. This would usually be done as part of initialization, but it is possible to change the configuration at any time. However, remember that the settings are not used until you call cameraApply(). Available functions include:

```
cameraLookAt( eyeX,eyeY,eyeZ, refX,refY,refZ, upX,upY,upZ );
    // Determines the viewing transform, just like gluLookAt
    // Default is cameraLookAt( 0,0,30, 0,0,0, 0,1,0 );
cameraSetLimits( xmin, xmax, ymin, ymax, zmin, zmax );
    // Sets the limits on the view volume, where zmin and zmax are
    // given with respect to the view reference point, NOT the eye,
    // and the xy limits are measured at the distance of the
    // view reference point, NOT the near distance.
    // Default is cameraSetLimits( -5,5, -5,5, -10,10 );
```

```
cameraSetScale( limit );
    // a convenience method, which is the same as calling
    // cameraSetLimits( -limit,limit, -limit,limit, -2*limit, 2*limit
);
cameraSetOrthographic( ortho );
    // Switch between orthographic and perspective projection.
    // The parameter should be 0 for perspective, 1 for
    // orthographic. The default is perspective.
cameraSetPreserveAspect( preserve );
    // Determine whether the aspect ratio of the viewport should
    // be respected. The parameter should be 0 to ignore and
    // 1 to respect the viewport aspect ratio. The default
    // is to preserve the aspect ratio.
```

In many cases, the default settings are sufficient. Note in particular how cameraLookAt and cameraSetLimits work together to set up the view and projection. The parameters to cameraLookAt represent three points in world coordinates. The view reference point, (ref*X*, ref*Y*, ref*Z*), should be somewhere in the middle of the scene that you want to render. The parameters to cameraSetLimits define a box about that view reference point that should contain everything that you want to appear in the image.

For use with JOGL in Java, the camera API is implemented as a class named Camera, defined in the file jogl/Camera.java. The camera is meant for use with a GLPanel or GLCanvas that is being used as an OpenGL drawing surface. To use a camera, create an object of type Camera as an instance variable:

```
camera = new Camera();
```

Before drawing the scene, call

```
camera.apply(gl2);
```

where *gl2* is the OpenGL drawing context of type GL2. (Note the presence of the parameter gl2, which was not necessary in C; it is required because the OpenGL drawing context in JOGL is implemented as an object.) As in the C version, this sets the viewing and projection transformations and can replace any other code that you would use for that purpose. The functions for configuring the camera are the same in Java as in C, except that they become methods in the camera object, and true/false parameters are boolean instead of int:

```
camera.lookAt( eyeX,eyeY,eyeZ, refX,refY,refZ, upX,upY,upZ );
camera.setLimits( xmin,xmax, ymin,ymax, zmin,zmax );
```

```
camera.setScale( limit );
camera.setOrthographic( ortho ); // ortho is of type boolean
camera.setPreserveAspect( preserve ); // preserve is of type boolean
```

The camera comes with a simulated "trackball." The trackball allows the user to rotate the view by clicking and dragging the mouse on the display. To use it with GLUT in C, you just need to install a mouse function and a mouse motion function by calling

```
glutMouseFunc( trackballMouseFunction );
glutMotionFunc( trackballMotionFunction );
```

The functions trackballMouseFunction and trackballMotionFunction are defined as part of the camera API and are declared and documented in camera.h. The trackball works by modifying the viewing transformation associated with the camera, and it only works if cameraApply() is called at the beginning of the display function to set the viewing and projection transformations. To install a trackball for use with a Camera object in JOGL, call

```
camera.installTrackball(drawSurface);
```

where drawSurface is the component on which the camera is used.

3.4 Polygonal Meshes and glDrawArrays

We have drawn only very simple shapes with OpenGL. In this section, we look at how more complex shapes can be represented in a way that is convenient for rendering in OpenGL, and we introduce a new, more efficient way to draw OpenGL primitives.

OpenGL can only directly render points, lines, and polygons. (In fact, in modern OpenGL, the only polygons that are used are triangles.) A polyhedron, the 3D analog of a polygon, can be represented exactly, since a polyhedron has faces that are polygons. On the other hand, if only polygons are available, then a curved surface, such as the surface of a sphere, can only be approximated. A polyhedron can be represented, or a curved surface can be approximated, as a polygonal mesh, that is, a set of polygons that are connected along their edges. If the polygons are small, the approximation can look like a curved surface. (We will see in the next chapter how lighting effects can be used to make a polygonal mesh look more like a curved surface and less like a polyhedron.)

So, our problem is to represent a set of polygons-most often a set of triangles. We start by defining a convenient way to represent such a set as a data structure.

3.4.1 Indexed Face Sets

The polygons in a polygonal mesh are also referred to as "faces" (as in the faces of a polyhedron), and one of the primary means for representing a polygonal mesh is as an indexed face set, or IFS.

The data for an IFS includes a list of all the vertices that appear in the mesh, giving the coordinates of each vertex. A vertex can then be identified by an integer that specifies its index, or position, in the list. As an example, consider this "house," a polyhedron with 10 vertices and 9 faces:

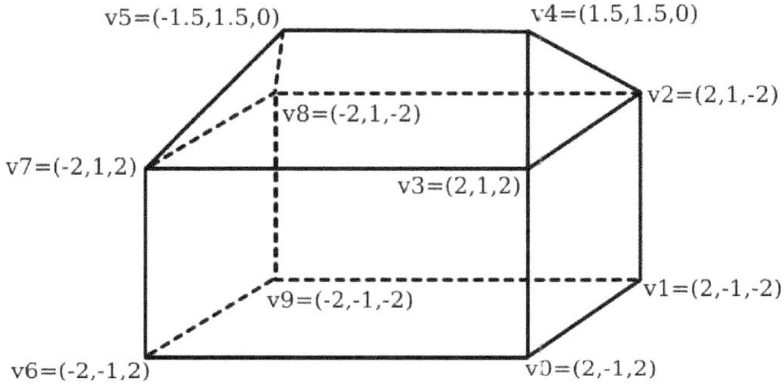

The vertex list for this polyhedron has the form

```
Vertex #0. (2, -1, 2)
Vertex #1. (2, -1, -2)
Vertex #2. (2, 1, -2)
Vertex #3. (2, 1, 2)
Vertex #4. (1.5, 1.5, 0)
Vertex #5. (-1.5, 1.5, 0)
Vertex #6. (-2, -1, 2)
Vertex #7. (-2, 1, 2)
Vertex #8. (-2, 1, -2)
Vertex #9. (-2, -1, -2)
```

The order of the vertices is completely arbitrary. The purpose is simply to allow each vertex to be identified by an integer.

To describe one of the polygonal faces of a mesh, we just have to list its vertices, in order going around the polygon. For an IFS, we can specify a vertex by giving its index in the list. For example, we can say that one of the triangular faces of the pyramid is the polygon formed by vertex #3, vertex #2, and vertex #4. So, we can complete our data for the mesh by giving a list of vertex indices for each face. Here is the face data for the house. Remember that the numbers in parenthese are indices into the vertex list:

```
Face #0: (0, 1, 2, 3)
Face #1: (3, 2, 4)
Face #2: (7, 3, 4, 5)
Face #3: (2, 8, 5, 4)
Face #4: (5, 8, 7)
Face #5: (0, 3, 7, 6)
Face #6: (0, 6, 9, 1)
Face #7: (2, 1, 9, 8)
Face #8: (6, 7, 8, 9)
```

Again, the order in which the faces are listed in arbitrary. There is also some freedom in how the vertices for a face are listed. You can start with any vertex. Once you've picked a starting vertex, there are two possible orderings, corresponding to the two possible directions in which you can go around the circumference of the polygon. For example, starting with vertex 0 , the first face in the list could be specified either as (0,1,2,3) or as (0,3,2,1). However, the first possibility is the right one in this case, for the following reason. A polygon in 3D can be viewed from either side; we can think of it as having two faces, facing in opposite directions. It turns out that it is often convenient to consider one of those faces to be the "front face" of the polygon and one to be the "back face." For a polyhedron like the house, the front face is the one that faces the outside of the polyhedron. The usual rule is that the vertices of a polygon should be listed in counterclockwise order when looking at the front face of the polygon. When looking at the back face, the vertices will be listed in clockwise order. This is the default rule used by OpenGL.

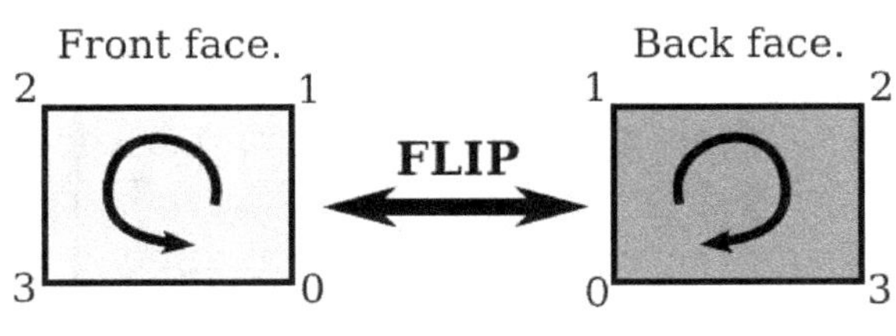

Vertex order 0,1,2,3 is counter-clockwise from the front and clockwise from the back

The vertex and face data for an indexed face set can be represented as a pair of twodimensional arrays. For the house, in a version for Java, we could use

```
double[] [] vertexList =
        { {2,-1,2}, {2,-1,-2}, {2,1,-2}, {2,1,2}, {1.5,1.5,0},
            {-1.5,1.5,0}, {-2,-1,2}, {-2,1,2}, {-2,1,-2}, {-2,-1,-2} };
int[] [] faceList =
        { {0,1,2,3}, {3,2,4}, {7,3,4,5}, {2,8,5,4}, {5,8,7},
            {0,3,7,6}, {0,6,9,1}, {2,1,9,8}, {6,7,8,9} };
```

In most cases, there will be additional data for the IFS. For example, if we want to color the faces of the polyhedron, with a different color for each face, then we could add another array, faceColors, to hold the color data. Each element of faceColors would be an array of three double values in the range 0.0 to 1.0 , giving the RGB color components for one of the faces. With this setup, we could use the following code to draw the polyhedron, using Java and JOGL:

```
for (int i = 0; i < faceList.length; i++) {
    gl2.glColor3dv( faceColors[i], 0 ); // Set color for face number i.
    gl2.glBegin(GL2.GL_TRIANGLE_FAN);
    for (int j = 0; j < faceList[i].length; j++) {
        int vertexNum = faceList[i][j]; // Index for vertex j of face
i.
        double[] vertexCoords = vertexList[vertexNum]; // The vertex
itself.
        gl2.glVertex3dv( vertexCoords, 0 );
    }
    gl2.glEnd();
}
```

Note that every vertex index is used three or four times in the face data. With the IFS representation, a vertex is represented in the face list by a single integer. This representation uses less memory space than the alternative, which would be to write out the vertex in full each time it occurs in the face data. For the house example, the IFS representation uses 64 numbers to represent the vertices and faces of the polygonal mesh, as opposed to 102 numbers for the alternative representation.

Indexed face sets have another advantage. Suppose that we want to modify the shape of the polygon mesh by moving its vertices. We might do this in each frame of an animation, as a way of "morphing" the shape from one form to another. Since only the positions of the vertices are changing, and not the way that they are connected together, it will only be necessary to update the 30 numbers in the vertex list. The values in the face list will remain unchanged.

There are other ways to store the data for an IFS. In C, for example, where two-dimensional arrays are more problematic, we might use one dimensional arrays for the data. In that case, we would store all the vertex coordinates in a single array. The length of the vertex array would be three times the number of vertices, and the data for vertex number *N* will begin at index 3**N* in the array. For the face list, we have to deal with the fact that not all faces have the same number of vertices. A common solution is to add a -1 to the array after the data for each face. In C, where it is not possible to determine the length of an array, we also need variables to store the number of vertices and the number of faces. Using this representation, the data for the house becomes:

```
int vertexCount = 10; // Number of vertices.
double vertexData[] =
        { 2,-1,2, 2,-1,-2, 2,1,-2, 2,1,2, 1.5,1.5,0,
                -1.5,1.5,0, -2,-1,2, -2,1,2, -2,1,-2, -2,-1,-2};
int faceCount = 9; // Number of faces.
int[] [] faceData =
            { 0,1,2,3,-1, 3,2,4,-1, 7,3,4,5,-1, 2,8,5,4,-1, 5,8,7,-1,
                0,3,7,6,-1, 0,6,9,1,-1, 2,1,9,8,-1, 6,7,8,9,-1};
```

After adding a faceColors array to hold color data for the faces, we can use the following C code to draw the house:

```
int i,j;
j = 0; // index into the faceData array
for (i = 0; i < faceCount; i++) {
    glColor3dv( &faceColors[ i*3 ] ); // Color for face number i.
    glBegin(GL_TRIANGLE_FAN);
    while ( faceData[j] != -1) { // Generate vertices for face number
i.
        int vertexNum = faceData[j]; // Vertex number in vertexData
array.
        glVertex3dv( &vertexData[ vertexNum*3 ] );
        j++;
    }
    j++; // increment j past the -1 that ended the data for this face.
```

```
    glEnd();
}
```

Note the use of the C address operator, &. For example, &faceColors [i*3] is a pointer to element number *i**3 in the faceColors array. That element is the first of the three color component values for face number *i*. This matches the parameter type for glColor3dv in C, since the parameter is a pointer type.

We could easily draw the edges of the polyhedron instead of the faces simply by using GL_LINE_LOOP instead of GL_TRIANGLE_FAN in the drawing code (and probably leaving out the color changes). An interesting issue comes up if we want to draw both the faces and the edges. This can be a nice effect, but we run into a problem with the depth test: Pixels along the edges lie at the same depth as pixels on the faces. As discussed in Subsection 3.1.4, the depth test cannot handle this situation well. However, OpenGL has a solution: a feature called "polygon offset." This feature can adjust the depth, in clip coordinates, of a polygon, in order to avoid having two objects exactly at the same depth. To apply polygon offset, you need to set the amount of offset by calling

```
glPolygonOffset(1,1);
```

The second parameter gives the amount of offset, in units determined by the first parameter. The meaning of the first parameter is somewhat obscure; a value of 1 seems to work in all cases. You also have to enable the GL_POLYGON_OFFSET_FILL feature while drawing the faces. An outline for the procedure is

```
glPolygonOffset(1,1);
glEnable( GL_POLYGON_OFFSET_FILL );
    .
    . // Draw the faces.
    .
glDisable( GL_POLYGON_OFFSET_FILL );
    .
    \mathrm{ - // Draw the edges.}
     -
```

There is a sample program that can draw the house and a number of other polyhedra. It uses drawing code very similar to what we have looked at here, including polygon offset. The program is also an example of using the camera and trackball API that was discussed in Subsection 3.3.5, so that the user can rotate a polyhedron by dragging it with the mouse. The program has menus that allow the user to turn rendering of edges and faces on and off, plus some other options. The Java version of the program is jogl/IFSPolyhedronViewer.java, and the C version is glut/ifs-polyhedron-viewer.c. To get at the menu in the C version, right-click on the display. The data for the polyhedra are created in jogl/Polyhedron.java and glut/polyhedron.c. There is also a live demo version of the program in this section on line.

3.4.2 glDrawArrays and glDrawElements

All of the OpenGL commands that we have seen so far were part of the original OpenGL 1.0. OpenGL 1.1 added some features to increase performance. One complaint about the original OpenGL was the large number of function calls needed to draw a primitive using functions such as glVertex2d and glColor3fv with glBegin/glEnd. To address this issue, OpenGL 1.1 introduced the functions glDrawArrays and glDrawElements. These functions are still used in modern OpenGL, including WebGL. We will look at glDrawArrays first. There are some differences between the C and the Java versions of the API. We consider the C version first and will deal with the changes necessary for the Java version in the next subsection.

When using glDrawArrays, all of the data that is needed to draw a primitive, including vertex coordinates, colors, and other vertex attributes, can be packed into arrays. Once that is done, the primitive can be drawn with a single call to glDrawArrays. Recall that a primitive such as a GL_LINE_LOOP or a GL_TRIANGLES can include a large number of vertices, so that the reduction in the number of function calls can be substantial.

To use glDrawArrays, you must store all of the vertex coordinates for a primitive in a single one-dimensional array. You can use an array of int, float, or double, and you can have 2,3 , or 4 coordinates for each vertex. The data in the array are the same numbers that you would pass as parameters to a function such as glVertex3f, in the same order. You need to tell OpenGL where to find the data by calling

```
void glVertexPointer(int size, int type, int stride, void* array)
```

The size parameter is the number of coordinates per vertex. (You have to provide the same number of coordinates for each vertex.) The type is a constant that tells the data type of each of the numbers in the array. The possible values are GL_FLOAT, GL_INT, and GL_DOUBLE. The constant that you provide here must match the data type of the numbers in the array. The stride is usually 0 , meaning that the data values are stored in consecutive locations in the array; if that is not the case, then stride gives the distance in bytes between the location of the data for one vertex and location for the next vertex. (This would allow you to store other data, along with the vertex coordinates, in the same array.) The final parameter is the array that contains the data. It is listed as being of type "void*", which is a C data type for a pointer that can point to any type of data. (Recall that an array variable in C is a kind of pointer, so you can just pass an array variable as the fourth parameter.) For example, suppose that we want to draw a square in the *xy*-plane. We can set up the vertex array with

```
float coords [8] = { - 0.5,-0.5, 0.5,-0.5, 0.5,0.5, -0.5,0.5};
glVertexPointer( 2, GL_FLOAT, 0, coords );
```

In addition to setting the location of the vertex coordinates, you have to enable use of the array by calling

```
glEnableClientState(GL_VERTEX_ARRAY);
```

OpenGL ignores the vertex pointer except when this state is enabled. You can use glDisableClientState to disable use of the vertex array. Finally, in order to actually draw the primitive, you would call the function

```
void glDrawArrays( int primitiveType, int firstVertex, int vertexCount)
```

This function call corresponds to one use of glBegin/glEnd. The primitiveType tells which primitive type is being drawn, such as GL_QUADS or GL_TRIANGLE_STRIP. The same ten primitive types that can be used with glBegin can be used here. The parameter firstVertex is the number of the first vertex that is to be used for drawing the primitive. Note that the position is given in terms of vertex number; the corresponding array index would be the vertex number times the number of coordinates per vertex, which was set in the call to glVertexPointer. The vertexCount parameter is the number of vertices to be used, just as if glVertex* were called vertexCount times. Often, firstVertex will be zero, and vertexCount will be the total number of vertices in the array. The command for drawing the square in our example would be

```
glDrawArrays( GL_TRIANGLE_FAN, 0, 4 );
```

Often there is other data associated with each vertex in addition to the vertex coordinates. For example, you might want to specify a different color for each vertex. The colors for the vertices can be put into another array. You have to specify the location of the data by calling

```
void glColorPointer(int size, int type, int stride, void* array)
```

which works just like *g* VertexPointer. And you need to enable the color array by calling

```
glEnableClientState(GL_COLOR_ARRAY);
```

With this setup, when you call glDrawArrays, OpenGL will pull a color from the color array for each vertex at the same time that it pulls the vertex coordinates from the vertex array.

Later, we will encounter other kinds of vertex data besides coordinates and color that can be dealt with in much the same way.

Let's put this together to draw the standard OpenGL red/green/blue triangle, which we drew using glBegin/glEnd in Subsection 3.1.2. Since the vertices of the triangle have different colors, we will use a color array in addition to the vertex array.

```
float coords[6] = { -0.9,-0.9, 0.9,-0.9, 0,0.7}; // two coords per
vertex.
float colors[9] = { 1,0,0, 0,1,0, 1,0,0}; // three RGB values per
vertex.
glVertexPointer( 2, GL_FLOAT, 0, coords ); // Set data type and
location.
glColorPointer( 3, GL_FLOAT, 0, colors );
glEnableClientState( GL_VERTEX_ARRAY ); // Enable use of arrays.
glEnableClientState( GL_COLOR_ARRAY );
glDrawArrays( GL_TRIANGLES, 0, 3 ); // Use 3 vertices, starting with
vertex 0.
```

In practice, not all of this code has to be in the same place. The function that does the actual drawing, glDrawArrays, must be in the display routine that draws the image. The rest could be in the display routine, but could also be done, for example, in an initialization routine.

The function glDrawElements is similar to glDrawArrays, but it is designed for use with data in a format similar to an indexed face set. With glDrawArrays, OpenGL pulls data from the enabled arrays in order, vertex 0 , then vertex 1 , then vertex 2 , and so on. With glDrawElements, you provide a list of vertex numbers. OpenGL will go through the list of vertex numbers, pulling data for the specified vertices from the arrays. The advantage of this comes, as with indexed face sets, from the fact that the same vertex can be reused several times.

To use glDrawElements to draw a primitive, you need an array to store the vertex numbers. The numbers in the array can be 8,16 , or 32 bit integers. (They are supposed to be unsigned integers, but arrays of regular positive integers will also work.) You also need arrays to store the vertex coordinates and other vertex data, and you must enable those arrays in the same way as for glDrawArrays, using functions such as glVertexArray and glEnableClientState. To actually draw the primitive, call the function

```
void glDrawElements( int primitiveType, vertexCount, dataType, void
*array)
```

Here, primitiveType is one of the ten primitive types such as GL_LINES, vertexCount is the number of vertices to be drawn, dataType specifies the type of data in the array, and array is the array that holds the list of vertex numbers. The dataType must be given as one of the constants GL_UNSIGNED_BYTE, GL_UNSIGNED_SHORT, or GL_UNSIGNED_INT to specify 8, 16, or 32 bit integers respectively.

As an example, we can draw a cube. We can draw all six faces of the cube as one primitive of type GL_QUADS. We need the vertex coordinates in one array and the vertex numbers for the faces in another array. I will also use a color array for vertex colors. The vertex colors will be interpolated to pixels on the faces, just like the red/green/blue triangle. Here is code that could be used to draw the cube. Again, all this would not necessarily be in the same part of a program:

```
float vertexCoords[24] = { // Coordinates for the vertices of a cube.
       1,1,1, 1,1,-1, 1,-1,-1, 1,-1,1,
    -1,1,1, -1,1,-1, -1,-1,-1, -1,-1,1};
float vertexColors[24] = { // An RGB color value for each vertex
    1,1,1, 1,0,0, 1,1,0, 0,1,0,
    0,0,1, 1,0,1, 0,0,0, 0,1,1 };
int elementArray[24] = { // Vertex numbers for the six faces.
    0,1,2,3, 0,3,7,4, 0,4,5,1,
    6,2,1,5, 6,5,4,7, 6,7,3,2 };


glVertexPointer( 3, GL_FLOAT, 0, vertexCoords );
glColorPointer( 3, GL_FLOAT, 0, vertexColors );
glEnableClientState( GL_VERTEX_ARRAY );
glEnableClientState( GL_COLOR_ARRAY );
glDrawElements( GL_QUADS, 24, GL_UNSIGNED_INT, elementArray );
```

Note that the second parameter is the number of vertices, not the number of quads. The sample program glut/cubes-with-vertex-arrays.c uses this code to draw a cube. It draws a second cube using glDrawArrays. The Java version is jogl/CubesWithVertexArrays.java, but you need to read the next subsection before you can understand it. There is also a JavaScript version, glsim/cubes-with-vertex-arrays.html.

3.4.3 Data Buffers in Java

Ordinary Java arrays are not suitable for use with glDrawElements and glDrawArrays, partly because of the format in which data is stored in them and partly because of inefficiency in transfer of data between Java arrays and the Graphics Processing Unit. These problems are solved by using direct nio buffers. The term "nio" here refers to the package java.nio, which contains classes for input/output. A "buffer" in this case is an object of the class java.nio.Buffer or one of its subclasses, such as FloatBuffer or IntBuffer. Finally, "direct" means that the buffer is optimized for direct transfer of data between memory and other devices such as the GPU. Like an array, an nio buffer is a numbered sequence of elements, all of the same type. A FloatBuffer, for example, contains a numbered sequence of values of type float. There are subclasses of Buffer for all of Java's primitive data types except boolean.

Nio buffers are used in JOGL in several places where arrays are used in the C API. For example, JOGL has the following glVertexPointer method in the GL2 class:

```
public void glVertexPointer(int size, int type, int stride, Buffer
buffer)
```

Only the last parameter differs from the C version. The buffer can be of type FloatBuffer, IntBuffer, or DoubleBuffer. The type of buffer must match the type parameter in the method. Functions such as glColorPointer work the same way, and glDrawElements takes the form

```
public void glDrawElements( int primitiveType, vertexCount,
    dataType, Buffer buffer)
```

where the buffer can be of type IntBuffer, ShortBuffer, or ByteBuffer to match the dataType UNSIGNED_INT, UNSIGNED_SHORT, or UNSIGNED_BYTE.

The class com.jogamp.common.nio.Buffers contains static utility methods for working with direct nio buffers. The easiest to use are methods that create a buffer from a Java array. For example, the method Buffers.newDirectFloatBuffer(array) takes a float array as its parameter and creates a FloatBuffer of the same length and containing the same data as the array. These methods are used to create the buffers in the sample program jogl/Cubes With VertexArrays.java. For example,

```
float[] vertexCoords = { // Coordinates for the vertices of a cube.
    1,1,1, 1,1,-1, 1,-1,-1, 1,-1,1,
    -1,1,1, -1,1,-1, -1,-1,-1, -1,-1,1};
int[] elementArray = { // Vertex numbers for the six faces.
    0,1,2,3, 0,3,7,4, 0,4,5,1,
    6,2,1,5, 6,5,4,7, 6,7,3,2 };
```

```
// Buffers for use with glVertexPointer and glDrawElements:
FloatBuffer vertexCoordBuffer =
Buffers.newDirectFloatBuffer(vertexCoords);
IntBuffer elementBuffer = Buffers.newDirectIntBuffer(elementArray);
```

The buffers can then be used when drawing the cube:

```
gl2.glVertexPointer( 3, GL2.GL_FLOAT, 0, vertexCoordBuffer );
gl2.glDrawElements( GL2.GL_QUADS, 24, GL2.GL_UNSIGNED_INT,
elementBuffer );
```

There are also methods such as Buffers.newDirectFloatBuffer (n), which creates a FloatBuffer of length n. Remember that an nio Buffer, like an array, is simply a linear sequence of elements of a given type. In fact, just as for an array, it is possible to refer to items in a buffer by their index or position in that sequence. Suppose that buffer is a variable of type FloatBuffer, i is an int and x is a float. Then

```
buffer.put(i,x);
```

copies the value of x into position number i in the buffer. Similarly, buffer.get (i) can be used to retrieve the value at index i in the buffer. These methods make it possible to work with buffers in much the same way that you can work with arrays.

3.4.4 Display Lists and VBOs

All of the OpenGL drawing commands that we have considered so far have an unfortunate inefficiency when the same object is going be drawn more than once: The commands and data for drawing that object must be transmitted to the GPU each time the object is drawn. It should be possible to store information on the GPU, so that it can be reused without retransmitting it. We will look at two techniques for doing this: display lists and vertex buffer objects (VBOs). Display lists were part of the original OpenGL 1.0, but they are not part of the modern OpenGL API. VBOs were introduced in OpenGL 1.5 and are still important in modern OpenGL; we will discuss them only briefly here and will consider them more fully when we get to WebGL.

Display lists are useful when the same sequence of OpenGL commands will be used several times. A display list is a list of graphics commands and the data used by those commands. A display list can be stored in a GPU. The contents of the display list only have to be transmitted once to the GPU. Once a list has been created, it can be "called." The key point is that calling a list requires only one OpenGL command. Although the same list of commands still has to be executed, only one command has to be transmitted from the CPU to the graphics card. and then the full power of hardware acceleration can be used to execute the commands at the highest possible speed.

Note that calling a display list twice can result in two different effects, since the effect can depend on the OpenGL state at the time the display list is called. For example, a display list that generates the geometry for a sphere can draw spheres in different locations, as long as different modeling transforms are in effect each time the list is called. The list can also produce spheres of different colors, as long as the drawing color is changed between calls to the list.

If you want to use a display list, you first have to ask for an integer that will identify that list to the GPU. This is done with a command such as

```
listID = glGenLists(1);
```

The return value is an int which will be the identifier for the list. The parameter to glGenLists is also an int, which is usually 1 . (You can actually ask for several list IDs at once; the parameter tells how many you want. The list IDs will be consecutive integers, so that if list A is the return value from glGenLists(3), then the identifiers for the three lists will be listA, list$A + 1$, and list $A + 2$.)

Once you've allocated a list in this way, you can store commands into it. If listID is the ID for the list, you would do this with code of the form:

```
glNewList(listID, GL_COMPILE);
     ... // OpenGL commands to be stored in the list.
 glEndList();
```

The parameter *GL_COMPILE* means that you only want to store commands into the list, not execute them. If you use the alternative parameter *GL_COMPILE_AND_EXECUTE*, then the commands will be executed immediately as well as stored in the list for later reuse.

Once you have created a display list in this way, you can call the list with the command

```
glCallList(listID);
```

The effect of this command is to tell the GPU to execute a list that it has already stored. You can tell the graphics card that a list is no longer needed by calling

```
gl.glDeleteLists(listID, 1);
```

The second parameter in this method call plays the same role as the parameter in glGenLists; that is, it allows you delete several sequentially numbered lists. Deleting a list when you are through with it allows the GPU to reuse the memory that was used by that list.

Vertex buffer objects take a different approach to reusing information. They only store data, not commands. A VBO is similar to an array. In fact, it is essentially an array that can be stored on the GPU for efficiency of reuse. There are OpenGL commands to create and delete VBOs and to transfer data from an array on the CPU side into a VBO on the GPU. You can configure glDrawArrays() and glDrawElements() to take the data from a VBO instead of from an ordinary array (in C) or from an nio Buffer (in JOGL). This means that you can send the data once to the GPU and use it any number of times.

I will not discuss how to use VBOs here, since it was not a part of OpenGL 1.1. However, there is a sample program that lets you compare different techniques for rendering a complex image. The C version of the program is glut/color-cube-of-spheres.c, and the Java version is jogl/ColorCubeOfSpheres.java. The program draws 1331 spheres, arranged in an 11-by-11-by11 cube. The spheres are different colors, with the amount of red in the color varying along one axis, the amount of green along a second axis, and the amount of blue along the third. Each sphere has 66 vertices, whose coordinates can be computed using the math functions sin and cos. The program allows you to select from five different rendering methods, and it shows the time that it takes to render the spheres using the selected method. (The Java version has a drop-down menu for selecting the method; in the C version, right-click the image to get the menu.) You can use your mouse to rotate the cube of spheres, both to get a better view and to generate more data for computing the average render time. The five rendering techniques are:

- Direct Draw, Recomputing Vertex Data - A remarkably foolish way to draw 1331 spheres, by recomputing all of the vertex coordinates every time a sphere is drawn.
- Direct Draw, Precomputed Data - The vertex coordinates are computed once and stored in an array. The spheres are drawn using glBegin/glEnd, but the data used in the calls to glVertex* are taken from the array rather than recomputed each time they are needed.
- Display List - A display list is created containing all of the commands and data needed to draw a sphere. Each sphere can then be drawn by a single call of that display list.
- DrawArrays with Arrays - The data for the sphere is stored in a vertex array (or, for Java, in an nio buffer), and each sphere is drawn using a call to glDrawArrays,

using the techniques discussed earlier in this section. The data has to be sent to the GPU every time a sphere is drawn.

- DrawArrays with VBOs - Again, glDrawArrays is used to draw the spheres, but this time the data is stored in a VBO instead of in an array, so the data only has to be transmitted to the GPU once.

In my own experiments, I found, as expected, that display lists and VBOs gave the shortest rendering times, with little difference between the two. There were some interesting differences between the results for the C version and the results for the Java version, which seem to be due to the fact that function calls in C are more efficient than method calls in Java. You should try the program on your own computer, and compare the rendering times for the various rendering methods.

3.5 Some Linear Algebra

Linear algebra is a branch of mathematics that is fundamental to computer graphics. It studies vectors, linear transformations, and matrices. We have already encountered these topics in Subsection 2.3.8 in a two-dimensional context. In this section, we look at them more closely and extend the discussion to three dimensions.

It is not essential that you know the mathematical details that are covered in this section, since they can be handled internally in OpenGL or by software libraries. However, you will need to be familiar with the concepts and the terminology. This is especially true for modern OpenGL, which leaves many of the details up to your programs. Even when you have a software library to handle the details, you still need to know enough to use the library. You might want to skim this section and use it later for reference.

3.5.1 Vectors and Vector Math

A vector is a quantity that has a length and a direction. A vector can be visualized as an arrow, as long as you remember that it is the length and direction of the arrow that are relevant, and that its specific location is irrelevant. Vectors are often used in computer graphics to represent directions, such as the direction from an object to a light source or the direction in which a surface faces. In those cases, we are more interested in the direction of a vector than in its length.

If we visualize a 3D vector V as an arrow starting at the origin, (0,0,0), and ending at a point P, then we can, to a certain extent, identify V with P-at least as long as we remember that an arrow starting at any other point could also be used to represent V. If P has coordinates (a, b, c), we can use the same coordinates for V. When we think of (a, b, c) as a vector, the value of a represents the change in the x-coordinate between the starting point of the arrow and its ending point, b is the change in the y-coordinate, and c is the change in the z-coordinate. For example, the 3D point $(x, y, z) = (3,4,5)$ has the same coordinates as the vector $(dx, dy, dz) = (3,4,5)$. For the point, the coordinates (3,4,5) specify a position in space in the xyz coordinate system. For the vector, the coordinates (3,4,5) specify the change in the x, y, and z coordinates along the vector. If we represent the vector with an arrow that starts at the origin (0,0,0), then the head of the arrow will be at (3,4,5). But we could just as well visualize the vector as an arrow that starts at the point (1,1,1), and in that case the head of the arrow would be at the point (4,5,6).

The distinction between a point and a vector is subtle. For some purposes, the distinction can be ignored; for other purposes, it is important. Often, all that we have is a sequence of numbers, which we can treat as the coordinates of either a vector or a point, whichever is more appropriate in the context.

One of the basic properties of a vector is its length. In terms of its coordinates, the length of a 3D vector (x, y, z) is given by $\text{sqrt}(x^2 + y^2 + z^2)$. (This is just the Pythagorean theorem in three dimensions.) If v is a vector, its length is denoted by $|v|$. The length of a vector is also called its norm. (We are considering 3D vectors here, but concepts and formulas are similar for other dimensions.)

Vectors of length 1 are particularly important. They are called unit vectors. If $v = (x, y, z)$ is any vector other than (0,0,0), then there is exactly one unit vector that points in the same direction as v. That vector is given by

```
( x/length, y/length, z/length )
```

where length is the length of v. Dividing a vector by its length is said to normalize the vector: The result is a unit vector that points in the same direction as the original vector.

Two vectors can be added. Given two vectors $v1 = (x1, y1, z1)$ and $v2 = (x2, y2, z2)$, their sum is defined as

```
v1+v2 = (x1+x2,y1+y2, z1+z2);
```

The sum has a geometric meaning:

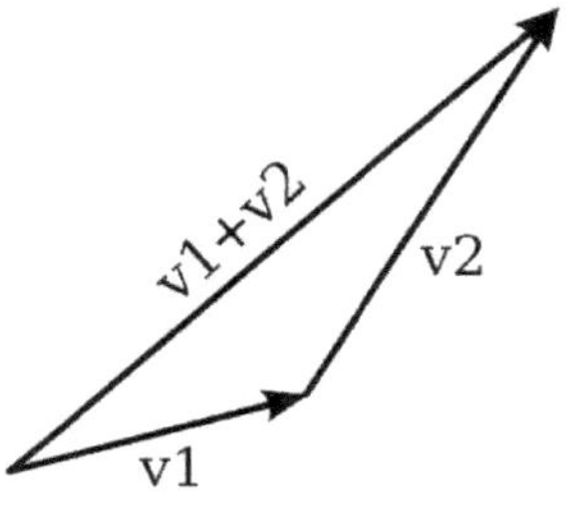

The vector sum of v 1 and v 2 can be obtained by placing the starting point of v 2 at the ending point of v 1 . The sum is the vector from the starting point of v 1 to the ending point of v 2 .

Remember that vectors have length and direction, but no set position.

Multiplication is more complicated. The obvious definition of the product of two vectors, similar to the definition of the sum, does not have geometric meaning and is rarely used. However, there are three kinds of vector multiplication that are used: the scalar product, the dot produt, and the cross product.

If $v = (x, y, z)$ is a vector and a is a number, then the scalar product of a and v is defined as

```
av = (a*x, a*y, a*z );
```

Assuming that a is positive and v is not zero, av is a vector that points in the same direction as v, whose length is a times the length of v. If a is negative, av points in the opposite direction from v, and its length is $|a|$ times the length of v. This type of product is called a scalar product because a number like a is also referred to as a "scalar," perhaps because multiplication by a scales v to a new length.

Given two vectors $v1 = (x1, y1, z1)$ and $v2 = (x2, y2, z2)$, the dot product of $v1$ and $v2$ is denoted by $v1 \cdot v2$ and is defined by

```
\mathrm { v1.v2 } \mathrm { = } \mathrm { x1*x2 } \mathrm { + } \mathrm
{ y1*y2 } \mathrm { + } \mathrm { z1*z2 }
```

Note that the dot product is a number, not a vector. The dot product has several very important geometric meanings. First of all, note that the length of a vector v is just the square root of $v \cdot v$. Furthermore, the dot product of two non-zero vectors $v1$ and $v2$ has the property that

```
cos(angle) = v1.v2 / (|v1|*|v2|)
```

where angle is the measure of the angle between $v1$ and v2. In particular, in the case of two unit vectors, whose lengths are 1 , the dot product of two unit vectors is simply the cosine of the angle between them. Furthermore, since the cosine of a 90 -degree angle is zero, two non-zero vectors are perpendicular if and only if their dot product is zero. Because of these properties, the dot product is particularly important in lighting calculations, where the effect of light shining on a surface depends on the angle that the light makes with the surface.

The scalar product and dot product are defined in any dimension. For vectors in 3D, there is another type of product called the cross product, which also has an important geometric meaning. For vectors $v1 = (x1, y1, z1)$ and $v2 = (x2, y2, z2)$, the cross product of $v1$ and $v2$ is denoted $v1 \times v2$ and is the vector defined by

```
v1)v2 = (y1*z2 - z1*y2, z1*x2 - x1*z2, x1*y2 - y1*x2)
```

If $v1$ and $v2$ are non-zero vectors, then $v1 \times v2$ is zero if and only if $v1$ and $v2$ point in the same direction or in exactly opposite directions. Assuming $v1 \times v2$ is non-zero, then it is perpendicular both to $v1$ and to $v2$; furthermore, the vectors $v1, v2, v1 \times v2$ follow the right-hand rule (in a right-handed coordinate system); that is, if you curl the fingers of your right hand from v1 to $v2$, then your thumb points in the direction of $v1 \times v2$. If $v1$ and $v2$ are perpendicular unit vectors, then the cross product $v1 \times v2$ is also a unit vector, which is perpendicular both to $v1$ and to $v2$.

Finally, I will note that given two points $P1 = (x1, y1, z1)$ and $P2 = (x2, y2, z2)$, the difference P2-P1 is defined by

$$\mathrm{P2} - \mathrm{P1} = (\mathrm{x2} - \mathrm{x1}, \mathrm{y2} - \mathrm{y1}, \mathrm{z2} - \mathrm{z1})$$

This difference is a vector that can be visualized as an arrow that starts at $P1$ and ends at $P2$.

Now, suppose that P1, P2, and P3 are vertices of a polygon. Then the vectors P1-P2 and P3-P2 lie in the plane of the polygon, and so the cross product

```
(P3-P2) × (P1-P2)
```

is a vector that is perpendicular to the polygon.

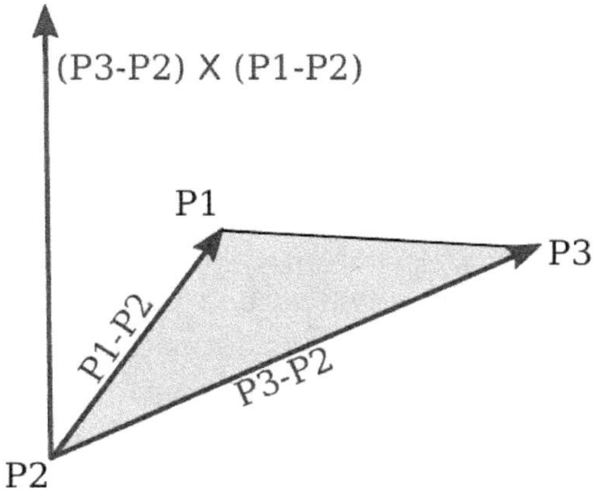

Try to visualize this in 3D! A vector that is perpendicular to the triangle is obtained by taking the cross product of P3-P2 and P1-P2, which are vectors that lie along two sides of the triangle.

This vector is said to be a normal vector for the polygon. A normal vector of length one is called a unit normal. Unit normals will be important in lighting calculations, and it will be useful to be able to calculate a unit normal for a polygon from its vertices.

3.5.2 Matrices and Transformations

A matrix is just a two-dimensional array of numbers. A matrix with r rows and c columns is said to be an r-by-c matrix. If A and B are matrices, and if the number of columns in A is equal to the number of rows in B, then A and B can be multiplied to give the matrix product AB. If A is an n-by- m matrix and B is an m-by- k matrix, then AB is an n-by- k matrix. In particular, two n-by- n matrices can be multiplied to give another n-by- n matrix.

An n-dimensional vector can be thought of an n-by- 1 matrix. If A is an n-by- n matrix and v is a vector in n dimensions, thought of as an n-by- 1 matrix, then the product Av is again an n-dimensional vector. The product of a 3 -by- 3 matrix A and a 3D vector $v = (x, y, z)$ is often displayed like this:

$$\begin{pmatrix} a1 & a2 & a3 \\ b1 & b2 & b3 \\ c1 & c2 & c3 \end{pmatrix} \begin{pmatrix} x \\ y \\ z \end{pmatrix} = \begin{pmatrix} a1^{*}x + a2^{*}y + a3^{*}z \\ b1^{*}x + b2^{*}y + b3^{*}z \\ c1^{*}x + c2^{*}y + c3^{*}z \end{pmatrix}$$

Note that the i-th coordinate in the product Av is simply the dot product of the i-th row of the matrix A and the vector v.

Using this definition of the multiplication of a vector by a matrix, a matrix defines a transformation that can be applied to one vector to yield another vector. Transformations that are defined in this way are linear transformations, and they are the main object of study in linear algebra. A linear transformation L has the properties that for two vectors v and w, $L(v+w)=L(v)+L(w)$, and for a number s, $L(sv)=sL(v)$.

Rotation and scaling are linear transformations, but translation is not a linear transformaton. To include translations, we have to widen our view of transformation to include affine transformations. An affine transformation can be defined, roughly, as a linear transformation followed by a translation. Geometrically, an affine transformation is a transformation that preserves parallel lines; that is, if two lines are parallel, then their images under an affine transformation will also be parallel lines. For computer graphics, we are interested in affine transformations in three dimensions. However-by what seems at first to be a very odd trickwe can narrow our view back to the linear by moving into the fourth dimension.

Note first of all that an affine transformation in three dimensions transforms a vector $(x1, y1, z1)$ into a vector $(x2, y2, z2)$ given by formulas

```
x2 = a1*x1 + a2*y1 + a3*z1 + t1
y2 = b1*x1 + b2*y1 + b3*z1 + t2
z2 = c1*x1 + c2*y1 + c3*z1 + t3
```

These formulas express a linear transformation given by multiplication by the 3 -by- 3 matrix

$$\begin{pmatrix} a1 & a2 & a3 \\ b1 & b2 & b3 \\ c1 & c2 & c3 \end{pmatrix}$$

followed by translation by $t1$ in the x direction, $t2$ in the y direction and $t3$ in the z direction. The trick is to replace each three-dimensional vector (x, y, z) with the four-dimensional vector $(x, y, z, 1)$, adding a " 1 " as the fourth coordinate. And instead of the 3 -by- 3 matrix, we use the 4-by-4 matrix

$$\begin{pmatrix} a1 & a2 & a3 & t1 \\ b1 & b2 & b3 & t2 \\ c1 & c2 & c3 & t3 \\ 0 & 0 & 0 & 1 \end{pmatrix}$$

If the vector $(x1, y1, z1, 1)$ is multiplied by this 4 -by-4 matrix, the result is precisely the vector $(x2, y2, z2, 1)$. That is, instead of applying an affine transformation to the 3D vector $(x1, y1, z1)$, we can apply a linear transformation to the 4D vector $(x1, y1, z1, 1)$.

This might seem pointless to you, but nevertheless, that is what is done in OpenGL and other 3D computer graphics systems: An affine transformation is represented as a 4 -by- 4 matrix in which the bottom row is (0,0,0,1), and a three-dimensional vector is changed into a four dimensional vector by adding a 1 as the final coordinate. The result is that all the affine transformations that are so important in computer graphics can be implemented as multiplication of vectors by matrices.

The identity transformation, which leaves vectors unchanged, corresponds to multiplication by the identity matrix, which has ones along its descending diagonal and zeros elsewhere. The OpenGL function glLoadIdentity() sets the current matrix to be the 4 -by- 4 identity matrix. An OpenGL transformation function, such as glTranslatef (tx, ty, tz), has the effect of multiplying the current matrix by the 4 -by- 4 matrix that represents the transformation. Multiplication is on the right; that is, if M is the current matrix and T is the matrix that represents the transformation, then the current matrix will be set to the product matrix MT. For the record, the following illustration shows the identity matrix and the matrices corresponding to various OpenGL transformation functions:

$$\begin{pmatrix} 1 & 0 & 0 & 0 \\ 0 & 1 & 0 & 0 \\ 0 & 0 & 1 & 0 \\ 0 & 0 & 0 & 1 \end{pmatrix}$$

Identity Matrix

$$\begin{pmatrix} 1 & 0 & 0 & tx \\ 0 & 1 & 0 & ty \\ 0 & 0 & 1 & tz \\ 0 & 0 & 0 & 1 \end{pmatrix}$$

glTranslatef(tx,ty,tz)

$$\begin{pmatrix} sx & 0 & 0 & 0 \\ 0 & sy & 0 & 0 \\ 0 & 0 & sz & 0 \\ 0 & 0 & 0 & 1 \end{pmatrix}$$

glScalef(sx,sy,sz)

$$\begin{pmatrix} 1 & 0 & 0 & 0 \\ 0 & \cos(d) & -\sin(d) & 0 \\ 0 & \sin(d) & \cos(d) & 0 \\ 0 & 0 & 0 & 1 \end{pmatrix}$$

glRotatef(d,1,0,0)

$$\begin{pmatrix} \cos(d) & 0 & \sin(d) & 0 \\ 0 & 1 & 0 & 0 \\ -\sin(d) & 0 & \cos(d) & 0 \\ 0 & 0 & 0 & 1 \end{pmatrix}$$

glRotatef(d,0,1,0)

$$\begin{pmatrix} \cos(d) & -\sin(d) & 0 & 0 \\ \sin(d) & \cos(d) & 0 & 0 \\ 0 & 0 & 1 & 0 \\ 0 & 0 & 0 & 1 \end{pmatrix}$$

glRotatef(d,0,0,1)

It is even possible to use an arbitrary transformation matrix in OpenGL, using the function glMultMatrixf (T) or glMultMatrixd (T). The parameter, T, is an array of numbers of type float or double, representing a transformation matrix. The array is a one-dimensional array of length 16. The items in the array are the numbers from the transformation matrix, stored in column-major order, that is, the numbers in the fist column, followed by the numbers in the second column, and so on. These functions multiply the current matrix by the matrix T, on the right. You could use them, for example, to implement a shear transform, which is not easy to represent as a sequence of scales, rotations, and translations.

3.5.3 Homogeneous Coordinates

We finish this section with a bit of mathematical detail about the implementation of transformations. There is one common transformation in computer graphics that is not an affine transformation: In the case of a perspective projection, the projection transformation is not affine. In a perspective projection, an object will appear to get smaller as it moves farther away from the viewer, and that is a property that no affine transformation can express, since affine transforms preserve parallel lines and parallel lines will seem to converge in the distance in a perspective projection.

Surprisingly, we can still represent a perspective projection as a 4 -by- 4 matrix, provided we are willing to stretch our use of coordinates even further than we have already. We have already represented 3D vectors by 4D vectors in which the fourth coordinate is 1 . We now allow the fourth coordinate to be anything at all, except for requiring that at least one of the four coordinates is non-zero. When the fourth coordinate, w, is non-zero, we consider the coordinates (x, y, z, w) to represent the three-dimensional vector $(x/w, y/w, z/w)$. Note that this is consistent with our previous usage, since it considers $(x, y, z, 1)$ to represent (x, y, z), as before. When the fourth coordinate is zero, there is no corresponding 3D vector, but it is possible to think of $(x, y, z, 0)$ as representing a 3D "point at infinity" in the direction of (x, y, z).

Coordinates (x, y, z, w) used in this way are referred to as homogeneous coordinates. If we use homogeneous coordinates, then any 4 -by- 4 matrix can be used to transform threedimensional vectors, including matrices whose bottom row is not (0,0,0,1). Among the transformations that can be represented in this way is the projection transformation for a perspective projection. And in fact, this is what OpenGL does internally. It represents all three-dimensional points and vectors using homogeneous coordinates, and it represents all transformations as 4 -by- 4 matrices. You can even specify vertices using homogeneous coordinates. For example, the command

$$\text{glVertex4f}\ (x, y, z, w)$$

with a non-zero value for w, generates the 3D point $(x/w, y/w, z/w)$. Fortunately, you will almost never have to deal with homogeneous coordinates directly. The only real exception to this is that homogeneous coordinates are used, surprisingly, when configuring OpenGL lighting, as we'll see in the next chapter.

3.6 Using GLUT and JOGL

Opengl is an api for graphics only, with no support for things like windows or events. OpenGL depends on external mechanisms to create the drawing surfaces on which it will draw. Windowing APIs that support OpenGL often do so as one library among many others that are used to produce a complete application. We will look at two cross-platform APIs that make it possible to use OpenGL in applications, one for C/C + + and one for Java.

For simple applications written in C or C++, one possible windowing API is ***GLUT*** (OpenGL Utility Toolkit). GLUT is a small API. It is used to create windows that serve as simple frames for OpenGL drawing surfaces. It has support for handling mouse and keyboard events, and it can do basic animation. It does not support controls such as buttons or input fields, but it does allow for a menu that pops up in response to a mouse action. The original version of GLUT is no longer actively supported, and a version called freeglut (http://freeglut.sourceforge.net/) is recommended instead. For example, the version included in Linux is actually freeglut. For details of the freeglut API, see http://freeglut.sourceforge.net/docs/api.php

JOGL (Java OpenGL) is a collection of classes that make it possible to use OpenGL in Java applications. JOGL is integrated into Swing and AWT, the standard Java graphical user interface APIs. With JOGL, you can create Java GUI components on which you can draw using OpenGL. These OpenGL components can be used in any Java application, in much the same way that you would use a Canvas or JPanel as a drawing surface. Like many things Java, JOGL is immensely complicated. We will use it only in fairly simple applications. JOGL is not a standard part of Java. It's home web site is http://jogamp.org/jogl/www/

This section contains information to get you started using GLUT and JOGL, assuming that you already know the basics of programming with C and Java. It also briefly discusses glsim.js, a JavaScript library that I have written to simulate the subset of OpenGL 1.1 that is used in this book.

3.6.1 Using GLUT

To work with GLUT, you will need a C compiler and copies of the OpenGL and GLUT (or freeglut) development libraries. I can't tell you exactly that means on your own computer. On my computer, which runs Linux Mint, for example, the free C compiler gcc is already available. To do OpenGL development, I installed several packages, including freeglut3-dev and libgl1-mesa-dev. (Mesa is a Linux implementation of OpenGL.) If glutprog.c contains a complete C program that uses GLUT, I can compile it using a command such as

```
gcc -o glutprog glutprog.c -lGL -lglut
```

The "-o glutprog" tells the compiler to use "glutprog" as the name of its output file, which can then be run as a normal executable file; without this option, the executable file would be named "a.out". The "-lglut" and "-lGL" options tell the compiler to link the program with the GLUT and OpenGL libraries. (The character after the "-" is a lower case "L".) Without these options, the linker won't recognize any GLUT or OpenGL functions. If the program also uses the GLU library, compiling it would require the option "-lGLU, and if it uses the math library, it would need the option "-lm". If a program requires additional .c files, they should be included as well. For example, the sample program glut/color-cube-of-spheres.c depends on camera.c, and it can be compiled with the Linux gcc compiler using the command:

```
gcc -o cubes color-cube-of-spheres.c camera.c -lGL -lglut -lGLU -lm
```

The sample program glut/glut-starter.c can be used as a starting point for writing programs that use GLUT. While it doesn't do anything except open a window, the program contains the framework needed to do OpenGL drawing, including doing animation, responding to mouse and keyboard events, and setting up a menu. The source code contains comments that tell you how to use it.

On Windows, you might consider installing the WSL, or Windows Subsystem for Linux, (https://docs.microsoft.com/en-us/windows/wsl/), which as I write this should soon include the ability to work with GUI programs. WSL is an official Microsoft system lets you install a version of Linux inside Windows. Another option is the older open source project, Cygwin (https://cygwin.com/). (Using Cygwin, I installed the packages gcc-core, xinit, xorg-server, libglut-devel, libGLU-devel, and libGL-devel. After starting the X11 window system with the startxwin command, I was able to compile and run OpenGL examples from this textbook in a Cygwin terminal window using the same commands that I would use in Linux.)

For MacOS, the situation is more complicated, because OpenGL has been deprecated in favor of Metal, Apple's own proprietary API. However, as I write this, OpenGL can still be used on MacOS with Apple's XCode developer tools. The examples from this textbook require some modification to work with XCode tools, since the OpenGL and GLUT libraries are not loaded in the same way on Mac as they are on Linux. Modified programs for use on MacOS can be found in the source folder glut/glut-mac. See the README.txt file in that folder for more information.

***

The GLUT library makes it easy to write basic OpenGL applications in C. GLUT uses event-handling functions. You write functions to handle events that occur when the display needs to be redrawn or when the user clicks the mouse or presses a key on the keyboard.

To use GLUT, you need to include the header file glut.h (or freeglut.h) at the start of any source code file that uses it, along with the general OpenGL header file, gl.h. The header files should be installed in a standard location, in a folder named *GL*. (But note that the folder name could be different, or omitted entirely.) So, the program usually begins with something like

```
#include <GL/gl.h>
#include <GL/glut.h>
```

On my computer, saying #include <GL/glut.h> actually includes the subset of FreeGLUT that corresponds to GLUT. To get access to all of FreeGLUT, I would substitute #include < GL/freeglut.h>. Depending on the features that it uses, a program might need other header files, such as #include <GL/glu.h> and #include <math.h>.

The program's main() function must contain some code to initialize GLUT, to create and open a window, and to set up event handling by registering the functions that should be called in response to various events. After this setup, it must call a function that runs the GLUT event-handling loop. That function waits for events and processes them by calling the functions that have been registered to handle them. The event loop runs until the program ends, which happens when the user closes the window or when the program calls the standard exit() function.

To set up the event-handling functions, GLUT uses the fact that in C, it is possible to pass a function name as a parameter to another function. For example, if display() is the function that should be called to draw the content of the window, then the program would use the command

```
glutDisplayFunc(display);
```

to install this function as an event handler for display events. A display event occurs when the contents of the window need to be redrawn, including when the window is first opened. Note that display must have been previously defined, as a function with no parameters:

```
void display() {
    \text { -}
    \mathrm{ . // OpenGL drawing code goes here!}
```

```
    -
}
```

Keep in mind that it's not the name of this function that makes it an OpenGL display function. It has to be set as the display function by calling glutDisplayFunc(display). All of the GLUT event-handling functions work in a similar way (except many of them do need to have parameters).

There are a lot of possible event-handling functions, and I will only cover some of them here. Let's jump right in and look at a possible main() routine for a GLUT program that uses most of the common event handlers:

```
int main(int argc, char** argv) {
    glutInit(&argc, argv); // Required initialization!
    glutInitDisplayMode(GLUT_DOUBLE | GLUT_DEPTH);
    glutInitWindowSize(500,500); // size of display area, in pixels
    glutInitWindowPosition(100,100); // location in screen coordinates
    glutCreateWindow("OpenGL Program"); // the parameter is the window
title
    glutDisplayFunc(display); // called when window needs to be redrawn
    glutReshapeFunc(reshape); // called when size of the window changes
    glutKeyboardFunc(keyFunc); // called when user types a character
    glutSpecialFunc(specialKeyFunc);// called when user presses a
special key
    glutMouseFunc(mouseFunc); // called for mousedown and mouseup
events
    glutMotionFunc(mouseDragFunc); // called when mouse is dragged
    glutIdleFunc(idleFun); // called when there are no other events
    glutMainLoop(); // Run the event loop! This function never returns.
    return 0; // (This line will never actually be reached.)
}
```

The first five lines do some necessary initialization, the next seven lines install event handlers, and the call to glutMainLoop() runs the GLUT event loop. I will discuss all of the functions that are used here. The first GLUT function call must be glutInit, with the parameters as shown. (Note that argc and argv represent command-line arguments for the program. Passing them to glutInit allows it to process certain command-line arguments that are recognized by GLUT. I won't discuss those arguments here.) The functions glutInitWindowSize and glutInitWindowPosition do the obvious things; size is given in pixels, and window position is given in terms of pixel coordinates on the computer screen, with (0,0) at the upper left corner of the screen. The function glutCreateWindow creates the window, but note that nothing can happen in that window until glutMainLoop is called. Often, an additional, user-defined function is called in main() to do whatever initialization of global variables and OpenGL state is required by the program. OpenGL initialization can be done after calling glutCreateWindow and before calling glutMainLoop. Turning to the other functions used in main(), glutInitDisplayMode(GLUT DOUBLE | GLUT DEPTH) - Must be called to define some characteristics of the OpenGL drawing context. The parameter specifies features that you would like the OpenGL context to have. The features are represented by constants that are OR'ed together in the parameter. GLUT_DEPTH says that a depth buffer should be created; without it, the depth test won't work. If you are doing 2D graphics, you wouldn't include this option. GLUT_DOUBLE asks for double buffering, which means that drawing is actually done off-screen, and the off-screen copy has to copied to the screen to be seen. The copying is done by glutSwapBuffers(), which must be called at the end of the display function. (You can use GLUT_SINGLE instead of GLUT_DOUBLE to get single buffering; in that case, you have to call glFlush() at the end of the display function instead of glutSwapBuffers(). However, all of the examples in this book use GLUT_DOUBLE.)

glutDisplayFunc(display) - The display function should contain OpenGL drawing code that can completely redraw the scene. This is similar to paintComponent() in the Java Swing API. The display function can have any name, but it must be declared as a void function with no parameters: void display(). glutReshapeFunc(reshape) - The reshape function is called when the user changes the size of the window. Its parameters tell the new width and height of the drawing area:

```
void reshape( int width, int height )
```

For example, you might use this method to set up the projection transform, if the projection depends only on the window size. A reshape function is not required, but if one is provided, it should always set the OpenGL viewport, which is the part of the window that is used for drawing. Do this by calling

```
glViewport(0,0,width,height);
```

The viewport is set automatically if no reshape function is specified. glutKeyboardFunc(keyFunc) - The keyboard function is called when the user types a character such as 'b' or 'A' or a space. It is not called for special keys such as arrow keys that do not produce characters when pressed. The keyboard function has a parameter of type unsigned char which represents the character that was typed. It also has two int parameters that give the location of the mouse when the key was pressed, in pixel coordinates with (0,0) at the upper left corner of the display area. So, the definition of the key function must have the form:

```
void keyFunc( unsigned char ch, int x, int y )
```

Whenever you make any changes to the program's data that require the display to be redrawn, you should call glutPostRedisplay(). This is similar to calling repaint() in Java. It is better to call glutPostRedisplay() than to call the display function directly. (I also note that it's possible to call OpenGL drawing commands directly in the event-handling functions, but it probably only makes sense if you are using single buffering; if you do this, call glFlush() to make sure that the drawing appears on the screen.) glutSpecialFunc(specialKeyFunc) - The "special" function is called when the user presses certain special keys, such as an arrow key or the Home key. The parameters are an integer code for the key that was pressed, plus the mouse position when the key was pressed:

```
void specialKeyFunc( int key, int x, int y )
```

GLUT has constants to represent the possible key codes, including GLUT_KEY_LEFT, GLUT_KEY_RIGHT, GLUT_KEY_UP, and GLUT_KEY_DOWN for the arrow keys and GLUT_KEY_HOME for the Home key. For example, you can check whether the user pressed the left arrow key by testing if (key == GLUT_KEY_LEFT). glutMouseFunc(mouseFunc) - The mouse function is called both when the user presses and when the user releases a button on the mouse, with a parameter to tell which of these occurred. The function will generally look like this:

```
void mouseFunc(int button, int buttonState, int x, int y) {
    if (buttonState == GLUT_DOWN) {
        // handle mousePressed event
    }
    else { // buttonState is GLUT_UP
        // handle mouseReleased event
    }
}
```

The first parameter tells which mouse button was pressed or released; its value is the constant GLUT_LEFT_BUTTON for the left, GLUT_MIDDLE_BUTTON for the middle, and GLUT_RIGHT_BUTTON for the right mouse button. The other two parameters tell the position of the mouse. The mouse position is given in pixel coordinates with (0,0) in the top left corner of the display area and with y increasing from top to bottom. glutMotionFunc(mouseDragFunc) - The motion function is called when the user moves the mouse while dragging, that is, while a mouse button is pressed. After the user presses the mouse in the OpenGL window, this function will continue to be called even if the mouse moves outside the window, and the mouse release event will also be sent to the same window. The function has two parameters to specify the new mouse position:

```
void mouseDragFunc(int x, int y)
```

glutIdleFunc(idleFunction) - The idle function is called by the GLUT event loop whenever there are no events waiting to be processed. The idle function has no parameters. It is called as often as possible, not at periodic intervals. GLUT also has a timer function, which schedules some function to be called once, after a specified delay. To set a timer, call

```
glutTimerFunc(delayInMilliseconds, timerFunction, userSelectedID)
```

and define timerFunction as

```
void timerFunction(int timerID) { ...
```

The parameter to timerFunction when it is called will be the same integer that was passed as the third parameter to glutTimerFunc. If you want to use glutTimerFunc for animation, then timerFunction should end with another call to glutTimerFunc.

A GLUT window does not have a menu bar, but it is possible to add a hidden popup menu to the window. The menu will appear in response to a mouse click on the display. You can set whether it is triggered by the left, middle, or right mouse button.

A menu is created using the function glutCreateMenu(menuHandler), where the parameter is the name of a function that will be called when the user selects a command from the menu. The function must be defined with a parameter of type int that identifies the command that was selected:

```
void menuHandler( int commandID ) { ...
```

Once the menu has been created, commands are added to the menu by calling the function glutAddMenuEntry (name,commandID). The first parameter is the string that will appear in the menu. The second is an int that identifies the command; it is the integer that will be passed to the menu-handling function when the user selects the command from the menu.

Finally, the function glutAttachMenu(button) attaches the menu to the window. The parameter specifies which mouse button will trigger the menu. Possible values are GLUT_LEFT_BUTTON, GLUT_MIDDLE_BUTTON, and GLUT_RIGHT_BUTTON. As far as I can tell, if a mouse click is used to trigger the popup menu, than the same mouse click will not also produce a call to the mouse-handler function.

Note that a call to glutAddMenuEntry doesn't mention the menu, and a call to glutAttachMenu doesn't mention either the menu or the window. When you call glutCreateMenu, the menu that is created becomes the "current menu" in the GLUT state. When glutAddMenuEntry is called, it adds a command to the current menu. When glutAttachMenu is called, it attaches the current menu to the current window, which was set by a call to glutCreateWindow.

All this is consistent with the OpenGL "state machine" philosophy, where functions act by modifying the current state.

As an example, suppose that we want to let the user set the background color for the display. We need a function to carry out commands that we will add to the menu. For example, we might define

```
function doMenu( int commandID ) {
    if ( commandID == 1)
        glClearColor(0,0,0,1); // BLACK
    else if ( commandID == 2)
        glClearColor(1,1,1,1); // WHITE
    else if ( commandID == 3)
        glClearColor(0,0,0.5,1); // DARK BLUE
    else if (commandID == 10)
        exit(0); // END THE PROGRAM
    glutPostRedisplay(); // redraw the display, with the new background
color
}
```

We might have another function to create the menu. This function would be called in main(), after calling glutCreateWindow:

```
function createMenu() {
    glutCreateMenu( doMenu ); // Call doMenu() in response to menu
commands.
    glutAddMenuEntry( "Black Background", 1 );
    glutAddMenuEntry( "White Background", 2 );
    glutAddMenuEntry( "Blue Background", 3 );
    glutAddMenuEntry( "EXIT", 10 );
```

```
    glutAttachMenu(GLUT_RIGHT_BUTTON); // Show menu on right-click.
}
```

It's possible to have submenus in a menu. I won't discuss the procedure here, but you can look at the sample program glut/ifs-polyhedron-viewer.c for an example of using submenus.

In addition to window and event handling, GLUT includes some functions for drawing basic 3D shapes such as spheres, cones, and regular polyhedra. It has two functions for each shape, a "solid" version that draws the shape as a solid object, and a wireframe version that draws something that looks like it's made of wire mesh. (The wireframe is produced by drawing just the outlines of the polygons that make up the object.) For example, the function

```
void glutSolidSphere(double radius, int slices, int stacks)
```

draws a solid sphere with the given radius, centered at the origin. Remember that this is just an approximation of a sphere, made up of polygons. For the approximation, the sphere is divided by lines of longitude, like the slices of an orange, and by lines of latitude, like a stack of disks. The parameters slices and stacks tell how many subdivisions to use. Typical values are 32 and 16 , but the number that you need to get a good approximation for a sphere depends on the size of the sphere on the screen. The function glutWireframeSphere has the same parameters but draws only the lines of latitude and longitude. Functions for a cone, a cylinder, and a torus (doughnut) are similar:

```
void glutSolidCone(double base, double height,
    int slices, int stacks)
void glutSolidTorus(double innerRadius, double outerRadius,
        int slices, int rings)
void glutSolidCylinder(double radius, double height,
        int slices, int stacks)
    // NOTE: Cylinders are available in FreeGLUT and in Java,
    // but not in the original GLUT library.
```

For a torus, the innerRadius is the size of the doughnut hole. The function

```
void glutSolidCube(double size)
```

draws a cube of a specified size. There are functions for the other regular polyhedra that have no parameters and draw the object at some fixed size: glutSolidTetrahedron(), glutSolidOctahedron(), glutSolidDodecahedron(), and glutSolidIcosahedron(). There is also glutSolidTeapot(size) that draws a famous object that is often used as an example. Here's what the teapot looks like:

Wireframe versions of all of the shapes are also available. For example, glutWireTeapot(size) draws a wireframe teapot. Note that GLUT shapes come with normal vectors that are required for lighting calculations. However, except for the teapot, they do not come with texture coordinates, which are required for applying textures to objects.

GLUT also includes some limited support for drawing text in an OpenGL drawing context. I won't discuss that possibility here. You can check the API documentation if you are interested, and you can find an example in the sample program glut/color-cube-of-spheres.c.

3.6.2 Using JOGL

JOGL is a framework for using OpenGL in Java programs. It is a large and complex API that supports all versions of OpenGL, but it is fairly easy to use for basic applications. You should use JOGL 2.4 or later. Version 2.4.0 is still under development, but I have used it to run the sample programs from this textbook without any problems. The previous version, Jogl 2.3.2, has some problems with modern versions of Java, but it might work for you.

The sample program jogl/JoglStarter.java can be used as a starting point for writing OpenGL programs using JOGL. While it doesn't do anything except open a window, the program contains the framework needed to do OpenGL drawing, including doing animation, responding to mouse and keyboard events, and setting up a menu. The source code contains comments that tell you how to use it.

To use JOGL, you will need two .jar files containing the Java classes for JOGL: jogl-all.jar and gluegen-rt.jar. In addition, you will need two native library files. A native library is a collection of routines that can be called from Java but are not written in Java. Routines in a native library will work on only one kind of computer; you need a different native library for each type of computer on which your program is to be used. The native libraries for JOGL are stored in additional .jar files, which are available in several versions for different computers. For example, for 64-bit Linux on Intel or AMD CPUs, you need jogl-all-natives-linux-amd64.jar and gluegen-rt-natives-linux-amd64.jar. It is unfortunate that there are different versions for different platforms, since many people don't know exactly which one they are using. However, if you are in doubt, you can get more than one version; JOGL will figure out which one to use.

JOGL software can be found at https://jogamp.org/. You can download the jar files from the most recent release, which can be found at the very end of the list at https://jogamp.org/deployment/archive/rc/
I downloaded the files from the release v2.4.0-rc-20210111. Click on the release name, then click on the jar/ link to see the full list of jar files. Find and download jogl-all.jar and gluegenrt.jar and the corresponding native library files. I have also made jogl-all.jar and gluegen-rt.jar available on my own web site, along with the native libraries for some of the most common platforms, at http://math.hws.edu/eck/cs424/jogl_2_4_support/

JOGL is open-source, and the files are freely redistributable, according to their license. To do JOGL development, you should create a directory somewhere on your computer to hold the jar files. Place the two JOGL jar files in that directory, along with the two native library jar files for your platform. (Having extra native library jar files doesn't hurt, as long as you have the ones that you need.)

It is possible to do JOGL development on the command line. You have to tell the javac command where to find the two JOGL jar files. You do that in the classpath ("-cp") option to the javac command. For example, if you are working in Linux or MacOS, and if the jar files happen to be in the same directory where you are working, you might say:

```
javac -cp jogl-all.jar:gluegen-rt.jar:. MyOpenGLProg.java
```

It's similar for Windows, except that the classpath uses a ";" instead of a ":" to separate the items in the list:

```
javac -cp jogl-all.jar;gluegen-rt.jar;. MyOpenGLProg.java
```

There is an essential period at the end of the classpath, which makes it possible for Java to find .java files in the current directory. If the jar files are not in the current directory, you can use full path names or relative path names to the files. For example,

```
javac -cp ../jogl/jogl-all.jar:../jogl/gluegen-rt.jar:.
MyOpenGLProg.java
```

Running a program with the java command is exactly similar. For example:

```
java -cp jogl-all.jar:gluegen-rt.jar:. MyOpenGLProg
```

Note that you don't have to explicitly reference the native library jar files. They just have to be in the same directory with the JOGL jar files.

I do most of my Java development using the Eclipse IDE (http://eclipse.org). To do development with JOGL in Eclipse, you will have to configure Eclipse with information about the jar files. To do that, start up Eclipse. You want to create a "User Library" to contain the jar files: Open the Eclipse Preferences window, and select "Java" / "Build Path" / "User Libraries" on the left. Click the "New" button on the right. Enter "JOGL" (or any name you like) as the name of the user library. Make sure that the new user library is selected in the list of libraries, then click the "Add External Jars" button. In the file selection box, navigate to the directory that contains the JOGL jar files, and select the two jar files that are needed for JOGL, jogl-all.jar and gluegen-rt.jar. (Again, you do not need to add the native libraries; they just need to be in the same directory as the JOGL jar files.) Click "Open." The selected jars will be added to the user library. (You could also add them one at a time, if you don't know how to select multiple files.) It should look something like this:

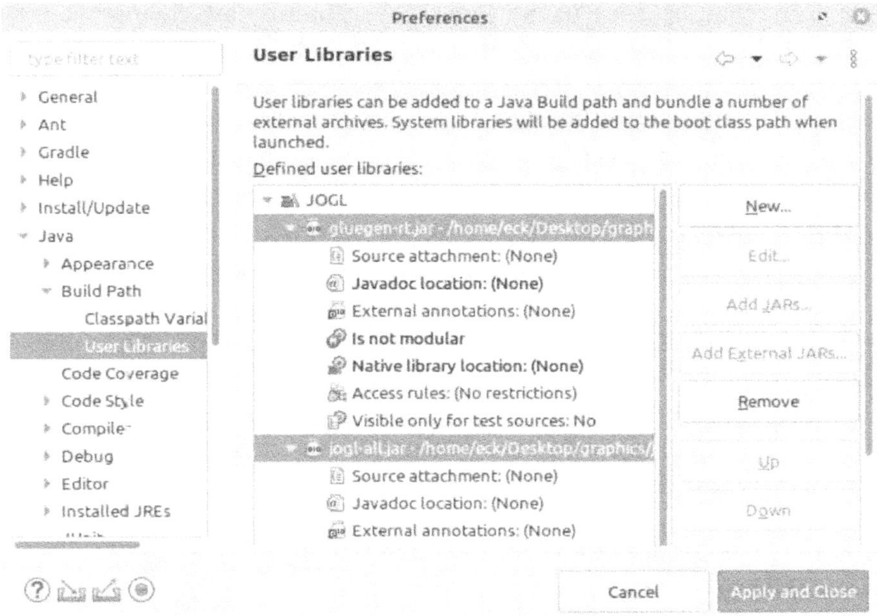

Click "OK." The user library has been created. You will only have to do this once, and then you can use it in all of your JOGL projects.

Now, to use OpenGL in a project, create a new Java project as usual in Eclipse. (If you are asked whether you want to create a module-info.java file for the project, say "Don't Create". Sample programs for this textbook do not use Java modules.) Right-click the new project in the Project Explorer view, and select "Build Path" / "Configure Build Path" from the menu. You will see the project Properties dialog, with "Java Build Path" selected on the left. (You can also access this through the "Properties" command in the "Project" menu.) Select the "Libraries" tab at the top of the window, and then click on "Class Path" in the "Libraries" tab to select it. Click the "Add Library" button, on the right. In the popup window, select "User Library" and click "Next." In the next window, select your JOGL User Library and click "Finish." Finally, click "Apply and Close" in the main Properties window. Your project should now be set up to do JOGL development. You should see the JOGL User Library listed as part of the project in the Project Explorer. Any time you want to start a new JOGL project, you can go through the same setup to add the JOGL User Library to the build path in the project.

With all that setup out of the way, it's time to talk about actually writing OpenGL programs with Java. With JOGL, we don't have to talk about mouse and keyboard handling or animation, since that can be done in the same way as in any Java Swing program. You will only need to know about a few classes from the JOGL API.

First, you need a GUI component on which you can draw using OpenGL. For that, you can use GLJPanel, which is a subclass of JPanel. (GLJPanel is for use in programs based on the Swing API; an alternative is GLCanvas, which is a subclass of the older AWT class Canvas.) The class is defined in the package com.jogamp.opengl.awt. All of the other classes that we will need for basic OpenGL programming are in the package com.jogamp.opengl.

JOGL uses Java's event framework to manage OpenGL drawing contexts, and it defines a custom event listener interface, GLEventListener, to manage OpenGL events. To draw on a GLJPanel with OpenGL, you need to create an object that implements the GLEventListener interface, and register that listener with your GLJPanel. The GLEventListener interface defines the following methods:

```
public void init(GLAutoDrawable drawable)
public void display(GLAutoDrawable drawable)
public void dispose(GLAutoDrawable drawable)
public void reshape(GLAutoDrawable drawable,
    int x, int y, int width, int height)
```

The drawable parameter in these methods tells which OpenGL drawing surface is involved. It will be a reference to the GLJPanel. (GLAutoDrawable is an interface that is implemented by GLJPanel and other OpenGL drawing surfaces.) The init() method is a place to do OpenGL initialization. (According to the documentation, it can actually be called several times, if the OpenGL context needs to be recreated for some reason. So init() should not be used to do initialization that shouldn't be done more than once.) The dispose() method will be called to give you a chance to do any cleanup before the OpenGL drawing context is destroyed. The reshape() method is called when the window first opens and whenever the size of the GLJPanel changes. OpenGL's glViewport() function is called automatically before reshape() is called, so you won't need to do it yourself. Usually, you won't need to write any code in dispose() or reshape(), but they have to be there to satisfy the definition of the GLEventListener interface.

The display() method is where the actual drawing is done and where you will do most of your work. It should ordinarily clear the drawing area and completely redraw the scene. Take a minute to study an outline for a minimal JOGL program. It creates a GLJPanel which also serves as the GLEventListener:

```
import com.jogamp.opengl.*;
import com.jogamp.opengl.awt.GLJPanel;
import java.awt.Dimension;
import javax.swing.JFrame;
public class JOGLProgram extends GLJPanel implements GLEventListener {
    public static void main(String[] args) {
        JFrame window = new JFrame("JOGL Program");
        JOGLProgram panel = new JOGLProgram();
        window.setContentPane(panel);
        window.pack();
        window.setLocation(50,50);
        window.setDefaultCloseOperation(JFrame.EXIT_ON_CLOSE);
        window.setVisible(true);
    }
    public JOGLProgram() {


        setPreferredSize( new Dimension(500,500) );
        addGLEventListener(this);
    }
    // --------------- Methods of the GLEventListener interface -------
---
    public void init(GLAutoDrawable drawable) {
            // called when the panel is created
        GL2 gl = drawable.getGL().getGL2();
        // Add initialization code here!
    }
    public void display(GLAutoDrawable drawable) {
            // called when the panel needs to be drawn
        GL2 gl = drawable.getGL().getGL2();
        // Add drawing code here!
    }
    public void reshape(GLAutoDrawable drawable,
                int x, int y, int width, int height) {
        // called when user resizes the window
    }
    public void dispose(GLAutoDrawable drawable) {
        // called when the panel is being disposed
```

```
    }
}
```

At this point, the only other thing you need to know is how to use OpenGL functions in the program. In JOGL, the OpenGL 1.1 functions are collected into an object of type GL2. (There are different classes for different versions of OpenGL; GL2 contains OpenGL 1.1 functionality, along with later versions that are compatible with 1.1.) An object of type GL2 is an OpenGL graphics context, in the same way that an object of type Graphics2D is a graphics context for ordinary Java 2D drawing. The statement

```
GL2 gl = drawable.getGL().getGL2();
```

in the above program obtains the drawing context for the GLAutoDrawable, that is, for the GLJPanel in that program. The name of the variable could, of course, be anything, but *gl* or gl2 is conventional.

For the most part, using OpenGL functions in JOGL is the same as in C, except that the functions are now methods in the object *gl*. For example, a call to glClearColor (r, g, b, a) becomes

```
gl.glClearColor(r,g,b,a);
```

The redundant "gl.gl" is a little annoying, but you get used to it. OpenGL constants such as GL_TRIANGLES are static members of GL2, so that, for example, GL_TRIANGLES becomes GL2.GL_TRIANGLES in JOGL. Parameter lists for OpenGL functions are the same as in the C API in most cases. One exception is for functions such as glVertex3fv() that take an array/pointer parameter in C. In JOGL, the parameter becomes an ordinary Java array, and an extra integer parameter is added to give the position of the data in the array. Here, for example, is how one might draw a triangle in JOGL, with all the vertex coordinates in one array:

```
float[] coords = { 0,0.5F, -0.5F,-0.5F, 0.5F,-0.5F };
gl.glBegin(GL2.GL_TRIANGLES);
gl.glVertex2fv(coords, 0); // first vertex data starts at index 0
gl.glVertex2fv(coords, 2); // second vertex data starts at index 2
gl.glVertex2fv(coords, 4); // third vertex data starts at index 4
gl.glEnd();
```

The biggest change in the JOGL API is the use of nio buffers instead of arrays in functions such as glVertexPointer. This is discussed in Subsection 3.4.3. We will see in Subsection 4.3.9 that texture images also get special treatment in JOGL.

The JOGL API includes a class named GLUT that makes GLUT's shape-drawing functions available in Java. (Since you don't need GLUT's window or event functions in Java, only the shape functions are included.) Class GLUT is defined in the package com.jogamp.opengl.util.gl2. To draw shapes using this class, you need to create an object of type GLUT. It's only necessary to make one of these for use in a program:

```
GLUT glut = new GLUT();
```

The methods in this object include all the shape-drawing functions from the GLUT C API, with the same names and parameters. For example:

```
glut.glutSolidSphere( 2, 32, 16 );
glut.glutWireTeapot( 5 );
glut.glutSolidIcosahedron();
```

(I don't know why these are instance methods in an object rather than static methods in a class; logically, there is no need for the object.)

The GLU library is available through the class com.jogamp.opengl.glu. *GLU*, and it works similarly to GLUT. That is, you have to create an object of type GLU, and the GLU functions will be available as methods in that object. We have encountered GLU only for the functions gluLookAt and gluPerspective, which are discussed in Section 3.3. For example,

```
GLU glu = new GLU();
glu.gluLookAt( 5,15,7, 0,0,0, 0,1,0 );
```

3.6.3 About glsim.js

The JavaScript library glsim.js was written to accompany and support this textbook. It implements the subset of OpenGL 1.1 that is discussed in Chapter 3 and Chapter 4, except for display lists (Subsection 3.4.4). It is used in the demos that appear in the on-line versions of those chapters. Many of the sample programs that are discussed in those chapters are available in JavaScript versions that use glsim.js.

If you would like to experiment with OpenGL 1.1, but don't want to go through the trouble of setting up a C or Java environment that supports OpenGL programming, you can consider writing your programs as web pages using glsim.js. Note that glsim is meant for experimentation and practice only, not for serious applications.

The OpenGL API that is implemented by glsim.js is essentially the same as the C API, although some of the details of semantics are different. Of course the techniques for creating a drawing surface and an OpenGL drawing context are specific to JavaScript and differ from those used in GLUT or JOGL.

To use glsim.js, you need to create an HTML document with a <canvas> element to serve as the drawing surface. The HTML file has to import the script; if glsim.js is in the same directory as the HTML file, you can do that with

```
<script src="glsim.js"></script>
```

To create the OpenGL drawing context, use the JavaScript command

```
glsimUse(canvas);
```

where canvas is either a string giving the id of the <canvas> element or is the JavaScript DOM object corresponding to the <canvas> element. Once you have created the drawing context in this way, any OpenGL commands that you give will apply to the canvas. To run the program, you just need to open the HTML document in a web browser that supports WebGL 1.0.

The easiest way to get started programming is to modify a program that already exists. The sample program glsim/first-triangle.html, from Subsection 3.1.2 is a very minimal example of using glsim.js. The sample web page glsim/glsim-starter.html can be used as a starting point for writing longer programs that use glsim.js. It provides a framework for doing OpenGL drawing, with support for animation and mouse and keyboard events. The code contains comments that tell you how to use it. Some documentation for the glsim.js library can be found in glsim/glsimdoc.html. All of these files are part of the web site for this textbook and can be found in the web site download in a folder named glsim inside the source folder.

Chapter-4

OpenGL 1.1: Light and Material

One of the goals of computer graphics is physical realism, that is, making images that look like they could be photographs of reality. This is not the only goal. For example, for scientific visualization, the goal is to use computer graphics to present information accurately and clearly. Artists can use computer graphics to create abstract rather than realistic art. However, realism is a major goal of some of the most visible uses of computer graphics, such as video games, movies, and advertising.

One important aspect of physical realism is lighting: the play of light and shadow, the way that light reflects from different materials, the way it can bend or be diffracted as it passes through translucent objects. The techniques that are used to produce the most realistic graphics can take all these factors and more into account.

However, another goal of computer graphics is speed. OpenGL, in particular, was designed for real-time graphics, where the time that is available for rendering an image is a fraction of a second. For an animated movie, it's OK if it takes hours to render each frame. But a video game is expected to render sixty frames every second. Even with the incredible speed of modern computer graphics hardware, compromises are necessary to get that speed. And thirty years ago, when OpenGL was still new, the compromises were a lot bigger.

In this chapter, we look at light and material in OpenGL 1.1. You will learn how to configure light sources and how to assign material properties to objects. Material properties determine how the objects interact with light. And you will learn how to apply an image to a surface as a texture. The support for light, material, and texture in OpenGL 1.1 is relatively crude and incomplete, by today's standards. But the concepts that it uses still serve as the foundation for modern real-time graphics and, to a significant extent, even for the most realistic computer graphics.

4.1 Introduction to Lighting

Lighting is one of the most important considerations for realistic 3D graphics. The goal is to simulate light sources and the way that the light that they emit interacts with objects in the scene. Lighting calculations are disabled by default in OpenGL. This means that when OpenGL applies color to a vertex, it simply uses the current color value as set by the one of the functions glColor*. In order to get OpenGL to do lighting calculations, you need to enable lighting by calling glEnable(GL_LIGHTING). If that's all you do, you will find that your objects are all completely black. If you want to see them, you have to turn on some lights.

The properties of a surface that determine how it interacts light are referred to as the material of the surface. A surface can have several different material properties. Before we study the OpenGL API for light and material, there are a few general ideas about light and material properties that you need to understand. Those ideas are introduced in this section. We postpone discussion of how lighting is actually done in OpenGL 1.1 until the next section.

4.1.1 Light and Material

When light strikes a surface, some of it will be reflected. Exactly how it reflects depends in a complicated way on the nature of the surface, what I am calling the material properties of the surface. In OpenGL 1.1, the complexity is approximated - very crudely-by two general types of reflection, specular reflection and diffuse reflection. These two types of reflection are important in other 3D graphics systems as well. (But see Section 8.2 for a more modern view of materials.)

Specular Reflection

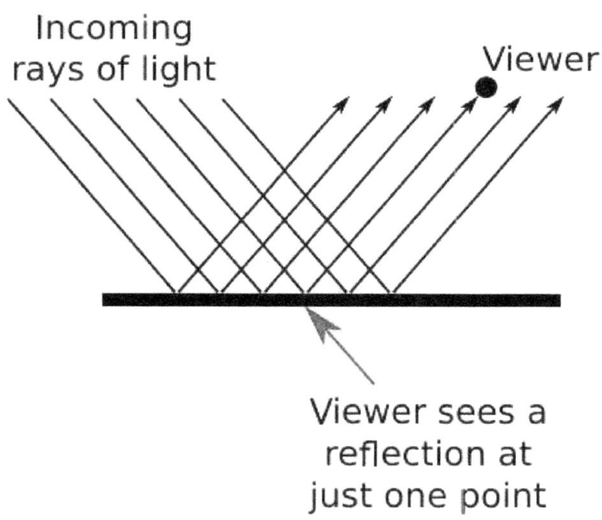

Diffuse Reflection

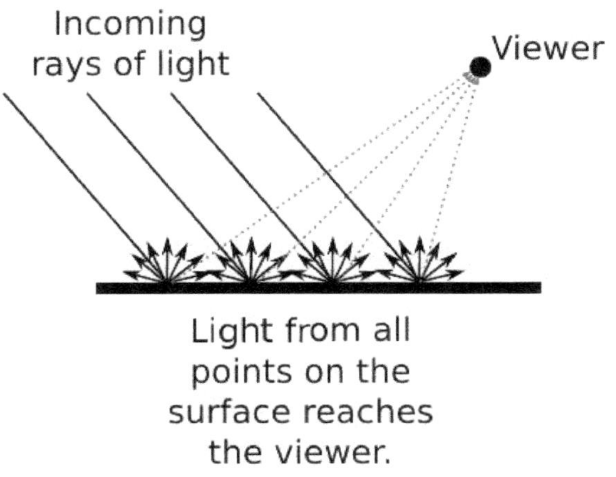

In perfect specular ("mirror-like") reflection, an incoming ray of light is reflected from the surface intact. The reflected ray makes the same angle with the surface as the incoming ray. A viewer can see the reflected ray only if the viewer is in exactly the right position, somewhere along the path of the reflected ray. Even if the entire surface is illuminated by the light source, the viewer will only see the reflection of the light source at those points on the surface where the geometry is right. Such reflections are referred to as specular highlights. In practice, we think of a ray of light as being reflected not as a single perfect ray, but as a cone of light, which can be more or less narrow.

Specular Reflection Cone

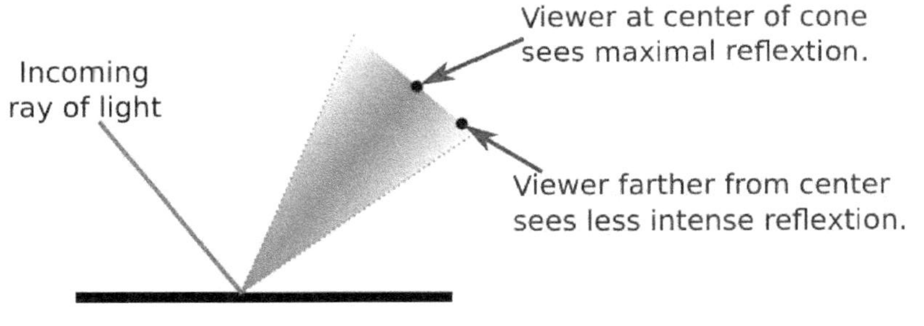

Specular reflection from a very shiny surface produces very narrow cones of reflected light; specular highlights on such a material are small and sharp. A duller surface will produce wider cones of reflected light and bigger, fuzzier specular highlights. In OpenGL, the material property that determines the size and sharpness of specular highlights is called shininess. Shininess in OpenGL is a number in the range 0 to 128 . As the number increases, specular highlights get smaller. This image shows eight spheres that differ only in the value of the shininess material property:

For the sphere on the left, the shininess is 0 , which leads to an ugly specular "highlight" that almost covers an entire hemisphere. Going from left to right, the shininess increases by 16 from one sphere to the next.

In pure diffuse reflection, an incoming ray of light is scattered in all directions equally. A viewer would see reflected light from all points on the surface. If the incoming light arrives in parallel rays that evenly illuminate the surface, then the surface would appear to the viewer to be evenly illuminated. (If different rays strike the surface at different angles, as they would if they come from a nearby lamp or if the surface is curved, then the amount of illumination at a point depends on the angle at which the ray hits the surface at that point, but not on the angle of the line from that point to the user.)

When light strikes a surface, some of the light can be absorbed, some can be reflected diffusely, and some can be reflected specularly. The amount of reflection can be different for different wavelengths. The degree to which a material reflects light of various wavelengths is what constitutes the color of the material. We now see that a material can have two different colors-a diffuse color that tells how the material reflects light diffusely, and a specular color that tells how it reflects light specularly. The diffuse color is the basic color of the object. The specular color determines the color of specular highlights. The diffuse and specular colors can be the same; for example, this is often true for metallic surfaces. Or they can be different; for example, a plastic surface will often have white specular highlights no matter what the diffuse color. (The demo c4/materials-demo.html in the on-line version of this section lets the user experiment with the material properties that we have discussed so far.)

OpenGL goes even further. In fact, there are two more colors associated with a material. The third color is the ambient color of the material, which tells how the surface reflects ambient light. Ambient light refers to a general level of illumination that does not come directly from a light source. It consists of light that has been reflected and re-reflected so many times that it is no longer coming from any particular direction. Ambient light is why shadows are not absolutely black. In fact, ambient light is only a crude approximation for the reality of multiply reflected light, but it is better than ignoring multiple reflections entirely. The ambient color of a material determines how it will reflect various wavelengths of ambient light. Ambient color is generally set to be the same as the diffuse color.

The fourth color associated with a material is an emission color, which is not really a color in the same sense as the first three color properties. That is, it has nothing to do with how the surface reflects light. The emission color is color that does not come from any external source, and therefore seems to be emitted by the material itself. This does not mean that the object is giving off light that will illuminate other objects, but it does mean that the object can be seen even if there is no source of light (not even ambient light). In the presence of light, the object will be brighter than can be accounted for by the light that illuminates it, and in that sense it appears to glow. The emission color is usually black; that is, the object has no emission at all.

Each of the four material color properties is specified in terms of three numbers giving the RGB (red, green, and blue) components of the color. Real light can contain an infinite number of different wavelengths. An RGB color is made up of just three components, but the nature of human color vision makes this a pretty good approximation for most purposes. (See Subsection 2.1.4.) Material colors can also have alpha components, but the only alpha component that is ever used in OpenGL is the one for the diffuse material color.

In the case of the red, blue, and green components of the ambient, diffuse, or specular color, the term "color" really means reflectivity. That is, the red component of a color gives the proportion of red light hitting the surface that is reflected by that surface, and similarly for green and blue. There are three different types of reflective color because there are three different types of light in OpenGL, and a material can have a different reflectivity for each type of light.

4.1.2 Light Properties

Leaving aside ambient light, the light in an environment comes from a light source such as a lamp or the sun. In fact, a lamp and the sun are examples of two essentially different kinds of light source: a point light and a directional light. A point light source is located at a point in 3D space, and it emits light in all directions from that point. For a directional light, all the light comes from the same direction, so that the rays of light are parallel. The sun is considered to be a directional light source since it is so far away that light rays from the sun are essentially parallel when they get to the Earth .

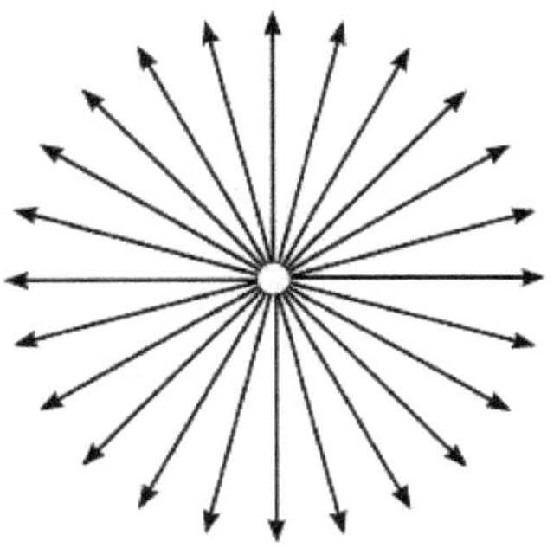

POINT LIGHT emits light in all directions.

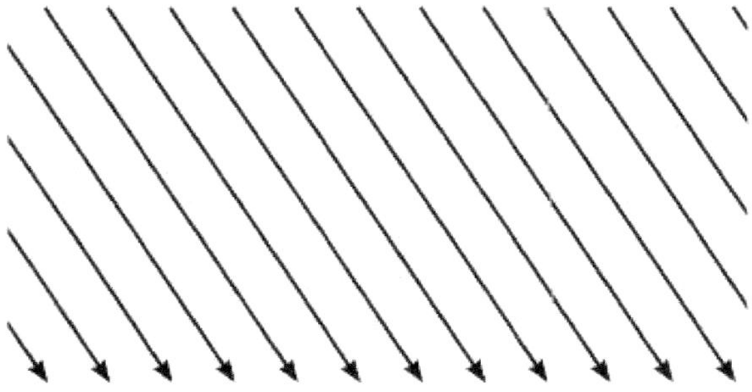

DIRECTIONAL LIGHT has parallel light rays, all from the same direction.

A light can have color. In fact, in OpenGL, each light source has three colors: an ambient color, a diffuse color, and a specular color. Just as the color of a material is more properly referred to as reflectivity, color of a light is more properly referred to as intensity or energy. More exactly, color refers to how the light's energy is distributed among different wavelengths. Real light can contain an infinite number of different wavelengths; when the wavelengths are separated, you get a spectrum or rainbow containing a continuum of colors. Light as it is usually modeled on a computer contains only the three basic colors, red, green, and blue. So, just like material color, light color is specified by giving three numbers representing the red, green, and blue intensities of the light.

The diffuse intensity of a light is the aspect of the light that interacts with diffuse material color, and the specular intensity of a light is what interacts with specular material color. It is common for the diffuse and specular light intensities to be the same.

The ambient intensity of a light works a little differently. Recall that ambient light is light that is not directly traceable to any light source. Still, it has to come from somewhere and we can imagine that turning on a light should increase the general level of ambient light in the environment. The ambient intensity of a light in OpenGL is added to the general level of ambient light. (There can also be global ambient light, which is not associated with any of the light sources in the scene.) Ambient light interacts with the ambient color of a material, and this interaction has no dependence on the position of the light sources or viewer. So, a light doesn't have to shine on an object for the object's ambient color to be affected by the light source; the light source just has to be turned on.

I should emphasize again that this is all just an approximation, and in this case not one that has a basis in the physics of the real world. Real light sources do not have separate ambient, diffuse, and specular colors, and many computer graphics systems model light sources using just one color.

4.1.3 Normal Vectors

The visual effect of a light shining on a surface depends on the properties of the surface and of the light. But it also depends to a great extent on the angle at which the light strikes the surface. The angle is essential to specular reflection and also affects diffuse reflection. That's why a curved, lit surface looks different at different points, even if its surface is a uniform color. To calculate this angle, OpenGL needs to know the direction in which the surface is facing. That direction is specified by a vector that is perpendicular to the surface. Another word for "perpendicular" is "normal," and a non-zero vector that is perpendicular to a surface at a given point is called a normal vector to that surface. When used in lighting calculations, a normal vector must have length equal to one. A normal vector of length one is called a unit normal. For proper lighting calculations in OpenGL, a unit normal must be specified for each vertex. However, given any normal vector, it is possible to calculate a unit normal from it by dividing the vector by its length. (See Section 3.5 for a discussion of vectors and their lengths.)

Since a surface can be curved, it can face different directions at different points. So, a normal vector is associated with a particular point on a surface. In OpenGL, normal vectors are actually assigned only to the vertices of a primitive. The normal vectors at the vertices of a primitive are used to do lighting calculations for the entire primitive.

Note in particular that you can assign different normal vectors at each vertex of a polygon. Now, you might be asking yourself, "Don't all the normal vectors to a polygon point in the same direction?" After all, a polygon is flat; the perpendicular direction to the polygon doesn't change from point to point. This is true, and if your objective is to display a polyhedral object whose sides are flat polygons, then in fact, all the normals of each of those polygons should point in the same direction. On the other hand, polyhedra are often used to approximate curved surfaces such as spheres. If your real objective is to make something that looks like a curved surface, then you want to use normal vectors that are perpendicular to the actual surface, not to the polyhedron that approximates it. Take a look at this example:

The two objects in this picture are made up of bands of rectangles. The two objects have exactly the same geometry, yet they look quite different. This is because different normal vectors are used in each case. For the top object, the band of rectangles is supposed to approximate a smooth surface. The vertices of the rectangles are points on that surface, and I really didn't want to see the rectangles at all-I wanted to see the curved surface, or at least a good approximation. So for the top object, when I specified the normal vector at each of the vertices, I used a vector that is perpendicular to the surface rather than one perpendicular to the rectangle. For the object on the bottom, on the other hand, I was thinking of an object that really is a band of rectangles, and I used normal vectors that were actually perpendicular to the rectangles. Here's a two-dimensional illustration that shows the normal vectors that were used for the two pictures:

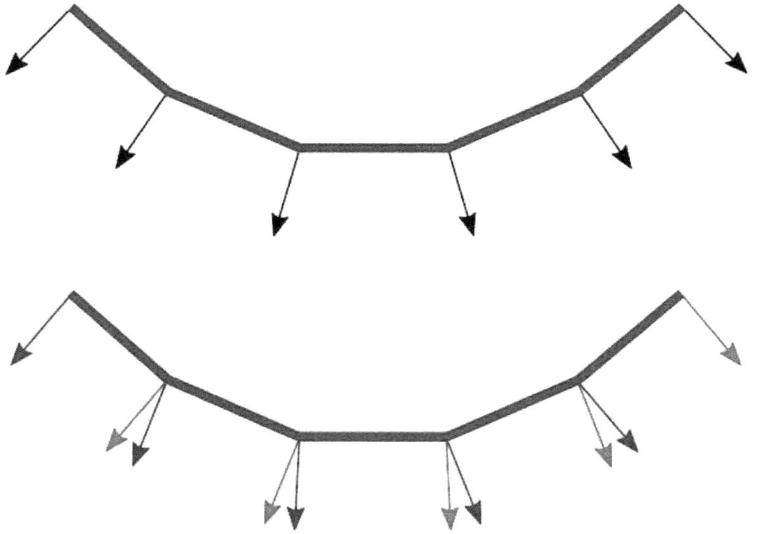

The thick blue lines represent the rectangles, as seen edge-on from above. The arrows represent the normal vectors. Each rectangle has two normals, one at each endpoint. Each vertex is part of two rectangles, and so two normal vectors are specified at each vertex.

In the bottom half of the illustration, two rectangles that meet at a point have different normal vectors at that point. The normal vectors for a rectangle are actually perpendicular to the rectangle. There is an abrupt change in direction as you move from one rectangle to the next, so where one rectangle meets the next, the normal vectors to the two rectangles are different. The visual effect on the rendered image is an abrupt change in shading that is perceived as a corner or edge between the two rectangles.

In the top half, on the other hand, the vectors are perpendicular to a curved surface that passes through the endpoints of the rectangles. When two rectangles share a vertex, they also share the same normal at that vertex. Visually, this eliminates the abrupt change in shading, resulting in something that looks more like a smoothly curving surface.

The two ways of assigning normal vectors are called flat shading and smooth shading. Flat shading makes a surface look like it is made of flat sides or facets. Smooth shading makes it look more like a smooth surface. The on-line demo c4/smooth-vs-flat.html can help you to understand the difference. It shows a polygonal mesh being used to approximate a sphere, with your choice of smooth or flat shading.

The upshot of all this is that you get to make up whatever normal vectors suit your purpose. A normal vector at a vertex is whatever you say it is, and it does not have to be literally perpendicular to the polygon. The normal vector that you choose should depend on the object that you are trying to model.

There is one other issue in choosing normal vectors: There are always two possible unit normal vectors at a point on a surface, pointing in opposite directions. A polygon in 3D has two faces, facing in opposite directions. OpenGL considers one of these to be the front face and the other to be the back face. OpenGL tells them apart by the order in which the vertices are specified. (See Subsection 3.4.1.) The default rule is that the order of the vertices is counterclockwise when looking at the front face and is clockwise when looking at the back face. When the polygon is drawn on the screen, this rule lets OpenGL tell whether it is the front face or the back face that is being shown. When specifying a normal vector for the polygon, the vector should point out of the front face of the polygon. This is another example of the right-hand rule. If you curl the fingers of your right hand in the direction in which the vertices of the polygon were specified, then the normal vector should point in the direction of your thumb. Note that when you are looking at the front face of a polygon, the normal vector should be pointing towards you. If you are looking at the back face, the normal vector should be pointing away from you.

It can be a difficult problem to come up with the correct normal vectors for an object. Complex geometric models often come with the necessary normal vectors included. This is true, for example, for the solid shapes drawn by the GLUT library.

4.1.4 The OpenGL 1.1 Lighting Equation

What does it actually mean to say that OpenGL performs "lighting calculations"? The goal of the calculation is to produce a color, (r, g, b, a), for a point on a surface. In OpenGL 1.1, lighting calculations are actually done only at the vertices of a primitive. After the color of each vertex has been computed, colors for interior points of the primitive are obtained by interpolating the vertex colors.

The alpha component of the vertex color, a, is easy: It's simply the alpha component of the diffuse material color at that vertex. The calculation of r, g, and b is fairly complex and rather mathematical, and you don't necessarily need to understand it. But here is a short description of how it's done...

Ignoring alpha components, let's assume that the ambient, diffuse, specular, and emission colors of the material have RGB components (ma_r, ma_g, ma_b), (md_r, md_g, md_b), (ms_r, ms_g, ms_b), and (me_r, me_g, me_b), respectively. Suppose that the global ambient intensity, which represents ambient light that is not associated with any light source in the environment, is (ga_r, ga_g, ga_b). There can be several point and directional light sources, which we refer to as light number 0 , light number 1, light number 2, and so on. With this setup, the red component of the vertex color will be:

$$\mathrm{r} = \mathrm{me}_r + \mathrm{ga}_r * \mathrm{ma}_r + \mathrm{I}_{0,r} + \mathrm{I}_{1,r} + \mathrm{I}_{2,r} + \cdots$$

where $I_{0,r}$ is the red component of the contribution to the color that comes from light number 0; $I_{1,r}$ is the contribution from light number 1 ; and so on. A similar equation holds for the green and blue components of the color. This equation says that the emission color, me_r, is simply added to any other contributions to the color. And the contribution of global ambient light is obtained by multiplying the global ambient intensity, ga_r, by the material ambient color, ma_r. This is the mathematical way of saying that the material ambient color is the fraction of the ambient light that is reflected by the surface.

The terms $\mathrm{I}_{0,r}$, $\mathrm{I}_{1,r}$, and so on, represent contributions to the final color from the various light sources in the environment. The contributions from the light sources are complicated. Consider just one of the light sources. Note, first of all, that if a light source is disabled (that is, if it is turned off), then the contribution from that light source is zero. For an enabled light source, we have to look at the geometry as well as the colors:

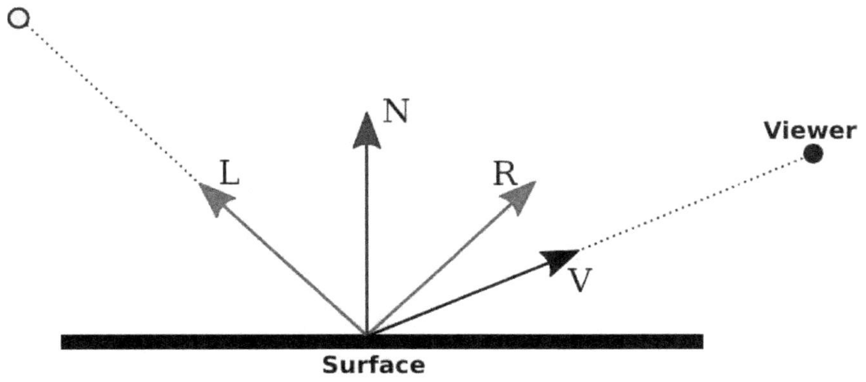

In this illustration, N is the normal vector at the point whose color we want to compute. L is a vector that points back along the direction from which the light arrives at the surface. V is a vector that points in the direction of the viewer. And R is the direction of the reflected ray, that is, the direction in which a light ray from the source would be reflected specularly when it strikes the surface at the point in question. The angle between N and L is the same as the angle between N and R; this is a basic fact about the physics of light. All of the vectors are unit vectors, with length 1 . Recall that for unit vectors A and B, the inner product $A \cdot B$ is equal to the cosine of the angle between the two vectors. Inner products occur at several points in the lighting equation, as the way of accounting for the angles between various vectors.

Now, let's say that the light has ambient, diffuse, and specular color components ($\mathrm{la}_r, \mathrm{la}_g, \mathrm{la}_b$), $(\mathrm{ld}_r, \mathrm{ld}_g, \mathrm{ld}_b)$, and $(\mathrm{ls}_r, \mathrm{ls}_g, \mathrm{ls}_b)$. Also, let mh be the value of the shininess property of the material. Then, assuming that the light is enabled, the contribution of this light source to the red component of the vertex color can be computed as

$$\mathrm{I}_r = l\mathrm{a}_r * \mathrm{ma}_r + \mathrm{f} * (l\ \mathrm{d}_r * \mathrm{md}_r * (\mathrm{L} \cdot \mathrm{N}) + l\ \mathrm{s}_r * \mathrm{ms}_r * \max(0, \mathrm{V} \cdot \mathrm{R})^{mh})$$

with similar equations for the green and blue components. The first term, $la_r * ma_r$ accounts for the contribution of the ambient light from this light source to the color of the surface. This term is added to the color whether or not the surface is facing the light.

The value of f is 0 if the surface is facing away from the light and is 1 if the surface faces the light; that is, it accounts for the fact that the light only illuminates one side of the surface. To test whether f is 0 or 1 , we can check whether $L \cdot N$ is less than 0 . This dot product is the cosine of the angle between L and N; it is less than 0 when the angle is greater than 90 degrees, which would mean that the normal vector is on the opposite side of the surface from the light. When f is zero, there is no diffuse or specular contribution from the light to the color of the vertex.

The diffuse component of the color, before adjustment by f, is given by ld_r *md_r *$(L \cdot N)$. This represents the diffuse intensity of the light times the diffuse reflectivity of the material, multiplied by the cosine of the angle between L and N. The angle is involved because for a larger angle, the same amount of energy from the light is spread out over a greater area:

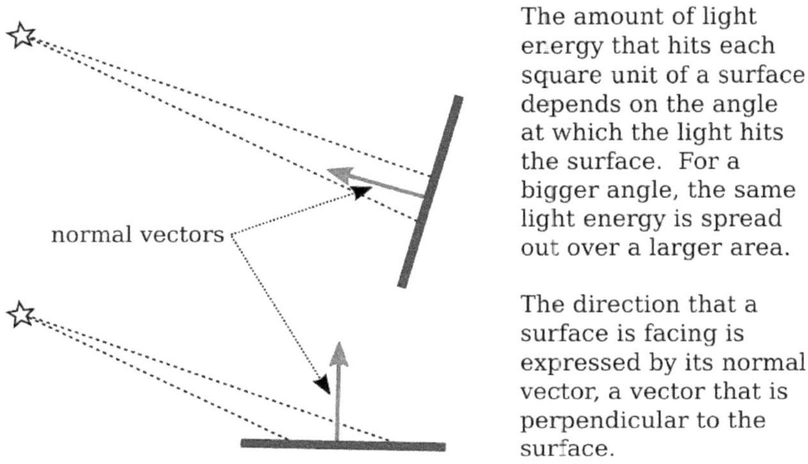

As the angle increases from 0 to 90 degrees, the cosine of the angle decreases from 1 to 0 , so the larger the angle, the smaller the value of ld_r *md_r *$(L \cdot N)$ and the smaller the contribution of diffuse illumination to the color.

For the specular component, recall that a light ray is reflected specularly as a cone of light. The reflection vector, R, is at the center of the cone. The closer the viewer is to the center of the cone, the more intense the specular reflection. The distance of the viewer from the center of the cone depends on the angle between V and R, which appears in the equation as the dot product $V \cdot R$. Mathematically, the specular contribution to the color is given by ls_r *ms_r *$\max(0, V \cdot R)^{mh}$. Taking the maximum of 0 and $V \cdot R$ ensures that the specular contribution is zero if the angle between V and R is greater than 90 degrees. Assuming that is not the case, $\max(0, V \cdot R)$ is equal to $V \cdot R$. Note that this dot product is raised to the exponent mh, which is the material's shininess property. When mh is $0, (V \cdot R)^{mh}$ is 1 , and there is no dependence on the angle; in that case, the result is the sort of huge and undesirable specular highlight that we have seen for shininess equal to zero. For positive values of shininess, the specular contribution is maximal when the angle between V and R is zero, and it decreases as the angle increases. The larger the shininess value, the faster the rate of decrease. The result is that larger shininess values give smaller, sharper specular highlights.

Remember that the same calculation is repeated for every enabled light and that the results are combined to give the final vertex color. It's easy, especially when using several lights, to end up with color components larger than one. In the end, before the color is used to color a pixel on the screen, the color components must be clamped to the range zero to one. Values greater than one are replaced by one. This makes it easy to produce ugly pictures in which large areas are a uniform white because all the color values in those areas exceeded one. All the information that was supposed to be conveyed by the lighting has been lost. The effect is similar to an over-exposed photograph. It can take some work to find appropriate lighting levels to avoid this kind of over-exposure. (My discussion of lighting in this section leaves out some factors. The equation as presented doesn't take into account the fact that the effect of a point light can depend on the distance to the light, and it doesn't take into account spotlights, which emit just a cone of light. Both of these can configured in OpenGL 1.1, but this book does not cover how to do that. There are also many aspects of light that are not captured by the simple model used in OpenGL. One of the most obvious omissions is shadows: Objects don't block light! Light shines right through them. We will encounter some extensions to the model in later chapters when we discuss other graphics systems.)

4.2 Light and Material in OpenGL 1.1

In this section, we will see how to use light and material in OpenGL. The functions that are discussed in this section are specific to older versions of OpenGL, and will not carry over directly to other graphics APIs. (But the general ideas that they implement, which were covered in the previous section are more generally applicable.)

In OpenGL 1.1, the use of light and material must be enabled by calling glEnable(GL_LIGHTING). When lighting is disabled, the color of a vertex is simply the current color as set by glColor*. When lighting is enabled, the color of a vertex is computed using a mathematical formula that takes into account the lighting of the scene and the material properties that have been assigned to the vertex, as discussed in the previous section. Now it's time to learn about the OpenGL commands that are used to configure lighting and to assign materials to objects.

It is common for lighting to be turned on for rendering some parts of a scene, but turned off for other parts. We will say that some objects are "lit" while others aren't. For example, wireframe objects are usually drawn with lighting disabled, even if they are part of a scene in which solid objects are lit. But note that it is illegal to call glEnable or glDisable between calls to glBegin and glEnd, so it is not possible for part of a primitive to be lit while another part of the same primitive is unlit. (I should note that when lighting is enabled, it is applied to point and line primitives as well as to polygons, even though it rarely makes sense to do so.) Lighting can be enabled and disabled by calling glEnable and glDisable with parameter GL_LIGHTING. Other light and material settings don't have to be modified when lighting is turned off, since they are simply ignored when lighting is disabled.

To light a scene, in addition to enabling GL_LIGHTING, you must configure at least one source of light. For very basic lighting, it often suffices to call

```
glEnable(GL_LIGHT0);
```

This command turns on a directional light that shines from the direction of the viewer into the scene. (Note that the last character in GL_LIGHT0 is a zero.) Since it shines from the direction of the viewer, it will illuminate everything that the user can see. The light is white, with no specular component; that is, you will see the diffuse color of objects, without any specular highlights. We will see later in this section how to change the characteristics of this light source and how to configure additional sources. But first, we will consider materials and normal vectors.

4.2.1 Working with Material

Material properties are vertex attributes in that same way that color is a vertex attribute. That is, the OpenGL state includes a current value for each of the material properties. When a vertex is generated by a call to one of the glVertex* functions, a copy of each of the current material properties is stored, along with the vertex coordinates. When a primitive that contains the vertex is rendered, the material properties that are associated with the vertex are used, along with information about lighting, to compute a color for the vertex.

This is complicated by the fact that polygons are two-sided, and the front face and back face of a polygon can have different materials. This means that, in fact, two sets of material property values are stored for each vertex: the front material and the back material. (The back material isn't actually used unless you turn on two-sided lighting, which will be discussed below.)

With all that in mind, we will look at functions for setting the current values of material properties. For setting the ambient, diffuse, specular, and emission material colors, the function is

```
void glMaterialfv( int side, int property, float* valueArray )
```

The first parameter can be $GL\_FRONT\_AND\_BACK, GL\_FRONT$, or GL_BACK. It tells whether you are setting a material property value for the front face, the back face, or both. The second parameter tells which material property is being set. It can be $GL\_AMBIENT$,

GL_DIFFUSE, GL_SPECULAR, GL_EMISSION, or GL_AMBIENT_AND_DIFFUSE. Note that it is possible to set the ambient and diffuse colors to the same value with one call to glMaterialfv by using GL_AMBIENT_AND_DIFFUSE as the property name; this is the most common case. The last parameter to glMaterialfv is an array containing four float numbers. The numbers give the RGBA color components as values in the range from 0.0 to 1.0 ; values outside this range are actually allowed, and will be used in lighting computations, but such values are unusual. Note that an alpha component is required, but it is used only in the case of diffuse color: When the vertex color is computed, its alpha component is set equal to the alpha component of the diffuse material color.

The shininess material property is a single number rather than an array, and there is a different function for setting its value (without the "v" at the end of the name):

```
void glMaterialf( int side, int property, float value )
```

Again, the side can be *GL_FRONT_AND_BACK*, *GL_FRONT*, or *GL_BACK*. The property must be *GL_SHININESS*. And the value is a float in the range 0.0 to 128.0 .

Compared to the large number of versions of glColor* and glVertex*, the options for setting material are limited. In particular, it is not possible to set a material color without defining an array to contain the color component values. Suppose for example that we want to set the ambient and diffuse colors to a bluish green. In C , that might be done with

```
float bgcolor[4] = { 0.0, 0.7, 0.5, 1.0};
glMaterialfv( GL_FRONT_AND_BACK, GL_AMBIENT_AND_DIFFUSE, bgcolor );
```

With my JavaScript simulator for OpenGL, this would look like

```
let bgcolor = [ 0.0, 0.7, 0.5, 1.0 ];
glMaterialfv( GL_FRONT_AND_BACK, GL_AMBIENT_AND_DIFFUSE, bgcolor );
```

And in the JOGL API for Java, where where methods with array parameters have an additional parameter to give the starting index of the data in the array, it becomes

```
float[] bgcolor = { 0.0F, 0.7F, 0.5F, 1.0F };
gl.glMaterialfv(GL2.GL_FRONT_AND_BACK, GL2.GL_AMBIENT_AND_DIFFUSE,
bgcolor, 0);
```

In C , the third parameter is actually a pointer to float, which allows the flexabilty of storing the values for several material properties in one array. Suppose, for example, that we have a C array

```
float gold[13] = { 0.24725, 0.1995, 0.0745, 1.0, /* ambient */
        0.75164, 0.60648, 0.22648, 1.0, /* diffuse */
        0.628281, 0.555802, 0.366065, 1.0, /* specular */
        50.0 /* shininess */
    };
```

where the first four numbers in the array specify an ambient color; the next four, a diffuse color; the next four, a specular color; and the last number, a shininess exponent. This array can be used to set all the material properties:

```
glMaterialfv( GL_FRONT_AND_BACK, GL_AMBIENT, gold );
glMaterialfv( GL_FRONT_AND_BACK, GL_DIFFUSE, &gold[4] );
glMaterialfv( GL_FRONT_AND_BACK, GL_SPECULAR, &gold[8] );
glMaterialf( GL_FRONT_AND_BACK, GL_SHININESS, gold[12] );
```

Note that the last function is glMaterialf rather than glMaterialfv, and that its third parameter is a number rather than a pointer. Something similar can be done in Java with

```
float[] gold = { 0.24725F, 0.1995F, 0.0745F, 1.0F, /* ambient */
        0.75164F, 0.60648F, 0.22648F, 1.0F, /* diffuse */
        0.628281F, 0.555802F, 0.366065F, 1.0F, /* specular */
        50.0F /* shininess */
    };
gl.glMaterialfv( GL2.GL_FRONT_AND_BACK, GL2.GL_AMBIENT, gold, 0 );
gl.glMaterialfv( GL2.GL_FRONT_AND_BACK, GL2.GL_DIFFUSE, gold, 4 );
gl.glMaterialfv( GL2.GL_FRONT_AND_BACK, GL2.GL_SPECULAR, gold, 8 );
gl.glMaterialf( GL2.GL_FRONT_AND_BACK, GL2.GL_SHININESS, gold[12] );
```

The functions glMaterialfv and glMaterialf can be called at any time, including between calls to glBegin and glEnd. This means that different vertices of a primitive can have different material properties.

So, maybe you like glColor* better than glMaterialfv? If so, you can use it to work with material as well as regular color. If you call

```
glEnable( GL_COLOR_MATERIAL );
```

then some of the material color properties will track the color. By default, setting the color will also set the current front and back, ambient and diffuse material properties. That is, for example, calling

```
glColor3f( 1, 0, 0 );
```

will, if lighting is enabled, have the same effect as calling

```
glMaterialfv( GL_FRONT_AND_BACK, GL_AMBIENT_AND_DIFFUSE, array );
```

where array contains the values 1,0,0,1. You can change the material property that tracks the color using

```
void glColorMaterial( side, property );
```

where side can be GL_FRONT_AND_BACK, GL_FRONT, or GL_BACK, and property can be GL_AMBIENT, GL_DIFFUSE, GL_SPECULAR, GL_EMISSION, or GL_AMBIENT_AND_DIFFUSE. Neither glEnable nor glColorMaterial can be called between calls to glBegin and glEnd, so all of the vertices of a primitive must use the same setting.

Recall that when glDrawArrays or glDrawElements is used to draw a primitive, the color values for the vertices of the primitive can be taken from a color array, as specified using glColorPointer. (See Subsection 3.4.2.) There are no similar arrays for material properties. However, if a color array is used while lighting is enabled, and if GL_COLOR_MATERIAL is also enabled, then the color array will be used as the source for the values of the material properties that are tracking the color.

4.2.2 Defining Normal Vectors

Normal vectors are essential to lighting calculations. (See Subsection 4.1.3.) Like color and material, normal vectors are attributes of vertices. The OpenGL state includes a current normal vector, which is set using functions in the family glNormal*. When a vertex is specified with glVertex*, a copy of the current normal vector is saved as an attribute of the vertex, and it is used as the normal vector for that vertex when the color of the vertex is computed by the lighting equation. Note that the normal vector for a vertex must be specified before glVertex* is called for that vertex.

Functions in the family glNormal* include glNormal3f, glNormal3d, glNormal3fv, and glNormal3dv. As usual, a "v" means that the values are in an array, " f " means that the values are floats, and "d" means that the values are doubles. (All normal vectors have three components). Some examples:

```
glNormal3f( 0, 0, 1 ); // (This is the default value.)
glNormal3d( 0.707, 0.707, 0.0 );
float normalArray[3] = { 0.577, 0.577, 0.577 };
glNormal3fv( normalArray );
```

For a polygon that is supposed to look flat, the same normal vector is used for all of the vertices of the polygon. For example, to draw one side of a cube, say the "top" side, facing in the direction of the positive y-axis:

```
glNormal3f( 0, 1, 0 ); // Points along positive y-axis
glBegin(GL_QUADS);
glVertex3fv(1,1,1);
glVertex3fv(1,1,-1);
glVertex3fv(-1,1,-1);
glVertex3fv(-1,1,1);
glEnd();
```

Remember that the normal vector should point out of the front face of the polygon, and that the front face is determined by the order in which the vertices are generated. (You might think that the front face should be determined by the direction in which the normal vector points, but that is not how its done. If a normal vector for a vertex points in the wrong direction, then lighting calculations will not give the correct color for that vertex.)

When modeling a smooth surface, normal vectors should be chosen perpendicular to the surface, rather than to the polygons that approximate the surface. (See Subsection 4.1.3.) Suppose that we want to draw the side of a cylinder with radius 1 and height 2 , where the center of the cylinder is at (0,0,0) and the axis lies along the z-axis. We can approximate the surface using a single triangle strip. The top and bottom edges of the side of a cylinder are circles. Vertices along the top edge will have coordinates $(\cos(a), \sin(a), 1)$ and vertices along the bottom edge will have coordinates $(\cos(a), \sin(a), -1)$, where a is some angle. The normal vector points in the same direction as the radius, but its z-coordinate is zero since it points directly out from the side of the cylinder. So, the normal vector to the side of the cylinder at both of these points will be $(\cos(a), \sin(a), 0)$. Looking down the z-axis at the top of the cylinder, it looks like this:

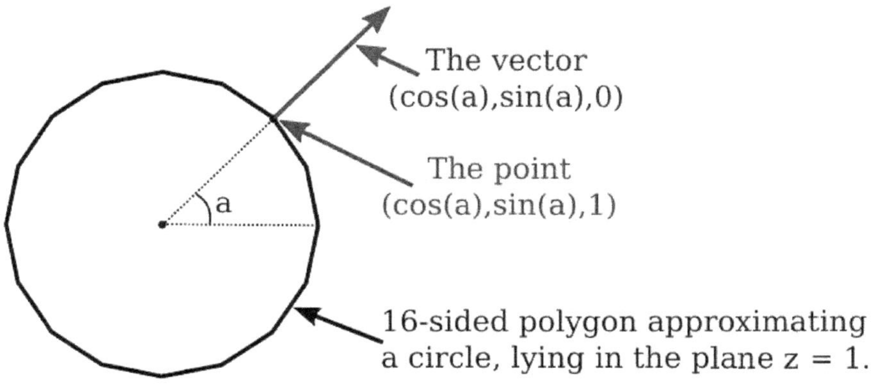

When we draw the side of the cylinder as a triangle strip, we have to generate pairs of vertices on alternating edges. The normal vector is the same for the two vertices in the pair, but it is different for different pairs. Here is the code:

```
glBegin(GL_TRIANGLE_STRIP);
for (i = 0; i <= 16; i++) {
    double angle = 2*3.14159/16 * i; // i 16-ths of a full circle
    double x = cos(angle);
    double y = sin(angle);
    glNormal3f( x, y, 0 ); // Normal for both vertices at this angle.
    glVertex3f( x, y, 1 ); // Vertex on the top edge.
    glVertex3f( x, y, -1 ); // Vertex on the bottom edge.
}
glEnd();
```

When we draw the top and bottom of the cylinder, on the other hand, we want a flat polygon, with the normal vector pointing in the direction (0,0,1) for the top and in the direction (0,0, −1) for the bottom:

```
glNormal3f( 0, 0, 1);
glBegin(GL_TRIANGLE_FAN); // Draw the top, in the plane z = 1.
for (i = 0; i <= 16; i++) {
    double angle = 2*3.14159/16 * i;
    double x = cos(angle);
    double y = sin(angle);
    glVertex3f( x, y, 1 );
}
glEnd();
```

```
glNormal3f( 0, 0, -1 );
glBegin(GL_TRIANGLE_FAN); // Draw the bottom, in the plane z = -1
for (i = 16; i >= 0; i--) {
    double angle = 2*3.14159/16 * i;
    double x = cos(angle);
    double y = sin(angle);
    glVertex3f( x, y, -1 );
}
glEnd();
```

Note that the vertices for the bottom are generated in the opposite order from the vertices for the top, to account for the fact that the top and bottom face in opposite directions. As always, vertices need to be enumerated in counterclockwise order, as seen from the front.

When drawing a primitive with glDrawArrays or glDrawElements, it is possible to provide a different normal for each vertex by using a normal array to hold the normal vectors. The normal array works in the same way as the color array and the vertex array. To use one, you need to enable the use of a normal array by calling

```
glEnableClientState(GL_NORMAL_ARRAY);
```

The coordinates for the normal vectors must be stored in an array (or in an nio buffer for JOGL), and the location of the data must be specified by calling

```
glNormalPointer( type, stride, data );
```

The type specifies the type of values in the array. It can be GL_INT, GL_FLOAT, or GL_DOUBLE. The stride is an integer, which is usually `0` , meaning that there is no extra data in the array between the normal vectors. And data is the array (or buffer) that holds the normal vectors, with three numbers for each normal.

With this setup, when glDrawArrays or glDrawElements is used to draw a primitive, the normal vectors for the primitive will be pulled from the array. Note that if GL_NORMAL_ARRAY is not enabled, then all of the normal vectors for the primitive will be the same, and will be equal to the current normal vector as set by glNormal*.

The lighting equation assumes that normal vectors are unit normals, that is, that they have length equal to one. The default in OpenGL is to use normal vectors as provided, even if they don't have length one, which will give incorrect results. However, if you call

```
glEnable(GL_NORMALIZE);
```

then OpenGL will automatically convert every normal vector into a unit normal that points in the same direction.

Note that when a geometric transform is applied, normal vectors are transformed along with vertices; this is necessary because a transformation can change the direction in which a surface is facing. A scaling transformation can change the length of a normal vector, so even if you provided unit normal vectors, they will not be unit normals after a scaling transformation. However, if you have enabled GL_NORMALIZE, the transformed normals will automatically be converted back to unit normals. My recommendation is to always enable GL_NORMALIZE as part of your OpenGL initialization. The only exception would be if all of the normal vectors that you provide are of length one and you do not apply any scaling transformations. (Translations and rotations are OK, because they do not modify lengths.)

4.2.3 Working with Lights

OpenGL 1.1 supports at least eight light sources, which are identified by the constants GL_LIGHT0, GL_LIGHT1, ..., GL_LIGHT7. (An OpenGL implementation might allow additional lights.) Each light source can be configured to be either a directional light or a point light, and each light can have its own diffuse, specular, and ambient intensities. (See Subsection 4.1.2.)

By default, all of the light sources are disabled. To enable a light, call glEnable (light), where light is one of the constants GL_LIGHT0, GL_LIGHT1, . . . However, just enabling a light does not give any illumination, except in the case of GL_LIGHT0, since all light intensities are zero by default, with the single exception of the diffuse color of light number 0 . To get any light from the other light sources, you need to change some of their properties. Light properties can be set using the functions

```
void glLightfv( int light, int property, float* valueArray );
```

The first parameter is one of the constants GL_LIGHT0, GL_LIGHT1, . . , GL_LIGHT7. It specifies which light is being configured. The second parameter says which property of the light is being set. It can be GL_DIFFUSE, GL_SPECULAR, GL_AMBIENT, or GL_POSITION. The last parameter is an array that contains at least four float numbers, giving the value of the property.

For the color properties, the four numbers in the array specify the red, green, blue, and alpha components of the color. (The alpha component is not actually used for anything.) The values generally lie in the range 0.0 to 1.0 , but can lie outside that range; in fact, values larger than 1.0 are occasionally useful. Remember that the diffuse and specular colors of a light tell how the light interacts with the diffuse and specular material colors, and the ambient color is simply added to the global ambient light when the light is enabled. For example, to set up light zero as a bluish light, with blue specular highlights, that adds a bit of blue to the ambient light when it is turned on, you might use:

```
float blue1[4] = { 0.4, 0.4, 0.6, 1};
float blue2[4] = { 0, 0, 0.8, 1 };
float blue3[4] = { 0, 0, 0.15, 1 };
glLightfv( GL_LIGHT1, GL_DIFFUSE, blue1 );
glLightfv( GL_LIGHT1, GL_SPECULAR, blue2 );
glLightfv( GL_LIGHT1, GL_AMBIENT, blue3 );
```

It would likely take some experimentation to figure out exactly what values to use in the arrays to get the effect that you want.

The GL_POSITION property of a light is quite a bit different. It is used both to set whether the light is a point light or a directional light, and to set its position or direction. The property value for *GL*_POSITION is an array of four numbers (x, y, z, w), of which at least one must be non-zero. When the fourth number, w, is zero, then the light is directional and the point (x, y, z) specifies the direction of the light: The light rays shine in the direction of the line from the point (x, y, z) towards the origin. This is related to homogeneous coordinates: The source of the light can be considered to be a point at infinity in the direction of (x, y, z).

On the other hand, if the fourth number, w, is non-zero, then the light is a point light, and it is located at the point $(x/w, y/w, z/w)$. Usually, w is 1. The value $(x, y, z, 1)$ gives a point light at (x, y, z). Again, this is really homogeneous coordinates.

The default position for all lights is (0,0,1,0), representing a directional light shining from the positive direction of the z-axis, towards the negative direction of the z-axis.

One important and potentially confusing fact about lights is that the position that is specified for a light is transformed by the modelview transformation that is in effect at the time the position is set using glLightfv. Another way of saying this is that the position is set in eye coordinates, not in world coordinates. Calling glLightfv with the property set to GL_POSITION is very much like calling glVertex*. The light position is transformed in the same way that the vertex coordinates would be transformed. For example,

```
float position[4] = { 1,2,3,1 }
glLightfv(GL_LIGHT1, GL_POSITION, position);
```

puts the light in the same place as

```
glTranslatef(1,2,3);
float position[4] = { 0,0,0,1 }
glLightfv(GL_LIGHT1, GL_POSITION, position);
```

For a directional light, the direction of the light is transformed by the rotational part of the modelview transformation.

There are three basic ways to use light position. It is easiest to think in terms of potentially animated scenes.

First, if the position is set before any modelview transformation is applied, then the light is fixed with respect to the viewer. For example, the default light position is effectively set to (0,0,1,0) while the modelview transform is the identity. This means that it shines in the direction of the negative *z*-axis, in the coordinate system of the viewer, where the negative *z*-axis points into the screen. Another way of saying this is that the light always shines from the direction of the viewer into the scene. It's like the light is attached to the viewer. If the viewer moves about in the world, the light moves with the viewer.

Second, if the position is set after the viewing transform has been applied and before any modeling transform is applied, then the position of the light is fixed in world coordinates. It will not move with the viewer, and it will not move with objects in the scene. It's like the light is attached to the world.

Third, if the position is set after a modeling transform has been applied, then the light is subject to that modeling transformation. This can be used to make a light that moves around in the scene as the modeling transformation changes. If the light is subject to the same modeling transformation as an object, then the light will move around with that object, as if it is attached to the object.

The sample program glut/four-lights.c or jogl/FourLights.java uses multiple moving, colored lights and lets you turn them on and off to see the effect. The image below is taken from the program. There is also a live demo version on-line. The program lets you see how light from various sources combines to produce the visible color of an object. The source code provides examples of configuring lights and using material properties.

4.2.4 Global Lighting Properties

In addition to the properties of individual light sources, the OpenGL lighting system uses several global properties. There are only three such properties in OpenGL 1.1. One of them is the global ambient light, which is ambient light that doesn't come from the ambient color property of any light source. Global ambient light will be present in the environment even if all of GL_LIGHT0, GL_LIGHT1, . . . are disabled. By default, the global ambient light is black (that is, its RGB components are all zero). The value can be changed using the function

```
void glLightModelfv( int property, float* value )
```

where the property must be GL_LIGHT_MODEL_AMBIENT and the value is an array containing four numbers giving the RGBA color components of the global ambient light as numbers in the range 0.0 to 1.0 . In general, the global ambient light level should be quite low. For example, in C :

```
float ambientLevel[] = { 0.15, 0.15, 0.15, 1 };
glLightModelfv( GL_LIGHT_MODEL_AMBIENT, ambientLevel );
```

The alpha component of the color is usually set to 1 , but it is not used for anything. For JOGL, as usual, there is an extra parameter to specify the starting index of the data in the array, and the example becomes:

```
float[] ambientLevel = { 0.15F, 0.15F, 0.15F, 0 };
gl.glLightModelfv( GL2.GL_LIGHT_MODEL_AMBIENT, ambientLevel, 0 );
```

The other two light model properties are options that can be either off or on. The properties are GL_LIGHT_MODEL_TWO_SIDE and GL_LIGHT_MODEL_LOCAL_VIEWER. They can be set using the function

```
void glLightModeli( int property, int value )
```

with a value equal to 0 or 1 to indicate whether the option should be off or on. You can use the symbolic constants *GL_FALSE* and *GL_TRUE* for the value, but these are just names for 0 and 1 .

GL_LIGHT_MODEL_TWO_SIDE is used to turn on two-sided lighting. Recall that a polygon can have two sets of material properties, a front material and a back material. When two-sided lighting is off, which is the default, only the front material is used; it is used for both the front face and the back face of the polygon. Furthermore, the same normal vector is used for both faces. Since those vectors point-or at least are supposed to point-out of the front face, they don't give the correct result for the back face. In effect, the back face looks like it is illuminated by light sources that lie in front of the polygon, but the back face should be illuminated by the lights that lie behind the polygon.

On the other hand, when two-sided lighting is on, the back material is used on the back face and the direction of the normal vector is reversed when it is used in lighting calculations for the back face.

You should use two-sided lighting whenever there are back faces that might be visible in your scene. (This will not be the case when your scene consists of "solid" objects, where the back faces are hidden inside the solid.) With two-sided lighting, you have the option of using the same material on both faces or specifying different materials for the two faces. For example, to put a shiny purple material on front faces and a duller yellow material on back faces:

```
glLightModeli( GL_LIGHT_MODEL_TWO_SIDE, 1 ); // Turn on two-sided
lighting.
float purple[] = { 0.6, 0, 0.6, 1 };
float yellow[] = { 0.6, 0.6, 0, 1};
float white[] = { 0.4, 0.4, 0.4, 1}; // For specular highlights.
float black [] = { 0, 0, 0, 1};


glMaterialfv( GL_FRONT, GL_AMBIENT_AND_DIFFUSE, purple ); // front
material
glMaterialfv( GL_FRONT, GL_SPECULAR, white );
glMaterialf( GL_FRONT, GL_SHININESS, 64 );
glMaterialfv( GL_BACK, GL_AMBIENT_AND_DIFFUSE, yellow ); // back
material
glMaterialfv( GL_BACK, GL_SPECULAR, black ); // no specular highlights
```

This picture shows what these materials look like on a cylinder that has no top, so that you can see the back faces on the inside surface:

The third material property, GL_LIGHT_MODEL_LOCAL_VIEWER, is much less important. It has to do with the direction from a surface to the viewer in the lighting equation. By default, this direction is always taken to point directly out of the screen, which is true for an orthographic projection but is not accurate for a perspective projection. If you turn on the local viewer option, the true direction to the viewer is used. In practice, the difference is usually not very noticeable.

4.3 Image Textures

Uniformly colored 3D objects look nice enough, but they are a little bland. Their uniform colors don't have the visual appeal of, say, a brick wall or a plaid couch. Threedimensional objects can be made to look more interesting and more realistic by adding a texture to their surfaces. A texture, in general, is some sort of variation from pixel to pixel within a single primitive. We will consider only one kind of texture: image textures. An image texture can be applied to a surface to make the color of the surface vary from point to point, something like painting a copy of the image onto the surface. Here is a picture that shows six objects with various image textures:

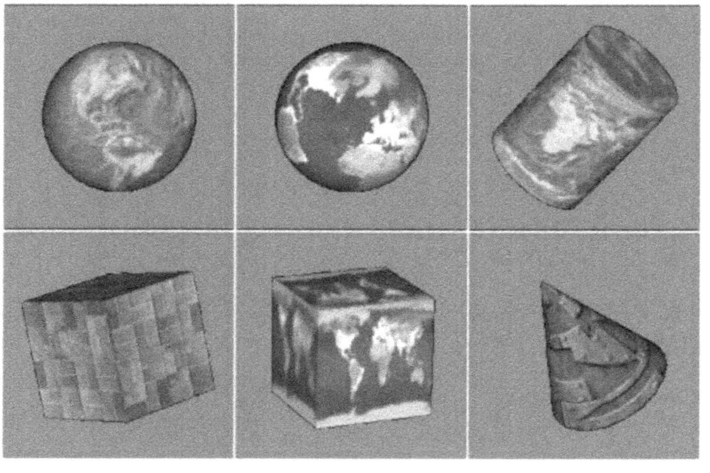

(Topographical Earth image, courtesy NASA/JPL-Caltech. The brick and metal are free textures (which were downloaded from a web site that no longer exists). EarthAtNight image taken from the Astronomy Picture of the Day web site; it is also a NASA/JPL image. Copies of the images can be found in the folder named textures in either the jogl or glut folder inside the source folder of the web site download. Images from that folder will be used in several examples in this book.)

Textures might be the most complicated part of OpenGL, and they are a part that has survived, and become more complicated, in the most modern versions since they are so vital for the efficient creation of realistic images. This section covers only part of the OpenGL 1.1 texture API. We will see more of textures in later chapters.

Note that an image that is used as a texture should have a width and a height that are powers of two, such as 128, 256, or 512. This is a requirement in OpenGL 1.1. The requirement is relaxed in some versions, but it's still a good idea to use power-of-two textures Some of the things discussed in this section will not work with non-power-of-two textures, even on modern systems.

When an image texture is applied to a surface, the default behavior is to multiply the RGBA color components of pixels on the surface by the color components from the image. The surface color will be modified by light effects, if lighting is turned on, before it is multiplied by the texture color. It is common to use white as the surface color. If a different color is used on the surface, it will add a "tint" to the color from the texture image.

4.3.1 Texture Coordinates

When a texture is applied to a surface, each point on the surface has to correspond to a point in the texture. There has to be a way to determine how this mapping is computed. For that, the object needs texture coordinates. As is generally the case in OpenGL, texture coordinates are specified for each vertex of a primitive. Texture coordinates for points inside the primitive are calculated by interpolating the values from the vertices of the primitive.

A texture image comes with its own 2D coordinate system. Traditionally, *s* is used for the horizontal coordinate on the image and *t* is used for the vertical coordinate. The *s* coordinate is a real number that ranges from 0 on the left of the image to 1 on the right, while *t* ranges from 0 at the bottom to 1 at the top. Values of *s* or *t* outside of the range 0 to 1 are not inside the image, but such values are still valid as texture coordinates. Note that texture coordinates are not based on pixels. No matter what size the image is, values of *s* and *t* between 0 and 1 cover the entire image.

To draw a textured primitive, we need a pair of numbers (s,t) for each vertex. These are the texture coordinates for that vertex. They tell which point in the image is mapped to the vertex. For example, suppose that we want to apply part of an EarthAtNight image to a triangular primitive. Let's say that the area in the image that is to be mapped onto the primitive is the triangle shown here outlined in thick orange:

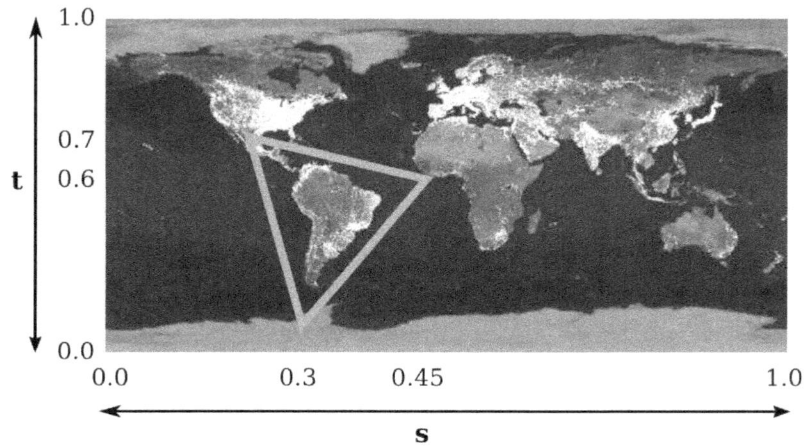

The vertices of this area have (s,t) coordinates (0.3,0.1), (0.45,0.6), and (0.25,0.7). These coordinates from the image should be used as the texture coordinates for the vertices of the triangular primitive.

The texture coordinates of a vertex are an attribute of the vertex, just like color, normal vectors, and material properties. Texture coordinates are specified by the family of functions glTexCoord*, including the functions glTexCoord2f(s,t), glTexCoord2d(s,t), glTexCoord2fv(array), and glTexCoord2dv(array). The OpenGL state includes a current set of texture coordinates, as specified by these functions. When you specify a vertex with glVertex*, the current texture coordinates are copied and become an attribute that is associated with the vertex. As usual, this means that the texture coordinates for a vertex must be specified before glVertex* is called. Each vertex of a primitive will need a different set of texture coordinates.

For example, to apply the triangular region in the image shown above to the triangle in the xy-plane with vertices at (0,0), (0,1), and (1,0), we can say:

```
glNormal3d(0,0,1); // This normal works for all three vertices.
glBegin(GL_TRIANGLES);
glTexCoord2d(0.3,0.1); // Texture coords for vertex (0,0)
```

```
glVertex2d(0,0);
glTexCoord2d(0.45,0.6); // Texture coords for vertex (0,1)
glVertex2d(0,1);
glTexCoord2d(0.25,0.7); // Texture coords for vertex (1,0)
glVertex2d(1,0);
glEnd();
```

Note that there is no particular relationship between the (x, y) coordinates of a vertex, which give its position in space, and the (s, t) texture coordinates associated with the vertex. In fact, in this case, the triangle that I am drawing has a different shape from the triangular area in the image, and that piece of the image will have to be stretched and distorted to fit. Such distortion occurs in most uses of texture images.

Sometimes, it's difficult to decide what texture coordinates to use. One case where it's easy is applying the complete texture to a rectangle. Here is a code segment that draws a square in the xy-plane, with appropriate texture coordinates to map the entire image onto the square:

```
glBegin(GL_TRIANGLE_FAN);
glNormal3f(0,0,1);
glTexCoord2d(0,0); // Texture coords for lower left corner
glVertex2d(-0.5,-0.5);
glTexCoord2d(1,0); // Texture coords for lower right corner
glVertex2d(0.5,-0.5);
glTexCoord2d(1,1); // Texture coords for upper right corner
glVertex2d(0.5,0.5);
glTexCoord2d(0,1); // Texture coords for upper left corner
glVertex2d(-0.5,0.5);
glEnd();
```

Unfortunately, the standard shapes in the GLUT library do not come with texture coordinates (except for the teapot, which does). I have written a set of functions for drawing similar shapes that do come with texture coordinates. The functions can be found in jogl/TexturedShapes.java for JOGL or in glut/textured-shapes.c (plus the corresponding header file glut/textured-shapes.h) for C. Of course, there are many ways of applying a texture to a given object. If you use my functions, you are stuck with my decision about how to do so.

The sample program jogl/TextureDemo.java or glut/texture-demo.c lets you view several different texture images on my textured shapes.

One last question: What happens if you supply texture coordinates that are not in the range from 0 to 1? It turns out that such values are legal. By default, in OpenGL 1.1, they behave as though the entire *st*-plane is filled with copies of the image. For example, if the texture coordinates for a square range from 0 to 3 in both directions, instead of 0 to 1 , then you get nine copies of the image on the square (three copies horizontally by three copies vertically).

To draw a textured primitive using glDrawArrays or glDrawElements, you will need to supply the texture coordinates in a vertex array, in the same way that you supply vertex coordinates, colors, and normal vectors. (See Subsection 3.4.2.) The details are similar: You have to enable the use of a texture coordinate array by calling

```
glEnableClientState(GL_TEXTURE_COORD_ARRAY);
```

and you have to tell OpenGL the location of the data using the function

```
void glTexCoordPointer( int size, int dataType, int stride, void* array)
```

The size, for us, will always be 2 . (OpenGL also allows 3 or 4 texture coordinates, but we have no use for them.) The dataType can be GL_FLOAT, GL_DOUBLE, or GL_INT. The stride will ordinarily be zero, to indicate that there is no extra data between texture coordinates in the array. The last parameter is an array or pointer to the data, which must be of the type indicated by the dataType. In JOGL, as usual, you would use an nio buffer instead of an array.

4.3.2 MipMaps and Filtering

When a texture is applied to a surface, the pixels in the texture do not usually match up one-to-one with pixels on the surface, and in general, the texture must be stretched or shrunk as it is being mapped onto the surface. Sometimes, several pixels in the texture will be mapped to the same pixel on the surface. In this case, the color that is applied to the surface pixel must somehow be computed from the colors of all the texture pixels that map to it. This is an example of "filtering"; in particular, it uses a minification filter because the texture is being shrunk. When one pixel from the texture covers more than one pixel on the surface, the texture has to be magnified, and we need a magnification filter.

One bit of terminology before we proceed: The pixels in a texture are referred to as texels, short for "texture pixel" or "texture element", and I will use that term from now on.

When deciding how to apply a texture to a pixel on a surface, OpenGL must deal with the fact that that pixel actually contains an infinite number of points, and each point has its own texture coordinates. So, how should a texture color for the pixel be computed? The easiest thing to do is to select one point from the pixel, say the point at the center of the pixel. OpenGL knows the texture coordinates for that point. Those texture coordinates correspond to one point in the texture, and that point lies in one of the texture's texels. The color of that texel could be used as the texture color for the pixel. This is called "nearest texel filtering." It is very fast, but it does not usually give good results. It doesn't take into account the difference in size between the pixels on the surface and the texels in the image. An improvement on nearest texel filtering is "linear filtering," which can take an average of several texel colors to compute the color that will be applied to the surface.

The problem with linear filtering is that it will be very inefficient when a large texture is applied to a much smaller surface area. In this case, many texels map to one pixel, and computing the average of so many texels becomes very inefficient. There is a neat solution for this: mipmaps.

A mipmap for a texture is a scaled-down version of that texture. A complete set of mipmaps consists of the full-size texture, a half-size version in which each dimension is divided by two, a quarter-sized version, a one-eighth-sized version, and so on. If one dimension shrinks to a single pixel, it is not reduced further, but the other dimension will continue to be cut in half until it too reaches one pixel. In any case, the final mipmap consists of a single pixel. Here are the first few images in the set of mipmaps for a brick texture:

You'll notice that the mipmaps become small very quickly. The total memory used by a set of mipmaps is only about one-third more than the memory used for the original texture, so the additional memory requirement is not a big issue when using mipmaps.

Mipmaps are used only for minification filtering. They are essentially a way of pre-computing the bulk of the averaging that is required when shrinking a texture to fit a surface. To texture a pixel, OpenGL can first select the mipmap whose texels most closely match the size of the pixel. It can then do linear filtering on that mipmap to compute a color, and it will have to average at most a few texels in order to do so.

In newer versions of OpenGL, you can get OpenGL to generate mipmaps automatically. In OpenGL 1.1, if you want to use mipmaps, you must either load each mipmap individually, or you must generate them yourself. (The GLU library has a method, gluBuild2DMipmaps that can be used to generate a set of mipmaps for a 2D texture.) However, my sample programs do not use mipmaps.

4.3.3 Texture Target and Texture Parameters

OpenGL can actually use one-dimensional and three-dimensional textures, as well as twodimensional. Because of this, many OpenGL functions dealing with textures take a texture target as a parameter, to tell whether the function should be applied to one, two, or three dimensional textures. For us, the only texture target will be GL_TEXTURE_2D.

There are a number of options that apply to textures, to control the details of how textures are applied to surfaces. Some of the options can be set using the glTexParameteri () function, including two that have to do with filtering. OpenGL supports several different filtering techniques for minification and magnification. The filters can be set using glTexParameteri():

```
glTexParameteri(GL_TEXTURE_2D, GL_TEXTURE_MAG_FILTER, magFilter);
glTexParameteri(GL_TEXTURE_2D, GL_TEXTURE_MIN_FILTER, minFilter);
```

The values of magFilter and minFilter are constants that specify the filtering algorithm. For the magFilter, the only options are GL_NEAREST and GL_LINEAR, giving nearest texel and linear filtering. The default for the MAG filter is GL_LINEAR, and there is rarely any need to change it. For minFilter, in addition to GL_NEAREST and GL_LINEAR, there are four options that use mipmaps for more efficient filtering. The default MIN filter is GL_NEAREST_MIPMAP_LINEAR, which does averaging between mipmaps and nearest texel filtering within each mipmap. For even better results, at the cost of greater inefficiency, you can use GL_LINEAR_MIPMAP_LINEAR, which does averaging both between and within mipmaps. The other two options are GL_NEAREST_MIPMAP_NEAREST and GL_LINEAR_MIPMAP_NEAREST.

One very important note: If you are not using mipmaps for a texture, it is imperative that you change the minification filter for that texture to GL_LINEAR or, less likely,

GL_NEAREST. The default MIN filter requires mipmaps, and if mipmaps are not available, then the texture is considered to be improperly formed, and OpenGL ignores it! Remember that if you don't create mipmaps and if you don't change the minification filter, then your texture will simply be ignored by OpenGL.

There is another pair of texture parameters to control how texture coordinates outside the range 0 to 1 are treated. As mentioned above, the default is to repeat the texture. The alternative is to "clamp" the texture. This means that when texture coordinates outside the range 0 to 1 are specified, those values are forced into that range: Values less than 0 are replaced by 0 , and values greater than 1 are replaced by 1 . Values can be clamped separately in the *s* and *t* directions using

```
glTexParameteri(GL_TEXTURE_2D, GL_TEXTURE_WRAP_S, GL_CLAMP);
glTexParameteri(GL_TEXTURE_2D, GL_TEXTURE_WRAP_T, GL_CLAMP);
```

Passing *GL_REPEAT* as the last parameter restores the default behavior. When clamping is in effect, texture coordinates outside the range 0 to 1 return the same color as a texel that lies along the outer edge of the image. Here is what the effect looks like on two textured squares:

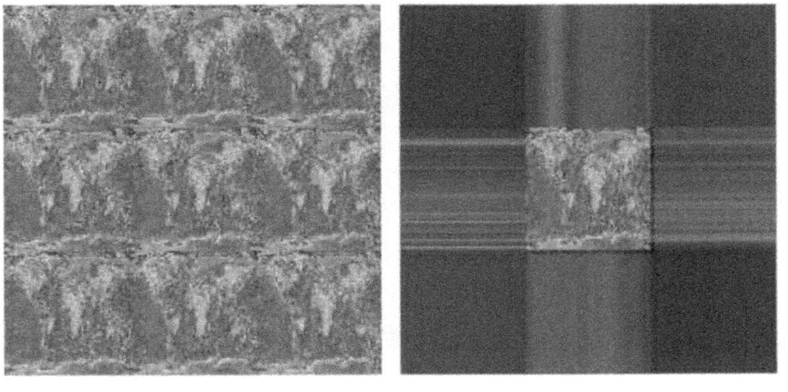

The two squares in this image have *s* and *t* texture coordinates that range from -1 to 2 . The original image lies in the center of the square. For the square on the left, the texture is repeated. On the right, the texture is clamped.

4.3.4 Texture Transformation

When a texture is applied to a primitive, the texture coordinates for a vertex determine which point in the texture is mapped to that vertex. Texture images are 2D, but OpenGL also supports one-dimensional textures and three-dimensional textures. This means that texture coordinates cannot be restricted to two coordinates. In fact, a set of texture coordinates in OpenGL is represented internally in the form of homogeneous coordinates, which are referred to as (s,t,r,q). We have used glTexCoord2* to specify texture s and t coordinates, but a call to glTexCoord2$f(s,t)$, for example, is really just shorthand for glTexCoord4$f(s,t,0,1)$.

Since texture coordinates are no different from vertex coordinates, they can be transformed in exactly the same way. OpenGL maintains a texture transformation as part of its state, along with the modelview and projection transformations. The current value of each of the three transformations is stored as a matrix. When a texture is applied to an object, the texture coordinates that were specified for its vertices are transformed by the texture matrix. The transformed texture coordinates are then used to pick out a point in the texture. Of course, the default texture transform is the identity transform, which doesn't change the coordinates.

The texture matrix can represent scaling, rotation, translation and combinations of these basic transforms. To specify a texture transform, you have to use glMatrixMode() to set the matrix mode to GL_TEXTURE. With this mode in effect, calls to methods such as glRotate*, glScale*, and glLoadIdentity are applied to the texture matrix. For example to install a texture transform that scales texture coordinates by a factor of two in each direction, you could say:

```
glMatrixMode(GL_TEXTURE);
glLoadIdentity(); // Make sure we are starting from the identity
matrix.
glScalef(2,2,1);
glMatrixMode(GL_MODELVIEW); // Leave matrix mode set to GL_MODELVIEW.
```

Since the image lies in the st-plane, only the first two parameters of glScalef matter. For rotations, you would use (0,0,1) as the axis of rotation, which will rotate the image within the st-plane.

Now, what does this actually mean for the appearance of the texture on a surface? In the example, the scaling transform multiplies each texture coordinate by 2 . For example, if a vertex was assigned 2D texture coordinates (0.4,0.1), then after the texture transform is applied, that vertex will be mapped to the point $(s,t) = (0.8,0.2)$ in the texture. The texture coordinates vary twice as fast on the surface as they would without the scaling transform. A region on the surface that would map to a 1 -by-1 square in the texture image without the transform will instead map to a 2 -by- 2 square in the image - so that a larger piece of the image will be seen inside the region. In other words, the texture image will be shrunk by a factor of two on the surface! More generally, the effect of a texture transformation on the appearance of the texture is the inverse of its effect on the texture coordinates. (This is exactly analogous to the inverse relationship between a viewing transformation and a modeling transformation.) If the texture transform is translation to the right, then the texture moves to the left on the surface. If the texture transform is a counterclockwise rotation, then the texture rotates clockwise on the surface.

I mention texture transforms here mostly to show how OpenGL can use transformations in another context. But it is sometimes useful to transform a texture to make it fit better on a surface. And for an unusual effect, you might even animate the texture transform to make the texture image move on the surface. To see the effect of texture transformations, try the on-line demo c4/texture-transform.html.

4.3.5 Loading a Texture from Memory

It's about time that we looked at the process of getting an image into OpenGL so that it can be used as a texture. Usually, the image starts out in a file. OpenGL does not have functions for loading images from a file. For now, we assume that the file has already been loaded from the file into the computer's memory. Later in this section, I will explain how that's done in C and in Java.

The OpenGL function for loading image data from the computer's memory into a 2D texture is glTexImage2D(), which takes the form:

```
glTexImage2D(target, mipmapLevel, internalFormat, width, height,
border,
    format, dataType, pixels);
```

The target should be GL_TEXTURE_2D. The mipmapLevel should ordinarily be 0 . The value 0 is for loading the main texture; a larger value is used to load an individual mipmap. The internalFormat tells OpenGL how you want the texture data to be stored in OpenGL texture memory. It can be *GL_RGB* to store an 8 -bit red/green/blue component for each pixel. Another possibility is *GL_RGBA*, which adds an alpha component. The width and height give the size of the image; the values should be powers of two. The value of border should be 0 ; the only other possibility is 1 , which indicates that a one-pixel border has been added around the image data for reasons that I will not discuss. The last three parameters describe the image data. The format tells how the original image data is represented in the computer's memory, such as *GL_RGB* or *GL_RGBA*. The dataType is usually GL_UNSIGNED_BYTE, indicating that each color component is represented as a one-byte value in the range 0 to 255 . And pixels is a pointer to the start of the actual color data for the pixels. The pixel data has to be in a certain format, but that need not concern us here, since it is usually taken care of by the functions that are used to read the image from a file. (For JOGL, the pointer would be replaced by a buffer.)

This all looks rather complicated, but in practice, a call to glTexImage2D generally takes the following form, except possibly with GL_RGB replaced with GL_RGBA.

```
glTexImage2D(GL_TEXTURE_2D,    0,    GL_RGB,    width,    height,    0,
    GL_RGB, GL_UNSIGNED_BYTE, pixels);
```

Calling this function will load the image into the texture, but it does not cause the texture to be used. For that, you also have to call

```
glEnable(GL_TEXTURE_2D);
```

If you want to use the texture on some objects but not others, you can enable $GL\_TEXTURE\_2D$ before drawing objects that you want to be textured and disable it before drawing untextured objects. You can also change the texture that is being used at any time by calling glTexImage2D.

4.3.6 Texture from Color Buffer

Texture images for use in an OpenGL program usually come from an external source, most often an image file. However, OpenGL is itself a powerful engine for creating images. Sometimes, instead of loading an image file, it's convenient to have OpenGL create the image internally, by rendering it. This is possible because OpenGL can read texture data from its own color buffer, where it does its drawing. To create a texture image using OpenGL, you just have to draw the image using standard OpenGL drawing commands and then load that image as a texture using the method

```
glCopyTexImage2D( target, mipmapLevel, internalFormat,
    x, y, width, height, border );
```

In this method, target will be GL_TEXTURE_2D; mipmapLevel should be zero; the internalFormat will ordinarily be GL_RGB or GL_RGBA; x and y specify the lower left corner of the rectangle from which the texture will be read; width and height are the size of that rectangle; and border should be 0 . As usual with textures, the width and height should ordinarily be powers of two. A call to glCopyTexImage2D will typically look like

```
glCopyTexImage2D(GL_TEXTURE_2D, 0, GL_RGB, x, y, width, height, 0);
```

The end result is that the specified rectangle from the color buffer will be copied to texture memory and will become the current 2D texture. This works in the same way as a call to glTexImage2D(), except for the source of the image data.

An example can be found in the JOGL program jogl/TextureFromColorBuffer.java or in the C version glut/texture-from-color-buffer.c. This program draws the windmill-and-cart scene from Subsection 2.4.1 and then uses that drawing as a texture on 3D objects. Here is an image from the program, showing the texture on a cylinder:

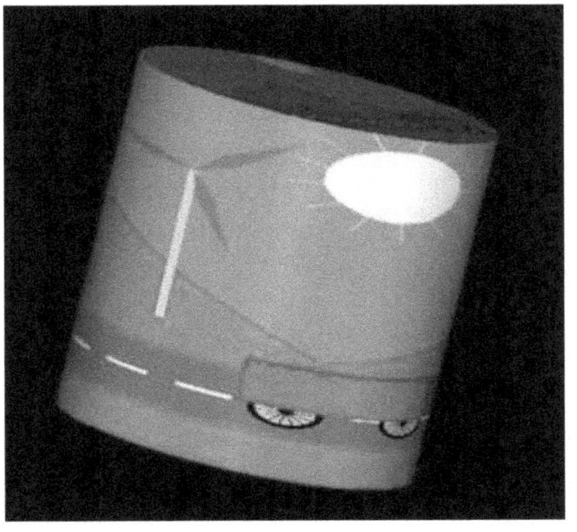

The texture can be animated! For the animation, a new texture is drawn for each frame. All the work is done in the program's display function. In that function, the current frame of the windmill-and-cart scene is first drawn as a 2D scene with lighting disabled. This picture is not shown on the computer screen; the drawing is done off-screen and the image will be erased and replaced with the 3D image before it's ever shown on screen. The glCopyTexImage2D() function is then called to copy the scene into the current texture. Then, the color buffer is cleared, lighting is enabled, and a 3D projection is set up, before finally drawing the 3D object that is seen on the computer screen.

4.3.7 Texture Objects

Everything that I've said so far about textures was already true for OpenGL 1.0. OpenGL 1.1 introduced a new feature called texture objects to make texture handling more efficient. Texture objects are used when you need to work with several texture images in the same program. The usual method for loading texture images, glTexImage2D, transfers data from your program into the graphics card. This is an expensive operation, and switching among multiple textures by using this method can seriously degrade a program's performance. Texture objects offer the possibility of storing texture data for multiple textures on the graphics card. With texture objects, you can switch from one texture object to another with a single, fast OpenGL command: You just have to tell OpenGL which texture object you want to use. (Of course, the graphics card has only a limited amount of memory for storing textures, and you aren't guaranteed that all of your texture objects will actually be stored on the graphics card. Texture objects that don't fit in the graphics card's memory are no more efficient than ordinary textures.)

Texture objects are managed by OpenGL and the graphics hardware. A texture object is identified by an integer ID number. To use a texture object, you need to obtain an ID number from OpenGL. This is done with the glGenTextures function:

```
void glGenTexures( int textureCount, int* array )
```

This function can generate multiple texture IDs with a single call. The first parameter specifies how many IDs you want. The second parameter says where the generated IDs will be stored. It should be an array whose length is at least textureCount. For example, if you plan to use three texture objects, you can say

```
int idList[3];
glGenTextures( 3, idList );
```

You can then use *id*List[0], idList[1], and idList[2] to refer to the textures. Because of the way pointers work in C , if you want to get a single texture ID, you can pass a pointer to an integer variable as the second parameter to glGenTextures(). For example,

```
int texID;
glGenTextures( 1, &texID );
```

The new texture ID will be stored in the variable texID. Every texture object has its own state, which includes the values of texture parameters such as GL_TEXTURE_MIN_FILTER as well as the texture image itself. To work with a specific texture object, you must first call

```
glBindTexture( GL_TEXTURE_2D, texID )
```

where texID is the texture ID returned by glGenTextures. After this call, any use of glTexParameteri, glTexImage2D, or glCopyTexImage2D will be applied to the texture object with ID texID.

Similarly, when a textured primitive is rendered, the texture that is used is the one that was most recently bound using glBindTexture. A typical pattern would be to load and configure a number of textures during program initialization:

```
glGenTextures( n, textureIdList );
for (i = 0; i < n; i++) {
    glBindTexture( textureIDList[i] );
        .
```

```
        \mathrm{ - // Load texture image number i}
        \mathrm{ - // Configure texture image number i}
}
```

Then, while rendering a scene, you would call glBindTexture every time you want to switch from one texture image to another texture image. This would be much more efficient than calling glTexImage2D every time you want to switch textures.

OpenGL 1.1 reserves texture ID zero as the default texture object, which is bound initially. It is the texture object that you are using if you never call glBindTexture. This means that you can write programs that use textures without ever mentioning glBindTexture. (However, I should note that when we get to WebGL, that will no longer be true.)

The small sample program glut/texture-objects.c shows how to use texture objects in C. In is available only in C since, as we will see, JOGL has its own way of working with texture objects.

4.3.8 Loading Textures in C

We have seen how to load texture image data from memory into OpenGL. The problem that remains is how to get the image data into memory before calling glTexImage2D. One possibility is to compute the data-you can actually have your program generate texture data on the fly. More likely, however, you want to load it from a file. This section looks at how that might be done in C . You will probably want to use a library of image-manipulation functions. Several free image processing libraries are available. I will discuss one of them, FreeImage, which can work with many image file formats. FreeImage can be obtained from http://freeimage.sourceforge.net/, but I was able to use it in Linux simply by installing the package libfreeimage-dev. To make it available to my program, I added #include "FreeImage.h" to the top of my C program, and I added the option -lfreeimage to the *gcc* command to make the library available to the compiler. (See the sample program glut/texture-demo.c for an example that uses this library.) Instead of discussing FreeImage in detail, I present a well-commented function that uses it to load image data from a file:

```
void* imgPixels; // Pointer to raw RGB data for texture in memory.
int imgWidth; // Width of the texture image.
int imgHeight; // Height of the texture image.
void loadTexture( char* fileName ) {
    // Loads a texture image using the FreeImage library, and stores
the
    // required info in global variables imgPixels, imgWidth,
```

```
imgHeight.
    // The parameter fileName is a string that contains the name of the
    // image file from which the image is to be loaded. If the image


        // can't be loaded, then imgPixels will be set to be a null
pointer.
    imgPixels = 0; // Null pointer to signal that data has not been
read.
    FREE_IMAGE_FORMAT format = FreeImage_GetFIFFromFilename(fileName);
        // FREE_IMAGE_FORMAT is a type defined by the FreeImage
library.
        // Here, the format is determined from the file extension in
        // the file name, such as .png, .jpg, or .gif. Many formats
        // are supported.
    if (format == FIF_UNKNOWN) {
        printf("Unknown file type for texture image file %s\n",
fileName);
        return;
    }
    FIBITMAP* bitmap = FreeImage_Load(format, fileName, 0);
            // FIBITMAP is a type defined by the FreeImage library,
representing
            // the raw image data plus some metadata such as width,
height,
            // and the format of the image data. This actually tries to
            // read the data from the specified file.
    if (!bitmap) {
        printf ("Failed to load image %s\n", fileName);
        return;
    }
    FIBITMAP* bitmap2 = FreeImage_ConvertTo24Bits(bitmap);
            // This creates a copy of the image, with the data
represented
            // in standard RGB (or BGR) format, for use with OpenGL.
    FreeImage_Unload(bitmap);
            // After finishing with a bitmap, it should be disposed.
            // We are finished with bitmap, but not with bitmap2, since
```

```
        // we will continue to use the data from bitmap2.
    imgPixels = FreeImage_GetBits(bitmap2); // Get the data we need!
    imgWidth = FreeImage_GetWidth(bitmap2);
    imgHeight = FreeImage_GetHeight(bitmap2);
    if (imgPixels) {
        printf("Texture image loaded from file %s, size %dx%d\n",
                fileName, imgWidth, imgHeight);
    }
    else {
        printf ("Failed to get texture data from %s\n", fileName);
    }
} // end loadTexture
```

After this function has been called, the data that we need for glTexImage2D() is in the global variables imgWidth, imgHeight, and imgPixels (or imgPixels is 0 to indicate that the attempt to load the image failed). There is one complication: FreeImage will store the color components for a pixel in the order red/green/blue on some platforms but in the order blue/green/red on other platforms. The second data format is called $GL - BGR$ in OpenGL. If you use the wrong format in glTextImage2D(), then the red and blue components of the color will be reversed. To tell the difference, you can use the FreeImage constant *FI_RGBA_RED*, which tells the position of the red color component in pixel data. This constant will be 0 if the format is *GL_RGB* and will be 2 if the format is *GL_BGR*. So, to use the texture in OpenGL, you might say:

```
if ( imgPixels ) { // The image data exists
    int format; // The format of the color data in memory
    if ( FI_RGBA_RED == 0 )
        format = GL_RGB;
    else
        format = GL_BGR;
    glTexImage2D(GL_TEXTURE_2D, 0, GL_RGBA, imgWidth, imgHeight, 0,
format,
            GL_UNSIGNED_BYTE, imgPixels);
    glEnable(GL_TEXTURE_2D);
}
else { // The image data was not loaded, so don't attempt to use the
texture.
    glDisable(GL_TEXTURE_2D);
}
```

To be even more careful, you could check that the width and the height of the image are powers of two. If not, you can resize it using the function FreeImage_Rescale() from the FreeImage library.

FreeImage is a large, complicated system that might not be easily made available on your computer. To make it easier for you to experiment with textures in C, I have also included a small C utility for reading textures from .rgb files. The rgb file format is fairly simple, but rgb files are generally much larger than the corresponding .png or .jpeg files. The format is not widely supported, but I have included .rgb versions of my sample texture images in the folder glut/textures-rgb. The small library for loading them into textures is glut/textures-rgb/readrgb.c and its header file glut/textures-rgb/readrgb.h. (The library is from http://paulbourke.net/dataformats/sgirgb/.) Sample programs that use the library are glut/texture-objects-rgb.c and glut/texture-demo-rgb.c.

4.3.9 Using Textures with JOGL

We turn finally to using texture images in Java. JOGL comes with several classes that make it fairly easy to use textures in Java, notably the classes Texture and TextureIO in package com.jogamp.opengl.util.texture and AWTTextureIO in package com.jogamp.opengl.util.texture.awt. For an example of using textures with JOGL, see the sample program jogl/TextureDemo.java.

An object of type Texture represents a texture that has already been loaded into OpenGL. Internally, it uses a texture object to store the texture and its configuration data. If tex is an object of type Texture, you can call

```
tex.bind(gl);
```

to use the texture image while rendering objects. The parameter, *gl*, as usual, is a variable of type GL2 the represents the OpenGL drawing context. This function is equivalent to calling glBindTexture for the OpenGL texture object that is used by the Java Texture. You still need to enable GL_TEXTURE_2D by calling gl.glEnable(GL2.GL_TEXTURE_2D) or, equivalently,

```
tex.enable(gl);
```

You can set texture parameters in the usual way, by calling gl.glTexParameteri() while the texture is bound, but it is preferable to use a method from the Texture class to set the parameters:

```
tex.setTexParameteri( gl, parameterName, value );
```

This will automatically bind the texture object before setting the texture parameter. For example,

```
tex.setTexParameteri(gl, GL2.GL_TEXTURE_MIN_FILTER,
GL2.LINEAR_MIPMAP_LINEAR);
```

So, once you have a Texture, it's pretty easy to use. But there remains the problem of creating Texture objects. For that, you can use static methods in the Texture/O and AWTTextureIO classes. For example, if fileName is the name of an image file (or a path to such a file), then you can say

```
tex = TextureIO.newTexture( new File(fileName), true );
```

to load a texture from the file into a Texture object, tex. The boolean parameter here, and in all the methods we will look at, tells JOGL whether or not to create mipmaps for the texture; by passing true, we automatically get a full set of mipmaps!

One important note: Java's texture creation functions will only work when an OpenGL context is "current." This will be true in the event-handling methods of a GLEventListener, including the init() and display() methods. However, it will not be true in ordinary methods and constructors.

Of course, in Java, you are more likely to store the image as a resource in the program than as a separate file. If resourceName is a path to the image resource, you can load the image into a texture with

```
URL textureURL;
textureURL = getClass().getClassLoader().getResource( resourceName );
texture = TextureIO.newTexture(textureURL, true, null);
```

The third parameter to this version of newTexture specifies the image type and can be given as a string containing a file suffix such as "png" or "jpg"; the value null tells OpenGL to autodetect the image type, which should work in general. (By the way, all the texture-loading code that I discuss here can throw exceptions, which you will have to catch or otherwise handle in some way.)

One problem with all this is that textures loaded in this way will be upside down! This happens because Java stores image data from the top row of the image to the bottom, whereas OpenGL expects image data to be stored starting with the bottom row. If this is a problem for you, you can flip the image before using it to create a texture. To do that, you have to load the image into a BufferedImage and then load that into a texture using the

AWTTextureIO class. For example, assuming resourceName is a path to an image resource in the program:

```
URL textureURL;
textureURL = getClass().getClassLoader().getResource( resourceName );
BufferedImage img = ImageIO.read( textureURL );
ImageUtil.flipImageVertically( img );
texture = AWTTextureIO.newTexture(GLProfile.getDefault(), img, true);
```

The ImageUtil class is defined in package com.jogamp.opengl.util.awt. Here, I obtained a BufferedImage by reading it from a resource. You could also read it from a file-or even draw it using Java 2D graphics.

4.4 Lights, Camera, Action

A scene in computer graphics can be a complex collection of objects, each with its own attributes. In Subsection 2.4.2, we saw how a scene graph can be used to organize all the objects in a 2D scene. Rendering a scene means traversing the scene graph, rendering each object in the graph as it is encountered. For 3D graphics, scene graphs must deal with a larger variety of objects, attributes, and transforms. For example, it is often useful to consider lights and cameras to be objects and to be able to include them in scene graphs. In this section, we consider scene graphs in 3D, and how to treat cameras and lights as objects.

When designing scene graphs, there are many options to consider. For example, should transforms be properties of object nodes, or should there be separate nodes to represent transforms? The same question can be asked about attributes. Another question is whether an attribute value should apply only to the node of which it is a property, or should it be inherited by the children of that node?

A fundamental choice is the shape of the graph. In general, a scene graph can be a directed acyclic graph, or "dag," which is a tree-like structure except that a node can have several parents in the graph. The scene graphs in Subsection 2.4.2 were dags. This has the advantage that a single node in the graph can represent several objects in the scene, since in a dag, a node can be encountered several times as the graph is traversed. On the other hand, representing several objects with one scene graph node can lead to a lack of flexibility, since those objects will all have the same value for any property encoded in the node. So, in some applications, scene graphs are required to be trees. In a tree, each node has a unique parent, and the node will be encountered only once as the tree in traversed.

The distinction between trees and dags will show up when we discuss camera nodes in scene graphs.

4.4.1 Attribute Stack

We have seen how the functions glPushMatrix and glPopMatrix are used to manipulate the transform stack. These functions are useful when traversing a scene graph: When a node that contains a transform is encountered during a traversal of the graph, glPushMatrix can be called before applying the transform. Then, after the node and its descendants have been rendered, glPopMatrix is called to restore the previous modelview transformation.

Something similar can be done for attributes such as color and material, if it is assumed that an attribute value in a scene graph node should be inherited as the default value of that attribute for children of the node. OpenGL 1.1 maintains an attribute stack, which is manipulated using the functions glPushAttrib and glPopAttrib. In addition to object attributes like the current color, the attribute stack can store global attributes like the global ambient color and the enabled state of the depth test. Since there are so many possible attributes, glPushAttrib does not simply save the value of every attribute. Instead, it saves a subset of the possible attributes. The subset that is to be saved is specified as a parameter to the function. For example, the command

```
glPushAttrib(GL_ENABLED_BIT);
```

will save a copy of each of the OpenGL state variables that can be enabled or disabled. This includes the current state of GL_DEPTH_TEST, GL_LIGHTING, GL_NORMALIZE, and others. Similarly,

```
glPushAttrib(GL_CURRENT_BIT);
```

saves a copy of the current color, normal vector, and texture coordinates. And

```
glPushAttrib(GL_LIGHTING_BIT);
```

saves attributes relevant to lighting such as the values of material properties and light properties, the global ambient color, color material settings, and the enabled state for lighting and each of the individual lights. Other constants can be used to save other sets of attributes; see the OpenGL documentation for details. It is possible to OR together several constants to combine sets of attributes. For example,

```
glPushAttrib(GL_LIGHTING_BIT | GL_ENABLED_BIT)
```

will save the attributes in both the GL_LIGHTING_BIT set and in the GL_ENABLED_BIT set.

Calling glPopAttrib() will restore all the values that were saved by the corresponding call to glPushAttrib. There is no need for a parameter to glPopAttrib, since the set of attributes that are restored is determined by the parameter that was passed to glPushAttrib.

It should be easy to see how glPushAttrib and glPopAttrib can be used while traversing a scene graph: When processing a node, before changing attribute values, call glPushAttrib to save a copy of the relevant set or sets of attributes. Render the node and its descendants. Then call glPopAttrib to restore the saved values. This limits the effect of the changes so that they apply only to the node and its descendants.

There is an alternative way to save and restore values. OpenGL has a variety of "get" functions for reading the values of various state variables. I will discuss just some of them here. For example,

```
glGetFloatv( GL_CURRENT_COLOR, floatArray );
```

retrieves the current color value, as set by glColor*. The floatArray parameter should be an array of float, whose length is at least four. The RGBA color components of the current color will be stored in the array. Note that, later, you can simply call glColor4fv (colorArray) to restore the color. The same function can be used with different first parameters to read the values of different floating-point state variables. To find the current value of the viewport, use

```
glGetIntegerv( GL_VIEWPORT, intArray );
```

This will set intArray [0] and intArray [1] to be the x and y coordinates of the lower left corner of the current viewport, intArray [2] to be its width, and intArray [3] to be its height. To read the current values of material properties, use

```
glGetMaterialfv( face, property, floatArray );
```

The face must be *GL_FRONT* or *GL_BACK*. The property must be *GL_AMBIENT*, GL_DIFFUSE, GL_SPECULAR, GL_EMISSION, or GL_SHININESS. The current value of the property will be stored in floatArray, which must be of length at least four for the color properties, or length at least one for GL-SHININESS. There is a similar command, glGetLightfv, for reading properties of lights.

Finally, I will mention glIsEnabled(name), which can be used to check the enabled/disabled status of state variables such as GL_LIGHTING and GL_DEPTH_TEST. The parameter should be the constant that identifies the state variable. The function returns 0 if the state variable is disabled and 1 if it is enabled. For example, glIsEnabled (GL_LIGHTING) tests whether lighting is enabled. Suppose that a node in a scene graph has an attribute lit to tell whether that node (and its descendants) should be rendered with lighting enabled. Then the code for rendering a node might include something like this:

```
int saveLit = glIsEnabled(GL_LIGHTING);
if (lit)
        glEnable(GL_LIGHTING);
else
        glDisable(GL_LIGHTING);
    .
    . // Render the node and its descendants
    .
if (saveLit)
    glEnable(GL_LIGHTING);
else
    glDisable(GL_LIGHTING);
```

Since glPushAttrib can be used to push large groups of attribute values, you might think that it would be more efficient to use glIsEnabled and the glGet* family of commands to read the values of just those state variables that you are planning to modify. However, recall that OpenGL can queue a number of commands into a batch to be sent to the graphics card, and those commands can be executed by the GPU at the same time that your program continues to run. A glGet command can require your program to communicate with the graphics card and wait for the response. This means that any pending OpenGL commands will have to be sent to the graphics card and executed before the glGet command can complete. This is the kind of thing that can hurt performance. In contrast, calls to glPushAttrib and glPopAttrib can be queued with other OpenGL commands and sent to the graphics card in batches, where they can be executed efficiently by the graphics hardware. In fact, you should generally prefer using glPushAttrib/glPopAttrib instead of a glGet command when possible.

4.4.2 Moving Camera

Let's turn to another aspect of modeling. Suppose that we want to implement a viewer that can be moved around in the world like other objects. Sometimes, such a viewer is thought of as a moving camera. The camera is used to take pictures of the scene. We want to be able to apply transformations to a camera just as we apply transformations to other objects. The position and orientation of the camera determine what should be visible when the scene is rendered. And the "size" of the camera, which can be affected by a scaling transformation, determines how large a field of view it has. But a camera is not just another object. A camera really represents the viewing transformation that we want to use. Recall that modeling and viewing transformations have opposite effects: Moving objects to the right with a modeling transform is equivalent to moving the viewer to the left with a viewing transformation. (See Subsection 3.3.4.) To apply a modeling transformation to the camera, we really want to apply a viewing transformation to the scene as a whole, and that viewing transformation is the inverse of the camera's modeling transformation.

The following illustration shows a scene viewed from a moving camera. The camera starts in the default viewing position, at the origin, looking in the direction of the negative z-axis. This corresponds to using the identity as the viewing transform. For the second image, the camera has moved forward by ten units. This would correspond to applying the modeling transformation glTranslatef $(0,0,-10)$ to the camera (since it is moving in the negative z direction). But to implement this movement as a change of view, we want to apply the inverse operation as a viewing transformation. So, the viewing transform that we actually apply is glTranslatef (0,0,10). This can be seen, if you like, as a modeling transformation that is applied to all the other objects in the scene: Moving the camera ten units in one direction is equivalent to moving all the other objects 10 units in the opposite direction.

Original View

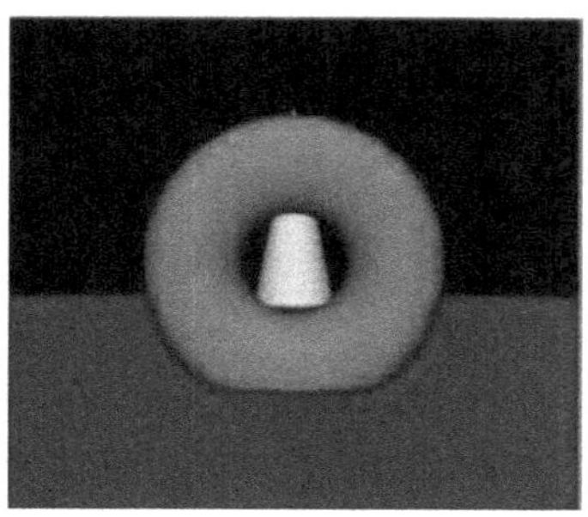

Afer moving forward ten units

After turning 21 degrees to the right

For the third image, the camera has rotated in place by 21 degrees to the right-a 21 -degree clockwise rotation about the y-axis-after it has been translated. This can be implemented by the transformation glRotatef(21,0,1,0)-a 21 -degree counterclockwise rotation about the y-axis-applied before the translation. Remember that the inverse of a composition of transformations is the composition of their inverses, in the opposite order. Mathematically, using T^{-1} to represent the inverse of a transformation T, we have that $(RS)^{-1} = S^{-1}R^{-1}$ for two transformations R and S.

The images in the illustration are from the demo c4/walkthrough.html, which you can try on-line. The demo lets you move around in a scene. More accurately, of course, it lets you change the viewing transformation to see the scene from different viewpoints.

When using scene graphs, it can be useful to include a camera object in the graph. That is, we want to be able to include a node in the graph that represents the camera, and we want to be able to use the camera to view the scene. It can even be useful to have several cameras in the scene, providing alternative points of view. To implement this, we need to be able to render a scene from the point of view of a given camera. From the previous discussion, we know that in order to do that, we need to use a viewing transformation that is the inverse of the modeling transformation that is applied to the camera object. The viewing transform must be applied before any of the objects in the scene are rendered.

When a scene graph is traversed, a modeling transformation can be applied at any node. The modeling transform that is in effect when a given node is encountered is the composition of all the transforms that were applied at nodes along the path that led to given node. However, if the node is a camera node, we don't want to apply that modeling transform; we want to apply its inverse as a viewing transform. To get the inverse, we can start at the camera node and follow the path backwards, applying the inverse of the modeling transform at each node.

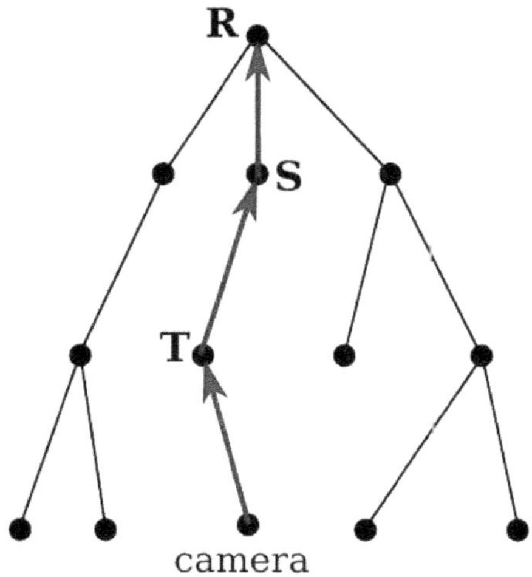

A scene graph, actually a tree, containing a camera node. R, S, and T represent modeling transformations applied to nodes in the graph. The modeling transformation applied to the camera is RST. The viewing transfomation is the inverse, $T^{-1} S^{-1} R^{-1}$, which can be obtained by following parent pointers from the camera node.

To easily implement this, we can add "parent pointers" to the scene graph data structure. A parent pointer for a node is a link to the parent of that node in the graph. Note that this only works if the graph is a tree; in a tree, each node has a unique parent, but that is not true in a general directed acyclic graph. It is possible to move up the tree by following parent pointers.

We this in mind, the algorithm for rendering the scene from the point of view of a camera goes as follows: Set the modelview transform to be the identity, by calling glLoadIdentity(). Start at the camera node, and follow parent pointers until you reach the root of the tree. At each node, apply the inverse of any modeling transformation in that node. (For example, if the modeling transform is translation by (a, b, c), call glTranslatef ($-a, -b, -c$).) Upon reaching the root, the viewing transform corresponding to the camera has been established. Now, traverse the scene graph to render the scene as usual. During this traversal, camera nodes should be ignored.

Note that a camera can be attached to an object, in the sense that the camera and the object are both subject to the same modeling transformation and so move together as a unit. In modeling terms, the camera and the object are sub-objects in a complex object. For example, a camera might be attached to a car to show the view through the windshield of that car. If the car moves, because its modeling transformation changes, the camera will move along with it.

4.4.3 Moving Light

It can also be useful to think of lights as objects, even as part of a complex object. Suppose that a scene includes a model of a lamp. The lamp model would include some geometry to make it visible, but if it is going to cast light on other objects in the scene, it also has to include a source of light. This means that the lamp is a complex object made up of an OpenGL light source plus some geometric objects. Any modeling transformation that is applied to the lamp should affect the light source as well as the geometry. In terms of the scene graph, the light is represented by a node in the graph, and it is affected by modeling transformations in the same way as other objects in the scene graph. You can even have animated lights-or animated objects that include lights as sub-objects, such as the headlights on a car.

Recall from Subsection 4.2.3 that a light source is subject to the modelview transform that is in effect at the time the position of the light source is set by glLightfv. If the light is represented as a node in a scene graph, then the modelview transform that we need is the one that is in effect when that node is encountered during a traversal of the scene graph. So, it seems like we should just traverse the graph and set the position of the light when we encounter it during the traversal.

But there is a problem: Before any geometry is rendered, all the light sources that might affect that geometry must already be configured and enabled. In particular, the lights' positions must be set before rendering any geometry. This means that you can't simply set the position of light sources in the scene graph as you traverse the graph in the usual way. If you do that, objects that are drawn before the light is encountered won't be properly illuminated by the light. Similarly, if the light node contains values for any other properties of the light, including the enabled/disabled state of the light, those properties must be set before rendering any geometry.

One solution is to do two traversals of the scene graph, the first to set up the lights and the second to draw the geometry. Since lights are affected by the modelview transformation, you have to set up the modeling transform during the first traversal in exactly the same way that you do in the second traversal. When you encounter the lights during the first traversal, you need to set the position of the light, since setting the position is what triggers the application of the current modelview transformation to the light. You also need to set any other properties of the light. During the first traversal, geometric objects in the scene graph are ignored. During the second traversal, when geometry is being rendered, light nodes can be ignored.

Chapter 5

Three.js: A 3D Scene Graph API

Chapter 3 and Chapter 4 introduced 3D graphics using OpenGL 1.1. Most of the ideas covered in those chapters remain relevant to modern computer graphics, but there have been many changes and improvements since the early days of OpenGL. In the remaining chapters, we will be using WebGL, a modern version of OpenGL that is used to create 3D graphics content for web pages.

WebGL is a low level language-even more so than OpenGL 1.1, since a WebGL program has to handle a lot of the low-level implementation details that were handled internally in the original version of OpenGL. This makes WebGL much more flexible, but more difficult to use. We will soon turn to working directly with WebGL. However, before we do that, we will look at a higher-level API for 3D web graphics that is built on top of WegGL: three.js. There are several reasons for starting at this high level. It will allow you to see how some of the things that you have learned are used in a modern object-oriented graphics package. It will allow me to introduce some new features such as shadows and environment mapping. It will let you work with a graphics library that you might use in real web applications. And it will be a break from the low-level detail we have been dealing with, before we move on to an even lower level.

You can probably follow much of the discussion in this chapter without knowing JavaScript. However, if you want to do any programming with three.js (or with WebGL), you need to know JavaScript.

5.1 Three.js Basics

Three.js is an object-oriented JavaScript library for 3D graphics. It is an open-source project created by Ricardo Cabello (who goes by the handle "mr.doob", https://mrdoob.com/), with contributions from other programmers. It seems to be the most popular open-source JavaScript library for 3D web applications. Three.js uses concepts that you are already familiar with, such as geometric objects, transformations, lights, materials, textures, and cameras. But it also has additional features that build on the power and flexibility of WegGL.

You can download three.js and read the documentation at its main web site, https://threejs.org. The download is quite large, since it includes many examples and support files. In this book, I use Release 129 of the software, from June, 2021. Version 1.2 of this book used Release 89. There have been a number of significant changes in the API since that release, and many programs written for older releases will not run under Release 129. You should be aware that some of the material about three.js that you might find on the Internet does not apply to the most recent version.

One of the changes in three.js is that it is now written as a "modular" JavaScript program. Modules are relatively independent components. A module only has access to an identifier from another module if the identifier is explicitly "exported" by one module and "imported" by the other. You will see modules used in many three.js examples, which include the appropriate input and export commands. However, modules are not used in this textbook. It is possible to build a non-modular Javascript program from modular source code, and it is the non-modular version of three.js that is used in this textbook.

The core features of three.js are defined in a single large JavaScript file named "three.js", which can be found in a build directory in the three.js download. This version is designed to be used with either modular or non-modular programs. There is also a smaller "minified" version, three.min.js, that contains the same definitions in a format that is not meant to be humanreadable. To use three.js on a web page, you can load either script with a <script> element on the page. For example, assuming that three.min.js is in the same folder as the web page, then the script element would be:

In addition to this core, the three.js download has a directory containing many examples and a variety of support files that are used in the examples. The examples use many features that are not part of the three.js core. These add-ons can be found in a folder named js inside the folder named examples in the download (or in a folder named *jsm* for the modular versions). Several of the add-ons are used in this textbook.

Copies of three.js, three.min.js, and several add-on scripts can be found in the threejs folder in the source folder of this textbook's web site. The three.js license allows these files to be freely redistributed. But if you plan to do any serious work with three.js, you should read the documentation on its web site about how to use it and how to deploy it.

5.1.1 Scene, Renderer, Camera

Three.js works with the HTML <canvas> element, the same thing that we used for 2D graphics in Section 2.6. In almost all web browsers, in addition to its 2D Graphics API, a canvas also supports drawing in 3D using WebGL, which is used by three.js and which is about as different as it can be from the 2D API.

Three.js is an object-oriented scene graph API. (See Subsection 2.4.2.) The basic procedure is to build a scene graph out of three.js objects, and then to render an image of the scene it represents. Animation can be implemented by modifying properties of the scene graph between frames.

The three.js library is made up of a large number of classes. Three of the most basic are THREE.Scene, THREE.Camera, and THREE.WebGLRenderer. (There are actually several renderer classes available. THREE. WebGLRenderer is by far the most common. It uses WebGL 2.0 if available, but can also use WebGL 1.0 if not. One alternative is THREE. WebGL1Renderer, with a " 1 " in the name, which forces the use of WebGL 1.0.) A three.js program will need at least one object of each type. Those objects are often stored in global variables let scene, renderer, camera; Note that almost all of the three.js classes and constants that we will use are properties of an object named THREE, and their names begin with "THREE.". I will sometimes refer to classes without using this prefix, and it is not usually used in the three.js documentation, but the prefix must always be included in actual program code.

A Scene object is a holder for all the objects that make up a 3D world, including lights, graphical objects, and possibly cameras. It acts as a root node for the scene graph. A Camera is a special kind of object that represents a viewpoint from which an image of a 3D world can be made. It represents a combination of a viewing transformation and a projection. A WebGLRenderer is an object that can create an image from a scene graph.

The scene is the simplest of the three objects. A scene can be created as an object of type THREE.Scene using a constructor with no parameters:

```
scene = new THREE.Scene();
```

The function scene.add(item) can be used to add cameras, lights, and graphical objects to the scene. It is probably the only scene function that you will need to call. The function scene.remove(item), which removes an item from the scene, is also occasionally useful.

There are two kinds of camera, one using orthographic projection and one using perspective projection. They are represented by classes THREE.OrthographicCamera and THREE.PerspectiveCamera, which are subclasses of THREE.Camera. The constructors specify the projection, using parameters that are familiar from OpenGL (see Subsection 3.3.3):

```
camera = new THREE.OrthographicCamera( left, right, top, bottom, near,
far );
```

or

```
camera = new THREE.PerspectiveCamera( fieldOfViewAngle, aspect, near, far );
```

The parameters for the orthographic camera specify the x, y, and z limits of the view volume, in eye coordinates - that is, in a coordinate system in which the camera is at (0,0,0) looking in the direction of the negative *z*-axis, with the *y*-axis pointing up in the view. The near and far parameters give the z -limits in terms of distance from the camera. For an orthographic projection, near can be negative, putting the "near" clipping plane in back of the camera. The parameters are the same as for the OpenGL function glOrtho(), except for reversing the order of the two parameters that specify the top and bottom clipping planes.

Perspective cameras are more common. The parameters for the perspective camera come from the function gluPerspective() in OpenGL's GLU library. The first parameter determines the vertical extent of the view volume, given as an angle measured in degrees. The aspect is the ratio between the horizontal and vertical extents; it should usually be set to the width of the canvas divided by its height. And near and far give the z -limits on the view volume as distances from the camera. For a perspective projection, both must be positive, with near less than far. Typical code for creating a perspective camera would be:

```
camera = new THREE.PerspectiveCamera( 45, canvas.width/canvas.height, 1, 100 );
```

where canvas holds a reference to the <canvas> element where the image will be rendered. The near and far values mean that only things between 1 and 100 units in front of the camera are included in the image. Remember that using an unnecessarily large value for far or an unnecessarily small value for near can interfere with the accuracy of the depth test.

A camera, like other objects, can be added to a scene, but it does not have to be part of the scene graph to be used. You might add it to the scene graph if you want it to be a parent or child of another object in the graph. In any case, you will generally want to apply a modeling transformation to the camera to set its position and orientation in 3D space. I will cover that later when I talk about transformations more generally.

A renderer is an instance of the class THREE.WebGLRenderer (or THREE.WebGL1Renderer, which is used in exactly the same way). Its constructor has one parameter, which is a JavaScript object containing settings that affect the renderer. The settings you are most likely to specify are canvas, which tells the renderer where to draw, and antialias, which asks the renderer to use antialiasing if possible:

```
renderer = new THREE.WebGLRenderer( {
        canvas: theCanvas,
        antialias: true
    } );
```

Here, theCanvas would be a reference to the <canvas> element where the renderer will display the images that it produces. (Note that the technique of having a JavaScript object as a parameter is used in many three.js functions. It makes it possible to support a large number of options without requiring a long list of parameters that must all be specified in some particular order. Instead, you only need to specify the options for which you want to provide non-default values, and you can specify those options by name, in any order.)

The main thing that you want to do with a renderer is render an image. For that, you also need a scene and a camera. To render an image of a given scene from the point of view of a given camera, call

```
renderer.render( scene, camera );
```

This is really the central command in any three.js application. (I should note that most of the examples that I have seen do not provide a canvas to the renderer; instead, they allow the renderer to create it. The canvas can then be obtained from the renderer and added to the page. Furthermore, the canvas typically fills the entire browser window. The sample program threejs/full-window.html shows how to do that. However, all of my other examples use an existing canvas, with the renderer constructor shown above.)

5.1.2 THREE.Object3D

A three.js scene graph is made up of objects of type THREE.Object3D (including objects that belong to subclasses of that class). Cameras, lights, and visible objects are all represented by subclasses of Object3D. In fact, THREE.Scene itself is also a subclass of Object3D.

Any Object3D contains a list of child objects, which are also of type Object3D. The child lists define the structure of the scene graph. If node and object are of type Object3D, then the method node.add(object) adds object to the list of children of node. The method node.remove(object) can be used to remove an object from the list.

A three.js scene graph must, in fact, be a tree. That is, every node in the graph has a unique parent node, except for the root node, which has no parent. An Object3D, obj, has a property obj.parent that points to the parent of obj in the scene graph, if any. You should never set this property directly. It is set automatically when the node is added to the child list of another node. If obj already has a parent when it is added as a child of node, then obj is first removed from the child list of its current parent before it is added to the child list of node.

The children of an Object3D, obj, are stored in a property named obj.children, which is an ordinary JavaScript array. However, you should always add and remove children of obj using the methods obj.add() and obj.remove().

To make it easy to duplicate parts of the structure of a scene graph, Object3D defines a clone() method. This method copies the node, including the recursive copying of the children of that node. This makes it easy to include multiple copies of the same structure in a scene graph:

```
let node = THREE.Object3D();
    .
    . // Add children to node.
    .
scene.add(node);
let nodeCopy1 = node.clone();
    .
    . // Modify nodeCopy1, maybe apply a transformation.
    .
scene.add(nodeCopy1)
let nodeCopy2 = node.clone();
    .
    . // Modify nodeCopy2, maybe apply a transformation.
    .
scene.add(nodeCopy2) ;
```

An Object3D, obj, has an associated transformation, which is given by properties obj.scale, obj.rotation, and obj.position. These properties represent a modeling transformation to be applied to the object and its children when the object is rendered. The object is first scaled, then rotated, then translated according to the values of these properties. (Transformations are actually more complicated than this, but we will keep things simple for now and will return to the topic later.)

The values of obj.scale and obj.position are objects of type THREE.Vector3. A Vector3 represents a vector or point in three dimensions. (There are similar classes THREE. Vector2 and THREE. Vector 4 for vectors in 2 and 4 dimensions.) A Vector 3 object can be constructed from three numbers that give the coordinates of the vector:

```
let v = new THREE.Vector3( 17, -3.14159, 42);
```

This object has properties $v.x$, $v.y$, and $v.z$ representing the coordinates. The properties can be set individually; for example: $v.x = 10$. They can also be set all at once, using the method $v.set(x, y, z)$. The Vector3 class also has many methods implementing vector operations such as addition, dot product, and cross product.

For an Object3D, the properties obj.scale.x, obj.scale.y, and obj.scale.z give the amount of scaling of the object in the x, y, and z directions. The default values, of course, are 1. Calling

```
obj.scale.set(2,2,2);
```

means that the object will be subjected to a uniform scaling factor of 2 when it is rendered. Setting

```
obj.scale.y = 0.5;
```

will shrink it to half-size in the y-direction only (assuming that obj.scale.x and obj.scale. z still have their default values).

Similarly, the properties obj.position.x, obj.position.y, and obj.position.z give the translation amounts that will be applied to the object in the x, y, and z directions when it is rendered. For example, since a camera is an Object3D, setting

```
camera.position.z = 20;
```

means that the camera will be moved from its default position at the origin to the point (0,0,20) on the positive z-axis. This modeling transformation on the camera becomes a viewing transformation when the camera is used to render a scene.

The object obj.rotation has properties obj.rotation.x, obj.rotation.y, and obj.rotation.z that represent rotations about the x -, y -, and z -axes. The angles are measured in radians. The object is rotated first about the x -axis, then about the y -axis, then about the z -axis. (It is possible to change this order.) The value of obj.rotation is not a vector. Instead, it belongs to a similar type, THREE.Euler, and the angles of rotation are called Euler angles.

5.1.3 Object, Geometry, Material

A visible object in three.js is made up of either points, lines, or triangles. An individual object corresponds to an OpenGL primitive such as GL_POINTS, GL_LINES, or GL_TRIANGLES (see Subsection 3.1.1). There are five classes to represent these possibilities: THREE.Points for points, THREE.Mesh for triangles, and three classes for lines: THREE.Line, which uses the GL_LINE_STRIP primitive; THREE.LineSegments, which uses the GL_LINES primitive; and THREE.LineLoop, which uses the GL_LINE_LOOP primitive.

A visible object is made up of some geometry plus a material that determines the appearance of that geometry. In three.js, the geometry and material of a visible object are themselves represented by JavaScript classes THREE.BufferGeometry and THREE.Material.

An object of type THREE.BufferGeometry can store vertex coordinates and their attributes. (In fact, the vertex coordinates are also considered to be an "attribute" of the geometry.) These values must be stored in a form suitable for use with the OpenGL functions glDrawArrays and glDrawElements (see Subsection 3.4.2). For JavaScript, this means that they must be stored in typed arrays. A typed array is similar to a normal JavaScript array, except that its length is fixed and it can only hold numerical values of a certain type. For example, a Float32Array holds 32 -bit floating point numbers, and a UInt16Array holds unsigned 16-bit integers. A typed array can be created with a constructor that specifies the length of the array. For example,

```
vertexCoords = new Float32Array(300); // Space for 300 numbers.
```

Alternatively, the constructor can take an ordinary JavaScript array of numbers as its parameter. This creates a typed array that holds the same numbers. For example,

```
data = new Float32Array( [ 1.3, 7, -2.89, 0, 3, 5.5 ] );
```

In this case, the length of data is six, and it contains copies of the numbers from the JavaScript array.

Specifying the vertices for a BufferGeometry is a multistep process. You need to create a typed array containing the coordinates of the vetices. Then you need to wrap that array inside an object of type THREE.BufferAttribute. Finally, you can add the attribute to the geometry. Here is an example:

```
let vertexCoords = new Float32Array([ 0,0,0, 1,0,0, 0,1,0 ]);
let vetexAttrib = new THREE.BufferAttribute(vertexCoords, 3);
let geometry = new THREE.BufferGeometry();
geometry.setAttribute( "position", vertexAttrib );
```

The second parameter to the BufferGeometry constructor is an integer that tells three.js the number of coordinates of each vertex. Recall that a vertex can be specified by 2 , 3, or 4 coordinates, and you need to specify how many numbers are provided in the array for each vertex. Turning to the setAttribute() function, a BufferGeometry can have attributes specifying color, normal vectors, and texture coordinates, as well as other custom attributes. The first parameter to setAttribute() is the name of the attribute. Here, "position" is the name of the attribute that specifies the coordinates, or position, of the vertices.

Similarly, to specify a color for each vertex, you can put the RGB components of the colors into a Float32Array, and use that to specify a value for the BufferGeometry attribute named "color".

For a specific example, suppose that we want to represent a primitive of type GL_POINTS, using a three.js object of type THREE.Points. Let's say we want 10000 points placed at random inside the unit sphere, where each point can have its own random color. Here is some code that creates the necessary BufferGeometry:

```
let pointsBuffer = new Float32Array( 30000 ); // 3 numbers per vertex!
let colorBuffer = new Float32Array( 30000 );
let i = 0;
while ( i < 10000 ) {
    let x = 2*Math.random() - 1;
    let y = 2*Math.random() - 1;
    let z = 2*Math.random() - 1;
    if ( x*x + y*y + z*z < 1 ) {
            // only use points inside the unit sphere
        pointsBuffer[3*i] = x;
        pointsBuffer[3*i+1] = y;
        pointsBuffer[3*i+2] = z;
        colorBuffer[3*i] = 0.25 + 0.75*Math.random();
        colorBuffer[3*i+1] = 0.25 + 0.75*Math.random();
        colorBuffer[3*i+2] = 0.25 + 0.75*Math.random();
        i++;
    }
}
let pointsGeom = new THREE.BufferGeometry();
pointsGeom.setAttribute("position",
                    new THREE.BufferAttribute(pointsBuffer,3));
pointsGeom.setAttribute("color",
                    new THREE.BufferAttribute(colorBuffer,3));
```

In three.js, to make some geometry into a visible object, we also need an appropriate material. For example, for an object of type THREE.Points, we can use a material of type

THREE.PointsMaterial, which is a subclass of Material. The material can specify the color and the size of the points, among other properties:

```
let pointsMat = new THREE.PointsMaterial( {
        color: "yellow",
        size: 2,
        sizeAttenuation: false
    } );
```

The parameter to the constructor is a JavaScript object whose properties are used to initialize the material. With the sizeAttenuation property set to false, the size is given in pixels; if it is true, then size represents the size in world coordinates and the point is scaled to reflect distance from the viewer. If the color is omitted, a default value of white is used. The default for size is 1 and for sizeAttenuation is true. The parameter to the constructor can be omitted entirely, to use all the defaults. A PointsMaterial is not affected by lighting; it simply shows the color specified by its color property.

It is also possible to assign values to properties of the material after the object has been created. For example,

```
let pointsMat = new THREE.PointsMaterial();
pointsMat.color = new THREE.Color("yellow");
pointsMat.size = 2;
pointsMat.sizeAttenuation = false;
```

Note that the color is set as a value of type THREE.Color, which is constructed from a string, "yellow". When the color property is set in the material constructor, the same conversion of string to color is done automatically.

Once we have the geometry and the material, we can use them to create the visible object, of type THREE.Points, and add it to a scene:

```
let sphereOfPoints = new THREE.Points( pointsGeom, pointsMat );
scene.add( sphereOfPoints );
```

This will show a cloud of yellow points. But we wanted each point to have its own color! Recall that the colors for the points are stored in the geometry, not in the material. We have to tell the material to use the colors from the geometry, not the material's own color property. This is done by setting the value of the material property vertexColors to true. So, we could create the material using

```
let pointsMat = new THREE.PointsMaterial( {
        color: "white",
        size: 2,
        sizeAttenuation: false,
        vertexColors: true
    } );
```

White is used here as the material color because the vertex colors are actually multiplied by the material color, not simply substituted for it.

The on-line demo c5/point-cloud.html shows an animated point cloud, where the user can choose between yellow points and randomly colored points.

The color parameter in the above material was specified by the string "yellow". Colors in three.js can be represented by values of type THREE.Color. The class THREE.Color represents an RGB color. A Color object *c* has properties *c.r*, *c.g*, and *c.b* giving the red, blue, and green color components as floating point numbers in the range from 0.0 to 1.0 . Note that there is no alpha component; three.js handles transparency separately from color.

There are several ways to construct a THREE. Color object. The constructor can take three parameters giving the RGB components as real numbers in the range 0.0 to 1.0 . It can take a single string parameter giving the color as a CSS color string, like those used in the 2D canvas graphics API; examples include "white", "red", " rgb(255,0,0) ", and "#FF0000". Or the color constructor can take a single integer parameter in which each color component is given as an eight-bit field in the integer. Usually, an integer that is used to represent a color in this way is written as a hexadecimal literal, beginning with "0x". Examples include 0xff0000 for red, 0x00ff00 for green, 0x0000ff for blue, and 0x007050 for a dark blue-green. Here are some examples of using color constructors:

```
let c1 = new THREE.Color("skyblue");
let c2 = new THREE.Color(1,1,0); // yellow
let c3 = new THREE.Color(0x98fb98); // pale green
```

In many contexts, such as the THREE.Points constructor, three.js will accept a string or integer where a color is required; the string or integer will be fed through the Color constructor. As another example, a WebGLRenderer object has a "clear color" property that is used as the background color when the renderer renders a scene. This property could be set using any of the following commands:

```
renderer.setClearColor( new THREE.Color(0.6, 0.4, 0.1) );
renderer.setClearColor( "darkgray" );
renderer.setClearColor( 0x99BBEE );
```

Turning next to lines, an object of type THREE.Line represents a a line strip-what would be a primitive of the type called GL_LINE_STRIP in OpenGL. To get the same strip of connected line segments, plus a line back to the starting vertex, we can use an object of type THREE. LineLoop. For the outline of a triangle, for example, we could provide a BufferGeometry holding coordinates for three points and use a LineLoop.

We will also need a material. For lines, the material can be represented by an object of type THREE.LineBasicMaterial. As usual, the parameter for the constructor is a JavaScript object, whose properties can include color and linewidth. For example:

```
let lineMat = new THREE.LineBasicMaterial( {
    color: 0xA000A0, // purple; the default is white
    linewidth: 2 // 2 pixels; the default is 1
} );
```

(The three.js documentation says that the linewidth property might not be respected. Curiously, on my computer, it was respected by a WebGL1Renderer but not by a WebGLRenderer.)

As with points, it is possible to specify a different color for each purpose by adding a "color" attribute to the geometry and setting the value of the vertexColors material property to true. Here is a complete example that makes a triangle with vertices colored red, green, and blue:

```
let positionBuffer = new Float32Array([
        -2, -2, // Coordinates for first vertex.
            2, -2, // Coordinates for second vertex.
            0, 2 // Coordinates for third vertex.
    ]);
let colorBuffer = new Float32Array([
        1, 0, 0, // Color for first vertex (red).
        0, 1, 0, // Color for second vertex (green).
        0, 0, 1 // Color for third vertex (blue).
    ]);
let lineGeometry = new THREE.BufferGeometry();
lineGeometry.setAttribute(
        "position",
```

```
        new THREE.BufferAttribute(positionBuffer,2)
    );
lireGeometry.setAttribute(
        "color",
        new THREE.BufferAttribute(colorBuffer,3)
    );

let      lineMaterial      =      new      THREE.LineBasicMaterial(      {
        linewidth:                                                        3,
        vertexColors:                                                  true
    }                                                                    );
let  triangle  =  new  THREE.LineLoop(  lineGeometry,  lineMaterial  );
scene.add(triangle);
```

This produces the image:

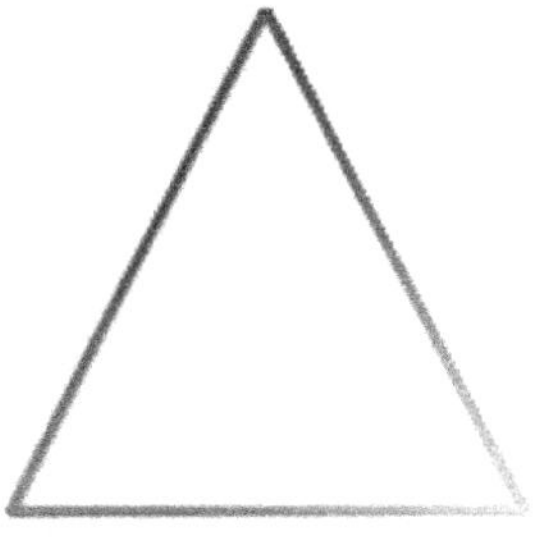

The "Basic" in LineBasicMaterial indicates that this material uses basic colors that do not require lighting to be visible and are not affected by lighting. This is generally what you want for lines.

A mesh object in three.js corresponds to the OpenGL primitive GL_TRIANGLES. The geometry object for a mesh must specify which vertices are part of which triangles. We will see how to do that in the next section. However, three.js comes with classes to represent common mesh geometries, such as a sphere, a cylinder, and a torus. For these built-in classes, you just need to call a constructor to create the appropriate geometry. For example, the class THREE. CylinderGeometry represents the geometry for a cylinder, and its constructor takes the form

```
new     THREE.CylinderGeometry(radiusTop,     radiusBottom,     height,
    radiusSegments, heightSegments, openEnded, thetaStart, thetaLength)
```

The geometry created by this constructor represents an approximation for a cylinder that has its axis lying along the y-axis. It extends from from - height /2 to height /2 along that axis. The radius of its circular top is radiusTop and of its bottom is radiusBottom. The two radii don't have to be the same; when the are different, you get a truncated cone rather than a cylinder as such. Using a value of zero for radiusTop makes an actual cone. The parameters radiusSegments and heightSegments give the number of subdivisions around the circumference of the cylinder and along its length respectively - what are called slices and stacks in the GLUT library for OpenGL. The parameter openEnded is a boolean value that indicates whether the top and bottom of the cylinder are to be drawn; use the value true to get an open-ended tube. Finally, the last two parameters allow you to make a partial cylinder. Their values are given as angles, measured in radians, about the y-axis. Only the part of the cylinder beginning at thetaStart and ending at thetaStart plus thetaLength is rendered. For example, if thetaLength is Math.PI, you will get a half-cylinder.

The large number of parameters to the constructor gives a lot of flexibility. The parameters are all optional. The default value for each of the first three parameters is one. The default for radiusSegments is 8 , which gives a poor approximation for a smooth cylinder. Leaving out the last three parameters will give a complete cylinder, closed at both ends.

Other standard mesh geometries are similar. Here are some constructors, listing all parameters (but keep in mind that most of the parameters are optional):

```
new THREE.BoxGeometry(width, height, depth,
    widthSegments, heightSegments, depthSegments)
new THREE.PlaneGeometry(width, height, widthSegments, heightSegments)
new THREE.RingGeometry(innerRadius, outerRadius, thetaSegments,
phiSegments,
    thetaStart, thetaLength)
new THREE.ConeGeometry(radiusBottom, height, radiusSegments,
    heightSegments, openEnded, thetaStart, thetaLength)
new THREE.SphereGeometry(radius, widthSegments, heightSegments,
    phiStart, phiLength, thetaStart, thetaLength)
new THREE.TorusGeometry(radius, tube, radialSegments, tubularSegments,
arc)
```

The class BoxGeometry represents the geometry of a rectangular box centered at the origin. Its constructor has three parameters to give the size of the box in each direction; their default value is one. The last three parameters give the number of subdivisions in each direction, with a default of one; values greater than one will cause the faces of the box to be subdivided into smaller triangles.

The class PlaneGeometry represents the geometry of a rectangle lying in the xy-plane, centered at the origin. Its parameters are similar to those for a cube. A RingGeometry represents an annulus, that is, a disk with a smaller disk removed from its center. The ring lies in the xy-plane, with its center at the origin. You should always specify the inner and outer radii of the ring.

The constructor for ConeGeometry has exactly the same form and effect as the constructor for CylinderGeometry, with the radiusTop set to zero. That is, it constructs a cone with axis along the y -axis and centered at the origin.

For SphereGeometry, all parameters are optional. The constructor creates a sphere centered at the origin, with axis along the y-axis. The first parameter, which gives the radius of the sphere, has a default of one. The next two parameters give the numbers of slices and stacks, with default values 32 and 16. The last four parameters allow you to make a piece of a sphere; the default values give a complete sphere. The four parameters are angles measured in radians. phiStart and phiLength are measured in angles around the equator and give the extent in longitude of the spherical shell that is generated. For example,

```
new THREE.SphereGeometry( 5, 32, 16, 0, Math.PI )
```

creates the geometry for the "western hemisphere" of a sphere. The last two parameters are angles measured along a line of latitude from the north pole of the sphere to the south pole. For example, to get the sphere's "northern hemisphere":

```
new THREE.SphereGeometry( 5, 32, 16, 0, 2*Math.PI, 0, Math.PI/2)
```

For TorusGeometry, the constructor creates a torus lying in the xy-plane, centered at the origin, with the z-axis passing through its hole. The parameter radius is the distance from the center of the torus to the center of the torus's tube, while tube is the radius of the tube. The next two parameters give the number of subdivisions in each direction. The last parameter, arc, allows you to make just part of a torus. It is an angle between 0 and 2* Math.PI, measured along the circle at the center of the tube.

There are also geometry classes representing the regular polyhedra: THREE. TetrahedronGeometry, THREE.OctahedronGeometry, THREE.DodecahedronGeometry, and THREE.IcosahedronGeometry. (For a cube use a BoxGeometry.) The constructors for these four classes take two parameters. The first specifies the size of the polyedron, with a default of 1 . The size is given as the radius of the sphere that contains the polyhedron.

The second parameter is an integer called detail. The default value, 0 , gives the actual regular polyhedron. Larger values add detail by adding additional faces. As the detail increases, the polyhedron becomes a better approximation for a sphere. This is easier to understand with an illustration:

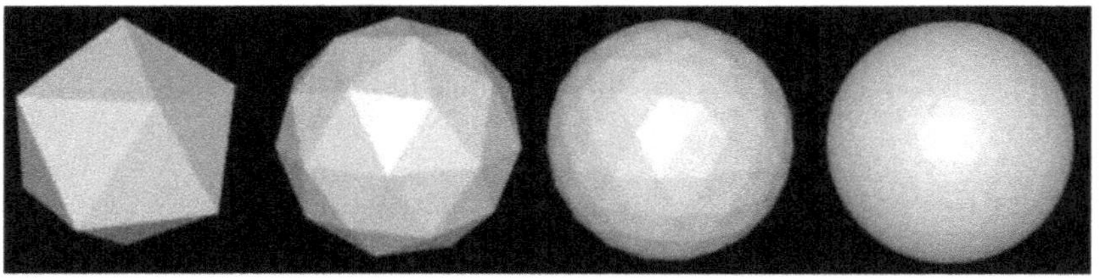

The image shows four mesh objects that use icosahedral geometries with detail parameter equal to 0,1,2, and 3 .

To create a mesh object, you need a material as well as a geometry. There are several kinds of material suitable for mesh objects, including THREE.MeshBasicMaterial, THREE.MeshLambertMaterial, and THREE.MeshPhongMaterial. (There are also two newer mesh materials, THREE.MeshStandardMaterial and THREE.MeshPhysicalMaterial, that implement techniques associated with physically based rendering, an approach to improved rendering that has become popular. However, I will not cover them here.)

A MeshBasicMaterial represents a color that is not affected by lighting; it looks the same whether or not there are lights in the scene, and it is not shaded, giving it a flat rather than 3D appearance. The other two classes represent materials that need to be lit to be seen. They implement models of lighting known as Lambert shading and Phong shading. The major difference is that MeshPhongMaterial has a specular color but MeshLambertMaterial does not. Both can have diffuse and emissive colors. For all three material classes, the constructor has one parameter, a JavaScript object that specifies values for properties of the material. For example:

```
let mat = new THREE.MeshPhongMaterial( {
        color: 0xbbbb00, // reflectivity for diffuse and ambient light
        emissive: 0, // emission color; this is the default (black)
        specular: 0x070707, // reflectivity for specular light
        shininess: 50 // controls size of specular highlights
    } );
```

This example shows the four color parameters for a Phong material. The parameters have the same meaning as the five material properties in OpenGL (Subsection 4.1.1). A Lambert material lacks specular and shininess, and a basic mesh material has only the color parameter.

There are a few other material properties that you might need to set in the constructor. Except for flatShading, these apply to all three kinds of mesh material:

- vertexColors - a boolean property that can be set to true to use vertex colors from the geometry. The default is false.
- wireframe - a boolean value that indicates whether the mesh should be drawn as a wireframe model, showing only the outlines of its faces. The default is false. A true value works best with MeshBasicMaterial.
- wireframeLinewidth - the width of the lines used to draw the wireframe, in pixels. The default is 1 . (Non-default values might not be respected.)
- visible - a boolean value that controls whether the object on which it is used is rendered or not, with a default of true.
- side - has value THREE.FrontSide, THREE.BackSide, or THREE.DoubleSide, with the default being THREE.FrontSide. This determines whether faces of the mesh are drawn or not, depending on which side of the face is visible. With the default value, THREE.FrontSide, a face is drawn only if it is being viewed from the front. THREE.DoubleSide will draw it whether it is viewed from the front or from the back, and THREE.BackSide only if it is viewed from the back. For closed objects, such as a cube or a complete sphere, the default value makes sense, at least as long as the viewer is outside of the object. For a plane, an open tube, or a partial sphere, the value should be set to THREE.DoubleSide. Otherwise, parts of the object that should be in view won't be drawn.
- flatShading - a boolean value, with the default being false. This works only for MeshPhongMaterial. For an object that is supposed to look "faceted," with flat sides, it is important to set this property to true. That would be the case, for example, for a cube or for a cylinder with a small number of sides.

As an example, let's make a shiny, blue-green, open, five-sided tube with flat sides:

```
let mat = new THREE.MeshPhongMaterial( {
        color: 0x0088aa,
        specular: 0x003344,
        shininess: 100,
        flatShading: true, // for flat-looking sides
        side: THREE.DoubleSide // for drawing the inside of the tube
    } );
```

```
let geom = new THREE.CylinderGeometry(3,3,10,5,1,true);
let obj = new THREE.Mesh(geom,mat);
scene.add(obj);
```

The on-line demo c5/mesh-objects.html lets you view a variety of three.js mesh objects with several different materials.

The demo can show a wireframe version of an object overlaid on a solid version. In three.js, the wireframe and solid versions are actually two objects that use the same geometry but different materials. Drawing two objects at exactly the same depth can be a problem for the depth test. You might remember from Subsection 3.4.1 that OpenGL uses polygon offset to solve the problem. In three.js, you can apply polygon offset to a material. In the demos, this is done for the solid materials that are shown at the same time as wireframe materials. For example,

```
mat = new THREE.MeshLambertMaterial({
    polygonOffset: true,
    polygonOffsetUnits: 1,
    polygonOffsetFactor: 1,
    color: "yellow",
    side: THREE.DoubleSide


});
```

The settings shown here for polygonOffset, polygonOffsetUnits, and polygonOffsetFactor will increase the depth of the object that uses this material slightly so that it doesn't interfere with the wireframe version of the same object.

One final note: You don't always need to make new materials and geometries to make new objects. You can reuse the same materials and geometries in multiple objects.

5.1.4 Lights

Compared to geometries and materials, lights are easy! Three.js has several classes to represent lights. Light classes are subclasses of THREE.Object3D. A light object can be added to a scene and will then illuminate objects in the scene. We'll look at directional lights, point lights, ambient lights, and spotlights.

The class THREE. DirectionalLight represents light that shines in parallel rays from a given direction, like the light from the sun. The position property of a directional light gives the direction from which the light shines. (This is the same position property, of type Vector3, that all scene graph objects have, but the meaning is different for directional lights.) Note that the light shines from the given position towards the origin. The default position is the vector (0,1,0), which gives a light shining down the *y*-axis. The constructor for this class has two parameters:

```
new THREE.DirectionalLight( color, intensity )
```

where color specifies the color of the light, given as a THREE. Color object, or as a hexadecimal integer, or as a CSS color string. Lights do not have separate diffuse and specular colors, as they do in OpenGL. The intensity is a non-negative number that controls the brightness of the light, with larger values making the light brighter. A light with intensity zero gives no light at all. The parameters are optional. The default for color is white (0 xffffff) and for intensity is 1 . The intensity can be greater than 1 , but values less than 1 are usually preferable, to avoid having too much illumination in the scene.

Suppose that we have a camera on the positive *z*-axis, looking towards the origin, and we would like a light that shines in the same direction that the camera is looking. We can use a directional light whose position is on the positive *z*-axis:

```
let light = new THREE.DirectionalLight(); // default white light
light.position.set( 0, 0, 1 );
scene.add(light);
```

The class THREE.PointLight represents a light that shines in all directions from a point. The location of the point is given by the light's position property. The constructor has three optional parameters:

```
new THREE.PointLight( color, intensity, cutoff )
```

The first two parameters are the same as for a directional light, with the same defaults. The cutoff is a non-negative number. If the value is zero-which is the default-then the illumination from the light extends to infinity, and intensity does not decrease with distance. While this is not physically realistic, it generally works well in practice. If cutoff is greater than zero, then the intensity falls from a maximum value at the light's position down to an intensity of zero at a distance of cutoff from the light; the light has no effect on objects that are at a distance greater than cutoff. This falloff of light intensity with distance is referred to as attenuation of the light source.

A third type of light is THREE.AmbientLight. This class exists to add ambient light to a scene. An ambient light has only a color:

```
new THREE.AmbientLight( color )
```

Adding an ambient light object to a scene adds ambient light of the specified color to the scene. The color components of an ambient light should be rather small to avoid washing out colors of objects.

For example, suppose that we would like a yellowish point light at (10,30,15) whose illumination falls off with distance from that point, out to a distance of 100 units. We also want to add a bit of yellow ambient light to the scene:

```
let light = new THREE.PointLight( 0xffffcc, 1, 100 );
light.position.set( 10, 30, 15 );
scene.add(light);
scene.add( new THREE.AmbientLight(0x111100) );
```

The fourth type of light, THREE.SpotLight, is something new for us. An object of that type represents a spotlight, which is similar to a point light, except that instead of shining in all directions, a spotlight only produces a cone of light. The vertex of the cone is located at the position of the light. By default, the axis of the cone points from that location towards the origin (so unless you change the direction of the axis, you should move the position of the light away from the origin). The constructor adds two parameters to those for a point light:

```
new THREE.SpotLight( color, intensity, cutoff, coneAngle, exponent )
```

The coneAngle is a number between 0 and Math.PI/2 that determines the size of the cone of light. It is the angle between the axis of the cone and the side of the cone. The default value is Math.PI/3. The exponent is a non-negative number that determines how fast the intensity of the light decreases as you move from the axis of the cone toward the side. The default value, 10, gives a reasonable result. An exponent of zero gives no falloff at all, so that objects at all distances from the axis are evenly illuminated.

The technique for setting the direction of a three.js spotlight is a little odd, but it does make it easy to control the direction. An object spot of type SpotLight has a property named spot.target. The target is a scene graph node. The cone of light from the spotlight is pointed in the direction from spotlight's position towards the target's position. When a spotlight is first created, its target is a new, empty Object3D, with position at (0,0,0). However, you can set the target to be any object in the scene graph, which will make the spotlight shine towards that object. For three.js to calculate the spotlight direction, a target whose position is anything other than the origin must actually be a node in the scene graph. For example, suppose we want a spotlight located at the point (0,0,5) and pointed towards the point (2,2,0):

```
spotlight = new THREE.SpotLight();
spotlight.position.set(0,0,5);
spotlight.target.position.set(2,2,0);
scene.add(spotlight);
scene.add(spotlight.target);
```

The interaction of spotlights with material illustrates an important difference between Phong and Lambert shading. With a MeshLambertMaterial, the lighting equation is applied at the vertices of a primitive, and the vertex colors computed by that equation are then interpolated to calculate colors for the pixels in the primitive. With MeshPhongMaterial, on the other hand, the lighting equation is applied at each individual pixel. The following illustration shows what can happen when we shine a spotlight onto a square that was created using THREE.PlaneGeometry:

Phong Shading No subdivision

Lambert Shading No subdivision

Lambert Shading 3 subdivisions

Lambert Shading 10 subdivisions

For the two squares on the left, the square was not subdivided; it is made up of two triangular faces. The square at the far left, which uses Phong shading, shows the expected spotlight effect. The spotlight is pointed at the center of the square. Note how the illumination falls off with distance from the center. When I used the same square and spotlight with Lambert shading in the second picture, I got no illumination at all! The vertices of the the square lie outside the cone of light from the spotlight. When the lighting equation is applied, the vertices are black, and the black color of the vertices is then applied to all the pixels in the square.

For the third and fourth squares in the illustration, plane geometries with horizontal and vertical subdivisions were used with Lambert shading. In the third picture, the square is divided into three subdivisions in each direction, giving 18 triangles, and the lighting equation is applied only at the vertices of those triangles. The result is still a very poor approximation for the correct illumination. In the fourth square, with 10 subdivisions in each direction, the approximation is better but still not perfect.

The upshot is, if you want an object to be properly illuminated by a spotlight, use a MeshPhongMaterial on the object, even if it has no specular reflection. A MeshLambertMaterial will only give acceptable results if the faces of the object are very small.

5.1.5 A Modeling Example

In the rest of this chapter, we will go much deeper into three.js, but you already know enough to build 3D models from basic geometric objects. An example is in the sample program threejs/diskworld-1.html, which shows a very simple model of a car driving around the edge of a cylindrical base. The car has rotating tires. The diskworld is shown in the picture on the left below. The picture on the right shows one of the axles from the car, with a tire on each end.

I will discuss some of the code that is used to build these models. If you want to experiment with your own models, you can use the program threejs/modeling-starter.html as a starting point.

To start with something simple, let's look at how to make a tree from a brown cylinder and a green cone. I use an Object3D to represent the tree as a whole, so that I can treat it as a unit. The two geometric objects are added as children of the Object3D.

```
let tree = new THREE.Object3D();
let trunk = new THREE.Mesh(
    new THREE.CylinderGeometry(0.2,0.2,1,16,1),
    new THREE.MeshLambertMaterial({
        color: 0x885522
    })
);
trunk.position.y = 0.5; // move base up to origin
let leaves = new THREE.Mesh(
    new THREE.ConeGeometry(.7,2,16,3),
    new THREE.MeshPhongMaterial({
        color: 0x00BB00,
        specular: 0x002000,
        shininess: 5
    })
);
leaves.position.y = 2; // move bottom of cone to top of trunk
tree.add(trunk);
tree.add(leaves);
```

The trunk is a cylinder with height equal to 1 . Its axis lies along the *y*-axis, and it is centered at the origin. The plane of the diskworld lies in the *xz*-plane, so I want to move the bottom of the trunk onto that plane. This is done by setting the value of trunk.position.y, which represents a translation to be applied to the trunk. Remember that objects have their own modeling coordinate system. The properties of objects that specify transformations, such as trunk.position, transform the object in that coordinate system. In this case, the trunk is part of a larger, compound object that represents the whole tree. When the scene is rendered, the trunk is first transformed by its own modeling transformation. It is then further transformed by any modeling transformation that is applied to the tree as a whole. (This type of hierarchical modeling was first covered in Subsection 2.4.1.)

Once we have a tree object, it can be added to the model that represents the diskworld. In the program, the model is an object of type Object3D named diskworldModel. The model will contain several trees, but the trees don't have to be constructed individually. I can make additional trees by cloning the one that I have already created. For example:

```
tree.position.set(-1.5,0,2);
tree.scale.set(0.7,0.7,0.7);
diskworldModel.add( tree.clone() );
```

```
tree.position.set(-1,0,5.2);
tree.scale.set(0.25,0.25,0.25);
diskworldModel.add( tree.clone() );
```

This adds two trees to the model, with different sizes and positions. When the tree is cloned, the clone gets its own copies of the modeling transformation properties, position and scale. Changing the values of those properties in the original tree object does not affect the clone.

Lets turn to a more complicated object, the axle and wheels. I start by creating a wheel, using a torus for the tire and using three copies of a cylinder for the spokes. In this case, instead of making a new Object3D to hold all the components of the wheel, I add the cylinders as children of the torus. Remember that any screen graph node in three.js can have child nodes.

```
let wheel = new THREE.Mesh( // the tire; spokes will be added as
children
    new THREE.TorusGeometry(0.75, 0.25, 16, 32),
    new THREE.MeshLambertMaterial({ color: 0x0000A0 })
);
let yellow = new THREE.MeshPhongMaterial({
        color: 0xffff00,
        specular: 0x101010,
        shininess: 16
    });
let cylinder = new THREE.Mesh( // a cylinder with height 1 and diameter
1
    new THREE.CylinderGeometry(0.5,0.5,1,32,1),
    yellow
);
cylinder.scale.set(0.15,1.2,0.15); // Make it thin and tall for use as
a spoke.
wheel.add( cylinder.clone() ); // Add a copy of the cylinder.
cylinder.rotation.z = Math.PI/3; // Rotate it for the second spoke.
wheel.add( cylinder.clone() );
cylinder.rotation.z = -Math.PI/3; // Rotate it for the third spoke.
wheel.add( cylinder.clone() );
```

Once I have the wheel model, I can use it along with one more cylinder to make the axle. For the axle, I use a cylinder lying along the z-axis. The wheel lies in the xy-plane. It is facing in the correct direction, but it lies in the center of the axle. To get it into its correct position at the end of the axle, it just has to be translated along the z-axis.

```
axleModel = new THREE.Object3D(); // A model containing two wheels and
an axle.
cylinder.scale.set(0.2,4.3,0.2); // Scale the cylinder for use as an
axle.
cylinder.rotation.set(Math.PI/2,0,0); // Rotate its axis onto the z-
axis.
axleModel.add( cylinder );
wheel.position.z = 2; // Wheels are positioned at the two ends of the
axle.
axleModel.add( wheel.clone() );
wheel.position.z = -2;
axleModel.add( wheel );
```

Note that for the second wheel, I add the original wheel model rather than a clone. There is no need to make an extra copy. With the axleModel in hand, I can build the car from two copies of the axle plus some other components.

The diskworld can be animated. To implement the animation, properties of the appropriate scene graph nodes are modified before each frame of the animation is rendered. For example, to make the wheels on the car rotate, the rotation of each axle about its z-axis is increased in each frame:

```
carAxle1.rotation.z += 0.05;
carAxle2.rotation.z += 0.05;
```

This changes the modeling transformation that will be applied to the axles when they are rendered. In its own coordinate system, the central axis of an axle lies along the z-axis. The rotation about the z-axis rotates the axle, with its attached tires, about its axis.

For the full details of the sample program, see the source code.

5.2 Building Objects

In three.js, a visible object is constructed from a geometry and a material. We have seen how to create simple geometries that are suitable for point and line primitives, and we have encountered a variety of standard mesh geometries, such as THREE.

CylinderGeometry and THREE.IcosahedronGeometry, that use the GL_TRIANGLES primitive. In this section, we will see how to create new mesh geometries from scratch. We'll also look at some of the other support that three.js provides for working with objects and materials.

5.2.1 Polygonal Meshes and IFSs

A mesh in three.js is what we called a polygonal mesh in Section 3.4, although in a three.js mesh, all of the polygons must be triangles. There are two ways to draw polygonal meshes in WebGL. One uses the function glDrawArrays(), which requires just a list of vertices. The other uses the representation that we called an indexed face set (IFS), which is drawn using the function glDrawElements(). In addition to a list of vertices, an IFS uses a list of face indices to specify the triangles. We will look at both methods, using this pyramid as an example:

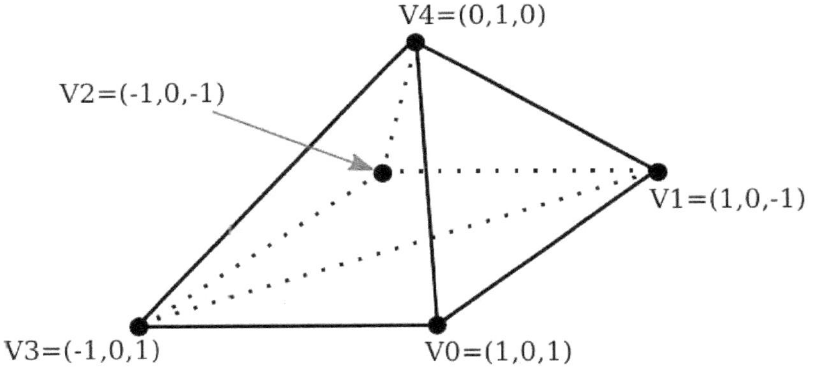

Note that the bottom face of the pyramid, which is a square, has to be divided into two triangles in order for the pyramid to be represented as a mesh geometry. The vertices are numbered from 0 to 4 . A triangular face can be specified by the three numbers that give the vertex numbers of the vertices of that triangle. As usual, the vertices of a triangle should be specified in counterclockwise order when viewed from the front, that is, from outside the pyramid. Here is the data that we need.

VERTEX COORDINATES:

Vertex 0:	1,0, 1
Vertex 1:	1,0, -1
Vertex 2:	−1,0, -1

Vertex 3:	−1,0,	1
Vertex 4:	0,	1,

FACE INDICES:

Face 1:	3,	2,	1
Face 2:	3,	1,	0
Face 3:	3,	0,	4
Face 4:	0,	1,	4
Face 5:	1,	2,	4
Face 6:	2,	3,	4

A basic polygonal mesh representation does not use face indices. Instead, it specifies each triangle by listing the coordinates of the vertices. This requires nine numbers - three numbers per vertex-for the three vertices of the triangle. Since a vertex can be shared by several triangles, there is some redundancy. For the pyramid, the coordinates for a vertex will be repeated three or four times.

A three.js mesh object requires a geometry and a material. The geometry is an object of type THREE.BufferedGeometry, which has a "position" attribute that holds the coordinates of the vertices that are used in the mesh. The attribute uses a typed array that holds the coordinates of the vertices of the triangles that make up the mesh. Geometry for the pyramid can be created like this:

```
let pyramidVertices = new Float32Array( [
            // Data for the pyramidGeom "position" attribute.
            // Contains the x,y,z coordinates for the vertices.
            // Each group of three numbers is a vertex;
            // each group of three vertices is one face.
        -1,0,1, -1,0,-1, 1,0,-1, // First triangle in the base.
        -1,0,1, 1,0,-1, 1,0,1, // Second triangle in the base.
        -1,0,1, 1,0,1, 0,1,0, // Front face.
            1,0,1, 1,0,-1, 0,1,0, // Right face.
```

```
            1,0,-1, -1,0,-1, 0,1,0, // Back face.
        -1,0,-1, -1,0,1, 0,1,0 // Left face.
    ] );
let pyramidGeom = new THREE.BufferGeometry();
pyramidGeom.setAttribute("position",
            new THREE.BufferAttribute(pyramidVertices,3) );
```

When this geometry is used with a Lambert or Phong material, normal vectors are required for the vertices. If the geometry has no normal vectors, Lambert and Phong materials will appear black. The normal vectors for a mesh have to be stored in another attribute of the BufferedGeometry. The name of the attribute is "normal", and it holds a normal vector for each vertex in the "position" attribute. It could be created in the same way that the "position" attribute is created, but a BufferedGeometry object includes a method for calculating normal vectors. For the pyramidGeom, we can simply call

```
pyramidGeom.computeVertexNormals();
```

For a basic polygonal mesh, this will create normal vectors that are perpendicular to the faces. When several faces share a vertex, that vertex will have a different normal vector for each face. This will produce flat-looking faces, which are appropriate for a polyhedron, whose sides are in fact flat. It is not appropriate if the polygonal mesh is being used to approximate a smooth surface. In that case, we should be using normal vectors that are perpendicular to the surface, which would mean creating the "normal" attribute by hand. (See Subsection 4.1.3.)

Once we have the geometry for our pyramid, we can use it in a three.js mesh object by combining it with, say, a yellow Lambert material:

```
pyramid = new THREE.Mesh(
        pyramidGeom,
        new THREE.MeshLambertMaterial({ color: "yellow" })
    );
```

But the pyramid would look a little boring with just one color. It is possible to use different materials on different faces of a mesh. For that to work, the vertices in the geometry must be divided into groups. The addGroup () method in the BufferedGeometry class is used to create the groups. The vertices in the geometry are numbered 0,1,2, ..., according their sequence in the "position" attribute. (This is not the same numbering used above.) The addGroup()
method takes three parameters: the number of the first vertex in the group, the number of vertices in the group, and a material index. The material index is an integer that

determines which material will be applied to the group. If you are using groups, it is important to put all of the vertices into groups. Here is how groups can be created for the pyramid:

```
pyramidGeom.addGroup(0,6,0); // The base (2 triangles)
pyramidGeom.addGroup(6,3,1); // Front face.
pyramidGeom.addGroup(9,3,2); // Right face.
pyramidGeom.addGroup(12,3,3); // Back face.
pyramidGeom.addGroup(15,3,4); // Left face.
```

To apply different materials to different groups, the materials should be put into an array. The material index of a group is an index into that array.

```
pyramidMaterialArray= [
            // Array of materials, for use as pyramids's material.
        new THREE.MeshLambertMaterial( { color: 0xffffff } ),
        new THREE.MeshLambertMaterial( { color: 0x99ffff } ),
        new THREE.MeshLambertMaterial( { color: 0xff99ff } ),
        new THREE.MeshLambertMaterial( { color: 0xffff99 } ),
        new THREE.MeshLambertMaterial( { color: 0xff9999 } )
    ];
```

This array can be passed as the second parameter to the THREE.Mesh constructor, where a single material would ordinarily be used.

```
pyramid = new THREE.Mesh( pyramidGeom, pyramidMaterialArray );
```

(But note that you can still use a single material on a mesh, even if the mesh geometry uses groups.)

A THREE.BoxGeometry comes with groups that make it possible to assign a different material to each face. The sample program threejs/vertex-groups.html uses the code from this section to create a pyramid, and it displays both the pyramid and a cube, using multiple materials on each object. Here's what they look like:

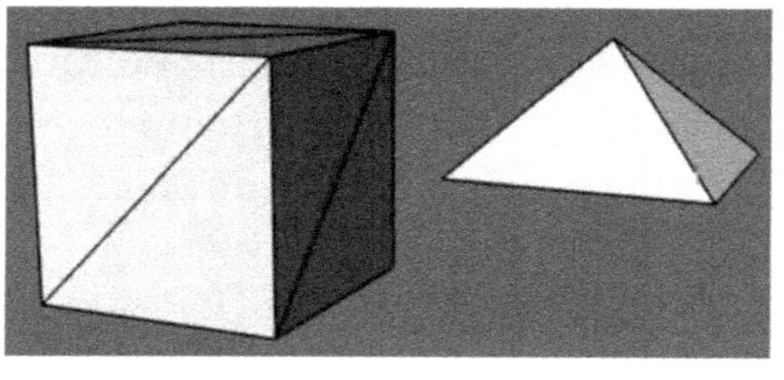

There is another way to assign different colors to different vertices. A BufferedGeometry can have an attribute named "color" that specifies a color for each vertex. The "color" attribute uses an array containing a set of three RGB component values for each vertex. The vertex colors are ignored by default. To use them, the geometry must be combined with a material in which the vertexColors property is set to true. Here is how vertex colors could be used to color the sides of the pyramid:

```
pyramidGeom.setAttribute(
            "color",
            new THREE.BufferAttribute( new Float32Array([
                    1,1,1, 1,1,1, 1,1,1, // Base vertices are white
                        1,1,1, 1,1,1, 1,1,1,
                        1,0,0, 1,0,0, 1,0,0, // Front face vertices are
red,
                        0,1,0, 0,1,0, 0,1,0, // Right face vertices are
green,
                        0,0,1, 0,0,1, 0,0,1, // Back face vertices are
blue,
                        1,1,0, 1,1,0, 1,1,0 // Left face vertices are
yellow.
                ]), 3)
    );
pyramid = new THREE.Mesh(
        pyramidGeom,
        new THREE.MeshLambertMaterial({
                color: "white",
                vertexColors: true
            })
    );
```

The color components of the vertex colors from the geometry are actually multiplied by the color components of the color in the Lambert material. It makes sense for that color to be white, with color components equal to one; in that case the vertex colors are not modified by the material color.

In this example, each face of the pyramid is a solid color. There is a lot of redundancy in the color array for the pyramid, because a color must be specified for every vertex, even if all of the vertex colors for a given face are the same. In fact, it's not required that all of the vertices of a face have the same color. If they are assigned different colors, colors will be interpolated from the vertices to the interior of the face. As an example, in this image, a random vertex color was specified for each vertex of an icosahedral approximation for a sphere:

The image is from a demo in the online version of this section. The demo can run two somewhat silly animations; the vertex colors and the vertex positions can be animated.

The glDrawElements() function is used to avoid the redundancy of the basic polygonal mesh representation. It uses the indexed face set pattern, which requires an array of face indices to specify the vertices for the faces of the mesh. In that array, a vertex is specified by a single number, rather than repeating all of the coordinates and other data for that vertex. Note that a given vertex number refers to all of the data for that vertex: vertex coordinates, normal vector, vertex color, and any other data that are provided in attributes of the geometry. Suppose that two faces share a vertex. If that vertex has a different normal vector, or a different value for some other attribute, in the two faces, then that vector will need to occur twice in the attribute arrays. The two occurrences can be combined only if the vertex has identical properties in the two faces. The IFS representation is most suitable for a polygonal mesh that is being used as an approximation for a smooth surface, since in that case a vertex has the same normal vector for all of the vertices in which it occurs. It can also be appropriate for an object that uses a MeshBasicMaterial, since normal vectors are not used with that type of material.

To use the IFS pattern with a BufferedGeometry, you need to provide a face index array for the geometry. The array is specified by the geometry's setIndex() method. The parameter can be an ordinary JavaScript array of integers. For our pyramid example the "position" attribute of the geometry would contain each vertex just once, and the face index array would refer to a vertex by its position in that list of vertices:

```
pyramidVertices = new Float32Array( [
            1, 0, 1, // vertex number 0
            1, 0, -1, // vertex number 1
        -1, 0, -1, // vertex number 2
        -1, 0, 1, // vertex number 3
            0, 1, 0 // vertex number 4
    ] );
pyramidFaceIndexArray = [
        3, 2, 1, // First triangle in the base.
        3, 1, 0, // Second Triangle in the base.
        3, 0, 4, // Front face.
        0, 1, 4, // Right face.
        1, 2, 4, // Back face.
        2, 3, 4 // Left face.
    ];
pyramidGeom = new THREE.BufferGeometry();
pyramidGeom.setAttribute("position",
                new THREE.BufferAttribute(pyramidVertices,3) );
pyramidGeom.setIndex( pyramidFaceIndexArray );
```

This would work with a MeshBasicMaterial. The sample program threejs/vertex-groupsindexed.html is a variation on threejs/vertex-groups.html that uses this approach.

The computeVertexNormals() method can still be used for a BufferedGeometry that has an index array. To compute a normal vector for a vertex, it finds all of the faces in which that vertex occurs. For each of those faces, it computes a vector perpendicular to the face. Then it averages those vectors to get the vertex normal. (I will note if you tried this for our pyramid, it would look pretty bad. It's really only appropriate for smooth surfaces.)

5.2.2 Curves and Surfaces

In addition to letting you build indexed face sets, three.js has support for working with curves and surfaces that are defined mathematically. Some of the possibilities are illustrated in the sample program threejs/curves-and-surfaces.html, and I will discuss a few of them here.

Parametric surfaces are the easiest to work with. A parametric surface is defined by a mathematical function of two parameters (u, v), where u and v are numbers, and each value of the function is a point in space. The surface consists of all the points that are values of the function for u and v in some specified ranges. For three.js, the function is a regular JavaScript function that takes three parameters: u, v, and an object of type

THREE.Vector3. The function must modify the vector to represent the point in space that corresponds to the values of the u and v parameters. A parametric surface geometry is created by calling the function at a grid of (u, v) points. This gives a collection of points on the surface, which are then connected to give a polygonal approximation of the surface. In three.js, the values of both u and v are always in the range 0.0 to 1.0 . The geometry is created by a constructor

```
new THREE.ParametricGeometry( func, slices, stacks )
```

where func is the JavaScript function that defines the surface, and slices and stacks determine the number of points in the grid; slices gives the number of subdivisions of the interval from 0 to 1 in the u direction, and stacks, in the v direction. Once you have the geometry, you can use it to make a mesh in the usual way. Here is an example, from the sample program:

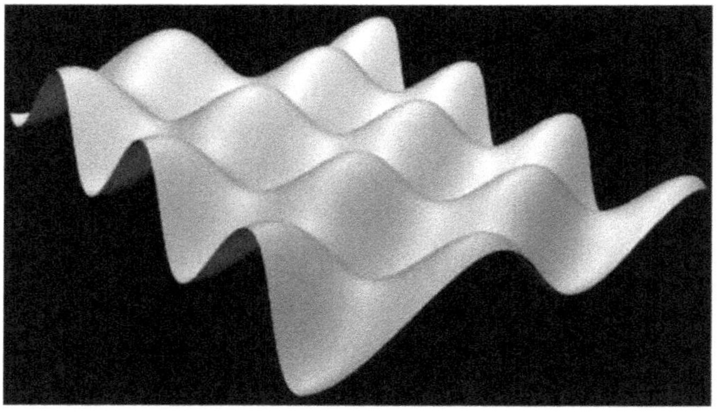

This surface is defined by the function

```
function surfaceFunction( u, v, vector ) {
    let x,y,z; // Coordinates for a point on the surface,
        // calculated from u,v, where u and v
        // range from 0.0 to 1.0.
    x = 20*(u-0.5); // x and z range from -10 to 10
    z = 20 * (v - 0.5);
    y = 2*(Math.sin(x/2) * Math.cos(z));
    vector.set( x, y, z );
}
```

and the three.js mesh that represents the surface is created using

```
let surfaceGeometry = new THREE.ParametricGeometry(surfaceFunction, 64,
64);
let surface = new THREE.Mesh( surfaceGeometry, material );
```

Curves are more complicated in three.js. The class THREE. Curve represents the abstract idea of a parametric curve in two or three dimensions. (It does not represent a three.js geometry.) A parametric curve is defined by a function of one numeric variable t. The value returned by the function is of type THREE. Vector2 for a 2D curve or THREE. Vector3 for a 3D curve. For an object, curve, of type THREE.Curve, the method curve.getPoint (t) should return the point on the curve corresponding to the value of the parameter t. The curve consists of points generated by this function for values of t ranging from 0.0 to 1.0 . However, in the Curve class itself, getPoint() is undefined. To get an actual curve, you have to define it. For example,

```
let helix = new THREE.Curve();
helix.getPoint = function(t) {
    let s = (t - 0.5) * 12*Math.PI;
        // As t ranges from 0 to 1, s ranges from -6*PI to 6*PI
    return new THREE.Vector3(
        5*Math.cos(s),
        s,
        5*Math.sin(s)
    );
}
```

Once getPoint is defined, you have a usable curve. One thing that you can do with it is create a tube geometry, which defines a surface that is a tube with a circular cross-section and with the curve running along the center of the tube. The sample program uses the helix curve, defined above, to create two tubes:

The geometry for the wider tube is created with

```
tubeGeometry1 = new THREE.TubeGeometry( helix, 128, 2.5, 32 );
```

The second parameter to the constructor is the number of subdivisions of the surface along the length of the curve. The third is the radius of the circular cross-section of the tube, and the fourth is the number of subdivisions around the circumference of the cross-section.

To make a tube, you need a 3D curve. There are also several ways to make a surface from a 2D curve. One way is to rotate the curve about a line, generating a surface of rotation. The surface consists of all the points that the curve passes through as it rotates. This is called lathing. This image from the sample program shows the surface generated by lathing a cosine curve. (The image is rotated 90 degrees, so that the y -axis is horizontal.) The curve itself is shown above the surface:

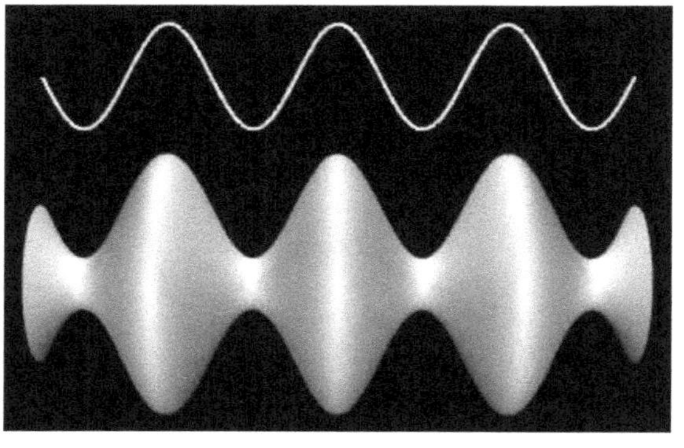

The surface is created in three.js using a THREE.LatheGeometry object. A LatheGeometry is constructed not from a curve but from an array of points that lie on the curve. The points are objects of type Vector2, and the curve lies in the xy-plane. The surface is generated by rotating the curve about the y -axis. The LatheGeometry constructor takes the form

```
new THREE.LatheGeometry( points, slices )
```

The first parameter is the array of Vector2. The second is the number of subdivisions of the surface along the circle generated when a point is rotated about the axis. (The number of "stacks" for the surface is given by the length of the points array.) In the sample program, I create the array of points from an object, cosine, of type Curve by calling cosine.getPoints(128). This function creates an array of 128 points on the curve, using values of the parameter that range from 0.0 to 1.0 .

Another thing that you can do with a 2D curve is simply to fill in the inside of the curve, giving a 2D filled shape. To do that in three.js, you can use an object of type THREE.Shape, which is a subclass of THREE. Curve. A Shape can be defined in the same way as a path in the 2D Canvas API that was covered in Section 2.6. That is, an object shape of type THREE.Shape has methods shape.moveTo, shape.ineTo, shape.quadraticCurveTo and shape.bezierCurveTo that can be used to define the path. See Subsection 2.6.2 for details of how these functions work. As an example, we can create a teardrop shape:

```
let path = new THREE.Shape();
path.moveTo(0,10);
path.bezierCurveTo( 0,5, 20,-10, 0,-10 );
path.bezierCurveTo( -20,-10, 0,5, 0,10 );
```

To use the path to create a filled shape in three.js, we need a ShapeGeometry object:

```
let shapeGeom = new THREE.ShapeGeometry( path );
```

The 2D shape created with this geometry is shown on the left in this picture:

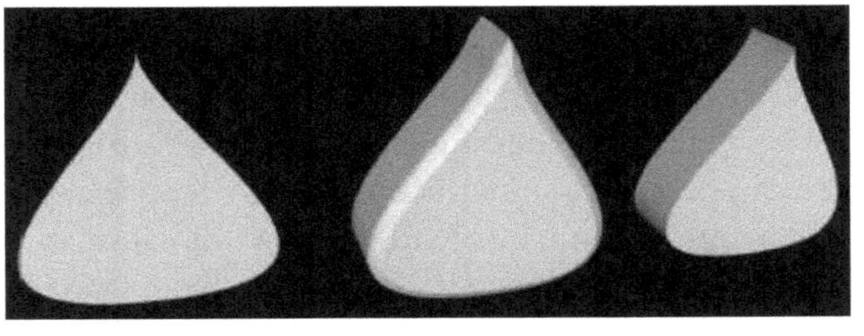

The other two objects in the picture were created by extruding the shape. In extrusion, a filled 2D shape is moved along a path in 3D. The points that the shape passes through make up a 3D solid. In this case, the shape was extruded along a line segement perpendicular to the shape, which is the most common case. The basic extruded shape is shown on the right in the illustration. The middle object is the same shape with "beveled" edges. For more details on extrusion, see the documentation for THREE.ExtrudeGeometry and the source code for the sample program.

5.2.3 Textures

A texture can be used to add visual interest and detail to an object. In three.js, an image texture is represented by an object of type THREE. Texture. Since we are talking about web pages, the image for a three.js texture is generally loaded from a web address. Image textures are usually created using the load function in an object of type THREE.

TextureLoader. The function takes a URL (a web address, usually a relative address) as parameter and returns a Texture object:

```
let loader = new THREE.TextureLoader();
let texture = loader.load( imageURL );
```

A texture in three.js is considered to be part of a material. To apply a texture to a mesh, just assign the Texture object to the map property of the mesh material that is used on the mesh:

```
material.map = texture;
```

The map property can also be set in the material constructor. All three types of mesh material (Basic, Lambert, and Phong) can use a texture. In general, the material base color will be white, since the material color will be multiplied by colors from the texture. A non-white material color will add a "tint" to the texture colors. The texture coordinates that are needed to map the image to a mesh are part of the mesh geometry. The standard mesh geometries such as THREE.SphereGeometry come with texture coordinates already defined.

That's the basic idea-create a texture object from an image URL and assign it to the map property of a material. However, there are complications. First of all, image loading is "asynchronous." That is, calling the load function only starts the process of loading the image, and the process can complete sometime after the function returns. Using a texture on an object before the image has finished loading does not cause an error, but the object will be rendered as completely black. Once the image has been loaded, the scene has to be rendered again to show the image texture. If an animation is running, this will happen automatically; the image will appear in the first frame after it has finished loading. But if there is no animation, you need a way to render the scene once the image has loaded. In fact, the load function in a TextureLoader has several optional parameters:

```
loader.load( imageURL, onLoad, undefined, onError );
```

The third parameter here is given as undefined because that parameter is no longer used. The onLoad and onError parameters are callback functions. The onLoad function, if defined, will be called once the image has been successfully loaded. The onError function will be called if the attempt to load the image fails. For example, if there is a function render() that renders the scene, then render itself could be used as the onLoad function:

```
texture = new THREE.TextureLoader().load( "brick.png", render );
```

Another possible use of onLoad would be to delay assigning the texture to a material until the image has finished loading. If you do change the value of material.map, be sure to set

```
material.needsUpdate = true;
```

to make sure that the change will take effect when the object is redrawn. A Texture has a number of properties that can be set, including properties to set the minification and magnification filters for the texture and a property to control the generation of mipmaps, which is done automatically by default. The properties that you are most likely to want to change are the wrap mode for texture coordinates outside the range 0 to 1 and the texture transformation. (See Section 4.3 for more information about these properties.)

For a Texture object tex, the properties tex.wrap *S* and tex.wrap *T* control how *s* and *t* texture coordinates outside the range 0 to 1 are treated. The default is "clamp to edge." You will most likely want to make the texture repeat in both directions by setting the property values to THREE.RepeatWrapping:

```
tex.wrapS = THREE.RepeatWrapping;
tex.wrapT = THREE.RepeatWrapping;
```

RepeatWrapping works best with "seamless" textures, where the top edge of the image matches up with the bottom edge and the left edge with the right. Three.js also offers an interesting variation called "mirrored repeat" in which every other copy of the repeated image is flipped. This eliminates the seam between copies of the image. For mirrored repetition, use the property value THREE.MirroredRepeatWrapping:

```
tex.wrapS = THREE.MirroredRepeatWrapping;
tex.wrapT = THREE.MirroredRepeatWrapping;
```

The texture properties repeat, offset, and rotation control the scaling, translation, and rotation that are applied to the texture as texture transformations. The values of repeat and offset are of type THREE. Vector2, so that each property has an *x* and a *y* component. The rotation is a number, measured in radians, giving the rotation of the texture about the point (0,0). (But the center of rotation is actually given by another property named center.) For a Texture, tex, the two components of tex.offset give the texture translation in the horizontal and vertical directions. To offset the texture by 0.5 horizontally, you can say either

```
tex.offset.x = 0.5;
```

or

```
tex.offset.set( 0.5, 0 );
```

Remember that a positive horizontal offset will move the texture to the left on the objects, because the offset is applied to the texture coordinates not to the texture image itself.

The components of the property tex.repeat give the texture scaling in the horizontal and vertical directions. For example,

```
tex.repeat.set(2,3);
```

will scale the texture coordinates by a factor of 2 horizontally and 3 vertically. Again, the effect on the image is the inverse, so that the image is shrunk by a factor of 2 horizontally and 3 vertically. The result is that you get two copies of the image in the horizontal direction where you would have had one, and three vertically. This explains the name "repeat," but note that the values are not limited to be integers.

The demo c5/textures.html shows image textures applied to a variety of three.js objects.

Suppose that we want to use an image texture on the pyramid that was created at the beginning of this section. In order to apply a texture image to an object, WebGL needs texture coordinates for that object. When we build a mesh from scratch, we have to supply the texture coordinates as part of the mesh's geometry object.

Let's see how to do this on our pyramid example. A BufferedGeometry object such as pyramidGeom in the example has an attribute named "uv" to hold texture coordinates. (The name "uv" refers to the coordinates on an object that are mapped to the *s* and *t* coordinates in a texture. The texture coordinates for a surface are often referred to as "uv coordinates.") The BufferAttribute for a "uv" attribute can be made from a typed array containing a pair of texture coordinates for each vertex.

Our pyramid example has six triangular faces, with a total of 18 vertices. We need an array containing vertex coordinates for 18 vertices. The coordinates have to be chosen to map the image in a reasonable way onto the faces. My choice of coordinates maps the entire texture image onto the square base of the pyramid, and it cuts a triangle out of the image to apply to each of the sides. It takes some care to come up with the correct coordinates. I define the texture coordinates for the pyramid geometry as follows:

```
let pyramidUVs = new Float32Array([
    0,0, 0,1, 1,1, // uv coords for first triangle in base.
```

```
    0,0, 1,1, 1,0, // uv coords for second triangle in base.
    0,0, 1,0, 0.5,1, // uv coords for front face.
    1,0, 0,0, 0.5,1, // uv coords for right face.
    0,0, 1,0, 0.5,1, // uv coords for back face.
    1,0, 0,0, 0.5,1 // uv coords for left face.
]);
pyramidGeom.setAttribute("uv",
        new THREE.BufferAttribute(pyramidUVs,2) );
```

The sample program threejs/textured-pyramid.html shows the pyramid with a brick texture. Here is an image from the program:

5.2.4 Transforms

In order to understand how to work with objects effectively in three.js, it can be useful to know more about how it implements transforms. I have explained that an Object3D, obj, has properties obj.position, obj.scale, and obj.rotation that specify its modeling transformation in its own local coordinate system. But these properties are not used directly when the object is rendered. Instead, they are combined to compute another property, obj.matrix, that represents the transformation as a matrix. By default, this matrix is recomputed automatically every time the scene is rendered. This can be inefficient if the transformation never changes, so obj has another property, obj.matrixAutoUpdate, that controls whether obj.matrix is computed automatically. If you set obj.matrixAutoUpdate to false, the update is not done. In that case, if you do want to change the modeling transformation, you can call obj.updateMatrix() to compute the matrix from the current values of obj.position, obj.scale, and obj.rotation.

We have seen how to modify obj's modeling transformation by directly changing the values of the properties obj.position, obj.scale, and obj.rotation. However, you can also change the position by calling the function obj.translate $X(dx)$, obj.translate $Y(dy)$, or obj.translate $Z(dz)$ to move the object by a specified amount in the direction of a coordinate axis. There is also a function obj.translateOnAxis(axis,amount), where axis is a

Vector3 and amount is a number giving the distance to translate the object. The object is moved in the direction of the vector, axis. The vector must be normalized; that is, it must have length 1 . For example, to translate obj by 5 units in the direction of the vector (1,1,1), you could say

```
obj.translateOnAxis( new THREE.Vector3(1,1,1).normalize(), 5 );
```

There are no functions for changing the scaling transform. But you can change the object's rotation with the functions obj.rotateX (angle), obj.rotateY (angle), and obj.rotateZ (angle) to rotate the object about the coordinate axes. (Remember that angles are measured in radians.) Calling obj.rotateX (angle) is not the same as adding angle onto the value of obj.rotation.x, since it applies a rotation about the x -axis on top of other rotations that might already have been applied.

There is also a function obj.rotateOnAxis(axis,angle), where axis is a Vector3. This function rotates the object through the angle angle about the vector (that is, about the line between the origin and the point given by axis). The axis must be a normalized vector. (Rotation is actually even more complicated. The rotation of an object, obj, is actually represented by the property obj.quaternion, not by the property obj.rotation. Quaternions are mathematical objects that are often used in computer graphics as an alternative to Euler angles, to represent rotations. However, when you change one of the properties obj.rotation or obj.quaterion, the other is automatically updated to make sure that both properties represent the same rotation. So, we don't need to work directly with the quaternions.)

I should emphasize that the translation and rotation functions modify the position and rotation properties of the object. That is, they apply in object coordinates, not world coordinates, and they are applied as the first modeling transformation on the object when the object is rendered. For example, a rotation in world coordinates can change the position of an object, if it is not positioned at the origin. However, changing the value of the rotation property of an object will never change its position.

The actual transformation that is applied to an object when it is rendered is a combination of the modeling transformation of that object, combined with the modeling transformation on all of its ancestors in the scene graph. In three.js, that transformation is stored in a property of the object named obj.matrix World.

There is one more useful method for setting the rotation: obj.lookAt(vec), which rotates the object so that it is facing towards a given point. The parameter, vec, is a Vector3, which must be expressed in the object's own local coordinate system. (For an object that has no parent, or whose ancestors have no modeling transformations, that will be the same as world coordinates.) The object is also rotated so that its "up" direction is equal to the value of the property obj.up, which by default is (0,1,0). This function can be used with any object, but it is most useful for a camera.

5.2.5 Loading Models

Although it is possible to create mesh objects by listing their vertices and faces, it would be difficult to do it by hand for all but very simple objects. It's much easier, for example, to design an object in an interactive modeling program such as Blender (Appendix B). Modeling programs like Blender can export objects using many different file formats. Three.js has utility functions for loading models from files in a variety of file formats. These utilities are not part of the three.js core, but JavaScript files that define them can be found in the examples folder in the three.js download.

The preferred format for model files is ***GLTF***. A GLTF model can be stored in a text file with extension .gltf or in a binary file with extension .glb. Binary files are smaller and more efficient, but not human-readable. A three.js loader for GLTF files is defined by the file GLTFLoader.js. from the three.js download. Copies of that script, as well as scripts for other model loaders, can be found in the threejs folder in the source folder for this textbook.

If loader is an object of type THREE.GTLFLoader, you can use its load() method to start the process of loading a model:

```
loader = new THREE.GLTFLoader()
loader.load( url, onLoad, onProgress, onError );
```

Only the first parameter is required; it is a URL for the file that contains the model. The other three parameters are callback functions: onLoad will be called when the loading is complete, with a parameter that represents the data from the file; onProgress is called periodically during the loading with a parameter that contains information about the size of the model and how much of it has be loaded; and onError is called if any error occurs. (I have not actually used onProgress myself.) Note that, as for textures, the loading is done asynchronously.

A GLTF file can be quite complicated and can contain an entire 3D scene, containing multiple objects, lights, and other things. The data returned by a GLTFLoader contains a three.js Scene. Any objects defined by the file will be part of the scene graph for that scene. All of the model files used in this textbook define a Mesh object that is the first child of the Scene object. This object comes complete with both geometry and material. The onLoad callback function can add that object to the scene and might look something like this:

```
function onLoad(data) { // the parameter is the loaded model data
    let object = data.scene.children[0];
    // maybe modify the modeling transformation or material...
    scene.add(object); // add the loaded object to our scene
    render(); // call render to show the scene with the new object
}
```

The sample program threejs/model-viewer.html uses GLTFLoader to load several models. It also uses loaders for models in two other formats, Collada and OBJ, that work much the same way. The technique for loading the models is actually a little more general that what I've described here. See the source code for the example program for details. (If you try to run the sample program from a download of the web site version of this textbook, it probably won't work because of security restrictions in most web browsers. See the section on running things locally in the three.js documentation. The same applies to the demo below.)

I'll also mention that GLTF models can include animations. Three.js has several classes that support animation, including THREE.AnimationMixer, THREE.AnimationAction, and THREE.AnimationClip. I won't discuss animation here, but these three classes are used to animate the horse and stork models in the on-line demo c5/mesh-animation.html.

5.3 Other Features

We will finish this chapter with a look at a few additional features of three.js. In the process, you will learn about some new aspects of 3D graphics.

5.3.1 Instanced Meshes

The class THREE.InstancedMesh makes it possible to quickly render several objects, possibly a large number of objects, that use the same geometry but differ in the transformations that are applied to them and, possibly, in their material color. Each copy of the object is called an "instance," and the process of creating all of the copies is called instanced drawing or instancing. In WebGL 2.0 (and in WebGL 1.0 with an extension), it is possible to draw all of the instances with a single function call, making it very efficient.

InstancedMesh is fairly easy to use. Along with the geometry and material for the mesh, the constructor specifies the maximum number of instances that it can support:

instances = new THREE.InstancedMesh(geometry, material, count)
To set the transformation for instance number i, you can call
instances.setMatrixAt(i, matrix);

where matrix is an object of type THREE.Matrix4 representing the modeling transformation. Similarly, you can set the color for instance number i with instances.setColorAt(i, color);

where color is of type THREE. Color. Instance colors are optional. If provided, they replace the color property of material.

The Matrix4 class includes methods that make it easy to create a transformation matrix. The constructor matrix = new THREE.Matrix4(); creates an identity matrix, which can then be modified. For example, the method matrix.makeTranslation (dx, dy, dz) replaces the current matrix with the transformation matrix for a translation by the vector (dx, dy, dz). There are functions for making scaling and rotation matrices. To make more complex transformations, there is a function for multiplying matrices.

The sample program threejs/instanced-mesh.html uses a single InstancedMesh to make 1331 spheres, arranged in an 11-by-11-by-11 cube. To move the spheres into position, different translations are applied to each instance. An instance color is also set for each instance.

5.3.2 User Input

Most real programs require some kind of user interaction. For a web application, of course, the program can get user input using HTML widgets such as buttons and text input boxes. But direct mouse interaction with a 3D world is more natural in many programs.

The most basic example is using the mouse to rotate the scene. In three.js, rotation can be implemented using the class THREE. TrackballControls or the class THREE.OrbitControls. Note that both classes support touchscreen as well as mouse interaction. The main difference between the classes is that with OrbitControls, the rotation is constrained so that the positive y-axis is always the up direction in the view. TrackballControls, on the other hand, allows completely free rotation. Another difference is that TrackballControls is meant to be used only with a scene that is continuously animated. OrbitControls is used for rotation in most of my sample programs and demos. TrackballControls is used only in threejs/full-window.html and threejs/curves-and-surfaces.html.

The two control classes are not part of the main three.js JavaScript file. To use one of them, you need the JavaScript file OrbitControls.js or TrackballControls.js, which can be found in the folder examples/js/controls in the three.js download.

The two classes are used in a similar way. I will discuss OrbitControls first. In my examples, I create a camera and move it away from the origin. I usually add a light object to the camera object, so that the light will move along with the camera, providing some illumination to anything that is visible to the camera. The OrbitControls object is used to rotate the camera around the scene. The constructor for the control object has two parameters, the camera and the canvas on which the scene is rendered. Here is typical setup:

```
camera = new THREE.PerspectiveCamera(45, canvas.width/canvas.height,
0.1, 100);
camera.position.set(0,15,35);
camera.lookAt( new THREE.Vector3(0,0,0) ); // camera looks toward
origin
let light = new THREE.PointLight(0xffffff, 0.6);
camera.add(light); // viewpoint light moves with camera
scene.add(camera);
controls = new THREE.OrbitControls( camera, canvas );
```

The constructor installs listeners on the canvas so that the controls can respond to mouse events. If an animation is running, the only other thing that you need to do is call

```
controls.update();
```

before rendering the scene. The user will be able to rotate the scene by dragging on it with the left mouse button. The controls will also do "panning" (dragging the scene in the plane of the screen) with the right mouse button and "zooming" (moving the camera forward and backward) with the middle mouse button or scroll wheel. To disable zooming and panning, you can set

```
controls.enablePan = false;
controls.enableZoom = false;
```

And you can return the original view of the scene by calling controls.reset(). If your program is not running a continuous animation, you need a way to re-render the scene in response to user actions. When the user drags the mouse, the controls object generates a "change" event. You can add a listener for that event, to respond to the event by redrawing the scene. To do that, just call

```
controls.addEventListener( "change", callback );
```

Where callback() is the function that should be called when the event occurs. If you have a function render() that renders your scene, you can simply pass render as the value of callback.

Unfortunately, a TrackballControls object does not emit "change" events, and there does not seem to be any way to use it without having an animation running. With an animation, TrackballControls are used in the same way as OrbitControls, except that the properties for panning and zooming are controls.noPan and controls.noZoom; they should be set to true to disable panning and zooming. One nice feature of TrackballControls is that they implement inertia: When the user releases the mouse after dragging, the motion of the scene will slow to a stop instead of stopping abruptly.

A much more interesting form of mouse interaction is to let the user select objects in the scene by clicking on them. The problem is to determine which object the user is clicking. The general procedure is something like this: Follow a ray from the camera through the point on the screen where the user clicked and find the first object in the scene that is intersected by that ray. That's the object that is visible at the point where the user clicked. Unfortunately, the procedure involves a lot of calculations. Fortunately, three.js has a class that can do the work for you: THREE.Raycaster.

A Raycaster can be used to find intersections of a ray with objects in a scene. (A ray is just half of a line, stretching from some given starting point in a given direction towards infinity.) You can make one raycaster object to use throughout your program:

```
raycaster = new THREE.Raycaster();
```

To tell it which ray to use, you can call

```
raycaster.set( startingPoint, direction );
```

where both of the parameters are of type THREE. Vector3. Their values are in terms of world coordinates, the same coordinate system that you use for the scene as a whole. The direction must be a normalized vector, with length equal to one. For example, suppose that you want to fire a laser gun.... The startingPoint is the location of the gun, and the direction is the direction that the gun is pointing. Configure the raycaster with those parameters, and you can use it to find out what object is struck by the laser beam.

Alternatively, and more conveniently for processing user input, you can express the ray in terms of the camera and a point on the screen:

```
raycaster.setFromCamera( screenCoords, camera );
```

The screenCoords are given as a THREE. Vector2 expressed in clip coordinates. This means the horizontal coordinate ranges from -1 on the left edge of the viewport to 1 on the right, and the vertical coordinate ranges from -1 at the bottom to 1 on the top. (Clip coordinates are called "normalized device coordinates" in three.js.) So, we need to convert from pixel coordinates on a canvas to clip coordinates. Here's one way to do it, given a mouse event, evt:

```
let r = canvas.getBoundingClientRect();
let x = evt.clientX - r.left; // convert mouse location to canvas pixel
coords
let y = evt.clientY - r.top;
let a = 2*x/canvas.width - 1; // convert canvas pixel coords to clip
coords
let b = 1 - 2*y/canvas.height;
raycaster.setFromCamera( new THREE.Vector2(a,b), camera );
```

Once you have told the raycaster which ray to use, it is ready to find intersections of that ray with objects in the scene. This can be done with the function

```
raycaster.intersectObjects( objectArray, recursive );
```

The first parameter is an array of Object3D. The raycaster will search for intersections of its current ray with objects in the array. If the second parameter is true, it will also search descendants of those objects in the scene graph; if it is false or is omitted, then only the objects in the array will be searched. For example, to search for intersections with all objects in the scene, use

```
raycaster.intersectObjects( scene.children, true );
```

The return value from intersectObjects is an array of JavaScript objects. Each item in the array represents an intersection of the ray with an Object3D. The function finds all such intersections, not just the first. If no intersection is found, the array is empty. The array is sorted by increasing distance from the starting point of the ray. If you just want the first intersection, use the first element of the array.

Each element in the array is an object whose properties contain information about the intersection. Suppose that item is one of the array elements. Then the most useful properties are: item.object, which is the Object3D that was intersected by the ray; and item.point, which is the point of intersection, given as a Vector3 in world coordinates. That information is enough to implement some interesting user interaction.

The demo c5/raycaster-input.html uses some basic mouse interaction to let the user edit a scene. The scene shows a number of tapered yellow cylinders standing on a green base. The user can drag the cylinders, add and delete cylinders, and rotate the scene. A set of radio buttons lets the user select which action should be performed by the mouse. Here's a screenshot from the program:

Let's look at how the actions are implemented. The only objects are the base and the cylinders. In the program, the base is referred to as ground, and all the objects are children of an Object3D named world. (I use the world object to make it easy to rotate the set of all visible objects without moving the camera or lights.) For all drag, add, and delete actions, I look for intersections of these objects with a ray that extends from the camera through the mouse position:

```
raycaster.setFromCamera( new THREE.Vector2(a,b), camera );
let intersects = raycaster.intersectObjects( world.children );
```

If intersects.length is zero, there are no intersections, and there is nothing to do. Otherwise, I look at intersects[0], which represents an intersection with the object that is visible at the mouse position. So, intersects [0].object is the object that the user clicked, and intersects [0].point is the point of intersection.

The Delete action is the simplest to implement: When the user clicks a cylinder, the cylinder should be removed from the scene. If the first intersection is with the ground, then nothing is deleted. Otherwise, the clicked object was a cylinder and should be deleted:

```
if ( intersects[0].object != ground ) {
    world.remove( intersects[0].object );
    render();
}
```

For an Add action, we should add a cylinder only if the user clicked the ground. In that case, the point of intersection tells where the cylinder should be added. An interesting issue here is that we get the point of intersection in world coordinates, but in order to add the cylinder as a child of world, I need to know the point of intersection in the local coordinate system for world. The two coordinate systems will be different if the world has been rotated. Fortunately, every Object3D has a method worldToLocal (v) that can be used to transform a Vector3, v, from world coordinates to local coordinates for that object. This method does not return a value; it modifies the coordinates of the vector v. (There is also a localTo World method.) So, the Add action can be implemented like this:

```
item = intersects[0];
if (item.object == ground) {
    let locationX = item.point.x; // world coords of intersection point
    let locationZ = item.point.z;
    let coords = new THREE.Vector3(locationX, 0, locationZ); // y is
always 0
    world.worldToLocal(coords); // transform to local coords
    addCylinder(coords.x, coords.z); // adds a cylinder at corrected
location
    render();
}
```

For a Drag action, we can determine which cylinder was clicked using the same test as for delete. However, the problem of moving the cylinder as the user drags the mouse raises a new issue: how do we know where to put the cylinder when the mouse moves? We somehow have to transform a new mouse position into a new position for the cylinder. For that, we can use the raycaster again. My first thought was to create a ray from the camera through the new mouse position, use that ray to find its intersection with the ground, and then to move the cylinder to that point of intersection. Unfortunately, this puts the base of the cylinder at the mouse position, and it made the cylinder jump to the wrong position as soon as I started moving the mouse. I realized that I didn't want to track the intersection with the ground; I needed to track the intersection with a plane that lies at the same height as the original point of intersection. To implement this, I add an invisible plane at that height just during dragging, and I use intersections with that plane instead of intersections with the ground. (You can have invisible objects in three.js-just set the visible property of the material to false.)

5.3.3 Shadows

One thing that has been missing in our 3D images is shadows. Even if you didn't notice the lack consciously, it made many of the images look wrong. Shadows can add a nice touch of realism to a scene, but OpenGL, including WebGL, cannot generate shadows automatically. There are ways to compute shadows that can be implemented in OpenGL, but they are tricky to use and they are not completely realistic physically. One method, which is called shadow mapping, is implemented in three.js. Shadow mapping in three.js is certainly not trivial to use, but it is easier than trying to do the same thing from scratch.

The online demo c5/shadows.html shows a three.js scene that uses shadow mapping. The lights that cast the shadows can be animated, so you can watch the shadows change as the lights move. Here is an image from the demo:

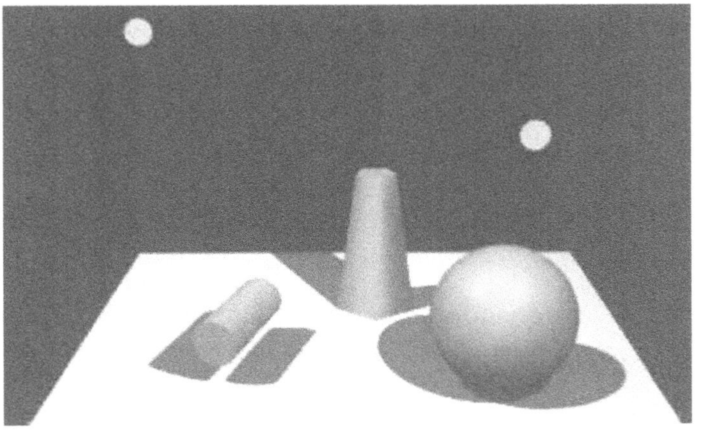

The basic idea of shadow mapping is fairly straightforward: To tell what parts of a scene are in shadow, you have to look at the scene from the point of view of the light source. Things that are visible from the point of view of the light are illuminated by that light. Things that are not visible from the light are in shadow. (This is ignoring the possibility of transparency and indirect, reflected light, which cannot be handled by shadow mapping.) To implement this idea, place a camera at the light source and take a picture. In fact, you don't need the picture itself. What you need is the depth buffer. After the picture has been rendered, the value stored in the depth buffer for a given pixel contains, essentially, the distance from the light to the object that is visible from the the light at that point. That object is illuminated by the light. If an object is at greater depth than the value stored in the depth buffer, then that object is in shadow. The depth buffer is the shadow map. Now, go back to the point of view of the camera, and consider a point on some object as it is rendered from the camera's point of view. Is that point in shadow or not? You just have to transform that point from the camera's viewing coordinates to the light's viewing coordinates and check the depth of the transformed point. If that depth is greater than the corresponding value in the shadow map, then the point is in shadow. Note that if there are several lights, each light casts its own shadows, and you need a shadow map for each light.

It is computationally expensive to compute shadow maps and to apply them, and shadows are disabled by default in three.js. To get shadows, you need to do several things. You need to enable shadow computations in the WebGL renderer by saying

```
renderer.shadowMap.enabled = true;
```

Only DirectionalLights and SpotLights can cast shadows. To get shadows from a light, even after enabling shadows in the renderer, you have to set the light's castShadow property to true:

```
light.castShadow = true; // This light will cast shadows.
```

Furthermore, shadows have to be enabled for each object that will cast or receive shadows. "Receiving" a shadow means that shadows will be visible on that object. Casting and receiving are enabled separately for an object.

```
object.castShadow = true; // This object will cast shadows.
object.receiveShadow = true; // Shadows will show up on this object.
```

Even this might not make any shadows show up, and if they do they might look pretty bad. The problem is that you usually have to configure the cameras that are used to make the shadow maps.

Each DirectionalLight or SpotLight has its own shadow camera, which is used to create the shadow map from the point of view of that light. (A DirectionalLight has a property named shadow of type THREE.DirectionalLightShadow, which in turn has a property named camera of type THREE.OrthographicCamera that holds the shadow camera. So, the shadow camera for a directional light *dl* is dl.shadow.camera.) The shadow camera for a directional light uses an orthographic projection. An orthographic projection is configured by view volume limits xmin, xmax, ymin, ymax, near, and far (see Subsection 3.3.3). For a directional light, *dl*, these limits correspond to the properties dl.shadow.camera.left, dl.shadow.camera.right, dl.shadow.camera.bottom, dl.shadow.camera.top, dl.shadow.camera.near, and dl.shadow.camera.far. These values are in view coordinates for the shadow camera; that is, they are relative to dl.position. It is important to make sure that all the objects in your scene, or at least those that cast shadows, are within the view volume of the shadow camera. Furthermore, you don't want the limits to be too big: If the scene occupies only a small part of the camera's view volume, then only a small part of the shadow map contains useful information-and then since there is so little information about shadows, your shadows won't be very accurate. The default values assume a very large scene. For a relatively small scene, you might set:

```
dl.shadow.camera.left = -20;
dl.shadow.camera.right = 20;
dl.shadow.camera.bottom = -20;
dl.shadow.camera.top = 20;
dl.shadow.camera.near = 1;
dl.shadow.camera.far = 30;
```

The shadow camera for a spotlight is of type THREE.PerspectiveCamera and uses a perspective projection. (The use of a camera with a limited view is why you can have shadows from spotlights but not from point lights.) For a spotlight *sl*, the shadow camera is configured by the properties sl.shadow.camera.near, sl.shadow.camera.far, and sl.shadow.camera.fov (where "fov" is the vertical field of view angle, given in degrees rather than radians). The default value for fov is probably OK, except that if you change the spotlight's cutoff angle, you will want to change the fov to match. But you should be sure to set appropriate values for near and far, to include all of your scene and as little extra as is practical. Again, near and far are distances from sl.position.

To get more accurate shadows, you might want to increase the size of the shadow map. The shadow map is a kind of texture image which by default is 512 by 512 pixels. You can increase the accuracy of the shadows by using a larger shadow map. To do that for a light, light, set the values of the properties light.shadow.mapSize.width and light.shadow.mapSize.height. For example,

```
light.shadow.mapSize.width = 1024;
light.shadow.mapSize.height = 1024;
```

I'm not sure whether power-of-two values are absolutely required here, but they are commonly used for textures.

5.3.4 Cubemap Textures and Skyboxes

We have created and viewed simple scenes, shown on a solid-colored background. It would be nice to put our scenes in an "environment" such as the interior of a building, a nature scene, or a public square. It's not practical to build representations of such complex environments out of geometric primitives, but we can get a reasonably good effect using textures. The technique that is used in three.js is called a skybox. A skybox is a large cube - effectively, infinitely large - where a different texture is applied to each face of the cube.

The textures are images of some environment. For a viewer inside the cube, the six texture images on the cube fit together to provide a complete view of the environment in every direction. The six texture images together make up what is called a cubemap texture. The images must match up along the edges of the cube to form a seamless view of the environment.

A cube map of an actual physical environment can be made by taking six pictures of the environment in six directions: left, right, up, down, forward, and back. (More realistically, it is made by taking enough photographs to cover all directions, with overlaps, and then using software to "stitch" the images together into a complete cube map.) The six directions are referred to by their relation to the coordinate axes as: positive x , negative x , positive y , negative y , positive z , and negative z , and the images must be listed in that order when you specify the cube map. Here is an example. The first picture shows the six images of a cube map laid out next to each other. The positive y image is at the top, the negative y image is at the bottom. In between are the negative x , positive z , positive x , and negative z images laid out in a row. The second picture shows the images used to texture a cube, viewed here from the outside. You can see how the images match up along the edges of the cube:

(This cube map, and others used in this section, are by Emil Persson, who has made a large number of cube maps available for download at http://www.humus.name/index.php?page=Textures under a creative commons license.) For a skybox, conceptually, a very large cube would be used. The camera, lights, and any objects that are to be part of the scene would be inside the cube. It is possible to construct a skybox by hand in just this way.

However, Three.js makes it very easy to use a skybox as the background for a scene. It has the class THREE. CubeTexture to represent cube maps, and you can enclose your scene in a skybox simply by assigning a CubeTexture as the value of the property scene.background. (The value of that property could also be a normal Texture or a Color.)

A CubeTexture can be created by a CubeTextureLoader, which can load the six images that make up the cube map. The loader has a method named load() that works in the same way as the load() method of a TextureLoader (Subsection 5.2.3), except that the first parameter to the method is an array of six strings giving the URLs of the six images for the cube map. For example:

```
let textureURLs = [ // URLs of the six faces of the cube map
        "cubemap-textures/park/posx.jpg", // Note: The order in which
        "cubemap-textures/park/negx.jpg", // the images are listed is
        "cubemap-textures/park/posy.jpg", // important!
        "cubemap-textures/park/negy.jpg",
        "cubemap-textures/park/posz.jpg",
        "cubemap-textures/park/negz.jpg"
    ];
loader = new THREE.CubeTextureLoader();
cubeTexture = loader.load( textureURLs, onLoad, undefined, onError );
```

Here, onLoad is a function that will be called after the texture has finished loading. The function could, for example, set scene.background equal to cubeTexture and re-render the scene with the new background. The last parameter onError is a function that will be called if the texture cannot be loaded. Only the first parameter is required.

The sample program threejs/skybox.html shows two WebGL scenes. The first scene shows a cube with the six images from a cube map applied as normal textures to the six faces of a cube. The second scene uses the same cube map as a skybox. If you rotate the view of the second scene, you can look at all parts of the skybox and see how it forms a seamless environment that completely encloses the scene.

5.3.5 Reflection and Refraction

A reflective surface shouldn't just reflect light-it should reflect its environment. Three.js can use environment mapping to simulate reflection. (Environment mapping is also called "reflection mapping.") Environment mapping uses a cube map texture. Given a point on a surface, a ray is cast from the camera position to that point, and then the ray is reflected off the surface. The point where the reflected ray hits the cube determines which point from the texture should be mapped to the point on the surface. For a simulation of perfect, mirror-like reflection, the surface point is simply painted with the color from the texture. Note that the surface does not literally reflect other objects in the scene. It reflects the contents of the cube map texture. However, if the same cube map texture is used on a skybox, and if the skybox is the only other object in the scene, then it will look like the surface is a mirror that perfectly reflects its environment.

This type of reflection is very easy to do in three.js. You only need to make a mesh material and set its envMap property equal to the cubemap texture object. For example, if cubeTexture is the texture object obtained using a THREE. CubeTextureLoader, as in the skybox example above, we can make a sphere that perfectly reflects the texture by saying:

```
let geometry = new THREE.SphereGeometry(1,32,16);
let material = new THREE.MeshBasicMaterial( {
        color: "white", // Color will be multiplied by the environment
map.
        envMap: cubeTexture // CubeTexture to be used as an environment
map.
    } );
let mirrorSphere = new THREE.Mesh( geometry, material );
```

For the effect to look good, you would want to use the same texture as the scene background. Note that no lighting would be necessary in the scene, since the sphere uses a MeshBasicMaterial. The colors seen on the sphere come entirely from the environment map and the basic color of the sphere material. The environment map color is multiplied by the basic color. In this example, the basic color of the material is white, and the sphere color is exactly equal to the color from the texture. With a different base color, the environment map texture would be "tinted" with that color. You could even apply a regular texture map to the sphere, to be used in place of the color, so that the reflection of the skybox would be combined with the texture.

The sample program threejs/reflection.html demonstrates environment mapping. It can show a variety of environment-mapped objects, with a variety of skybox textures, and it has several options for the base color of the object. Here are two images from that program. The one on the left shows a reflective arrowhead shape with a white base color. On the right, the object is a model of a horse (taken from the three.js download) whose base color is pink:

A very similar program is available as a demo in the on-line version of this section. Three.js can also do refraction. Refraction occurs when light passes through a transparent or translucent object. A ray of light will be bent as it passes between the inside of the object and the outside. The amount of bending depends on the so-called "indices of refraction" of the material outside and the material inside the object. More exactly, it depends on the ratio between the two indices. Even a perfectly transparent object will be visible because of the distortion induced by this bending (unless the ratio is 1 , meaning that there is no bending of light at all).

In three.js, refraction is implemented using environment maps. As with reflection, a refracting object does not show its actual environment; it refracts the cubemap texture that is used as the environment map. For refraction, a special "mapping" must be used for the environment map texture. The mapping property of a texture tells how that texture will be mapped to a surface. For a cubemap texture being used for refraction, it should be set to THREE.CubeRefractionMapping. (The default value of this property in a cubemap texture is appropriate for reflection rather than refraction.) Here is an example of loading a cubemap texture and setting its mapping property for use with refraction:

```
cubeTexture = new THREE.CubeTextureLoader().load( textureURLs );
cubeTexture.mapping = THREE.CubeRefractionMapping;
```

In addition to this, the refractionRatio property of the material that is applied to the refracting object should be set. The value is a number between 0 and 1 ; the closer to 1 , the less bending of light. The default value is so close to 1 that the object will be almost invisible. This example uses a value of 0.6 :

```
let material = new THREE.MeshBasicMaterial( {
        color: "white",
        envMap: cubeTexture,
```

```
        refractionRatio: 0.6
    } );
```

This gives a strong refractive effect. If you set the material color to something other than white, you will get something that looks like tinted glass. Another property that you might set is the reflectivity. For a refractive object, this value tells how much light is transmitted through the object rather than reflected from its surface. The default value, 1 , gives 100% transmission of light; smaller values make objects look like they are made out of "cloudy" glass that blocks some of the light.

The sample program threejs/refraction.html is a copy of reflection.html that has been modified to do refraction instead of reflection. The objects look like they are made of glass instead of mirrors. The program has a checkbox that makes the glass look cloudy and one that increases the refractionRatio from 0.6 to 0.9 . The following images are from that program. A perfectly transmissive arrowhead is shown in the first image, and a cloudy sphere in the second. Notice how the sphere shows an inverted image of the objects behind it:

In my reflection and refraction examples, the environment is a skybox, and there is a single object that reflects or refracts that environment. But what if a scene includes more than one object? The objects won't be in the cubemap texture. If you use the cubemap texture on the objects, they won't reflect or refract each other. There is no complete solution to this problem in WebGL. However, you can make an object reflect or refract other objects by making an environment map that includes those objects. If the objects are moving, this means that you have to make a new environment map for every frame. Recall that an environment map can be made by taking six pictures of the environment from different directions. Three.js has a kind of camera that can do just that, THREE.CubeCamera. I won't go into the full details, but a CubeCamera can take a six-fold picture of a scene from a given point of view and make a cubemap texture from those images. To use the camera, you have to place it at the location of an object - and make the object invisible so it doesn't show up in the pictures. Snap the picture, and apply it as an environment map on the object. For animated scenes, you have to do this in every frame, and you need to do it for every reflective/refractive object in the scene. Obviously, this can get very computationally expensive! And the result still isn't perfect. For one thing, you won't see multiple reflections, where objects reflect back and forth on each other several times. For that, you need a different kind of rendering from the one used by OpenGL. We will return to the topic of dynamic cubemaps in Subsection 7.4.4 and to alternative rendering techniques in Chapter 8.

Chapter 6

Introduction to WebGL

In this chapter, we turn to ***WebG***, the version of OpenGL for the Web. Three.js, which was covered in the previous chapter, uses WebGL for 3D graphics. Of course, it is more difficult to use WebGL directly, but doing so gives you full control over the graphics hardware. And learning it will be a good introduction to modern graphics programming. WebGL is very different from OpenGL 1.1, which we studied in Chapter 3 and Chapter 4. Nevertheless, it will turn out that much of what you learned in previous chapters will carry over to WebGL.

It is not my intention to cover WebGL in its entirety. There are many WebGL features that I will not even mention, and many of those are important for more advanced computer graphics. However, I will cover the core features that are needed for 2D and 3D graphics, along with a few of the more advanced aspects, as a bonus.

There are two versions of WebGL, both of them still in use. WebGL 1.0 is based on OpenGL ES 2.0, a version of OpenGL designed for use on embedded systems such as smart phones and tablets. OpenGL ES 1.0, the original OpenGL for embedded systems, was very similar to OpenGL 1.1. However, the 2.0 version of OpenGL ES introduced major changes. It is actually a smaller, simpler API that puts more responsibility on the programmer. For example, functions for working with transformations, such as glRotatef and glPushMatrix, were eliminated from the API, making the programmer responsible for keeping track of transformations. WebGL does not use glBegin/glEnd to generate geometry, and it doesn't use function such as glColor* or glNormal* to specify attributes of vertices. WebGL 1.0 is supported in almost every web browser. (On some devices, WebGL might be disabled because of hardware limitations.)

WebGL 2.0, which is based on OpenGL ES 3.0, is already supported in many devices, but is still not as widely supported as the 1.0 version. Most programs written for WebGL 1.0 will also work under WebGL 2.0, so almost everything that you learn about the 1.0 version will carry over to the newer version. In this textbook, I will concentrate on WebGL 1.0, but I will also cover some of the new features of WebGL 2.0. I will try to make it clear when I am talking about features that only apply to WebGL 2.0.

There are two sides to any WebGL program. Part of the program is written in JavaScript, the programming language for the web. The second part is written in GLSL, a language for writing "shader" programs that run on the GPU. WebGL 1.0 uses GLSL ES 1.00 (the OpenGL

Shader Language for Embedded Systems, version 1.00). WebGL 2.0 can use shader programs written in GLSL ES 1.00, but it can also use GLSL ES 3.00, which has some significant differences as well as new features. I will try to always be clear about which language I am discussing.

For this introductory chapter about WebGL, we will stick to basic 2D graphics. You will learn about the structure of WebGL programs. You will learn most of the JavaScript side of the API, and you will learn how to write and use simple shaders. In the next chapter, we will move on to 3D graphics, and you will learn a great deal more about GLSL.

6.1 The Programmable Pipeline

Opengl 1.1 uses a fixed-function pipeline for graphics processing. Data is provided by a program and passes through a series of processing stages that ultimately produce the pixel colors seen in the final image. The program can enable and disable some of the steps in the process, such as the depth test and lighting calculations. But there is no way for it to change what happens at each stage. The functionality is fixed.

OpenGL 2.0 introduced a programmable pipeline. It became possible for the programmer to replace certain stages in the pipeline with their own programs. This gives the programmer complete control over what happens at that stage. In OpenGL 2.0, the programmability was optional; the complete fixed-function pipeline was still available for programs that didn't need the flexibility of programmability. WebGL uses a programmable pipeline, and it is mandatory. There is no way to use WebGL without writing programs to implement part of the graphics processing pipeline.

The programs that are written as part of the pipeline are called shaders. For WebGL, you need to write a vertex shader, which is called once for each vertex in a primitive, and a fragment shader, which is called once for each pixel in the primitive. Aside from these two programmable stages, the WebGL pipeline also contains several stages from the original fixed-function pipeline. For example, the depth test is still part of the fixed functionality, and it can be enabled or disabled in WebGL in the same way as in OpenGL 1.1.

In this section, we will cover the basic structure of a WebGL program and how data flows from the JavaScript side of the program into the graphics pipeline and through the vertex and fragment shaders.

I should note that later versions of OpenGL have introduced new programmable stages, in addition to the vertex and fragment shaders, but they are not part of WebGL 1.0 or 2.0, and they are not covered in this book.

6.1.1 The WebGL Graphics Context

To use WebGL, you need a WebGL graphics context. The graphics context is a JavaScript object whose methods implement the JavaScript side of the WebGL API. WebGL draws its images in an HTML canvas, the same kind of <canvas> element that is used for the 2D API that was covered in Section 2.6. A graphics context is associated with a particular canvas. A graphics context for WebGL 1.0 can be obtained by calling the function canvas.getContext("webgl"), where canvas is a DOM object representing the canvas. For WebGL 2.0, you would simply use canvas.getContext("webgl2") instead. The return value of getContext() will be null if the context cannot be created. So, getting a WebGL graphics context often looks something like this:

```
canvas = document.getElementById("webglcanvas");
gl = canvas.getContext("webgl"); // or maybe
canvas.getContext("webgl2")
if ( ! gl ) {
    throw new Error("WebGL not supported; can't create graphics
context.");
}
```

Here, the first line gets a reference to the HTML canvas that WebGL will used throughout the program for drawing. The name *gl* for the variable is up to you, but I will always use *gl* for the WebGL graphics context in my discussion. This code assumes that the HTML source for the web page includes a canvas element with id="webglcanvas", such as

```
<canvas width="800" height="600" id="webglcanvas"></canvas>
```

In the second line of the above code, canvas.getContext("webgl") will return null if the web browser does not support "webgl" as a parameter to getContext. Since null is considered to be false in JavaScript when used in a boolean context, the third line tests whether the return value is null. In that case, the code throws an error, which can be handled elsewhere, probably by showing an error message to the user. Furthermore, the code will throw an exception if the browser has no support at all for <canvas>. My programs often use an initialization function of the form

```
function init() {
    try {
        canvas = document.getElementById("webglcanvas");
        gl = canvas.getContext("webgl"); // or "webgl2"
        if ( ! gl ) {
            throw new Error("WebGL not supported.");
```

```
        }
    }
    catch (e) {
            .
            \mathrm{ - // report the error}
            -
        return;
    }
    initGL(); // a function that initializes the WebGL graphics context
        .
        \mathrm{ - // other JavaScript initialization}
}
```

In this function, canvas and *gl* are global variables. And *initGL*() is a function defined elsewhere in the script that initializes the graphics context, including creating and installing the shader programs. The init() function should be called when the page is loaded. This can be arranged, for example, by assigning "window.onload = init;" in the script.

Once the graphics context, *gl*, has been created, it can be used to call functions in the WebGL API. For example, the command for enabling the depth test, which was written as glEnable(GL_DEPTH_TEST) in OpenGL, becomes

```
gl.enable( gl.DEPTH_TEST );
```

Note that both functions and constants in the API are referenced through the graphics context. The name "gl" for the graphics context is conventional, but remember that it is just an ordinary JavaScript variable whose name is up to the programmer. (Some very old browsers required canvas.getContext("experimental-webgl") to create a WebGL 1.0 context. This includes Internet Explorer 11, but at this point, no one should be using Internet Explorer.)

6.1.2 The Shader Program

Drawing with WebGL requires a shader program, which consists of a vertex shader and a fragment shader. Shaders are written in some version of the GLSL programming language. WebGL 1.0 used GLSL ES 1.00, while WebGL 2.0 can use either GLSL ES 1.00 or GLSL ES 3.00. The discussion here is about GLSL ES 1.00 ; I will explain some of the changes in the 3.00 version later.

GLSL is based on the C programming language. The vertex shader and fragment shader are separate programs, each with its own main() function. The two shaders are compiled separately and then "linked" to produce a complete shader program. The JavaScript API for WebGL includes functions for compiling the shaders and then linking them. To use the functions, the source code for the shaders must be JavaScript strings. Let's see how it works. It takes three steps to create the vertex shader.

```
let vertexShader = gl.createShader( gl.VERTEX_SHADER );
gl.shaderSource( vertexShader, vertexShaderSource );
gl.compileShader( vertexShader );
```

The functions that are used here are part of the WebGL graphics context, *gl*, and the parameter vertexShaderSource is the string that contains the source code for the shader. Errors in the source code will cause the compilation to fail silently. You need to check for compilation errors by calling the function

```
gl.getShaderParameter( vertexShader, gl.COMPILE_STATUS )
```

which returns a boolean value to indicate whether the compilation succeeded. In the event that an error occurred, you can retrieve an error message with

```
gl.getShaderInfoLog( vertexShader )
```

which returns a string containing the result of the compilation. (The exact format of the string is not specified by the WebGL standard. The string is meant to be human-readable.)

The fragment shader can be created in a similar way. With both shaders in hand, you can create and link the program. The shaders need to be "attached" to the program object before linking. The code takes the form:

```
let prog = gl.createProgram();
gl.attachShader( prog, vertexShader );
gl.attachShader( prog, fragmentShader );
gl.linkProgram( prog );
```

Even if the shaders have been successfully compiled, errors can occur when they are linked into a complete program. For example, the vertex and fragment shader can share certain kinds of variable. If the two programs declare such variables with the same name but with different types, an error will occur at link time. Checking for link errors is similar to checking for compilation errors in the shaders.

The code for creating a shader program is always pretty much the same, so it is convenient to pack it into a reusable function. Here is the function that I use for the examples in this chapter:

```
/**
    * Creates a program for use in the WebGL context gl, and returns
the
    * identifier for that program. If an error occurs while compiling
or
    * linking the program, an exception of type Error is thrown. The
error
    * string contains the compilation or linking error.


*/
function createProgram(gl, vertexShaderSource, fragmentShaderSource) {
    let vsh = gl.createShader( gl.VERTEX_SHADER );
    gl.shaderSource( vsh, vertexShaderSource );
    gl.compileShader( vsh );
    if ( ! gl.getShaderParameter(vsh, gl.COMPILE_STATUS) ) {
        throw new Error("Error in vertex shader: " +
gl.getShaderInfoLog(vsh));
    }
    let fsh = gl.createShader( gl.FRAGMENT_SHADER );
    gl.shaderSource( fsh, fragmentShaderSource );
    gl.compileShader( fsh );
    if ( ! gl.getShaderParameter(fsh, gl.COMPILE_STATUS) ) {
        throw new Error("Error in fragment shader: " +
gl.getShaderInfoLog(fsh));
    }
    let prog = gl.createProgram();
    gl.attachShader( prog, vsh );
    gl.attachShader( prog, fsh );
    gl.linkProgram( prog );
    if ( ! gl.getProgramParameter( prog, gl.LINK_STATUS) ) {
        throw new Error("Link error in program: " +
gl.getProgramInfoLog(prog));
    }
    return prog;
}
```

There is one more step: You have to tell the WebGL context to use the program. If prog is a program identifier returned by the above function, this is done by calling

```
gl.useProgram( prog );
```

It is possible to create several shader programs. You can then switch from one program to another at any time by calling gl.useProgram, even in the middle of rendering an image. (Three.js, for example, uses a different program for each type of Material.)

It is advisable to create any shader programs that you need as part of initialization. Although gl.useProgram is a fast operation, compiling and linking are rather slow, so it's better to avoid creating new programs while in the process of drawing an image.

Shaders and programs that are no longer needed can be deleted to free up the resources they consume. Use the functions gl.deleteShader(shader) and gl.deleteProgram(program).

6.1.3 Data Flow in the Pipeline

The WebGL graphics pipeline renders an image. The data that defines the image comes from JavaScript. As it passes through the pipeline, it is processed by the current vertex shader and fragment shader as well as by the fixed-function stages of the pipeline. You need to understand how data is placed by JavaScript into the pipeline and how the data is processed as it passes through the pipeline.

The basic operation in WebGL is to draw a geometric primitive. WebGL uses just seven of the OpenGL primitives that were introduced in Subsection 3.1.1. The primitives for drawing quads and polygons have been removed. The remaining primitives draw points, line segments, and triangles. In WegGL, the seven types of primitive are identified by the constants gl.POINTS, gl.LINES, gl.LINE_STRIP, gl.LINE_LOOP, gl.TRIANGLES, gl.TRIANGLE_STRIP, and gl.TRIANGLE_FAN, where *gl* is a WebGL graphics context.

When WebGL is used to draw a primitive, there are two general categories of data that can be provided for the primitive. The two kinds of data are referred to as attribute variables (or just "attributes") and uniform variables (or just "uniforms"). A primitive is defined by its type and by a list of vertices. The difference between attributes and uniforms is that a uniform variable has a single value that is the same for the entire primitive, while the value of an attribute variable can be different for different vertices.

One attribute that should always be specified is the coordinates of the vertex. The vertex coordinates must be an attribute since each vertex in a primitive will have its own set of coordinates. Another possible attribute is color. We have seen that OpenGL allows you to specify a different color for each vertex of a primitive. You can do the same thing in WebGL, and in that case the color will be an attribute. On the other hand, maybe you want the entire primitive to have the same, "uniform" color; in that case, color can be a uniform variable. Other quantities that could be either attributes or uniforms, depending on your needs, include normal vectors and material properties. Texture coordinates, if they are used, are almost certain to be an attribute, since it doesn't really make sense for all the vertices in a primitive to have the same texture coordinates. If a geometric transform is to be applied to the primitive, it would naturally be represented as a uniform variable.

It is important to understand, however, that WebGL does not come with any predefined attributes, not even one for vertex coordinates. In the programmable pipeline, the attributes and uniforms that are used are entirely up to the programmer. As far as WebGL is concerned, attributes are just values that are passed into the vertex shader. Uniforms can be passed into the vertex shader, the fragment shader, or both. WebGL does not assign a meaning to the values. The meaning is entirely determined by what the shaders do with the values. The set of attributes and uniforms that are used in drawing a primitive is determined by the source code of the shaders that are in use when the primitive is drawn.

To understand this, we need to look at what happens in the pipeline in a more detail. When drawing a primitive, the JavaScript program specifies values for any attributes and uniforms in the shader program. For each attribute, it will specify an array of values, one for each vertex. For each uniform, it will specify a single value. It must send these values to the to the GPU before drawing the primitive. The primitive can then be drawn by calling a single JavaScript function. At that point, the GPU takes over, and executes the shader programs. When drawing the primitive, the GPU calls the vertex shader once for each vertex. The attribute values for the vertex that is to be processed are passed as input into the vertex shader. Values of uniform variables are also passed to the vertex shader. The way this works is that both attributes and uniforms are represented as global variables in the vertex shader program. Before calling the shader for a given vertex, the GPU sets the values of those variables appropriately for that specific vertex.

As one of its outputs, the vertex shader must specify the coordinates of the vertex in the clip coordinate system (see Subsection 3.3.1). It does that by assigning a value to a special variable named gl_Position. The position is often computed by applying a transformation to the attribute that represents the coordinates in the object coordinate system, but exactly how the position is computed is up to the programmer.

After the positions of all the vertices in the primitive have been computed, a fixed-function stage in the pipeline clips away the parts of the primitive whose coordinates are outside the range of valid clip coordinates (-1 to 1 along each coordinate axis). The primitive is then rasterized; that is, it is determined which pixels lie inside the primitive. The GPU then calls the fragment shader once for each pixel that lies in the primitive. The fragment shader has access to uniform variables (but not attributes). It can also use a special variable named gl_FragCoord that contains the clip coordinates of the pixel. Pixel coordinates are computed by interpolating the values of gl_Position that were specified by the vertex shader. The interpolation is done by another fixed-function stage that comes between the vertex shader and the fragment shader.

Other quantities besides coordinates can work in much that same way. That is, the vertex shader computes a value for the quantity at each vertex of a primitive. An interpolator takes the values at the vertices and computes a value for each pixel in the primitive. The value for a given pixel is then input into the fragment shader when the shader is called to process that pixel. For example, color in OpenGL follows this pattern: The color of an interior pixel of a primitive is computed by interpolating the color at the vertices. In GLSL, this pattern is implemented using varying variables.

A varying variable is declared both in the vertex shader and in the fragment shader. The vertex shader is responsible for assigning a value to the varying variable. Each vertex of a primitive can assign a different value to the variable. The interpolator takes all the values produced by executing the vertex shader for each vertex of the primitive, and it interpolates those values to produce a value for each pixel. When the fragment shader is executed for a given pixel, the value of the varying variable is the interpolated value for that pixel. The fragment shader can use the value in its own computations.

Varying variables exist to communicate data from the vertex shader to the fragment shader. They are defined in the shader source code. They are not used or referred to in the JavaScript side of the API. Note that it is entirely up to the programmer to decide what varying variables to define and what to do with them.

We have almost gotten to the end of the pipeline. After all that, the job of the fragment shader is simply to specify a color for the pixel. It does that by assigning a value to a special variable named gl_FragColor. That value will then be used in the remaining fixed-function stages of the pipeline.

To summarize: The JavaScript side of the program sends values for attributes and uniform variables to the GPU and then issues a command to draw a primitive. The GPU executes the vertex shader once for each vertex. The vertex shader can use the values of attributes and uniforms. It assigns values to gl_Position and to any varying variables that exist in the shader. After clipping, rasterization, and interpolation, the GPU executes the fragment shader once for each pixel in the primitive. The fragment shader can use the values of varying variables, uniform variables, and gl_FragCoord. It computes a value for gl_FragColor. This diagram summarizes the flow of data:

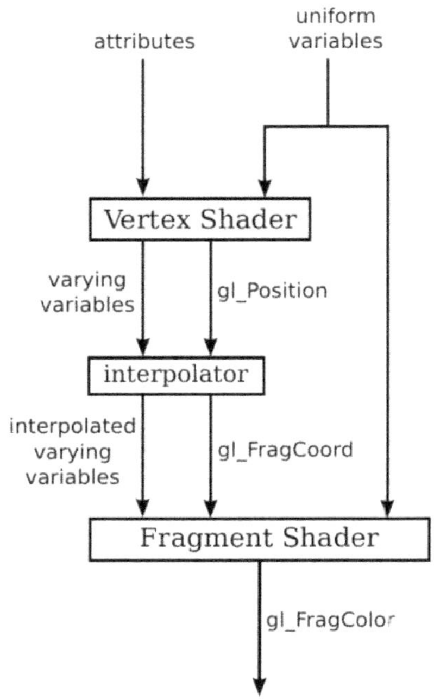

The diagram is not complete. There are a few more special variables that I haven't mentioned. And there is the important question of how textures are used. But if you understand the diagram, you have a good start on understanding WebGL.

For GLSL ES 3.00, the same diagram applies, except that there is no special variable gl_FragColor. Instead, the fragment shader must define its own output variable to represent the color. In GLSL ES 1.00, the words "attribute" and "varying" are used when declaring variables in the actual shader program source code. In source code for the 3.00 version, attribute variables become "in" variables, since they are inputs to the vertex shader, and varying variables become "out" variables in the vertex shader and "in" variables in the fragment shader. And the variable gl_FragColor is replaced by an "out" variable in the fragment shader. The use of the terms "in" and "out" are actually more appropriate to systems with additional pipeline stages, where "out" variables from one stage can become "in" variables to the next stage. In any case, people still use the terms attribute and varying when discussing WebGL, even if it is using GLSL ES 3.00.

6.1.4 Values for Uniform Variables

It's time to start looking at some actual WebGL code. We will concentrate on the JavaScript side first, but you need to know a little about GLSL. GLSL has some familiar basic data types: float, int, and bool. But it also has some new predefined data types to represent vectors and matrices. For example, the data type vec3 represents a vector in 3D. The value of a vec3 variable is a list of three floating-point numbers. Similarly, there are data types vec2 and vec4 to represent 2D and 4D vectors.

Global variable declarations in a vertex shader can be marked as attribute, varying, or uniform (or as in, out, or uniform in GLSL ES 3.00, but again, we will stick to the 1.00 version for the time being). A variable declaration with none of these modifiers defines a variable that is local to the vertex shader. Global variables in a fragment can optionally be uniform or varying, or they can be declared without a modifier. A varying variable should be declared in both shaders, with the same name and type. This allows the GLSL compiler to determine what attribute, uniform, and varying variables are used in a shader program.

The JavaScript side of the program needs a way to refer to particular attributes and uniform variables. The function gl.getUniformLocation can be used to get a reference to a uniform variable in a shader program, where *gl* refers to the WebGL graphics context. It takes as parameters the identifier for the compiled program, which was returned by gl.createProgram, and the name of the uniform variable in the shader source code. For example, if prog identifies a shader program that has a uniform variable named color, then the location of the color variable can be obtained with the JavaScript statement

```
colorUniformLoc = gl.getUniformLocation( prog, "color" );
```

The location colorUniformLoc can then be used to set the value of the uniform variable. For example:

```
gl.uniform3f( colorUniformLoc, 1, 0, 0 );
```

The function gl.uniform 3*f* is one of a family of functions that can be referred to as a group as gl.uniform*. This is similar to the family glVertex* in OpenGL 1.1. The * represents a suffix that tells the number and type of values that are provided for the variable. In this case, gl.uniform3f takes three floating point values, and it is appropriate for setting the value of a uniform variable of type vec3. The number of values can be 1,2,3, or 4 . The type can be " f " for floating point or " i " for integer. (For a boolean uniform, you should use gl.uniform1i and pass 0 to represent false or 1 to represent true.) If a " v " is added to the suffix, then the values are passed in an array. For example,

```
gl.uniform3fv( colorUniformLoc, [ 1, 0, 0 ] );
```

There is another family of functions for setting the value of uniform matrix variables. We will get to that later.

The value of a uniform variable can be set any time after the shader program has been compiled, and the value remains in effect until it is changed by another call to gl.uniform*.

If the string that is passed as the second parameter gl.getUniformLocation is not the name of a uniform variable in the shader programs, then the return value is null. The return value can also be null if the uniform variable is declared in the shader source code but is not "active" in the program. A variable that is declared but not actually used is not active, and it does not get a location in the compiled program. This has occasionally caused problems for me, when I commented out part of a shader program for debugging purposes, and accidently made a variable inactive by doing so.

6.1.5 Values for Attributes

Turning now to attributes, the situation is more complicated, because an attribute can take a different value for each vertex in a primitive. The basic idea is that the complete set of data for the attribute is copied in a single operation from a JavaScript array into memory that is accessible to the GPU. Unfortunately, setting things up to make that operation possible is non-trivial.

First of all, a regular JavaScript array is not suitable for this purpose. For efficiency, we need the data to be in a block of memory holding numerical values in successive memory locations, and regular JavaScript arrays don't have that form. To fix this problem, a new kind of array, called typed arrays, was introduced into JavaScript. We encountered typed arrays when working with three.js in the Chapter 5. There is a short introduction to typed arrays in Subsection 5.1.3. A typed array has a fixed length, which is assigned when it is created, and it can only hold numbers of a specified type. There are different kinds of typed array for different kinds of numerical data. For now we will use Float32Array, which holds 32-bit floating point numbers. Once you have a typed array, you can use it much like a regular array, but when you assign any value to an element of a Float32Array, the value is converted into a 32 -bit floating point number. If the value cannot be interpreted as a number, it will be converted to NaN, the "not-a-number" value.

Before data can be transferred from JavaScript into an attribute variable, it must be placed into a typed array. When possible, for efficiency, you should work with typed arrays directly, rather than working with regular JavaScript arrays and then copying the data into typed arrays.

For use in WebGL, the attribute data must be transferred into a VBO (vertex buffer object). VBOs were introduced in OpenGL 1.5 and were discussed briefly in Subsection 3.4.4. A VBO is a block of memory that is accessible to the GPU. To use a VBO, you must first call the function gl.createBuffer() to create it. For example,

```
colorBuffer = gl.createBuffer();
```

Before transferring data into the VBO, you must "bind" the VBO:

```
gl.bindBuffer( gl.ARRAY_BUFFER, colorBuffer );
```

The first parameter to gl.bindBuffer is called the "target." It specifies how the VBO will be used. The target gl.ARRAY_BUFFER is used when the buffer is being used to store values for an attribute. Only one VBO at a time can be bound to a given target.

The function that transfers data into a VBO doesn't mention the VBO - instead, it uses the VBO that is currently bound. To copy data into that buffer, use gl.bufferData(). For example:

```
gl.bufferData(gl.ARRAY_BUFFER, colorArray, gl.STATIC_DRAW);
```

The first parameter is, again, the target. The data is transferred into the VBO that is bound to that target. The second parameter is the typed array that holds the data on the JavaScript side. All the elements of the array are copied into the buffer, and the size of the array determines the size of the buffer. Note that this is a straightforward transfer of raw data bytes; WebGL does not remember whether the data represents floats or ints or some other kind of data.

The third parameter to gl.bufferData is one of the constants gl.STATIC_DRAW, gl.STREAM_DRAW, or gl.DYNAMIC_DRAW. It is a hint to WebGL about how the data will be used, and it helps WebGL to manage the data in the most efficient way. The value gl.STATIC_DRAW means that you intend to use the data many times without changing it. For example, if you will use the same data throughout the program, you can load it into a buffer once, during initialization, using $gl.STATIC\_DRAW$. WebGL will probably store the data on the graphics card itself where it can be accessed most quickly by the graphics hardware. The second value, gl.STEAM_DRAW, is for data that will be used only once, or at most a few times. (It can be "streamed" to the card when it is needed.) The value gl.DYNAMIC_DRAW is somewhere between the other two values; it is meant for data that will be used multiple times, but with modifications.

Getting attribute data into VBOs is only part of the story. You also have to tell WebGL to use the VBO as the source of values for the attribute. To do so, first of all, you need to know the location of the attribute in the shader program. You can determine that using gl.getAttribLocation. For example,

```
colorAttribLoc = gl.getAttribLocation(prog, "a_color");
```

This assumes that prog is the shader program and "a_color" is the name of the attribute variable in the vertex shader. This is entirely analogous to gl.getUniformLocation (except that the return value is an integer, and is -1 if the requested attribute does not exist or is not active).

Although an attribute usually takes different values at different vertices, it is possible to use the same value at every vertex. In fact, that is the default behavior. The single attribute value for all vertices can be set using the family of functions gl.vertexAttrib*, which work similarly to gl.uniform*. In the more usual case, where you want to take the values of an attribute from a VBO, you must enable the use of a VBO for that attribute. This is done by calling

```
gl.enableVertexAttribArray( colorAttribLoc );
```

where the parameter is the location of the attribute in the shader program, as returned by a call to gl.getAttribLocation () . This command has nothing to do with any particular VBO. It just turns on the use of buffers for the specified attribute. Often, it is reasonable to call this method just once, during initialization. Use of data from the VBO can be turned off by calling

```
gl.disableVertexAttribArray( colorAttribLoc );
```

Finally, before you draw a primitive that uses the attribute data from a VBO, you have to tell WebGL which buffer contains the data and how the bits in that buffer are to be interpreted. This is done with gl.vertexAttribPointer(). The VBO must be bound to the ARRAY_BUFFER target when this function is called. For example,

```
gl.bindBuffer( gl.ARRAY_BUFFER, colorBuffer );
gl.vertexAttribPointer( colorAttribLoc, 3, gl.FLOAT, false, 0, 0 );
```

Assuming that colorBuffer refers to the VBO and colorAttribLoc is the location of the attribute, this tells WebGL to take values for the attribute from that buffer. Often, you will call gl.bindBuffer() just before calling gl.vertexAttribPointer(), but that is not necessary if the desired buffer is already bound.

The first parameter to gl.vertexAttribPointer is the attribute location. The second is the number of values per vertex. For example, if you are providing values for a vec2, the second parameter will be 2 and you will provide two numbers per vertex; for a vec3, the second parameter would be 3 ; for a float, it would be 1 . The third parameter specifies the type of each value. Here, gl.FLOAT indicates that each value is a 32 -bit floating point number. Other values include gl.BYTE, gl.UNSIGNED_BYTE, gl.UNSIGNED_SHORT, and gl.SHORT for integer values. Note that in WebGL 1.0, all attributes are floating point values; if you provide integer values for an attribute, they will be converted to floating point. The parameter value should match the data type in the buffer. For example, if the data came from a Float32Array, then the parameter should be gl.FLOAT. For the last three parameters in a call to gl.vertexAttribPointer, I will always use false, 0 , and 0 . These parameters add flexibility that I won't need; you can look them up in the documentation if you are interested. (The false parameter has to do with how integer values are converted into floating point values.)

In WebGL 2.0, attribute variables can have integer type. When gl.vertexAttribPointer() is used to configure an attribute, the values provided for the attribute will always be converted to floating point, so it is inappropriate for integer-valued attributes. For use with integer-valued attributes, WebGL 2.0 introduces a new function, gl.vertexAttribIPointer() that works correctly with integer data.

There is a lot to take in here. Using a VBO to provide values for an attribute requires six separate commands, and that is in addition to generating the data and placing it in a typed array. Here is the full set of commands:

```
colorAttribLoc = gl.getAttribLocation( prog, "a_color" );
colorBuffer = gl.createBuffer();
gl.enableVertexAttribArray( colorAttribLoc );
gl.bindBuffer( gl.ARRAY_BUFFER, colorBuffer );
gl.vertexAttribPointer( colorAttribLoc, 3, gl.FLOAT, false, 0, 0 );
gl.bufferData( gl.ARRAY_BUFFER, colorArray, gl.STATIC_DRAW );
```

However, the six commands will not always occur at the same point in the JavaScript code. The first three commands are often done as part of initialization. gl.bufferData would be called whenever the data for the attribute needs to be changed; it might be used just once during initialization, or it might be used whenever the data needs to be modified. gl.bindBuffer must be called before gl.vertexAttribPointer or gl.bufferData, since it establishes the VBO that is used by those two commands. Remember that all of this must be done for every attribute that is used in the shader program.

6.1.6 Drawing a Primitive

After the shader program has been created and values have been set up for the uniform variables and attributes, it takes just one more command to draw a primitive. One way to do that is with the function gl.drawArrays:

```
gl.drawArrays( primitiveType, startVertex, vertexCount );
```

The first parameter is one of the seven constants that identify WebGL primitive types, such as gl.TRIANGLES, gl.LINE_LOOP, and gl_POINTS. The second and third parameters are integers that determine which subset of available vertices is used for the primitive. Before calling gl.drawArrays, you will have placed attribute values for some number of vertices into one or more VBOs. When the primitive is rendered, the attribute values for enabled attributes are pulled from the VBOs. The startVetex is the starting vertex number of the data within the VBOs, and vertexCount is the number of vertices in the primitive. Often, startVertex is zero, and vertexCount is the total number of vertices for which data is available. For example, the command for drawing a single triangle might be

```
gl.drawArrays( gl.TRIANGLES, 0, 3 );
```

The use of the word "array" in gl.drawArrays and gl.ARRAY_BUFFER might be a little confusing, since the data is stored in vertex buffer objects rather than in JavaScript arrays. When glDrawArrays was first introduced in OpenGL 1.1, it used ordinary arrays rather than VBOs. Starting with OpenGL 1.5, glDrawArrays could be used either with ordinary arrays or VBOs. In WebGL, support for ordinary arrays was dropped, and gl.drawArrays can only work with VBOs, even though the name still refers to arrays.

We encountered the original version of glDrawArrays in Subsection 3.4.2. That section also introduced an alternative function for drawing primitives, glDrawElements, which can be used for drawing indexed face sets. A gl.drawElements function is also available in WebGL. With gl.drawElements, attribute data is not used in the order in which it occurs in the VBOs. Instead, there is a separate list of indices that determines the order in which the data is accessed.

To use gl.drawElements, an extra VBO is required to hold the list of indices. When used for this purpose, the VBO must be bound to the target gl.ELEMENT_ARRAY_BUFFER rather than *gl.ARRAY_BUFFER*. The VBO will hold integer values, which can be of type gl.UNSIGNED_BYTE or gl.UNSIGNED_SHORT (or, for WebGL 2.0, gl.USIGNED_INT). The values can be loaded from a JavaScript typed array of type Uint8Array, for gl.UNSIGNED_BYTE, or Uint16Array, for gl.UNSIGNED_SHORT. Creating the VBO and filling it with data is again a multistep process. For example,

```
elementBuffer = gl.createBuffer();
gl.bindBuffer( gl.ELEMENT_ARRAY_BUFFER, elementBuffer );
let data = new Uint8Array( [ 2,0,3, 2,1,3, 1,4,3 ] );
gl.bufferData( gl.ELEMENT_ARRAY_BUFFER, data, gl.STREAM_DRAW );
```

Assuming that the attribute data has also been loaded into VBOs, gl.drawElements can then be used to draw the primitive. A call to gl.drawElements takes the form

```
gl.drawElements( primitiveType, count, dataType, startByte );
```

The VBO that contains the vertex indices must be bound to the ELEMENT_ARRAY_BUFFER target when this function is called. The first parameter to gl.drawElements is a primitive type such as gl.TRIANGLE_FAN. The count is the number of vertices in the primitive. The dataType specifies the type of data that was loaded into the VBO; it will be either gl.UNSIGNED_SHORT or gl.UNSIGNED_BYTE. The startByte is the starting point in the VBO of the data for the primitive; it is usually zero. (Note that the starting point is given in terms of bytes, not vertex numbers.) A typical example would be

```
gl.drawElements( gl.TRIANGLES, 9, gl.UNSIGNED_BYTE, 0 );
```

We will have occasion to use this function later. If you find it confusing, you should review Subsection 3.4.2. The situation is much the same in WebGL as it was in OpenGL 1.1.

6.1.7 WebGL 2.0: Vertex Array Objects

The large number of functions needed to work with attributes can seem excessive. The situation is worse in a program that draws several different objects. Each object can require its own buffers and its own settings for attribute pointers. Before drawing each object, it would be necessary to call gl.bindBuffer() and gl.vertexAttribPointer() for each attribute. A typical 3D graphics program would use attributes for vertex coordinates, normal vectors, material properties, and texture coordinates. So, there would be a lot of function calls for each object.

To help with this situation, WebGL 2.0 introduced Vertex Array Objects (VAOs). A VAO is a section of memory, typically stored on the graphics card. It holds settings that are used by rendering functions such as gl.drawArrays(). This includes the enabled state of each attribute, references to the buffers used for the attribute data, and the values of all properties that are set by calling gl.vertexAttribPointer(). It also includes the settings and a reference to the buffer used by gl.drawElements(), as well as the attribute divisors that are discussed in the next subsection.

WebGL 2.0 has a default VAO, which it uses when no other VAO has been selected. To use an alternative VAO, you first have to create it, by calling gl.createVertexArray():

```
vao = gl.createVertexArray();
```

The return value, vao, is an identifier for the VAO that has been created. In the new VAO, all properties have their default values. In particular, all vertex attributes are disabled and have no associated buffers. To actually use a VAO, you need to bind it:

```
gl.bindVertexArray(vao);
```

Functions that affect or use attributes apply to the VAO that is currently bound. For example, the settings in a call to gl.vertexAttribPointer() are stored in the current VAO. And a call to gl.drawArrays () gets all the data that it needs to draw a primitive from the current VAO. A program can switch from one VAO to another at any time simply by calling gl.bindVertexArray. To go back to using the default VAO, a program can call gl.bindVertexArray (0).

The idea is that a program that draws several objects can use a different VAO for each object. The VAO for an object must be bound when the settings for the object are configured. But before drawing the object, the program simply needs to bind the VAO for that object. That single function call replaces a potentially a large number of function calls that would be needed to restore the appropriate settings for each attribute individually. The advantage is more than just a more nicely organized program-it is also much more efficient, since only one command needs to be sent to the GPU to configure all of the attributes.

The sample WebGL 2.0 program webgl/VAO-test-webgl2.html uses a different VAO for each of six different objects. That program uses many techniques that we have not yet covered, but you can look at the drawModel() function to see how it uses VAOs and VBOs.

6.1.8 WebGL 2.0: Instanced Drawing

It's common for a scene to contain multiple copies of the same primitive (that is, using the same vertex coordinates), but with different transformations, colors, or other properties for each copy. WebGL 2.0 makes it possible to draw all those copies with a single function call. This is called instanced drawing or instancing, and the individual copies of the primitive are called instances. The functions that use instanced drawing are gl.drawArraysInstanced () and gl.drawElementsInstanced().

Instanced properties - the properties that vary from one instance to another-are things that would likely be uniform variables when drawing each instance separately. That is, each instance gets just one value of the property that applies to all the vertices of the instance. Nevertheless, the properties are represented by attribute variables in the shader program, not uniform variables, and they are configured as attributes.

To specify that an attribute is an instanced property, you just need to specify a "divisor" for that attribute. This is done by calling gl.vertexAttribDivisor:

```
g.vertexAttribDivisor( attribID, divisor );
```

Here, attribID is the identifier for the attribute, as returned by gl.getAttribLocation(). The divisor is a non-negative integer. Passing zero as the divisor will turn off instancing for the attribute. If divisor is positive, then each value of the attribute will apply to that many instances. For example, if divisor is 3 , then the first entry in the attribute value array applies to the first, second, and third instances; the second value in the array applies to the fourth, fifth, and sixth instances; and so on. In practice, the value of divisor is usually one, meaning that each instance has its own entry in the attribute value array.

For an instanced property, in addition to setting the divisor, it is still necessary to enable the attribute, load data for it into a VBO, and configure it with gl.vertexAttribPointer. And, of course, it is necessary to draw the primitive using gl.drawArraysInstanced() or gl.drawElementsInstanced(), and not with gl.drawArrays() or gl.drawElements().

The sample WebGL 2.0 program webgl/instancing-test-webgl2.html is an example of instanced drawing. (Again, there is a lot in the program that you won't understand until we have covered more of WebGL). The program draws 30 colored disks, where a disk is approximated by a primitive of type gl.TRIANGLE_FAN. Three attributes are used: an attribute that holds the coordinates of the vertices, an instanced attribute that holds the colors for the disks, and an instanced attribute that holds a different translation for each disk.

Another point of interest in the program is its used of vertex buffer objects. The disks can be animated. The disks move, but their colors don't change. Since the colors don't change, the color values for the disks are loaded into a VBO once, during program initialization. The usage parameter in gl.bufferData is set to gl.STATIC_DRAW because the data will not be modified. However, because the disks are moving, the values for the translations of the disks have to change in each frame. So, new data is loaded into the corresponding VBO for each frame, with usage gl.STREAM_DRAW because the data that is being loaded will only be used once.

Finally, I should note that VAOs and instancing require WebGL 2.0, but the same functionality is available in many implementations of WebGL 1.0 as optional extensions. Webgl extensions will be discussed in Section 7.5.

6.2 First Examples

We are ready to start working towards our first WebGL programs. This section begins with a few more details about the WebGL graphics context, followed by a short introduction to GLSL, the programming language for WebGL shaders. With that in hand, we can turn to the standard first example: the RGB color triangle.

6.2.1 WebGL Context Options

We saw in Subsection 6.1.1 that a WebGL graphics context is created by the function canvas.getContext, where canvas is a reference to the <canvas> element where the graphics context will draw. This function takes an optional second parameter that can be used to set the value of certain options in the graphics context. The second parameter is only needed if you want to give a non-default value to at least one of the options. The parameter is a JavaScript object whose properties are the names of the options. Here is an example of context creation with options:

```
let options = {
    alpha: false,
    depth: false
};
gl = canvas.getContext( "webgl", options ); // (or "webgl2")
```

All of the options are boolean-valued. I will discuss the most useful ones here: alpha - determines whether the drawing buffer has an alpha component. This is the alpha component for the image canvas as a whole. If there is an alpha component, then it is possible for pixels in the canvas to be transparent or translucent, letting the background (on the web page behind the canvas) show through. The default value is true. It is safe to set the value to false, if you want the canvas to be fully opaque. Setting it to false does not stop you from doing alpha blending of the drawing color with the image color; the RGB color components can still be computed by blending. However, setting the value to false is only necessary if your program outputs pixels with alpha component less than 1.0 , and you don't want your image to blend with the background of the canvas. (Note however that a graphics context with an alpha component might be handled more efficiently, because web pages use RGBA colors for their display.) depth - determines whether a depth buffer is allocated. The default value is true. You only need a depth buffer if you enable the depth test. The depth buffer is generally not needed for 2D graphics. If your application doesn't need it, eliminating the depth buffer can save some memory in the GPU. antialias - is used to request that antialiasing be applied to the image. A WebGL implementation might ignore the request, for example if antialiasing is not supported by the GPU. The default value is true. Antialiasing can improve the quality of an image, but it can also significantly increase the computation time. preserveDrawingBuffer - determines whether the contents of the drawing buffer are discarded after the image has been copied to the web page. The default value is false. The drawing buffer is internal to WebGL. Its contents only become visible on the screen when the web browser copies the image onto the web page. The default value for preserveDrawingBuffer means that once that happens, WebGL can discard its own copy of the image, which allows the GPU to free up resources for other operations. As long as your rendering functions completely redraw the image every time they called, the default is fine. You should set the value to true only if you need to keep the image around so that you can add to it incrementally over time.

6.2.2 A Bit of GLSL

The next section will cover GLSL more thoroughly. But you will need to know something about the language to understand the examples in this section. This section discusses GLSL ES 1.00 only, but remember that that language can be used with both WebGL 1.0 and WebGL 2.0.

A vertex or fragment shader can contain global variable declarations, type definitions, and function definitions. One of the functions must be main(), which is the entry point for the shader; that is, it is the function that is called by the GPU to process the vertex or fragment. The main() routine takes no parameters and does not return a value, so it takes the form

```
void main() {
    .
    .
    .
}
```

(Alternatively, it can be declared as void main(void).) Control structures are limited. If statements take the same form as in C or Java. But some limitations are placed on the for loop syntax, and while and do...while loops are not allowed. Data structures include arrays and structs, again with some limitations. We will cover all this in some detail in the next section.

GLSL's strength lies in its built-in data types and functions for working with vectors and matrices. In this section, we will only need the data types float, vec2, vec3, and vec4. These types represent, respectively, 1,2,3, or 4 floating point numbers. Variable declarations are similar to C . Some examples are:

```
attribute vec3 a_coords; // (only in vertex shader)
vec3 rgb;
float width, height;
uniform vec2 u_size;
varying vec4 v_color;
```

Attribute, uniform, and varying variables were discussed in Section 6.1. They are used for communication between JavaScript and the shader program and between the vertex shader and the fragment shader. In the above examples, I used the prefixes " a_", " u_", and " v_" in the names of the variables, but that is not required.

It is common to construct a value for a vector from individual numbers or from shorter vectors. GLSL has a flexible notation for doing this. Using the variables declared in the above examples, we can write

```
rgb = vec3( 1.0, 0.7, 0.0 ); // construct a vec3 from constants
v_color = vec4( rgb, 1.0 ); // construct a vec4 from a vec3 and a
constant
gl_Position = vec4( a_coords, 0.0, 1.0 ); // vec4 from a vec2 and 2
constants
```

In the last assignment statement, gl_Position is the special built-in variable that is used in the vertex shader to give the coordinates of the vertex. gl_Position is of type vec4, requiring four numbers, because the coordinates are specified as homogeneous coordinates (Subsection 3.5.3). The special variable gl_FragCoord in the fragment shader is also a vec4, giving the coordinates of the pixel as homogeneous coordinates. And gl_FragColor is a vec4, giving the four RGBA color components for the pixel.

A vertex shader needs, at a minimum, an attribute to give the coordinates of the vertex. For 2D drawing, it's natural for that attribute to be of type vec2. If we assume that the values for the attribute are already expressed in clip coordinates, then the complete source code for the vertex shader could be as simple as:

```
attribute vec2 coords;
void main() {
    gl_Position = vec4( coords, 0.0, 1.0 );
}
```

For a corresponding minimal fragment shader, we might simply draw everything in yellow.

```
precision mediump float;
void main() {
    glFragColor = vec4( 1.0, 1.0, 0.0, 1.0 );
}
```

The strange first line in this fragment shader has not been explained, but something like it is required. It will be explained in the next section.

6.2.3 The RGB Triangle in WebGL

We are ready to look at our first full WebGL example, which will draw the usual RGB color triangle, as shown here:

The source code can be found in webgl/webgl-rgb-triangle.html. The code includes the usual init() and createProgram() functions as discussed in Subsection 6.1.1 and Subsection 6.1.2, except that I have turned off the "alpha" and "depth" options in the WebGL context. I won't discuss those two functions further.

The example uses an attribute of type vec2 to specify the coordinates of the vertices of the triangle. Coordinates range from -1 to 1 in the default WebGL coordinate system. For the triangle, the vertex coordinates that I use are in that range, so no coordinate transformation is needed. Since the color is different at each vertex of the triangle, the vertex color is also an attribute. I use an attribute of type vec3 for the vertex colors, since no alpha component is needed in this program.

The color of interior pixels in the triangle is interpolated from the colors at the vertices. The interpolation means that we need a varying variable to represent the color. A varying variable is assigned a value in the vertex shader, and its value is used in the fragment shader.

It looks like we need two color variables: an attribute and a varying variable. We can't use the same variable for both purposes. The attribute carries the vertex color from JavaScript into the vertex shader; the varying variable carries the color from the vertex shader to the fragment shader. In this case, the color value going out of the vertex shader is the same as the value coming in, so the shader just has to copy the value from the color attribute to the varying variable. This pattern is actually fairly common. Here is the vertex shader:

```
attribute vec2 a_coords;
attribute vec3 a_color;
varying vec3 v_color;
void main() {
    gl_Position = vec4(a_coords, 0.0, 1.0);
    v_color = a_color;
}
```

The fragment shader only has to copy the incoming color value from the varying variable into gl_FragColor, which specifies the outgoing color for the fragment:

```
precision mediump float;
varying vec3 v_color;
void main() {
    gl_FragColor = vec4(v_color, 1.0);
}
```

In order to compile the shader program, the source code for the shaders has to be in JavaScript strings. In this case, I construct the strings by concatenating constant strings representing the individual lines of code. For example, the fragment shader source code is included in the JavaScript script as the global variable

```
const fragmentShaderSource =
    "precision mediump float;\n" +
    "varying vec3 v_color;\n" +
    "void main() {\n" +
    "  gl_FragColor = vec4(v_color, 1.0);\n" +
    "}\n";
```

The line feed character, " n ", at the end of each line is not required, but it allows the GLSL compiler to include a meaningful line number in any error message that it generates.

Also on the JavaScript side, we need a global variable for the WebGL context. And we need to provide values for the attribute variables. The rather complicated process was discussed in Subsection 6.1.5. We need global variables to represent the location of each attribute in the shader program, and to represent the VBOs that will hold the attribute values. I use the variables

```
let gl; // The WebGL graphics context.
let attributeCoords; // Location of the attribute named "a_coords".
let bufferCoords; // A vertex buffer object to hold the values for
a_coords.
let attributeColor; // Location of the attribute named "a_color".
let bufferColor; // A vertex buffer object to hold the values for
a_color.
```

The graphics context is created in the init() function. The other variables are initialized in a function *initGL*() that is called from *init*(). That function also creates the shader program, using the createProgram() function from Subsection 6.1.2:

```
function initGL() {
    let prog = createProgram( gl, vertexShaderSource,
fragmentShaderSource );
```

```
    gl.useProgram(prog);
    attributeCoords = gl.getAttribLocation(prog, "a_coords");
    bufferCoords = gl.createBuffer();
    attributeColor = gl.getAttribLocation(prog, "a_color");
    bufferColor = gl.createBuffer();
}
```

To set up the values for an attribute, we need six different JavaScript commands (and more if you count placing the attribute values into a typed array). The commands getAttribLocation and createBuffer will most likely be called just once for each attribute, so I put them in my initialization routine. The other four commands are in draw(), the function that draws the image. In this program, draw() is called just once, so the division of the code into two functions is not really necessary, but in general, a draw function is meant to be called many times. (It would be a particularly bad idea to create a new VBO every time draw() is called!)

Before drawing the triangle, the draw() function fills the canvas with a black background. This is done using the WebGL functions gl.clearColor and gl.clear, which have exactly the same functionality as the OpenGL 1.1 functions glClearColor and glClear. Here is the code:

```
function draw() {
    gl.clearColor(0,0,0,1); // specify the color to be used for
clearing
    gl.clear(gl.COLOR_BUFFER_BIT); // clear the canvas (to black)
    /* Set up values for the "a_coords" attribute */
    let coords = new Float32Array( [ -0.9,-0.8, 0.9,-0.8, 0,0.9 ] );
    gl.bindBuffer(gl.ARRAY_BUFFER, bufferCoords);
    gl.bufferData(gl.ARRAY_BUFFER, coords, gl.STREAM_DRAW);
    gl.vertexAttribPointer(attributeCoords, 2, gl.FLOAT, false, 0, 0);
    gl.enableVertexAttribArray(attributeCoords);
    /* Set up values for the "a_color" attribute */
    let color = new Float32Array( [ 0,0,1, 0,1,0, 1,0,0 ] );
    gl.bindBuffer(gl.ARRAY_BUFFER, bufferColor);
    gl.bufferData(gl.ARRAY_BUFFER, color, gl.STREAM_DRAW);
    gl.vertexAttribPointer(attributeColor, 3, gl.FLOAT, false, 0, 0);
    gl.enableVertexAttribArray(attributeColor);
```

```
    /* Draw the triangle. */
    gl.drawArrays(gl.TRIANGLES, 0, 3);
}
```

In this function, the variable coords contains values for the attribute named "a_coords" in the vertex shader. That attribute represents the x and y coordinates of the vertex. Since the attribute is of type vec2, two numbers are required for each vertex. The value for coords is created here with a Float32Array constructor that takes an ordinary JavaScript array as its parameter; the values from the JavaScript array are copied into the newly created typed array. Similarly, the variable color contains values for the "a_color" attribute in the vertex shader, with three numbers per vertex.

We have now accounted for all the pieces of the RGB triangle program. Read the complete source code to see how it fits together.

6.2.4 Shape Stamper

Our next example will introduce a few new features. The example is a simple interactive program where the user can place shapes in a canvas by clicking the canvas with the mouse. Properties of the shape are taken from a set of popup menus. The properties include the color and degree of transparency of the shape, as well as which of several possible shapes is drawn. The shape is centered at the point where the user clicks.

The sample program is webgl/shape-stamper.html. There is also a demo version the program, c6/shape-stamper-demo.html, which you can find in the on-line version of this section.

In the RGB triangle example, color is an attribute, since a different color is assigned to each vertex of the triangle primitive. In the shape-stamper program, all vertices, and in fact all pixels, in a primitive have the same color. That means that color can be a uniform variable. The example also allows transparency, so colors need an alpha component as well as the RGB components. It was convenient in the program to treat the alpha and RGB components as separate quantities, so I represent them as two separate uniform variables in the shader program. The color and alpha uniforms are used in the fragment shader to assign the fragment's color. In fact, that's the only thing the fragment shader does, so the complete source code is as follows:

```
precision mediump float;
uniform vec3 u_color;
uniform float u_alpha;
void main() {
```

```
    gl_FragColor = vec4(u_color, u_alpha);
}
```

To work with a uniform variable on the JavaScript side, we need to know its location in the shader program. The program gets the locations of the two uniform variables in the intiGL() function using the commands

```
uniformColor = gl.getUniformLocation(prog, "u_color");
uniformAlpha = gl.getUniformLocation(prog, "u_alpha");
```

The program has two popup menus that let the user select the color and alpha that are to be used for drawing a primitive. When a shape is drawn, the values from the menus determine the values of the uniforms:

```
let colorNumber = Number(document.getElementById("colorChoice").value);
let alpha = Number(document.getElementById("opacityChoice").value);
gl.uniform3fv( uniformColor, colorList[colorNumber] );
gl.uniform1f( uniformAlpha, alpha );
```

Values for uniform variables are set using the gl.uniform* family of functions. In this case, colorList [colorNumber] is an array of three numbers holding the RGB color components for the color, so the function gl.uniform3fv is used to set the value: The " 3 f" means that 3 floating point values are provided, and the "v" means that the three values are in an array. Note that three floating point values are required to match the type, vec3, of the uniform variable in the shader. The value of alpha is a single floating point number, so the corresponding uniform variable is set using gl.uniform1f.

In order for the alpha component of the color to have any effect, alpha blending must be enabled. This is done as part of initialization with the two commands

```
gl.enable( gl.BLEND );
gl.blendFunc( gl.SRC_ALPHA, gl.ONE_MINUS_SRC_ALPHA );
```

The first line enables use of the alpha component. The second tells how the alpha component is to be used. The "blendFunc" used here is appropriate for transparency in 2D. The same commands were used in Subsection 3.1.2 in OpenGL 1.1.

When the program starts, the user sees a blank white canvas. When the user clicks the canvas, a shape is added. When the user clicks again, a second shape is added-and the first shape better still be there! However, this is not the default behavior for WebGL!

When the user clicks the canvas, an event-handler function for the mousedown event is called. The shape is drawn in that function. When the function returns, WebGL tells the web browser that the image has been modified, and the web browser copies the new image to the screen. Once that happens, as discussed earlier in this section, the default behavior for WebGL is to discard the image. But this means that the second mouse click is drawing on a blank canvas, since the shape from the first mouse click has been erased.

To fix this problem, the preserveDrawingBuffer option in the WebGL graphics context must be set to true. The shape-stamper program creates the context with

```
let options = { // No need for alpha channel or depth buffer, but we
            // need to preserve the image in the drawing buffer.
        alpha: false,
        depth: false,
        preserveDrawingBuffer: true
    };
gl = canvas.getContext("webgl", options);
```

Note that this program does not have a draw() function that redraws the entire image. All the drawing is done in the mouse-handling function, doMouseDown. Things could have been done differently. The program could have used a data structure to store information about the shapes that have been drawn. Clicking the canvas would add an item to the list, and the entire image would then be redrawn, including the new shape. In the actual program, however, the only record of what's in the image is the image itself. (In the terminology of Section 1.1, it is a painting program rather than a drawing program.)

WebGL uses a default coordinate system in which each of the coordinates ranges from -1 to 1 . Of course, we would like to use a more convenient coordinate system, which means that we need to apply a coordinate transformation to transform the coordinates that we use into the default coordinate system. In the shape-stamper program, the natural coordinate system is pixel coordinates on the canvas. In the pixel coordinate system, the x-coordinate ranges from 0 at the left to canvas.width at the right, and y ranges from 0 at the top to canvas.height at the bottom. The equations for transforming pixel coordinates $(x1, y1)$ to default coordinates $(x2, y2)$ are

```
x2 = -1 + 2*( x1 / canvas.width );
y2 = 1 - 2*( y1 / canvas.height );
```

In WebGL, the coordinate transformation is usually applied in the vertex shader. In this case, to implement the transformation, the vertex shader just needs to know the width and height of the canvas. The program provides the width and height to the vertex shader as uniform variables. The original pixel coordinates of the vertex are input to the vertex shader as an attribute. The shader applies the coordinate transformation to compute the value of gl_Position, which must be expressed in the default coordinate system. Here is the vertex shader source code:

```
attribute vec2 a_coords; // pixel coordinates
uniform float u_width; // width of canvas
uniform float u_height; // height of canvas
void main() {
    float x = -1.0 + 2.0*(a_coords.x / u_width);
    float y = 1.0-2.0*(a_coords.y / u_height);
    gl_Position = vec4(x, y, 0.0, 1.0);
}
```

Transformations can be much more complicated than this, especially in 3D, but the general pattern holds: Transformations are represented by uniform variables and are applied in the vertex shader. In general, transformations are implemented as matrices. We will see later that uniform variables can be matrices and that the shader language GLSL has good support for matrix operations.

In order to draw a shape, we need to store the pixel coordinates for that shape in a Float32Array; then, we have to load the values from that array into the buffer associated with the "a_coords" attribute; and finally, we must call gl.drawArrays to do the actual drawing. The coordinates for the shape can be computed based on what type of shape is being drawn and on the point where the user clicked. For example, the coordinate array for a circle is created by the following code, where x and y are the pixel coordinates for the point that was clicked:

```
coords = new Float32Array(64);
k = 0;
for (let i = 0; i < 32; i++) {
    let angle = i/32 * 2*Math.PI;
    coords[k++] = x + 50*Math.cos(angle); // x-coord of vertex i
    coords[k++] = y + 50*Math.sin(angle); // y-coord of vertex i
}
```

The circle is approximated as a 32 -sided regular polygon, with a radius of 50 pixels. Two coordinates are required for each vertex, so the length of the array is 64 . The code for the other shapes is similar. Once the array has been created, the shape is drawn using

```
gl.bindBuffer(gl.ARRAY_BUFFER, bufferCoords);
gl.bufferData(gl.ARRAY_BUFFER, coords, gl.STREAM_DRAW);
```

```
gl.vertexAttribPointer(attributeCoords, 2, gl.FLOAT, false, 0, 0);
gl.drawArrays(gl.TRIANGLE_FAN, 0, coords.length/2);
```

In the last line, coords.length /2 is the number of vertices in the shape, since the array holds two numbers per vertex. Note also that the last parameter to gl.bufferData is gl.STREAM_DRAW, which is appropriate when the data in the VBO will only be used once or a few times before being discarded.

Although the demo version of the sample program has the same functionality, I implemented shape drawing differently in the two versions. Notice that all circles in the program are the same; they are just in different locations. It should be possible to draw the circle in its own object coordinates, and then apply a modeling transformation to move the circle to its desired position in the scene. This is the approach that I take in the demo version of the program.

There are four kinds of shape: circles, squares, triangles, and stars. In the demo version, I create a separate VBO for each kind of shape. The VBO for a shape contains vertex coordinates for that shape in object coordinates, with the shape centered at (0,0). Since the object coordinates will never change, the VBO can be created once and for all as part of program initialization. For example, the VBO for the circle is created with

```
coords = new Float32Array(64);
let k = 0; // index into the coords array
for (let i = 0; i < 32; i++) {
    let angle = i/32 * 2*Math.PI;
    coords[k++] = 50*Math.cos(angle); // x-coord of vertex
    coords[k++] = 50*Math.sin(angle); // y-coord of vertex
}
bufferCoordsCircle = gl.createBuffer();
gl.bindBuffer( gl.ARRAY_BUFFER, bufferCoordsCircle );
gl.bufferData(gl.ARRAY_BUFFER, coords, gl.STATIC_DRAW);
```

Note the use of gl.STATIC_DRAW in the last line. It is appropriate since the data can be reused to draw many different circles.

To draw a shape with its center at (x, y), a translation must be applied to the coordinates in the VBO. I added the translation to the vertex shader, with a new uniform variable to represent the translation amount:

```
attribute vec2 a_coords;
uniform float u_width;
uniform float u_height;
```

```
uniform vec2 u_translation;
void main() {
    float x = -1.0 + 2.0*((a_coords.x + u_translation.x) / u_width);
    float y = 1.0-2.0*((a_coords.y + u_translation.y) / u_height);
    gl_Position = vec4(x, y, 0.0, 1.0);
}
```

You would probably find it worthwhile to read the full source code for the demo as well as the sample program.

6.2.5 The POINTS Primitive

The final example in this section demonstrates the gl.POINTS primitive. A POINTS primitive is basically a set of disconnected vertices. By default, each vertex is rendered as a single pixel. However, a program can specify a larger size. In OpenGL 1.1, this was done with the function gl_PointSize(). In WebGL, that function does not exist. Instead, the size is under the control of the vertex shader.

When working on one of the vertices of a POINTS primitive, the vertex shader should assign a value to the special built-in variable gl_PointSize. The variable is of type float. It gives the size of the vertex, in pixels. The vertex is rendered as a square, centered at the vertex position, whose width and height are given by gl_PointSize. What this really means is that the fragment shader will be called once for each pixel in that square. Note that there is an implementation-dependent limit on the size of points, which can be fairly small. The only size that is guaranteed to exist is one pixel, but most implementations seem to support point sizes at least up to 64 pixels, and possibly much larger.

When the fragment shader is called for a POINTS primitive, it is processing one pixel in the square of pixels surrounding the vertex. The special fragment shader variable gl_PointCoord tells the shader the location of the pixel within that square. The value of gl_PointCoord is an input to the shader. The type of gl_PointCoord is vec2, so it has two floating point components. The value of each component is in the range 0 to 1 . The first component, gl_PointCoord.x, is 0 at the left edge of the square and 1 at the right. The second component, gl_PointCoord.y, is 0 at the top of the square and 1 at the bottom. So, for example, the value is (0,0) at the top-left corner, (1,0) at the top-right corner, and (0.5,0.5) at the center of the square. (That, at least, is what the specification says, but I have encountered implementations that incorrectly put (0,0) at the bottom left corner. Hopefully that is fixed in modern web browsers.)

If the fragment shader uses gl_PointCoord in its computation, the color of the square can vary from pixel to pixel. As a simple example, setting

```
gl_FragColor = vec4( gl_PointCoord.x, 0.0, 0.0, 1.0 );
```

would render each vertex in the primitive as a square color gradient whose color varies horizontally from black on the left edge of the square to red on the right edge. In the sample program, I use gl_PointCoord to render the vertex as a disk instead of a square. The technique uses a new GLSL statement, discard, which is available only in the fragment shader. When the fragment shader executes the statement

```
discard;
```

the fragment shader terminates, and all further processing of the pixel is prevented. In particular, the color of the pixel in the image does not change. I use discard if the distance from *gl*_PointCoord to the center, (0.5,0.5), is greater than 0.5 . This discards pixels that do not lie in the disk of radius 0.5 . GLSL has a function for computing the distance between two vectors, so the test in the fragment shader is written

```
float distanceFromCenter = distance( gl_PointCoord, vec2(0.5,0.5) );
if ( distanceFromCenter >= 0.5 ) {
    discard; // don't draw this pixel!
}
```

The sample program is webgl/moving-points.html. It shows an animation of colored disks moving in the canvas and bouncing off the edges. All of the disks are drawn in one step as a single primitive of type gl.POINTS. The size of the disks is implemented as a uniform variable, so that all the disks have the same size, but the uniform size can be different in different frames of the animation. In the program, the user controls the size with a popup menu. There is also a demo version of the program, in the on-line version of this section.

In the program, the user can select whether the disks have random colors or are all colored red. Since each disk is a vertex of a single POINTS primitive, the fact that the disks can have different colors means that the color has to be given by an attribute variable. To implement random colors, a Float32Array is filled with random numbers, three for each vertex. The values are loaded into a VBO, and the values for the color attribute are taken from the VBO. But what happens when all the disks are red? Do we have to fill an array with multiple copies of " 1,0,0 " and use that data for the attribute? In fact, we don't. If we disable the VertexAttribArray for the color attribute, then that attribute will have the same value for every vertex. The value is specified by the gl.vertexAttrib* family of functions. So, in the sample program, the code for providing values for the color attribute is

```
if ( randomColors ) {
        // Use the attribute values from the color VBO,
```

```
        // which was filled during initialization.
    gl.enableVertexAttribArray( attributeColor );
}
else {
        // Turn off VertexAttribArray,
        // and set a constant attribute color.
    gl.disableVertexAttribArray( attributeColor );
    gl.vertexAttrib3f( attributeColor, 1, 0, 0 );
}
```

See the source code for full details of the example.

6.2.6 WebGL Error Handling

It is a sad fact that OpenGL programmers often find themselves looking at a blank screen, with no clear indication of what went wrong. In many cases, this is due to a programming logic error, such as accidently drawing a region of 3D space that contains no geometry. However, sometimes it's due to an error in the use of the API. In WebGL, and in OpenGL more generally, an error such as an illegal parameter value will not in general crash the program or produce any automatic notification of the error. Instead, when WebGL detects such an error, it ignores the illegal function call, and it sets the value of an error code that gives some indication of the nature of the error.

A program can check the current value of the error code by calling gl.getError (). This function returns an integer error code. The return value is *gl.NO_ERROR* if no error has occurred. Any other return value means that an error has occurred. Once an error code has been set, it stays set until gl.getError() is called, even if other, correct WebGL operations have been executed in the meantime. Calling gl.getError() retrieves the value of the error code and resets its value to gl.NO_ERROR. (So, if you call gl.getError() twice in a row, the second call will always return gl.NO_ERROR.) This means that when gl.getError() returns an error, the error might actually have been generated by an instruction that was executed some time ago.

As an example, consider a call to gl.drawArrays(primitive,first,count). If primitive is not one of the seven legal WebGL primitives, then WebGL will set the error code to gl.INVALID_ENUM. If first or count is negative, the error code is set to gl.INVALID_VALUE. If no shader program has been installed with gl.useProgram, the error is gl.INVALID_OPERATION. If no data has been specified for an enabled vertex attribute, an error of type gl.INVALID_STATE occurs. These four error codes are, in fact, the most common.

It is both impractical and inefficient to call gl.getError after each WebGL function call. However, when something goes wrong, it can be used as a debugging aid. When I suspect an error, I might insert code such as

```
console.log("Error code is " + gl.getError());
```

at several points in my code. The numeric value of *gl.NO_ERROR* is zero. Any non-zero value means that an error occurred at some point before the call to gl.getError. By moving the output statements around in the code, I can narrow in on the statement that actually produced the error.

Note that some browsers automatically output certain information about incorrect use of WebGL to their JavaScript console, which is part of the development tools built into many browsers. That console is also the destination for messages written using console.log () . It's always a good idea to check the console when running a WebGL program that is under development!

6.3 GLSL

You have seen a few short, simple examples of shader programs written in GLSL. In fact, shader programs are often fairly short, but they are not always so simple. To understand the more complex shaders that we will be using in the rest of this book, you will need to know more about GLSL. This section aims to give a short introduction to the major features of the language. This is a rather technical section. You should read it to get some familiarity with GLSL, and then use it as a reference when needed.

For WebGL 1.0, shaders must be written in version 1.00 of GLSL ES. WebGL 2.0 can use either version 1.00 or version 3.00, but some features of WebGL 2.0 are only available when shaders are written in GLSL ES 3.00. Although the two versions of GLSL are very similar, there are major differences and incompatibilities. Unless otherwise noted, the discussion here applies to both versions.

The vertex shader and the fragment shader in a shader program must be written using the same version of GLSL. A GLSL ES 3.00 shader program must begin with the line

```
#version 300 es
```

This must be the very first line of the shader source code. It cannot even be preceded by blank lines or comments. A shader program that does not start with this line is a version 1.00 shader. A version 1.00 shader does not include a declaration of the version number.

6.3.1 Basic Types

Variables in GLSL must be declared before they are used. GLSL is a strictly typed language, and every variable is given a type when it is declared.

GLSL has built-in types to represent scalars (that is, single values), vectors, and matrices. The scalar types are float, int, and bool. Version 3.00 adds an unsigned integer type, uint. A GPU might not support integers or booleans on the hardware level, so it is possible that the int and bool types are actually represented as floating point values.

The types vec2, vec3, and vec4 represent vectors of two, three, and four floats. There are also types to represent vectors of ints (ivec2, ivec3, and ivec4) and bools (bvec2, bvec3, and bvec4) - and, in version 3.00 , of unsigned integers (uvec2, uvec3, and uvec4). GLSL has very flexible notation for referring to the components of a vector. One way to access them is with array notation. For example, if v is a four-component vector, then its components can be accessed as $v[0], v[1], v[2]$, and $v[3]$. But they can also be accessed using the dot notation as $v.x, v.y, v.z,$ and$v.w$. The component names x, y, z, and w are appropriate for a vector that holds coordinates. However, vectors can also be used to represent colors, and the components of v can alternatively be referred to as $v.r, v.g, v.b$, and $v.a$. Finally, they can be referred to as $v.s, v.t, v.p$, and v.q - names appropriate for texture coordinates.

Furthermore, GLSL allows you to use multiple component names after the dot, as in v.rgb or $v.zx$ or even v.yyy. The names can be in any order, and repetition is allowed. This is called swizzling, and $v.zx$ is an example of a swizzler. The notation $v.zx$ can be used in an expression as a two-component vector. For example, if v is vec4 (1.0,2.0,3.0,4.0), then $v.zx$ is equivalent to $vec2$(3.0,1.0), and v.yyy is like vec3(2.0,2.0,2.0). Swizzlers can even be used on the left-hand side of an assignment, as long as they don't contain repeated components. For example,

```
vec4 coords = vec4(1.0, 2.0, 3.0, 4.0);
vec3 point = vec3(5.0, 6.0, 7.0);
coords.yzw = coords.wyz; // Now, coords is (1.0, 4.0, 2.0, 3.0)
point.xy = coords.xx; // Now, point is (1.0, 1.0, 7.0)
```

A notation such as vec2(1.0,2.0) is referred to as a "constructor," although it is not a constructor in the sense of Java or C++, since GLSL is not object-oriented, and there is no new operator. A constructor in GLSL consists of a type name followed by a list of expressions in parentheses, and it represents a value of the type specified by the type name. Any type name can be used, including the scalar types. The value is constructed from the values of the expressions in parentheses. An expression can contribute more than one value to the constructed value; we have already seen this in examples such as

```
vec2 v = vec2( 1.0, 2.0 );
vec4 w = vec4( v, v ); // w is ( 1.0, 2.0, 1.0, 2.0 )
```

Note that the expressions can be swizzlers:

```
vec3 v = vec3( 1.0, 2.0, 3.0 );
vec3 w = vec3( v.zx, 4.0 ); // w is ( 3.0, 1.0, 4.0 )
```

Extra values from the last parameter will be dropped. This makes is possible to use a constructor to shorten a vector. However, it is not legal to have extra parameters that contribute no values at all to the result:

```
vec4 rgba = vec4( 0.1, 0.2, 0.3, 0.4);
vec3 rgb = vec3( rgba ); // takes 3 items from rgba; rgb is (0.1, 0.2,
0.3)
float r = float( rgba ); // r is 0.1
vec2 v = vec2( rgb, rgba ); // ERROR: No values from rgba are used.
```

As a special case, when a vector is constructed from a single scalar value, all components of the vector will be set equal to that value:

```
vec4 black = vec4( 1.0 ); // black is ( 1.0, 1.0, 1.0, 1.0 )
```

When constructing one of the built-in types, type conversion will be applied if necessary. For purposes of conversion, the boolean values true/false convert to the numeric values zero and one; in the other direction, zero converts to false and any other numeric value converts to true. As far as I know, constructors are the only context in which GLSL does automatic type conversion. For example, you need to use a constructor to assign an int value to a float variable, and it is illegal to add an int to a float:

```
int k = 1;
float x = float(k); // OK; "x = k" would be a type mismatch error
x = x + 1.0; // OK
x = x + 1; // ERROR: Can't add values of different types.
```

The built-in matrix types are mat2, mat3, and mat4. They represent, respectively, two-by-two, three-by-three, and four-by-four matrices of floating point numbers. (There are no matrices of integers or booleans, but there are some additional matrix types for representing non-square matrices.) The elements of a matrix can be accessed using array notation, such as $M[2][1]$. If a single index is used, as in $M[2]$, the result is a vector. For example, if M is of type mat4, then $M[2]$ is a vec4. Arrays in GLSL, as in OpenGL, use column-major order. This means that $M[2]$ is column number 2 in M rather than row number 2 (as it would be in Java), and $M[2][1]$ is the element in column 2 and row 1.

A matrix can be constructed from the appropriate number of values, which can be provided as scalars, vectors or matrices. For example, a mat3 can be constructed from nine float or from three vec3 parameters:

```
mat3 m1 = mat3( 1.0, 2.0, 3.0, 4.0, 5.0, 6.0, 7.0, 8.0, 9.0 );
vec3 v = vec3( 1, 2, 3 );
mat3 m2 = mat3( v, v, v );
```

Keep in mind that the matrix is filled in column-major order; that is, the first three numbers go into column 0 , the next three into column 1 , and the last three into column 2.

As a special case, if a matrix M is constructed from a single scalar value, then that value is put into all the diagonal elements of $M(M[0][0], M[1][1]$, and so on). The non-diagonal elements are all set equal to zero. For example, mat4(1.0) constructs the four-by-four identity matrix.

The only other built-in types are the so-called "sampler types", which are used for accessing textures. The sampler types can be used only in limited ways. They are not numeric types and cannot be converted to or from numeric types. The will be covered in the next section.

6.3.2 Data Structures

A GLSL program can define new types using the struct keyword. The syntax is the same as in C, with some limitations. A struct is made up of a sequence of named members, which can be of different types. The type of a member can be any of the built-in types, an array type, or a previously defined struct type. For example,

```
struct LightProperties {
    vec4 position;
    vec3 color;
    float intensity;
};
```

This defines a type named LightProperties. The type can be used to declare variables:

```
LightProperties light;
```

The members of the variable light are then referred to as light.position, light.color, and light.intensity. Struct types have constructors, but their constructors do not support type conversion: The constructor must contain a list of values whose types exactly match the types of the corresponding members in the struct. For example,

```
light = LightProperties( vec4(0.0, 0.0, 0.0, 1.0), vec3(1.0), 1.0);
```

GLSL also supports arrays. Only one-dimensional arrays are allowed. The base type of an array can be any of the basic types or it can be a struct type. The size of the array must be specified in the variable declaration as an integer constant. For example

```
int A[10];
vec3 palette[8];
LightProperties lights[3];
```

In version 1.00, there are no array constructors, and it is not possible to initialize an array as part of its declaration. Version 3.00 does have array constructors, and it allows type names such as "int [10], representing an array of 10 integers:

```
int[4] B; // B is an array of 4 ints; GLSL ES 3.00 only!
B = int[4] (2, 3, 5, 7); // Array constructor; GLSL ES 3.00 only!
```

Array indexing uses the usual syntax, such as $A[0]$ or palette $[i+1]$ or lights [3]. color. In GLSL ES 1.00, there are some strong limitations on the expressions that can be used as array indices. With one exception, an expression that is used as the index for an array can contain only integer constants and for loop variables (that is, variables that are used as loop control variables in for loops). For example, the expression palette $[i+1]$ would only be legal inside a for of the form for (int $i = \cdots$. The single exception is that arbitrary index expressions can be used for arrays of uniforms in a vertex shader (and then only if the array does not contain samplers). Note that these restrictions do not apply in GLSL ES 3.00.

Just as in C, there is no check for array index out of bounds errors. It is up to the programmer to make sure that array indices are valid.

6.3.3 Qualifiers

Variable declarations can be modified by various qualifiers. You have seen examples of the qualifiers attribute, uniform, and varying. These are called storage qualifiers. The qualifiers attribute and varying do not exist in version 3.00 ; instead, an attribute is declared in the vertex shader using the storage qualifier in, and a varying variable is declared using out in the vertex shader and in in the fragment shader. The uniform qualifier is used in both versions. Only global variables, not local variables in function definition, can be attribute, uniform, or varying variables.

The attribute qualifier can only be used in a GLSL ES 1.00 vertex shader, and it only applies to the built-in floating point types float, vec2, vec3, vec4, mat2, mat3, and mat4. (Matrix attributes are not supported directly on the JavaScript side. A matrix attribute has to be treated as a set of vector attributes, one for each column. The attribute locations for the columns are successive integers, and the WebGL function gl.getAttribLocation will return the location for the first column. Matrix attributes would be rare, though perhaps useful for instanced drawing, and I won't go into further detail about them here.)

In GLSL ES 3.00, the in qualifier on a vertex shader variable defines it to be an attribute variable, and it can be applied to integer and unsigned integer scalars and vectors, as well as to the floating point types.

Also in GLSL ES 3.00, the out qualifier can be used on integer and floating point scalars and vectors in the fragment shader. In version 1.00, a fragment shader has the predefined variable gl_FragColor of type vec4 to specify the color of the pixel. In version 3.00, a fragment shader can have multiple outputs, and the outputs are not necessarily colors. Because the output type does not have to be vec4, it is not possible to have a predefined output variable. For now, we will only use one fragment shader output representing a color. So, a version 3.00 fragment shader will have one out variable of type vec4. (When we discuss framebuffers in Section 7.4, we will see how multiple outputs can be used.)

Both the vertex shader and the fragment shader can use uniform variables. The same variable can occur in both shaders, as long as the types in the two shaders are the same. Uniform variables can be of any type, including array and structure types. Now, JavaScript only has functions for setting uniform values that are scalar variables, vectors, or matrices. There are no functions for setting the values of structs or arrays. The solution to this problem requires treating every component of a struct or array as a separate uniform value. For example, consider the declarations

```
struct LightProperties {
    vec4 position;
    vec3 color;
    float intensity;
};
uniform LightProperties light[4];
```

The variable light contains twelve basic values, which are of type vec4, vec3, or float. To work with the light uniform in JavaScript, we need twelve variables to represent the locations of the 12 components of the uniform variable. When using gl.getUniformLocation to get the location of one of the 12 components, you need to give the full name of the component in the GLSL program. For example: gl.getUniformLocation(prog, "light[2].color"). It is natural to store the 12 locations in an array of JavaScript objects that parallels the structure of the array of structs on the GLSL side. Here is typical JavaScript code to create the structure and use it to initialize the uniform variables:

```
lightLocations = new Array(4);
for (i = 0; i < light.length; i++) {
    lightLocations[i] = {
        position: gl.getUniformLocation(prog, "light[" + i +
"].position" );
        color: gl.getUniformLocation(prog, "light[" + i + "].color" );
        intensity: gl.getUniformLocation(prog, "light[" + i +
"].intensity" );
    };
}
for (i = 0; i < light.length; i++) {
    gl.uniform4f( lightLocations[i].position, 0, 0, 0, 1);
    gl.uniform3f( lightLocations[i].color, 1, 1, 1);
    gl.uniform1f( lightLocations[i].intensity, 0 );
}
```

For uniform shader variables that are matrices, the JavaScript function that is used to set the value of the uniform is gl.uniformMatrix2fv for a mat2, gl.uniformMatrix3fv for a mat3, or gl.uniformMatrix $4fv$ for a mat4. Even though the matrix is two-dimensional, the values are stored in a one dimensional array. The values are loaded into the array in column-major order. For example, if transform is a uniform mat3 in the shader, then JavaScript can set its value to be the identity matrix with

```
transformLoc = gl.getUniformLocation(prog, "transform");
gl.uniformMatrix3fv( transformLoc, false, [ 1,0,0, 0,1,0, 0,0,1 ] );
```

In Version 1.00, the second parameter must be false. In Version 3.00, the second parameter can be true to indicate that the entries of the matrix are provided in row-major rather than column-major order. Note that the 3 in uniformMatrix3fv refers to the number of rows and columns in the matrix, not to the length of the array, which must be 9 . (By the way, it is OK to use a typed array rather than a normal JavaScript array for the value of a uniform.)

A varying variable should be declared with the same name and type in both the vertex shader and fragment shader. In version 1.00, the storage qualifier for declaring varying variables is varying, and it can only be used for for the built-in floating point types (float, vec2, vec3, vec4, mat2, mat3, and mat4) and for arrays of those types.

In version 3.00, a varying variable can also be an integer or unsigned integer scalar or vector. But there is a complication because it doesn't make sense to apply interpolation to integer values. So, a varying variable of integer type must be declared with the additional qualifier flat, which means it will not be interpolated. Instead, the value from the first vertex of a triangle or line segment will be used for every pixel. (Floating point varying variables can also, optionally, be declared as flat.) For example: flat in ivec3 A; // GLSL ES 3.00 fragment shader only! Another possible storage qualifier is const, which means that the value of the variable cannot be changed after it has been initialized. The declaration of a const variable must include initialization.

A variable declaration can also be modified by precision qualifiers. The possible precision qualifiers are highp, mediump, and lowp. A precision qualifier sets the minimum range of possible values for an integer variable or the minimum range of values and number of decimal places for a floating point variable. GLSL doesn't assign a definite meaning to the precision qualifiers, but mandates some minimum requirements. For example, in version 1.00 , lowp integers must be able to represent values in at least the range -2^8 to 2^8; mediump integers, in the range -2^{10} to 2^{10}; and highp integers, in the range -2^{16} to 2^{16}. For version 3.00 , highp variables always use 32 bits, and the requirements for mediump and lowp are higher. It is even possible that all values are 32 -bit values and the precision qualifiers have no real effect. But GPUs in embedded systems can be more limited.

A precision qualifier can be used on any variable declaration, including local variables and function parameters. If the variable also has a storage qualifier, the storage qualifier comes first. For example

```
lowp int n;
varying highp float v;
uniform mediump vec3 colors[3];
```

A varying variable can have different precisions in the vertex and in the fragment shader. The default precision for integers and floats in the vertex shader is highp. Fragment shaders are not required to support highp, although it is likely that they do so, except perhaps on older mobile hardware. In the fragment shader, the default precision for integers is mediump, but floats do not have a default precision. This means that every floating point variable in the fragment shader has to be explicitly assigned a precision. Alternatively, it is possible to set a default precision for floats with the statement

```
precision mediump float;
```

This statement was used at the start of each of the fragment shaders in the previous section. Of course, if the fragment shader does support highp, this restricts the precision unnecessarily. You can avoid that by using this code at the start of the fragment shader:

```
#ifdef GL_FRAGMENT_PRECISION_HIGH
    precision highp float;
#else
    precision mediump float;
#endif
```

This sets the default precision to highp if it is available and to mediump if not. The lines starting with "#" are preprocessor directives - an aspect of GLSL that I don't want to get into.

The next qualifier, invariant, is even more difficult to explain, and it has only a limited use. Invariance refers to the requirement that when the same expression is used to compute the value of the same variable (possibly in different shaders), then the value that is assigned to the variable should be exactly the same in both cases. This is not automatically the case. For example, the values can be different if a compiler uses different optimizations or evaluates the operands in a different order in the two expressions. The invariant qualifier on the variable will force the compiler to use exactly the same calculations for the two assignment statements. The qualifier can only be used on declarations of varying variables. It must be the first qualifier in the declaration. For example,

```
invariant varying mediump vec3 color;
```

It can also be used to make the predefined variables such as gl_Position and gl_FragCoord invariant, using a statement such as

```
invariant gl_Position;
```

Invariance can be important in a multi-pass algorithm that applies two or more shader programs in succession to compute an image. It is important, for example, that both shaders get the same answer when they compute gl_Position for the same vertex, using the same expression in both vertex shaders. Making gl_Position invariant in the shaders will ensure that.

The last type of qualifier, a "layout" qualifier, is only available in version 3.00. It can be used to specify the integer ID of an attribute variable, as an alternative to using the JavaScript function gl.getAttribLocation() to query the ID. An example would be

```
layout(location = 0) in vec3 a_coords; // GLSL ES 3.00 vertex shader
only!
```

The same kind of layout qualifier can be used on an out variable in a GLSL ES 3.00 fragment shader that has multiple outputs. In that case, it specifies which of several output destinations should be used for that variable.

6.3.4 Expressions

Expressions in GLSL can use the arithmetic operators $+, -, *, /, ++$ and -- for integer and floating point values. In version 3.00, the remainder operator, %, as well as left and right shift and bitwise logical operators, are also available for integer types. There is no automatic type conversion in expressions. If x is of type float, the expression $x + 1$ is illegal. You have to say $x + 1.0$ or x + float(1).

The arithmetic operators have been extended in various ways to work with vectors and matrices. If you use * to multiply a matrix and a vector, in either order, it multiplies them in the linear algebra sense, giving a vector as the result. The types of the operands must match in the obvious way; for example, a vec3 can only be multiplied by a mat3, and the result is a vec3. When used with two matrices of the same size, $*$ does matrix multiplication.

If,,+ $-*$, or / is used on a vector and a scalar of the same basic type, then the operation is performed on each element of the vector. For example, vec2(3.0,3.0) / 2.0 is the vector vec2 (1.5,1.5), and 2 $*$ ivec 3(1,2,3) is the vector ivec3(2,4,6). When one of these operators is applied to two vectors of the same type, the operation is applied to each pair of components, and the result is a vector. For example, the value of

```
vec3( 1.0, 2.0, 3.0) + vec3( 4.2, -7.0, 1.7)
```

is the vector vec3 (5.2, $-$5.0,4.7). Note in particular that the usual vector arithmetic operationsaddition and subtraction of vectors, multiplication of a vector by a scalar, and multiplication of a vector by a matrix-are written in the natural way is GLSL.

The relational operators <, >, <=, and >= can only be applied to integer and floating point scalars, and the types of the two operands must match exactly. However, the equality operators $==$ and $!=$ have been extended to work on all of the built-in types except sampler types. Two vectors are equal only if the corresponding pairs of components are all equal. The same is true for matrices. The equality operators cannot be used with arrays, but they do work for structs, as long as the structs don't contain any arrays or samplers; again, every pair of members in two structs must be equal for the structs to be considered equal.

GLSL has logical operators !, &&, ||, and ↑ (the last one being an exclusive or operation). The operands must be of type bool.

Finally, there are the assignment operators $=, +=, -=, *=$, and $/=$, with the usual meanings.

GLSL also has a large number of predefined functions, more than I can discuss here. All of the functions that I will mention here require floating-point values as parameters, even if the function would also make sense for integer values.

Most interesting, perhaps, are functions for vector algebra. See Section 3.5 for the definitions of these operations. These functions have simple formulas, but they are provided as functions for convenience and because they might have efficient hardware implementations in a GPU. The function dot(x, y) computes the dot product $x \cdot y$ of two vectors of the same length. The return value is a float; cross(x, y) computes the cross product $x \times y$, where the parameters and return value are of type vec3; length (x) is the length of the vector x and distance (x, y) gives the distance between two vectors; normalize (x) returns a unit vector that points in the same direction as x. There are also functions named reflect and refract that can be used to compute the direction of reflected and refracted light rays; I will cover them when I need to use them.

The function mix (x, y, t) computes $x * (1 - t) + y * t$. If t is a float in the range 0.0 to 1.0 , then the return value is a linear mixture, or weighted average, of x and y. This function might be used, for example, to do alpha-blending of two colors. The function clamp(x, low, high) clamps x to the range low to high; the return value could be computed as $\min(\max(x, low), high)$. If rgb is a vector representing a color, we could ensure that all of the components of the vector lie in the range 0 to 1 with the command

```
rgb = clamp( rgb, 0.0, 1.0 );
```

If s and t are floats, with $s < t$, then smoothstep (s, t, x) returns 0.0 for x less than s and returns 1.0 for x greater than t. For values of x between s and t, the return value is smoothly interpolated from 0.0 to 1.0 . Here is an example that might be used in a fragment shader for rendering a gl.POINTS primitive, with transparency enabled:

```
float dist = distance( gl_PointCoord, vec2(0.5) );
float alpha = 1.0 - smoothstep( 0.45, 0.5, dist );
if (alpha == 0.0) {
    discard; // discard fully transparent pixels
```

```
}
gl_FragColor = vec4( 1.0, 0.0, 0.0, alpha );
```

This would render the point as a red disk, with the color fading smoothly from opaque to transparent around the edge of the disk, as dist increases from 0.45 to 0.5 . Note that for the functions mix, clamp, and smoothstep, the x and y parameters can be vectors as well as floats. In that case, they operate on each component of the vector individually.

The usual mathematical functions are available in GLSL, including sin, cos, tan, asin, acos, atan, log, exp, pow, sqrt, abs, floor, ceil, min, and max. (In version 3.00, abs, min, and max also apply to integer types.) For these functions, the parameters can be any of the types float, vec2, vec3, or vec4. The return value is of the same type, and the function is applied to each component separately. For example, the value of sqrt(vec3(16.0,9.0,4.0)) is the vector vec3(4.0,3.0,2.0). For min and max, there is also a second version of the function in which the first parameter is a vector and the second parameter is a float. For those versions, each component of the vector is compared to the float; for example, max(vec3(1.0,2.0,3.0),2.5) is vec3(2.5, 2.5,3.0).

The function mod(x, y) computes the modulus, or remainder, when x is divided by y. The return value is computed as $x - y *$ floor (x/y). As with min and max, y can be either a vector or a float. The mod function can be used as a substitute for the % operator, which is not supported in GLSL ES 1.00.

There are also functions for working with sampler variables. I will discuss some of them in the next section.

6.3.5 Function Definitions

A GLSL program can define new functions, with a syntax similar to C. Unlike C, function names can be overloaded; that is, two functions can have the same name, as long as they have different numbers or types of parameters. A function must be declared before it is used. As in C , it can be declared by giving either a full definition or a function prototype.

Function parameters can be of any type. The return type for a function can be any type except for array types. A struct type can be a return type, as long as the structure does not include any arrays. When an array is used a formal parameter, the length of the array must be specified by an integer constant. For example,

```
float arraySum10( float A[10] ) {
    float sum = 0.0;
    for ( int i = 0; i < 10; i++ ) {
        sum += A[i];
```

```
    }
    return sum;
}
```

Function parameters can be modified by the qualifiers in, out, or inout. The default, if no qualifier is specified, is in. The qualifier indicates whether the parameter is used for input to the function, output from the function, or both. For input parameters, the value of the actual parameter in the function call is copied into the formal parameter in the function definition, and there is no further interaction between the formal and actual parameters. For output parameters, the value of the formal parameter is copied to the actual parameter when the function returns. For an inout parameter, the value is copied in both directions. This type of parameter passing is referred to as "call by value/return." Note that the actual parameter for an out or inout parameter must be something to which a value can be assigned, such as a variable or swizzler. (All parameters in C, Java, and JavaScript are input parameters, but passing a pointer as a parameter can have an effect similar to an inout parameter. GLSL, of course, has no pointers.) For example,

```
void cumulativeSum( in float A[10], out float B[10]) {
    B[0] = A[0] ;
    for ( int i = 1; i < 10; i++ ) {
        B[i] = B[i-1] + A[i] ;
    }
}
```

Note that recursion is not supported for functions in GLSL.

6.3.6 Control Structures

The only control structures in GLSL ES 1.00 for WebGL are the if statement and a very restricted form of the for loop. There is no while or do..while loop, and there is no switch statement. However, all of these are supported in GLSL ES 3.00.

If statements are supported with the full syntax from C, including else and else if. In version 3.00, the syntax for all control structures is pretty much the same as in C .

In a for loop in a version 1.00 shader, the loop control variable must be declared in the loop, and it must be of type int or float. The initial value for the loop control variable must be a constant expression (that is, it can include operators, but all the operands must be literal constants or const variables) The code inside the loop is not allowed to change the value of the loop control variable. The test for ending the loop can only have the form var op expression, where var is the loop control variable, the *op* is one of the relational or equality operators, and the expression is a constant expression. Finally, the update expression must have one of the forms var ++, var--, var +=expression, or var- = expression, where var is the loop control variable, and expression is a constant expression. Of course, this is the most typical form for for loops in other languages. Some examples of legal first lines for for loops:

```
for (int i = 0; i < 10; i++)
for (float x = 1.0; x < 2.0; x += 0.1)
for (int k = 10; k != 0; k -= 1)
```

In version 3.00, these restrictions do not apply. Note that all loops can include break and continue statements.

6.3.7 Limits

WebGL puts limits on certain resources that are used by WebGL and its GLSL programs, such as the number of attribute variables or the size of a texture image. The limits are due in many cases to hardware limits in the GPU, and they depend on the device on which the program is running, and on the implementation of WebGL on that device. The hardware limits can be lower on mobile devices such as tablets and phones, but modern tablets and phones have pretty impressive GPUs. Although the limits can vary, WebGL imposes a set of minimum requirements that all implementations must satisfy. I will give the minimums for WebGL 1.0 . The minimums for WebGL 2.0 are greater.

For example, any WebGL implementation must allow at least 8 attributes in a vertex shader. The actual limit for a particular implementation might be more, but cannot be less. The actual limit is available in a GLSL program as the value of a predefined constant, gl_MaxVertexAttribs. More conveniently, it is available on the JavaScript side as the value of the expression

```
gl.getParameter( gl.MAX_VERTEX_ATTRIBS )
```

Attribute variables of type float, vec2, vec3, and vec4 all count as one attribute against the limit. For a matrix-valued attribute, each column counts as a separate attribute as far as the limit goes.

Similarly, there are limits on varying variables, and there are separate limits on uniform variables in the vertex and fragment shaders. (The limits are on the number of four-component "vectors." There can be some packing of separate variables into a single vector, but the packing that is used does not have to be optimal. No packing is done for attribute variables.) The limits must satisfy

```
gl_MaxVertexAttribs >= 8;
gl_MaxVertexUniformVectors >= 128;
gl_MaxFragmentUniformVectors >= 16;
gl_MaxVaryingVectors >= 8;
```

There are also limits in GLSL on the number of texture units, which means essentially the number of textures that can be used simultaneously. These limits must satisfy

```
gl_MaxTextureImageUnits >= 8; // limit for fragment shader
gl_MaxVertexTextureImageUnits >= 0; // limit for vertex shader
gl_MaxCombinedTextureImageUnits >= 8; // total limit for both shaders
```

Textures are usually used in fragment shaders, but they can sometimes be useful in vertex shaders. Note however, that gl_MaxVertexTextureImageUnits can be zero, which means that implementations are not required to allow texture units to be used in vertex shaders. (This possibility is for WebGL 1.0 only.)

There are also limits on other things, including viewport size, texture image size, line width for line primitives, and point size for the POINTS primitive. All of the limits can be queried from the JavaScript side using gl.getParameter().

At the end of the on-line version of this section, you will find a live demo that shows the actual values of the resource limits on the device on which it is running. The demo shows the limits for a WebGL 1.0 graphics context. You can use it to check the capabilities of various devices on which you want your WebGL programs to run. In general, the actual limits will be significantly larger than the required minimum values.

6.4 Image Textures

Textures play an essential role in 3D graphics, and support for image textures is built into modern GPUs on the hardware level. In this section, we look at the WebGL API for image textures. Image textures in OpenGL 1.1 were covered in Section 4.3. Much of that section is still relevant in modern OpenGL, including WebGL. So, as we cover image textures in WebGL, much of the material will not be new to you. However, there is one feature that is new since OpenGL 1.1: texture units.

One of the significant differences between WebGL 1.0 and WebGL 2.0 is an increase in support for different types of textures and for different ways of using textures. Access to most of the new features requires using GLSL ES 3.00 for the shader programs. We will stick to WebGL 1.0 for most of this section, but will discuss some of the new WebGL 2.0 features in the final subsection.

6.4.1 Texture Units and Texture Objects

A texture unit, also called a texture mapping unit (***TMU***) or a texture processing unit (TPU), is a hardware component in a GPU that does sampling. Sampling is the process of computing a color from an image texture and texture coordinates. Mapping a texture image to a surface is a fairly complex operation, since it requires more than just returning the color of the texel that contains some given texture coordinates. It also requires applying the appropriate minification or magnification filter, possibly using mipmaps if available. Fast texture sampling is one of the key requirements for good GPU performance.

Texture units are not to be confused with texture objects. We encountered texture objects in Subsection 4.3.7. A texture object is a data structure that contains the color data for an image texture, and possibly for a set of mipmaps for the texture, as well as the values of texture properties such as the minification and magnification filters and the texture repeat mode. A texture unit must access a texture object to do its work. The texture unit is the processor; the texture object holds the data that is processed. (By the way, I should really be more careful about throwing around the terms "GPU" and "hardware." Although a texture unit probably does use an actual hardware component in the GPU, it could also be emulated, more slowly, in software. And even if there is hardware involved, having eight texture units does not necessarily mean that there are eight hardware components; the texture units might share time on a smaller number of hardware components. Similarly, I said previously that texture objects are stored in memory in the GPU, which might or might not be literally true in a given case. Nevertheless, you will probably find it conceptually easier to think of a texture unit as a piece of hardware and a texture object as a data structure in the GPU.)

In GLSL, texture lookup is done using sampler variables. A sampler variable is a variable in a shader program. In GLSL ES 1.00, the only sampler types are sampler2D and samplerCube. A sampler2D is used to do lookup in a standard texture image; a samplerCube is used to do lookup in a cubemap texture (Subsection 5.3.4). The value of a sampler variable is a reference to a texture unit. The value tells which texture unit is invoked when the sampler variable is used to do texture lookup. Sampler variables must be declared as global uniform variables. It is not legal for a shader program to assign a value to a sampler variable. The value must come from the JavaScript side.

On the JavaScript side, the available texture units are numbered 0,1,2, ..., where the maximum value is implementation dependent. The number of units can be determined as the value of the expression

```
gl.getParameter ( gl.MAX_COMBINED_TEXTURE_IMAGE_UNITS )
```

(Please remember, again, that *gl* here is the name of a JavaScript variable that refers to the WebGL context, and that the name is up to the programmer.)

As far as JavaScript is concerned, the value of a sampler variable is an integer. If you want a sampler variable to use texture unit number 2 , then you set the value of the sampler variable to 2 . This can be done using the function gl.uniform1i (Subsection 6.1.4). For example, suppose a shader program declares a sampler variable

```
uniform sampler2D u_texture;
```

To set its value from JavaScript, you need the location of the variable in the shader program. If prog is the shader program, the location is obtained by calling

```
u_texture_location = gl.getUniformLocation( prog, "u_texture" );
```

Then, you can tell the sampler variable to use texture unit number 2 by calling

```
gl.uniform1i( u_texture_location, 2 );
```

Note that the integer value is not accessible in GLSL. The integer tells the sampler which texture unit to use, but there is no way for the shader program to find out the number of the unit that is being used.

To use an image texture, you also need to create a texture object, and you need to load an image into the texture object. You might want to set some properties of the texture object, and you might want to create a set of mipmaps for the texture. And you will have to associate the texture object with a texture unit. All this is done on the JavaScript side.

The command for creating a texture object is gl.createTexture(). The command in OpenGL 1.1 was glGenTextures. The WebGL command is easier to use. It creates a single texture object and returns a reference to it. For example,

```
textureObj = gl.createTexture();
```

This just allocates some memory for the object. In order to use it, you must first "bind" the texture object by calling gl.bindTexture. For example,

```
gl.bindTexture( gl.TEXTURE_2D, textureObj );
```

The first parameter, gl.TEXTURE_2D, is the texture target. This target is used for working with an ordinary texture image. There is a different target for cubemap textures.

The function gl.texImage2D is used to load an image into the currently bound texture object. We will come back to that in the next subsection. But remember that this command

and other commands always apply to the currently bound texture object. The texture object is not mentioned in the command; instead, the texture object must be bound before the command is called.

You also need to tell a texture unit to use the texture object. Before you can do that, you need to make the texture unit "active," which is done by calling the function gl.activeTexture. The parameter is one of the constants gl.TEXTURE0, gl.TEXTURE1, gl.TEXTURE2, ..., which represent the available texture units. (The values of these constants are not 0,1,2, ...) Initially, texture unit number 0 is active. To make texture unit number 2 active, for example, use

```
gl.activeTexture( gl.TEXTURE2 );
```

(This function should really have been called activeTextureUnit, or maybe bindTextureUnit, since it works similarly to the various WebGL "bind" functions.) If you then call

```
gl.bindTexture( gl.TEXTURE_2D, textureObj );
```

to bind a texture object, while texture unit 2 is active, then the the texture object texture *Obj* is bound to texture unit number 2 for gl.TEXTURE_2D operations. The binding just tells the texture unit which texture object to use. That is, when texture unit 2 does TEXTURE_2D lookups, it will do so using the image and the settings that are stored in textureObj. A texture object can be bound to several texture units at the same time. However, a given texture unit can have only one bound TEXTURE_2D at a time.

So, working with texture images in WebGL involves working with texture objects, texture units, and sampler variables. The relationship among the three is illustrated in this picture:

A sampler variable uses a texture unit, which uses a texture object, which holds a texture image. The JavaScript commands for setting up this chain are shown in the illustration. To apply a texture image to a primitive, you have to set up the entire chain. Of course, you also have to provide texture coordinates for the primitive, and you need to use the sampler variable in the shader program to access the texture.

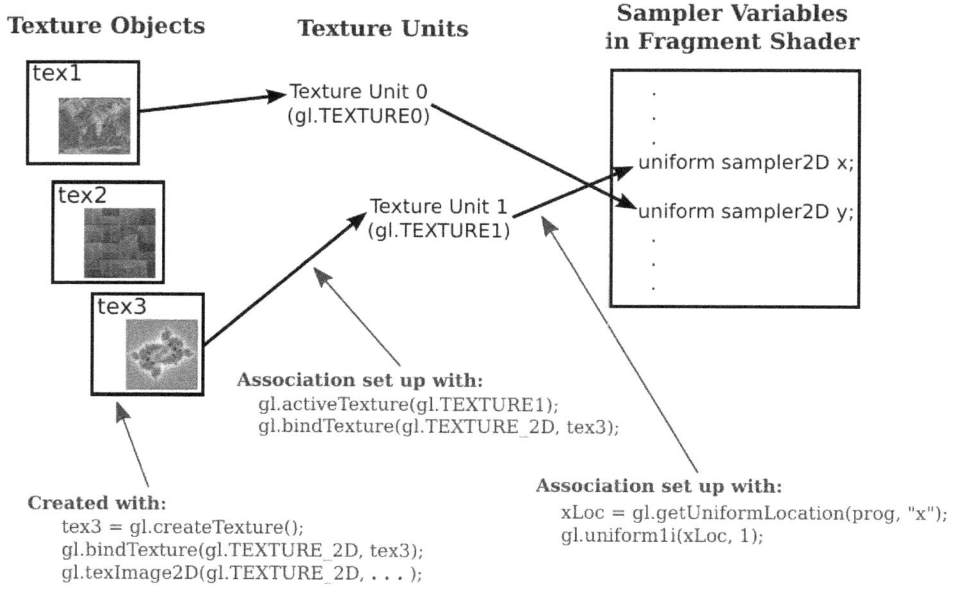

Suppose that you have several images that you would like to use on several different primitives. Between drawing primitives, you need to change the texture image that will be used. There are at least three different ways to manage the images in WebGL:

1. You could use a single texture object and a single texture unit. The bound texture object, the active texture unit, and the value of the sampler variable can be set once and never changed. To change to a new image, you would use gl.texImage2D to load the image into the texture object. This is essentially how things were done in OpenGL 1.0. It's very inefficient, except when you are going to use each image just once. That's why texture objects were introduced.

2. You could use a different texture object for each image, but use just a single texture unit. The active texture and the value of the sampler variable will never have to be changed. You would switch to a new texture image using gl.bindTexture to bind the texture object that contains the desired image.

3. You could use a different texture unit for each image. You would load each image into its own texture object and bind that object to one of the texture units. You would switch to a new texture image by changing the value of the sampler variable.

I don't know how options 2 and 3 compare in terms of efficiency. Note that you are only forced to use more than one texture unit if you want to apply more than one texture image to the same primitive. To do that, you will need several sampler variables in the shader program. They will have different values so that they refer to different texture units, and the color of a pixel will somehow depend on samples from both images. This picture shows two textures being combined in simple ways to compute the colors of pixels in a textured square:

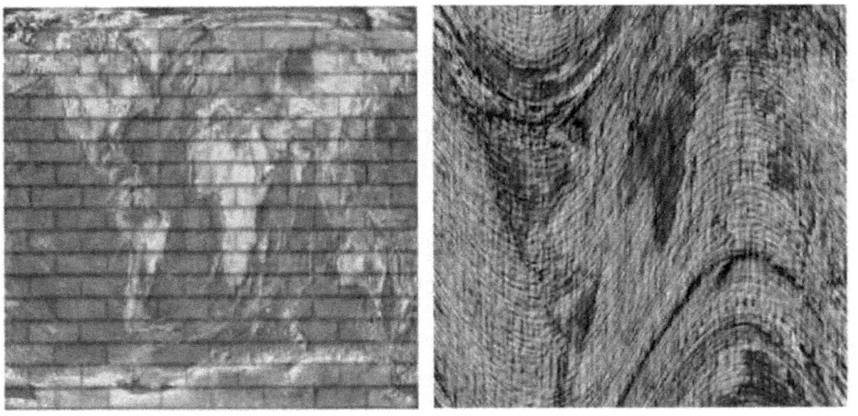

In the image on the left, a grayscale "brick" image is multiplied by an "Earth" image; that is, the red component of a pixel is computed by multiplying the red component from the brick texture by the red component from the Earth texture, and same for green and blue. On the right, the same Earth texture is subtracted from a "cloth" texture. Furthermore, the pattern is distorted because the texture coordinates were modified before being used to sample the textures, using the formula texCoords. $y += 0.25 * \sin(6.28^{*}$ texCoords. x). That's the kind of thing that could only be done with programmable shaders! The images are taken from the on-line demo c6/multi-texture.html. Try it out!

You might want to view the source code to see how the textures are programmed. Two texture units are used. The values of two uniform sampler variables, u_texture1 and u_texture2, are set during initialization with the code

```
u_texture1_location = gl.getUniformLocation(prog, "u_texture1");
u_texture2_location = gl.getUniformLocation(prog, "u_texture2");
gl.uniform1i(u_texture1_location, 0);
gl.uniform1i(u_texture2_location, 1);
```

The values are never changed. The program uses several texture images. There is a texture object for each image. On the JavaScript side, the IDs for the texture objects are stored in an array, textureObjects. Two popup menus allow the user to select which texture images are applied to the primitive. This is implemented in the drawing routine by binding the two selected texture objects to texture units 0 and 1 , which are the units used by the two sampler variables. The code for that is:

```
let tex1Num = Number(document.getElementById("textureChoice1").value);
gl.activeTexture( gl.TEXTURE0 );
gl.bindTexture( gl.TEXTURE_2D, textureObjects[tex1Num] );
let tex2Num = Number(document.getElementById("textureChoice2").value);
gl.activeTexture( gl.TEXTURE1 );
gl.bindTexture( gl.TEXTURE_2D, textureObjects[tex2Num] );
```

Getting images into the texture objects is another question, which we turn to next.

6.4.2 Working with Images

An image can be loaded into a texture object using the function gl.texImage2D. For use with WebGL, this function usually has the form

```
gl.texImage2D( target, 0, gl.RGBA, gl.RGBA, gl.UNSIGNED_BYTE, image );
```

The target is gl.TEXTURE_2D for ordinary textures; there are other targets for loading cubemap textures. The second parameter is the mipmap level, which is 0 for the main image. Although it is possible to load individual mipmaps, that is rarely done. The next two parameters give the format of the texture inside the texture object and in the original image. In WebGL 1.0, the two format parameters should have the same value. Since web images are stored in RGBA format, gl.RGBA is probably the most efficient choice, and there is rarely a need to use anything else. But you can use gl. *RGB* if you don't need the alpha component. And by using gl.LUMINANCE or gl.LUMINANCE_ALPHA, you can convert the image to grayscale. (Luminance is a weighted average of red, green, and blue that approximates the perceived brightness of a color.) The fourth parameter is always going to be gl.UNSIGNED_BYTE, indicating that the colors in the image are stored using one byte for each color component. Although other values are possible, they don't really make sense for web images.

The last parameter in the call to gl.texImage2D is the image. Ordinarily, image will be a DOM image element that has been loaded asynchronously by JavaScript. The image can also be a <canvas> element. This means that you can draw on a canvas, using the HTML canvas 2D graphics API, and then use the canvas as the source for a texture image. You can even do that with an off-screen canvas that is not visible on the web page.

The image is loaded into the texture object that is currently bound to target in the currently active texture unit. There is no default texture object; that is, if no texture has been bound when gl.texImage2D is called, an error occurs. The active texture unit is the one that has been selected using gl.activeTexture, or is texture unit 0 if gl.activeTexture has never been called. A texture object is bound to the active texture unit by gl.bindTexture. This was discussed earlier in this section.

Using images in WebGL is complicated by the fact that images are loaded asynchronously. That is, the command for loading an image just starts the process of loading the image. You can specify a callback function that will be executed when the loading completes. The image won't actually be available for use until after the callback function is called. When loading an image to use as a texture, the callback function should load the image into a texture object. Often, it will also call a rendering function to draw the scene, with the texture image.

The sample program webgl/simple-texture.html is an example of using a single texture on a triangle. Here is a function that is used to load the texture image in that program. The texture object is created before the function is called.

```
/**
* Loads a texture image asynchronously. The first parameter is the url
* from which the image is to be loaded. The second parameter is the
* texture object into which the image is to be loaded. When the image
* has finished loading, the draw() function will be called to draw the
* triangle with the texture. (Also, if an error occurs during loading,
* an error message is displayed on the page, and draw() is called to
* draw the triangle without the texture.)
*/


function loadTexture( url, textureObject ) {
    const img = new Image(); // A DOM image element to represent the
image.
    img.onload = function() {
        // This function will be called after the image loads
successfully.
        // We have to bind the texture object to the TEXTURE_2D target
before
        // loading the image into the texture object.
        gl.bindTexture(gl.TEXTURE_2D, textureObject);
        try {

gl.texImage2D(gl.TEXTURE_2D,0,gl.RGBA,gl.RGBA,gl.UNSIGNED_BYTE,img);
            gl.generateMipmap(gl.TEXTURE_2D); // Create mipmaps; you
```

```
must either
                        // do this or change the minification filter.
        }
        catch (e) { // Probably a security exception, because this page
has been
                    // loaded through a file:// URL.
            document.getElementById("headline").innerHTML =
                "Sorry, couldn't load texture.<br>" +
                "Some web browsers won't use images from a local disk";
        }
        draw(); // Draw the canvas, with or without the texture.
    };
    img.onerror = function() {
        // This function will be called if an error occurs while
loading.
        document.getElementById("headline").innerHTML =
                        "<p>Sorry, texture image could not be
loaded.</p>";
        draw(); // Draw without the texture; triangle will be black.
    };
    img.src = url; // Start loading of the image.
                    // This must be done after setting onload and
onerror.
}
```

Note that image textures for WebGL 1.0 should be power-of-two textures. That is, the width and the height of the image should each be a power of 2 , such as 128 , 256 , or 512 . You can, in fact, use non-power-of-two textures, but you can't use mipmaps with such textures, and the only texture repeat mode that is supported by such textures is gl.CLAMP_TO_EDGE. (WebGL 2.0 does not have these restrictions.) (The try..catch statement is used in this function because most web browsers will throw a security exception when a page attempts to use an image from the local file system as a texture. This means that if you attempt to run a program that uses textures from a downloaded version of this book, the programs that use textures might not work.)

There are several parameters associated with a texture object, including the texture repeat modes and the minification and magnification filters. They can be set using the function gl.texParameteri. The setting applies to the currently bound texture object. Most of the details are the same as in OpenGL 1.1 (Subsection 4.3.3). For example, the minification filter can be set to LINEAR using

```
gl.texParameteri( gl.TEXTURE_2D, gl.TEXTURE_MIN_FILTER, gl.LINEAR);
```

Recall that the default minification filter won't work without mipmaps. To get a working texture, you have to change the minification filter or install a full set of mipmaps. Fortunately, WebGL has a function that will generate the mipmaps for you:

```
gl.generateMipmap( gl.TEXTURE_2D );
```

The texture repeat modes determine what happens when texture coordinates lie outside the range 0.0 to 1.0 . There is a separate repeat mode for each direction in the texture coordinate system. In WebGL, the possible values are gl.REPEAT, gl.CLAMP_TO_EDGE, and gl.MIRRORED_REPEAT. The default is gl.REPEAT. The mode CLAMP_TO_EDGE was called CLAMP in OpenGL 1.1, and MIRRORED_REPEAT is new in WebGL. With MIRRORED_REPEAT, the texture image is repeated to cover the entire plane, but every other copy of the image is reflected. This can eliminate visible seams between the copies. To set a texture to use mirrored repeat in both directions, use

```
gl.texParameteri( gl.TEXTURE_2D, gl.TEXTURE_WRAP_S,
gl.MIRRORED_REPEAT);
gl.texParameteri( gl.TEXTURE_2D, gl.TEXTURE_WRAP_T,
gl.MIRRORED_REPEAT);
```

In WebGL, texture coordinates are usually input to the vertex shader as an attribute of type vec2. They are communicated to the fragment shader in a varying variable. Often, the vertex shader will simply copy the value of the attribute into the varying variable. Another possibility is to apply an affine texture transformation to the coordinates in the vertex shader before passing them on to the fragment shader. In the fragment shader, the texture coordinates are used to sample a texture. The GLSL ES 1.00 function for sampling an ordinary texture is

```
texture2D( samplerVariable, textureCoordinates );
```

where samplerVariable is the uniform variable of type sampler *2D* that represents the texture, and textureCoordinates is a vec2 containing the texture coordinates. The return value is an RGBA color, represented as a value of type vec4. As a very minimal example, here is a fragment shader that simply uses the sampled value from the texture as the color of the pixel.

```
precision mediump float;
uniform sampler2D u_texture;
varying vec2 v_texCoords;
void main() {
    vec4 color = texture2D( u_texture, v_texCoords );
    gl_FragColor = color;
}
```

This shader is from the sample program webgl/simple-texture.html. Textures are sometimes used on primitives of type gl.POINTS. In that case, it's natural to get the texture coordinates for a pixel from the special fragment shader variable gl_PointCoord. A point is rendered as a square, and the coordinates in gl_PointCoord range from 0.0 to 1.0 over that square. So, using gl_PointCoord means that one copy of the texture will be pasted onto the point. If the POINTS primitive has more than one vertex, you will see a copy of the texture at the location of each vertex. This is an easy way to put an image, or multiple copies of an image, into a scene. The technique is sometimes referred to as "point sprites."

Here is an example of a textured primitive of type gl.POINTS. Only a circular cutout from each square point is drawn. The picture is from an on-line demo, c6/textured-points.html.

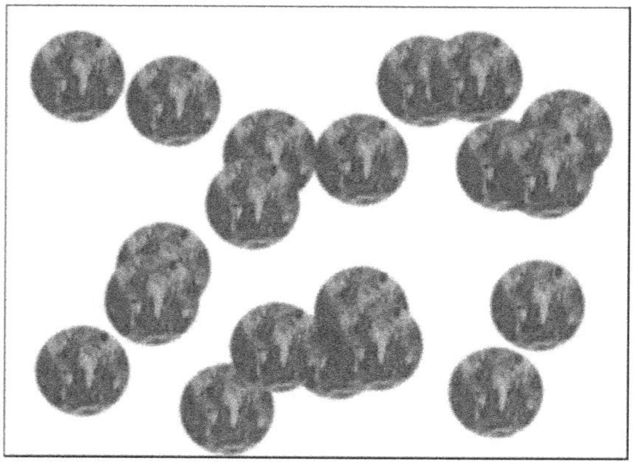

The pixel data for a texture image in WebGL is stored in memory starting with the row of pixels at the bottom of the image and working up from there. When WebGL creates the texture by reading the data from an image, it assumes that the image uses the same format. However, images in a web browser are stored in the opposite order, starting with the pixels in the top row of the image and working down. The result of this mismatch is that texture images will appear upside down. You can account for this by modifying your texture coordinates. However, you can also tell WebGL to invert the images for you as it "unpacks" them. To do that, call

```
gl.pixelStorei( gl.UNPACK_FLIP_Y_WEBGL, 1 );
```

Generally, you can do this as part of initialization. Note however that for gl.POINTS primitives, the coordinate system used by gl_PointCoord is already upside down, with the *y*-coordinate increasing from top to bottom. So, if you are loading an image for use on a POINTS primitive, you might want to set gl. UNPACK_FLIP_ Y_WEBGL to its default value, 0 .

6.4.3 More Ways to Make Textures

We have seen how to create a texture from an image or canvas element using gl.texImage2D. There are several more ways to make an image texture in WebGL. First of all, the function

```
glCopyTexImage2D( target, mipmapLevel, internalFormat,
    x, y, width, height, border );
```

which was covered in Subsection 4.3.6 also exists in WebGL. This function copies data from the color buffer (where WebGL renders its images) into the currently bound texture object. The data is taken from the rectangular region in the color buffer with the specified width and height and with its lower left corner at (x, y). The internalFormat is usually $gl.RGBA$. For WebGL, the border must be zero. For example,

```
glCopyTexImage2D( gl.TEXTURE_2, 0, gl.RGBA, 0, 0, 256, 256, 0);
```

This takes the texture data from a 256 -pixel square in the bottom left corner of the color buffer. (In a later chapter, we will see that it is actually possible, and more efficient, for WebGL to render an image directly to a texture object, using something called a "framebuffer.")

More interesting, perhaps, is the ability to take the texture data directly from an array of numbers. The numbers will become the color component values for the pixels in the texture. The function that is used for this is an alternative version of texImage2D:

```
texImage2D( target, mipmapLevel, internalFormat, width, height,
    border, dataFormat, dataType, dataArray )
```

and a typical function call would have the form

```
gl.texImage2D(gl.TEXTURE_2D, 0, gl.RGBA, 16, 16,
    0, gl.RGBA, gl.UNSIGNED_BYTE, pixels);
```

Compared to the original version of texImage2D, there are three extra parameters, width, height, and border. The width and height specify the size of the texture image. For WebGL, the border must be zero, and for WebGL 1.0, the internalFormat and dataFormat must be the same.

The last parameter in this version of texImage2D must be a typed array of type Uint8Array or Uint16Array, depending on the dataFormat of the texture. My examples will use Uint8Array and texture format gl.RGBA or gl.LUMINANCE.

For an RGBA texture, four color component values are needed for each pixel. The values will be given as unsigned bytes, with values ranging from 0 to 255 , in a Uint8Array. The length of the array will be 4 $*$ width $*$ height (that is, four times the number of pixels in the image). The data for the bottom row of pixels comes first in the array, followed by the row on top of that, and so on, with the pixels in a given row running from left to right. And within the data for one pixel, the red component comes first, followed by the blue, then the green, then the alpha.

As an example of making up texture data from scratch, let's make a 16-by-16 texture image, with the image divided into four 8 -by- 8 squares that are colored red, white, and blue. The code uses the fact that when a typed array is created, it is initially filled with zeros. We just have to change some of those zeros to 255 .

```
let pixels = new Uint8Array( 4*16*16 ); // four bytes per pixel
for (let i = 0; i < 16; i++) {
    for (let j = 0; j < 16; j++) {
        let offset = 64*i + 4*j ; // starting index of data for this
pixel
        pixels[offset + 3] = 255; // alpha value for the pixel
        if ( i < 8 && j < 8) { // bottom left quadrant is red
            pixels[offset] = 255; // set red component to maximum
        }
        else if ( i >= 8 && j >= 8 ) { // top right quadrant is blue
            pixels[offset + 2] = 255; // set blue component to maximum
        }
        else { // the other two quadrants are white
            pixels[offset] = 255; // set all components to maximum
            pixels[offset + 1] = 255;
            pixels[offset + 2] = 255;
        }
    }
}
texture = gl.createTexture();
```

```
gl.bindTexture(gl.TEXTURE_2D, texture);
gl.texImage2D(gl.TEXTURE_2D, 0, gl.RGBA, 16, 16,
                0, gl.RGBA, gl.UNSIGNED_BYTE, pixels);
gl.texParameteri(gl.TEXTURE_2D, gl.TEXTURE_MIN_FILTER, gl.LINEAR);
```

The last line is there because the default minification filter won't work without mipmaps. The texture uses the default magnification filter, which is also gl.LINEAR. This texture is used on the leftmost square in the image shown below. The image is from the sample program webgl/texture-from-pixels.html.

Note the blending along the edges between colors in the leftmost square. The blending is caused by the gl.LINEAR magnification filter. The second square uses the same texture, but with the gl.NEAREST magnification filter, which eliminates the blending. The same effect can be seen in the next two squares, which use a black/white checkerboard pattern, one with gl.Linear as the magnification filter and one using gl.NEAREST. The texture is repeated ten times horizontally and vertically on the square. In this case, the texture is a tiny 2 -by- 2 image with two black and two white pixels.

As another example, consider the rightmost square in the image. The gradient effect on that square comes from a texture. The texture size is 256 -by- 1 pixels, with the color changing from black to white along the length of the texture. One copy of the texture is mapped to the square. For the gradient texture, I used gl.LUMINANCE as the texture format, which means that the data consists of one byte per pixel, giving the grayscale value for that pixel. The texture can be created using

```
let pixels = new Unit8Array( 256 ); // One byte per pixel
for ( let i = 0; i < 256; i++ ) {
    pixels[i] = i; // Grayscale value for pixel number i is i.
}
gl.texImage2D(gl.TEXTURE_2D, 0, gl.LUMINANCE, 256, 1,
        0, gl.LUMINANCE, gl.UNSIGNED_BYTE, pixels);
```

See the sample program for more detail.

6.4.4 Cubemap Textures

We encountered cubemap textures in Subsection 5.3.4, where saw how they are used in three.js for skyboxes and environment mapping. WebGL has built-in support for cubemap textures. Instead of representing an ordinary image texture, a texture object can hold a cubemap texture. And two texture objects can be bound to the same texture unit simultaneously, one holding an ordinary texture and one holding a cubemap texture. The two textures are bound to different targets, gl.TEXTURE_2D and gl.TEXTURE_CUBE_MAP. A texture object, texObj, is bound to the cubemap target in the currently active texture unit by calling

```
gl.bindTexture( gl.TEXTURE_CUBE_MAP, texObj );
```

A given texture object can be either a regular texture or a cubemap texture, not both. Once it has been bound to one texture target, it cannot be rebound to the other target.

A cubemap texture consists of six images, one for each face of the cube. A texture object that holds a cubemap texture has six image slots, identified by the constants

```
gl.TEXTURE_CUBE_MAP_NEGATIVE_X
gl.TEXTURE_CUBE_MAP_POSITIVE_X
gl.TEXTURE_CUBE_MAP_NEGATIVE_Y


gl.TEXTURE_CUBE_MAP_POSITIVE_Y
gl.TEXTURE_CUBE_MAP_NEGATIVE_Z
gl.TEXTURE_CUBE_MAP_POSITIVE_Z
```

The constants are used as the targets in gl.texImage2D and gl.copyTexImage2D, in place of gl.TEXTURE_2D. (Note that there are six targets for loading images into a cubemap texture object, but only one target, gl.TEXTURE_CUBE_MAP, for binding the texture object to a texture unit.) A cubemap texture is often stored as a set of six images, which must be loaded separately into a texture object. Of course, it is also possible for WebGL to create a cubemap by rendering the six images.

As usual for images on the web, there is the problem of asynchronous image loading to be dealt with. Here, for example, is a function that creates a cubemap texture in my sample program webgl/cubemap-fisheye.html:

```
function loadCubemapTexture() {
    const tex = gl.createTexture();
```

```
    let imageCt = 0; // Number of images that have finished loading.
    load( "cubemap-textures/park/negx.jpg",
gl.TEXTURE_CUBE_MAP_NEGATIVE_X );
    load( "cubemap-textures/park/posx.jpg",
gl.TEXTURE_CUBE_MAP_POSITIVE_X );
    load( "cubemap-textures/park/negy.jpg",
gl.TEXTURE_CUBE_MAP_NEGATIVE_Y );
    load( "cubemap-textures/park/posy.jpg",
gl.TEXTURE_CUBE_MAP_POSITIVE_Y );
    load( "cubemap-textures/park/negz.jpg",
gl.TEXTURE_CUBE_MAP_NEGATIVE_Z );
    load( "cubemap-textures/park/posz.jpg",
gl.TEXTURE_CUBE_MAP_POSITIVE_Z );
    function load(url, target) {
        let img = new Image();
        img.onload = function() {
            gl.bindTexture(gl.TEXTURE_CUBE_MAP, tex);
            try {
                gl.texImage2D(target, 0, gl.RGBA, gl.RGBA,
gl.UNSIGNED_BYTE, img);
            }
            catch (e) {
                document.getElementById("headline").innerHTML =
                    "Can't access texture. Note that some browsers" +
                    " can't use a texture from a local file.";
                return;
            }
            imageCt++;
            if (imageCt === 6) { // all 6 images have been loaded
                gl.generateMipmap( gl.TEXTURE_CUBE_MAP );
                document.getElementById("headline").innerHTML =
                        "Funny Cubemap (Fisheye Camera Effect)";
                textureObject = tex;
                craw();
            }
        };
        img.onerror = function() {
            document.getElementById("headline").innerHTML =
```

```
                                    "SORRY, COULDN'T LOAD TEXTURES";
        };
        img.src = url;
    }
}
```

The images for a cubemap must all be the same size. They must be square. The size should, as usual, be a power of two. For a cubemap texture, texture parameters such as the minification filter are set using the target gl.TEXTURE_CUBE_MAP, and they apply to all six faces of the cube. For example,

```
gl.texParameteri(gl.TEXTURE_CUBE_MAP, gl.TEXTURE_MIN_FILTER,
gl.LINEAR);
```

Similarly, gl.generateMipmap will generate mipmaps for all six faces (so it should not be called until all six images have been loaded).

In a shader program, a cube map texture is represented by a uniform variable of type samplerCube. In GLSL ES 1.00, the texture is sampled using function textureCube. For example,

```
vec4 color = textureCube( u_texture, vector );
```

The first parameter is the samplerCube variable that represents the texture. The second parameter is a vec3. Cube map textures are not sampled using regular texture coordinates. Instead, a 3D vector is used. The goal is to pick out a point in the texture. The texture lies on the surface of a cube. To use a vector to pick out a point in the texture, cast a ray from the center of the cube in the direction given by the vector, and check where that ray intersects the cube. That is, if you put the starting point of the vector at the center of the cube, it points to the point on the cube where the texture is to be sampled.

Since we aren't doing 3D graphics in this chapter, we can't use cube maps in the ordinary way. The sample program webgl/cubemap-fisheye.html uses a cube map in an interesting, if not very useful way. The program uses 2D texture coordinates. The fragment shader transforms a pair of 2D texture coordinates into a 3D vector that is then used to sample the cubemap texture. The effect is something like a photograph produced by a fisheye camera. Here's what it looks like.

The picture on the left imitates a fisheye camera with a 170 -degree field of view. On the right the field of view is 330 -degrees, so that pixels near the edge of the disk actually show parts of the cube that lie behind the camera.

For each picture, the program draws a square with texture coordinates ranging from 0.0 to 1.0. In the texture coordinate system, pixels at a distance greater than 0.5 from the point (0.5,0.5) are colored white. Within the disk of radius 0.5 , each circle around the center is mapped to a circle on the unit sphere. That point is then used as the direction vector for sampling the cubemap texture. The point in the texture that appears at the center of the disk is the point where the cube intersects the positive z -axis, that is, the center of the "positive z" image from the cube map. You don't actually need to understand this, but here, for your information, is the fragment shader that does the work:

```
#ifdef GL_FRAGMENT_PRECISION_HIGH
    precision highp float;
#else
    precision mediump float;
#endif
uniform samplerCube u_texture;
uniform float u_angle; // field of view angle
varying vec2 v_texCoords;
void main() {
    float dist = distance( v_texCoords, vec2(0.5) );
    if (dist > 0.5)
        gl_FragColor = vec4(1.0); // white
    else {
        float x,y; // coords relative to a center at (0.5,0.5)
        x = v_texCoords.x - 0.5;
        y = v_texCoords.y - 0.5;
```

```
        vec2 circ = normalize(vec2(x,y)); // on the unit circle
        float phi = radians(u_angle/2.0)*(2.0*dist); // "latitude"
        vec3 vector = vec3(sin(phi)*circ.x, sin(phi)*circ.y, cos(phi));
        gl_FragColor = textureCube( u_texture, vector );
    }
}
```

6.4.5 A Computational Example

A GPU can offer an immense amount of processing power. Although GPUs were originally designed to apply that power to rendering images, it was quickly realized that the same power could be harnessed to do much more general types of programming. Not every programming task can take advantage of the highly parallel architecture of the typical GPU, but if a task can be broken down into many subtasks that can be run in parallel, then it might be possible to speed up the task significantly by adapting it to run on a GPU. Modern GPUs have become much more computationally versatile, but in GPUs that were designed to work only with colors, that might mean somehow representing the data for a computation as color values. The trick often involves representing the data as colors in a texture, and accessing the data using texture lookup functions.

The sample program webgl/webgl-game-of-life.html is a simple example of this approach. The program implements John Conway's well-known Game of Life (which is not really a game). A Life board consists of a grid of cells that can be either alive or dead. There is a set of rules that takes the current state, or "generation," of the board and produces a new generation. Once some initial state has been assigned to each cell, the game can play itself, producing generation after generation, according to the rules. The rules compute the state of a cell in the next generation from the states of the cell and its eight neighboring cells in the current generation. To apply the rules, you have to look at each neighboring cell and count the number of neighbors that are alive. The same process is applied to every cell, so it is a highly parallelizable task that can be easily adapted to run on a GPU.

In the sample program, the Life board is a 1024-by-1024 canvas, with each pixel representing a cell. Living cells are colored white, and dead cells are black. The program uses WebGL to compute the next generation of the board from the current board. The work is done in a fragment shader. To trigger the computation, a single square is drawn that covers the entire canvas, which causes the fragment shader to be called for every pixel in the canvas. The fragment shader needs access to the current color of the fragment and of its eight neighbors, but it has no way to query those colors directly. To give the shader access to that information, the program copies the board into a texture object, using the function gl.copyTexImage2D(). The fragment shader can then get the information that it needs using the GLSL texture lookup function texture2D().

An interesting point is that the fragment shader needs the texture coordinates not just for itself but for its neighbors. The texture coordinates for the fragment itself are passed into the fragment shader as a varying variable, with values in the range 0 to 1 for each coordinate. It can get the texture coordinates for a neighbor by adding an offset to its own texture coordinates. Since the texture is 1024-by-1024 pixels, the texture coordinates for a neighbor need to be offset by 1.0/1024.0. Here is the complete GLSL ES 1.00 fragment shader program:

```
#ifdef GL_FRAGMENT_PRECISION_HIGH
    precision highp float;
#else
    precision mediump float;
#endif
varying vec2 v_coords; // texture coordinates for this cell
const float scale = 1.0/1024.0; // 1.0 / canvas_size; (offset between
            // neighboring cells, in texture coords)
uniform sampler2D source; // the texture holding the previous
generation
void main() {
        int alive; // is this cell alive ?
        if (texture2D(source,v_coords).r > 0.0)
            alive = 1;
    else
            alive = 0;
        // Count the living neighbors. To check for living, just test
        // the red component of the color, which will be 1.0 for a
        // living cell and 0.0. for a dead cell.
        int neighbors = 0; // will be the number of neighbors that are
alive
        if (texture2D(source,v_coords+vec2(scale,scale)).r > 0.0)
            neighbors += 1;
        if (texture2D(source,v_coords+vec2(scale,0)).r > 0.0)
            neighbors += 1;
        if (texture2D(source,v_coords+vec2(scale,-scale)).r > 0.0)
            neighbors += 1;
        if (texture2D(source,v_coords+vec2(0,scale)).r > 0.0)
```

```
            neighbors += 1;
        if (texture2D(source,v_coords+vec2(0,-scale)).r > 0.0)
            neighbors += 1;
        if (texture2D(source,v_coords+vec2(-scale,scale)).r > 0.0)
            neighbors += 1;
        if (texture2D(source,v_coords+vec2(-scale,0)).r > 0.0)
            neighbors += 1;
        if (texture2D(source,v_coords+vec2(-scale,-scale)).r > 0.0)

        neighbors                            +=                          1;
    // Output the new color for this cell. using the rules of Life.
    float     color     =     0.0;     //     color     for     dead     cell
    if               (alive                ==               1)              {
        if     (neighbors     ==     2     ||     neighbors     ==     3)
            color = 1.0; // color for living cell; cell stays alive
    }
    else         if         (         neighbors         ==         3         )
        color = 1.0; // color for living cell; cell comes to life
    gl_FragColor       =       vec4(color,       color,       color,       1);
}
```

There are some other points of interest in the program. When the WebGL graphics context is created, anti-aliasing is turned off to make sure that every pixel is either perfectly black or perfectly white. Antialiasing could smear out the colors by averaging the colors of nearby pixels. Similarly, the magnification and minification filters for the texture are set to gl.NEAREST to avoid averaging of colors. Also, there is the issue of setting the initial configuration onto the board-that's done by drawing onto the board using another shader program with a different fragment shader.

On my computer, the webgl/webgl-game-of-life.html can easily compute 360 generations per second. I urge you to try it. It can be fun to watch.

General purpose programming on GPUs has become more and more important. Modern GPUs can do computations that have nothing to do with color, using various numerical data types. WebGL 2.0, as we'll see, has moved a bit in that direction, but accessing the full computational power of GPUs from the Web will require a new API. WebGPU, currently under development and already available as an experimental feature in some web browsers, is an attempt to fulfill that need. (However, unlike WebGL, it is not based on OpenGL.)

6.4.6 Textures in WebGL 2.0

One of the major changes in WebGL 2.0 is greatly increased support for textures. A large number of new texture formats have been added. RGBA color components in OpenGL are represented as floating point values in the range zero to one, but in practice are often stored as one-byte unsigned integers, with values in the range 0 to 255 , which matches the format that is used for displaying colors on most screens. In fact, you don't really have control over how colors are represented internally for use on displays. There have been computer displays that used only 16 bits per pixel instead of 32, and new HDR (High Dynamic Range) displays can use even more bits per pixel. But when storing data in a texture, it's not really necessary to match the color format that is used on a physical display.

WebGL 2.0 introduced a large number of so-called "sized" texture formats, which give the programmer control over how the data in the texture is represented. For example, if the format is gl.RGBA32F, then the texture contains four 32-bit floating point numbers for each pixel, one for each of the four RGBA color components. The format gl.R32UI indicates one 32-bit unsigned integer per pixel. And gl.RG8I means two 8-bit integers per pixel. And gl.RGBA8 corresponds to the usual format, using one 8 -bit unsigned integer for each color component. These sized formats are used for the internal format of a texture, the internalFormat parameter in a call to a function like gl.texImage2D(), which specifies how the data is actually stored in the texture. You can use textures with sized internal formats as image textures for rendering. But 32 bits for a color component encodes far more different colors than could ever be distinguished visually. These data formats are particularly useful for computational applications, where you really need to control what kind of data you are working with. But to effectively compute with data stored in textures, we really need to be able to write data to textures, as well as read from textures. And for that, we need framebuffers, which won't be covered until Section 7.4. For now, we will just look at a few aspects of the WebGL 2.0 API for working with textures.

Various versions of the texImage2D() function can be used to initialize a texture from an image or from an array of data-or to zero, when no data source is provided. WebGL 2.0 has another, potentially more efficient, function for allocating the storage for a texture and initializing it to zero:

```
gl.texStorage2D( target, levels, internalFormat, width, height );
```

The first parameter is gl.TEXTURE_2D or gl.TEXTURE_CUBE_MAP. The second parameter specifies the number of mipmap level that should be generated; generally, this will be 1 . The width and height give the size of the texture, and of course the internalFormat specifies the data format for the texture. The internalFormat must be one of the sized internal formats, such as gl.RGBA8.

WebGL 2.0 has support for 3D textures, which hold data for a 3D grid of texels, with functions gl.texImage3D() and gl.texStorage3D(). It has depth textures, which store depth values like those used in the depth test and are commonly used for shadow mapping. And it can work with compressed textures, which can decrease the amount of data that needs to be transferred between the CPU and the GPU. However, I will leave you to explore these capabilities on your own if you need them.

Shader programs use sampler variables to read data from textures. The shader programming language GLSL ES 3.00 introduces a number of new sampler types to deal with the new texture formats in WebGL 2.0. Where GLSL ES 1.00 had only sampler2D and samplerCube, the newer language adds types such as sampler3D for 3D textures, isampler2D for sampling textures whose values are signed integers, and sampler2DShadow for sampling depth textures. For example, for sampling a texture with a 32 -bit integer format, you might declare a sampler variable such as

```
uniform highp isampler2D datatexture;
```

The precision qualifier, highp, must be specified because isampler2D variables do not have a default precision. Using high precision ensures that you can read 32-bit integers exactly. (The sampler2D type has default precision lowp, which is sufficient when color components are really 8-bit integers but which might not be what you want for floating point data textures.)

GLSL ES 1.00 uses the function texture2D() to sample a 2D texture and textureCube() for sampling a cubemap texture. Rather than have a separate function for each sampler type, GLSL ES 3.00 removes texture2D and textureCube and replaces them with a single overloaded function texture(), which can be used to sample any kind of texture. So, the datatexture defined above might be sampled using

```
highp ivec4 data = texture( datatexture, coords );
```

where coords is a vec2 holding the texture coordinates. But in fact, you might want to access texel values more directly. There is a new texelFecth() function that fetches texel values from a texture, treating the texture as an array of texels. Texels are accessed using integer coordinates that range from 0 up to the size of the texture. Applied to datatexture, this could look like

```
highp ivec4 data = texelFetch( datatexture, 0, ivec2(i,j) );
```

where i ranges from 0 to the width of the texture minus one, and j ranges from 0 to the height minus one. The second parameter, 0 here, specifies the mipmap level that is being accessed. (For integer textures, you are not likely to be using mipmaps.) (The sample program webgl/texelFetch-MonaLisa-webgl2.html is a rather fanciful example of using texelFetch(), though with an ordinary image texture rather than a data texture.)

There is a lot more that could be said about WebGL 2.0 textures, but it would take us well beyond what I need for this introductory textbook.

6.5 Implementing 2D Transforms

This chapter uses WebGL for 2D drawing. Of course, the real motivation for using WebGL is to have high-performance 3D graphics on the web. We will turn to that in the next chapter. With WebGL, implementing transformations is the responsibility of the programmer, which adds a level of complexity compared to OpenGL 1.1. But before we attempt to deal with that complexity in three dimensions, this short section shows how to implement transforms and hierarchical modeling in a 2D context.

6.5.1 Transforms in GLSL

Transforms in 2D were covered in Section 2.3. To review: The basic transforms are scaling, rotation, and translation. A sequence of such transformations can be combined into a single affine transform. A 2D affine transform maps a point $(x1, y1)$ to the point $(x2, y2)$ given by formulas of the form

$$x2 = a * x1 + c * y1 + e$$
$$y2 = b * x1 + d * y1 + f$$

where $a, b, c, d, e,$ and f are constants. As explained in Subsection 2.3.8, this transform can be represented as the 3 -by- 3 matrix

$$\begin{pmatrix} a & c & e \\ b & d & f \\ 0 & 0 & 1 \end{pmatrix}$$

With this representation, a point (x, y) becomes the three-dimensional vector $(x, y, 1)$, and the transformation can be implemented as multiplication of the vector by the matrix.

To apply a transformation to a primitive, each vertex of the primitive has to be multiplied by the transformation matrix. In GLSL, the natural place to do that is in the vertex shader. Technically, it would be possible to do the multiplication on the JavaScript side, but GLSL can do it more efficiently, since it can work on multiple vertices in parallel, and it is likely that the GPU has efficient hardware support for matrix math. (It is, by the way, a property of affine transformations that it suffices to apply them at the vertices of a primitive. Interpolation of the transformed vertex coordinates to the interior pixels of the primitive will give the correct result; that is, it gives the same answer as interpolating the original vertex coordinates and then applying the transformation in the fragment shader.)

In GLSL, the type mat3 represents 3 -by-3 matrices, and vec3 represents three-dimensional vectors. When applied to a mat3 and a vec3, the multiplication operator * computes the product. So, a transform can applied using a simple GLSL assignment statement such as

```
transformedCoords = transformMatrix * originalCoords;
```

For 2D drawing, the original coordinates are likely to come into the vertex shader as an attribute of type vec2. We need to make the attribute value into a vec3 by adding 1.0 as the z-coordinate. The transformation matrix is likely to be a uniform variable, to allow the JavaScript side to specify the transformation. This leads to the following minimal GLSL ES 1.00 vertex shader for working with 2D transforms. (For a GLSL ES 3.00 version, the "attribute" qualifier is replaced by "in", and a first line "#version 300 es" is added.)

```
attribute vec2 a_coords;
uniform mat3 u_transform;
void main() {
    vec3 transformedCoords = u_transform * vec3(a_coords,1.0);
    gl_Position = vec4(transformedCoords.xy, 0.0, 1.0);
}
```

The input coordinates are given as a vec2, (x, y), but we need a vec3, $(x, y, 1)$, to multiply by the matrix, so the first line of main () adds 1.0 as the z-coordinate. In the next line, the value for gl_Position must be a vec4. For a 2D point, the z-coordinate should be 0.0 , not 1.0 , so we use only the x - and y-coordinates from transformedCoords.

On the JavaScript side, the function gl.uniformMatrix3fv is used to specify a value for a uniform of type mat3 (Subsection 6.3.3). To use it, the nine elements of the matrix should be stored in an array in column-major order. For loading an affine transformation matrix into a mat3, the command would be something like this:

```
gl.uniformMatrix3fv(u_transform_location, false, [ a, b, 0, c, d, 0, e,
f, 1 ]);
```

6.5.2 Transforms in JavaScript

To work with transforms on the JavaScript side, we need a way to represent the transforms. We also need to keep track of a "current transform" that is the product all the individual modeling transformations that are in effect. The current transformation changes whenever a transformation such as rotation or translation is applied. We need a way to save a copy of the current transform before drawing a complex object and to restore it after drawing. Typically, a stack of transforms is used for that purpose. You should be well familiar with this pattern from both 2D and 3D graphics. The difference here is that the data structures and operations that we need are not built into the standard API, so we need some extra JavaScript code to implement them.

As an example, I have written a JavaScript class, AffineTransform2D, to represent affine transforms in 2D. This is a very minimal implementation. The data for an object of type AffineTransform2D consists of the numbers a, b, c, d, e and f in the transform matrix. There are methods in the class for multiplying the transform by scaling, rotation, and translation transforms. These methods modify the transform to which they are applied, by multiplying it on the right by the appropriate matrix. Here is a full description of the API, where transform is an object of type AffineTransform2D:

- transform = new AffineTransform2D(a,b,c,d,e,f) - creates a AffineTransform2D with the matrix shown at the beginning of this section.
- transform = new AffineTransform2D() - creates an AffineTransform2D representing the identity transform.
- transform = new AffineTransform2D(original) - where original is an AffineTransform2D, creates a copy of original.
- transform.rotate(r) - modifies transform by composing it with the rotation matrix for a rotation by r radians.
- transform.translate(dx , dy) - modifies transform by composing it with the translation matrix for a translation by (dx, dy).
- transform.scale(sx,sy) - modifies transform by composing it with the scaling matrix for scaling by a factor of sx horizontally and sy vertically.
- transform.scale(s) - does a uniform scaling, the same as transform.scale(s, s).
- array = transform.getMat3() - returns an array of nine numbers containing the matrix for transform in column-major order.

In fact, an AffineTransform2D object does not represent an affine transformation as a matrix. Instead, it stores the coefficients a, b, c, d, e, and f as properties of the object. With this representation, the scale method in the AffineTransform2D class can defined as follows:

```
scale(sx, sy = sx) { // Default value for sy is the value of sx.
    this.a *= sx;
    this.b *= sx;
    this.c *= sy;
    this.d *= sy;
    return this;
}
```

This code multiplies the transform represented by "this" object by a scaling matrix, on the right. Other methods have similar definitions, but you don't need to understand the code in order to use the API.

Before a primitive is drawn, the current transform must be sent as a mat3 into the vertex shader, where the mat3 will be used to transform the vertices of the primitive. The method transform.getMat3() returns the transform as an array that can be passed to gl.uniformMatrix3fv, which sends it to the shader program.

To implement the stack of transformations, we can use an array of objects of type AffineTransform2D. In JavaScript, an array does not have a fixed length, and it comes with *push*() and *pop*() methods that make it possible to use the array as a stack. For convenience, we can define functions pushTransform() and popTransform() to manipulate the stack. Here, the current transform is stored in a global variable named transform:

```
let transform = new AffineTransform2D(); // Initially the identity.
const transformStack = []; // An array to serve as the transform stack.
/**
    * Push a copy of the current transform onto the transform stack.
    */
function pushTransform() {
        transformStack.push( new AffineTransform2D(transform) );
}
/**
    * Remove the top item from the transform stack, and set it to be
the current
    * transform. If the stack is empty, nothing is done (and there is
```

```
no error).

*/
function popTransform() {
    if (transformStack.length > 0) {
        transform = transformStack.pop();
    }
}
```

This code is from the sample program webgl/simple-hierarchy2D.html, which demonstrates using AffineTransform2D and a stack of transforms to implement hierarchical modeling. Here is a screenshot of one of the objects drawn by that program:

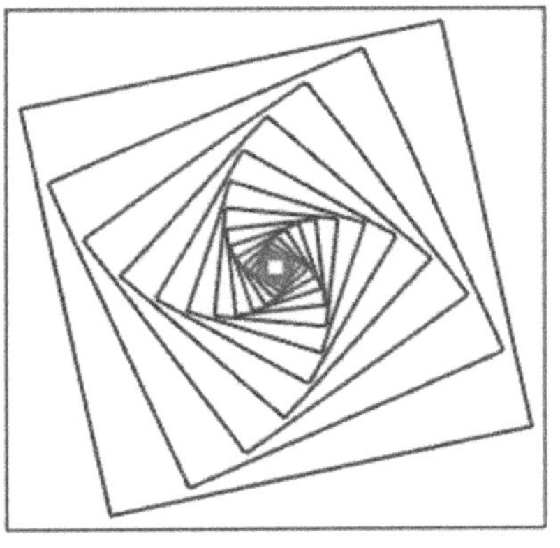

and here's the code that draws it:

```
function square() {
    gl.uniformMatrix3fv(u_transform_loc, false, transform.getMat3());
    gl.bindBuffer(gl.ARRAY_BUFFER, squareCoordsVBO);
    gl.vertexAttribPointer(a_coords_loc, 2, gl.FLOAT, false, 0, 0);
    gl.drawArrays(gl.LINE_LOOP, 0, 4);
}
function nestedSquares() {
    gl.uniform3f( u_color_loc, 0, 0, 1); // Set color to blue.
    square();
    for (let i = 1; i < 16; i++) {
        gl.uniform3f( u_color_loc, i/16, 0, 1 - i/16); // Red/Blue
mixture.
        transform.scale(0.8);
```

```
        transform.rotate(framenumber / 200);
        square();
    }
}
```

The function square() draws a square that has size 1 and is centered at (0,0) in its own object coordinate system. The coordinates for the square have been stored in a buffer, squareCoordsVBO, and a_coords_loc is the location of an attribute variable in the shader program. The variable transform holds the current modeling transform that must be applied to the square. It is sent to the shader program by calling

```
gl.uniformMatrix3fv(u_transform_loc, false, transform.getMat3());
```

The second function, nestedSquares(), draws 16 squares. Between the squares, it modifies the modeling transform with

```
transform.scale(0.8);
transform.rotate(framenumber / 200);
```

The effect of these commands is cumulative, so that each square is a little smaller than the previous one, and is rotated a bit more than the previous one. The amount of rotation depends on the frame number in an animation.

The nested squares are one of three compound objects drawn by the program. The function draws the nested squares centered at (0,0). In the main *draw*() routine, I wanted to move them and make them a little smaller. So, they are drawn using the code:

```
pushTransform();
transform.translate(-0.5,0.5); // Move center of squares to (-0.5, 0.5).
transform.scale(0.85);    //    Reduce    size    from    1    to    0.85.
nestedSquares();
popTransform();
```

The pushTransform() and popTransform() ensure that all of the changes made to the modeling transform while drawing the squares will have no effect on other objects that are drawn later. Transforms are, as always, applied to objects in the opposite of the order in which they appear in the code.

I urge you to read the source code and take a look at what it draws. The essential ideas for working with transforms are all there. It would be good to understand them before we move on to 3D.

Chapter-7

3D Graphics with WebGL

The previous chapter covered WebGL, but only in the context of two-dimensional graphics. As we move into 3D, we will have to work with more complex transformations. For that, we will rely mainly on an open-source JavaScript library for vector and matrix math. We will also need to implement lighting and material, which we will do directly in GLSL.

We begin the chapter by duplicating most of the capabilities of OpenGL 1.1 that were covered in Chapter 3 and Chapter 4. But we will soon move beyond that by adding features such as spotlights, Phong shading, and environment mapping.

7.1 Transformations in 3D

We have already seen in Chapter 6 how to draw primitives using WebGL, and how to implement 2D transformations. Drawing primitives is the same in 3D, except that there are three coordinates per vertex instead of two. Transformations in 3D are also similar to 2D, but for transformations the increase in complexity that comes with the third dimension is substantial. This section covers the geometric side of 3D graphics with WebGL. In the next section, we will move on to the question of lighting and materials.

7.1.1 About Shader Scripts

But before we begin working more seriously with WebGL, it will be nice to have a better way to include shader source code on a web page. Up until now, I have created the source code strings by concatenating a bunch of JavaScript string literals, one for each line of code. That format is hard to read and very hard to edit. There are at least two other techniques that are often used. One is to put the GLSL shader source code inside <script> elements. Here is an example for a vertex shader:

```
<script type="x-shader/x-vertex" id="vshader">
    attribute vec3 a_coords;
    uniform mat4 modelviewProjection;
    void main() {
        vec4 coords = vec4(a_coords,1.0);
        gl_Position = modelviewProjection * coords;
```

```
    }
</script>
```

This relies on the fact that a web browser will not recognize the type listed in the <script> element, so it will not try to execute the script. However, it does store the content of the <script> element in the DOM data structure that represents the web page. The content can be retrieved as a string using the standard DOM API. I won't explain the API functions that are used, but here is a function that takes the id of the script element as its parameter and returns a string containing the text from inside the element:

```
function getTextContent( elementID ) {
    let element = document.getElementById(elementID);
    let node = element.firstChild;
    let str = "";
    while (node) {
        if (node.nodeType == 3) // this is a text node
            str += node.textContent;
        node = node.nextSibling;
    }
    return str;
}
```

The sample program webgl/glmatrix-cube-unlit.html uses this technique. The other idea is to define the source code as a JavaScript template string. (See Subsection A.3.1). A template string is enclosed between single backquote characters and can span multiple lines. (The "backquote" is also called a "backtick.") Template strings were only introduced into JavaScript as part of ES6. They can include the values of JavaScript expressions, but we don't need that capability here. Here is how the above shader could be defined as a template string:

```
const vertexShaderSource = '
attribute vec3 a_coords;
uniform mat4 modelviewProjection;
void main() {
    vec4 coords = vec4(a_coords,1.0);
    gl_Position = modelviewProjection * coords;
}';
```

This technique is used in many of the sample programs in this chapter. Note that if you define a GLSL ES 3.00 shader as a template string, you should be sure to include the required first line, #version 3.00 es, immediately after the opening backquote, since that line cannot be preceded by a blank line.

7.1.2 Introducing glMatrix

Transformations are essential to computer graphics. The WebGL API does not provide any functions for working with transformations. In Section 6.5, we used a simple JavaScript class to represent modeling transformations in 2D. Things get more complex in three dimensions. For 3D graphics with WebGL, the JavaScript side will usually have to create both a modelview transform and a projection transform, and it will have to apply rotation, scaling, and translation to the modelview matrix, all without help from WebGL. Doing so is much easier if you have a JavaScript library to do the work. One commonly used library is glMatrix, a free JavaScript library for vector and matrix math written by Brandon Jones and Colin MacKenzie IV. It is available from https://glmatrix.net. This textbook uses Version 2.3 of the library, from 2015, although newer versions are available. According to its license, this file can be freely used and distributed. My programs use the script gl-matrix-min.js. You can find a copy in the source folder in the web site download of this book. This file is a "minified" JavaScript file, which is not meant to be human-readable. (You can also read the full source for version 2.2, in humanreadable form including comments, in the file webgl/gl-matrix.js, which can be found in the directory source/webgl in the web-site download of this book, and more information can be found on the glmatrix web site.)

The glMatrix API can be made available for use on a web page with a script element such as

```
<script src="gl-matrix-min.js"></script>
```

This assumes that *gl*-matrix-min.js is in the same directory as the web page. The glMatrix library defines what it calls "classes" named vec2, vec3, and vec4 for working with vectors of 2,3 , and 4 numbers. It defines mat3 for working with 3 -by- 3 matrices and mat4 for 4-by-4 matrices. The names should not be confused with the GLSL types of the same names; glMatrix in entirely on the JavaScript side. However, a glMatrix mat4 can be passed to a shader program to specify the value of a GLSL mat4, and similarly for the other vector and matrix types.

Each glMatrix class defines a set of functions for working with vectors and matrices. In fact, however, although the documentation uses the term "class," glMatrix is not object-oriented. Its classes are really just JavaScript objects, and the functions in its classes are what would be called static methods in Java. Vectors and matrices are represented in glMatrix as arrays, and the functions in classes like vec4 and mat4 simply operate on those arrays. There are no objects of type vec4 or mat4 as such, just arrays of length 4 or 16 respectively. The arrays can be either ordinary JavaScript arrays or typed arrays of type Float32Array. If you let glMatrix create the arrays for you, they will be Float32Arrays, but all glMatrix functions will work with either kind of array. For example, if the glMatrix documentation says that a parameter should be of type vec3, it is OK to pass either a Float32Array or a regular JavaScript array of three numbers as the value of that parameter.

Note that it is also the case that either kind of array can be used in WebGL functions such as gl.uniform3fv() and gl.uniformMatrix4fv(). glMatrix is designed to work with those functions. For example, a mat4 in glMatrix is an array of length 16 that holds the elements of a 4-by-4 array in column-major order, the same format that is used by gl.uniformMatrix 4 fv.

Each glMatrix class has a create() function which creates an array of the appropriate length and fills it with default values. For example,

```
transform = mat4.create();
```

sets transform to be a new Float32Array of length 16, initialized to represent the identity matrix. Similarly,

```
vector = vec3.create();
```

creates a Float32Array of length 3, filled with zeros. Each class also has a function clone (x) that creates a copy of its parameter x. For example:

```
saveTransform = mat4.clone(modelview);
```

Most other functions do not create new arrays. Instead, they modify the contents of their first parameter. For example, mat4.multiply (A, B, C) will modify A so that it holds the matrix product of B and C. Each parameter must be a mat4 (that is, an array of length 16) that already exists. It is OK for some of the arrays to be the same. For example, mat4.multiply (A, A, B) has the effect of multiplying A times B and modifying A so that it contains the answer.

There are functions for multiplying a matrix by standard transformations such as scaling and rotation. For example if A and B are mat4s and v is a vec3, then mat4.translate (A, B, v) makes A equal to the product of B and the matrix that represents translation by the vector v. In practice, we will use such operations mostly on a matrix that represents the modelview transformation. So, suppose that we have a mat4 named modelview that holds the current modelview transform. To apply a translation by a vector [dx, dy, dz], we can say

```
mat4.translate( modelview, modelview, [dx,dy,dz] );
```

This is equivalent to calling glTranslatef (dx, dy, dz) in OpenGL. That is, if we draw some geometry after this statement, using modelview as the modelview transformation, then the geometry will first be translated by [dx, dy, dz] and then will be transformed by whatever was the previous value of modelview. Note the use of a vector to specify the translation in this command, rather than three separate parameters; this is typical of glMatrix. To apply a scaling transformation with scale factors sx, sy, and sz, use

```
mat4.scale( modelview, modelview, [sx,sy,sz] );
```

For rotation, glMatrix has four functions, including three for the common cases of rotation about the x, y, or z axis. The fourth rotation function specifies the axis of rotation as the line from (0,0,0) to a point (dx, dy, dz). This is equivalent to glRotatef(angle, dx, dy, dz) Unfortunately, the angle of rotation in these functions is specified in radians rather than in degrees:

```
mat4.rotateX( modelview, modelview, radians );
mat4.rotateY( modelview, modelview, radians );
mat4.rotateZ( modelview, modelview, radians );
mat4.rotate( modelview, modelview, radians, [dx,dy,dz] );
```

These functions allow us to do all the basic modeling and viewing transformations that we need for 3D graphics. To do hierarchical graphics, we also need to save and restore the transformation as we traverse the scene graph. For that, we need a stack. We can use a regular JavaScript array, which already has push and pop operations. So, we can create the stack as an empty array:

```
const matrixStack = [];
```

We can then push a copy of the current modelview matrix onto the stack by saying

```
matrixStack.push( mat4.clone(modelview) );
```

and we can remove a matrix from the stack and set it to be the current modelview matrix with

```
modelview = matrixStack.pop();
```

These operations are equivalent to glPushMatrix() and glPopMatrix() in OpenGL.

The starting point for the modelview transform is usually a viewing transform. In OpenGL, the function gluLookAt is often used to set up the viewing transformation (Subsection 3.3.4). The glMatrix library has a "lookAt" function to do the same thing:

```
mat4.lookAt( modelview, [eyex,eyey,eyez], [refx,refy,refz],
[upx,upy,upz] );
```

Note that this function uses three vec3's in place of the nine separate parameters in gluLookAt, and it places the result in its first parameter instead of in a global variable. This function call is actually equivalent to the two OpenGL commands

```
glLoadIdentity();
gluLookAt( eyex,eyey,eyez,refx,refy,refz,upx,upy,upz );
```

So, you don't have to set modelview equal to the identity matrix before calling mat4.lookAt, as you would usually do in OpenGL. However, you do have to create the modelview matrix at some point before using mat4.lookAt, such as by calling

```
let modelview = mat4.create();
```

If you do want to set an existing mat4 to the identity matrix, you can do so with the mat4.identity function. For example,

```
mat4.identity( modelview );
```

You could use this as a starting point if you wanted to compose the view transformation out of basic scale, rotate, and translate transformations.

Similarly, glMatrix has functions for setting up projection transformations. It has functions equivalent to glOrtho, glFrustum, and gluPerspective (Subsection 3.3.3), except that the field-of-view angle in mat4.perspective is given in radians rather than degrees:

```
mat4.ortho( projection, left, right, bottom, top, near, far );
mat4.frustum( projection, left, right, bottom, top, near, far );
mat4.perspective( projection, fovyInRadians, aspect, near, far );
```

As with the modelview transformation, you do not need to load projection with the identity before calling one of these functions, but you must create projection as a mat4 (or an array of length 16).

7.1.3 Transforming Coordinates

Of course, the point of making a projection and a modelview transformation is to use them to transform coordinates while drawing primitives. In WebGL, the transformation is usually done in the vertex shader. The coordinates for a primitive are specified in object coordinates. They are multiplied by the modelview transformation to covert them into eye coordinates and then by the projection matrix to covert them to the final clip coordinates that are actually used for drawing the primitive. Alternatively, the modelview and projection matrices can be multiplied together to get a matrix that represents the combined transformation; object coordinates can then be multiplied by that matrix to transform them directly into clip coordinates.

In the shader program, coordinate transforms are ususally represented as GLSL uniform variables of type mat4. The shader program can use either separate projection and modelview matrices or a combined matrix (or both). Sometimes, a separate modelview transform matrix is required, because certain lighting calculations are done in eye coordinates, but here is a minimal GLSL ES 1.00 vertex shader that uses a combined matrix:

```
attribute vec3 a_coords; // (x,y,z) object coordinates of vertex.
uniform mat4 modelviewProjection; // Combined transformation matrix.
void main() {
    vec4 coords = vec4(a_coords,1.0); // Add 1.0 for the w-coordinate.
    gl_Position = modelviewProjection * coords; // Transform the
coordinates.
}
```

This shader is from the sample program webgl/glmatrix-cube-unlit.html. That program lets the user view a colored cube, using just basic color with no lighting applied. The user can select either an orthographic or a perspective projection and can rotate the cube using the keyboard. The rotation is applied as a modeling transformation consisting of separate rotations about the $x-, y-$, and z-axes. For transformation matrices on the JavaScript side, the program uses the mat4 class from the glMatrix library to represent the projection, modelview, and combined transformation matrices:

```
const projection = mat4.create(); // projection matrix
const modelview = mat4.create(); // modelview matrix
const modelviewProjection = mat4.create(); // combined matrix
```

(These variables can be const since the same matrix objects will be used throughout the program, even though the numbers in the objects will change.) Only modelviewProjection corresponds to a shader variable. The location of that variable in the shader program is obtained during initialization using

```
u_modelviewProjection = gl.getUniformLocation(prog,
"modelviewProjection");
```

The transformation matrices are computed in the draw() function, using functions from the glMatrix mat4 class. The value for modelviewProjection is sent to the shader program using gl.uniformMatrix $4fv$ before the primitives that make up the cube are drawn. Here is the code that does it:

```
/* Set the value of projection to represent the projection
transformation */
if (document.getElementById("persproj").checked) {
    mat4.perspective(projection, Math.PI/5, 1, 4, 8);
}
else {
    mat4.ortho(projection, -2, 2, -2, 2, 4, 8);
}
/* Set the value of modelview to represent the viewing transform. */
mat4.lookAt(modelview, [2,2,6], [0,0,0], [0,1,0]);
/* Apply the modeling tranformation to modelview. */
mat4.rotateX(modelview, modelview, rotateX);
mat4.rotateY(modelview, modelview, rotateY);
mat4.rotateZ(modelview, modelview, rotateZ);
/* Multiply the projection matrix times the modelview matrix to give
the
    combined transformation matrix, and send that to the shader
program. */
mat4.multiply( modelviewProjection, projection, modelview );
gl.uniformMatrix4fv(u_modelviewProjection, false, modelviewProjection
);
```

If separate modelview and projection matrices are used in the shader program, then the modelview matrix can be applied to transform object coordinates to eye coordinates, and the projection can then be applied to the eye coordinates to compute gl_Position. Here is a minimal vertex shader that does that:

```
attribute vec3 a_coords; // (x,y,z) object coordinates of vertex.
uniform mat4 modelview; // Modelview transformation.
```

```
uniform mat4 projection; // Projection transformation
void main() {

    vec4 coords = vec4(a_coords,1.0); // Add 1.0 for w-coordinate.
    vec4 eyeCoords = modelview * coords; // Apply modelview transform.
    glPosition = projection * eyeCoords; // Apply projection transform.
}
```

7.1.4 Transforming Normals

Normal vectors are essential for lighting calculations (Subsection 4.1.3). When a surface is transformed in some way, it seems that the normal vectors to that surface will also change. However, that is not true if the transformation is a translation. A normal vector tells what direction a surface is facing. Translating the surface does not change the direction in which the surface is facing, so the nomal vector remains the same. Remember that a vector doesn't have a position, just a length and a direction. So it doesn't even make sense to talk about moving or translating a vector.

Your first guess might be that the normal vector should be transformed by just the rotation/scaling part of the transformation. The guess is that the correct transformation is represented by the 3 -by- 3 matrix that is obtained by dropping the right column and the bottom row from the 4 -by- 4 coordinate transformation matrix. (The right column represents the translation part of the transformation, and the bottom row is only there because implementing translation in a matrix requires the use of homogeneous coordinates to represent vectors. Normal vectors, where translation is not an issue, do not use homogeneous coordinates.) But that can't be correct in all cases. Consider, for example, a shear transform. As this illustration shows, if the normal vectors to an object are subjected to the same shear transformation as the object, the resulting vectors will not be perpendicular to the object:

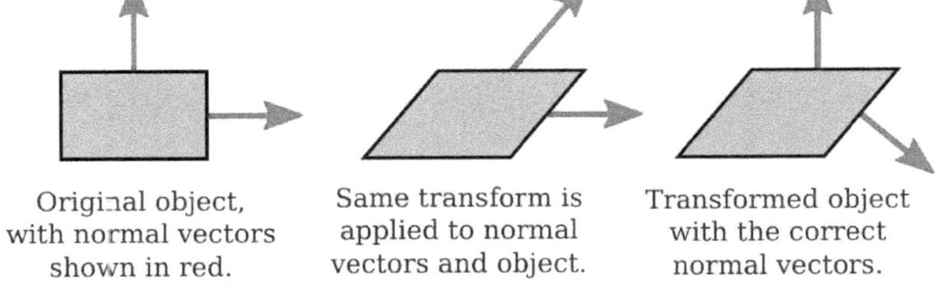

Nevertheless, it is possible to get the correct transformation matrix for normal vectors from the coordinate transformation matrix. It turns out that you need to drop the fourth row and the fourth column and then take something called the "inverse transpose" of the resulting 3-by-3 matrix. You don't need to know what that means or why it works. The glMatrix library will compute it for you. The function that you need is normalFromMat4, and it is defined in the mat3 class:

```
mat3.normalFromMat4( normalMatrix, coordinateMatrix );
```

In this function call, coordinateMatrix is the mat4 that represents the transformation that is applied to coordinates, and normalMatrix is a mat3 that already exists. This function computes the inverse transpose of the rotation/scale part of coordinateMatrix and places the answer in normalMatrix. Since we need normal vectors for lighting calculations, and lighting calculations are done in eye coordinates, the coordinate transformation that we are interested in is usually the modelview transform.

The normal matrix should be sent to the shader program, where it is needed to transform normal vectors for use in lighting calculations. Lighting requires unit normal vectors, that is, normal vectors of length one. The normal matrix does not in general preserve the length of a vector to which it is applied, so it will be necessary to normalize the transformed vector. GLSL has a built-in function for normalizing vectors. A vertex shader that implements lighting might take the form:

```
attribute vec3 a_coords; // Untransformed object coordinates.
attribute vec3 normal; // Normal vector.
uniform mat4 projection; // Projection transformation matrix.
uniform mat4 modelview; // Modelview transformation matrix.
uniform mat3 normalMatrix; // Transform matrix for normal vectors.
    .
    . // Variables to define light and material properties.
    .
void main() {
        vec4 coords = vec4(a_coords,1.0); // Add a 1.0 for the w-
coordinate.
        vec4 eyeCoords = modelview * coords; // Transform to eye
coordinates.
        gl_Position = projection * eyeCoords; // Transform to clip
coordinates.
        vec3 transformedNormal = normalMatrix*normal; // Transform
normal vector.
        vec3 unitNormal = normalize(transformedNormal); // Normalize.
```

```
        .
        . // Use eyeCoords, unitNormal, and light and material
        . // properties to compute a color for the vertex.
}
```

We will look at several specific examples in the next section. I will note that GLSL ES 3.00 (but not GLSL ES 1.00) has built-in functions for computing the inverse and the transpose of a matrix, making it fairly easy to compute the normal matrix in the shader. However, it might still be more efficient to compute the matrix once on the JavaScript side, rather than computing it in every execution of the vertex shader.

7.1.5 Rotation by Mouse

Computer graphics is a lot more interesting when there is user interaction. The 3D experience is enhanced considerably just by letting the user rotate the scene, to view it from various directions. The unlit cube example lets the user rotate the scene using the keyboard. But using the mouse for rotation gives the user much better control. I have written two JavaScript classes, SimpleRotator and TrackballRotator, to implement two different styles of rotation-by-mouse.

The SimpleRotator class is defined in the file webgl/simple-rotator.js. To use it on a web page, you need to include that file in a <script> tag, and you need to create an object of type SimpleRotator:

```
rotator = new SimpleRotator( canvas, callback, viewDistance );
```

The first parameter must be a DOM <canvas> element. It should be the canvas where WebGL renders the scene. The SimpleRotator constructor adds a listener for mouse events to the canvas; it also handles touch events on a touchscreen. The second parameter to the constructor is optional. If it is defined, it must be a function. The function is called, with no parameters, each time the rotation changes. Typically, the callback function is the function that renders the image in the canvas. The third parameter is also optional. If defined, it must be a non-negative number. It gives the distance of the viewer from the center of rotation. The default value is zero, which can be OK for an orthographic projection but is usually not correct.

A SimpleRotator keeps track of a viewing transformation that changes as the user rotates the scene. The most important function is rotator.getViewMatrix(). This function returns an array of 16 numbers representing the matrix for the viewing transformation in column-major order. The matrix can be sent directly to the shader program using gl.uniformMatrix $4fv$, or it can be used with functions from the glMatrix library as the initial value of the modelview matrix.

The sample program webgl/cube-with-simple-rotator.html is an example of using a SimpleRotator. The program uses a perspective projection defined by the glMatrix function

```
mat4.perspective(projection, Math.PI/8, 1, 8, 12);
```

The viewDistance for the rotator has to be between the near and far distances in the projection. Here, near is 8 and far is 12, and the viewDistance can be set to 10. The rotator is created during initialization using the statement

```
rotator = new SimpleRotator(canvas, draw, 10);
```

In the draw() function, the viewing transformation is obtained from the rotator before drawing the scene. There is no modeling transformation in this program, so the view matrix is also the modelview matrix. That matrix is multiplied by the projection matrix using a glMatrix function, and the combined transformation matrix is sent to the shader program:

```
let modelview = rotator.getViewMatrix();
mat4.multiply( modelviewProjection, projection, modelview );
gl.uniformMatrix4fv(u_modelviewProjection, false, modelviewProjection
);
```

That's really all that you need to know if you just want to use SimpleRotator in your own programs. I have also written an alternative rotator class, TrackballRotator, which is defined in the JavaScript file webgl/trackball-rotator.js. A TrackballRotator can be used in the same way as a SimpleRotator. The main difference is that a TrackballRotator allows completely free rotation while a SimpleRotator has the constraint that the y-axis will always remain vertical in the image.

The sample program webgl/cube-with-trackball-rotator.html uses a TrackballRotator, but is otherwise identical to the SimpleRotator example. Also, the demo c7/rotators.html in the online version of this section lets you try out both kinds of rotator.

By default, the center of rotation for either type of rotator is the origin, even if the origin is not at the center of the image. However, you can change the center of rotation to be the point (a, b, c) by calling rotation.setRotationCenter ([a, b, c]). The parameter must be an array of three numbers. Typically, (a, b, c) would be the point displayed at the center of the image (the point that would be the view reference point in gluLookAt).

You don't need to understand the mathematics that is used to implement a rotator. In fact, TrackballRotator uses some advanced techniques that I don't want to explain here. However, SimpleRotator is, well, more simple, and it's nice to know how it works. So, I will explain how the view transformation is computed for a SimpleRotator. Actually, it will be easier to think in terms of the corresponding modeling transformation on the scene as a whole. (Recall the equivalence between modeling and viewing (Subsection 3.3.4).)

The modeling transformation includes a rotation about the y-axis followed by a rotation about the x-axis. The sizes of the rotations change as the user drags the mouse. Left/right motion controls the rotation about the y-axis, while up/down motion controls the rotation about the x-axis. The rotation about the x-axis is restricted to lie in the range -85 to 85 degrees. Note that a rotation about the y-axis followed by a rotation about the x-axis always leaves the y-axis pointing in a vertical direction when projected onto the screen.

Suppose the center of rotation is (tx, ty, tz) instead of $(0,0,0)$. To implement that, before doing the rotations, we need to translate the scene to move the point (tx, ty, tz) to the origin. We can do that with a translation by $(-tx, -ty, -tz)$. Then, after doing the rotation, we need to translate the origin back to the point (tx, ty, tz).

Finally, if the viewDistance is not zero, we need to push the scene viewDistance units away from the viewer. We can do that with a translation by (0,0, -viewDistance). If d is the view distance, ry is the rotation about the y-axis, and rx is the rotation about the x-axis, then the sequence of modeling transformations that we need to apply to the scene is as follows:

1. Move the view center to the origin: Translate by $(-tx, -ty, -tz)$.
2. Rotate the scene by ry radians about the y-axis.
3. Rotate the scene by rx radians about the x-axis.
4. Move the origin back to view center: Translate by (tx, ty, tz).
5. Move the scene away from the viewer: Translate by $(0,0,-d)$.

Keeping in mind that modeling transformations are applied to objects in the opposite of the order in which they occur in the code, the view matrix could be created by the following glMatrix commands:

```
viewmatrix = mat4.create();
mat4.translate(viewmatrix, viewmatrix, [0,0,-d]);
mat4.translate(viewmatrix, viewmatrix, [tx,ty,tz]);
mat4.rotateX(viewmatrix, viewmatrix, rx);
mat4.rotateY(viewmatrix, viewmatrix, ry);
mat4.translate(viewmatrix, viewmatrix, [-tx,-ty,-tz]);
```

In fact, in my code, I create the view matrix directly, based on the matrices for the individual transformations. The 4-by-4 matrices for rotation and translation are given in

Subsection 3.5.2. The view matrix for a SimpleRotator is the matrix product of five translation and rotation matrices:

$$
\underbrace{\begin{pmatrix} 1 & 0 & 0 & 0 \\ 0 & 1 & 0 & 0 \\ 0 & 0 & 1 & -d \\ 0 & 0 & 0 & 1 \end{pmatrix}}_{\text{Translate by - viewDistance in z direction}}
\underbrace{\begin{pmatrix} 1 & 0 & 0 & tx \\ 0 & 1 & 0 & ty \\ 0 & 0 & 1 & tz \\ 0 & 0 & 0 & 1 \end{pmatrix}}_{\text{Translate origin to rotationCenter}}
\underbrace{\begin{pmatrix} 1 & 0 & 0 & 0 \\ 0 & \cos(rx) & -\sin(rx) & 0 \\ 0 & \sin(rx) & \cos(rx) & 0 \\ 0 & 0 & 0 & 1 \end{pmatrix}}_{\text{Rotate by rx radians about the x-axis}}
\underbrace{\begin{pmatrix} \cos(ry) & 0 & \sin(ry) & 0 \\ 0 & 1 & 0 & 0 \\ -\sin(ry) & 0 & \cos(ry) & 0 \\ 0 & 0 & 0 & 1 \end{pmatrix}}_{\text{Rotate by ry radians about the y-axis}}
\underbrace{\begin{pmatrix} 1 & 0 & 0 & -tx \\ 0 & 1 & 0 & -ty \\ 0 & 0 & 1 & -tz \\ 0 & 0 & 0 & 1 \end{pmatrix}}_{\text{Translate rotationCenter to origin}}
$$

It's actually not too difficult to implement the multiplication. See the JavaScript file, webgl/simple-rotator.js, if you are curious.

7.2 Lighting and Material

In this section, we turn to the question of lighting and material in WebGL. We will continue to use the basic OpenGL model that was covered in Section 4.1 and Section 4.2, but now we are responsible for implementing the lighting equation in our own GLSL shader programs. That means being more aware of the implementation details. It also means that we can pick and choose which parts of the lighting equation we will implement for a given application.

The goal of the lighting equation is to compute a color for a point on a surface. The inputs to the equation include the material properties of the surface and the properties of light sources that illuminate the surface. The angle at which the light hits the surface plays an important role. The angle can be computed from the direction to the light source and the normal vector to the surface. Computation of specular reflection also uses the direction to the viewer and the direction of the reflected ray. The four vectors that are used in the computation are shown in this lighting diagram from Subsection 4.1.4:

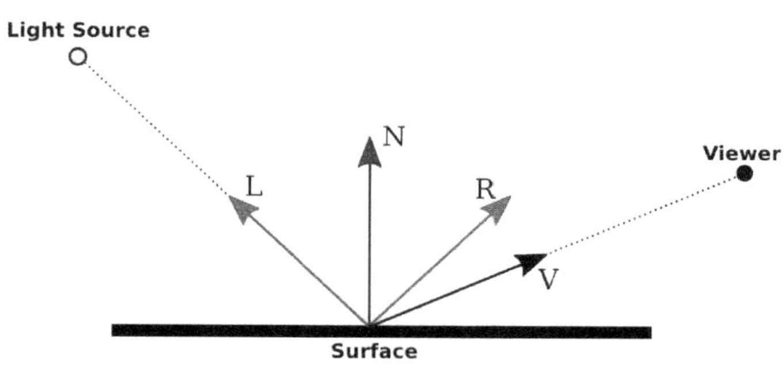

The vectors L, N, R, and V should be unit vectors. Recall that unit vectors have the property that the cosine of the angle between two unit vectors is given by the dot product of the two vectors.

The lighting equation also involves ambient and emission color, which do not depend the direction vectors shown in the diagram.

You should keep this big picture in mind as we work through some examples that use various aspects of the lighting model.

7.2.1 Minimal Lighting

Even very simple lighting can make 3D graphics look more realistic. For minimal lighting, I sometimes use what I call a "viewpoint light," a white light that shines from the direction of the viewer into the scene. In the simplest case, a directional light can be used. In eye coordinates, a directional viewpoint light shines in the direction of the negative z-axis. The light direction vector (L in the above diagram), which points towards the light source, is (0,0,1).

To keep things minimal, let's consider diffuse reflection only. In that case, the color of the light reflected from a surface is the product of the diffuse material color of the surface, the color of the light, and the cosine of the angle at which the light hits the surface. The product is computed separately for the red, green, and blue components of the color. We are assuming that the light is white, so the light color is 1 in the formula. The material color will probably come from the JavaScript side as a uniform or attribute variable.

The cosine of the angle at which the light hits the surface is given by the dot product of the normal vector N with the light direction vector L. In eye coordinates, L is (0,0,1). The dot product, $N \cdot L$ or $N \cdot (0,0,1)$, is therefore simply $N.z$, the z-component of N. However, this assumes that N is also given in eye coordinates. The normal vector will ordinarily come from the JavaScript side and will be expressed in object coordinates. Before it is used in lighting calculations, it must be transformed to the eye coordinate system. As discussed in Subsection 7.1.4, to do that we need a normal transformation matrix that is derived from the modelview matrix. Since the normal vector must be of length one, the GLSL code for computing N would be something like

```
vec3 N = normalize( normalMatrix * normal );
```

where normal is the original normal vector in object coordinates, normalMatrix is the normal transformation matrix, and normalize is a built-in GLSL function that returns a vector of length one pointing in the same direction as its parameter.

There is one more complication: The dot product $N \cdot L$ can be negative, which would mean that the normal vector points away from the light source (into the screen in this case). Ordinarily, that would mean that the light does not illuminate the surface. In the case of a viewpoint light, where we know that every visible surface is illuminated, it means that we are looking at the "back side" of the surface (or that incorrect normals were specified). Let's assume that we want to treat the two sides of the surface the same. The correct normal vector for the back side is the negative of the normal vector for the front side, and the correct dot product is $(-N) \cdot L$. We can handle both cases if we simply use $abs(N \cdot L)$. For $L = (0,0,1)$, that would be $abs(N.z)$. If color is a vec3 giving the diffuse color of the surface, the visible color can be computed as

```
vec3 visibleColor = abs(N.z) * color;
```

If color is instead a vec4 giving an RGBA color, only the RGB components should be multiplied by the dot product:

```
vec4 visibleColor = vec4( abs(N.z)*color.rgb, color.a );
```

The sample program webgl/cube-with-basic-lighting.html implements this minimal lighting model. The lighting calculations are done in the vertex shader. Part of the scene is drawn without lighting, and the vertex shader has a uniform bool variable to specify whether lighting should be applied. Here is the vertex shader source code from that program:

```
attribute vec3 a_coords; // Object coordinates for the vertex.
uniform mat4 modelviewProjection; // Combined transformation matrix.
uniform bool lit; // Should lighting be applied?
uniform vec3 normal; // Normal vector (in object coordinates).
uniform mat3 normalMatrix; // Transformation matrix for normal vectors.
uniform vec4 color; // Basic (diffuse) color.
varying vec4 v_color; // Color to be sent to fragment shader.
void main() {
    vec4 coords = vec4(a_coords,1.0);
    gl_Position = modelviewProjection * coords;
    if (lit) {
        vec3 N = normalize(normalMatrix*normal); // Transformed unit
normal.
        float dotProduct = abs(N.z);
        v_color = vec4( dotProduct*color.rgb, color.a );
    }
```

```
    else {
        v_color = color;
    }
}
```

It would be easy to add ambient light to this model, using a uniform variable to specify the ambient light level. Emission color is also easy.

The directional light used in this example is technically only correct for an orthographic projection, although it will also generally give acceptable results for a perspective projection.

But the correct viewpoint light for a perspective projection is a point light at (0,0,0)-the position of the "eye" in eye coordinates. A point light is a little more difficult than a directional light.

Remember that lighting calculations are done in eye coordinates. The vector *L* that points from the surface to the light can be computed as

```
vec3 L = normalize( lightPosition - eyeCoords.xyz );
```

where lightPosition is a vec3 that gives the position of the light in eye coordinates, and eyeCoords is a vec4 giving the position of the surface point in eye coordinates. For a viewpoint light, the lightPosition is (0,0,0), and *L* can be computed simply as normalize(-eyeCoords.xyz). The eye coordinates for the surface point must be computed by applying the modelview matrix to the object coordinates for that point. This means that the shader program needs to know the modelview matrix; it's not sufficient to know the combined modelview and projection matrix. The vertex shader shown above can modified to use a point light at (0,0,0) as follows:

```
attribute vec3 a_coords; // Object coordinates for the vertex.
uniform mat4 modelview; // Modelview transformation matrix
uniform mat4 projection; // Projection transformation matrix.
uniform bool lit; // Should lighting be applied?
uniform vec3 normal; // Normal vector (in object coordinates).
uniform mat3 normalMatrix; // Transformation matrix for normal vectors.
uniform vec4 color; // Basic (diffuse) color.
varying vec4 v_color; // Color to be sent to fragment shader.
void main() {
    vec4 coords = vec4(a_coords,1.0);
    vec4 eyeCoords = modelview * coords;
    gl_Position = projection * eyeCoords;
```

```
    if (lit) {
        vec3 L = normalize( - eyeCoords.xyz ); // Points to light.
        vec3 N = normalize(normalMatrix*normal); // Transformed unit
normal.
        float dotProduct = abs( dot(N,L) );
        v_color = vec4( dotProduct*color.rgb, color.a );
    }
    else {
        v_color = color;
    }
}
```

(Note, however, that in some situations, it can be better to move the lighting calculations to the fragment shader, as we will soon see.)

7.2.2 Specular Reflection and Phong Shading

To add specular lighting to our basic lighting model, we need to work with the vectors R and V in the lighting diagram. In perfect specular reflection, the viewer sees a specular highlight only if R is equal to V, which is very unlikely. But in the lighting equation that we are using, the amount of specular reflection depends on the dot product $R \cdot V$, which represents the cosine of the angle between R and V. The formula for the contribution of specular reflection to the visible color is

```
(R.V) s * specularMaterialColor * lightIntensity
```

where s is the specular exponent (the material property called "shininess" in OpenGL). The formula is only valid if $R \cdot V$ is greater than zero; otherwise, the specular contribution is zero.

The unit vector R can be computed from L and N. (Some trigonometry shows that R is given by $2^{*}(N \cdot L) * N - L$.) GLSL has a built-in function reflect (I, N) that computes the reflection of a vector I through a unit normal vector N; however, the value of reflect(L, N) is $-R$ rather than R. (GLSL assumes a light direction vector that points from the light toward the surface, while my L vector does the reverse.)

The unit vector V points from the surface towards the position of the viewer. Remember that we are doing the calculations in eye coordinates. For an orthographic projection, the viewer is essentially at infinite distance, and V can be taken to be (0,0,1). For a perspective projection, the viewer is at the point (0,0,0) in eye coordinates, and V is given by normalize(-eyeCoords) where eyeCoords contains the xyz coordinates of the surface point in the eye coordinate system. Putting all this together, and assuming that we already have *N* and *L*, the GLSL code for computing the color takes the form:

```
R = -reflect(L,N);
V = normalize( -eyeCoords.xyz ); // (Assumes a perspective projection.)
vec3 color = dot(L,N) * diffuseMaterialColor.rgb * diffuseLightColor;
if (dot(R,V) > 0.0) {
    color = color + ( pow(dot(R,V),specularExponent) *
        specularMaterialColor * specularLightColor );
}
```

The sample program webgl/basic-specular-lighting.html implements lighting with diffuse and specular reflection. For this program, which draws curved surfaces, normal vectors are given as a vertex attribute rather rather than a uniform variable. To add some flexibility to the lighting, the light position is specified as a uniform variable rather than a constant. Following the OpenGL convention, lightPosition is a vec4. For a directional light, the *w*-coordinate is 0 , and the eye coordinates of the light are lightPosition.xyz. If the *w*-coordinate is non-zero, the light is a point light, and its eye coordinates are lightPosition.xyz/lightPosition.w. (The division by lightPosition.w is the convention for homogeneous coordinates, but in practice, lightPosition. *w* will usually be either zero or one.) The program allows for different diffuse and specular material colors, but the light is always white, with diffuse intensity 0.8 and specular intensity 0.4 . You should be able to understand all of the code in the vertex shader:

```
attribute vec3 a_coords;
attribute vec3 a_normal;
uniform mat4 modelview;
uniform mat4 projection;
uniform mat3 normalMatrix;
uniform vec4 lightPosition;
uniform vec4 diffuseColor;
uniform vec3 specularColor;
uniform float specularExponent;
varying vec4 v_color;
void main() {
    vec4 coords = vec4(a_coords,1.0);
    vec4 eyeCoords = modelview * coords;
    gl_Position = projection * eyeCoords;
    vec3 N, L, R, V; // Vectors for lighting equation.
    N = normalize( normalMatrix*a_normal );
```

```
    if ( lightPosition.w == 0.0 ) { // Directional light.

        L = normalize( lightPosition.xyz );
    }
    else { // Point light.
        L = normalize( lightPosition.xyz/lightPosition.w -
eyeCoords.xyz );
    }
    R = -reflect(L,N);
    V = normalize( -eyeCoords.xyz); // (Assumes a perspective
projection.)
    if ( dot(L,N) <= 0.0 ) {
        v_color = vec4(0,0,0,1); // The vertex is not illuminated.
    }
    else {
        vec3 color = 0.8 * dot(L,N) * diffuseColor.rgb;
        if (dot(R,V) > 0.0) {
            color += 0.4 * pow(dot(R,V),specularExponent) *
specularColor;
        }
        v_color = vec4(color, diffuseColor.a);
    }
}
```

The fragment shader just assigns the value of v_color to gl_FragColor.

This approach imitates OpenGL 1.1 in that it does lighting calculations in the vertex shader. This is sometimes called per-vertex lighting. It is similar to Lambert shading in three.js, except that Lambert shading only uses diffuse reflection. But there are many cases where pervertex lighting does not give good results. We saw in Subsection 5.1.4 that it can give very bad results for spotlights. It also tends to produce bad specular highlights, unless the primitives are very small.

If a light source is close to a primitive, compared to the size of the primitive, the the angles that the light makes with the primitive at the vertices can have very little relationship to the angle of the light at an interior point of the primitive:

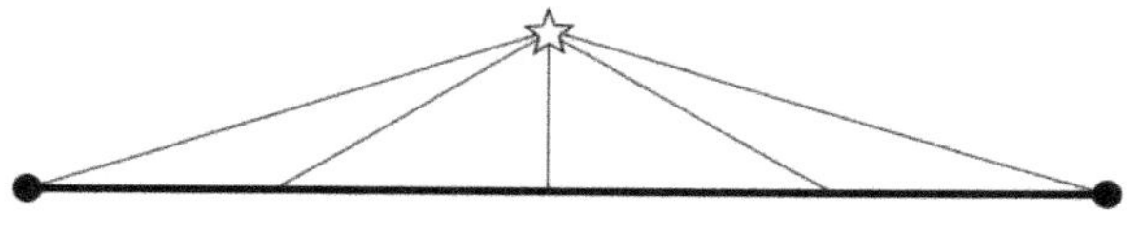

Since lighting depends heavily on the angles, per-vertex lighting will not give a good result in this case. To get better results, we can do per-pixel lighting. That is, we can move the lighting calculations from the vertex shader into the fragment shader.

To do per-pixel lighting, certain data that is available in the vertex shader must be passed to the fragment shader in varying variables. This includes, for example, either object coordinates or eye coordinates for the surface point. The same might apply to properties such as diffuse color, if they are attributes rather then uniform variables. Of course, uniform variables are directly accessible to the fragment shader. Light properties will generally be uniforms, and material properties might well be.

And then, of course, there are the normal vectors, which are so essential for lighting. Although normal vectors can sometimes be uniform variables, they are usually attributes. Perpixel lighting generally uses interpolated normal vectors, passed to the fragment shader in a varying variable. (Phong shading is just per-pixel lighting using interpolated normals.) An interpolated normal vector is in general only an approximation for the geometrically correct normal, but it's usually good enough to give good results. Another issue is that interpolated normals are not necessarily unit vectors, even if the normals in the vertex shader are unit vectors. So, it's important to normalize the interpolated normal vectors in the fragment shader. The original normal vectors in the vertex shader should also be normalized, for the interpolation to work properly.

The sample program webgl/basic-specular-lighting-Phong.html uses per-pixel lighting. I urge you to read the shader source code in that program. Aside from the fact that lighting calculations have been moved to the fragment shader, it is identical to the previous sample program.

The on-line demo c7/per-pixel-vs-per-vertex.html lets you view objects drawn using pervertex lighting side-by-side with objects drawn using per-pixel lighting. It uses the same shader programs as the two sample programs. Here is an example from that demo:

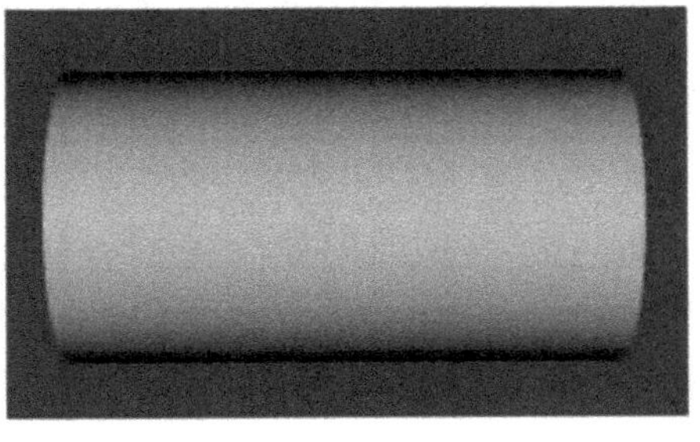

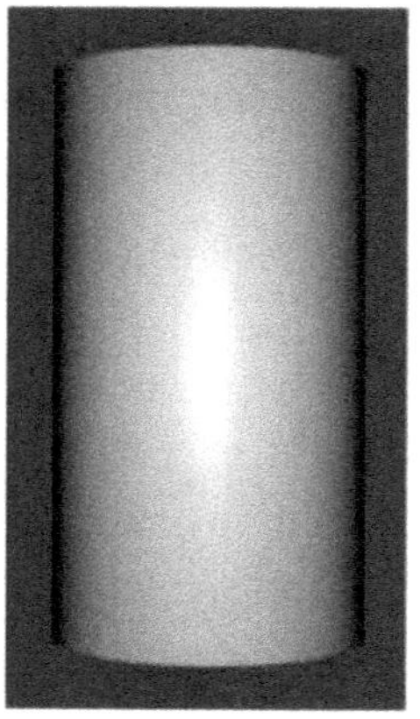

For this cylinder, all of the vertices are along the top and bottom edges, and the light source is fairly close to the cylinder. In this example, per-pixel lighting misses the specular highlight on the cylinder entirely. On the other hand, for a torus, which is made up of very small triangles, the per-vertex lighting in the demo gives a fairly good approximation of the correct specular highlights.

The sample program webgl/basic-specular-lighting-Phong-webgl2.html is a port of the original WebGL 1.0 Phong lighting program to WebGL 2.0. It shows what the shader program looks like in GLSL ES 3.00. The changes are minimal. Attribute variables become "in" variables, varying variables become "out" variables in the vertex shader and "in" variables in the fragment shader, and the built-in fragment shader variable gl_FragColor is replaced with a custom "out" variable. The JavaScript side would not have to be changed at all, but as an example, it has been modified to use vertex array objects to organize the data for the various objects that can be drawn in the in program.

7.2.3 Adding Complexity

Our shader programs are getting more complex. As we add support for multiple lights, additional light properties, two-sided lighting, textures, and other features, it will be useful to use data structures and functions to help manage the complexity. GLSL data structures were introduced in Subsection 6.3.2, and function definitions in Subsection 6.3.5. Let's look briefly at how they can be used to work with light and material.

It makes sense to define a struct to hold the properties of a light. The properties will usually include, at a minimum, the position and color of the light. Other properties can be added, depending on the application and the details of the lighting model that are used. For example, to make it possible to turn lights on and off, a bool variable might be added to say whether the light is enabled:

```
struct LightProperties {
    bool enabled;
    vec4 position;
    vec3 color;
};
```

A light can then be represented as a variable of type LightProperties. It will likely be a uniform variable so that its value can be specified on the JavaScript side. Often, there will be multiple lights, represented by an array; for example, to allow for up to four lights:

```
uniform LightProperties lights[4];
```

Material properties can also be represented as a struct. Again, the details will vary from one application to another. For example, to allow for diffuse and specular color:

```
struct MaterialProperties {
    vec3 diffuseColor;
    vec3 specularColor;
    float specularExponent;
};
```

With these data types in hand, we can write a function to help with the lighting calculation. The following function computes the contribution of one light to the color of a point on a surface. (Some of the parameters could be global variables in the shader program instead.)

```
vec3 lightingEquation( LightProperties light,
                MaterialProperties material,
                vec3 eyeCoords, // Eye coordinates for the point.
                vec3 N, // Normal vector to the surface.
                vec3 V // Direction to viewer.
            ) {
    vec3 L, R; // Light direction and reflected light direction.
    if ( light.position.w == 0.0 ) { // directional light
        L = normalize( light.position.xyz );
    }
    else { // point light
        L = normalize( light.position.xyz/light.position.w - eyeCoords
);
    }
    if (dot(L,N) <= 0.0) { // light does not illuminate the surface
        return vec3(0.0);
```

```
    }
    vec3 reflection = dot(L,N) * light.color * material.diffuseColor;
    R = -reflect(L,N);

if (dot(R,V) > 0.0) { // ray is reflected toward the the viewer

        float    factor   =    pow(dot(R,V),material.specularExponent);
        reflection  +=  factor  *  material.specularColor  *  light.color;
    }
    return                                                   reflection;
}
```

Then, assuming that there are four lights, the full calculation of the lighting equation might look like this:

```
vec3 color = vec3(0.0); // Start with black (all color components
zero).
for (int i = 0; i < 4; i++) { // Add in the contribution from light i.
    if (lights[i].enabled) { // Light can only contribute color if
enabled.
        color += lightingEquation( lights[i], material,
            eyeCoords, normal, viewDirection );
    }
}
```

7.2.4 Two-sided Lighting

The sample program webgl/parametric-function-grapher.html uses GLSL data structures similar to the ones we have just been looking at. It also introduces a few new features. The program draws the graph of a parametric surface. The (x, y, z) coordinates of points on the surface are given by functions of two variables u and v. The definitions of the functions can be input by the user. There is a viewpoint light, but two extra lights have been added in an attempt to provide more even illumination. The graph is considered to have two sides, which are colored yellow and blue. The program can, optionally, show grid lines on the surface. Here's what the default surface looks like, with grid lines:

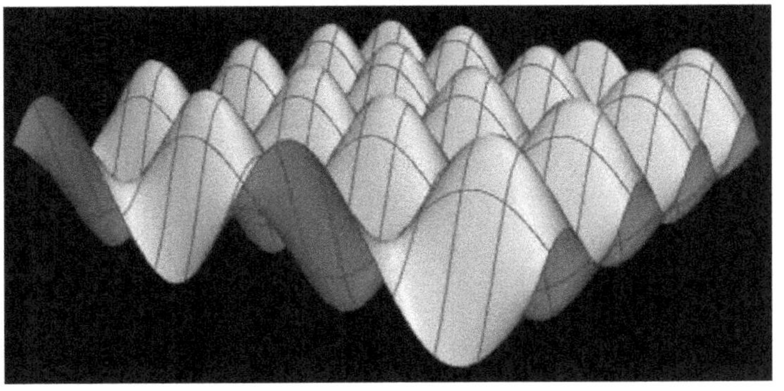

This is an example of two-sided lighting (Subsection 4.2.4). We need two materials, a front material for drawing front-facing polygons and a back material for drawing back-facing polygons. Furthermore, when drawing a back face, we have to reverse the direction of the normal vector, since normal vectors are assumed to point out of the front face.

But when the shader program does lighting calculations, how does it know whether it's drawing a front face or a back face? That information comes from outside the shader program: The fragment shader has a built-in boolean variable named gl_FrontFacing whose value is set to true before the fragment shader is called, if the shader is working on the front face of a polygon. When doing per-pixel lighting, the fragment shader can check the value of this variable to decide whether to use the front material or the back material in the lighting equation. The sample program has two uniform variables to represent the two materials. It has three lights. The normal vectors and eye coordinates of the point are varying variables. And the normal transformation matrix is also applied in the fragment shader:

```
uniform MaterialProperties frontMaterial;
uniform MaterialProperties backMaterial;
uniform LightProperties lights[3];
uniform mat3 normalMatrix;
varying vec3 v_normal;
varying vec3 v_eyeCoords;
```

A color for the fragment is computed using these variables and the lightingEquation function shown above:

```
vec3 normal = normalize( normalMatrix * v_normal );
vec3 viewDirection = normalize( -v_eyeCoords);
vec3 color = vec3(0.0);
for (int i = 0; i < 3; i++) {
```

```
    if (lights[i].enabled) {
        if (gl_FrontFacing) { // Computing color for a front face.
            color += lightingEquation( lights[i], frontMaterial,
v_eyeCoords,
                    normal, viewDirection);
        }
        else { // Computing color for a back face.
            color += lightingEquation( lights[i], backMaterial,
v_eyeCoords,
                    -normal, viewDirection);
        }
    }
}
gl_FragColor = vec4(color,1.0);
```

Note that in the second call to lightEquation, the normal vector is given as -normal. The negative sign reverses the direction of the normal vector for use on a back face.

If you want to use two-sided lighting when doing per-vertex lighting, you have to deal with the fact that gl_FrontFacing is not available in the vertex shader. One option is to compute both a front color and a back color in the vertex shader and pass both values to the fragment shader as varying variables. The fragment shader can then decide which color to use, based on the value of gl_FrontFacing.

There are a few WebGL settings related to two-sided lighting. Ordinarily, WebGL determines the front face of a triangle according to the rule that when the front face is viewed, vertices are listed in counterclockwise order around the triangle. The JavaScript command gl.frontFace(gl. CW) reverses the rule, so that vertices are listed in clockwise order when the front face is viewed. The command gl.frontFace(gl. CCW) restores the default rule.

In some cases, you can be sure that no back faces are visible. This will happen when the objects are closed surfaces seen from the outside, and all the triangles face towards the outside. In such cases, it is wasted effort to draw back faces, since you can be sure that they will be hidden by front faces. The JavaScript command gl.enable(gl.CULL_FACE) tells WebGL to discard triangles without drawing them, based on whether they are front-facing or back-facing. The commands gl.cullFace(gl.BACK) and gl.cullFace(gl.FRONT) determine whether it is backfacing or front-facing triangles that are discarded when $CULL\_FACE$ is enabled; the default is to discard back-facing triangles.

The sample program can display a set of grid lines on the surface. As always, drawing two objects at exactly the same depth can cause a problem with the depth test. As we have already seen at the end of Subsection 3.4.1 and in Subsection 5.1.3, OpenGL uses polygon offset to solve the problem. The same solution is available in WebGL. Polygon offset can be turned on with the commands

```
gl.enable(gl.POLYGON_OFFSET_FILL);
gl.polygonOffset(1,1);
```

and turned off with

```
gl.disable(gl.POLYGON_OFFSET_FILL);
```

In the sample program, polygon offset is turned on while drawing the graph and is turned off while drawing the grid lines.

7.2.5 Moving Lights

In our examples so far, lights have been fixed with respect to the viewer. But some lights, such as the headlights on a car, should move along with an object. And some, such as a street light, should stay in the same position in the world, but change position in the rendered scene as the point of view changes.

Lighting calculations are done in eye coordinates. When the position of a light is given in object coordinates or in world coordinates, the position must be transformed to eye coordinates, by applying the appropriate modelview transformation. The transformation can't be done in the shader program, because the modleview matrix in the shader program represents the transformation for the object that is being rendered, and that is almost never the same as the transformation for the light. The solution is to store the light position in eye coordinates. That is, the shader's uniform variable that represents the position of the light must be set to the position in eye coordinates.

For a light that is fixed with respect to the viewer, the position of the light is already expressed in eye coordinates. For example, the position of a point light that is used as a viewpoint light is (0,0,0), which is the location of the viewer in eye coordinates. For such a light, the appropriate modelview transformation is the identity.

For a light that is at a fixed position in world coordinates, the appropriate modelview transformation is the viewing transformation. The viewing transformation must be applied to the world-coordinate light position to transform it to eye coordinates. In WebGL, the transformation should be applied on the JavaScript side, and the output of the transformation should be sent to the uniform variable in the shader program that represents the light position in eye coordinates. Similarly, for a light that moves around in the world, the combined modeling and viewing transform should be applied to the light position on the JavaScript side. The glMatrix library (Subsection 7.1.2) defines the function

```
vec4.transformMat4( transformedVector, originalVector, matrix );
```

which can be used to do the transformation. The matrix in the function call will be the modelview transformation matrix. Recall, by the way, that light position is given as a vec4, using homogeneous coordinates. (See Subsection 4.2.3.) Multiplication by the modelview matrix will work for any light, whether directional or point, whose position is represented in this way. Here is a JavaScript function that can be used to set the position:

```
/* Set the position of a light, in eye coordinates.
    * @param u_position_loc The uniform variable location for
    * the position property of the light.
    * @param modelview The modelview matrix that transforms light
    * position to eye coordinates.
    * @param lightPosition The location of the light, in object
    * coordinates (a vec4).
    */
function setLightPosition( u_position_loc, modelview, lightPosition ) {
        let transformedPosition = new Float32Array(4);


    vec4.transformMat4( transformedPosition, lightPosition, modelview
);
    gl.uniform4fv( u_position_loc, transformedPosition );
}
```

The appropriate modelview matrix is the identity, for a light fixed with respect to the viewer; just the viewing transformation, for a light that has a fixed position in the world; or a combined viewing and modeling transformation, for a light that moves around in the world.

Remember that the light position, like other light properties, must be set before rendering any geometry that is to be illuminated by the light.

7.2.6 Spotlights

We encountered spotlights in three.js in Subsection 5.1.4. In fact, although I didn't mention it, spotlights already existed in OpenGL 1.1. Instead of emitting light in all directions, a spotlight emits only a cone of light. A spotlight is a kind of point light. The vertex of the cone is located at the position of the light. The cone points in some direction, called the spot direction. The spot direction is specified as a vector. The size of the cone is specified by a cutoff angle; light is only emitted from the light position in directions whose angle with the spot direction is less than the cutoff angle. Furthermore, for angles less than the cutoff angle, the intensity of the light ray can decrease as the angle between the ray and spot direction increases. The rate at which the intensity decreases is determined by a non-negative number called the spot exponent. The intensity of the ray is given by $I * c^s$ where I is the basic intensity of the light, c is the cosine of the angle between the ray and the spot direction, and s is the spot exponent.

This illustration shows three spotlights shining on a surface; the images are taken from the sample program webgl/spotlights.html:

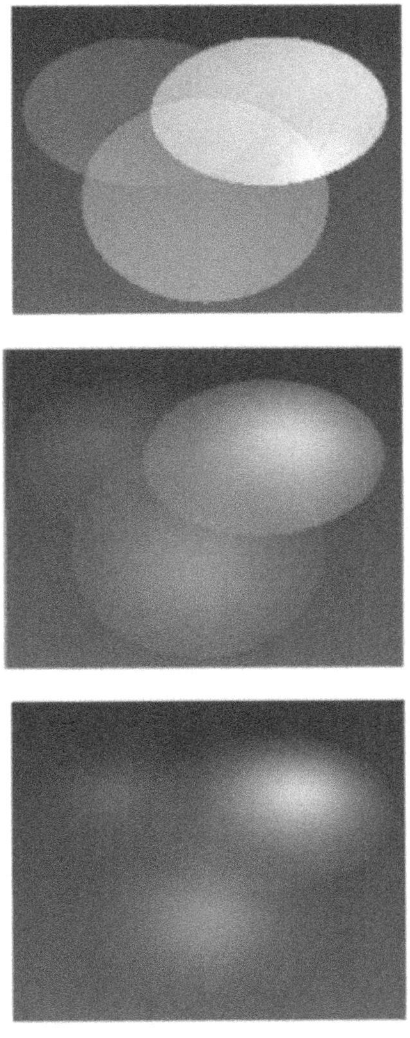

The cutoff angle for the three spotlights is 30 degrees. In the image on the left, the spot exponent is zero, which means there is no falloff in intensity with increasing angle from the spot direction. For the middle image, the spot exponent is 10 , and for the image on the right, it is 20.

Suppose that we want to apply the lighting equation to a spotlight. Consider a point **P** on a surface. The lighting equation uses a unit vector, L, that points from **P** towards the light source. For a spotlight, we need a vector that points from the light source towards **P**; for that we can use $-L$. Consider the angle between $-L$ and the spot direction. If that angle is greater than the cutoff angle, then **P** gets no illumination from the spotlight. Otherwise, we can compute the cosine of the angle between $-L$ and the spot direction as the dot product $-D \cdot L$, where D is a unit vector that points in the spot direction.

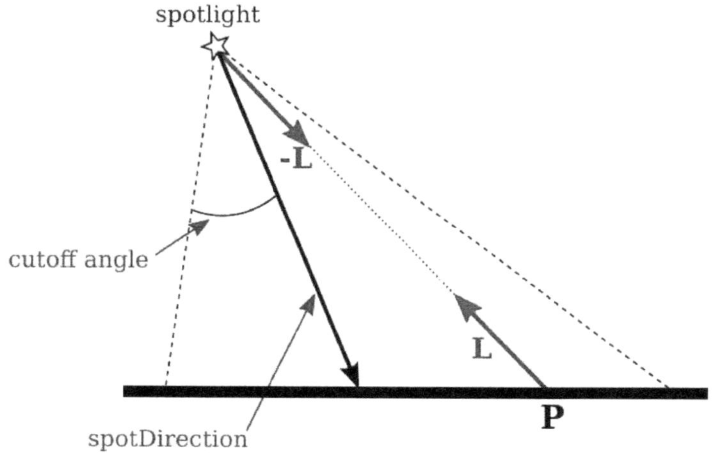

To implement spotlights in GLSL, we can add uniform variables to represent the spot direction, cutoff angle, and spot exponent. My implementation actually uses the cosine of the cutoff angle instead of the angle itself, since I can then compare the cutoff value using the dot product, $-D \cdot L$, that represents the cosine of the angle between the light ray and the spot direction. The LightProperties struct becomes:

```
struct LightProperties {
    bool enabled;
    vec4 position;
    vec3 color;
    vec3 spotDirection;
    float spotCosineCutoff;
    float spotExponent;
};
```

If position. z is zero, then the light is directional and cannot be a spotlight. For a point light, if spotCosineCutoff is less than or equal to zero, then the light is a regular point light, not a spotlight. For a spotlight, we need to compute the factor c^e that is multiplied by the basic light color to give the effective light intensity of the spotlight at a point on a surface. The following code for the computation is from the fragment shader in the sample program. For a spotlight, the value of c^e is assigned to spotFactor:

```
float spotFactor = 1.0; // multiplier to account for spotlight
if ( light.position.w == 0.0 ) {
    L = normalize( light.position.xyz );
}
else {
    L = normalize( light.position.xyz/light.position.w - v_eyeCoords );
    if (light.spotCosineCutoff > 0.0) { // the light is a spotlight
        vec3 D = -normalize(light.spotDirection);
        float spotCosine = dot(D,L);
        if (spotCosine >= light.spotCosineCutoff) {
            spotFactor = pow(spotCosine,light.spotExponent);
        }
        else { // The point is outside the cone of light from the
spotlight.
            spotFactor = 0.0; // The light will add no color to the
point.
        }
    }
}
// Light intensity will be multiplied by spotFactor
```

You should try the sample program, and read the source code. Or try the demo in the on-line version of this section, which is similar to the sample program, but with an added option to animate the spotlights.

* * *

The spotDirection uniform variable gives the direction of the spotlight in eye coordinates. For a moving spotlight, in addition to transforming the position, we also have to worry about transforming the direction in which the spotlight is facing. The spot direction is a vector, and it transforms in the same way as normal vectors. That is, the same normal transformation matrix that is used to transform normal vectors is also used to transform the spot direction. Here is a JavaScript function that can be used to apply a modelview transformation to a spot direction vector and send the output to the shader program:

```
/* Set the direction vector of a light, in eye coordinates.
    * @param modelview the matrix that does object-to-eye coordinate
transforms
    * @param u_direction_loc the uniform variable location for the
spotDirection
    * @param lightDirection the spot direction in object coordinates (a
vec3)
    */
function setSpotlightDirection( u_direction_loc, modelview,
lightDirection ) {
        let normalMatrix = mat3.create();
        mat3.normalFromMat4( normalMatrix,modelview );
        let transformedDirection = new Float32Array(3);
        vec3.transformMat3( transformedDirection, lightDirection,
normalMatrix );
        gl.uniform3fv( u_direction_loc, transformedDirection );
}
```

Of course, the position of the spotlight also has to be transformed, as for any moving light.

7.2.7 Light Attenuation

There is one more general property of light to consider: attenuation. This refers to the fact that the amount of illumination from a light source should decrease with increasing distance from the light. Attenuation applies only to point lights, since directional lights are effectively at infinite distance. The correct behavior, according to physics, is that the illumination is proportional to one over the square of the distance. However, that doesn't usually give good results in computer graphics. In fact, for all of my light sources so far, there has been no attenuation with distance.

OpenGL 1.1 supports attenuation. The light intensity can be multiplied by $1.0/(a + b * d + c * d^2)$, where d is the distance to the light source, and a, b, and c are properties of the light. The numbers a, b, and c are called the "constant attenuation," "linear attenuation," and "quadratic attenuation" of the light source. By default, a is one, and b and c are zero, which means that there is no attenuation.

Of course, there is no need to implement exactly the same model in your own applications. For example, quadratic attenuation is rarely used. In the next sample program, I use the formula $1/(1 + a * d)$ for the attenuation factor. The attenuation constant a is added as another property of light sources. A value of zero means no attenuation. In the lighting computation, the contribution of a light source to the lighting equation is multiplied by the attenuation factor for the light.

7.2.8 Diskworld 2

The sample program webgl/diskworld-2.html is our final, more complex, example of lighting in WebGL. The basic scene is the same as the three.js example threejs/diskworld-1.html from Subsection 5.1.5, but I have added several lighting effects.

The scene shows a red "car" traveling around the edge of a disk-shaped "world." In the new version, there is a sun that rotates around the world. The sun is turned off at night, when the sun is below the disk. (Since there are no shadows, if the sun were left on at night, it would shine up through the disk and illuminate objects from below.) At night, the headlights of the car turn on. They are implemented as spotlights that travel along with the car; that is, they are subject to the same modelview transformation that is used on the car. Also at night, a lamp in the center of the world is turned on. Light attenuation is used for the lamp, so that its illumination is weak except for objects that are close to the lamp. Finally, there is dim viewpoint light that is always on, to make sure that nothing is ever in absolute darkness. Here is a night scene from the program, in which you can see how the headlights illuminate the road and the trees, and you can probably see that the illumination from the lamp is stronger closer to the lamp:

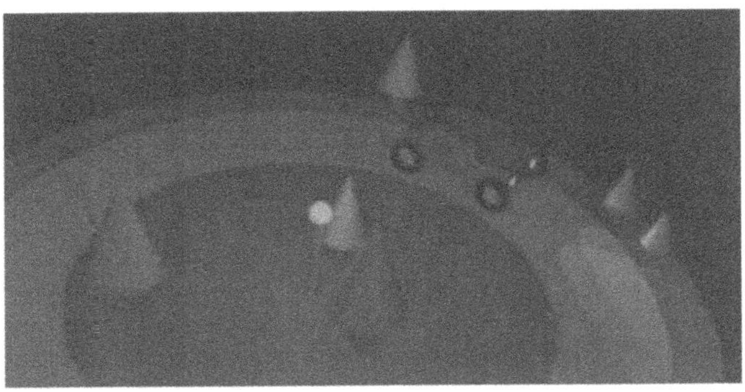

But you should run the program to see it in action! And read the source code to see how it's done.

My diskworld example uses per-pixel lighting, which gives much better results than pervertex lighting, especially for spotlights. However, with multiple lights, spotlights, and attenuation, per-pixel lighting requires a lot of uniform variables in the fragment shader - possibly more than are supported in some implementations. (See Subsection 6.3.7 for information about limitations in shader programs.) That's not really serious for a sample program in a textbook and not really likely on modern GPUs; it just means that there is some possibility that the example won't work in some browsers on some devices. But for more serious applications, using even more complex lighting, an alternative approach would be desirable, hopefully better than simply moving the calculation to the vertex shader. One option is to use a multi-pass algorithm in which the scene is rendered several times, with each pass doing the lighting calculation for a smaller number of lights. See Subsection 7.5.4 for a technique that can be used to implement this idea efficiently.

7.3 Textures

Most of the WebGL API for working with textures was already covered in Section 6.4. In this section, we look at several examples and techniques for using textures.

7.3.1 Texture Transforms with glMatrix

In Subsection 4.3.4, we saw how to apply a texture transformation in OpenGL. OpenGL maintains a texture transform matrix that can be manipulated to apply scaling, rotation, and translation to texture coordinates before they are used to sample a texture. It is easy to program the same operations in WebGL. We need to compute the texture transform matrix on the JavaScript side. The transform matrix is then sent to a uniform matrix variable in the the shader program, where it can be applied to the texture coordinates. Note that as long as the texture transformation is affine, it can be applied in the vertex shader, even though the texture is sampled in the fragment shader. That is, doing the transformation in the vertex shader and interpolating the transformed texture coordinates will give the same result as interpolating the original texture coordinates and applying the transformation to the interpolated coordinates in the fragment shader.

Since we are using glMatrix for coordinate transformation in 3D, it makes sense to use it for texture transforms as well. If we use 2D texture coordinates, we can implement scaling, rotation, and translation on the JavaScript side using the mat3 class from glMatrix. The functions that we need are

- mat3.create() - Returns a new 3 -by-3 matrix (represented as an array of length 9). The new matrix is the identity matrix.
- mat3.identity(A) - Sets *A* to be the identity matrix, where *A* is an already-existing mat3.

- mat3.translate(A, B, [dx, dy]) - Multiplies the matrix B by a matrix representing translation by (dx, dy), and sets A to be the resulting matrix. A and B must already exist.

- mat3.scale(A,B,[sx,sy]) - Multiplies B by a matrix representing scaling by (sx, sy), and sets A to be the resulting matrix.

- mat3.rotate(A,B,angle) - Multiplies B by a matrix representing rotation by angle radians about the origin, and sets A to be the resulting matrix.

For implementing texture transformations, the parameters A and B in these functions will be the texture transform matrix. For example, to apply a scaling by a factor of 2 to the texture coordinates, we might use the code:

```
var textureTransform = mat3.create();
mat3.scale( textureTransform, textureTransform, [2,2] );
gl.uniformMatrix3fv( u_textureTransform, false, textureTransform );
```

The last line assumes that u_textureTransform is the location of a uniform variable of type mat3 in the shader program. (And remember that scaling the texture coordinates by a factor of 2 will shrink the texture on the surfaces to which it is applied.)

The sample WebGL program webgl/texture-transform.html uses texture transformations to animate textures. In the program, texture coordinates are input into the vertex shader as an attribute named a_texCoords of type vec2, and the texture transformation is a uniform variable named textureTransform of type mat3. The transformed texture coordinates are computed in the vertex shader with the GLSL commands

```
vec3 texcoords = textureTransform * vec3(a_texCoords,1.0);
v_texCoords = texcoords.xy;
```

Read the source code to see how all this is used in the context of a complete program.

7.3.2 Generated Texture Coordinates

Texture coordinates are typically provided to the shader program as an attribute variable. However, when texture coordinates are not available, it is possible to generate them in the shader program. While the results will not usually look as good as using texture coordinates that are customized for the object that is being rendered, they can be acceptable in some cases.

Generated texture coordinates should usually be computed from the object coordinates of the object that is being rendered. That is, they are computed from the original vertex coordinates, before any transformation has been applied. Then, when the object is transformed, the texture will be transformed along with the object so that it will look like the texture is attached to the object. The texture coordinates could be almost any function of the object coordinates. If an affine function is used, as is usually the case, then the texture coordinates can be computed in the vertex shader. Otherwise, you need to send the object coordinates to the fragment shader in a varying variable and do the computation there.

The simplest idea for generated texture coordinates is simply to use the x and y coordinates from the object coordinate system as the texture coordinates. If the vertex coordinates are given as the value of the attribute variable a_coords, that would mean using a_coords.xy as texture coordinates. This has the effect of projecting the texture onto the surface from the direction of the positive z-axis, perpendicular to the xy-plane. The mapping works OK for a polygon that is facing, more-or-less, in the direction of positive z, but it doesn't give good results for polygons that are edge-on to the xy-plane. Here's what the mapping looks like on a cube:

The texture projects nicely onto the front face of the cube. It also works OK on the back face of the cube (not visible in the image), except that it is mirror-reversed. On the other four faces, which are exactly edge-on to the xy-plane, you just get lines of color that come from pixels along the border of the texture image. (In this example, one copy of the texture image exactly fills the front face of the cube. That doesn't happen automatically; you might need a texture transform to adapt the texture image to the surface.)

Of course, we could project in other directions to map the texture to other faces of the cube. But how to decide which direction to use? Let's say that we want to project along the direction of one of the coordinate axes. We want to project, approximately at least, from the direction that the surface is facing. The normal vector to the surface tells us that direction. We should project in the direction where the normal vector has its greatest magnitude. For example, if the normal vector is (0.12,0.85,0.51), then we should project from the direction of the positive y-axis. And a normal vector equal to $(-0.4,0.56,-0.72)$ would tell us to project from the direction of the negative z-axis. This resulting "cubical" generated texture coordinates are perfect for a cube, and it looks pretty good on most objects, except that there can be a seam where the direction of projection changes. Here, for example, the technique is applied to a teapot:

When using flat shading, so that all of the normals to a polygon point in the same direction, the computation can be done in the vertex shader. With smooth shading, normals at different vertices of a polygon can point in different directions. If you project texture coordinates from different directions at different vertices and interpolate the results, the result is likely to be a mess. So, doing the computation in the fragment shader is safer. Suppose that the interpolated normal vectors and object coordinates are provided to the fragment shader in varying variables named v_normal and v_objCoords. Then the following code can be used to generate "cubical" texture coordinates:

```
if ( (abs(v_normal.x) > abs(v_normal.y)) &&
        (abs(v_normal.x) > abs(v_normal.z)) ) {
    // project along the x-axis
    texcoords = (v_normal.x > 0.0) ? v_objCoords.yz : v_objCoords.zy;
}
```

```
else if ( (abs(v_normal.z) > abs(v_normal.x)) &&
        (abs(v_normal.z) > abs(v_normal.y)) ) {
    // project along the z-axis
    texcoords = (v_normal.z > 0.0) ? v_objCoords.xy : v_objCoords.yx;
}
else {
    // project along the y-axis
    texcoords = (v_normal.y > 0.0) ? v_objCoords.zx : v_objCoords.xz;
}
```

When projecting along the x-axis, for example, the y and z coordinates from $v_$objCoords are used as texture coordinates. The coordinates are computed as either v_objCoords.yz or v_objCoords.zy, depending on whether the projection is from the positive or the negative direction of x. The order of the two coordinates is chosen so that a texture image will be projected directly onto the surface, rather than mirror-reversed.

You can experiment with generated textures using the demo c7/generated-texcoords.html in the on-line version of this section. The demo shows a variety of textures and objects using cubical generated texture coordinates, as discussed above. You can also try texture coordinates projected just onto the xy or zx plane, as well as a cylindrical projection that wraps a texture image once around a cylinder. A final option is to use the x and y coordinates from the eye coordinate system as texture coordinates. That option fixes the texture on the screen rather than on the object, so the texture doesn't rotate with the object. The effect is interesting, but probably not very useful.

7.3.3 Procedural Textures

Up until now, all of our textures have been image textures. With an image texture, a color is computed by sampling the image, based on a pair of texture coordinates. The image essentially defines a function that takes texture coordinates as input and returns a color as output. However, there are other ways to define such functions besides looking up values in an image. A procedural texture is defined by a function whose value is computed rather than looked up. That is, the texture coordinates are used as input to a code segment whose output is the corresponding color value for the texture.

In WebGL, procedural textures can be defined in the fragment shader. The idea is simple: Take a vec2 representing a set of texture coordinates. Then, instead of using a sampler2D to look up a color, use the vec2 as input to some mathematical computation that computes a vec4 representing a color. In theory any computation could be used, as long as the components of the vech are in the range 0.0 to 1.0 .

We can even extend the idea to 3D textures. 2D textures use a vec2 as texture coordinates. For 3D texture coordinates, we use a vec3. Instead of mapping points on a plane to color, a 3D texture maps points in space to colors. It's possible to have 3D textures that are similar to image textures. That is, a color value is stored for each point in a 3D grid, and the texture is sampled by looking up colors in the grid. However, a 3D grid of colors takes up a lot of memory. On the other hand, 3D procedural textures use no memory resources and use very little more computational resources than 2D procedural textures.

So, what can be done with procedural textures? In fact, quite a lot. There is a large body of theory and practice related to procedural textures. We will look at a few of the possibilities. Here's a torus, textured using four different procedural textures. The images are from the demo mentioned at the end of this subsection:

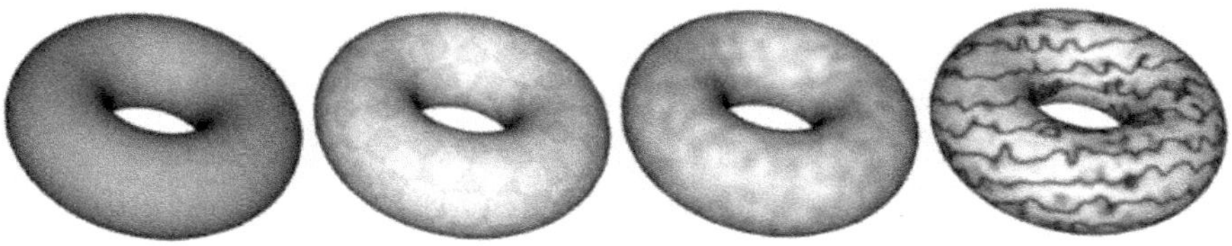

The torus on the left uses a 2D procedural texture representing a checkerboard pattern. The 2D texture coordinates were provided, as usual, as values of a vertex attribute variable in the shader program. The checkerboard pattern is regular grid of equal-sized colored squares, but, as with any 2D texture, the pattern is stretched and distorted when it is mapped to the curved surface of the torus. Given texture coordinates in the varying variable v_texCoords, the color value for the checkerboard texture can be computed as follows in the fragment shader:

```
vec4 color;
float a = floor(v_texCoords.x * scale);
float b = floor(v_texCoords.y * scale);
if (mod(a+b, 2.0) > 0.5) { // a+b is odd
    color = vec3(1.0, 0.5, 0.5, 1.0); // pink
}
else { // a+b is even
    color = vec3(0.6, 0.6, 1.0, 1.0); // light blue
}
```

The scale in the second and third lines represents a texture transformation that is used to adapt the size of the texture to the object that is being textured. (The texture coordinates for the torus range from 0 to 1 ; without the scaling, only one square in the checkerboard pattern would be mapped to the torus. For the torus in the picture, scale is 8 .) The floor function computes the largest integer less than or equal to its parameter, so a and b are integers. The value of $\text{mod}(a + b, 2.0)$ is either 0.0 or 1.0 , so the test in the fourth line tests whether $a + b$ is even or odd. The idea here is that when either a or b increases or decreases by $1, a + b$ will change from even to odd or from odd to even; that ensures that neighboring squares in the pattern will be differently colored.

The second torus in the illustration uses a 3D checkerboard pattern. The 3D pattern is made up of a grid of cubes that alternate in color in all three directions. For the 3D texture coordinates on the cube, I use object coordinates. That is, the 3D texture coordinates for a point are the same as its position in space, in the object coordinate system in which the torus is defined. The effect is like carving the torus out of a solid block that is colored, inside and out, with a 3D checkerboard pattern. Note that you don't see colored squares or rectangles on the surface of the torus; you see the intersections of that surface with colored cubes. The intersections have a wide variety of shapes. That might be a disadvantage for this particular 3D texture, but the advantage is that there is no stretching and distortion of the texture. The code for computing the 3D checkerboard is the same as for the 2D case, but using three object coordinates instead of two texture coordinates.

Natural-looking textures often have some element of randomness. We can't use actual randomness, since then the texture would look different every time it is drawn. However, some sort of pseudo-randomness can be incorporated into the algorithm that computes a texture. But we don't want the colors in the texture to look completely random - there has to be some sort of pattern in the pattern! Many natural-looking procedural textures are based on a type of pseudo-randomness called Perlin noise, named after Ken Perlin who invented the algorithm in 1983. The third torus in the above illustration uses a 3D texture based directly on Perlin noise. The "marble" texture on the fourth torus uses Perlin noise as a component in the computation. Both textures are 3D, but similar 2D versions are also possible. (I don't know the algorithm for Perlin noise. I copied the GLSL code from https://github.com/ashima/webgl-noise. The code is published under an MIT-style open source license, so that it can be used freely in any project.)

In the sample program, 3D Perlin noise is computed by a function snoise (v), where v is a vec3 and the output of the function is a float in the range -1.0 to 1.0 . Here is the computation:

```
float value = snoise( scale*v_objCoords );
value = 0.75 + value*0.25; // map to the range 0.5 to 1.0
color = vec3(1.0,value,1.0);
```

Here, v_objCoords is a varying variable containing the 3D object coordinates of the point that is being textured, and scale is a texture transformation that adapts the size of the texture to the torus. Since the output of snoise() varies between -1.0 and 1.0 , value varies from 0.5 to 1.0 , and the color for the texture ranges from pale magenta to white. The color variation that you see on the third torus is characteristic of Perlin noise. The pattern is somewhat random, but it has regular, similarly sized features. With the right scaling and coloration, basic Perlin noise can make a decent cloud texture.

The marble texture on the fourth torus in the illustration is made by adding some noise to a regular, periodic pattern. The basic technique can produce a wide variety of useful textures. The starting point is a periodic function of one variable, with values between 0.0 and 1.0 . To get a periodic pattern in 2D or 3D, the input to the function can be computed from the texture coordinates. Different functions can produce very different effects. The three patterns shown here use the functions $(1.0 + \sin(t))/2.0, abs(\sin(t))$ and $(t - \text{floor}(t))$, respectively:

In the second image, taking the absolute value of $\sin(t)$ produces narrower, sharper dark bands than the plain sine function in the first image. This is the function that is used for the marble texture in the illustration. The sharp discontinuity in the third image can be an interesting visual effect.

To get the 2D pattern from a function $f(t)$ of one variable, we can use a function of a vec2, v, defined as $f(a * v.x + b * v.y)$, where a and b are constants. The values of a and b determine the orientation and spacing of the color bands in the pattern. For a 3D pattern, we would use $f(a * v.x + b * v.y + c * v.z)$.

To add noise to the pattern, add a Perlin noise function to the input of the function. For a 3D pattern, the function would become

```
f( a*v.x + b*v.y + c*v.z + d*snoise(e*v))
```

The new constants d and e determine the size and intensity of the perturbations to the pattern. As an example, the code that creates the marble texture for the torus is:

```
vec3 v = v_objCoords*scale;
float t = (v.x + 2.0*v.y + 3.0*v.z);
t += 1.5*snoise(v);
float value = abs(sin(t));
color = vec3(sqrt(value));
```

(The sqrt at the end was added to make the color bands even sharper than they would be without it.)

The demo c7/procedural-textures.html in the on-line version of this section lets you apply a variety of 3D textures to different objects. The procedural textures used in the demo are just a small sample of the possibilities.

7.3.4 Bumpmaps

So far, the only textures that we have encountered have affected color. Whether they were image textures, environment maps, or procedural textures, their effect has been to vary the color on the surfaces to which they were applied. But, more generally, texture can refer to variation in any property. One example is bumpmapping, where the property that is modified by the texture is the normal vector to the surface. A normal vector determines how light is reflected by the surface, which is a major visual clue to the direction that the surface faces. Modifying the normal vectors has the effect of modifying the apparent orientation of the surface, as least with respect to the way it reflects light. It can add the appearance of roughness or "bumps" to the surface. The effect can be visually similar to changing the positions of points on the surface, but with bumpmapping the change in appearance is achieved without actually changing the surface geometry. The alternative approach of modifying the actual geometry, which is called "displacement mapping," can give better results but requires a lot more computational and memory resources.

The typical way to do bumpmapping is with a height map. A height map, is a grayscale image in which the variation in color is used to specify the amount by which points on the surface are (or appear to be) displaced. A height map is mapped to a surface in the same way as an image texture, using texture coordinates that are supplied as an attribute variable or generated computationally. But instead of being used to modify the color of a pixel, the color value from the height map is used to modify the normal vector that goes into the lighting equation that computes the color of the pixel. A height map that is used in this way is also called a bump map. I'm not sure that my implementation of this idea is optimal, but it can produce pretty good results.

Here are two examples. For each example, a bumpmapped torus is shown next to the height map that was applied to the torus:

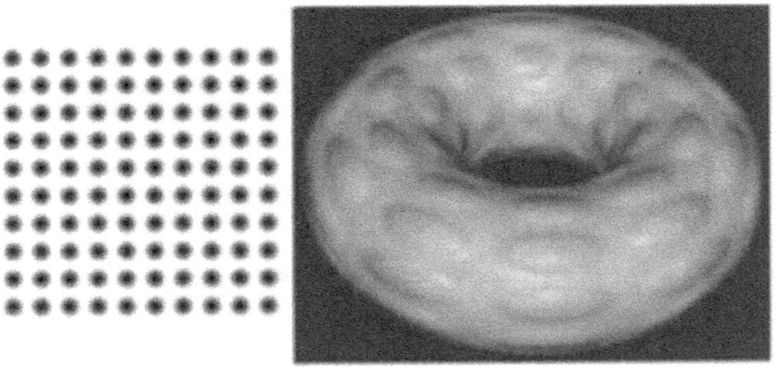

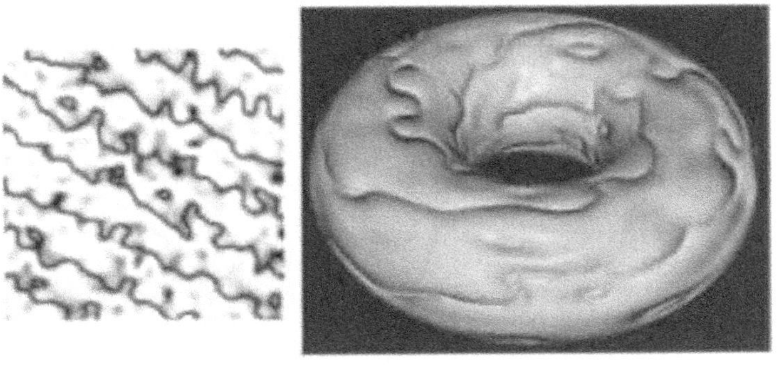

In the first example, the gray dots in the height map produce the appearance of bumps on the torus. The darker the color from the map, the greater apparent displacement of the point on the surface. The black centers of the dots map to the tops of the bumps. For the second example, the dark curves in the height map seem to produce deep grooves in the surface. As is usual for textures, the height maps have been stretched to cover the torus, which distorts the shape of the features from the map.

To see how bumpmapping can be implemented, let's first imagine that we want to apply it to a one-dimensional "surface." Consider a normal vector to a point on the surface, and suppose that a height map texture is applied to the surface. Take a vector, shown in black in the following illustration, that points in the direction in which the height map grayscale value is decreasing.

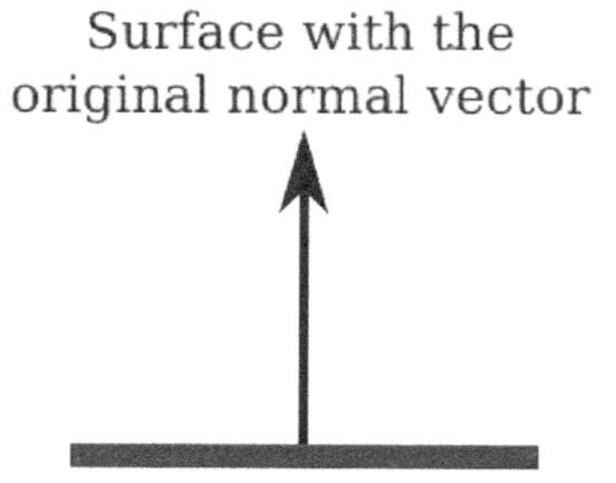

Height Map, with a vector that points in the direction height should decrease.

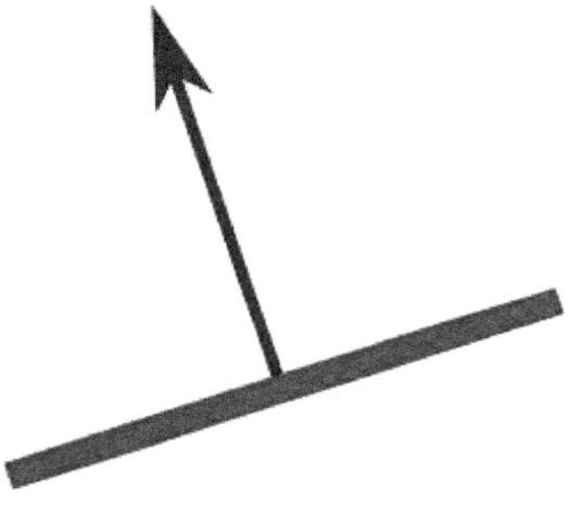

We want the surface to look as if it's tilted, like this.

Modifying the normal.

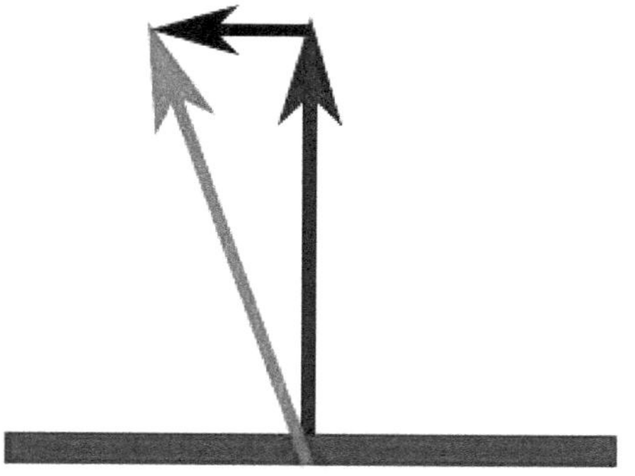

To achieve the effect, add a muliple of the vector from the height map to the normal. The new normal is shown in green.

We want the surface to appear as if it is tilted, as shown in the middle of the illustration. (I'm assuming here that darker colors in the height map correspond to smaller heights.) Literally tilting the surface would change the direction of the normal vector. We can get the same change in the normal vector by adding some multiple of the vector from the height map to the original normal vector, as shown on the right above. Changing the number that is multiplied by the height map vector changes the degree of tilting of the surface. Increasing the mulitplier gives a stronger bump effect. Using a negative multiple will tilt the surface in the opposite direction, which will transform "bumps" into "dimples," and vice versa. I will refer to the multiplier as the bump strength.

Things get a lot more complicated for two-dimensional surfaces in 3D space. A 1D "surface" can only be tilted left or right. On a 2D surface, there are infinitely many directions to tilt the surface. Note that the vector that points in the direction of tilt points along the surface, not perpendicular to the surface. A vector that points along a surface is called a tangent vector to the surface. To do bump mapping, we need a tangent vector for each point on the surface. Tangent vectors will have to be provided, along with normal vectors, as part of the data for the surface. For my version of bumpmapping, the tangent vector that we need should be coordinated with the texture coordinates for the surface: The tangent vector should point in the direction in which the s coordinate in the texture coordinates is increasing.

In fact, to properly account for variation in the height map, we need a second tangent vector. The second tangent vector is perpendicular both to the normal and to the first tangent vector. It is commonly called the "binormal" vector, and it can be computed from the normal and the tangent. (The binormal should point in the direction in which the t texture coordinate is increasing, but whether that can be exactly true will depend on the texture mapping. As long as it's not too far off, the result should be OK.)

Now, to modify the normal vector, proceed as follows: Sample the height maps at two points, separated by a small difference in the s coordinate. Let a be the difference between the two values; a represents the rate at which the height value is changing in the direction of the tangent vector (which, remember, points in the s direction along the surface). Then sample the height map at two points separated by a small difference in the t coordinate, and let b be the difference between the two values, so that b represents the rate at which the height value is changing in the direction of the binormal vector. Let D be the vector $a * \mathrm{T} + b * \mathrm{B}$, where T is the tangent vector and B is the binormal. Then add D, or a multiple of D, to the original normal vector to produce the modified normal that will be used in the lighting equation. (If you know multivariable calculus, what we are doing here amounts to using approximations for directional derivatives and the gradient vector of a height function on the surface.)

I have tried to explain the procedure in the following illustration. You need to visualize the situation in 3D, noting that the normal, tangent, and binormal vectors are perpendicular to each other. The white arrows on the left are actually multiples of the binormal and tangent vectors, with lengths given by the change in color between two pixels.

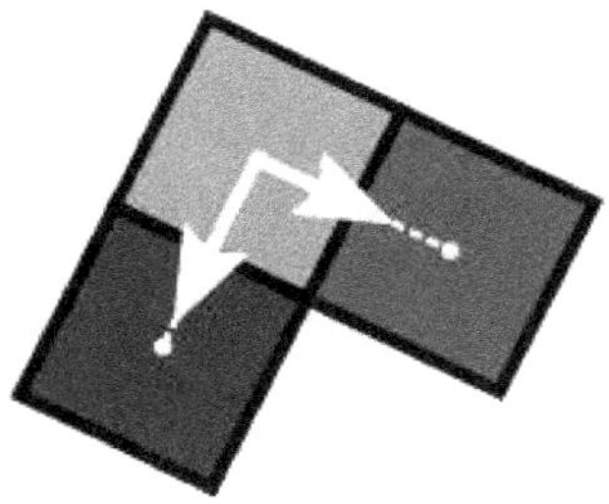

A pixel in the height map (light gray) and two neighboring pixels. The change in color between the pixels defines the two vectors shown in white.

The tangent, normal, and binormal vectors at the pixel on the surface that corresponds to the pixel in the bumpmap texture.

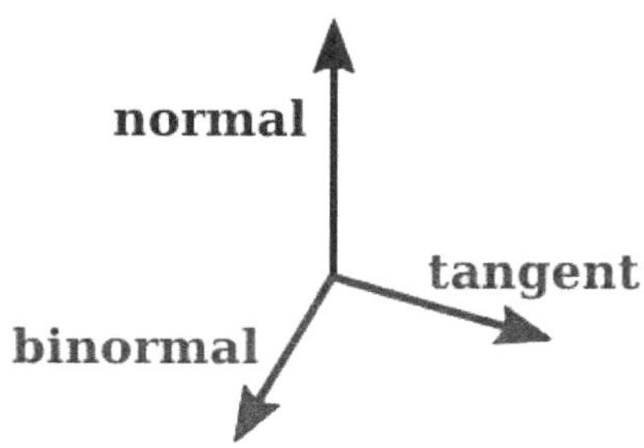

The small black vectors are some multiple of the white vectors from the height map.

They are added to the normal vector to produce the new normal vector, shown in green.

The sample program webgl/bumpmap.html demonstrates bumpmapping. The two bumpmapped toruses in the above illustration are from that program. When you run the program, pay attention to the specular highlights! They will help you to see how a bumpmap texture differs from an image texture. The effect might be more obvious if you change the "Diffuse Color" from white to some other color. The specular color is always white.

(For this program, I had to add tangent vectors to my objects. I chose three objects-a cube, a cylinder, and a torus-for which tangent vectors were relatively easy to compute. But, honestly, it took me a while to get all the tangent vectors pointing in the correct directions.)

The bumpmapping is implemented in the fragment shader in the sample program. The essential problem is how to modify the normal vector. Let's examine the GLSL code that does the work:

```
vec3 normal = normalize( v_normal );
vec3 tangent = normalize( v_tangent );
vec3 binormal = cross(normal,tangent);
float bm0, bmUp, bmRight; // Samples from the bumpmap at three texels.
bm0 = texture2D( bumpmap, v_texCoords ).r;
bmUp = texture2D( bumpmap, v_texCoords + vec2(0.0, 1.0/bumpmapSize.y)
).r;
bmRight = texture2D( bumpmap, v_texCoords + vec2(1.0/bumpmapSize.x,
0.0) ).r;
vec3 bumpVector = (bmRight - bm0)*tangent + (bmUp - bm0)*binormal;
normal += bumpmapStrength*bumpVector;
normal = normalize( normalMatrix*normal );
```

The first three lines compute the normal, tangent, and binormal unit vectors. The normal and tangent come from varying variables whose values are interpolated from attribute variables, which were in turn input to the shader program from the JavaScript side. The binormal, which is perpendicular to both the normal and the tangent, is computed as the cross product of the normal and tangent (Subsection 3.5.1).

The next four lines get the values of the height map at the pixel that corresponds to the surface point that is being processed and at two neighboring pixels. bm0 is the height map value at the current pixel, whose coordinates in the texture are given by the texture coordinates, $v\_texCoords$. The value for $bm0$ is the red color component from the bumpmap texture; since the texture is grayscale, all of its color components have the same value. $bmUp$ is the value from the pixel above the current pixel in the texture; the coordinates are computed by adding 1.0/bumpmapSize. y to the y-coordinate of the current pixel, where bumpmapSize is a uniform variable that gives the size of the texture image, in pixels. Since texture coordinates in the image run from 0.0 to 1.0 , the difference in the y-coordinates of the two pixels is 1.0/ bumpmapSize.y. Similarly, bmRight is the height map value for the pixel to the right of the current pixel in the bumpmap texture. I should note that the minification filter for the bumpmap texture was set to gl.NEAREST, because we need to read the actual value from the texture, not a value averaged from several pixels, as would be returned by the default minification filter.

The two vectors $(bmRight - bm0) *$ tangent and $(bmUp - bm0) *$ binormal are the two white vectors in the above illustration. Their sum is bumpVector. A multiple of that sum is added to the normal vector to give the modified normal vector. The multiplier, bumpmapStrength, is a uniform float variable.

All of the calculations so far have been done in the object coordinate system. The resulting normal depends only on the original object coordinates, not on any transformation that has been applied. The normal vector still has to be transformed into eye coordinates before it can be used in the lighting equation. That transformation is done in the last line of code shown above.

7.3.5 Environment Mapping

Subsection 5.3.5 showed how to use environment mapping in three.js to make it look like the surface of an object reflects an environment. Environment mapping uses a cubemap texture, and it is really just a way of mapping a cubemap texture to the surface. It doesn't make the object reflect other objects in its environment. We can make it look as if the object is reflecting its environment by adding a skybox-a large cube surrounding the scene, with the cubemap mapped onto its interior. However, the object will only seem to be reflecting the skybox. And if there are other objects in the environment, they won't be part of the reflection.

The sample program webgl/skybox-and-env-map.html implements environment mapping in WebGL. The program shows a single fully reflective object inside a skybox. No lighting is used in the scene; the colors for both the skybox and the object are taken directly from the cubemap texture. The object looks like a perfect mirror. This is not the only way of using an environment map. For example, a basic object color could be computed using the lighting equation-perhaps even with an image texture-and the environment map could be blended with the basic color to give the appearance of a shing but not fully reflective surface. However, the point of the sample program is just to show how to use a skybox and environment map in WebGL. The shader programs that are used to do that are actually quite short.

As for the cubemap texture itself, Subsection 6.4.4 showed how to load a cubemap texture as six separate images and how to access that texture in GLSL using a variable of type samplerCube. Remember that a cubemap texture is sampled using a 3D vector that points from the origin towards the point on the cube where the texture is to be sampled.

It's easy to render the skybox: Draw a large cube, centered at the origin, enclosing the scene and the camera position. To color a pixel in the fragment shader, sample the cubemap texture using a vector that points from the origin through the point on the cube that is being rendered, so that the color of a point on the cube is the same as the color of the corresponding point in the cubemap. Note that it is the cube's object coordinates that are used to sample the texture, since the texture should be attached to the cube when we rotate the view.

In the shader program for rendering a skybox, the vertex shader just needs to compute gl_Position as usual and pass the object coordinates on to the fragment shader in a varying variable. Here is the vertex shader source code for the skybox:

```
uniform mat4 projection;
uniform mat4 modelview;
attribute vec3 coords;
varying vec3 v_objCoords;
void main() {
    vec4 eyeCoords = modelview * vec4(coords,1.0);
    gl_Position = projection * eyeCoords;
    v_objCoords = coords;
}
```

And the fragment shader simply uses the object coordinates to get the fragment color by sampling the cubemap texture:

```
precision mediump float;
varying vec3 v_objCoords;
uniform samplerCube skybox;
void main() {
    gl_FragColor = textureCube(skybox, v_objCoords);
}
```

Note that the vector that is used to sample a cubemap texture does not have to be a unit vector; it just has to point in the correct direction.

To understand how a cube map texture can be applied to an object as a reflection map, we have to ask what point from the texture should be visible at a point on the object? If we think of the texture as an actual environment, then a ray of light would come from the environment, hit the object, and be reflected towards the viewer. We just have to trace that light ray back from the viewer to the object and then to the environment. The direction in which the light ray is reflected is determined, as always, by the normal vector. Consider a 2D version of the geometry. You can think of this as a cross-section of the 3D geometry:

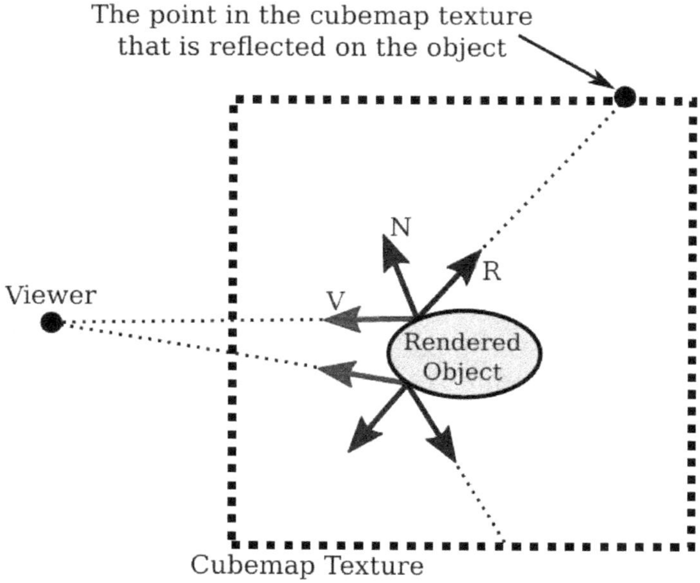

In this illustration, the dotted box represents the cubemap texture. (You really should think of it as being at infinite distance.) V is a vector that points from the object towards the viewer. N is the normal vector to the surface. And R is the reflection of V through N. R points to the texel in the cubemap texture that is visible to the viewer at the point on the surface; it is the vector that is needed to sample the cubemap texture. The picture shows the three vectors at two different points on the surface. In GLSL, R can be computed as - reflect (V, N).

If the same cubemap texture is also applied to a skybox, it will look as if the object is reflecting the skybox-but only if no transformation has been applied to the skybox cube. The reason is that transforming the skybox does not automatically transform the cubemap texture. Since we want to be able to rotate the view, we need to be able to transform the skybox. And we want the reflected object to look like it is reflecting the skybox in its transformed position, not in its original position. That viewing transformation can be thought of as a modeling transformation on the skybox, as well as on other objects in the scene. We have to figure out how to make it apply to the cubemap texture. Let's think about what happens in the 2D case when we rotate the view by -30 degrees. That's the same as rotating the skybox and object by 30 degrees. In the illustration, I've drawn the viewer at the same position as before, and I have rotated the scene. The square with the fainter dotted outline is the skybox. The cubemap texture hasn't moved:

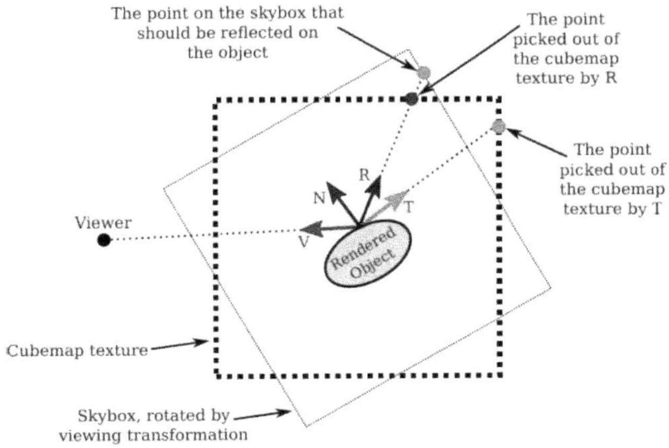

If we compute *R* as before and use it to sample the cubemap texture, we get the wrong point in the texture. The viewer should see the point where *R* intersects the skybox, not the point where *R* intersects the texture. The correct point in the texture is picked out by the vector *T*. *T* is computed by transforming *R* by the inverse of the viewing transformation. *R* was rotated by the viewing transformation; the inverse viewing transformation undoes that transformation, putting *T* into the same coordinate system as the cube map. In this case, since *R* was rotated by 30 degrees, a rotation of -30 degrees is applied to compute *T*. (This is just one way to understand the geometry. If you prefer to think of the cubemap as rotating along with the skybox, then we need to apply a texture transformation to the texture-which is another way of saying that we need to transform *R* before using it to sample the texture.)

In the sample program, the shader program that is used to represent the object is different from the one used to render the skybox. The vertex shader is very typical. Note that the modelview transformation can include modeling transforms that are applied to the object in addition to the viewing transform that is applied to the entire scene. Here is the source code:

```
uniform mat4 projection;
uniform mat4 modelview;
attribute vec3 coords;
attribute vec3 normal;
varying vec3 v_eyeCoords;
```

```
varying vec3 v_normal;
void main() {
    vec4 eyeCoords = modelview * vec4(coords,1.0);
    gl_Position = projection * eyeCoords;
    v_eyeCoords = eyeCoords.xyz;
    v_normal = normalize(normal);
}
```

The vertex shader passes eye coordinates to the fragment shader in a varying variable. In eye coordinates, the viewer is at the point (0,0,0), and the vector V that points from the surface to the viewer is simply - v_eyeCoords.

The source code for the fragment shader implements the algorithm discussed above for sampling the cubemap texture. Since we are doing perfect reflection, the color for the fragment comes directly from the texture:

```
precision mediump float;
varying vec3 vCoords;
varying vec3 v_normal;
varying vec3 v_eyeCoords;
uniform samplerCube skybox;
uniform mat3 normalMatrix;
uniform mat3 inverseViewTransform;
void main() {
    vec3 N = normalize(normalMatrix * v_normal);
    vec3 V = -v_eyeCoords;
    vec3 R = -reflect(V,N);
    vec3 T = inverseViewTransform * R;
    gl_FragColor = textureCube(skybox, T);
}
```

The inverseViewTransform is computed on the JavaScript side from the modelview matrix, after the viewing transform has been applied but before any addition modeling transformation is applied, using the commands

```
mat3.fromMat4(inverseViewTransform, modelview);
mat3.invert(inverseViewTransform,inverseViewTransform);
```

We need a mat3 to transform a vector. The first line discards the translation part of the modelview matrix, putting the result in inverseViewTransorm. Translation doesn't affect vectors, but the translation part is zero in any case since the viewing transformation in this program is just a rotation. The second line converts inverseViewTransform into its inverse.

7.4 Framebuffers

The term "frame buffer" traditionally refers to the region of memory that holds the color data for the image displayed on a computer screen. In WebGL, a framebuffer is a data structure that organizes the memory resources that are needed to render an image. A WebGL graphics context has a default framebuffer, which is used for the image that appears on the screen. The default framebuffer is created by the call to canvas.getContext() that creates the graphics context. Its properties depend on the options that are passed to that function and cannot be changed after it is created. However, additional framebuffers can be created, with properties controlled by the WebGL program. They can be used for off-screen rendering, and they are required for certain advanced rendering algorithms.

A framebuffer can use a color buffer to hold the color data for an image, a depth buffer to hold a depth value for each pixel, and something called a stencil buffer (which is not covered in this textbook). The buffers are said to be "attached" to the framebuffer. For a non-default framebuffer, buffers can be attached and detached by the WebGL program at any time. A framebuffer doesn't need a full set of three buffers, but you need a color buffer, a depth buffer, or both to be able to use the framebuffer for rendering. If the depth test is not enabled when rendering to the framebuffer, then no depth buffer is needed. And some rendering algorithms, such as shadow mapping (Subsection 5.3.3) use a framebuffer with a depth buffer but no color buffer. In WebGL 2.0, it is also possible to attach several color buffers to the same framebuffer, which can be useful for certain advanced algorithms and computational applications. (Also, see Subsection 7.5.4.)

The rendering functions gl.drawArrays () and gl.drawElements () affect the current framebuffer, which is initially the default framebuffer. The current framebuffer can be changed by calling

```
gl.bindFramebuffer( gl.FRAMEBUFFER, frameBufferObject );
```

The first parameter to this function is always gl.FRAMEBUFFER. The second parameter can be null to select the default framebuffer for drawing, or it can be a non-default framebuffer created by the function gl.createFramebuffer(), which will be discussed below.

7.4.1 Framebuffer Operations

Before we get to examples of using non-default framebuffers, we look at some WebGL settings that affect rendering into whichever framebuffer is current. Examples that we have already seen include the clear color, which is used to fill the color buffer when gl.clear () is called, and the enabled state of the depth test.

Another example that affects the use of the depth buffer is the depth mask, a boolean value that controls whether values are written to the depth buffer during rendering. (The enabled state of the depth test determines whether values from the depth buffer are used during rendering; the depth mask determines whether new values are written to the depth buffer.) Writing to the depth buffer can be turned off with the command

```
gl.depthMask( false );
```

and can be turned back on by calling gl.depthMask(true). The default value is true. One example of using the depth mask is for rendering translucent geometry. When some of the objects in a scene are translucent, then all of the opaque objects should be rendered first, followed by the translucent objects. Suppose that you rendered a translucent object, and then rendered an opaque object that lies behind the translucent object. The depth test would cause the opaque object to be hidden by the translucent object. But "translucent" means that the opaque object should be visible through the translucent object. So it's important to render all the opaque objects first. And it's important to turn off writing to the depth buffer, by calling gl.depthMask(false), while rendering the translucent objects. The reason is that a translucent object that is drawn behind another translucent object should be visible through the front object. Note, however, that the depth test must still be enabled while the translucent objects are being rendered, since a translucent object can be hidden by an opaque object. Also, alpha blending must be on while rendering the translucent objects.

For fully correct rendering of translucent objects, the translucent primitives should be sorted into back-to-front order before rendering, as in the painter's algorithm (Subsection 3.1.4).

However, that can be difficult to implement, and acceptable results can sometimes be obtained by rendering the translucent primitives in arbitrary order (but still after the opaque primitives). In fact that was done in the demos c3/rotation-axis.html from Subsection 3.2.2 and c3/transform-equivalence-3d.html from Subsection 3.3.4.

It is also possible to control writing to the color buffer, using the color mask. The color buffer has four "channels" corresponding to the red, green, blue, and alpha components of the color. Each channel can be controlled separately. You could, for example, allow writing to the red and alpha color channels, while blocking writing to the green and blue channels. That would be done with the command

```
gl.colorMask( true, false, false, true );
```

The colorMask function takes four parameters, one for each color channel. A true value allows writing to the channel; a false value blocks writing. When writing is blocked for a channel during rendering, the value of the corresponding color component is simply ignored.

One use of the color mask is for anaglyph stereo rendering (Subsection 5.3.1). An anaglyph stereo image contains two images of the scene, one intended for the left eye and one for the right eye. One image is drawn using only shades of red, while the other uses only combinations of green and blue. The two images are drawn from slightly different viewpoints, corresponding to the views from the left and the right eye. So the algorithm for anaglyph stereo has the form

```
gl.clearColor(0,0,0,1);
gl.clear( gl.COLOR_BUFFER_BIT | gl.DEPTH_BUFFER_BIT );
gl.colorMask( true, false, false, false ); // write to red channel only
... // set up view from left eye
... // render the scene
gl.clear( gl.DEPTH_BUFFER_BIT ); // clear only the depth buffer
gl.colorMask( false, true, true, false ); // write to green and blue
channels
... // set up view from right eye
... // render the scene
```

One way to set up the views from the left and right eyes is simply to rotate the view by a few degrees about the y-axis. Note that the depth buffer, but not the color buffer, must be cleared before drawing the second image, since otherwise the depth test would prevent some parts of the second image from being written.

Finally, I would like to look at blending in more detail. Blending refers to how the fragment color from the fragment shader is combined with the current color of the fragment in the color buffer. The default, assuming that the fragment passes the depth test, is to replace the current color with the fragment color. When blending is enabled, the current color can be replaced with some combination of the current color and the fragment color. Previously, I have only discussed turning on alpha blending for transparency with the commands

```
gl.enable( gl.BLEND );
gl.blendFunc( gl.SRC_ALPHA, gl.ONE_MINUS_SRC_ALPHA );
```

The function gl.blendFunc() determines how the new color is computed from the current color and the fragment color. With the parameters shown here, the formula for the new color, using GLSL syntax, is

```
(src * src.a) + (dest * (1-src.a))
```

where src is the "source" color (that is, the color that is being written, the fragment color) and dest is the "destination" color (that is, the color currently in the color buffer, which is the destination of the rendering operation). And src.a is the alpha component of the source color. The parameters to gl.blendFunc () determine the coefficients- src.a and (1 − src.a) - in the formula. The default coefficients for the blend function are given by

```
gl.blendFunc( gl.ONE, gl.ZERO );
```

which specifies the formula

```
(src * 1) + (dest * 0)
```

That is, the new color is equal to the source color; there is no blending. Note that blending applies to the alpha component as well as the RGB components of the color, which is probably not what you want. When drawing with a translucent color, it means that the color that is written to the color buffer will have an alpha component less than 1 . When rendering to a canvas on a web page, this will make the canvas itself translucent, allowing the background of the canvas to show through. (This assumes that the WebGL context was created with an alpha channel, which is the default.) To avoid that, you can set the blend function with the alternative command

```
gl.blendFuncSeparate( gl.SRC_ALPHA, gl.ONE_MINUS_SRC_ALPHA,
    gl.ZERO, gl.ONE );
```

The two extra parameters specify separate coefficients to be used for the alpha component in the formula, while the first two parameters are used only for the RGB components. That is, the new color for the color buffer is computed using the formula

```
vec4( (src.rgb*src.a) + (dest.rgb*(1-src.a)), src.a*0 + dest.a*1 );
```

With this formula, the alpha component in the destination (the color buffer) remains the same as its original value.

The blend function set by gl.blendFunc(gl.ONE,gl.ONE) can sometimes be used in multipass algorithms. In a multi-pass algorithm, a scene is rendered several times, and the results are combined somehow to produce the final image. (Anaglyph stereo rendering is an example.) If you simply want to add up the results of the various passes, then you can fill the color buffer with zeros, enable blending, and set the blend function to (gl.ONE,gl.ONE) during rendering.

As a simple example, the sample program webgl/image-blur.html uses a multi-pass algorithm to implement blurring. The scene in the example is just a texture image applied to a rectangle, so the effect is to blur the texture image. The technique involves drawing the scene nine times. In the fragment shader, the color is divided by nine. Blending is used to add the fragment colors from the nine passes, so that the final color in the color buffer is the average of the colors from the nine passes. For eight of the nine passes, the scene is offset slightly from its original position, so that the color of a pixel in the final image is the average of the colors of that pixel and the surrounding pixels from the original scene.

7.4.2 Render to Texture

The previous subsection applies to any framebuffer. But we haven't yet used a non-default framebuffer. We turn to that topic now.

One use for a non-default framebuffer is to render directly into a texture. That is, the memory occupied by a texture image can be attached to the framebuffer as its color buffer, so that rendering operations will send their output to the texture image. This technique, which is called render-to-texture, is used in the sample program webgl/render-to-texture.html.

Texture memory is normally allocated when an image is loaded into the texture using the function gl.texImage2D or gl.copyTexImage2D. (See Section 6.4.) However, there is a version of gl.texImage2D that can be used to allocate memory without loading an image into that memory. Here is an example, from the sample program:

```
texture = gl.createTexture();
gl.bindTexture(gl.TEXTURE_2D, texture);
gl.texImage2D(gl.TEXTURE_2D, 0, gl.RGBA, 512, 512,
    0, gl.RGBA, gl.UNSIGNED_BYTE, null);
```

It is the null parameter at the end of the last line that tells gl.texImage2D to allocate new memory without loading existing image data to fill that memory. Instead, the new memory is filled with zeros. The first parameter to gl.texImage2D is the texture target. The target is gl.TEXTURE_2D for normal textures, but other values are used for working with cubemap textures. The fourth and fifth parameters specify the height and width of the image; they should be powers of two. The other parameters usually have the values shown here; their meanings are the same as for the version of gl.texImage2D discussed in

Subsection 6.4.3. Note that the texture object must first be created and bound; gl.texImage2D applies to the texture that is currently bound to the active texture unit. (In WebGL 2.0, the same thing can also be accomplished using the gl.texStorage2D() function discussed in Subsection 6.4.6.)

To attach the texture to a framebuffer, you need to create a framebuffer object and make that object the current framebuffer by binding it. For example,

```
framebuffer = gl.createFramebuffer();
gl.bindFramebuffer(gl.FRAMEBUFFER, framebuffer);
```

Then the function gl.framebufferTexture2D can be used to attach the texture to the framebuffer:

```
gl.framebufferTexture2D( gl.FRAMEBUFFER, gl.COLOR_ATTACHMENT0,
    gl.TEXTURE_2D, texture, 0 );
```

The first parameter is always gl.FRAMEBUFFER. The second parameter says a color buffer is being attached. The last character in gl.COLOR_ATTACHMENT0 is a zero, which allows the possibility of having more than one color buffer attached to a framebuffer (although in standard WebGL 1.0, only one color buffer is allowed). The third parameter is the same texture target that was used in gl.texImage2D, and the fourth is the texture object. The last parameter is the mipmap level; it will usually be zero, which means rendering to the texture image itself rather than to one of its mipmap images.

With this setup, you are ready to bind the framebuffer and draw to the texture. After drawing the texture, call

```
gl.bindFramebuffer( gl.FRAMEBUFFER, null );
```

to start drawing again to the default framebuffer. At that point, the texture is ready for use in subsequent rendering operations. The texture object can be bound to a texture unit, and a sampler2D variable can be used in the shader program to read from the texture.

You are very likely to use different shader programs for drawing to the texture and drawing to the screen. Recall that the function gl.useProgram() is used to specify the shader program.

In the sample program, the texture can be animated. During the animation, a new image is drawn to the texture for each frame of the animation. The texture image is 2D, so the depth test is disabled while rendering it. This means that the framebuffer doesn't need a depth buffer. In outline form, the rendering function in the sample program has the form

```
function draw() {
    /* Draw the 2D image into a texture attached to a framebuffer. */
    gl.bindFramebuffer(gl.FRAMEBUFFER,framebuffer);
    gl.useProgram(prog_texture); // shader program for the texture
    gl.clearColor(1,1,1,1);
    gl.clear(gl.COLOR_BUFFER_BIT); // clear the texture to white
    gl.enable(gl.BLEND); // Use transparency while drawing 2D image.
    gl.disable(gl.DEPTH_TEST); // framebuffer doesn't even have a depth
buffer!
    gl.viewport(0,0,512,512); // Viewport is not set automatically!
        |
        . // draw the texture image, which changes in each frame
        -
    gl.disable(gl.BLEND);
    /* Now draw the main scene, which is 3D, using the texture. */
    gl.bindFramebuffer(gl.FRAMEBUFFER,null); // Draw to default
framebuffer.
    gl.useProgram(prog); // shader program for the on-screen image
    gl.clearColor(0,0,0,1);
    gl.clear(gl.COLOR_BUFFER_BIT | gl.DEPTH_BUFFER_BIT);
    gl.enable(gl.DEPTH_TEST);
    gl.viewport(0,0,canvas.width,canvas.height); // Reset the viewport!
    .
    \mathrm{ - // draw the scene}
    |
}
```

Note that the viewport has to be set by hand when drawing to a non-default frame buffer. It then has to be reset when drawing the on-screen image to match the size of the canvas where the on-screen image is rendered. I should also note that only one texture object is used in this program, so it can be bound once and for all during initialization. In this case, it is not necessary to call gl.bindTexture() in the draw() function.

This example could be implemented without using a framebuffer, as was done for the example in Subsection 4.3.6. In that example, the texture image was drawn to the default framebuffer, then copied to the texture object. However, the version in this section is more efficient because it does not need to copy the image after rendering it.

7.4.3 Renderbuffers

It is often convenient to use memory from a texture object as the color buffer for a framebuffer. However, sometimes its more appropriate to create separate memory for the buffer, not associated with any texture. For the depth buffer, that is the typical case. For such cases, the memory can be created as a renderbuffer. A renderbuffer represents memory that can be attached to a framebuffer for use as a color buffer, depth buffer, or stencil buffer. To use one, you need to create the renderbuffer and allocate memory for it. Memory is allocated using the function gl.renderbufferStorage(). The renderbuffer must be bound by calling $gl.bindRenderbuffer$() before allocating the memory. Here is an example that creates a renderbuffer for use as a depth buffer:

```
let depthBuffer = gl.createRenderbuffer();
gl.bindRenderbuffer(gl.RENDERBUFFER, depthBuffer);
gl.renderbufferStorage(gl.RENDERBUFFER, gl.DEPTH_COMPONENT16, 512,
512);
```

The first parameter to both gl.bindRenderbuffer and gl.renderbufferStorage must be gl.RENDERBUFFER. The second parameter to gl.renderbufferStorage specifies how the renderbuffer will be used. The value gl.DEPTH_COMPONENT16 is for a depth buffer with 16 bits for each pixel. (Sixteen bits is the only option in WebGL 1.0.) For a color buffer holding RGBA colors with four eight-bit values per pixel, the second parameter would be gl.RGBA8. Other values are possible, such as gl.RGB565, which uses 16 bits per pixel with 5 bits for the red color channel, 6 bits for green, and 5 bits for blue. For a stencil buffer, the value would be gl.STENCIL_INDEX8. The last two parameters to gl.renderbufferStorage are the width and height of the buffer.

The function gl.framebufferRenderbuffer() is used to attach a renderbufffer to be used as one of the buffers in a framebuffer. It takes the form

```
gl.framebufferRenderbuffer(gl.FRAMEBUFFER, gl.DEPTH_ATTACHMENT,
    gl.RENDERBUFFER, renderbuffer);
```

The framebuffer must be bound by calling gl.bindFramebuffer before this function is called. The first and third parameters to gl.framebufferRenderbuffer must be as shown. The last parameter is the renderbuffer. The second paramter specifies how the renderbuffer will be used. It can be, for example, gl.COLOR_ATTACHMENT0, gl.DEPTH_ATTACHMENT, or gl.STENCIL_ATTACHMENT.

7.4.4 Dynamic Cubemap Textures

To render a 3D scene to a framebuffer, we need both a color buffer and a depth buffer. An example can be found in the sample program webgl/cube-camera.html. This example uses render-to-texture for a cubemap texture. The cubemap texture is then used as an environment map on a reflective surface. In addition to the environment map, the program uses another cubemap texture for a skybox. (See Subsection 6.3.5.) Here's an image from the program:

The environment in this case includes the background skybox, but also includes several colored cubes that are not part of the skybox texture. The reflective sphere in the center of the image reflects the cubes as well as the skybox, which means that the environment map texture can't be the same as the skybox texture - it has to include the cubes. Furthermore, the scene can be animated and the cubes can move. The reflection in the sphere has to change as the cubes move. This means that the environment map texture has to be recreated in each frame. For that, we can use a framebuffer to render to the cubemap texture.

A cubemap texture consists of six images, one each for the positive and negative direction of the *x*, *y*, and *z* axes. Each image is associated with a different texture target (similar to gl.TEXTURE_2D). To render a cubemap, we need to allocate storage for all six sides. Here's the code from the sample program:

```
cubemapTargets = [
        // store texture targets in an array for convenience
```

```
    gl.TEXTURE_CUBE_MAP_POSITIVE_X, gl.TEXTURE_CUBE_MAP_NEGATIVE_X,
    gl.TEXTURE_CUBE_MAP_POSITIVE_Y, gl.TEXTURE_CUBE_MAP_NEGATIVE_Y,
    gl.TEXTURE_CUBE_MAP_POSITIVE_Z, gl.TEXTURE_CUBE_MAP_NEGATIVE_Z
];
dynamicCubemap = gl.createTexture(); // Create the texture object.
gl.bindTexture(gl.TEXTURE_CUBE_MAP, dynamicCubemap); // bind it as a
cubemap
for (i = 0; i < 6; i++) {
    gl.texImage2D(cubemapTargets[i], 0, gl.RGBA, 512, 512,
            0, gl.RGBA, gl.UNSIGNED_BYTE, null);
}
```

We also need to create a framebuffer, as well as a renderbuffer for use as a depth buffer, and we need to attach the depth buffer to the framebuffer. The same framebuffer can be used to render all six images for the texture, changing the color buffer attachment of the framebuffer as needed. To attach one of the six cubemap images as the color buffer, we just specify the corresponding cubemap texture target in the call to gl.framebufferTexture2D(). For example, the command

```
gl.framebufferTexture2D(gl.FRAMEBUFFER, gl.COLOR_ATTACHMENT0,
    gl.TEXTURE_CUBE_MAP_NEGATIVE_Z, dynamicCubemap, 0);
```

attaches the negative z image from the texture object dynamicCubemap to be used as the color buffer in the currently bound framebuffer.

After the six texture images have been rendered, the cubemap texture is ready to be used. Aside from the fact that six 3D images are rendered instead of one 2D image, this is all very similar to the render-to-texture example from earlier in this section.

The question remains of how to render the six images of the scene that are needed for the cubemap texture. To make an environment map for a reflective object, we want images of the environment that surrounds that object. The images can be made with a camera placed at the center of the object. The basic idea is to point the camera in the six directions of the positive and negative coordinate axes and snap a picture in each direction, but it's tricky to get the details correct. (And note that when we apply the result to a point on the surface, we will only have an approximation of the correct reflection. For a geometrically correct reflection at the point, we would need the view from that very point, not the view from the center of the object, but we can't realistically make a different environment map for each point on the surface. The approximation will look OK as long as other objects in the scene are not too close to the reflective surface.)

A "camera" really means a projection transformation and a viewing transformation. The projection needs a ninety-degree field of view, to cover one side of the cube, and its aspect ratio will be 1 , since the sides of the cube are squares. We can make the projection matrix with a glMatrix command such as

```
mat4.projection( projection, Math.PI/2, 1, 1, 100 );
```

where the last two parameters, the near and far clipping distances, should be chosen to include all the objects in the scene. If we apply no viewing transformation, the camera will be at the origin, pointing in the direction of the negative *z*-axis. If the reflective object is at the origin, as it is in the sample program, we can use the camera with no viewing transformation to take the negative-z image for the cubemap texture.

But, because of the details of how the images must be stored for cubemap textures, it turns out that we need to apply one transformation. Let's look at the layout of images for a cubemap texture:

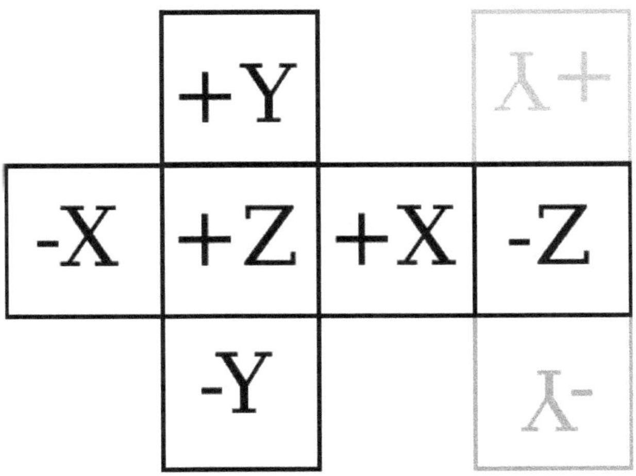

The six sides of the cube are shown in black, as if the sides of the cube have been opened up and laid out flat. Each side is marked with the corresponding coordinate axis direction. Duplicate copies of the plus and minus y sides are shown in gray, to show how those sides attach to the negative z side. The images that we make for the cubemap must fit together in the same way as the sides in this layout. However, the sides in the layout are viewed from the outside of the cube, while the camera will be taking a picture from the inside of the cube. To get the correct view, we need to filp the picture from the camera horizontally. After some experimentation, I found that I also need to flip it vertically, perhaps because web images are stored upside down with respect to the OpenGL convention. We can do both flips with a scaling transformation by (−1,−1,1). Putting this together, the code for making the cubemap's negative z image is

```
gl.bindFramebuffer(gl.FRAMEBUFFER, framebuffer); // Draw to offscreen
buffer.
gl.viewport(0,0,512,512); // Match size of the texture images.
/* Set up projection and modelview matrices for the virtual camera
mat4.perspective(projection, Math.PI/2, 1, 1, 100);
mat4.identity(modelview);
mat4.scale(modelview,modelview,[-1,-1,1]);
/* Attach the cubemap negative z image as the color buffer in the
framebuffer,
    and "take the picture" by rendering the image. */
gl.framebufferTexture2D(gl.FRAMEBUFFER, gl.COLOR_ATTACHMENT0,
        gl.TEXTURE_CUBE_MAP_NEGATIVE_Z, dynamicCubemap, 0);
renderSkyboxAndCubes();
```

The function in the last line renders the scene, except for the central reflective object itself, and is responsible for sending the projection and modelview matrices to the shader programs.

For the other five images, we need to aim the camera in a different direction before taking the picture. That can be done by adding an appropriate rotation to the viewing transformation. For example, for the positive x image, we need to rotate the camera by -90 degrees about the y-axis. As a viewing transform, we need the command

```
mat4.rotateY(modelview, modelview, Math.PI/2);
```

It might be easier to think of this as a modeling transformation that rotates the positive x side of the cube into view in front of the camera.

In the sample program, the six cubemap images are created in the function createDynamicCubemap(). Read the source code of that function for the full details.

This dynamic cubemap program is a nice example, since it makes use of so many of the concepts and techniques that we have covered. You should run the program and think about everything that is going on, and how it was all implemented.

7.5 WebGL Extensions

WebGL is designed to run on a wide variety of devices, including mobile devices that have relatively limited graphical capabilities. Because of this, only a minimal set of features is required of all WebGL implementations. However, WebGL has a mechanism for activating additional, optional features. The optional features are defined in WebGL extensions. A web page that requires a WebGL extension is not guaranteed to work in every implementation of WebGL. However, in many cases, it is fairly easy to write a page that can work with or without the extension, though perhaps with some missing feature when the extension is not available. There are several dozen extensions whose definitions have been standardized. These standard extensions are documented at https://www.khronos.org/registry/webgl/extensions/.

Standard OpenGL also has an extension mechanism. Historically, many features from extensions in one version of OpenGL have become required features in later versions. The same is true for WebGL extensions: Some of the WebGL 1.0 extensions have been incorporated as required features in WebGL 2.0.

This section covers the WebGL extension mechanism, and it discusses a few of the standard extensions.

7.5.1 Anisotropic Filtering

We start with a simple extension that can improve the appearance of textures in some scenes. The standard filtering methods for sampling an image texture give poor results when the texture is viewed at an oblique angle. In that case, a pixel on the surface corresponds to a trapezoidal region in the texture, and the standard minification and magnification filter rules such as gl.LINEAR don't handle that case very well. (Filtering was covered in Subsection 4.3.2.) A better result can be obtained, at the cost of additional computation, using something called anisotropic filtering, which samples the texture taking the trapezoidal shape into account. Many GPUs can do anisotropic filtering. It is not a required feature in WebGL implementations, but it is commonly available as an extension. The anisotropic filtering extension can be used with both WebGL 1.0 and WebGL 2.0, in the same way.

The sample program webgl/anisotropic-filtering.html shows how to use the anisotropic filtering extension. It shows a large plane textured with a brick image that can be viewed from a sharp, oblique angle. If the extension is available, then the user can turn anisotropic filtering on and off. If it is not available, the program will still draw the scene, but only using standard filtering. Here are two images from the program. Anisotropic filtering is used in the image on the right. On the left, without anisotropic filtering, the texture is blurred even at moderate distanced from the viewer:

Each WebGL extension has a name. The function gl.getExtension(name) is used to activate an extension, where name is a string containing the name of the extension. The return value of the function is null if the extension is not available, and you should always check the return value before attempting to use the extension. If the return value is not null, then it is a JavaScript object. The object might contain, for example, constants that are meant to be passed to WebGL functions in order to make use of the capabilities of the extension. It can also contain completely new functions.

The name of the anisotropic filtering extension is "EXT_texture_filter_anisotropic." To test for the availability of the extension and to activate it, a program can use a statement such as

```
anisotropyExtension                                              =
gl.getExtension("EXT_texture_filter_anisotropic");
```

If anisotropyExtension is null, then the extension is not available. If it is not null, then the object has a property named TEXTURE_MAX_ANISOTROPY_EXT that can be used as a parameter to gl.texParameteri to set the level, or amount, of anisotropic filtering that will be applied to the texture. For example, after creating and binding a texture, a program might say

```
gl.texParameteri(gl.TEXTURE_2D,
    anisotropyExtension.TEXTURE_MAX_ANISOTROPY_EXT, 16);
```

The third parameter is the anisotropic filtering level. Setting the level to 1 will turn off anisotropic filtering. Higher values give better results. There is an implementation-dependent maximum level, but asking for a level greater than the maximum is not an error-you will simply get the maximum level. To find out the maximum, you can use

```
max = gl.getParameter(
anisotropyExtension.MAX_TEXTURE_MAX_ANISOTROPY_EXT );
```

It is recommended to use gl.LINEAR_MIPMAP_LINEAR as the minification filter and gl.LINEAR as the magnification filter when using anisotropic filtering. A texture would typically be configured using code similar to the following:

```
gl.bindTexture(gl.TEXTURE_2D);
gl.generateMipmap(gl.TEXTURE_2D); // Need mipmaps for the minification
filter!
gl.texParameteri(gl.TEXTURE_2D,gl.TEXTURE_MIN_FILTER,gl.LINEAR_MIPMAP_L
INEAR);
gl.texParameteri(gl.TEXTURE_2D,gl.TEXTURE_MAG_FILTER,gl.LINEAR);
if (anisotropyExtension != null) {
        // turn on anisotropic filtering only if it is available.
    max =
gl.getParameter(anisotropyExtension.MAX_TEXTURE_MAX_ANISOTROPY_EXT);
    gl.texParameteri(gl.TEXTURE_2D,
            anisotropyExtension.TEXTURE_MAX_ANISOTROPY_EXT, max);
}
```

If the extension is not available, the texture might not look as good as it might have, but it will still work (and only a very observant user is likely to notice).

7.5.2 Floating-Point Colors

As a second example, we consider a pair of extensions that are named "OES_texture_float" and "WEBGL_color_buffer_float". The first of these makes it possible to use textures in which color component values are floating-point numbers, instead of eight-bit integers. The second makes it possible to render to such a texture by using it as the color buffer in a framebuffer. (These extensions are only for WebGL 1.0, but there is a similar WebGL 2.0 extension, EXT_color_buffer_float.)

Why would someone want to do this? Eight-bit integers are fine for representing colors visually, but they don't have enough precision for doing accurate calculations. For applications that do significant numerical processing with color components, floating-point values are essential.

As an example, consider finding the average color value of an image, which requires adding up the color values from a large number of pixels. This is something that can be speeded up by using the parallel processing power of a GPU. My technique for doing so uses two framebuffers, with two textures serving as color buffers. I assume that the image width and height are powers of two. Start by drawing the image to the first texture. Think of the image as divided in half, horizontally and vertically, giving four equal-sizes rectangles. As a first step, compute a half-size image that is the average of those four rectangles. That is, the color of a pixel in the half-size image is the average of the colors of four pixels in the original. The averaged image can be computed by drawing a half-size rectangle to the second framebuffer, using multiple samples from the image in the first texture. Here is a fragment shader that does the work:

```
#ifdef GL_FRAGMENT_PRECISION_HIGH
    precision highp float;
#else
    precision mediump float;
#endif
varying vec2 v_coords; // Texture coordinates, same as object coords.
uniform sampler2D texture; // A texture containing the original image.
uniform float offset; // Size of square in texture coordinate space.
void main() {
        vec4 a = texture2D(texture, v_coords);
        vec4 b = texture2D(texture, v_coords + vec2(offset,0));
        vec4 c = texture2D(texture, v_coords + vec2(0,offset));
        vec4 d = texture2D(texture, v_coords + vec2(offset,offset));
        gl_FragColor = (a + b + c + d)/4.0; // Color is average of four
samples.
}
```

In this first pass, the square with vertices at (0,0) and (0.5,0.5) is rendered, and offset is 0.5 . The drawing is done in a coordinate system in which the square with vertices (0,0) and (1,1) covers the entire drawing area. In that coordinate system, the square with vertices at (0,0) and (0.5,0.5) covers the lower left quarter of the drawing area. The first sample in the fragment shader comes from that quarter of the texture image, and the other three samples come from corresponding points in the other three quarters of the the image.

In a second pass, the roles of the two framebuffers are swapped, and a square with vertices at (0,0) and (0.25,0.25) is drawn, using the same fragment shader with offset equal to 0.25.

Since the framebuffers were swapped, the second pass is sampling the half-sized image that was produced in the first pass. The result is a quarter-sized image that is the average of four rectangles that cover the half-sized image - and therefore of 16 rectangles that cover the original image. This can be repeated, with smaller and smaller squares, until the resulting image is small enough that its colors can be efficiently read back into the CPU and averaged there. The result is a color value that is the average of all the pixels from the original image. We expect that, because a lot of the work is done in parallel by the GPU, we can get the answer much faster using this technique than if we had simply done all the computations on the CPU.

The point here is that for an accurate result, we want the color components to be represented as floating point values in the GPU, not as eight-bit integers.

I use this technique in the sample program webgl/image-evolver.html. In that program, the problem is to find the average difference in color between two images. I start by drawing the two images to two textures. I then render a difference image, in which the color of a pixel is the absolute value of the difference between the colors of the same pixel in the two textures. This is done with another special-purpose shader program. I then apply the above averaging process to the difference image.

The actual point of the sample program is to try to "evolve" an approximation to a given image, using a "genetic algorithm." (It was inspired by two students from my Fall, 2015 class, Felix Taschbach and Pieter Schaap, who worked on a similar program for their final project, though they didn't use the GPU.) In the program, the average difference between the original image and an approximation is used as a measure of how good the approximation is. I used a very simple grayscale image as the goal, with approximations made from small squares. You don't need to know anything about the genetic algorithm, especially since the program has no practical purpose. However, the source code is heavily commented if you want to try to understand it. Here is a screenshot from one particularly successful run of the program, showing the original image and the best approximation produced after running the genetic algorithm for 7500 generations:

Original Image:

Best Approximation So Far:

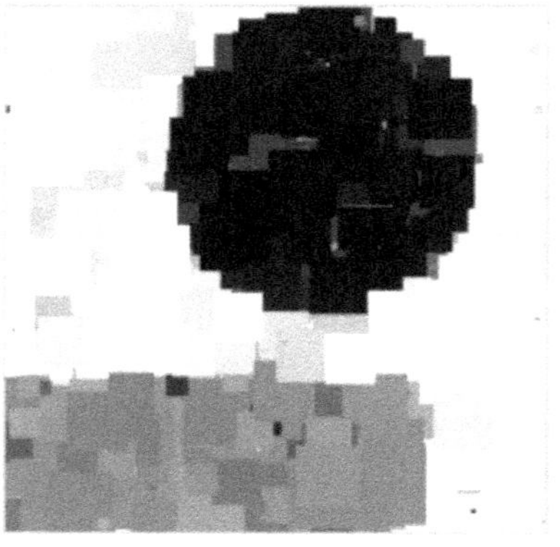

But what interests us here is how the program uses the WebGL floating-point color extensions. The program attempts to activate the extensions during initialization using the following code:

```
let EXTcbf = gl.getExtension("WEBGL_color_buffer_float");
let EXTtf = gl.getExtension("OES_texture_float");
if (!EXTcbf || !EXTtf) {
    throw new Error("This program requires the WebGL extension" +
        "WEBGL_color_buffer_float, which is not available in this
browser.");
}
```

The program requires the extensions, so an exception is thrown if they can't be activated. The extension objects, EXTcbf and EXTtf, dont't have any properties that are needed in this program; however, it is still necessary to call gl.getExension to activate the extensions.

The program creates two floating-point textures that are attached to framebuffers for use as color buffers. (See Subsection 7.4.2.) Here is the code that creates one of those textures:

```
tex1 = gl.createTexture();
gl.bindTexture(gl.TEXTURE_2D, tex1);
gl.texImage2D(gl.TEXTURE_2D, 0, gl.RGBA, 256, 256, 0, gl.RGBA,
gl.FLOAT, null);
```

The parameter gl. FLOAT in the last line specifies that the data type for the color components in the texture is float. That data type would be an error if the extensions had not been activated.

When the GPU does the averaging computation with these textures, it is doing floatingpoint calculations. The program computes a series of smaller and smaller averaged images, stopping with a 4 -by- 4 pixel image. It then reads the 16 pixel colors back from the texture using the following code:

```
let data = new Float32Array( 4*4*4 ); // 16 pixels, 4 numbers per pixels
gl.readPixels(0,0,4,4,gl.RGBA,gl.FLOAT,data)
```

The call to gl.readPixels reads the color data for the 16 pixels into the array, data. Again, the gl.FLOAT parameter specifies the data type, and that parameter value is legal in gl.readPixels only because the extensions have been activated.

7.5.3 Instanced Drawing in WebGL 1.0

Subsection 6.1.7 and Subsection 6.1.8 discussed two features of WebGL 2.0, Vertex Array Objects and instanced drawing. Although these features are not a standard part of WebGL 1.0, both are available as optional WebGL 1.0 extensions. VAOs are enabled by the extension "OES_vertex_array_object", while instanced drawing is enabled by "ANGLE_instanced_arrays". As an example, we look briefly at instanced drawing in WebGL 1.0.

The sample WebGL 1.0 program webgl/instancing-test-webgl1.html uses the instanced drawing extension. It is a copy of the sample WebGL 2.0 program from Subsection 6.1.8, modified to use version 1.0, but with exactly the same functionality. To use instanced drawing in WebGL 1.0, the appropriate extension has to be enabled:

```
instancedDrawExt = gl.getExtension("ANGLE_instanced_arrays");
if (!instancedDrawExt) {
    throw new Error("WebGL 1.0 Instanced Arrays extension is
required.");
}
```

The extension object, instancedDrawExt, contains functions that are equivalent to the WebGL 2.0 functions for instanced drawing: gl.vertexAttribDivisor(). gl.drawArraysInstanced(), and gl.drawElementsInstanced(). However, the functions are properties of the extension object, not of the graphics context *gl*, and their names have the word "ANGLE" appended. So, the command

```
gl.drawArraysInstanced(gl.TRIANGLE_FAN, 0, 64, DISK_COUNT);
```

from the original WebGL 2.0 program is replaced by

```
instancedDrawExt.drawArraysInstancedANGLE(gl.TRIANGLE_FAN,          0,
64,DISK_COUNT);
```

in the WebGL 1.0 program. And

```
gl.vertexAttribDivisor(a_color_loc,1);
```

becomes

```
instancedDrawExt.vertexAttribDivisorANGLE(a_color_loc,1);
```

Note that, in general, a WebGL 1.0 program that does not use any extensions will work as a WebGL 2.0 program without any modifications. However, if the WebGL 1.0 program uses extensions that are no longer available or no longer needed in WebGL 2.0, some work will be required to convert the program to WebGL 2.0.

7.5.4 Deferred Shading

I will discuss one more WebGL 1.0 extension, one that is useful for an important rendering technique called deferred shading. I don't have a sample program for deferred rendering, and I will only discuss it in general terms.

Deferred shading is used as an optimization when rendering complex scenes, and it is often used to speed up rendering in video games. It is most closely associated with lighting, since it can be used to render scenes with large numbers of light sources, but it can also be useful for other effects.

Recall that the number of lights that can be represented in OpenGL or in a WebGL shader is limited. But scenes with many lights can be rendered using a multi-pass algorithm: Each pass computes the contribution of one light, or a small number of lights, and the results of the passes are added together to give the complete scene. The problem is that, if the rendering in each pass is done in the normal way, then there are a lot of things that have to be recomputed, in exactly the same way, in each pass. For example, assuming that per-pixel lighting is used, that includes computing material properties and a unit normal vector for each pixel in the image. Deferred shading aims to avoid the duplicated effort.

In deferred shading, a first pass is used to compute material properties, normal vectors, and whatever other data is needed, for each pixel in the image. All of that data is saved, to be used in additional passes that will compute lighting and possibly other effects. For a given pixel, only the data for the object that is actually visible at the pixel is saved, since data for hidden surfaces is not needed to render the scene. The first pass uses the geometry and attributes of objects in the scene. Everything that the later passes need to know about geometry and attributes is in the saved data.

The saved data can be stored in texture objects. (Floating point textures are ideal for this, since the data will be used in further calculations.) In this case, the values in the textures don't necessarily represent images. For example, the RGB color components in one texture might represent the x, y, and z coordinates of a normal vector. And if a depth value is needed in later passes, it might be stored in the alpha color component of the same texture. Another texture might hold a diffuse color, while a third holds a specular color in its RGB components and a shininess value in its alpha component. Shader programs are free to interpret data in a texture however they like.

A WebGL shader can write data to a texture, using a framebuffer. But standard WebGL 1.0 can only write to one framebuffer at a time. Now, it would be possible to use a separate pass for each texture that we need to compute, but that would involve a lot of redundant calculations, which is what we are trying to avoid. What we need is a WebGL extension that makes it possible for a shader to write to several framebuffers simultaneously. The extension that we need is named "WEBGL_draw_buffers". When that extension is activated, it becomes possible to attach several textures (or renderbuffers) to a framebuffer, and it becomes possible for a shader to write data to all of the attached shaders simultaneously. The extension is relatively complicated to use. It must be activated, as usual, with a statement of the form EXTdb = gl.getExtension("WEBGL_draw_buffers");

Assuming that the extension is available, the maximum number of color buffers that can be used in a shader is given by *EXTdb.MAX_DRAW_BUFFERS_WEBGL*, which will be at least four. With the extension in place, you can attach multiple textures as color buffers for a framebuffer, using code of the form

```
gl.bindFramebuffer(gl.FRAMEBUFFER, framebuffer);
gl.framebufferTexture2D(gl.FRAMEBUFFER,
    EXTdb.COLOR_ATTACHMENT0_WEBGL, gl.TEXTURE_2D, texture1, 0);
gl.framebufferTexture2D(gl.FRAMEBUFFER,
    EXTdb.COLOR_ATTACHMENT1_WEBGL, gl.TEXTURE_2D, texture2, 0);
```

and so on, using constants such as EXTdb.COLOR_ATTACHMENT1_WEBGL from the extension object to specify the attachment points.

Usually in a fragment shader, the color that is output to the color buffer is specified by assigning a value to the special variable gl_FragColor. That changes when multiple color buffers are used. In that case, instead of gl_FragColor, the fragment shader has a special variable gl_FragData which is an array of vec4, one for each possible color buffer. Colors are output to the color buffers by assigning values to gl_FragData[0], gl_FragData [1], ...

Because this is a change in the legal syntax of the shader, the extension must also be activated in the fragment shader source code by adding the line

```
#extension GL_EXT_draw_buffers : require
```

to the beginning of the code. Suppose, for example, that we want to store a normal vector, a diffuse color, a specular color, and object coordinates in the color buffers. Let's say that these values are input to the fragment shader as varying variables or uniform variables, except for the diffuse color, which is sampled from a texture. Then the fragment shader might take the form

```
#extension GL_EXT_draw_buffers : require
precision highp float;
varying vec3 v_normal, v_objectCoords;
varying vec2 v_texCoords;
uniform vec3 u_specular;
uniform float u_shininess;
uniform sampler2D texture;
void main() {
    gl FragData[0] = vec4( normalize(v_normal), 0 );
    gl_FragData[1] = vec4( v_object_coords, 1 );
    glFragData[2] = texture2D( texture, v_texCoords );
    gl_fragData[3] = vec4( u_specular, u_shininess );
}
```

The final requirement for using the extension is to specify the correspondence between the indices that are used in gl_FragData and the color buffers that have been attached to the framebuffer. It seems like the correspondence should be automatic, but it's not. You have to specify it using the JavaScript function, EXTdb.drawBuffersWEBGL from the extension object. This function takes an array as parameter, and the values in the array are chosen from the constants EXTdb.COLOR_ATTACHMENT0_WEBGL, EXTdb.COLOR_ATTACHMENT1_WEBGL, . . . These are the same constants that are used to specify the color buffer attachment points in a framebuffer. For example, if for some reason you wanted a fragment shader to output to the color buffers that are attached at attachment points 2 and 3, you would call

```
EXTdb.drawBuffersWEBGL( [
    EXTdb.COLOR_ATTACHMENT2_WEBGL,
    EXTdb.COLOR_ATTACHMENT3_WEBGL
] );
```

After all that setup, you are ready to do the first pass for deferred shading. For the subsequent passes, you would use a different shader, with a single color buffer. For those passes, you want to run the fragment shader once for each pixel in the image. The fragment shader will use the pixel data that was saved in the first pass, together with other information such as light properties, to compute the output color for the pixel. You can trigger a call to the fragment shader for each pixel simply by drawing a single rectangle that covers the image.

The theory behind deferred shading is not all that complicated, but there are a lot of details to get right in the implementation. Deferred shading is just one of many tricks that are used by video game programmers to improve the rendering speed for their games.

7.5.5 Multiple Draw Buffers in WebGL 2.0

The ability to write to multiple draw buffers is a standard part of WebGL 2.0. The sample program webgl/multiple-draw-buffers-webgl2.html is a simple demonstration. This program takes a sample image and breaks it up into three separate images that show the red, green, and blue color components from the original image. It does that by attaching three textures to a framebuffer, and writing each color component to one of the textures. The image from each texture is then copied to the screen as a grayscale image.

The program has to create and allocate storage for three texture objects, and bind them to a frame buffer as color buffers. Here is the code that does this:

```
framebuffer = gl.createFramebuffer();
gl.bindFramebuffer(gl.FRAMEBUFFER,framebuffer);
texture0 = gl.createTexture();
gl.bindTexture(gl.TEXTURE_2D, texture0);
gl.texStorage2D(gl.TEXTURE_2D, 1, gl.R8, 320, 399);
gl.framebufferTexture2D(gl.FRAMEBUFFER,
    gl.COLOR_ATTACHMENT0, gl.TEXTURE_2D, texture0, 0);
texture1 = gl.createTexture();
gl.bindTexture(gl.TEXTURE_2D, texture1);
gl.texStorage2D(gl.TEXTURE_2D, 1, gl.R8, 320, 399);
gl.framebufferTexture2D(gl.FRAMEBUFFER,
    gl.COLOR_ATTACHMENT1, gl.TEXTURE_2D, texture1, 0);
texture2 = gl.createTexture();
gl.bindTexture(gl.TEXTURE_2D, texture2);
gl.texStorage2D(gl.TEXTURE_2D, 1, gl.R8, 320, 399);
gl.framebufferTexture2D(gl.FRAMEBUFFER,
    gl.COLOR_ATTACHMENT2, gl.TEXTURE_2D, texture2, 0);
```

The textures are created with format gl.R8, which stores one eight-bit unsigned integer per pixel; that is sufficient for a grayscale image. (For this format, an 8-bit integer is considered to be scaled to represent a color value in the range 0.0 to 1.0 .)

The function gl.drawBuffers() must be called to enable writing to multiple draw buffers and to specify the output destinations. The destinations are specified as an array of attachment points on the framebuffer:

```
gl.drawBuffers( [
    gl.COLOR_ATTACHMENT0, gl.COLOR_ATTACHMENT1, gl.COLOR_ATTACHMENT2
] );
```

The shader programs for this example are written in GLSL ES 3.00, which uses out variables in the fragment shader to send output to draw buffers. When there is a single out variable, it automatically sends output to the first draw buffer (draw buffer number zero). When there is more than one out variable, the destination number must be specified for every out variable using a layout qualifier. The location specified for an out variable in the fragment shader is an index into the array of attachment points that was passed to gl.drawBuffers(). As an example, here is the fragment shader from the sample program:

```
#version 300 es
precision mediump float;
uniform sampler2D u_picture; // texture containing original image
in vec2 v_coords;
layout(location = 0) out float red; // write to draw buffer 0
layout(location = 1) out float green; // write to draw buffer 1
layout(location = 2) out float blue; // write to draw buffer 2
void main() {
    vec4 color = texture(u_picture, v_coords);
    red = color.r;


    green = color.g;
    blue = color.b;
}
```

This fragment shader sends the separate RGB color components from the original image to the three textures that are attached to the framebuffer.

This is a fairly simple and not-very-useful example of using multiple draw buffers, but it does illustrate all the steps that are required to do so.

Chapter-8

Beyond Basic 3D Graphics

The first seven chapters of this textbook have covered basic real-time computer graphics, that is, graphics systems in which an image can be generated in a fraction of a second. The typical case is a video game, where new frames can be rendered as many as sixty times per second. Very complex and realistic-looking scenes can be rendered in real time, using techniques covered in this book and the immense processing power of modern GPUs, plus some tricks and advanced algorithms. Modern high-end GPUs have begun adding some direct hardware support for ray tracing and global illumination, but real-time graphics still can't match the realism of the very highest quality computer graphics, such as what can be found in movies. In fact, the CGI (computer generated imagery) in today's movies is sometimes indistinguishable from reality. Getting graphics of that quality can require hours of computing time to render a single frame.

This chapter is a very brief look at some techniques that can be used for very high quality graphics. The discussion will be in general terms. I won't be giving sample code or detailed discussions of the mathematics behind the techniques, but I hope to provide at least a basic conceptual understanding.

The first thing that you should understand, though, is that most of what you have leaned so far still applies. Scenes are still composed using geometric primitives, transformations, materials, textures, and light sources (although perhaps using more advanced material properties and lighting than we have encountered so far). The graphic designers working on CGI for a movie can see real time previews of their work that are rendered using techniques that we have covered. The final scene that you see in the movie is just rendered using different, much more computation-intensive techniques.

8.1 Ray Tracing

Ray tracing is probably the best known technique for higher quality graphics. The idea behind it is not complicated: To find out what you see when you look in a given direction, consider a ray of light that arrives at your location from that direction, and follow that light ray backwards to see where it came from. Or, as it is usually phrased, cast a ray from your location in a given direction, and see what it hits. That's what you see when you look in that direction. The operation of determining what is hit by a ray is called ray casting. It is fundamental to ray tracing and to other advanced graphics techniques.

8.1.1 Ray Casting

We have already seen ray casting used by objects of type THREE.RayCaster in the three.js API (Subsection 5.3.2). A Raycaster takes an initial point and a direction, given as a vector. The point and vector determine a ray, that is, a half-infinite line that extends from a starting point, in some direction, to infinity. The Raycaster can find all the intersections of the ray with a given set of objects in a three.js scene, sorted by order of distance from the rays's starting point. In this chapter, we are interested in the first intersection, the one that is closest to the starting point.

To apply ray casting to rendering, let's say that we have a scene consisting of objects in three-dimensional space, using point lights and directional lights for illumination. We want to render an image of the scene from a given point of view. It's convenient to imagine the image as a kind of rectangular window through which the scene is being viewed. Given a point in the image, we need to know how to color that point. To compute a color for the point, we begin by casting a ray from the position of the viewer through the point and into the scene. We want to find the first intersection of that ray with an object in the scene:

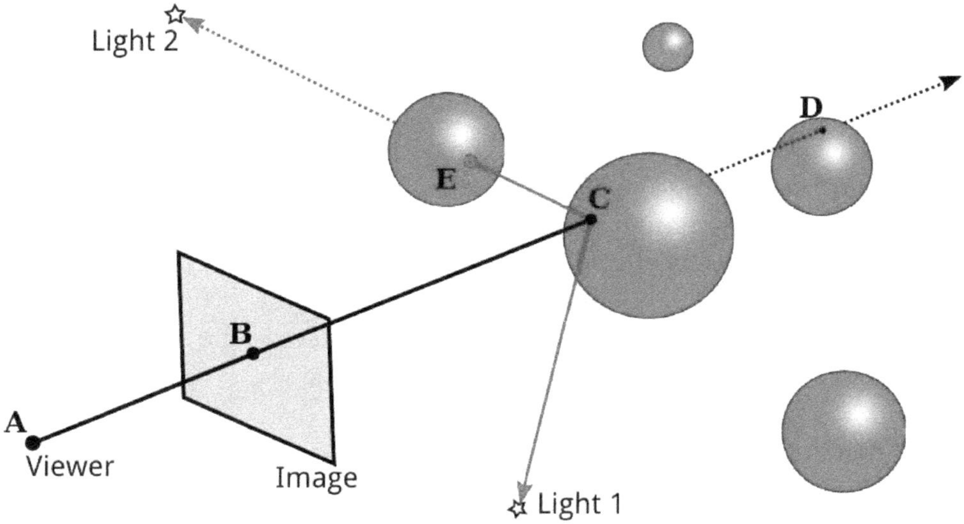

In this illustration, the scene contains several red spheres and two point lights. A ray is cast from the viewpoint (A) through a point (B) in the image. The ray intersects two of the spheres, but we are only interested in the intersection point (C) that is closest to the viewpoint. That's the point that is visible at B in the image.

We need to compute the color that the viewer will see at point B . For that, just as in OpenGL, we need a normal vector at point C , and we need the material properties of the surface at C . That data has to be computable from the scene description. The visible color also depends on the light that is illuminating the surface. Consider a light source, and let L be the vector that points from C in the direction of the light. If the angle between L and the normal vector is greater than 90 degrees, then the light source lies behind the surface and so does not add any illumination. Otherwise, we can use ray casting again: Cast a ray from C in the direction L. If that ray hits an object before it gets to the light, then that object will block light from that source from reaching C. That's the case for Light 2 in the illustration: The ray from C in the direction of Light 2 intersects an object at point E before it gets to the light. On the other hand, the point C is illuminated by Light 1. A ray from a point on a surface in the direction of a light source is called a shadow ray, because it can be used to determine whether the surface point lies in the shadow of another object.

With all this information, we can color point B in the image using the same lighting equation that is used in OpenGL (Subsection 4.1.4). Ray casting solves the hidden surface problem with no need for a depth buffer. And, as a bonus, we get shadows, which are hard to do in OpenGL! (If the ray from the viewpoint through B doesn't hit any objects in the scene, then B would be assigned a background color or a "sky" color that varies with different directions. Or maybe the entire scene is surrounded by a skybox, and a ray that doesn't hit any other object will hit the skybox.)

Ray casting is conceptually simple, but implementation details can be tricky. Spheres are actually fairly easy. There is a formula for finding the intersections of a line with a sphere, and a normal vector at a point on a sphere has the same direction as the line from the center of the sphere to that point. Assuming that the sphere has a uniform material, we have all the data we need.

However, surfaces are often given as triangular meshes, with properties specified only at the vertices of the triangles. Suppose that the intersection point found by our ray caster lies in one of those triangles. We will have to compute the properties of that intersection point by interpolating the property values that were specified at the vertices of the triangle.

The interpolation algorithm typically uses something called barycentric coordinates on the triangle: If A, B, and C are the vertices of a triangle, and P is a point in the triangle, then P can be written uniquely in the form a^* A + b^* B + c^*C, where a, b, and c are numbers in the range zero to one, and $a + b + c = 1$. The coefficients a, b, and c are called the barycentric coordinates of the point P in the triangle. If some quantity has values

V(A), V(B), and V(C) at the vertices of the triangle, then we can use the barycentric coordinates of P to get an interpolated value at P :

$$V(P) = a * V(A) + b * V(B) + c * V(C)$$

The quantity might be, for example, diffuse color, texture coordinates, or a normal vector. (Of course, I'm still leaving out a lot of the math here - how to test whether a line intersects a triangle and how to find barycentric coordinates of the point of intersection. There are formulas, but conceptually, they wouldn't add much to the discussion.)

8.1.2 Recursive Ray Tracing

Basic ray casting can be used to compute OpenGL-style rendering and, with the addition of shadow rays, to implement shadows as well. More features can be implemented by casting a few more rays. The improved algorithm is called ray tracing.

Consider specular reflection. In OpenGL, specular reflection can make an object look shiny in the sense that specular highlights can be seen where the object reflects light from a light source towards the viewer. But in reality, an object that has a mirror-like surface doesn't just reflect light sources; it also reflects other objects. If we are trying to compute a color for a point, *A*, on a mirror-like surface, we need to consider the contribution to that color from mirror-like reflection of other objects. To do that, we can cast a "reflected ray" from *A*. The direction of the reflected ray is determined by the normal vector to the surface at *A* and by the direction from *A* to the viewer. This illustration shows a 2D version. Think of it as a cross-section of the situation in 3D:

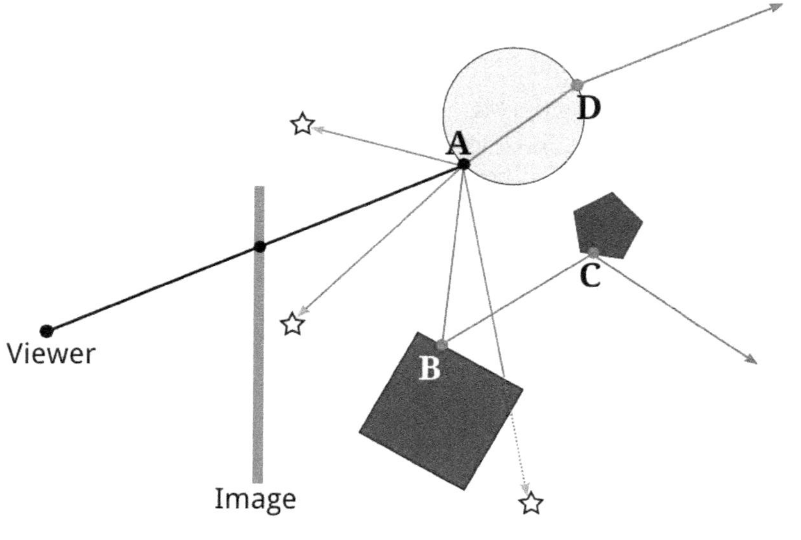

Here, the reflected ray from point A hits the purple square at point B, and the viewer will see a reflection of point B at A. (Remember that in ray tracing, we follow the path of light rays backwards from the viewer, to find out where they came from.)

To find out what the reflection of B looks like, we need to know the color of the the ray that arrives at A from B. But finding a color for B is the same sort of problem as finding a color for A, and we should solve it in the same way: by applying the ray-tracing algorithm to B ! That is, we use the material properties of the surface at B, we cast shadow rays from B towards light sources to determine how B is illuminated, and - if the purple square has a mirror-like surfacewe cast a reflected ray from B to find out what it reflects. In the illustration, the reflected ray from B hits a pentagon at point C, so the square reflects an image of the pentagon, and the disk reflects an image of the square, including its reflection of the pentagon. Ray-tracing can handle multiple mirror-like reflections between objects in a scene!

Because applying the ray-tracing algorithm at one point can involve applying the same algorithm at additional points, ray tracing is a recursive algorithm. To distinguish this from simple ray casting, ray tracing is often referred to as "recursive ray tracing."

Ray tracing can be extended in a similar way to handle transparency or, more properly, translucency. When computing a color for a point on a translucent object, we need to take into account light that arrives at that point through the object. To do that, we can cast yet another ray from that point, this time into the object. When a light ray passes from one medium, such as air, into another medium, such as glass, the path of the light ray can bend. This bending is called refraction, and the ray that is cast through a translucent object is called the "refracted ray." The above illustration shows the refracted ray from point A passing through the object and emerging from the object at D. To find a color for that ray, we would need to find out what, if anything, it hits, and we would need to apply ray tracing recursively at the point of intersection. (The degree of bending of a light ray that passes from one medium to another depends on a property of the two media called the "index of refraction." More exactly, it depends on the ratio between the two indices of refraction. In practice, the index of refraction outside objects is often taken to be equal to one, so that the bending depends only on the index of refraction of an object. The index of refraction is another material property for translucent objects. It is often abbreviated ***IOR***.)

We should look at the computations in a little more detail. The goal is to compute a color for a point on an image. We cast a ray from the viewpoint through the image and into the scene, and determine the first intersection point of the ray with an object. The color of that point is computed by adding up the contributions from different sources.

First, there is diffuse, specular, and possibly ambient reflection of light from various light sources. These contributions are based on the diffuse, specular, and ambient colors of the object, on the normal vector to the object, and on the properties of the light sources. Note that some color properties of the object, usually the ambient and diffuse colors, might come from a texture. The specular contribution can produce specular highlights, which are essentially the reflections of light sources. Shadow rays are used to determine which directional and point lights illuminate the object; aside from that, this part of the calculation is similar to OpenGL.

Next, if the surface has mirror-like reflection, then a reflected ray is cast and ray tracing is applied recursively to find a color for that ray. The contribution from that ray is combined with other contributions to the color of the surface, depending on the strength of the mirror reflection. For a perfect mirror, the reflected ray contributes 100% of the color, but in general the contribution is less. Mirror reflectivity is a new material property. It is responsible for reflections of one object on the surface of another, while specular color is responsible for specular highlights.

Finally, if the object is translucent, then a refracted ray is cast, and ray tracing is used to find its color. The contribution of that ray to the color of the object depends on the degree of transparency of the object, since some of the light can be absorbed rather than transmitted. The degree of transparency can depend on the wavelength of the light - as it does, for example, in colored glass.

And, of course, all of these calculations need to be done three times, for the red, the green, and the blue components of the color.

The ray tracing algorithm is recursive, and, as every programmer knows, recursion needs a base case. That is, there has to come a time when, instead of calling itself, the algorithm simply returns a value. A base case occurs whenever a casted ray does not intersect any objects. Another kind of base case can occur when it is determined that casting more rays cannot contribute any significant amount to the color of the image. For example, whenever a ray is reflected, some of that ray is absorbed rather than reflected, depending on the color of the object from which it is reflected. After reflecting many times, a ray would have very little color left to contribute to the final result. A ray can also lose energy because of attenuation of light with distance, and a ray-tracing algorithm might take that into account. In addition, a ray tracing algorithm should always be run with a maximum recursion depth, to put an absolute limit on the number of times the algorithm will call itself.

8.1.3 Limitations of Ray Tracing

Although ray tracing can produce very realistic images, there are some things that it can't do. For example, while ray tracing works well for point lights and directional lights, it can't handle area lights. An area light is one that has area. That is, it is an object that emits light from its entire surface area rather than from a single point. Of course, real lights are area lights. A fluorescent light emits light from the surface of a cylinder. A brightly lit window can be considered to be a kind of area light. Even a light bulb does not really radiate light from a single point. Ray tracing uses shadow rays to tell whether a light source illuminates an object. But a shadow ray is cast in only one direction, and can only hit one point on an area light. To implement area lights exactly, a different shadow ray would be needed for each point on the surface of the light.

A ray tracer can handle area lights in an approximate way, by replacing the area light with a grid of point lights. It can then cast a shadow ray towards each point in the grid. Using more point lights in the grid will give a better approximation. Of course, casting all those shadow rays can add significantly to the computation time.

Another problem with lighting in ray tracing is that it doesn't take into account illumination by reflected light. For example, light from a light source should reflect off a mirror, and the reflected light should illuminate other objects. Ray tracing uses shadow rays to tell whether a light source illuminates an object. But that won't work for reflected light, since the algorithm doesn't know where to aim the shadow ray-reflected light could come from any direction.

This is not just a problem with mirrors. Any reflected light, even from diffuse reflection, should illuminate nearby objects. For example, light that is reflected diffusely from a green object should add a green tint to nearby objects. This effect is called "color bleeding." In reality, light can be reflected and re-reflected many times, contributing a bit of color to each object that it hits. As with area lights, approximate methods can be added to ray tracing to simulate this effect. For example, "photon mapping" adds a pre-processing phase to ray tracing which simulates the emission of a large number of light rays, or "photons," from light sources, and tracks their paths through the scene to see how they add color to the objects that they hit. The information from this "photon map" is then used during the ray tracing phase to produce more realistic colors.

OpenGL uses ambient light as an approximation for light that has been reflected and rereflected many times. Ambient light is assumed to illuminate every object equally. However, that is a poor approximation. A better approximation uses ambient occlusion, the idea that ambient light heading towards a surface can be blocked, or "occluded," by nearby objects. Like ambient light, ambient occlusion is not physically realistic, but in practice, it can make lighting look more realistic and objects look more three-dimensional. One technique for estimating ambient occlusion uses ray casting. We assume that the ambient light comes from the background of the scene. To estimate ambient occlusion at a point, cast a number of rays from that point in random directions, and count how many of those rays are blocked by geometry in the scene and how many reach the sky. The more rays that are blocked, the greater the degree of ambient occlusion at that point.

Algorithms that attempt to take into account all of the interactions of light with objects in a scene are said to use global illumination. Approximate methods such as those mentioned above can be added on to ray tracing to increase its realism, at the cost of significantly increased complexity and a potentially large amount of extra computing. We begin to see why very realistic images can take so long to compute! In the next section we will look at a method that attempts to handle global illumination exactly.

8.2 Path Tracing

We have seen how ray tracing can be extended to approximate a variety of effects that are not handled by the basic algorithm. We look next at an algorithm that accounts for all those effects and more in a fairly straightforward and unified way: path tracing. Like ray tracing, path tracing computes colors for points in an image by tracing the paths of light rays backwards from the viewer through points on the image and into the scene. But in path tracing, the idea is to account for all possible paths that the light could have followed. Of course, that is not literally possible, but following a large number of paths can give a good approximation-one that gets better as the number of paths is increased ("Forward path tracing," where paths of light rays emitted from light sources are traced forward in time, is also sometimes used.)

8.2.1 BSDF's

In order to model a wide variety of physical phenomena, path tracing uses a generalization of the idea of material property. In OpenGL, a material is a combination of ambient, diffuse, specular, and emission colors, plus shininess. These properties, except for emission color, model how the surface interacts with light. Material properties can vary from point to point on a surface; that's an example of a texture.

OpenGL material is only a rough approximation of reality. In path tracing, a more general notion is used that is capable of more accurately representing the properties of almost any real physical surface or volume. The replacement for materials is call a ***BSDF***, or Bidirectional Scattering Distribution Function.

Think about how light that arrives at some point can be affected by the physical properties of whatever substance exists at that point. Some of the light might be absorbed. Some might pass through the point without being affected at all. And some might be "scattered," that is, sent off in another direction. In fact, we consider passing through the point as a special case of scattering. A BSDF describes how light is scattered from each point on a surface or in a volume.

Think of a single ray, or photon, of light that arrives at some point. What happens to it can depend on the direction from which it arrives. In general, assuming that it is not absorbed, the light is more likely to be scattered in some directions than in others. (As in specular reflection, for example.) The BSDF at the point gives the probability that the ray will leave the point heading in a given direction. It is a "bidirectional" function because the answer is a function of two directions, the direction from which the light arrives and the outgoing direction that you are asking about. (It is a "distribution function" in the sense of the mathematical theory of continuous probability distributions, but you don't need to understand that to get the general idea. For us, it's enough to understand that the function says how light coming in from a given direction is distributed among possible outgoing directions.) Note that a BSDF is also a function of the point that you are talking about, and it is generally a function of the wavelength of the light as well.

Any point in space can be assigned a BSDF. For empty space, the BSDF is trivial: It simply says that light arriving at a point has a 100% probability of continuing in the same direction. But light passing through fog or dusty air or dirty water has some probability of being absorbed and some probability of being scattered to a random direction. Similar remarks apply to light passing through the interior of a translucent solid object.

Traditionally, though, computer graphics has been mostly concerned with what happens to light at the surface of an object. Light can be absorbed or reflected or, if the object is translucent, transmitted through the surface. The function that describes the reflection of light from a surface is sometimes called a BRDF (Bidirectional Reflectance Distribution Function), and the formula for transmission of light is a BTDF (Bidirectional Transmission Distribution function). The BSDF for a surface is a combination of the two.

Let's consider OpenGL materials in terms of BSDFs. In basic OpenGL, light can only be reflected or absorbed. For diffuse reflection, light has an equal probability of being reflected in every direction that makes an angle of less than 90 degrees with the normal vector to the surface, and there is no dependence on the direction from which the light arrives. For specular reflection, the incoming light direction matters. In OpenGL, the possible outgoing directions for specularly reflected light form a cone, where the angle between the axis of the cone and the normal vector is equal to the angle between the normal vector and the incoming light direction. The axis of the cone is the most likely direction for outgoing light, and the probability falls off as the angle between the outgoing direction and the direction of the axis increases. The rate of falloff is specified by the shininess property of the material. The BRFD for the surface combines the diffuse and specular reflection. (The ambient material property doesn't fit well into the BSDF framework, since physically there is no such thing as an "ambient light" that is somehow different from regular light.)

Ray tracing adds two new possibilities to the interaction of light with a surface: perfect, mirror-like reflection, where the outgoing light makes exactly the same angle with the normal vector as the incoming light, and transmission of light into a translucent object, where the outgoing angle is determined by the indices of refraction outside and inside the object.

But BSDFs can provide even more realistic models of the interaction of light with surfaces. For example, the distinction between mirror-like reflection of an object and specular reflection of a light source is artificial. A perfect mirror should reflect both light sources and objects in a mirror-like way. For a shiny but rough surface, all specular reflection would send the light in a cone of directions, giving fuzzy images of objects and lights alike. A BSFD should handle both cases, and it shouldn't distinguish between light from light sources and light reflected off other objects.

BSDFs can also correctly handle a phenomenon called subsurface scattering, which can be an important visual effect for materials that are just a bit translucent, such as milk, jade, and skin. In sub-surface scattering, light that hits a surface can be transmitted into the object, be scattered a few times internally inside the object, and then emerge from the surface at another point. How the light behaves inside the object is determined by the BSDF of the material in the interior of the object. The BSDF in this case would be similar to the one for fog, except that the probability of scattering would be larger.

The point is that just about any physically realistic material can be modeled by a correctly chosen BSDF.

8.2.2 The Path Tracing Algorithm

Path tracing is based on a formula known as the "rendering equation." The formula says that the amount of light energy leaving a given point in a given direction is equal to the amount of light energy emitted by the point in that direction plus the amount of light energy arriving at the point from other sources that is then scattered in that direction.

Here, emitted light means light that is created, as by a light source. In the rendering equation, any object can be an emitter of light. In OpenGL terms, it's as if an object with an emission color actually emits light that can illuminate other objects. An area light is just an extended object that emits light from every point, and it is common to illuminate scenes with large light-emitting objects. (In fact, in a typical path tracing setup, point lights and directional lights have to be assigned some area to make them work correctly in the algorithm, or some forward path tracing has to be used.)

As for scattered light, the BSDF at a point determines how light arriving at that point is scattered. Light can, in general, arrive from any direction and can originate from any other point in the scene. The rendering equation holds at every point. It relates the light arriving at and departing from each point to the light arriving at and departing from every other point. It describes, in other words, an immensely complicated system, one for which you are unlikely to be able to find an exact solution. A rendering algorithm can be thought of as an attempt to find a good approximate solution to the rendering equation.

Path tracing is a probabilistic rendering algorithm. It looks at possible paths that might have been followed by light arriving at the position of the viewer. Each possible path has a certain probability. Path tracing generates a random sample of possible paths, choosing paths in the sample according to their probabilities. It uses those paths to create an image that approximates a solution to the rendering equation. It can be shown that as the size of the random sample increases, the image that is generated will approach the true solution. To get a good quality image, the algorithm will have to trace thousands of paths for each pixel in the image, but the result can be an almost shocking level of realism.

Let's think about how it should work. First, consider the case where light is only emitted and reflected by surfaces. As with ray tracing, we start at the position of the viewer and cast a ray in the direction of a point on the image, into the scene. (See Subsection 8.1.1.) We find the first intersection of that ray with an object in the scene. Our goal to trace one possible path that the ray could have followed from its point of origin until it arrives at the viewer, and we want the probability that we select a given path to be the probability that the light actually followed that path. This means that each time the light is scattered from a surface, we should choose the direction of the next segment of the path based on the BSDF for the surface. That is, the direction is chosen at random, using the probability distribution that is encoded in the BSDF. We construct the next segment of the path by casting a ray in the selected direction.

We continue to trace the path, backwards in time, possibly through multiple reflections, until it encounters an object that emits light. That object serves as the original source of the light. The color that the path contributes to the image is determined by the color and intensity of the emitter, by the colors of surfaces that the light hits along the way, and by the angles at which the light hits each surface. If the path escapes from the scene before it hits a light emitting object, then it does not contribute any color to the image. (It might be desirable to have a light-emitting background, like a sky, that emits light over a large area.) Note that it is possible for an object to be both an emitter and a reflector of light. In that case, a path can continue even after it gets to a light source.

Of course, we have to trace many such paths. The color for a pixel in the image is computed as an average of the colors obtained for all the paths that pass through that pixel.

The algorithm can be extended to handle the case where light can be scattered at arbitrary points in space, and not just at surfaces. For light traveling in a medium in 3D space, the question is, how far will the light travel before it is scattered? The BSDF for the medium will determine a probability distribution on possible travel distances between scatterings. When light enters a medium, that probability distribution is used to select a random distance that the light will travel before it is scattered (unless it hits a surface or enters a new medium before it has traveled that distance). When it scatters from a point in the medium, a new direction and length are chosen at random for the next segment of the path, according to the BSDF of the medium. For a light fog, the average distance between scatterings would be quite large; for a dense medium like milk, it would be quite short.

A great deal of computation is required to trace enough light paths to get a high-quality image. Although path tracing was invented in the 1980s, it is only recently that it has become practical for general use, and it can still take many hours to get high quality rendering. In fact, you can do path tracing on your desktop computer using the 3D modeling program Blender, which is discussed in Appendix B. Blender has a rendering engine called Cycles that uses path tracing.

Index

L

M

N

O

P

Q

R

S

www.ingramcontent.com/pod-product-compliance
Lightning Source LLC
LaVergne TN
LVHW081942200926
848484LV00009B/2493
9781787156500